THE VIOLENCE
AND ADDICTION EQUATION

THE VIOLENCE AND ADDICTION EQUATION

Theoretical and Clinical Issues
in Substance Abuse
and Relationship Violence

edited by

Christine Wekerle, Ph.D. and Anne-Marie Wall, Ph.D.

USA	Publishing Office:	BRUNNER-ROUTLEDGE
		A member of the Taylor & Francis Group
		29 West 35th Street
		New York, NY 10001
		Tel: (212) 216-7800
		Fax: (212) 564-7854
	Distribution Center:	BRUNNER-ROUTLEDGE
		A member of the Taylor & Francis Group
		7625 Empire Drive
		Florence, KY 41042
		Tel: 1-800-634-7064
		Fax: 1-800-248-4724
UK		BRUNNER-ROUTLEDGE
		A member of the Taylor & Francis Group
		27 Church Road
		Hove
		E. Sussex, BN3 2FA
		Tel: +44 (0) 1273 207411
		Fax: +44 (0) 1273 205612

THE VIOLENCE AND ADDICTION EQUATION: Theoretical and Clinical Issues in Substance Abuse and Relationship Violence

1 2 3 4 5 6 7 8 9 0

Printed by Edwards Brothers, Lillington, NC, 2001.
Cover design by Nancy Abbott.
Cover photo ® copyright 2001 PhotoDisc, Inc.

A CIP catalog record for this book is available from the British Library.
∞ The paper in this publication meets the requirements of the ANSI Standard Z39.48-1984 (Permanence of Paper).

Library of Congress Cataloging-in-Publication Data
Wekerle, Christine.
    The violence and addiction equation : theoretical and clinical issues in substance abuse and relationship violence / Christine Wekerle, Anne-Marie Wall.
        p. cm.
    Includes bibliographical references and index.
    ISBN 0-87630-959-7 (case : alk. paper)
    1. Substance abuse. 2. Family violence. 3. Violence. I. Wall, Anne-Marie. II. Title.

HV4998 .W45 2001
362.82'92—dc21

                                                                    2001037778

ISBN 0-87630-959-7

CONTENTS

Contributors   vii

Preface   xi

Chapter 1   *Christine Wekerle and Anne-Marie Wall*

**Introduction: The Overlap between Relationship
Violence and Substance Abuse**   1

I. THEORETICAL FRAMEWORKS

Chapter 2   *Robert O. Pihl and Peter N. S. Hoaken*

**Biological Bases of Addiction and Aggression
in Close Relationships**   25

Chapter 3   *Patricia McKinsey Crittenden and Angelika Hartl Claussen*

**Developmental Psychopathology Perspectives
on Substance Abuse and Relationship Violence**   44

Chapter 4   *Gordon L. Flett and Paul L. Hewitt*

**Personality Factors and Substance Abuse in Relationship
Violence and Child Abuse: A Review and Theoretical Analysis**   64

Chapter 5   *Sherry H. Stewart and Anne L. Israeli*

**Substance Abuse and Co-Occurring Psychiatric Disorders
in Victims of Intimate Violence**   98

Chapter 6   *Anne-Marie Wall and Sherry McKee*

**Cognitive Social Learning Models of Substance Use
and Intimate Violence**   123

II. RELATIONSHIP VIOLENCE AND ADDICTION ACROSS THE LIFESPAN

Chapter **7**   Debra J. Pepler, Wendy M. Craig, Jennifer Connolly,
and Kathryn Henderson

**Bullying, Sexual Harassment, Dating Violence, and
Substance Use among Adolescents**   153

Chapter **8**   Mark D. Wood and Kenneth J. Sher

**Sexual Assault and Relationship Violence among College
Students: Examining the Role of Alcohol and Other Drugs**   169

Chapter **9**   Kenneth E. Leonard

**Alcohol and Substance Abuse in Marital Violence
and Child Maltreatment**   194

Chapter **10**   Mandra L. Rasmussen Hall and Victoria M. Follette

Substance Abuse and Interpersonal Violence in Older Adults   220

III. CLINICAL ISSUES IN INTERVENTION FOR INTIMATE VIOLENCE AND ADDICTION PROBLEMS

Chapter **11**   John Schafer and Raul Caetano

**Violence and Alcohol: Cultural Issues and
Barriers to Treatment**   239

Chapter **12**   William R. Downs and Brenda A. Miller

**Treating Dual Problems of Partner Violence and
Substance Abuse**   254

Chapter **13**   Caroline Easton and Rajita Sinha

**Treating the Addicted Male Batterer: Promising Directions
for Dual-Focused Programming**   275

Chapter **14**   Timothy J. O'Farrell and Christopher M. Murphy

**Behavioral Couples Therapy for Alcoholism and Drug Abuse:
Encountering the Problem of Domestic Violence**   293

Chapter **15**   Anna-Lee Pittman and David A. Wolfe

**Bridging the Gap: Prevention of Adolescent Risk Behaviors
and Development of Healthy Nonviolent Dating Relationships**   304

Chapter **16**   Christine Wekerle and Anne-Marie Wall

**Conclusion: Clinical and Research Issues in Relationship
Violence and Substance Abuse**   324

Index   349

CONTRIBUTORS

Raul Caetano, M.D., Ph.D., M.Ph.
Houston School of Public Health, University of Texas, Houston, Texas

Angelika Hartl Claussen, Ph.D.
Department of Psychology, University of Miami, Coral Gables, Florida

Jennifer Connolly, Ph.D.
Department of Psychology, York University, Toronto, Ontario

Wendy M. Craig, Ph.D.
Department of Psychology, Queen's University, Kingston, Ontario

Patricia McKinsey Crittenden, Ph.D.
Institute of Family Relations, Miami, Florida

William R. Downs, Ph.D.
Department of Social Work, University of Northern Iowa, Cedar Falls, Iowa

Caroline Easton, Ph.D.
Department of Psychiatry, Yale University School of Medicine, New Haven, Connecticut

Gordon L. Flett, Ph.D.
Department of Psychology, York University, Toronto, Ontario

Victoria M. Follette, Ph.D.
Department of Psychology, University of Nevada—Reno, Reno, Nevada

Mandra L. Rasmussen Hall, B.A.
Department of Psychology, University of Nevada—Reno, Reno, Nevada

Kathryn Henderson, M.A.
Department of Psychology, Queen's University, Kingston, Ontario

Paul L. Hewitt, Ph.D.
Department of Psychology, University of British Columbia, British Columbia, Canada

Peter N. S. Hoaken, Ph.D.
Department of Psychology, Dalhousie University, Halifax, Nova Scotia

Anne L. Israeli, Ph.D.
Centre for Addiction and Mental Health, Toronto, Ontario

Kenneth E. Leonard, Ph.D.
Department of Psychiatry, State University of New York at Buffalo Medical School,Buffalo, New York, and The Research Institute on Addictions, Buffalo, New York

Sherry McKee, Ph.D.
Department of Psychiatry, Yale University School of Medicine, New Haven, Connecticut

Brenda A. Miller, Ph.D.
Center for Research on Urban Social Work Practice, State University of New York at Buffalo, Buffalo, New York

Christopher M. Murphy, Ph.D.
Department of Psychology, University of Maryland—Baltimore, Baltimore, Maryland

Timothy J. O'Farrell, Ph.D.
Department of Psychiatry, Harvard Medical School, Boston, Massachusetts, and Veterans Affairs Medical Center, Brockton, Massachusetts

Debra J. Pepler, Ph.D.
Department of Psychology, York University, Toronto, Ontario

Robert O. Pihl, Ph.D.
Department of Psychology, McGill University, Montreal, Quebec

Anna-Lee Pittman, M.L.I.S.
Department of Psychology, University of Western Ontario, London, Ontario

John Schafer, Ph.D.
Department of Psychology, University of Cincinnati, Cincinnati, Ohio

Kenneth J. Sher, Ph.D.
Department of Psychology, University of Missouri—Columbia, Columbia, Missouri

Rajita Sinha, Ph.D.
Department of Psychiatry, Yale University School of Medicine, New Haven, Connecticut

Sherry H. Stewart, Ph.D.
Department of Psychology, Dalhousie University, Halifax, Nova Scotia

Anne-Marie Wall, Ph.D.
York University, Toronto, Ontario and The LaMarsh Centre for Research on Violence and Conflict Resolution, York University, Toronto, Ontario

Christine Wekerle, Ph.D.
University of Toronto, Toronto, Ontario and The LaMarsh Centre for Research on Violence and Conflict Resolution, York University, Toronto, Ontario

David A. Wolfe, Ph.D.
Department of Psychology, University of Western Ontario, London, Ontario

Mark D. Wood, Ph.D.
Department of Psychology, University of Rhode Island, Kingston, Rhode Island

PREFACE

In our modern world, violence and substance use are commonplace. Persons in close relationships—our partners and children—are too often put in the position of victim, the recipients of aggression and neglect. While many victims recover well and repair their hurt selves, such victimization experiences contribute to subsequent struggles with alcohol and other drugs. It is further recognized that the perpetrators of abuse may be entangled in their own struggles with addictive substances. As policy makers, educators, researchers, clinicians, and other service providers, we are confronted with the separate public health issues of child maltreatment, partner violence, and addictions. There remains an undeniable need to integrate these distinct literatures so that a fund of research-based knowledge can be compiled and guide our future work. This volume exists to suggest that we are impelled to consider how and why relationship violence overlaps with substance abuse, and how and when interventions should be delivered. In reality, the violence and addiction equation is being computed on a daily basis in child protective services, juvenile justice, battered women's shelters, treatment services, courts, and addiction treatment agencies. This volume is one effort to assist us in grappling with what the overlap between relationship violence and addictions may be about.

The goal for the current volume, first and foremost, is to document this dual problem and to examine estimates of their overlap across the lifespan and subpopulations. In varying degrees, the weight of the data point to the overlap among child maltreatment, partner violence, alcohol abuse, illicit drug abuse, and polysubstance abuse. A main goal for the present volume is to direct scholarly attention to theoretical frameworks that could guide our understanding of this emergent field and inform the development of dual-focused prevention and treatment programs. Violence and addiction-related problems may exert an impact across development. In the absence of a large body of dual-focused longitudinal research, another goal for this volume is to attempt to address these overlapping problems at different stages across the lifespan, from adolescence, where partner relationships become initiated, to older adults, where violence and addiction issues may persist or emerge. Finally, attention to the clinical reality for the dual problem of relationship violence and addiction created a need to examine prevention and treatment efforts. In addition to discussing important issues for intervention, this volume seeks to profile novel and promising prevention and treatment approaches, and to present more established, empirically-validated interventions. Within this clinical reality, important contextual questions need to be addressed such as cultural differences and access to treatment, and conceptual models informing intervention need to be presented. These are complex issues to consider. For instance, while treatment goals of abstinence and harm reduction may be applied within the substance abuse and relationship violence fields, many of these behaviors are illegal. This creates unique challenges for integration across the problems of relationship violence and addiction, where disconnected systems are in need of greater cross-referencing and collaboration. In spite of the complexity and seeming intractability of some of these overlapping problems for some persons, such a collaborative endeavor may well be essential to obtaining better outcomes for individuals and their families.

As editors, we are indebted to many individuals who worked with us to bring this volume to fruition. It has been a privilege and a pleasure to work alongside our contributors. We thank the outstanding group of scholars who have brought the violence and addiction equation into sharper focus. Also, we extend our gratitude to the staff at the Taylor and Francis Publishing Group, including Katherine Mortimer, our Developmental Editor and, gratefully, a rapid responder to our queries on the details. We reserve special thanks for Bernadette Cappelle, our Acquisitions Editor, who provided an unwavering commitment to and belief in the importance of this work. The support at Taylor and Francis has been motivational to us and we are indebted for the opportunity, shepherding, and heralding of this book. We hope this book will be useful to students, researchers, educators, clinicians, and policy-makers. We want to express our admiration for those on the frontline in the addiction and violence fields. We want to acknowledge their clients, who have struggled with the problems of relationship violence and substance abuse. Their willingness to share their experiences, both in research and clinical practice, enables us to build a body of knowledge from which to better address these dual problems. Child maltreatment, partner violence, and alcohol and other drug abuse are areas of growth and priority. May the dialogue between these fields continue and flourish.

On a personal note, we acknowledge the considerable assistance of our exceptional secretary, Sandra Locke. We thank our friends and colleagues who have enthusiastically supported our efforts with this volume. We are pleased that our students have embraced the issue of the violence and addiction overlap and are appreciative of their assistance in various aspects related to this work. In alphabetical order, they are: Jana Atkins, Effie Avgoustis, Michelle Bissonnette, Ashley Glickman, Abby Goldstein, Lynn Hawkins, Benedicte Lovald, Goldie Millar, and Arlin Torrington. We conclude with our heartfelt thanks to our families for understanding the demands and importance of this project to us and their high levels of support and dedication. We remain grateful for all their love that surrounds us.

CHAPTER 1

Christine Wekerle
Anne-Marie Wall

Introduction: The Overlap between Relationship Violence and Substance Abuse

Most parents say they love their children; most husbands say they love their wives. Even so, children are most harmed by parents and women are most injured by partners. In 1997, over three million reports of child abuse were received by social service agencies (Wang & Daro, 1998); over 1,000 children died as a result of abuse or neglect (United States Department of Health and Human Services [USDHHS], 1998). Based on a survey of a nationally representative sample, nearly one million violent crimes were committed by partners against women (Rennison & Welchans, 2000). Results from the annual National Household Survey on Drug Abuse (NHSDA) indicate that in 1999 report approximately 10.3 million Americans (4.7%) age 12 or older were dependent on either alcohol or illicit drugs (Office of Applied Studies, 2000). It has been estimated that one in four children in the United States are exposed to parental alcohol dependence, alcohol abuse, or both (Grant, 2000), rendering this a prevalent concern. The presence of both substance abuse and aggressive tendencies in the perpetrator may be especially toxic, and the consequences for the child and adult female victims may be especially deleterious.

This chapter examines the extent to which alcohol and drug use, abuse, and dependence coexist with violence among intimates (parent-to-child and adult partner-to-partner). Understanding the true nature of the overlap between substance abuse and relationship violence, however, is an elusive endeavour. Variation in definitions and sampling methods necessitate a piecemeal approach to articulating prevalence, drawing upon epidemiological studies, forensic reports (e.g., child protective services, police reports), and data from self-selected clinical (e.g., addiction services and mental health clients) and community samples. The most general conclusion is that the prevalence of the overlap be-

We acknowledge the support of research funding to both authors from the Canadian Institutes of Health Research and the Social Sciences and Humanities Research Council of Canada, the Alcoholic Beverage Medical Research Foundation (A.-M. Wall), and an Ontario Mental Health Foundation New Investigator Fellowship (C. Wekerle). The authors thank D. Lynn Hawkins and Michelle Bissonnette for their research assistance and Sherry A. McKee, Regina A. Schuller, and David A. Wolf for their helpful comments on an earlier version of this chapter.

tween substance abuse and relationship violence is generally high, and that this is most evident in high-risk samples (i.e., those that are positive on either relationship violence [e.g., maltreating parents] or substance abuse [e.g., addicted partners]). The specific estimate depends on many factors, including definitional criteria (e.g., diagnostic, legal), sampling procedures (e.g., self-referred, court-ordered), data-gathering method (e.g., interview, questionnaire), and information source (e.g., parent, partner, child, professional).

In attempting to integrate findings across diverse studies, a myriad of conceptual and methodological issues arise in assessing the violence and addiction overlap (see Leonard, 1993; Leonard & Jacob, 1988; Roizen, 1993, 1997). Vast differences exist in the degree of specificity with which abuse of substances and intimates is quantified; to date, no study has comprehensively assessed both constructs and their overlap simultaneously. A particular concern is the accuracy of estimates. Underestimation may arise when community surveys have small samples, low participation rate, and underreporting by respondents. Official reports may underestimate when reporting is deemed as of low benefit or as disruptive to families already receiving services. Further underestimation may stem from the absence of policies, training, and procedures for these dual problems within investigatory agencies (Wolock & Magura, 1996). Overall, there are indisputable factors deflating overlap estimates, including potential for legal ramifications (e.g., legal action concerning child custody, procuring and use of illicit drugs), social stigma (e.g., a double standard for female alcoholism), private nature of events (i.e., the secret of family violence; solitary use in chemical dependency), and individuals' tendencies to deny or minimize substance and violence problems.

Conversely, other factors exist that may inflate the overlap between drug and intimate abuse. Official reports are widely thought to capture greater severity and, therein, may yield misleading estimates when considering the general population (Widom, 1993). Official reports reflect both a product (the illegal event) and a process (evaluating the probability of successful prosecution), and are subject to biases from professionals (e.g., selective reporting by ethnicity, gender, socioeconomic status [SES], multiproblem family status), clients (e.g., maltreating parents reporting greater substance abuse in an attempt to present a socially acceptable justification or mitigating circumstance), and agencies (e.g., priority to younger abused children, higher visibility problems). Considering these issues, it has been recommended that selected risk sample studies not be extrapolated to the general population, nor should the general population be considered the most suitable control group (Roizen, 1993, 1997). Both these data sources inform the violence and addiction equation.

With the above concerns as a caveat, this chapter considers literature reviews and recent work with improved methodology. First, the overlap between child abuse and parental substance use and abuse is presented, followed by a discussion of the contribution of child abuse to adult addiction. Next, the role of alcohol and drugs in domestic violence is examined. Finally, conclusions regarding the overlap between substance and intimate abuse and directions for future work are considered.

☐ Child Abuse and Substance-Abusing Parents

Children are vulnerable. Historically, demonstrable child physical injury from parents labeled the "battered-child syndrome," was noted by formal health systems in the 1960s (Kempe, Silverman, Steele, Droegemueller, & Silver, 1962). Subsequently, researchers have highlighted that various forms of child abuse (physical, sexual, emotional abuse, and neglect) overlap substantially with each other (Wekerle & Wolfe, 1996), with exposure to marital violence (Straus & Gelles, 1990), and with pediatric populations such as child accidental injury (Peterson & Brown, 1994) and failure-to-thrive infants (Benoit, 1993). One consistent contextual factor to all these forms of child abuse is parental substance abuse.

The general definition of child abuse involves the "physical or mental injury, sexual abuse or exploitation or maltreatment of a child under the age of eighteen . . . by a person . . . who is responsible for the child's welfare" (The Child Abuse Prevention and Treatment Act, 1984). Physical abuse refers to behaviors such as striking, shaking, or scalding that leave some evidence of physical injury (e.g., bruising, bleeding, burns). Sexual abuse ranges from adult-to-child exposure (of body, pornography, etc.) to more invasive assaults such as fondling, oral sex, and penetration. Neglect represents a range of acts of omission, including failure to provide the child with basic health care, nutrition, education, and protection from danger and injury. Emotional abuse includes such behaviors as verbal and emotional assaults (e.g., rejection, ridicule, isolation), as well as inappropriate confinement (e.g., physical restraint); it is commonly thought to coincide with other forms of abuse (Wekerle & Wolfe, 1996).

Parental substance abuse, alone, is not considered child abuse and, consequently, is not generally a cause in and of itself for mandatory protective services intervention (Wolock & Magura, 1996). Many states have laws requiring the reporting of drug- or alcohol-exposed infants. In some states, prenatal exposure itself constitutes neglect and is grounds for removing children from the custody of their parents (US General Accounting Office, 1997; USDHHS, 1994). Further, many chemically-involved parents remain invisible to child welfare agencies. This may be due to perceived greater overall functioning (e.g., nonsubstance-abusing spouse, employment of substance-abusing parent, "parentified" children, family and friend support) that may dampen immediate risk concerns. As a result of a parent's preoccupation with substances, however, a child's health and safety may be so seriously jeopardized as to capture the attention of child protective services (CPS). Child neglect may be a function of depletion of household budget on drugs and alcohol that would otherwise cover a child's basic needs. Abuse and neglect may be related to a parent's disappearance for hours or days, or a drug-related reduced emotional and physical availability and cognitive capacity (e.g., impaired judgment, reduced behavioral inhibition, reduced monitoring and supervising capacity). Further, exposure to criminal activity (e.g., drug or sex trade to obtain funds, manufacture or distribution of illicit drugs) to dangerous persons and high levels of household traffic increase child risk.

CPS reports are a valuable data source for considering the general question of the overlap between parental substance abuse and child abuse in that specified criteria (for child abuse) are applied. It provides unique information from community surveys and clinic-based studies, given that the majority of referrals are other-report, particularly professional report. For example, in 1996, two thirds of official reports were from professional sources; while 77% of perpetrators were parents, less than 7% were reporters to CPS (USDHHS, 1998). While CPS-based statistics and empirical studies move away from self-report biases such as social desirability, they remain subject to the biases of other-report. For instance, children in families with annual incomes below $15,000/year were 25 times more likely to have been noted by community professionals as being abused, as compared to those in families with annual incomes above $30,000 (USDHHS, 1996). Clearly, poverty overlaps with formal system entry. Nonetheless, it is widely regarded that national rates of reported child abuse are conservative, if not dramatic underestimates, given the data from cross-sectional and retrospective surveys (McCurdy & Daro, 1994). This is thought to be due, in part, to underreporting of professionals to CPS, a necessary reliance on evidenciary criteria to classify cases as "confirmed," and that silence enforced by the perpetrators is more often than not a successful strategy. Also, differing statistics are recorded by agencies, which complicates making any determination concerning the number of child victims versus incidents (McCurdy & Daro, 1994).

In 1990, child abuse was identified by the U.S. Advisory Board on Child Abuse and Neglect as an emergency. In 1996, close to one million children were identified by CPS as abuse and neglect victims in the United States, either substantiated or indicated (i.e., reasonable grounds, but insufficient evidence for prosecution) (USDHHS, 1998). The national rate of maltreatment was 15 victims per 1,000 children in the population. Neglect emerged as the most prevalent form (52% of children), and is the major reason for child removal from parent substance-abusing homes, as these children suffer more injuries and poisonings than those in the general population (Bijur, Kurzon, Overpeck, & Scheidt, 1992). Neglect is predominantly committed by adult females (69%). Victimization decreases with child age (the majority of victims are under age 8) and with similar proportions of male and female children. To a lesser extent than neglect, are physical abuse (23%) and sexual abuse (14%). While similar proportions of males and females are represented in both the perpetrators and victims of physical abuse, males predominantly perpetrate sexual abuse (82%), with females being predominantly victimized (77%). Emotional abuse is a rarer cause for reporting (approximately 6% of cases).

State child welfare records indicate that substance abuse is one of the top two problems in 81% of reported families; among confirmed cases, 40% involve the use of alcohol or other drugs (USDHHS, 1996). Substance abuse by the primary caretaker represented 26% of families on the open child welfare caseloads in 1994; of these, 23% were not offered substance abuse treatment services (Westat, 1997). These overall figures, though, mask variations in different locales; for example, the proportion of previously reported child welfare cases involving substance abuse were 50% in Illinois, 80% in Washington, D.C., and 64% in Boston (Feig, 1990). One study found that children in alcohol-abusing families were approximately four times more likely to be maltreated overall, five times more likely to be physically neglected, and ten times more likely to be emotionally neglected than children in nonalcohol-abusing families (USDHHS, 1993). Although parental substance abuse has been implicated in child abuse-related fatalities, it does not appear to be more prevalent than in nonfatal child abuse cases. Based on data available from 11 states, parental substance abuse was linked to 19% of child abuse fatalities (McCurdy & Daro, 1994).

While parental substance abuse represents a significant proportion of official child abuse reports, there are other issues to be addressed. For instance, it is not clear what percentage of specific types of child abuse is related directly to a substance-abusing parent, as compared to an indirect relationship through exposure to greater vulnerability. The risk to the child likely increases when there is no supporting adult to diffuse parental stress and occupy the parental role abdicated by the substance-abusing single parent. Also, the contribution of maternal and paternal substance abuse to reported child abuse across types remains unclear. For instance, research indicates that mothers who are classified as problem drinkers are more likely to be married to problem drinking fathers, and their children are at highest risk of serious physical injury (head injuries, fractures), as compared to problem drinking single mothers (Bijur et al., 1992). Also, epidemiological research with women randomly selected from the community found that for those women who reported child sexual abuse (i.e., perpetrator five years older than victim and coercive actions ranging from fondling to intercourse), having an alcoholic mother or father was a significant predictor. When child abuse was categorized by perpetrator, extrafamilial child sexual abuse was predicted by having an alcoholic mother, while familial sexual abuse was predicted by having an alcoholic father (Fleming, Mullen, & Bammer, 1997).

Further, substance use and abuse tends to be assessed globally in CPS investigations, without referencing quantity, frequency, and type of substance to the specific child abuse behavior. One report that did consider this issue found that among substance-abusing child welfare families, alcohol was dominant, with a substantial number of parents using marijuana, cocaine, crack, and, to a much lesser extent, heroin. According to caseworker reports, 65% of children with substance-abusing perpetrators were maltreated while the perpetrator was intoxicated (Westat, 1992, as cited in Magura & Laudet, 1996). In addition to acute intoxication, it is important to assess lifetime substance abuse (i.e., chronicity and cumulative problems that may persist even beyond recovery) and withdrawal effects, as all may have a negative impact (e.g., irritability, depression, impaired judgment) on the parent and may facilitate child abuse and neglect.

Moving from CPS statistics to empirical studies, early reviews of the research on alcoholism and child abuse (Hamilton & Collins, 1982; Orme & Rimmer, 1981) noted conflicting results, with no strong evidence to support such an association. These authors pointed to sampling and measurement issues, as well the failure of child abuse groups to exceed general population prevalence rates for alcoholism. Widom (1993) reviewed improved methodological work. Of the seven studies cited, four used control groups (pediatric patients), where abuse was determined from hospital file review or referral status (to court or abuse intervention program). As compared to controls, greater percentages of parents of abused and neglected children (from 18 to 45% of the identified sample) reported alcohol problems. In one study (Kaplan, Pelcovitz, Salzinger, & Ganeles, 1983), 25% of abusive parents, as compared to 5% of parents of pediatric patients, were given a diagnosis of alcoholism, based on a structured interview. Similarly, using a random sample from the courts and formal diagnostic and assessment criteria, 52% of court-referred families ($n = 31$) had at least one parent with a current or past history of alcoholism, as compared to 12% of control families ($n = 24$ pediatric patients) (Famularo, Stone, Barnum, & Wharton, 1986).

Subsequently, other studies more strongly support a link between parental alcohol problems and child maltreatment. For example, one study ($N = 705$) in which sexual abuse was deemed positive by a medical facility receiving state cases under investigation, found documented evidence of alcohol problems (e.g., a driving while intoxicated offense, addiction treatment history) in 75% of cases (Shah, Dail, & Heinrichs, 1995). Recently, Sher, Gershuny, Peterson, and Raskin (1997) found that, among college students, paternal alcoholism was consistently associated with all childhood family stressors (e.g., divorce, job instability, legal difficulties, etc.) and multiple forms of abuse (physical, sexual, emotional, witnessing violence, neglect) assessed; stressors such as experiencing public embarrassment, as well emotional, physical, and sexual abuse were most strongly related to paternal alcoholism. Miller, Smyth, and Mudar (1999) found that maternal past or current alcohol or other drug problems predicted verbal and physical aggression toward their child, as well as their child abuse potential score, even after controlling for maternal age, SES, marital status, and child age. These findings tended to remain when maternal partner violence and maternal history of childhood sexual and physical abuse were considered. Taken together, these studies identify an association between parental alcohol abuse and child abuse, with limited work considering differential effects by perpetrators.

Additional research has addressed the issue of substance use, beyond alcohol. In a study of child welfare cases before the courts on a care and protection petition ($N = 206$), about half of the sample had at least one substance-abusing parent, with alcohol, cocaine, and heroin being the most frequently misused substances for both mothers and fathers (Murphy et al., 1991). Further, substance abuse was noted by a professional for the majority of mothers in this sample (fathers were present in less than half the sample). Specifically, substance abuse was noted for mothers only (41%, $n = 36$), both mothers and fathers (45%, $n = 40$), and for fathers only (14%, $n = 12$). Both drug and alcohol use were more prevalent

(40%) than either drug or alcohol abuse alone. The association of polysubstance abuse and child maltreatment is echoed in other court sample studies. A current diagnosis of alcohol abuse, past diagnoses of alcohol, cocaine, or other drug abuse was found to differentiate maltreating mothers (court and substantiated hospital samples) from their nonmaltreating, sociodemographically-matched controls (Famularo, Kinscherff, & Fenton, 1992b).

Although CPS-based studies are frequently taken to reflect severe child abuse and, hence, more likely to involve substances, in fact, CPS receive a range of referrals. Wolock and Magura (1996) examined recidivism in mild to moderate CPS cases that were closed after investigation (i.e., judged to be a mild, resolved, or isolated event; family receiving services from other community agency). Based on interview data, drug and alcohol abuse by one or both caretakers was the strongest direct predictor of re-reports to protective services; parental drug or alcohol abuse only were also significant predictors. Overall, substance abuse in these court cases of abusive parents was associated with greater recidivism, danger to the child, permanent removal of the child by courts, and noncompliance with treatment.

The issue of an association between type of child abuse and type of substance abuse has been considered only in a limited way. No such association emerged in the Murphy et al. (1991) study, but in another court-based study, parental alcohol abuse was linked to physical abuse, whereas parental cocaine abuse was linked to sexual abuse (Famularo, Kinscherff, & Fenton, 1992a). Maternal and paternal substance abuse was not considered separately in the latter study, however, and substance abuse was gleaned from case records. Epidemiological studies (e.g., Egami, Ford, Greenfield, & Crum, 1996) have found alcohol dependence is related to both abuse and neglect, whereas drug disorders are related to neglect, but not abuse. No conclusions can be drawn at this point; exploring such matching among substance and maltreatment type would seem important.

Taken together, these studies suggest that formal systems may capture the multiproblem family most adeptly, wherein parental substance abuse and child abuse are integral comorbid features. The recent increase in children placed into substitute care for reasons of abuse and neglect has been attributed to the empirical association of parental substance abuse and child maltreatment (Takayam, Wolfe, & Coulter, 1998). While removal of the substance abuse is unlikely to solve the child abuse issue, mandatory substance abuse screening in all cases of serious child maltreatment is regarded as necessary to risk assessment and coordinated intervention efforts (Murphy et al., 1991).

Clinic-based research also has shown an association between parental substance abuse and abusive parenting. Miller, Maguin, and Downs (1997) reviewed the literature from self-referred clinic and community (e.g., college) samples and concluded that parental alcohol problems are related to childhood physical and sexual abuse. While many studies controlled for relevant background variables, used diagnostic criteria for labeling alcohol problems, and included community controls, parental alcohol problems and child abuse are based solely on retrospective reporting by adults self-nominated for study participation. Self-report is limited by the absence of any corroboration (e.g., extensive history-taking, other-report, or direct diagnostic testing). Further, parental illicit drug use was not typically assessed and parental aggression was not paired with any harm or endangerment standard (other than that inherent to the item, i.e., "hit with object"). While the latter clearly identifies harsh disciplinary practices, it may not identify "reportable" abuse per se. Critically, these studies should be considered complementary, but not directly comparable, to CPS-based studies because of dramatic sample differences. For instance, a nonfamilial member was the majority perpetrator of child sexual abuse in these studies, which stands in marked contrast to CPS cases (in many states, perpetrators by definition must be in a child caretaking role and stranger abuse may be diverted to other investigatory agencies like police [USDHHS, 1998]). Consequently, these studies address indirect effects of parental substance abuse (i.e., failure to protect), as subjects could not report on nonfamilial alcohol problems (Miller et al., 1997).

Finally, data from epidemiological studies are consistent with the above research in supporting a consistent and substantial association between child physical abuse and neglect and parental drug and alcohol abuse. A province-wide Ontario community survey ($N = 9,953$) found that respondents who reported a childhood history of physical punishment and physical abuse ("often" kicked/bit/punched; "any" choked/burned/scalded), or sexual abuse (exposure to intercourse), were more likely to report that their parents had a drinking or drug problem (MacMillan, Galimidi, Walsh, & Wong, 1999). Similar findings emerge from U.S. epidemiological work. The National Institute of Mental Health (NIMH) Catchment Area study sampled five sites, using a face-to-face structured diagnostic interview; a total of 11,662 interviewees were identified as caretakers (Kelleher, Chaffin, Hollenberg, & Fischer, 1994). One interview question queried child physical abuse (resulting in bruises, bed days, or medical care) and four queried neglect (e.g., leaving young children unattended for extended periods, inadequate feeding, etc.). A positive response on any item classified the respondent as either abusive, neglecting, or both. Not surprisingly, self-reported rates of child abuse were lower than accepted population estimates: 1.4% ($n = 169$) endorsed physical abuse, 1.8% ($n = 209$) reported neglect, and .1% ($n = 16$) noted both physical abuse and neglect. Adults reporting abusive or neglectful parenting were matched on sociodemographic factors to those not reporting abuse. Significantly more abusive (40%) and neglectful (56%) adults had a lifetime alcohol or drug disorder when compared to controls (16%). Adults with an alcohol or drug disorder were 2.7 times more likely to have reported physically abusing their child and 4.2 times more likely to neglect their child. The contribution of substance abuse disorders to predicting maltreatment remained significant after controlling for adult depressive and antisocial personality disorders, household size, and social support. The finding that self-identified child abusers have increased substance abuse diagnoses are supported by two other community-sampled, retrospective studies (i.e., Dinwiddie & Bucholz, 1993; Egami et al., 1996). The outstanding issue in these studies is the temporal association between parental abuse of substances and children, given the reliance on retrospective lifetime diagnoses.

One study attempted to address this temporal issue. This study involved a survey of 7,103 parents who did not identify physical abuse or neglect of their children at the first wave of data collection (Chaffin, Kelleher, & Hollenberg, 1996). In this second sampling, one year later, .9% of parents "newly" endorsed the physical abuse item, while 1.2% endorsed at least one of the neglect items (only a few parents endorsed both abuse and neglect). Parents classified as having a substance abuse disorder in the first wave endorsed significantly more child abuse items in the second wave, as compared to parents not similarly diagnosed. Substance abuse remained a significant predictor when controlling for sociodemographic variables. While these data may reflect onset of child abuse, they may also reflect onset of reporting. Given the issues with self-reported child abuse and limited assessment of child abuse, however, it is unclear what unique sample features may be operative.

At present, it seems that whether one considers studies based on official abuse reports, clinic-based studies, or epidemiological work, thorough assessment of *both* child abuse and parental substance abuse (including both alcohol and illicit drugs) and the use of multimethod assessment are lacking. Considering (and in spite of) this limitation, a consistent, substantial association between parental alcohol, polysubstance abuse, and child abuse emerges across these diverse samples. As causality cannot be inferred from this data, prospective studies are required. One prospective study did follow a birth cohort of more than 1,000 children; however, childhood sexual abuse reports (before age 16) were queried retrospectively at age 18 (Fergusson, Lynskey, & Horwood, 1996). Parental response to questions about illegal drug use ("marijuana and other drugs") and history of "alcoholism" or "problems with alcohol" were obtained when the child was age 11 (drug use) and 15 (alcohol use). Sexual abuse was reported by 17% of female and 3% of male adolescents, with parental alcoholism or alcohol problems emerging as a significant predictor. Ideally, though, a prospective study needs to examine parental substance abuse and child abuse, in tandem, over time.

Ongoing clinical and research work that considers substance-abusing parents as an at-risk population for child abuse is clearly warranted. One conceptual question, though, is whether to consider parental substance problems an integral part of a parent-child relationship disorder. Child abuse, as a relational psychopathology, suggests a poor fit between the child, parent, and environment (Cicchetti & Olson, 1990). Parental substance abuse may play a dynamic role in a violent parent-child relationship, wherein single incidents of child abuse underlie a patterned victim-victimizer interactional style, characterized by parental power abuse (Wekerle & Wolfe, 1998). Whether (or when) parental substance abuse is causal, comorbid, or a dynamic feature with respect to child abuse remains an empirical question.

☐ Child Abuse as a Predictor of Adult Substance Abuse

The long-term deleterious impact of childhood maltreatment on psychological adjustment is well documented (Miller-Perrin & Perrin, 1999; Wekerle & Wolfe, 1996). While childhood maltreatment has been identified as a risk factor for substance abuse in adolescence (Dembo, Dertke, laVoie, Borders, Washburn, & Schmeidler, 1987; Fergusson, Horwood, & Lynskey, 1996), this research has tended to concentrate on sexual abuse. For example, using self-report measures with a large sample of high school students in grades 7 through 12 ($N = 36,000$), females endorsing a sexual abuse item were more likely to report weekly use of alcohol and marijuana than randomly selected females who did not endorse the sexual abuse item (Chandy, Blum, & Resnick, 1996a). When comparing sexually abused males with females, males reported greater substance use before and during school, greater weekly alcohol and marijuana use, and more binge-drinking episodes (5 or more drinks/occasion) than females (Chandy, Blum, & Resnick, 1996b). Similar results on the greater deleterious effects of sexual abuse on male versus female youth, with respect to alcohol and drug use, was found in a Netherlands school study (Garnefski & Arends, 1998). Further, being physically abused, in addition to experiencing sexual abuse, increased the likelihood of binge drinking (Luster & Small, 1997) and the use of multiple substances (Chandy et al., 1996b) in large statewide school surveys.

The literature on adult survivors shows an elevated risk for substance abuse or dependence, as compared to nonvictims (for reviews, see Langeland & Hartgers, 1998; Miller et al., 1997; Polusny & Follette, 1995; Stewart, 1996). Several issues cloud this general conclusion, though, including varying definitions of childhood (e.g., ages of victimization range from under age 12 to, typically, under age 18), victimization (a label of "abused" versus specific behavioral definitions; combining types of abuse), uneven attention to maternal and paternal perpetration, and lack of prospective work and research on male survivors. With respect to childhood physical abuse (CPA) and adult alcohol use disorders, Miller et al. (1997) suggest that a complex relationship may exist, at least among women. For instance, Downs, Miller, and Gondoli (1987) found that alcoholic women, in comparison to a nonclinical community sample, reported experiencing significantly greater levels of paternal verbal aggression, as well as paternal moderate and severe violence; no differences in the degree of maternal abuse experienced across groups were observed. Although Miller, Downs, and Testa (1993) found that alcoholic women also reported higher levels of maternal abuse (verbal aggression, moderate and severe abuse), differences were not apparent when demographic variables and parental alcoholism were statistically controlled. Unfortunately, many studies have not considered the gender of the perpetrator in analyses and have combined child physical abuse with other forms of victimization.

Based on female patients seen in primary care practices, McCauley et al. (1997) found that women with a history of victimization (physical or sexual abuse queried prior to age 18) were more likely to currently (or ever) use street drugs and have a past drinking problem than never victimized women. As part of a national survey, Duncan, Saunders, Kilpatrick, Hanson, and Resnick (1996) found that women who reported physical assaults prior to age 18 (boyfriends were perpetrators 12.5% of the time; fathers/stepfathers 38.5% of the time) were more likely to have begun drinking earlier, to have more intoxicated days in the previous year, to be current users of marijuana and cocaine, and to have experienced more alcohol and drug-related problems (e.g., driving while intoxicated) as compared to nonvictims. These findings are echoed in a national survey of male and female adolescents (ages 12–17), where victimized adolescents with alcohol abuse or dependence tended to show an earlier age of onset for nonexperimental alcohol use, and significantly earlier use of marijuana as compared to nonvictimized dependent adolescents (Kilpatrick et al., 2000). These results held when considering different types of victimization (physical abuse, sexual abuse, witnessing violence). Further, the average age of victimization for sexual or physical assault was substantially earlier (11.6 years), as compared to the average ages of substance use (13.1–14.4 years), suggesting indirect evidence that child abuse preceded substance abuse and dependence. However, prospective work based on court-substantiated CPA cases (prior to age 12) failed to find any relationship to adulthood alcohol problems when compared to matched controls (Widom, Ireland, & Glynn, 1995).

In an attempt to consider the prospective versus retrospective reporting issues, Widom, Weiler, and Cottler (1999) compared their sample of official court-substantiated abuse cases (dominantly neglect was reported) and demographically matched nonvictims for self-reported victimization (in contrast, dominantly physical abuse was reported) obtained in young adulthood. As well, drug abuse and dependence diagnostic interviewing was conducted in adulthood. While significant associations were found among official CPA and neglect and current drug diagnosis, as well as cocaine abuse and dependence diagnosis (for women only), these disappeared with Bonferroni corrections. So, at best, trends were noted with the prospective data. In contrast, self-reported victimization showed a robust pattern of association between all forms of victimization (physical, sexual abuse, and neglect) and lifetime and current drug abuse and dependence diagnoses. Further, individuals who had no self-report (both official report and no official report groups) had similar rates of current drug abuse. Since child abuse was age limited to before age 12, it is possible that some subjects had official reporting at a young age (e.g., infancy), of a less viscerally dramatic nature (e.g., neglect) and, therefore, may be less likely to self-report. Individuals with both official and self-reports of childhood victimization had the highest rates of current drug abuse diagnoses, as compared to the no self-report/no official report group. Thus, while CPA prospective studies remain few in number to reach a consensus, cross-sectional and self-report data clearly support an association between CPA and substance abuse problems.

In their review of the literature on childhood sexual abuse (CSA) and adult addiction, Polunsy and Follette (1995) note that, within psychiatric samples, investigators have consistently found that alcohol and drug problems are higher among survivors of childhood sexual abuse (27–37% for alcohol; 21–57% for drugs), in comparison to nonvictims (4–20% for alcohol; 2–27% for drugs). Within addiction samples, the percentage of self-identified CSA survivors is significantly higher than that observed in the general population, with estimates ranging from 49–75% for women (Rohsenow, Corbett, & Devine, 1988; Windle, Windle, Scheidt, & Miller, 1995) and 12% for men (Windle et al., 1995). Windle et al.'s (1995) study of inpatient alcoholics, which included males and females and examined both childhood sexual and physical abuse, revealed gender differences with respect to the *specific* type of child abuse. Consistent with the child abuse literature, these investigators found that physical abuse did not differ among male and female alcoholics, but that the ratio of childhood sexual abuse and dual abuse (physical and sexual) for females and males was 4:1.

Although the relationship between CSA and adult substance abuse may be overestimated in clinical samples, similar results have emerged from large national surveys of women. After controlling for age, ethnicity, and parental education, Wilsnack, Vogeltanz, Klassen, and Harris (1997) found that women with a history of childhood (before age 18) sexual abuse, in comparison to nonvictims, were significantly more likely to report recent alcohol use, intoxication, alcohol-related problems, and alcohol dependence symptoms in the past year, as well as lifetime use of prescription and illicit drugs. In a community survey in New Zealand, CSA (before age 16) was related to heavy drinking (14 or more drinks/week), with women experiencing CSA involving intercourse showing higher rates of excessive alcohol use than nonvictim controls (Mullen, Martin, Anderson, Romans, & Herbison, 1993, 1996). Taken together, there is clear support for the overlap between child sexual abuse and adult, female addiction. As noted by Miller et al. (1997), the few studies that have examined this link in men have yielded equivocal findings.

Surprisingly, given the overlap between alcohol and partner aggression, few studies have examined the long-term impact of witnessing violence in one's family of origin on adult substance use patterns. Based on national surveys, estimates of children exposed to marital violence has been advanced as at least 3.3 million annually (Carlson, 1984). It remains an empirical question whether alcohol and drug use (i.e., either habitual patterns or acute intoxication at the time of parental violence) influences the frequency or severity (or both) of domestic violence witnessed by children. Moreover, relatively little is known about the relationship between witnessing parental violence and adult alcohol and drug problems. Two recent studies (Fergusson & Horwood, 1998; Sher et al., 1997) suggest that exposure to violence in one's family of origin significantly elevates the risk for alcohol-related problems in adulthood. Specifically, Sher et al. (1997) found that exposure to parental verbal and physical abuse directed at spouses or siblings or both were associated with a lifetime alcohol use disorder among college students. Witnessing such verbal and physical abuse, however, only partially mediated the relationship between family history of alcoholism and adult alcohol use disorders, thus suggesting the mediational influence of nonenvironmental factors (e.g., personality, alcohol sensitivity). As part of a longitudinal study, Fergusson and Horwood (1998) examined the relationship between 18 year olds' retrospective accounts of exposure to interparental violence and psychological maladjustment, including substance abuse and dependence, they experienced between the ages 16–18. In this investigation, father- and mother-perpetrated spousal violence, although significantly correlated, were examined separately. Increased reports of interparental violence (both mother and father initiated) were associated with alcohol and other drug (e.g., nicotine, cannabis) abuse and dependence; alcohol and drug dependence was 2–7 times higher among participants reporting high exposure to interparental violence, in comparison to individuals who did not witness such abuse. After controlling for socioeconomic status, family functioning, and other types of child abuse (i.e., sexual abuse, use of physical punishment), maternal (but not paternal) perpetrated parental aggression was, however, only associated with alcohol abuse and dependence. This finding was observed for both males and females.

Overall, research examining the overlap between childhood victimization and adult substance abuse problems is still developing, especially in regard to male survivors. Converging evidence has emerged from these diverse studies in support of an overlap between childhood physical abuse, sexual abuse, and to a much more limited extent, witnessing parental violence and adult alcohol and drug problems. However, several issues remain. Most of the work in this area has failed to consider that male and female children suffer multiple forms of abuse, especially in studying prevalent forms of abuse (i.e., witnessing abuse of others and neglect). To date, researchers have not carried out fine grain analyses concerning the potential impact of victim (e.g., gender, attributions concerning the meaning of abuse), abuse (e.g., age of onset, duration, type, severity), and perpetrator (e.g., extra versus intrafamilial, multiple abusers, mother versus father) characteristics on the development of adult addiction (Miller et al., 1997). Finally, follow-up studies of offspring of chemically-involved, child-abusing parents are needed to better understand the unique and combined contributions of these distal risk factors to adult addiction.

☐ Substance Use and Abuse and Domestic Violence

Violence by adult intimate partners can be defined as aggressive or controlling behavior that ranges from mild to severe, spanning physical, sexual, and emotional abuse. Acknowledging that domestic violence can include husband-to-wife and wife-to-husband aggression, it is generally accepted that women are the targets of spousal violence (but see Malone, Tyree, & O'Leary, 1989; O'Leary, Barling, Arias, Rosenbaum, Malone, & Tryee, 1989), particularly of a severe, physically injurious nature (Stets & Straus, 1990). This has led to the recent distinction between reciprocal, "common" couple violence and the male-to-female form likely dominating battered women's shelter populations, labeled "patriarchal terrorism" (Johnson, 1995). Unlike child abuse, acts of spousal violence are not generally subject to mandatory reporting procedures (Gelles, 1997). Thus, estimates concerning the overlap between partner aggression and substance use and abuse are typically obtained from studies that rely on self-report. Despite methodological concerns, it is generally agreed that drugs, particularly alcohol, are associated with domestic violence.

Results from the National Crime Victimization Study (NCVS), a large annual household survey of criminal victimization of individuals aged 12 and over, estimate that, in 1998, approximately 1 million violent crimes were committed by intimate partners, with 85% of these being perpetrated against women (Rennison & Welchans, 2000). Women were 5 times more likely than men to experience victimization from partners. Approximately half of female victims of intimate violence reported sustaining an injury, and 40% sought professional medical treatment. Restricting definitions of "violence" to physical and sexual assault, as defined by the Criminal Code of Canada, the 1993 National Survey on Violence Against Women (VAW) found 29% of women (aged 18 or older) had been assaulted at some point during adult relationships. Three percent reported an assault in the past year, with the distribution of violent acts varying as a function of the number of years married and age. Assault rates in the past year were highest among couples married two years or less (8%) and those in the 18–24 age range (12% and 13% for female victims and male perpetrators, respectively). This study underscored wife assault as patterned behavior, with two thirds of cases involving repeat assaults (Rodgers, 1994).

While these studies show severe husband-to-wife assaults occurring at a high rate in North American families, Gelles (1997) notes that restricting definitions of "domestic violence" to legal parameters may underestimate the number of aggressive acts women experience across a continuum of severity. Accordingly, large-scale studies examining specific behavioral acts yield higher prevalence rates of husband-to-wife aggression. Specifically, lifetime prevalence rates for husband-to-wife physical abuse range from 11–46% (National Family Violence Study [NFVS], 1985; Straus & Gelles, 1990; VAW, Rodgers, 1994) with milder forms of violence (e.g., pushed, grabbed, shoved) being most common. As compared with physical aggression, greater emotional abuse (33–74%; VAW, Rodgers, 1994; Straus & Sweet, 1992) and less sexual abuse (5–17%; Gelles, 1997; VAW, Rodgers, 1994) is noted. Types of intimate violence overlap, with most physical assaults coinciding with emotional abuse (VAW, Rodgers, 1994) and sexual assault (Browne, 1987; see Schuller & Hastings, 1997). Husband-to-wife aggression tends to occur repeatedly (Gelles, 1997; VAW, Rodgers, 1994), and is most prevalent among younger, newly-married couples (Cazenave & Straus, 1990; Leonard, this volume; McLaughlin, Leonard, & Senchak, 1992; O'Leary et al., 1989; VAW, Rodgers, 1994).

Habitual Substance Use and Husband-to-Wife Physical Abuse

Research over the past 20 years has confirmed that substance use and abuse is a significant correlate of domestic physical violence. To date, the majority of studies, that have been cross-sectional in nature, have focused on husbands' habitual use of alcohol. Previous reviews show a substantial overlap, particularly within subgroups in which domestic violence or substance abuse and dependence has been identified (Hotaling & Sugarman, 1986; Lee & Weinstein, 1997; Leonard, 1993; Leonard & Jacob, 1988; Murphy & O'Farrell, 1996; Tolman & Bennett, 1990). For example, 20–93% of battered women consider their partners to be problem drinkers or alcoholics (Leonard, 1993; Leonard & Jacob, 1988; Tolman & Bennett, 1990). Among male alcoholics presenting for behavioral marital therapy, husband-to-wife violence described approximately two thirds of these men's current relationships (O'Farrell, Van Hutton, & Murphy, 1999). O'Farrell and Murphy (1995) found that significantly more wives of alcoholics, in comparison to a matched, community sample, experienced husband-perpetrated violence, particularly of a severe nature; wife-to-husband violence also was more prevalent among wives of alcoholics. Problematic drinking by husbands predicts intimate, male-to-female physical aggression in community samples, even after controlling for confounding variables (e.g., see Leonard & Blane, 1992; Leonard, Bromet, Parkinson, Day, & Ryan, 1985; Leonard & Senchak, 1993). There is some evidence, however, that the relationship between husbands' heavy use of alcohol and the perpetration of physical violence against wives is moderated by individual difference (e.g., hostility and tolerance for intoxicated aggressive behavior) and relationship (e.g., marital satisfaction) variables (Leonard & Senchak, 1993). Finally, examining the overlap between victims' dependence on alcohol and domestic violence, investigators have found that alcoholic women, in comparison to a community sample, experience higher levels of partner violence, after controlling for demographic variables and intimate involvement with a problem drinker (e.g., see Downs, Miller, & Panek, 1993; Miller, Downs, & Gondoli, 1989). Overall, results of cross-sectional studies suggest a consistent relationship exists between husband-to-wife physical abuse and habitual, problematic alcohol consumption patterns.

Longitudinal investigations carried out in this area have yielded strong support for the causal role of husbands' heavy use of alcohol in the perpetration of male-to-female partner violence during the early years of marriage. Specifically, Leonard and Senchak (1996) found that, after controlling for demographic variables and premarital aggression, husbands' heavy use of alcohol strongly and prospectively predicted husband-to-wife physical violence during the first year of marriage. While Heyman, Jouriles, and O'Leary (1995) reported similar findings for the first year of marriage from their longitudinal investigation, the relationship between husbands' use of alcohol and the perpetration of wife physical abuse, as assessed at 18 months postmarriage, was moderated by husbands' aggressive personality style; neither husbands' use of alcohol, aggressive personality style, nor their interaction prospectively predicted husband-to-wife violence assessed at 30 months. Heyman et al. (1995), however, did not assess the contribution of wive's use of alcohol to their victimization experiences, which may account for the apparent lack of relationship observed between husbands' use of alcohol and the perpetration of male-to-female physical abuse beyond the first two years of marriage.

While most of the work in this area has focused on male partners' use of alcohol, some investigators have examined the unique and relative contribution of each member of the dyad's general alcohol and, to a lesser extent, drug use patterns to the perpetration of male-to-female partnership violence. There is some evidence that victims' general use of alcohol and drugs elevates their risk for intimate violence, particularly of a severe nature. Analysis of data collected from the 1985 NFVS study, for example, found that women who were severely physically abused (e.g., hit, assaulted with weapon) by their husbands were, in comparison to nonvictims, six times more likely to have reported being "high on marijuana or other drugs" at least once in the previous year. A comparable six-fold increase also was observed among victims of severe violence who reported that their husbands engaged in similar drug use. Also, victims' reports of being "drunk" on more than one occasion in the previous year constituted a three-fold increase in their likelihood of experiencing severe physical violence, whereas a two-fold increase was noted when considering victims' reports of husband drunkenness. Similar results were obtained in the 1992 parallel study, The National Alcohol and Family Violence Survey (NAFVS), which employed more precise measures of alcohol and drug use (Kaufman Kantor & Asdigian, 1997). In this study, the highest rates of victimization were observed among heavy drinking women who also used marijuana and among women whose husbands used alcohol and "hard drugs" (i.e., nonprescription amphetamines, barbiturates, tranquillizers, cocaine, and heroin) in the previous year. This finding echoes the child abuse work in highlighting polysubstance use as a possible domain of high risk for the perpetration of aggression within families.

The relative contribution of husband and wife drug and alcohol use to women's victimization experiences of partnership violence appears to vary as a function of abuse severity. Specifically, the 1985 NFVS study found that husbands' use of "marijuana or other drugs" and both partners' being drunk in the previous year predicted mild occurrences of violence, whereas severe violence was predicted solely by the husband's use of "marijuana or other drugs" (Kaufman Kantor & Straus, 1989). In the 1992 NAFVS study, husbands' use of illicit drugs and problematic use of alcohol, as well as wives' use of marijuana predicted incidents of mild husband-to-wife physical abuse. Comparable analyses concerning predictors of severe violence were not reported (Kaufman Kantor & Asdigian, 1997). Importantly, while the use of alcohol and illicit drugs by each partner appeared to significantly elevate women's risk of victimization, it is important to note that most women and many aggressors did not report any heavy drinking (54% and 30% for women and men, respectively) or drug use (76% and 69% for women and men, respectively) in the previous year (Kaufman Kantor & Straus, 1989).

Research conducted by Leonard and colleagues suggest that husbands', but not wives', heavy use of alcohol is a significant predictor of male-to-female physical violence. Over the course of marriages however, the dyadic interplay between both partners' drinking patterns may play a more critical role. Specifically, after controlling for demographic and individual difference variables, Leonard and Senchak (1993) found that, among engaged couples, excessive alcohol use by men and women was associated with male-to-female physical aggression prior to marriage. Victims' alcohol use, however, failed to remain a significant predictor once the aggressor's use was statistically controlled. Following these couples, Leonard and Senchak (1996) similarly found, once again controlling for demographic variables, as well as premarital aggression, that husbands', but not wives', premarital drinking was a direct predictor of husband perpetrated marital aggression during the first year of marriage. Most recently, Quigley and Leonard (2000) examined whether husbands' and wives' heavy drinking during their first year of marriage prospectively predicted husband-to-wife physical aggression during the second and third years of marriage. After statistically controlling for demographic and individual difference variables, as well as premarital aggression, husbands' heavy use of alcohol did not emerge as a significant predictor of male perpetrated physical violence during the second or third years of marriage. Interestingly, however, husbands' heavy drinking patterns were predictive of violence in years two and three of marriage when considered in concert with wives' drinking behavior during the first year. Specifically, these investigators reported that husband alcohol consumption was not predictive of marital violence in the second and third years when the wife was a heavy drinker. Husbands' use of alcohol was, however, prospectively predictive of violence in years two and three when wives were light drinkers. These authors concluded that "The fact that premarital husband alcohol use had a strong main effect in predicting first year marital violence, but that husband and wife first year alcohol use interact to predict violence in the second and third years of marriage, suggests that the mechanisms by which early husband alcohol use is related to violence may change over time" (Leonard & Senchak, 1996, p. 1007).

Acute Alcohol and Drug Intoxication and Episodes of Husband-to-Wife Physical Abuse

Research attempting to examine the contribution of acute intoxication to episodes of violence has found that alcohol, as opposed to other drugs, is most commonly associated with intoxicated aggression (Kaufman Kantor & Asdigian, 1997; VAW, Rodgers, 1994). This is likely due to the fact that alcohol use is ubiquitous in society. Results from the National Crime Victimization Study (NCVS) collected between 1992 and 1995 indicate that, on average, two thirds of victims who suffered intimate violence reported that alcohol had been a factor. Among victims of spousal abuse, three quarters of offenders were perceived by victims to have been drinking at the time of the offense. In contrast, in instances of stranger aggression where the victim was able to discern whether the perpetrator had been drinking at the time of the offence, 31% reported that the aggressor had been drinking (Greenfeld, 1998). Similar estimates, derived from retrospective accounts, have been found in other national surveys (Kaufman Kantor & Asdigian, 1997; Rodgers, 1994).

It appears that the perpetrator's, as opposed to the victim's, use of alcohol is more proximally associated with physical abuse, particularly of a more severe nature. In general, it is uncommon for female victims of domestic violence to be solely intoxicated at the time of the assault, with solitary male or mutual consumption being more frequently reported (Kaufman Kantor & Asdigian, 1997; Leonard & Quigley, 1999). Alcohol intoxication on the part of the perpetrator is positively associated with the victim's risk of sustaining injuries as a result of intimate violence (Martin & Bachman, 1997; Rodgers, 1994, but see Pernanen, 1991). Using both between- and within-group strategies, Leonard and Quigley (1999) examined the relative contribution of husband and wife acute alcohol intoxication to specific types of marital abuse. For the between-group comparison, these investigators examined the presence of husband and wife intoxication (as reported by both partners) among couples whose most serious marital conflict during their first year of marriage involved either a verbal argument, mild physical abuse (e.g., slapped, pushed, grabbed, shoved), or severe physical abuse (e.g., kicked, hit with a fist, beat up). Couples reporting both verbal and physical altercations were included in the within-group comparison; across the most serious verbal and physical episodes that participants experienced, both members of the couple reported on both husband and wife intoxication. After controlling for individual differences (e.g., sociodemographic, personality attributes, and general drinking patterns) and episode context information (e.g., presence of others, location where the aggressive event occurred), these investigators found, both in the between- and within-group analyses, that husband drinking was more likely to occur in physical versus verbal episodes of aggression; overall, wife intoxication was generally unrelated to the severity of marital violence experienced. Leonard and Quigley (1999) cautioned, however, that while their findings suggest an association between acute intoxication by husbands and the severity of abuse perpetrated against wives, over 50% of severe episodes and at least 73% (according to wives' reports) of moderate episodes did not involve husband drinking, thus leading them to conclude that drinking is neither a necessary nor sufficient cause of marital violence.

To summarize, the association between habitual substance use patterns, especially with alcohol, and husband-to-wife physical abuse is well substantiated. Polysubstance users may be a particularly high-risk group for both offending and being victimized. Of the limited longitudinal work that has been conducted, husbands' heavy use of alcohol appears to be an important prospective predictor of physical domestic violence. Additional longitudinal research with samples other than young, newly-married couples is needed to further clarify the temporal sequencing of substance use and adult partnership violence. While the bulk of this research has focused on only one member of the dyad, it would appear that, in the first year of marriage, it is the perpetrator's use of alcohol that is critical; over time, however, its influence is moderated by the victim's level of consumption. Acute alcohol intoxication, as opposed to illicit drug use, is a common situational variable in specific incidents of husband-to-wife aggression. Furthermore, husbands', but not wives', acute intoxication appears to contribute to the perpetration of male-to-female aggression, particularly of a more severe nature. Additional research is needed to clarify whether alcohol-related spousal violence represents a deviation from habitual consumption patterns observed within families (for a more complete discussion, see Leonard, 1999). Clearly, however, the absence of alcohol (or other drugs) in many episodes of domestic physical violence confirms that intoxication is neither necessary nor sufficient for wife assault to ensue (Gelles, 1993, 1997; Lee & Weinstein, 1997; Leonard & Quigley, 1999). Finally, very little is known about the overlap between partners' substance use and wife-to-husband violence or other forms of spousal abuse (namely, emotional and sexual) that are commonly experienced by many adults.

☐ Conclusion

The overlap between intimate violence and addiction is real. Both child and woman abuse are consistently and substantially related to substance use and abuse, with alcohol more commonly examined than illicit drugs. Given the complexity of parameters inherent in determining the overlap between addiction and intimate violence, an accurate estimate of the *degree* of overlap remains elusive. Considering the many factors that influence the overlap, in both a positive and negative direction, the current state of the literature warrants a conservative approach. Adopting this strategy, it is clear that, whether one considers formal child welfare cases or community, self-identified abusers, at least 40% of parents suffer from alcohol or drug problems. With respect to woman abuse, 20% or more of partner perpetrators exhibit problematic drinking patterns and are intoxicated at the time of the assault. Although a more recent focus, female victims of childhood abuse and domestic violence appear to be over represented in addiction samples. Among high-risk groups, the overlap describes the majority (child abuse [Shah et al., 1995], battered women [Brookoff et al., 1997], female survivors of sexual assault in addiction treatment [Rohsenow et al., 1988]).

Ultimately, greater specificity in estimation is contingent upon future work utilizing more complete and multiple measurement domains. To date, no single study has comprehensively assessed substance abuse in tandem with child or partner abuse. For example, studies have yet to capture the context across the range of problem behaviors (e.g., pairing a harm/endangerment standard across intimate abuse types). The vast majority of studies have focused on alcohol, despite more recent indications of the importance of polysubstance abuse to intimate violence (child abuse [Murphy et al., 1991], woman abuse [Kaufman Kantor & Asdigian, 1997]). Other issues clouding global estimates include (1) failure to incorporate gender in perpetration and substance use and abuse; in perpetration and victimization of domestic violence and dyadic substance use and abuse; and in childhood maltreatment as a risk factor for addiction; (2) the lack of attention to temporal sequencing of substance-related intimate abuse (within specific episodes and patterning over time); (3) reliance on individual self-report of substance-related, relationship violence that, by definition, is dyadic in nature; and (4) the need for multifactorial designs to rule out third variable explanations.

In recognition of the overlap between addiction and intimate violence, there is a clear imperative to elucidate underlying, theoretical mechanisms, to consider distinct populations across the lifespan, and to address prevention and treatment needs. In the first section of this volume, major theoretical frameworks spanning developmental to biological processes are presented. Subsequently, this issue of overlap is explored within specific populations in the second section. Finally, prevention and treatment issues for this dual problem are considered in the last section of this volume. Emerging themes across this volume and directions for further work are presented in the concluding chapter.

☐ References

Benoit, D. (1993). Failure to thrive and feeding disorders. In C. H. Zeanah, Jr. (Ed.), *Handbook of infant mental health* (pp. 317–331). New York: Guilford.

Bijur, P. E., Kurzon, M., Overpeck, M. D., & Scheidt, P. C. (1992). Parental alcohol use, problem drinking, and children's injuries. *Journal of the American Medical Association, 267*, 3166–3171.

Brookoff, D., O'Brien, K., Cook, C. C., Thompson, T. D., and Williams, C. (1997). Characteristics of participants in domestic violence. *Journal of the American Medical Association, 277*, 1369–1393.

Browne, A. (1987). *When battered women kill.* New York: Free Press.

Carlson, B. E. (1984). Children's observations of interparental violence. In A. R. Roberts (Ed.), *Battered women and their families* (pp. 147–167). New York: Springer.

Cazenave, N., & Straus, M. (1990). Race, class, network embeddedness, and family violence: A search for potent support systemts. In M. A. Straus & R. J. Gelles (Eds.), *Physical violence in American families: Risk factors and adaptions to violence in 8,145 families* (pp. 321– 339). New Brunswick, NJ: Transaction.

Chaffin, M., Kelleher, K., & Hollenberg, J. (1996). Onset of physical abuse and neglect: Psychiatric, substance abuse, and social risk factors from prospective community data. *Child Abuse and Neglect, 20,* 191–203.

Chandy, J. M., Blum, R. W., & Resnick, M. D. (1996a). Female adolescents with a history of sexual abuse. *Journal of Interpersonal Violence, 11,* 503–518.

Chandy, J. M., Blum, R. W., & Resnick, M. D. (1996b). Gender-specific outcomes for sexually abused adolescents. *Child Abuse and Neglect, 20,* 1219–1231.

Cicchetti, D., & Olson, K. (1990). The developmental psychopathology of child maltreatment. In M. Lewis & S. M. Miller (Eds.), *Handbook of developmental psychopathology* (pp. 261–279). New York: Plenum.

Dembo, R. Dertke, M., la Voie, L., Borders, S., Washburn, M., & Schmeider, J. (1987). Physical abuse, sexual victimization and illicit drug use: A structural analysis among high risk adolescents. *Journal-of-Adolescence, 10,* 13–34.

Dinwiddie, S. H., & Bucholz, K. K. (1993). Psychiatric diagnoses of self-reported child abusers. *Child Abuse & Neglect, 17,* 465–476.

Downs, W. R., Miller, B. A., & Gondoli, D. M. (1987). Childhood experiences of parental physical violence for alcoholic women as compared with a randomly selected household sample of women. *Violence and Victims, 2,* 225–240.

Downs, W. R., Miller, B. A., & Panek, D. D. (1993). Differential patterns of partner-to-woman violence: A comparison of samples of community, alcohol-abusing and battered women. *Journal of Family Violence, 8,* 113–135.

Duncan, R. D., Saunders, B. E., Kilpatrick, D. G., Hanson, R. F., & Resnick, H. S. (1996). Childhood physical assault as a risk factor for PTSD, depression, and substance abuse: Findings from a national survey. *American Journal of Orthopsychiatry, 66,* 437–448.

Egami, Y., Ford, D. E., Greenfield, S. F., & Crum, R. M. (1996). Psychiatric profile and sociodemographic characteristics of adults who report physically abusing or neglecting children. *American Journal of Psychiatry, 153,* 921–928.

Famularo, R., Kinscherff, R., & Fenton, T. (1992a). Parental substance abuse and the nature of child maltreatment. *Child Abuse & Neglect, 16,* 475–483.

Famularo, R., Kinscherff, R., & Fenton, T. (1992b). Psychiatric diagnoses of abusive mothers: A preliminary report. *Journal of Nervous and Mental Disease, 180,* 658–661.

Famularo, R., Stone, K., Barnum, R., & Wharton, R. (1986). Alcoholism and severe child maltreatment. *American Journal of Orthopsychiatry, 56,* 481–485.

Feig, L. (1990). *Drug exposed infants and children: Service needs and policy questions.* Washington, DC: United States Department of Health and Human Services.

Fergusson, D. M., & Horwood, L. J. (1998). Exposure to interparental violence in childhood and psychological adjustment in young adulthood. *Child Abuse and Neglect, 22,* 339–357.

Fergusson, D. M., Horwood, L. J., & Lynskey, M. T. (1996). Childhood sexual abuse and psychiatric disorder in young adulthood: II. Psychiatric outcomes of childhood sexual abuse. *Journal of the American Academy of Child and Adolescent Psychiatry, 34,* 1365–1374.

Fergusson, D. M., Lynskey, M. T., & Horwood, L. J. (1996). Childhood sexual abuse and psychiatric disorder in young adulthood: I. Prevalence of sexual abuse and factors associated with sexual abuse. *Journal of the American Academy of Child and Adolescent Psychiatry, 34,* 1355–1364.

Fleming, J., Mullen, P., & Bammer, G. (1997). A study of potential risk factors for sexual abuse in childhood. *Child Abuse & Neglect, 21,* 49–58.

Garnefski, N., & Arends, E. (1998). Sexual abuse and adolescent maladjustment: Differences between male and female victims. *Journal of Adolescence, 21,* 99–107.

Gelles, R. J. (1993). Alcohol and other drugs are associated with violence—they are not its cause. In R. J. Gelles & D. R. Loseke (Eds.), *Current controversies on family violence* (pp. 182–196). New York: Sage.

Gelles, R. J. (1997). *Intimate violence in families* (3rd ed.). Thousand Oaks, CA: Sage.

Grant, B. F. (2000). Estimates of US children exposed to alcohol abuse and dependence in the family. *American Journal of Public Health, 90,* 112–115.

Greenfeld, L. A. (1998). *Alcohol and crime: An analysis of national data on the prevalence of alcohol involvement in crime.* Washington, DC: U.S. Deparment of Justice, Bureau of Justice Statistics.

Hamilton, C. J., & Collins, J. J. (1982). The role of alcohol in wife beating and child abuse: A review of the literature. In J. J. Collins (Ed.), *Drinking and crime: Perspectives on the relationship between alcohol consumption of parents and criminal behavior* (pp. 253–287). London: Guilford.

Heyman, R. E., Jouriles, E. N., & O'Leary, K. D. (1995). Alcohol and aggressive personality styles: Potentiators of serious physical aggression against wives? *Journal of Family Psychology, 9,* 44–57.

Hotaling, G. T., & Sugarman, D. B. (1986). An analysis of risk markers in husband to wife violence. The current state of knowledge. *Violence and Victims, 1,* 101–124.

Johnson, M. P. (1995). Patriarchal terrorism and common couple violence: Two forms of violence against women. *Journal of Marriage and the Family, 57,* 283–294.

Kaplan, S. J., Pelcovitz, D., Salzinger, S., & Ganelles, D. (1983). Psychopathology of parents of abused and neglected children and adolescents. *Journal of the American Academy of Child Psychiatry, 22,* 238–244.

Kaufman Kantor, G., & Asdigian, N. (1997). When women are under the influence: Does drinking or drug use by women provoke beatings by men? In M. Galanter (Ed.), *Recent developments in alcoholism: Vol. 13, Alcohol and Violence* (pp. 315–336). New York: Plenum.

Kaufman Kantor, G., & Straus, M. A. (1989). Substance abuse as a precipitant of wife abuse victimization. *American Journal of Drug & Alcohol Abuse, 15,* 173–189.

Kelleher, K., Chaffin, M., Hollenberg, J., & Fischer, E. (1994). Alcohol and drug disorders among physically abusive and neglectful parents in a community-based sample. *American Journal of Public Health, 84,* 1586–1590.

Kempe, C., Silverman, F., Steele, B., Droegemueller, W., & Silver, H. (1962). The battered child syndrome. *Journal of the American Medical Association, 181,* 17–24.

Kilpatrick, D. G., Acierno, R., Saunders, B., Resnick, H. S., Best, C. L., & Schnurr, P. P. (2000). Risk factors for adolescent substance abuse and dependence: Data from a national sample. *Journal of Consulting and Clinical Psychology, 68,* 19–30.

Largelard, W., & Hartogers, C. (1998). Child sexual and physical abuse and alcoholism: A review. *Journal of Studies in Alcohol, 59,* 336–348.

Lee, W. V., & Weinstein, S. P. (1997). How far have we come? A critical review of the research on men who batter. In M. Galanter (Ed.), *Recent developments in alcoholism: Vol. 13, Alcohol and Violence* (pp. 337–356). New York: Plenum.

Leonard, K. E. (1993). Drinking patterns and intoxication in marital violence: Review, critique, and future directions for research. In S. E. Martin (Ed.), *Alcohol and interpersonal violence: Fostering interdisciplinary research* (NIAAA Research Monograph No. 24, NIH Pub. No. 93-3496) (pp. 253–280). Rockville, MD: National Institutes of Health.

Leonard, K. E. (1999). Alcohol use and husband marital aggression among newlywed couples. In X. B. Arriga & S. Oskamp (Eds.), *Violence in intimate relationships* (pp. 113–135). Thousand Oaks, CA: Sage.

Leonard, K. E., & Blane, H. T. (1992). Alcohol and marital aggression in a national sample of young men. *Journal of Interpersonal Violence, 7,* 19–30.

Leonard, K. E., Bromet, E. J., Parkinson, D. K., Day, N. L., & Ryan, C. M. (1985). Patterns of alcohol use and physically aggressive behavior in men. *Journal of Studies on Alcohol, 46,* 279–282.

Leonard, K. E., & Jacob, T. (1988). Alcohol, alcoholism, and family violence. In V. B. Van Hasselt, R. L. Morrision, A. S. Bellack, & M. Hersen (Eds.), *Handbook of family violence* (pp. 383–406). New York: Plenum Press.

Leonard, K. E., & Quigley, B. M. (1999). Drinking and marital aggression in newlyweds: An event-based analysis of drinking and the occurrence of husband marital aggression. *Journal of Studies on Alcohol, 60,* 537–545.

Leonard, K. E., & Senchak, M. (1993). Alcohol and premarital aggression among newlywed couples. *Journal of Studies on Alcohol, 11,* 96–108.

Leonard, K. E., & Senchak, M. (1996). Prospective prediction of husband marital aggression within newlywed couples. *Journal of Abnormal Psychology, 105,* 369–380.

MacMillan, H. L., Galimidi, L., Walsh, C., & Wong, M. (1999, October). *Relationship between parental substance abuse and child maltreatment.* Paper presented at the Joint Annual Meeting of the American

Academy of Child and Adolescent Psychiatry and the Canadian Academy of Child Psychiatry, Chicago, IL.

Magura, S., & Laudet, A. B. (1996). Parental substance abuse and child maltreatment: Review and implications for intervention. *Child and Youth Services Review, 18*, 193–220.

Malone, J., Tryee, A., & O'Leary, K. D. (1989). Generalization and containment: Different effects of aggressive histories for wives and husbands. *Journal of Marriage and the Family, 51*, 687–697.

Martin, S. E., & Bachman, R. (1997). The relationship of alcohol to injury in assault cases. In M. Galanter (Ed.), *Recent developments in alcoholism: Vol. 13, Alcohol and Violence* (pp. 42–56). New York: Plenum Press.

McCauley, J., Kern, D. E., Kolodner, K., Dill, L., Schroeder, A. F., DeChant, H. K., Ryden, J., Derogatis, L. R., & Bass, E. B. (1997). Clinical characteristics of women with a history of child abuse. *Journal of the American Medical Association, 277*, 1362–1368.

McCurdy, K., & Daro, D. (1994). Child maltreatment. *Journal of Interpersonal Violence, 9*, 75–94.

McLaughlin, I. G., Leonard, K. E., & Senchak, M. (1992). Prevalence and distribution of premarital aggression among couples applying for a marriage license. *Journal of Family Violence, 7*, 309–319.

Miller, B. A., Downs, W. R., & Gondoli, D. M. (1989). Spousal violence among alcoholic women as compared to a random sample of women. *Journal of Studies on Alcohol, 50*, 533–540.

Miller, B. A., Downs, W. R., & Testa, M. (1993). Interrelationships between victimization experiences and women's alcohol use. *Journal of Studies on Alcohol Supplement, 11*, 109–117.

Miller, B. A., Maguin, E., & Downs, W. R. (1997). Alcohol, drugs, and violence in children's lives. In M. Galanter (Ed.), *Recent developments in alcoholism: Vol. 13, Alcohol and Violence* (pp. 357–385). New York: Plenum.

Miller, B. A., Smyth, N. J., & Mudar, P. (1999). Mothers' alcohol and other drug problems and their punitiveness toward their children. *Journal of Studies on Alcohol, 60*, 632–642.

Miller-Perrin, C. L., & Perrin, R. D. (1999). *Child maltreatment. An introduction.* Thousand Oaks, CA: Sage.

Mullen, P.E., Martin, J.L., Anderson, J.C., Romans, S.E., & Herbison, G.P. (1993). Childhood sexual abuse and mental health in adult life. *British Journal of Psychiatry, 163*, 721–732.

Mullen, P. E., Martin, J. L., Anderson, J. C., Romans, S. E., & Herbison, G. P. (1996). The long-term impact of physical, emotional, and sexual abuse of children: A community study. *Child Abuse and Neglect, 20*, 7–21

Murphy, C. M., Jellinek, M., Quinn, D., Smith, G., Poitrast, F. G., & Goshko, M. (1991). Substance abuse and serious child mistreatment: Prevalence, risk, and outcome in a court sample. *Child Abuse & Neglect, 15*, 197–211.

Murphy, C. M., & O'Farrell, T. J. (1996). Marital violence among alcoholics. *Current Directions in Psychological Science, 5*, 183–186.

O'Farrell, T. J., & Murphy, C. M. (1995). Marital violence before and after alcoholism treatment. *Journal of Consulting and Clinical Psychology, 63*, 256–262.

O'Farrell, T. J., Van Hutton, V., & Murphy, C. M. (1999). Domestic violence before and after alcoholism treatment: A two-year longitudinal study. *Journal of Studies on Alcohol, 60*, 317–321.

Office of Applied Studies, Substance Abuse and Mental Health Statistics. (2000). *Highlights from the latest OAS report* [On-line]. Available: http://www.drugabusestatistics.samhsa.gov.

O'Leary, K. D., Barling, J., Arias, I., Rosenbaum, A., Malone, J., & Tyree, A. (1989). Prevalence and stability of physical aggression between spouses: A longtitudinal analysis. *Journal of Consulting and Clinical Psychology, 57*, 263–268.

Orme, T. C., & Rimmer, J. (1981). Alcoholism and child abuse: A review. *Journal of Studies on Alcohol, 42*, 273–287.

Pernanen, K. (1991). *Alcohol in human violence.* New York: Guilford.

Peterson, L.. & Brown, D. (1994). Integrating child injury and abuse-neglect research: Common histories, etiologies, and solutions. *Psychological Bulletin, 116*, 293–315.

Polusny, M. A., & Follette, V. M. (1995). Long-term correlates of child sexual abuse: Theory and review of the empirical literature. *Applied & Preventive Psychology, 4*, 143–166.

Quigley, B. M., & Leonard, K. E. (2000). Alcohol and the continuation of early marital aggression. *Alcoholism: Clinical and Experimental Research, 24*, 1003–1010.

Rennison, C. M., & Welchans, S. (2000). *Intimate partner violence*. Washington, DC: U.S. Department of Justice, Bureau of Justice Statistics Special Report.

Rodgers, K. (1994). Wife assault: The findings of a national survey. *Juristat Service Bulletin, 14*, 1-22.

Rohsenow, D. J., Corbett, R., & Devine, D. (1988). Molested as children: A hidden contribution to substance abuse? *Journal of Substance Abuse Treatment, 5*, 13–18.

Roizen, J. (1993). Issues in the epidemiology of alcohol and violence. In S. E. Martin (Ed.), *Alcohol and interpersonal violence: Fostering interdisciplinary research* (NIAAA Research Monograph No. 24, NIH Pub. No. 93-3496) (pp. 3–36). Rockville, MD: National Institutes of Health.

Roizen, J. (1997). Epidemiological issues in alcohol-related violence. In M. Galanter (Ed.), *Recent developments in alcoholism: Vol. 13, Alcohol and Violence* (pp. 7–40). New York: Plenum.

Schuller, R. A., & Hastings, P. A. (1997). The scientific status of research on domestic violence against women. In D. L. Faignman, D. H. Kaye, M. J. Saks, J. Sanders (Eds.), *Modern scientific evidence: The law and science of expert testimony* (pp. 351–379). St. Paul, MN: West.

Shah, R. Z., Dail, P. W., & Heinrichs, T. (1995). Familial influences upon the occurrence of childhood sexual abuse. *Journal of Child Sexual Abuse, 4*, 45–61.

Sher, K. J., Gershuny, B. S., Peterson, L., & Raskin, G. (1997). The role of childhood stressors in the intergenerational transmission of alcohol use disorders. *Journal of Studies on Alcohol, 58*, 414–427.

Stets, J. E., & Straus, M. A. (1990). Gender differences in reporting marital violence and its medical and psychological consequences. In M. A. Straus & R. J. Gelles (Eds.), *Physical violence in American families: Risk factors and adaptations to violence in 8,145 families* (pp. 151–164). New Brunswick, NJ: Transaction.

Stewart, S. H. (1996). Alcohol abuse in individuals exposed to trauma: A critical review. *Psychological Bulletin, 120*, 83–112.

Straus, M. A., & Gelles, R. J. (1990). *Physical violence in American families: Risk factors and adaptations to violence in 8,145 families*. New Brunswick, NJ: Transaction.

Straus, M. A., & Sweet, S. (1992). Verbal aggression in couples: Incidence rates and relationships to personal characteristics. *Journal of Marriage and the Family, 54*, 346–357.

Takayama, J. I., Wolfe, E., & Coulter, K. P. (1998). Relationship between reason for placement and medical findings among children in foster care. *Pediatrics, 101*, 201–207.

Tolman, R. M., & Bennett, L. W. (1990). A review of quantitative research on men who batter. *Journal of Interpersonal Violence, 5*, 87–118.

United States Department of Health and Human Services. (1993). *A Report on child maltreatment in alcohol-abusing families*. Washington, DC: U.S. Government Printing Office.

United States Department of Health and Human Services. (1994). *Protecting children in sustance-abusing families*. Washington, DC: U.S. Government Printing Office.

United States Department of Health and Human Services. (1996). *Third national incidence study of child abuse and neglect: Final report (NIS-3)*. Washington, DC: U.S. Government Printing Office.

United States Department of Health and Human Services. (1998). *Child maltreatment 1996: Reports from the States to the National Child Abuse and Neglect Data System*. Washington, DC: U.S. Government Printing Office.

United States General Accounting Office. (1997). Parental substance abuse: Implications for children, the child welfare system, and foster care outcomes. Report available online: http:\\ info@www.gao.gov.

Wang, C. T., & Daro, D. (1998). *Current trends in child abuse reporting and fatalities: The results of the 1997 annual fifty state survey*. Chicago: National Center on Child Abuse Prevention Research.

Wekerle, C., & Wolfe, D. A. (1996). Child maltreatment. In E. J. Mash & R. A. Barkley (Eds.), *Child psychopathology* (pp. 492–540). New York: Guilford.

Wekerle, C., & Wolfe, D. A. (1998). Windows for preventing child and partner abuse: Early childhood and adolescence. In P. K. Trickett & C. J. Schellenbach (Eds.), *Violence against women and children in the family and in the community* (pp. 338–400). Washington, DC: American Psychological Association.

Westat (1997). *National study of preventive, protective, and reunification services delivered to children and their families*. Washington, DC: United States Department of Health and Human Services, Children's Bureau.

Widom, C. S. (1993). Child abuse and alcohol use and abuse. In S. E. Martin (Ed.), *Alcohol and interpersonal violence: Fostering interdisciplinary research* (NIAAA Research Monograph No. 24, NIH Pub. No. 93-3496) (pp. 291–314). Rockville, MD: National Institutes of Health.

Widom, C. S., Ireland, T., & Glynn, P. J. (1995). Alcohol abuse in abused and neglected children followed-up: Are they at increased risk? *Journal of Studies on Alcohol, 56,* 207–217.

Widom, C. S., Weiler, B. L., & Cottler, L. B. (1999). Childhood victimization and drug abuse: A comparison of prospective and retrospective findings. *Journal of Consulting and Clinical Psychology, 67,* 867–880.

Wilsnack, S. C., Vogeltanz, N. D., Klassen, A. D., & Harris, T. R. (1997). Childhood sexual abuse and women's substance abuse: National Survey Findings. *Journal of Studies on Alcohol, 58,* 264–271.

Windle, M., Windle, R. C., Scheidt, D. M., & Miller, G. B. (1995). Physical and sexual abuse and associated mental disorders among alcoholic inpatients. *American Journal of Psychiatry, 152,* 1322–1328.

Wolock, I., & Magura, S. (1996). Parental substance abuse as a predictor of child maltreatment re-reports. *Child Abuse and Neglect, 20,* 1183–1193.

THEORETICAL FRAMEWORKS

2 Biological Bases of Addiction and Aggression
in Close Relationships
Robert O. Pihl and Peter N. S. Hoaken

3 Developmental Psychopathology Perspectives
on Substance Abuse and Relationship Violence
*Patricia McKinsey Crittenden and
Angelika Hartl Claussen*

4 Personality Factors and Substance Abuse
in Relationship Violence and Child Abuse:
A Review and Theoretical Analysis
Gordon L. Flett and Paul L. Hewitt

5 Substance Abuse and Co-Occurring Psychiatric
Disorders in Victims of Intimate Violence
Sherry H. Stewart and Anne L. Israeli

6 Cognitive Social Learning Models
of Substance Use and Intimate Violence
Anne-Marie Wall and Sherry McKee

CHAPTER

Robert O. Pihl
Peter N. S. Hoaken

Biological Bases of Addiction and Aggression in Close Relationships

Numerous current and substantive reviews of the biology of drug addiction exist (Pihl & Peterson, 1992). Less evident, but still plentiful, are those related to drug-involved aggression, although often the focus is specific to a single neurotransmitter (Pihl & Lemarquand, 1998) or an aspect of cognitive functioning (Hoaken, Giancola, & Pihl, 1998). All of these reviews are consistent with the relatively recent trend, driven by rapid methodological innovation and daily discovery, of drawing upon biology to explain psychological and social phenomena. For example, the current head of the National Institute of Drug Abuse illustrates this view in an article titled "Addiction is a Brain Disease, and it Matters," where he notes, "Addiction as a chronic, relapsing disease of the brain is a totally new concept for much of the general public, for many policy makers, and, sadly, for many health care professionals" (Leshner, 1997, p. 46).

The present chapter will not be a collectively exhaustive review, covering already well worn ground; rather its goals are to present a structure that integrates information for both the biology of addictions and drug-related aggression, and to link relevant information to the focus of this chapter, "close relationships." The latter goal is particularly challenging as at face value what the biology of addiction and drug-related aggression has to do with close relationships is not apparent. There is, of course, the obvious: Aggression in humans and other primates is primarily a social behavior. But beyond the blatant, just what is particular to close relationships that might interact with the biology of various drugs requires speculation. The two relevant literatures appear almost mutually exclusive: the former dealing with social psychological and sociological theories on addiction and aggression in close or family relationships; the latter on the biology of addiction and violence. For example, research on biological factors in marital aggression is virtually nonexistent. Thus, writing a chapter on biological factors in close relationships poses a challenge.

This chapter thus begins by reviewing and synthesising the extant literature on the biology of addiction and aggression within the framework of putative motivation systems. This is followed by a discussion of a new focus of attention in addiction and aggression research, the frontal cortex. The chapter concludes by examining how these biological factors impact close relationships and vice versa.

This work was supported in part by the Medical Research Council of Canada.

25

☐ Biology and the Risk for Addictions and Aggression

There are many ways to organize an examination of the contribution of biology to addiction and to the drug-aggression relationship. The perspective of level, that is, genetic, biochemical-physiological, and neurobiological, is a common approach. Each of these levels offers many facts that demonstrate how each, in turn, contributes to increased risk. Often lacking, however, is an explanatory model of how these facts interrelate and interact in what are highly complex causative equations. The approach of asking how these facts—genetic, biochemical, physiological, and so forth—impact biological systems demands integration and presents a more functional representation. General questions, such as what factors impact degree of risk for abuse, as well as specific ones, such as which alcohol-affected biological mechanisms alter provocation threshold in the alcohol-aggression relationship, can be addressed.

We have previously hypothesized the existence of at least four relevant biological systems, important to risk for drug abuse (Pihl & Peterson, 1995a) and drug-related aggression (Pihl & Peterson, 1995b), which are differentially responsive to various drugs and to which, for a myriad of reasons, individuals differ in their responsivity. Although these systems are theoretical, they synthesize and model current drug effect information from all levels, and further begin to allow for some understanding of perplexing questions such as Why do only some individuals develop abuse and dependency problems?; Why do some individuals appear more susceptible to some drugs and not others?; and Why do individuals aggress when under the influence of a drug or drugs? Currently, the four systems are labeled: (1) the cue for reward system, (2) the cue for punishment system, (3) the pain system, and (4) the satiation system. Each system encompasses the operative interaction of biological and experiential factors. This is essential as biological contributions are likely meaningful only in terms of what has happened, what is happening, and will happen to the individual. In this regard, it needs to be said that the nature-nurture debate, in the extreme (which invariably arises when biological explanations for a social phenomenon like drug abuse and drug-related aggression are considered) is a perversity of logic. Patently, we do not exist without a body nor in a vacuum. Thus, the following discussion and speculation regarding the interaction between drugs and brain mechanisms which increase the likelihood of addiction and aggression should be viewed as only part of the story. The explanations are not reductionistic; rather, they depend on contextual factors—past, present, and future. On the other hand, it is equally incongruous but, unfortunately, common that some psychosocial explanations and adherents thereof seem to ignore the fact that the drugs of concern affect brain functioning. We now consider how drugs and alcohol affect these four systems, in susceptible individuals, and how the likelihood of addiction and aggression is, therefore, altered.

The Cue for Reward System

It is common to refer to legal and illegal drugs that are abused as rewarding. Why else, the argument goes, would individuals steadfastly, and in the face of great negative consequences, continue their seemingly single-minded, drug-taking, abusing behavior? There exists vast animal and human literatures that have delineated the reinforcement properties of many drugs. Yet, to simply note that certain drugs are rewarding obscures complex relationships and even totally opposite reasons why different individuals abuse the same drug. The obvious conundrum regarding simple reward explanations is that primary reinforcers like food, water, and sex, to which some drug effects are often compared, actually result in satiation so that these reinforcers are no longer temporarily effective. Satiation typically does not occur with, for example, drugs that increase stimulation by activating certain dopaminergic mechanisms. Thus, the hypothesized cue for reward system becomes important. A cue for reward is anything that has previously been contiguously associated with something basically rewarding, that is satiating, or with something that produces the cessation of punishment, threat, or anything novel. Cues of reward (or promise) in themselves result in psychological states of excitement, curiosity, pleasure, and hope. This "system" is often referred to as the psychomotor system as its stimulation results in an activation of involvement, that is, movement toward biologically relevant stimuli. In addition, accompanying important subjective feelings of excitement, curiosity, and euphoria, and increased power and energy also occur. The seemingly biological purpose of these effects is to force us to approach that which may be primarily reinforcing. Animals will work to activate electrodes or chemicals that stimulate this system, and such stimulation reinforces learning such as condition place learning (Fibiger & Phillips, 1988). It also is known that the degree of these effects depends on the density of dopamine receptors. Specifically implicated is the dopaminergic pathway of the ventral tegmental-nucleus accumbens area (Koob, 1992; Wise & Bozarth, 1987). Stimulant drugs such as cocaine and amphetamine, in particular, activate this system but so do alcohol, THC, nicotine, PCP, and some prescribed drugs. Cocaine, for example, seems to slow dopamine reuptake as does amphetamine, which also releases dopamine (Koob & Bloom, 1988). Use of these drugs in particular can result in sensitization where other similar drugs become more effective (Wise, 1988). For example, the high correlation ($r = .84$) between cocaine and alcohol abuse is relevant (Helzer & Pryzbeck, 1988). When cocaine and alcohol are combined, there is a substantial increase in cocaine-related euphoria, improvement in alcohol psychomotor performance, and an overall increase in heart rate (Farre et al., 1993). In fact, cocaine and alcohol interact to produce a metabolite, cocaethylene that significantly increases dopaminergic effects on the cue for reward system, which seems responsible for the enhanced euphoria-inducing effects when these drugs are combined (Jatlow et al., 1991; McCance-Katz et al., 1993).

Alcohol alone can and does affect this reward system. Alcohol produces effects on locomotor activity, which have been shown to be dopamine mediated (Dudek & Abbott, 1984) and like other stimulant drugs, can result in place preference learning, particularly on the rising limb of the blood alcohol curve (for a review, see Wise & Bozarth, 1987). One notable outcome, like the other stimulants, is that alcohol can cause an increase in resting heart rate (Finn & Pihl, 1987), along with concomitant positive subjective feelings (Conrod, Pihl, & Vassileva, 1998; Earleywine & Martin, 1993). In general, these effects are time and dose limited (Stewart, Finn, & Pihl, 1992) and, more importantly, they are individually differential. In fact, genetic factors have been implicated in determining the degree of response to the stimulating or sedating effects of alcohol (Dudek, Phillips, & Hahn, 1991). For example, particular alcohol preferring strains of rats, when compared with other especially bred strains, demonstrate heightened dopaminergic activity to alcohol, more sensitivity to the locomotor activity enhancing effects, and more resistance to the sedating effects of alcohol (Gordon, Meehan, & Schechter, 1993). These effects may be both direct or indirect when the activity of other biochemical systems that operate on the dopamine system are altered (Harris, Brody, & Dunwiddle, 1992). In humans, a substantive increase in heart rate from alcohol has been found in alcoholics (Peterson et al., 1996) and in some multigenerational sons of alcoholics who are at a four to nine times increased risk for developing the disorder (Conrod, Pihl, & Ditto, 1995; Conrod et al., 1998). Recently, Bruce, Shestowsky, Mayerovitch, and Pihl (1999) demonstrated additional positive effects of this response. Twenty four hours after intoxication, individuals who showed this high heart rate response recalled more positive and fewer negative words than low heart rate responders from a list of words learned while intoxicated the previous day.

The above findings illustrate how variability in the functioning of the cue for reward system would affect susceptibility to addiction. However, how this variability is relevant to a biological explanation of drug-related aggression is less clear. An answer comes from both data and theory. In a recent study, young men who had been part of a longitudinal study that began when they were age six in kindergarten consumed an intoxicating dose of alcohol (Assaad, Pihl, Séguin, & Tremblay, 1999). These individuals were selected for the study by their teachers on the basis of their level of demonstrated aggressive school behavior. Continuous testing throughout the years, in school, at home, and in laboratory studies, confirmed the stability of behavior for those individuals who were highly and continuously aggressive, in comparison to others who were consistently nonaggressive. What the alcohol challenge data shows is that those individuals who display a high heart rate response to alcohol are more likely to have a history of delinquent behavior, engage in more fighting, and, in general, display a gamut of antisocial acts when compared with other subjects. Further, these individuals are more likely to display sensation-seeking, particularly disinhibited personality characteristics. These results might be interpreted to suggest that individuals with a heightened sensitivity of the cue for reward system are at risk for aggression and related behaviors. These results also replicate the well known fact that conduct disorder/Anti-Social Personality Disorder (ASPD) and alcohol and drug abuse are frequent comorbid disorders (see Flett & Hewitt, this volume). The question of whether drugs or alcohol intoxication will increase or decrease aggression in these subjects is the focus of a current laboratory investigation. It is known that sons from a male-limited, dense family history of alcoholism (Type 2; Cloninger, 1987) are prone to aggression when intoxicated, as are women diagnosed with ASPD (Conrod, Pihl, Stewart, & Doniger, 2000). Finally, the literature, (detailed later in this chapter) that relates frontal lobe functioning deficits frequent in these subjects and alcohol-produced frontal dysfunction in increased aggressivity is relevant. Substantial data exists detailing the inhibitory control that frontal structures play over the cues for reward system by affecting the release of dopamine and subsequent psychomotor behavior.

Theoretically, how alcohol specifically affects the cues for reward system to potentiate the increased likelihood of aggression is illustrated in Figure 2.1. First, simply promoting exploration and raising the excitement and curiosity stimulation of this system increases the likelihood of confrontation. Additionally, and importantly, the effects of this system and the concomitant subjective responses are likely analgesic to that which is externally threatening and inhibitory to aggression. In that omnipresent valence between action/ promise and inhibition/threat activating cues for reward diminishes cues for threat. In a sense, then, the breaking of rules which, by definition, often leads to the unexpected, becomes exciting and initiates activity. Further, in the extreme, it is the diminishment of sensitivity to threat and punishment by the activation of this approach behavior that results in aggressive behaviors that are dangerous to the self and others.

The Cue for Punishment (Threat) System

The majority of problem drinkers when asked why they drink will give an answer that fundamentally translates as, "to reduce stress." Indeed, like benzodiazepines and barbiturates, alcohol has anxiolytic effects. Pharmacologically, alcohol and other anxiolytics operate on the major brain inhibitory neurotransmitter, GABA. It has been shown, for example, that alcohol affects the chloride ion channels at the GABA benzodiazepine receptor (Warnecke, 1991), increases the firing rate of GABA and, thus, increases inhibitory action

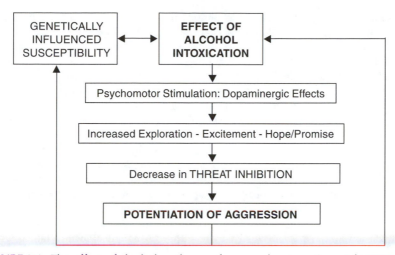

FIGURE 2.1. The effect of alcohol on the cue for reward system. Copyright 2001 by R. O. Pihl.

on other neurons. Stress often represents threat that can be operationalized as a cue for punishment, as are pain, depriving situations, sensory overstimulation, frustration, disappointments, social isolation, and the occurrence of novelty. It appears a great deal of the mammalian brain is hard-wired to deal with threat as the continued survival of the organism can rest on the speed of reactivity. It is a jungle out there, at least it used to be, and not reacting fast enough can quickly result in death. Thus, the purpose of the threat system is to inhibit ongoing behavior and stop us from getting hurt. This responsivity can take the form of specific fears or, more, generally, anxiety. Fear protects us from that which has previously produced harm, and anxiety results in caution to cues of threat. For example, isolation from others is a threatening condition and it is anxiety that leads us to be careful and appropriate in the presence of others, alerting us to our possible, current, past, and future faux pas.

As with cues of reward, there appears to be a differential individual sensitivity to cues of threat. Clearly, this reactivity can become pathological as witnessed in anxiety disorders. This individual sensitivity can be genetic; it has been shown that the high alcohol sensitive strain of rats and the long sleep strain of mice are much more responsive to the sedative effects of alcohol than their counterpart strains (Crabbe, 1989). This sensitivity to the sedative effect of alcohol also is exhibited by the fact that these animals will die from a lower dosage than controls. In humans, the abuse of alcohol correlates with anxiety sensitivity in both clinical (Cox, Swinson, Shulman, Kuck, & Reichman, 1993) and nonclinical (Stewart & Pihl, 1994) samples. Additionally, anxiety sensitive individuals have been shown to display a decrease in their stress response (called response dampening) when intoxicated (Stewart & Pihl, 1994). It is logical to assume, therefore, that the heightened abuse pattern found in these individuals reflects a form of self-medication with alcohol activating the brain's inhibitory mechanisms and, thus, decreasing responsivity to threatening stimuli. Most notable in these threatening stimuli for anxiety-sensitive individuals are cues attacking the integrity of the self (Stewart, Conrod, Pihl, & Doniger, 1999). Some sons of alcoholics show stress response dampening, but in their sober states they are overreactive to novel stimuli, likely related to a cognitive problem. For both these groups, the modification of the threat response, albeit for different reasons, explains the increased abuse potential these groups reflect. This dampening of the threat system also explains more generally the increased likelihood of aggression when intoxicated.

Figure 2.2 illustrates how threat inhibits aggression. Even given intense provocation, the possibility of retaliatory pain and injury (physical, psychological, social) controls the response. We have demonstrated this effect in numerous laboratory studies where knowledge of likely consequences, and the determined motivation of the attacker, inhibit retaliation when sober (Zeichner & Pihl, 1979, 1980). Indeed, this inhibitory control is likely to a large degree what the socialization process is all about. The presumed threat of retaliation and conscience even when provoked by the aggressor is what likely keeps most of us in check. This control, however, is somewhat soluble with alcohol. As Figure 2.2 illustrates, an intoxicating dose of alcohol is seen as restraining this inhibition. This specific conclusion is derived from numerous animal and human studies. Intoxicated rats typically venture from hiding even knowing a cat is present, which increases the likelihood of their demise (Blanchard, Veniegas, Elloran, & Blanchard, 1993). This diminishment of inhibition of control also explains the frequent role of drug intoxication in victims of violence. Intoxicated humans, even when aware of the consequences, will retaliate when provoked (i.e., knowing that a fight will likely erupt) (Zeichner, Pihl, Niaura, & Zacchia, 1982). Thus, it is not the absence of knowledge (i.e., drug-induced stupidity) that is the operative mechanism, but the inhibition of threat control.

The Pain System

The pain or punishment system refers to where and how the negative consequences of behavior that decrease the future likelihood of that behavior operate. Neuroanatomically, there appears to be considerable overlap between structures that affect the affective aspects of pain and aggressive behavior, including the prefrontal and orbital frontal cortex,

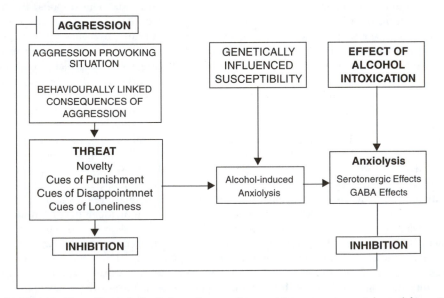

FIGURE 2.2. The effect of alcohol on the cue for punishment system. Adapted from "A biosocial model of the alcohol-aggression relationship" by R. O. Pihl, J. Peterson, and M. A. Lau, 1993, *Journal of Studies on Alcohol, Suppl. 11,* pp. 128–139. Copyright 1993 by R. O. Pihl. Adapted and reprinted with permission.

the amygdala, various hypothalmic nuclei, and the dorsal raphe nucleus (Albert, Walsh, & Jonik, 1993; Chapman 1996; Raine, Stoddard, Bibule, & Buchsbaum, 1998; Willis & Westlund, 1997). Negative consequences that affect this system are many and divergent. They include not just the obvious (e.g., simple physical pain), but also states of deprivation, sensory overstimulation, frustration, disappointment, and social isolation. The response to pain can be both inhibitory and anger-inducing. Inhibition occurs in the sense of "once hurt, twice shy," and anger and aggression can often result into the putative purpose of the elimination of the presumed source of pain. Thus, fear and hate are coexisting emotional responses to a painful stimulus, and those drugs that decrease pain are negatively reinforcing. Analgesics (e.g., opiates) operate on the periaqueductal gray brain area which is directly related to the mediation of pain (Panksepp, Jalowiec, DeEskinazi, & Bishop, 1985), although these drugs also affect the cue for reward area (Wise, 1988). Further, their administration not only reduces physical pain but also social distress (Knowles, Conner, & Panksepp, 1987) developed in maternally deprived stress induced animals. Interestingly, this effect can be reversed by the opiate antagonist nalexone (Knowles et al., 1987).

Alcohol also impacts the pain system through that system's neurotransmitters, the endorphins. It has been shown that C57 BL/6J alcohol-preferring mice have a particularly low pain threshold that is increased by opiate agonists. This concomitantly decreases alcohol consumption (Gianoulakis & Gupta, 1985). In our research, we have shown that sons from families with multigenerational male alcoholism reflect greater sober pain sensitivity (ratings to electric shock) than men with no family history of alcoholism (Stewart, Finn, & Pihl, 1995). We have also shown that these individuals display a substantive increase in plasma beta endorphin on the rising limb of the blood alcohol curve (Peterson et al., 1996). We obtained a correlation of .91 between blood alcohol and plasma endorphin levels in individuals who showed a high heart rate response versus one of .26 for negative family history controls. We have recently demonstrated that naltrexone blocks this response (Peterson, Conrod, Pihl, & Gianoulakis, 1999).

The putative relationships among alcohol, the pain system, and aggression, are highly complex. First, there is the situation where alcohol acts much like it does on the threat system, decreasing or inhibiting the withdrawal response inherent in the pain response. Thus, a shift in the fear-anger valance occurs in favor of anger, and a retaliatory attack occurs. Certainly, in many species, non-avoidable pain is perhaps the most common and reliable procedure for eliciting aggression, both direct and indirect. To reiterate, substantial provocation with negative stimuli is usually required to produce aggression in humans. Although there are a myriad of different forms of aggression, retaliatory/defensive aggression predominates. In this sense, drugs like alcohol also affect sensitivity to pain. While it is true that alcohol is seen by many as a sedative and has in the past been used as a surgical anaesthetic (Mullen & Lockhart, 1934), this effect is dose- and individual-dependent. At moderate dosages, and on the rising limb of the curve, alcohol has been shown to result in heightened ratings of pain sensitivity in a general population (Gustafson, 1985), a response also seen in lowered pain thresholds in alcohol intoxicated rats (Gray, 1982). Thus, alcohol and other drugs may contribute to aggression simply by increasing reactivity to pain (i.e., the significance of provocation).

The complexity of this situation, however, is demonstrated in some individuals who even on the rising limb of the blood alcohol curve seem to show less responsivity to pain. We have demonstrated (Pihl, Peterson, & Finn, 1990) on our laboratory aggression task that some men with a positive family history for alcoholism who tend to be more aggressive when sober, and putatively more pain sensitive, are less aggressive and reactive when intoxicated.

The Satiation System

The biological systems involved in unconditioned positive reinforcement comprise what we view as the satiation system. The neurotransmitter serotonin (5HT) is uniquely involved in a wide range of basic functions including food and water intake, sexual behavior, and sleep. It appears that serotonin operates on these systems by generally providing a moderating influence on the activity of other neurotransmitters. For example, serotonin has been shown to inhibit behavior to threat (Sobrie, 1986), release dopamine, and increase locomotion (Kriem, Abraini, & Rostain, 1996). Indeed, the functioning of serotonin in the brain has been analogized as the maestro of an orchestra organizing and controlling talented individuals and melding them into a harmonious unit (Pihl & Peterson, 1995a). At appropriate optimum levels of the functioning of the neurostransmitter, neuro-synchrony is thought to result, while at insufficient levels of functioning, dys-synchrony results (Spoont, 1992).

Low or insufficient serotonergic functioning has been linked to aggression in both animals and humans (see Pihl & Lemarquand, 1998 for a review). For example, mice bred to lack a specific serotonergic receptor are more aggressive when provoked than controls (Saudou et al., 1994), and when serotonergic activity is less, as measured by spinal fluid metabolites, monkeys are spontaneously more aggressive, have a higher mortality (Higley, Mehlman, Higley, & Fernald, 1996), and take more risks (Mehlman, Higley, Faucher, & Lilly, 1995). Conversely, with higher serotonin levels monkeys display greater prosocial behavior (Mehlman, Higley, Faucher, & Lilly, 1995), and are more dominant (Higley, Mehlman, Taub, & Higley, 1992). In a study where we manipulated the serotonergic precursor tryptophan, functionally depleting brain serotonin levels, we increased level of aggression in vervet monkeys (Chamberlain, Ervin, Pihl, & Young, 1987) and humans (Pihl et al., 1995). The general disinhibiting effect of manipulating serotonin also is seen where drugs that produce low levels of release result in increased impulsivity, whereas at higher levels (and thus increased 5HT functioning) there is a decrease in impulsivity (Poulos, Parker, & Le, 1998). The literature with humans reflects a very similar story, with low serotonergic functioning—also measured in terms of cerebral spinal fluid metabolite levels—being related to individual histories of aggressive impulsive behavior (Brown et al., 1982), homicide (Lidberg, 1985), children with impulsive and aggressive behaviors (Kruesi, Swedo, Leonard, & Rubinow, 1990), impulsive violent offenders (Virkunnen et al., 1994), individuals with serious suicide attempts (Virkunnen, De Jong, Bartko, & Linnoia, 1989), impulsive individuals with alcoholic fathers (Linnoila, De Jong, & Vikkunen, 1989), self-reported aggression in normals (Roy, Adinoff, & Linnoila, 1988), and in alcoholic violent offenders (Virkunnen et al., 1994). That low levels or dysfunction of 5HT is involved in the expression of aggression and impulsivity is supported by a large number of studies showing blunted hormonal responses to 5HT agonists. Lower receptor numbers or functioning in platelet 5HT reuptake studies in impulsive and aggressive patient populations has been demonstrated (see Pihl & LeMarquand, 1998 for review). In experimental investigations involving acute tryptophan depletion, similar conclusions are possible. What the data suggests is that 5HT is involved in controlling responsivity to stimuli, for it is specifically the response to provocation that is altered by reducing the serotonin levels. This is illustrated in Figure 2.3 (Pihl et al., 1995).

Alcohol does affect serotonin levels, although the relationship is complex (see LeMarquand, Pihl, & Benkelfat 1994a, 1994b for reviews). In numerous studies with various methodologies, increased serotonergic function leads to decreased ethanol consumption. A low level of serotonergic functioning seems to be a risk factor for alcohol abuse in that, while acute alcohol intake increases brain 5HT functioning, chronic intake may actu-

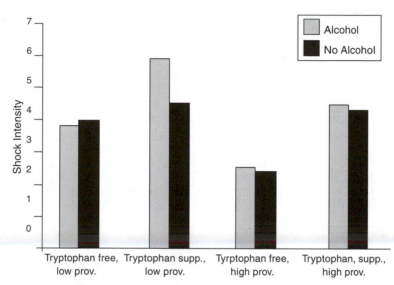

FIGURE 2.3. The effect of altered tryptophan levels and alcohol under low and high provocation on the intensity of shock administered to subjects. Data from "Serotonin and aggression and the alcohol-aggression relationship," by R. O. Pihl and D. Lemarquand, 1998, *Alcohol & Alcoholism, 33,* pp. 55–65. Figure copyright 2001 by R. O. Pihl.

ally decrease it. We have speculated (Pihl & LeMarquand, 1998) that such chronic consumption might lead to a general state of lowered 5HT functioning and, thus, a greater incidence of impulsivity and aggressive behavior. Recent attention has focused on subtypes of individuals, particularly individuals with early onset of drinking problems or antisocial characteristics. The serotonin autoreceptor 5-HTIB has been implicated in mouse (Saudou et al., 1994) and human studies (Lappalainier et al., 1998), for both drinking and aggression. It is precisely this specificity upon which the system's approach presented in this review is based.

☐ The Frontal Cortex: Executive Cognitive Function and Drug-Related Aggression

Figure 2.4 illustrates the relationship between the two most important systems regarding drug-related aggression, the cue for reward and threat systems, and another biological variable that has recently begun to garner significant research interest in those interested by addiction and aggression: the function of the prefrontal cortex. The importance of this brain area for human behavior is, simplistically, illustrated by its larger size relative to other cortical lobes, a fact that differentiates humans from other primates. In fact, research has demonstrated that disruption by drugs or preexisting dysfunction of the cognitive capacities mediated by this brain area (capacities often labeled executive functions) impact directly on the likelihood of aggression.

The executive cognitive functions comprise higher-order cognitive activities, including attention, planning, cognitive flexibility, abstract reasoning, self-monitoring, and the ability to integrate external and internal feedback in order to adaptively modulate further behavior. Executive functioning is commonly conceptualized as the ability to use these

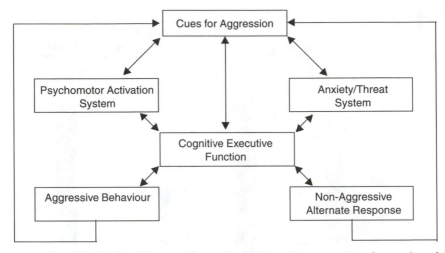

FIGURE 2.4. Schematic of the interrelationship between two systems and centrality of the executive function in the determination of aggressive and nonaggressive responding. Adapted from "Executive cognitive functions as mediators of alcohol-related aggression," by P. N. S. Hoaken, P. R. Giancola, and R. O. Pihl, 1998, *Alcohol & Alcoholism*, *33*(1), pp. 47–54. Copyright 1998 by R. O. Pihl. Adapted and reprinted with permission.

functions to plan, initiate, and regulate goal-directed behavior (Giancola & Zeichner, 1994). The prefrontal cortex represents the neural substrate that subserves these functions (Giancola, 1995; Stuss & Benson, 1984), with the dorsolateral prefrontal-subcortical circuit being the neuroanatomical pathway of considerable interest (Cummings, 1995). This pathway consists of dorsolateral prefrontal cortex and projections to and from several subcortical structures, including the caudate nucleus, globus pallidus, substantia nigra, and several thalamic nuclei, thus interacting directly with the cue for reward and threat systems.

There is considerable evidence that associates frontal lobe deficits with decreased regulation of human social behavior. Individuals with frontal lobe damage often manifest a disinhibition syndrome (Hecaen & Albert, 1978) and, even in nonlesioned individuals, there is evidence of this relationship. One study demonstrated a substantial relationship between aggressivity and scores on carefully selected tests of executive functioning in boys (Séguin, Pihl, Harden, Boulerice, & Tremblay, 1995). Further, from a neuroimaging standpoint, a study employing positron emmission tomography demonstrated that, while not lesioned per se, murderers demonstrated more prefrontal abnormalities than did matched controls (Raine et al., 1994). There have been a series of studies that show psychiatric disorders characterized by antisocial behavior such as conduct disorder (Moffitt, 1993), antisocial personality disorder (Gorenstein, 1987), and attention-deficit hyperactivity disorder (Barkley, 1997; Benson, 1991) are all also characterised by poorer performance on tests of executive function, relative to controls.

It is widely agreed that these cognitive capacities are related to a heightened propensity for aggression, and there is substantial evidence that alcohol and other drugs interfere with these capacities. Peterson and colleagues (1990) were among the first to hypothesize that the prefrontal cortex may be particularly susceptible to alcohol intoxication. In order to test this hypothesis, the experimenters administered low, moderate, and high doses of alcohol to participants in a balanced-placebo design, intended to eliminate the effects of expectancy, and then administered a battery of cognitive tests. The results, illustrated in Figure 2.5, show that high doses of alcohol detrimentally affected a number of functions associated with the frontal lobes, including planning, memory, and complex motor control, but appeared to have a lesser effect on other nonfrontal tests. In a subsequent study (Hoaken, Assaad, & Pihl, 1998), it was shown, through a repeated measures design, that alcohol significantly and specifically interfered with tests of executive function, even at a moderate dose. It is apparent, then, that alcohol produces cognitive deficits reminiscent of prefrontal damage. We have begun to examine the effects of both alcohol and executive functioning on behavioral measures of aggression in a series of laboratory studies. In the first study of this relationship (Lau, Pihl, & Peterson, 1995), two tests of executive functioning were used to screen male participants. Participants falling into either the highest or the lowest quartile of executive function were retained; half of each of these groups were administered alcohol, the other half remained sober. In this study, as provocation increased, the participants in the lower quartile became progressively and significantly more aggressive than those in the highest quartile. This led to the conclusion that alcohol intoxication and frontal lobe dysfunction were both involved in the disinhibition of ag-

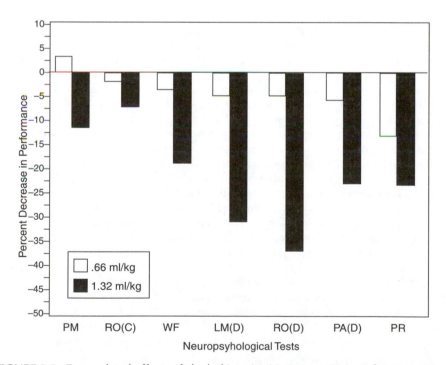

FIGURE 2.5. Dose-related effects of alcohol intoxication on cognitive performance: Tests associated with frontal function: PM (Porteus Maze). RO(C) (Rey-Osterreith, copy), WF (Thurstone Word Fluency); tests associated with hippocampal function: LM(D) (Logical Memory, Delayed), RO(D) (Rey-Osterreith, dealy, PA(D) (Paired Associated, Delay); tests assocated with motor function: PR (Pursuit Rotor). Data from "Acute alcohol intoxication and cognitive functioning," by J. P. Peterson, J. Rothfleisch, P. D. Zelazo, and R. O Pihl, 1990, *Journal of Studies on Alcohol, 51,* pp. 114–122. Figure copyright 2001 by R. O. Pihl.

gressive impulses. Giancola and Zeichner (1994) also reached this conclusion in a similar study.

In a subsequent study, Lau and Pihl (1996), in order to test their hypothesis that heightened aggression was due to an inability to inhibit impulsive behavior, tested whether participants with poor executive functioning would be able to inihibit aggressive responses if offered contingent monetary reward for not responding aggressively. Again, participants were classified into highest and lowest quartiles of executive function and tested while sober for aggression. The results of this study showed that the men in the lower quartile, when highly provoked and paid to inhibit, nonetheless responded aggressively, whereas the men in the upper quartile inhibited aggression. It appears as if lower quartile men are impulsive and respond aggressively when provoked, without being able to switch to other, more appropriate behaviors.

We know from decades of studies that drinking alcohol makes individuals more likely to manifest aggression. We also know that the vast majority of drinkers do not aggress when they become intoxicated. It may well be that sound executive functioning underlies this reality. It has been demonstrated that, even when acutely alcohol-intoxicated, men with above-average executive functioning will inhibit aggression in order to gain reward. That is, even when legally drunk, subjects seem to retain sufficient residual executive function to identify and utilize more appropriate behavioral responses to provocation (Hoaken et al., 1998). Although the aforementioned studies used men as participants, there is accumulating evidence that executive functioning may be related to aggression in women. Hoaken, Strickler, and Pihl (2000) conducted a study in which two groups of women, one sober, the other acutely alcohol intoxicated were tested on the aggression paradigm. What was surprising about this study was that alcohol intoxication did not appear to be as important as in previous studies with men; sober women were as aggressive as their intoxicated peers in the face of heightened provocation. What did appear to be consequential for predicting who would and who would not become aggressive was executive functioning. Measures of executive functioning taken before drink administration correlated very highly with aggression, irrespective of alcohol intoxication.

There also are studies that seem to suggest that poor executive functioning seems to predispose one to alcohol and drug use and abuse (Peterson & Pihl, 1990; Pihl et al., 1990). What is important to consider regarding executive functioning is that this cortical area provides the context for integrating and interpreting stimuli. Expectancies and cognitive schemas blend past learning, including language and imitation, to color event appraisal and determine behavioural outcome, which is a very social-, culture-specific process. One's general expectancy set subsumes the regulation of anxiety or threat and psychomotor activity, as well as beliefs regarding drug effects and interpersonal aggression. Historically, an individually determined behavior, and the behavior's dysfunction, due to prior programming (or lack thereof), incapacity, or drug insult (albeit temporary), can readily place the individual out of context and cause him or her to behave inappropriately.

☐ Specific Mediating Factors of the Close Relationship

The reader may now wonder what is specific about a close relationship that may somehow alter the seemingly deterministic biological factors delineated above. Three foci for consideration are assortative mating, genetic factors, and the saliency of provocation.

Assortative Mating

Many studies, dating back decades, have observed that there appears to be a high incidence of shared morbidity of various forms of psychological distress within married couples (Galbaud du Fort, Kovess, & Boivin, 1994). What this observation means, however, is arguable. Possible explanations are that a husband and wife living together apply profound influences on one another and, as such, one partner may infect the other with abnormal behaviors or reactions; it may be the case that the breakdown of the (shared) social environment may lead to pathology in both partners; or it may simply be the case that when one partner enters treatment, treatment for the second becomes facilitated (Neilsen, 1964). Alternatively, there may be some tendency of couples to attract each other on the basis of some preexisting similitude. This tendency for couples to be more similar for some phenotype or behavior than would be expected if they were paired randomly has been referred to as spouse similarity (assortative mating). This description appears to be particularly true for alcoholics where mutual partner diagnoses far exceed what would be expected by random pairing (Jacob & Bremer, 1986; Stabenau & Hesselbrock, 1983). One study, for example, demonstrated that adult children of alcoholics marry other adult children of alcoholics at a rate more than twice that found in the general population (Black, Bucky, & Wilder-Padilla, 1986). This is important because if both members of a couple share a predisposition for alcoholism, they likely share underlying biological characteristics, which are a basis for the increased risk of addiction, and also possibly aggressive behavior. Furthermore, if both members of a couple are intoxicated, provocation becomes that much more salient for both members and, as such, aggression becomes that much more likely. It has been demonstrated that more than half of all perpetrators and nearly half of all victims of violent crime are acutely intoxicated at the time of the crime; this certainly seems to support the contention that dual intoxication is a strong risk factor for aggressive interaction (Murdoch, Pihl, & Ross, 1990).

Evidence of assortative mating also has been found in heroin addiction (Anglin, Kao, Harlow, Peters, & Booth, 1987), schizophrenia (Alanen & Kinnunen, 1975), and antisocial personality (Cloninger, Reich, & Guze, 1975; Guze, Goodwin, & Crane, 1970; Kreuger, Moffitt, Caspi, Bleske, & Silva, 1998), with the latter being associated with both polydrug abuse and aggressive behavior. Thus, spousal similarity may be an element of a close relationship that leads to increased probability of both addiction and aggressive behavior.

Genetic Considerations

Another aspect of close relations is the heritability of risk for addiction and aggression passed from parents to offspring. It is critical to view the family as an interacting unit and not explicitly focus on the couple/parents. Stated succinctly, "The child acts; the environment reacts; and the child reacts back in mutually interlocking-evocative interaction" (Caspi, Elder, & Bem, 1987, p. 308). Bidirectionality of causality is likely as the added difficulties of a problematic offspring create and exacerbate existing parental relationship and individual problems. The literature on the heritability of risk for addiction and aggression is compelling. For example, regarding alcoholism, family, twin, and adoption studies place the contribution of genes for both men and women at approximately 60% (Cloninger, Bohman, & Sigvardsson, 1981; Cotton, 1979; Heath et al., 1996). The search for candidate genes is currently exuberant with many and divergent findings reported. However, at this juncture, only very preliminary speculation can be drawn, and conclusions must wait considerable replication. Yet, what is well known is that phenotypic expression presents a pattern of high risk for addiction and aggression. We and others have previously reviewed the behavioral characteristics of sons of alcoholics (Pihl et al., 1990; Sher, Walitzer, Wood, & Brent, 1991; Windle & Searles, 1990), particularly the behavioral dysregulation, electro-physiological, and biochemical idiosyncracies they display. Typically found in these individuals are disciplinary problems with histories of impulsivity, rebellion, conduct disorder, and antisociality. Very frequently, aggressive behavior, both sober and intoxicated, has been noted (Cloninger, 1987). In addition, there is evidence that offspring of alcoholics have a greater rate of crime and violent crime than do controls and that violence in the father is related to addiction in the offspring. For example, one Swedish adoption study showed a significant correlation between violent offenses in the biological fathers and alcohol dependence in the male adoptees (Bohman, Cloninger, Sigvardsson, & von Knorring, 1982).

The Saliency of Provocation

Mentioned previously is the increased saliency of provocation if both members of a close relationship are intoxicated. Numerous laboratory studies of the alcohol-aggression relationship clearly underscore the increased impact of provocation when intoxicated (Pihl, Peterson, & Lau, 1993). In fact, seemingly all putative variables that impact the relationship seem to interact with level of provocation. Specifically, drugs that enhance aggression appear to lower the reactivity/retaliation threshold of the individual. Even where particular neurotransmitters such as serotonin are involved, the interaction with level of provocation has been demonstrated. (Pihl et al., 1995; Smith, Pihl, Young, & Ervin, 1987). Both these studies used a tryptophan depletion paradigm (which dramatically decreases brain serotonin), with similar subjects participating on the same aggression task. The earlier study used noise as the aversive stimulus and found no effect, whereas the latest research provoked with a brief electric shock and produced a strong tryptophan depletion effect when compared with two control conditions.

However, it might be that the saliency of the provocation in a potentially violent altercation between two individuals in a close relationship would serve to *decrease* the likelihood of aggression. One of the most important aspects of the executive functions is a behavior-inhibition capacity. In light of this, we suggest that the inhibitory aspects of the frontal cortex may well mitigate aggression in close relationships more so than in other relationships. Plainly said, we are suggesting that in a close relationship, the salience of provocation makes situations less likely to become violent because of the increased involvement of the inhibitory aspects of the frontal cortex.

☐ Conclusion

From a biological point of view, there are several factors that may place individuals at risk for either addiction or aggression, or, often, both. As we have indicated in some detail, several biological motivational systems, constantly interacting with each other, and mediated by the inhibitory aspects of the prefrontal cortex, mediate the likelihood of these kinds of impulsive, maladaptive, disregulated behaviors. However, what we can say about the extent to which these factors are more or less in evidence in the context of a close relationship is limited. From a biological point of view, we hold the individual and his or her personal biological makeup to be the most predictive addictive or aggressive propensity, and suggest that an individual "wired just right," will manifest the problematic behaviours irrespective of social milieu. However, that is *not* to say that the social milieu is unimportant. Future research would do well to attempt to elucidate the relative contributions of biology and social environment in the manifestation of addiction and aggression in close relationships.

☐ References

Albert, D. J., Walsh, M., & Jonik, R. (1993). Aggression in humans: What is its biological foundation? *Neuroscience and Biobehavioral Reviews, 17*, 405–425.

Alanen, Y. O., & Kinnunen, P. (1975). Marriage and the development of schizophrenia. *British Journal of Psychiatry, 117*, 59–67.

Anglin, M. D., Kao, C. F., Harlow, L. L., Peters, K., & Booth, M. W. (1987). Similarity of behavior within addict couples. Part I. Methodology and narcotics patterns. *International Journal of the Addictions, 22*, 497–524.

Assaad, J. M., Pihl, R. O., Séguin, J., & Tremblay, R. (1999, June). *Heart rate response to alcohol challenge and history of aggression and antisociality.* Paper presented at the meeting of the Research Society on Alcoholism. Santa Barbara, California.

Barkley, R. A. (1997). Behavioral inhibition, sustained attention, and executive functions: Constructing a unifying theory of ADHD. *Psychological Bulletin, 121*, 65–94.

Benson, D. F. (1991). The role of frontal dysfunction in attention deficit hyperactivity disorder. *Journal of Child Neurology, 6*, S9–S12.

Black, C., Bucky, S. F., & Wilder-Padilla, S. (1986). The interpersonal and emotional consequences of being an adult child of an alcoholic. *International Journal of the Addictions, 21*(2), 213–231.

Blanchard, D. C., Veniegas, R., Elloran, I., & Blanchard, R. J. (1993). Alcohol and anxiety: Effects on offensive and defensive aggression. *Journal of Studies on Alcohol, 11*(Suppl.), 9–19.

Bohman, M., Cloninger, C. R., Sigvardsson, S., & von Knorring, A. (1982). Predisposition to petty criminality in Swedish adoptees: I. Genetic and environmental heterogeneity. *Archives of General Psychiatry, 39*, 1233–1241.

Brown, G. L., Ebert, M. H., Goyer, P. F., Jimerson, D. C., Klein, W. J., Bunney, W. E., & Goodwin, F. K. (1982). Aggression, suicide, and serotonin: Relationships to CSF amine metabolites. *American Journal of Psychiatry, 139*, 741–746.

Bruce, K., Shestowsky, J., Mayerovitch, J., & Pihl, R. (1999). Concomitant psychomotor stimulation and differentially-enhanced consolidation of emotionally charged memory following alcohol consumption. *Alcoholism: Clinical and Experimental Research, 23*, 693–701.

Caspi, A., Elder, G. H., & Bem, D. J. (1987). Moving against the world: Life-course patterns of explosive children. *Developmental Psychology, 23*, 308–313.

Chamberlain, B., Ervin, F., Pihl, R. O, & Young, S. N. (1987). The effect of raising or lowering tryptophan levels on aggression in vervet monkeys. *Pharmacology, Biochemistry and Behavior, 27*, 503–510.

Chapman, C. R. (1996). Limbic processes and the affective dimensions of pain. In G. Carli & M. Zimmerman (Eds.), *Towards the neurobiology of chronic pain* (pp. 53–81). Amsterdam: Elsevier.

Cloninger, C. R. (1987). Neurogenetic adaptive mechanisms in alcoholism. *Science, 23*, 410–415.

Cloninger, C., Bohman, M., & Sigvardsson, S. (1981). Inheritance of alcohol abuse: Cross-fostering analysis of adopted men. *Archives of General Psychiatry, 38*, 861–868.

Cloninger, C. R., Reich, T., & Guze, S. B. (1975). The multifactorial model of disease transmission and assortative mating II. Sex differences in the familial transmission of sociopathy (antisocial personality). *British Journal of Psychiatry, 127*, 11–22.

Conrod, P. J., Pihl, R., & Ditto, B. (1995). Autonomic reactivity and alcohol-induced dampening in men at risk for alcoholism and men at risk for hypertension. *Alcoholism: Clinical & Experimental Research, 19*, 482–489.

Conrod, P. J., Pihl, R. O., Stewart, S., & Dongier, M. (2000). Validation of a system of classifying female substance abusers on personality and motivational risk factors for substance abuse. *Psychology of Addictive Behaviors, 14*, 243–256.

Conrod, P. J., Pihl, R., & Vassileva, J. (1998). Differential sensitivity to alcohol reinforcement in groups of men at risk for distinct alcoholic syndrome. *Alcoholism: Clinical & Experimental Research, 22*, 585–597.

Cotton, N. S. (1979). The familial incidence of alcoholism. *Journal of Studies on Alcoholism,* 40, 89–116.

Cox, B. J., Swinson, R. P., Shulman, I. D., Kuck, K., & Reichman, J. (1993). Gender effects and alcohol use in panic disorder with agoraphobia. *Behaviour Research and Therapy, 31,* 413–416.

Crabbe, J. C. (1989). Genetic animal models in the study of alcoholism. *Alcoholism: Clinical & Experimental Research, 13,* 120–128.

Cummings, J. L. (1995). Anatomic and behavioral aspects of frontal-subcortical circuits. In J. Grafman, K. J. Holyoak, & F. Boiler (Eds.), *Structure and function of the human prefrontal cortex* (pp. 1–13). New York: Annals of the New York Academy of Sciences.

Dudek, B. C., & Abbott, M. E. (1984). The relationship between ethanol-induced locomotor activity and narcosis in long-sleep and short-sleep mice. *Alcoholism: Clinical and Experimental Research, 8,* 272–276.

Dudek, B. C., Phillips, T. J., & Hahn, M. E. (1991). Genetic analyses of the biphasic nature of the alcohol dose-response curve. *Alcoholism, Clinical & Experimental Research, 15*(2), 262–269.

Earleywine, M., & Martin, C. S. (1993). Anticipated stimulant and sedative effects of alcohol vary with dosages and limb of the blood alcohol curve. *Alcoholism: Clinical and Experimental Research, 17,* 135–139.

Farré, M., De Le Torre, R., Llorente, M., Lawas, X., Ugena, B., Segura, J., & Cami, J. (1993). Alcohol and cocaine interactions in humans. *Journal of Pharmacology and Experimental Therapeutics, 266,* 1364–1373.

Fibiger, H. C., & Phillips, A. C. (1988). Mesocorticolimbic dopamine systems and reward. *Annals of the New York Academy of Sciences, 537,* 206–215.

Finn, P. R., & Pihl, R. O. (1987). Men at high risk for alcoholism: The effects of alcohol on cardiovascular response to unavoidable shock. *Journal of Abnormal Psychology, 96,* 230–236.

Galbaud du Fort, G., Kovess, V., & Boivin, J.-F. (1994). Spouse similarity for psychological distress and well-being: A population study. *Psychological Medicine, 24,* 431–447.

Giancola, P. R. (1995). Evidence for dorsolateral and orbital prefrontal cortical involvement in the expression of aggressive behavior. *Aggressive Behavior, 21,* 431–450.

Giancola, P. R., & Zeichner, A. (1994). Neuropsychological performance on tests of frontal-lobe functioning and aggression in human males. *Journal of Abnormal Psychology, 103,* 832–835.

Gianoulakis, C., & Gupta, A. (1985). Inbred strains of mice with variable sensitivity to ethanol: Effect of acute ethanol treatment. *Neuropeptology, 5,* 579–582.

Gordon, T., Meehan, S. M., & Schechter, M. D. (1993). Differential effect of nicotine but not cathinone on motor activity of P and NP rats. *Pharmacology, Biochemistry & Behavior, 44,* 657–659.

Gorenstein, E. E. (1987). Cognitive-perceptual deficit in an alcoholism spectrum disorder. *Journal of Studies on Alcohol, 48,* 310–318.

Gray, J. A. (1982). *The neuropsychology of anxiety: An enquiry into the function of the septo-hippocampal system.* New York: Oxford University Press.

Gustafson, R. (1985). Alcohol and aggression: A validation study of the Taylor aggression paradigm. *Psychological Reports, 57,* 667–676.

Guze, S. B., Goodwin, D. W., & Crane, J. B. (1970). A psychiatric study of the wives of convicted felons: An example of assortative mating. *American Journal of Psychiatry, 126,* 1773–1776.

Harris, R. A., Brody, M. S., & Dunwiddle, T. V. (1992). Possible substrates of ethanol reinforcement: GABA and dopamine. *The neurobiology of drug and alcohol addiction. 654* (pp. 61–69). New York: Annals of the New York Academy of Sciences.

Heath, A., Bucholz, K., Madden, P., Dinwiddie, S., Slutske, W., Statham, D., Dunne, M., Whitfield, J.. & Martin, N. (1996). Genetic and environmental contributions to alcohol dependence risk in a national twin sample: Of findings in men and women. *Psychological Medicine, 27,* 1371–1396.

Hecaen, H., & Albert, M. L. (1978). *Human neuropsychology.* New York: Wiley.

Helzer, J. E., & Pryzbeck, T. R. (1988). The co-occurrence of alcoholism with other psychiatric disorders in the general population and its impact on treatment. *Journal of Studies on Alcohol, 49*(3), 219–224.

Higley, J. D., Mehlman, P. T., Higley, S. B., & Fernald, B. (1996). Excessive mortality in young free-ranging male nonhuman primates with low cerebrospinal fluid 5-hydroxyindoleacetic acid concentrations. *Archives of General Psychiatry, 53*(6), 537–543.

Higley, J. D., Mehlman, P. T., Taub, D. M., & Higley, S. B. (1992). Cerebrospinal fluid monoamine and adrenal correlates of aggression in free-ranging rhesus monkeys. *Archives of General Psychiatry, 49*(6), 436–441.

Hoaken, P. N. S., Assaad, J. M., & Pihl, R. O. (1998). Cognitive functioning and the inhibition of alcohol-induced aggression. *Journal of Studies on Alcohol, 59,* 599–607.

Hoaken, P. N. S., Giancola, P., & Pihl, R. O. (1998). Executive cognitive functions as mediators of alcohol-related aggression. *Journal of Alcohol and Alcoholism, 33*(1), 47–54.

Hoaken, P. N. S., Strickler, W. L. A., & Pihl, R. O. (2000). Alcohol intoxication and aggression in women: Mechanisms and predictive variables. Manuscript submitted for publication.

Jacob, T., & Bremer, D. A. (1986). Assortative mating among men and women alcoholics. *Journal of Studies on Alcohol, 47*(3), 219–222.

Jatlow, P., Elsworth, J., Brodberry, C., Winger, G., Taylor, J., Russell, R. & Roth, R. (1991). Cocaethyline: A neuropharmacologically ingestion. *Life Science, 48,* 1787–1794.

Knowles, P. A., Conner, R. L., & Panksepp, J. (1987). Opiate effects on social behaviour of juvenile dogs as a function of social deprivation. *Pharmacology, Biochemistry & Biobehavior, 33,* 533–537.

Koob, G. (1992). Drugs of abuse: Anatomy, pharmacology, and function of reward pathways. *Trends in Pharmacology, Science, 13,* 177–184.

Koob, G., & Bloom, F. E. (1988). Cellular and molecular mechanisms of drug dependence. *Science, 242*(4879), 715–723.

Kreuger, R. F., Moffitt, T. E., Caspi, A., Bleske, A., & Silva, P. A. (1998). Assortative mating   for antisocial behaviour: Developmental and methodological implications. *Behavior Genetics, 28,* 173–186.

Kriem, B., Abraini, J. H., & Rostain, J. C. (1996). Role of 5-HT-sub (lb) receptor in the pressure-induced behavioral and neurochemical disorders in rats. *Pharmacology, Biochemistry & Behavior, 53*(2), 257–264.

Kruesi, M. J., Swedo, S., Leonard, H., & Rubinow, D. R. (1990). CSF somatostatin in childhood psychiatric disorders: A preliminary investigation. *Psychiatry Research, 33*(3), 277–284.

Lappalainer, J., Long, J., Eggert, M., Ozaki, N., Robin, R., Brown, E., Nankkarinen, H., Virkkunen, M., Linnoila, M., & Goldman, D. (1998). Linkage of antisocial alcoholism to the serotonin 5-HTIB receptor gene in 2 populations. *Archives of General Psychiatry, 55,* 989–994.

Lau, M. A., & Pihl, R. O. (1996). Cognitive performance, monetary incentive, and aggression. *Aggressive Behaviour, 22,* 417–430.

Lau, M. A., Pihl, R. O., & Peterson, J. B. (1995). Provocation, acute alcohol intoxication, cognitive performance, and aggression. *Journal of Abnormal Psychology, 104,* 150–155.

LeMarquand, D., Pihl, R. O., & Benkelfat, C. (1994a). Serotonin and alcohol intake, abuse and dependence: Clinical evidence. *Biological Psychiatry, 36,* 326–337.

LeMarquand, D., Pihl, R. O., & Benkelfat, C. (1994b). Serotonin and alcohol intake, abuse and dependence: Findings of animal studies. *Biological Psychiatry, 36,* 395–421.

Leshner, A. (1997). Addiction is a Brain Disease, and it matters. *Science, 278,* 45–47.

Lidberg, L. (1985). Platelet monoamine oxidase activity and psychopathy. *Psychiatry Research, 16*(4), 339–343.

Linnoila, M., De Jong, J., & Virkkunen, M. (1989). Family history of alcoholism in violent offenders and impulsive fire starters. *Archives of General Psychiatry, 46,* 613–616.

McCance-Katz, E., Price, L., McDougle, C., Kostens, T., Black, J., & Jatlow, P. (1993). Concurrent cocaine-ethanol infections in humans, pharmacology, physiology, behavior, and the role of cocaethyline. *Psychopharmacology, 117,* 39–46.

Mehlman, P. T., Higley, J. D., Faucher, I., & Lilly, A. A. (1995). Low CSF 5-HIAA concentrations and severe aggression and impaired impulse control in nonhuman primates. *American Journal of Psychiatry, 151*(10), 1485–1491.

Moffitt, T. E. (1993). The neuropsychology of conduct disorder. *Developmental Psychopathology, 5,* 135–151.

Mullen, F. J., & Luckhardt, A. B. (1934). The effect of alcohol on cutaneous tactile and pain   sensitivity. *American Journal of Physiology, 109,* 77–78.

Murdoch, D., Pihl, R. O., Ross, D. (1990). Alcohol and crimes of violence: Present issues. *International Journal of Addictions, 25,* 1059–1075.

Neilson, J. (1964). Mental disorders in married couples (assortative mating). *British Journal of Psychiatry, 110,* 683–697.

Panksepp, J., Jalowiec, J., DeEskinazi, F. G., & Bishop, P. (1985). Opiates and play dominance in juvenile rats. *Behavioral Neuroscience, 99*(3), 441–453.

Peterson, J., Conrod, P., Pihl, R., & Gianoulakis, C. (1999). *Ethanol's stimulating effect on resting baseline heart rate is eliminated by naltrexone.* Paper presented at the Research Society on Alcoholism. Santa Barbara, California, June.

Peterson, J. B., & Pihl, R. O. (1990). Information processing, neuropsychological function, and the inherited predisposition to alcoholism. *Neuropsychological Review, 1,* 343–369.

Peterson, J., Pihl, R., Gianoulakis, C., Conrod, P., Finn, P., Stewart, S., LeMarquand, D., & Bruce, K. (1996). Ethanol-induced change in cardiac and endogenous opiate function and risk for alcoholism. *Alcoholism: Clinical and Experimental Research, 20,* 1542–1552.

Peterson, J. B., Rothfleisch, J., Zelazo, P. D., & Pihl, R. O. (1990). Acute alcohol intoxication and cognitive functioning. *Journal of Studies on Alcohol, 51,* 114–122.

Pihl, R., & LeMarquand, D. (1998). Serotonin and aggression and the alcohol-aggression relationship. *Alcohol and Alcoholism, 33,* 55–65.

Pihl, R. O., & Peterson, J. B. (1992). Etiology. *Annual Review of Addiction Research & Treatment, 21,* 153–175.

Pihl, R., & Peterson, J. (1995a). Alcoholism: The role of different motivational systems. *Journal of Psychiatry and Neuroscience, 20,* 372–376.

Pihl, R. O., & Peterson, J. B. (1995b). Drugs and aggression: Correlations, crime and human manipulative studies and some proposed mechanisms. *Journal of Psychiatric Neurosciences, 20*(2), 141–149.

Pihl, R. O., Peterson, J., & Finn, P. (1990). Inherited predisposition to alcoholism: Characteristics of sons of male alcoholics. *Journal of Abnormal Psychology, 99,* 291–301.

Pihl, R. O., Peterson, J. B., & Lau, M. A. (1993). A biosocial model of the alcohol-aggression relationship. *Journal of Studies on Alcohol, 11*(Suppl.), 128–139.

Pihl, R. O., Young, S. N., Harden, P., Plotnick, S., Chamberlain, B., & Ervin, F. R. (1995). Acute effect of altered tryptophan levels and alcohol on aggression in normal human males. *Psychopharmacology, 119,* 353–360.

Poulos, C. X., Parker, J. L., & Le, D. A. (1998). Increased impulsivity after injected alcohol predicts later alcohol consumption in rats: Evidence for "loss-of-control drinking" and marked individual differences. *Behavioral Neuroscience, 112*(5), 1247–1257.

Raine, A., Buchsbaum, M. S., Stanley, J., Lottenberg, S., Abel, L., & Stoddard, J. (1994). Selective reductions in prefrontal glucose metabolism in murderers. *Biological Psychiatry, 36,* 365–373.

Raine, A., Stoddard, J., Bibule, S., & Buchsbaum, M. (1998). Prefrontal glucose deficits in murderers lacking psychosocial deprivation. *Neuropsychiatry, Neuropsychology, & Behavioral Neurology, 11,* 1–7.

Roy, A., Adinoff, B., & Linnoila, M. (1988). Acting out hostility in normal volunteers: Negative correlation with levels of 5HIAA in cerebrospinal fluid. *Psychiatry Research, 24,* 187–194.

Saudou, F., Djamei, A., Dierich, A., LeMeur, M., Ramboz, S., Segu, L., Buhot, M., & Hen, R. (1994). Enhanced aggressive behavior in mice lacking 5-HT1B receptor. *Science, 265,* 1875–1878.

Séguin, J., Pihl, R., Harden, P., Boulerice, B., & Tremblay, R. (1995). Cognitive and neuropsychological characteristics of aggressive boys. *Journal of Abnormal Psychology, 104,* 614–624.

Sher, K. J., Walitzer, K. S., Wood, P. K., & Brent, E. (1991). Characteristics of children of alcoholics: Putative risk factors for substance use and abuse and psychopathology. *Journal of Abnormal Psychology, 100,* 427–448.

Smith, S. E., Pihl, R. O., Young, S. N., & Ervin, F. R. (1987). Elevation and reduction of plasma tryptophan and their effects on aggression and perceptual sensitivity in normal males. *Aggressive Behavior, 12,* 393–407.

Sobrie, P. (1986). Reconciling the role of central serotonin neurons in human and animal behaviour. *Behavior & Brain Science, 9,* 319–364.

Spoont, M. R. (1992). Modulatory role of serotonin in neural information processing: Implications for human psychopathology. *Psychological Bulletin, 112*(2), 330–350.

Stabenau, J. R., & Hesselbrock, V. M. (1983). Family pedigree of alcoholic and control patients. *International Journal of the Addictions, 18,* 351–363.

Stewart, S. H., Conrod, P. J., Pihl, R. O., & Doniger, M. (1999). Relations between posttraumatic stress symptom dimensions and substance dependence in a community-recruited sample of substance-abusing women. *Psychology of Addictive Behaviors, 13,* 78–88.

Stewart, S. H., Finn, P. R., & Pihl, R. O. (1992). The effects of alcohol on the cardiovascular response in men at high risk for alcoholism: A dose response study. *Journal of Studies on Alcoholism, 53,* 499–506.

Stewart, S. H., Finn, P. R., & Pihl, R. O. (1995). A dose-response study of the effects of alcohol on the perceptions of pain and discomfort due to electric shock in men at high familial-genetic risk for alcholism. *Psychopharmacology, 199,* 261–267.

Stewart, S. H., & Pihl, R. O. (1994). Effects of alcohol administration on psycophysiological and subjective emotional responses to aversive stimulation in anxiety-sensitive women. *Psychology & Addictive Behaviors, 8,* 29–42.

Stuss, D., & Benson, D. (1984). Neuropsychological studies of the frontal lobes. *Psychological Bulletin, 95,* 3–28.

Virkkunen, M., De Jong, J., Bartko, J. & Linnoia, M. (1989). Psychobiological concomitants of history of suicide attempts among violent offenders and impulsive fire starters. *Archives of General Psychiatry, 46,* 604–606.

Virkkunen, M., Rawlings, R., Tokola, R., Poland, R. E., Guidotti, A., Nemeroff, C., Bissette, G., Kalogeras, K., Karonen, S.-L., & Linnoila, M. (1994). CSF biochemistries, glucose metabolism, and diurnal activity rhythms in alcoholic violent offenders, fire setters, and healthy volunteers. *Archives of General Psychiatry, 51,* 20–27.

Warneke, L. B. (1991). Benzodiazepines: Abuse and new use. *Canadian Journal of Psychiatry, 36,* 194–205.

Willis, W. D., & Westlund, K. N. (1997). Neuroanatomy of the pain system and of the pathways that modulate pain. *Journal of Clinical Neurophysiology, 14,* 2–31.

Windle, M., & Searles, J. S. (1990). Children of alcoholics: Critical perspectives. In M. Windle & S. Searles (Eds.), *The Guilford substance abuse series* (pp. 217–238). New York: Guilford.

Wise, R. A. (1988). Psychomotor stimulant properties of addictive drugs. *Annals of the New York Academy of Sciences, 537,* 228–234.

Wise, R., & Bozarth, M. (1987). A psychomotor stimulant theory of addiction. *Psychological Review, 94,* 469–492.

Zeichner, A., & Pihl, R. O. (1979). Effects of alcohol and behavior contingencies on human aggression. *Journal of Abnormal Psychology, 88,* 153–160.

Zeichner, A., & Pihl, R. O. (1980). The effects of alcohol and instigator intent on human aggression. *Journal of Studies on Alcoholism, 41,* 265–276.

Zeichner, A., Pihl, R. O., Niaura, R., & Zacchia, C. (1982). Attentional processes in alcohol-mediated aggression. *Journal of Studies on Alcoholism, 43,* 714–724.

3

CHAPTER

Patricia McKinsey Crittenden
Angelika Hartl Claussen

Developmental Psychopathology Perspectives on Substance Abuse and Relationship Violence

This chapter is concerned with the developmental pathways that increase the probability of drug use, relationship violence, and the co-occurrence of these conditions. That is, the developmental antecedents of these two threats to adequate adult functioning are explored. Two central ideas form the underlying structure of this chapter. The first is developmental: the assumption that, in most cases, risk for maladaptation and maladaptation itself are not random events, but rather follow a series of developmental experiences that increase the probability of specific risk outcomes. The second is that both substance abuse and relationship violence can be considered strategies albeit rather drastic ones, for resolving problems. The question becomes why some individuals select these strategies, while others do not.

Most of the existing literature on the antecedents and correlates of substance abuse focuses on stressful life conditions and diagnoses of mental or personality disorder in either the affected individual or their caregivers and spouses. Not surprisingly, the array of predisposing and concurrent conditions is quite wide and consistently negative in impact (Doweiko, 1999). The same is true for the literature on interpersonal violence, although in general this literature, especially that on child maltreatment, is somewhat more developed. That is, attempts have been made to view violent behavior from a developmental perspective, as an aspect of distorted interpersonal processes, and in terms of its function in individuals' lives and relationships (Crittenden, 1996, 1998a; Kolko, 1996; Trickett & Putnam, 1998). Such a developmental approach to substance abuse is more recent (Cicchetti & Rogosch, 1999; Weinberg & Glantz, 1999). This chapter expands that approach to consideration of substance abuse and its co-occurrence with interpersonal violence.

The chapter begins with a review of research on the antecedents and correlates of substance abuse and on interpersonal violence and its effects on development. Both discussions include a brief overview of theories regarding each. Then, a theoretical model for describing context-adapted coping strategies, together with predisposing developmental conditions, is presented. We conclude by linking the empirical evidence to these strategies to suggest several developmental pathways that carry risk for substance abuse and interpersonal violence.

☐ Antecedents and Correlates of Substance Abuse and Relationship Violence

Substance Abuse

It is necessary to differentiate substance abuse from substance use, which is a normative behavior (Cicchetti & Rogosch, 1999). Approximately 90% of adults consume some alcohol during their lives (Schuckit, 1999), and half of all adults admit to illicit dug use at least once (Warner, Kessler, Hughes, Anthony, & Nelson, 1995), whereas an estimated 10% of the population abuses substances (Doweiko, 1999). Substance abuse and addiction appear to be highly correlated with other risk factors, with substance users in the community being similar to the normative population and in-patient substance abusers showing the most negative precursors, symptoms, and pathology (Newcomb, Bentler, & Fahy, 1987). This discussion focuses on the relation of substance abuse to (1) family, individual, and life event precursors and (2) psychiatric and personality disorders. Because some risk factors are relevant to all forms of substance abuse and others to specific substances, studies that focus on the latter are given special consideration. A review by Hawkins, Catalano, and Miller (1992) classified risk factors into two domains: contextual (e.g., availability of drugs) and individual-interpersonal. We focus on the latter, and specifically on those influences that are amenable to modification, rather than on genetic and biological factors that influence substance abuse and addiction (Schuckit, 1999; see also Pihl & Hoaken, this volume).

Interpersonal Precursors. Environmental factors, including childhood experiences, play a strong role in determining whether a person will abuse substances (Ammerman, Ott, Tarter, & Blackson, 1999). Although substance use is clearly related to concurrent environmental factors such as peers' use, childhood factors account for at least as much variance (Aseltine, Gore, & Colten, 1998; Dobkin, Tremblay, Masse, & Vitaro, 1995; Hoffman, 1998; Masse & Tremblay, 1997; Swaim, 1991). Childhood factors include unsupportive parents, problematic and conflicted family relationships, negativity, stress, isolation, and lack of family cohesion and structure (Aseltine et al., 1998; Baumrind, 1991; Dobkin, Tremblay, & Sacchitelle, 1997; Friedman, Bransfield, Tomko, & Katz, 1991; Hoffman, 1998; Johnson & Leff, 1999; Wekerle & Wall, this volume; Wills, Vaccaro, & McNamara, 1992). An important precursor of substance abuse is being raised by a substance-abusing parent (Caudill, Hoffman, Hubbard, Flynn, & Luckey, 1994; Hoffman, 1998; Risser, Bonsch, & Schneider, 1996; Swaim, 1991). Indeed, specific substances have been associated with the same substance abused by adolescents (Andrews, Hops, Ary, Tildesley, & Harris, 1993). Parental substance abuse has a particular impact when there are other risks present such as detrimental parent-child relationships (Dobkin et al., 1997; Johnson & Leff, 1999).

In general, one of the most consistent findings is that substance abuse is associated with prior traumatic events, particularly physical and sexual abuse, which are themselves outcomes of substance abuse (Clark, Lesnick, & Hegedus, 1997; Hoffman, 1998; Jantzen, Ball, Leventhal, & Schottenfeld, 1998; Langeland & Hartgers, 1998; Risser et al., 1996; Wills et al., 1992; see also Stewart & Israeli, this volume). Of those whose drug abuse resulted in death, 80% had experienced parental divorce or death during childhood (Risser et al., 1996).

It is clear that substance abuse is associated with poor parenting (e.g., Burns, Chethik, Burns, & Clark, 1991; Kelley, 1992, 1998) and is strongly linked to child abuse and neglect (Beeghly & Tronick, 1994; Chaffin, Kelleher, & Hollenberg, 1996; Kelley, 1992, 1998; Murphy et al., 1991; Singer et al., 1997). Less is known about specific patterns of parenting impairment (May & Bernstein, 1995), particularly for substances other than alcohol and in parenting children beyond early infancy (Johnson & Leff, 1999). In infancy, parental substance abuse, in conjunction with other risk factors, results in inattentive, intrusive and unresponsive mother-infant interaction (Bernstein, Jeremy, Hans, & Marcus, 1994; Burns et al., 1991; May et al., 1997) although not all studies find direct effects for substance use (Bernstein & Hans, 1994; Hagan & Myers, 1997). Anxious attachment, particularly the disorganized and extreme subpatterns, also is associated with maternal drug use (Claussen & Anderson, 1997; O'Connor, Sigman, & Brill, 1987; O'Connor, Sigman, & Kasari, 1992; Rodning, Beckwith, & Howard, 1992). This effect is in addition to that of prenatal exposure (Bernstein & Hans, 1994; Blackwell, Kirkhart, Schmitt, & Kaiser, 1998; Eiden & Leonard, 1996; Goodman, Hans, & Cox, 1999). Anxious attachment is also prevalent in adult offspring of substance users (Jaeger, Hahn, & Weinraub, 2000) and in adolescent drug users and their mothers (Rosenstein & Horowitz, 1996).

Certain child characteristics have been linked to later substance abuse. A review points to a cluster of developmental problems beginning with a "difficult" temperament in infancy, conduct problems in preschool and younger school years, and antisocial or delinquent behavior by high school age (Swaim, 1991). Specific childhood problems in this cluster include behavioral and emotional dysregulation, impulsivity, novelty-seeking, low harm avoidance, and childhood aggression and conduct problems (e.g., Brook, Whiteman, Cohen, Shapiro, & Balka, 1995; Brook, Whiteman, Finch, & Cohen, 1996; Dobkin et al., 1997; Friedman et al, 1991; Martin et al., 1994; Masse & Tremblay, 1997; Shedler & Block, 1990; Wills et al., 1992). Some forms of anxiety and social problems may actually protect against substance use (Cicchetti & Rogosch, 1999). In contrast to the previous cluster of externalizing behaviors, recent evidence indicates a relation between early inhibition and later alcohol abuse (Caspi, Moffitt, Newman, & Silva, 1998).

Although studies often focus on singular causes, multiple risk mechanisms for substance abuse are likely (Cicchetti & Rogosch, 1999). Further, it is possible that childhood problems may be related to substance abuse through underlying third factors (Weinberg & Glantz, 1999). A process suggested by the findings is that parents' inability to regulate conflict (with or without substance abuse) leads to distressed children, who display characteristics that combine with their parents' limited parenting skills to produce traumatic events in which the children are unprotected and feel uncomforted. When interpersonal strategies fail to elicit protection and reduce anxiety, some adolescents cope by using drugs, thus taking on the risks of abuse and addiction.

Psychiatric and Personality Disorders.   Many studies of substance abusers have identified increased comorbidity with personality disorders, using DSM Axis II diagnostic criteria (American Psychiatric Association, 1994), but, because most use inpatient samples, there is a bias toward very serious levels of substance abuse. Although substance use itself is not directly associated with personality disorder (Newcomb et al., 1987), chronic or severe substance abuse is. The direction of the findings, but not the severity of symptoms, may be relevant to the general population of substance users.

In spite of the difficulty of distinguishing between the symptoms of personality disorder and substance abuse (Weinberg & Glantz, 1999), more than half of substance abusing inpatients also show an Axis II diagnosis, most frequently antisocial or borderline personality disorder (Rounsaville et al., 1998). Specific problems associated with substance abuse include sensation seeking, poor problem solving skills, and impulse control (Ball, Carroll, & Rounsaville, 1994; Lejoyeux, Feuche, Loi, Solomon, & Ades, 1999; Pfefferbaum & Wood, 1994; Platt & Husband, 1993). Depression co-occurring with substance abuse was associated with far more serious family and peer problems than substance abuse alone (Aseltine et al., 1998).

The evidence regarding the relation of particular drugs to particular personality disorders is mixed (Campbell & Stark, 1990; Skodol, Oldham, & Gallagher, 1999). Alcohol abusing outpatients with a personality disorder were more likely to have intense negative emotions, interpersonal conflict, a pattern of testing personal control, and emotion-oriented coping styles than those without such a disorder (Smyth & Washousky, 1995). Affective disorder was also associated with alcohol abuse (Aseltine et al., 1998). A prospective study of college students found a strong association of alcoholism and anxiety disorders, with a reciprocal causal relation over time (Kushner, Sher, & Erickson, 1999). Severe cocaine abuse was associated with both personal and familial antisocial attention deficit disorder, conduct disorder, and personality disorder (Ball et al., 1994). A comparison of opiate and cocaine abusers found only limited differences between the groups, with cocaine relating to antisocial personality and opiates to anxiety and somatic distress (Craig & Olson, 1990). This is consistent with the findings that bipolar/cyclothymic and attention deficit disorder were associated with cocaine abuse and anxiety and panic disorder with sedative-hypnotic (opiate) abuse (Aseltine et al., 1998). Sedative-hypnotic abusers were the most likely to meet other Axis I criteria (Mirin, Weiss, Griffin, & Michael, 1991). Significantly, schizotypal and compulsive disorders are notably absent among substance abusers (Campbell & Stark, 1990; Craig & Olson, 1990).

Theoretical Perspectives.   Several theoretical perspectives have been offered ranging from the almost purely physiological/genetic to the purely experiential. Probably the best conclusion is that "causality in substance abuse apparently resides in genetic determinism modulated by the environment" (Miller & Giannini, 1990, p. 84). Given the absence of specific genetic determinants and the presence of considerable environmental evidence, it is the latter that can be explored more productively at this moment.

An outcomes-oriented review of intervention efforts finds that training in problem solving and social skills reduced the recurrence of substance abuse (Platt & Husband, 1993), suggesting at least a catalytic role for the management of interpersonal relationships. Others point more directly at relationships, particularly sexual relationships, as being critical to the decision to use drugs (Rhodes & Quirk, 1998). This is consistent with the high rates of sexual abuse reported among substance abusers. Others suggest that particular substances are used to achieve particular effects on affect regulation (Doweiko, 1999). Specifically, alcohol and central nervous system (CNS) depressants are hypothesized to counteract loneliness, opiates (heroine, morphine) to reduce rage and aggression, and CNS stimulants (cocaine, amphetamines) to reduce depression, anergia, and low self-esteem. This approach, while intriguing, seems premature at present. Another approach that accounts for some data, but simplifies what is probably a complex process, postulates three pathways for responding to a potential stressor (Shiffman & Wills, 1985). One involves failure to perceive the event or its significance; this leads to low physiological arousal and lethargy, which, in turn, lead to low subjective arousal and, thus, the desire for stimulants. A second pathway involves appropriate problem identification, leading to appropriate arousal and a moderate reaction without a need for psychoactive substances. The third pathway involves exaggerated perception of threat, intense physiological and affective arousal, and thus strong behavioral reactions that can be calmed and modulated by drugs that depress neurological activity. This theory accounts well for the types of disorders associated with substance abuse, that is, depression and Axis II disorders. The developmental data on precursors and symptoms suggest a pathway that could increase the probability of individuals using these maladaptive coping patterns. The goal of this chapter is to integrate these components in a theory of how experience in relationships prepares individuals to identify and respond to threatening events.

Relationship Violence

In contrast to the more recent interest in developmental aspects of substance abuse, there is an empirical literature on family violence, especially child abuse, covering almost four decades. There has been a development of theoretical perspectives from micro-theories of very narrow scope to multilayered systemic theories that begin to capture the complexity of this intense human phenomenon (e.g., Azar, 1991; Belsky, 1993; Crittenden, 1998a; Crittenden & Ainsworth, 1989; Emery & Laumann-Billings, 1998). Contributing factors to family violence are best presented in terms of a nested hierarchy that range from genetically-based species attributes to intrapersonal characteristics, dyadic relationships (especially attachment relationships), aspects of family functioning, and cultural and community influences. Similar to the recognition that substance use is a common behavior, interpersonal violence is no longer viewed as an aberrant condition affecting only a few deviant individuals. To the contrary, it is viewed on a continuum of severity and frequency on which every individual can be described in terms of both their use of violent behavior and also their probability of eliciting violence from others. Research and clinical questions, thus, can be organized around the conditions under which violent behavior becomes more frequent and extreme.

Cultural and Community Violence.   Violence in children's wider developmental context has detrimental effects on them. For example, children exposed to war develop symptoms of anxiety (e.g., sleep disorders, psychosomatic symptoms, anxiety, attentional problems, and fear of recurrence of violence) (Garmezy & Rutter, 1985). Children exposed to community violence (e.g., shootings, kidnappings, robberies), display a range of symptoms, including anxiety, fear, thought suppression, reliving experiences, depression, aggression, low self-esteem, oppositional behavior, apprehension, intensely experienced negative affect, and morbid or pessimistic thoughts (Horn & Trickett, 1998). Of course, not all children show these effects or the same effects. Further, the effects are not associated specifically with the type of violence experienced. On the other hand, the more closely and intensively the child experienced violence (i.e., to the self versus a stranger; a shooting versus a robbery), the greater were the effects (Horn & Trickett, 1998). Many symptoms were co-occurring, but, in one study, oppositional and anxious behaviors were mutually exclusive (Hill & Madhere, 1996). As for substance abuse, different developmental pathways among affected children are possible. Nevertheless, the implicit theory underlying most studies is simple-effects theory in which increasing stress yields increasingly negative effects. As Horn and Trickett point out, great complexity is possible, with some children experiencing few effects from similar stressors and others experiencing different patterns of effects. Theory to describe this developmental process has yet to be articulated.

Family Violence.   Violence in families takes several forms. The two most studied are spousal (or partner) abuse and child abuse (both physical and sexual). Like substance use, marital violence is relatively common, with an estimated third to half of children being exposed over the course of childhood, usually in multiple events (Margolin, 1998). Also, like substance abuse, marital violence is associated with other forms of violence, particularly child abuse, with an estimated 50% overlap between the two (Hughes, Parkinson, & Vargo, 1989; Margolin, 1998). Children living with an abused mother are at a substantially increased risk for sexual abuse from the mother's partner or an extrafamilial person (McCloskey, Figueredo, & Koss, 1995). There is also a relation between community violence and marital violence (Bell & Jenkins, 1993; Garbarino, Dubrow, Kostelny, & Pardo, 1992). Further, both forms of family violence are associated with other threats to children's development, particularly mental illness, personality problems, and substance use (Rosenbaum & O'Leary, 1981; Spaccarelli, Sandler, & Roosa, 1994). Finally, both forms of family violence initiate a cascade of stressful events tied to separation, including divorce, foster placement, incarceration, death, and changes of home and school. Thus, it becomes very difficult, if not impossible, to isolate the effects of family violence from those of other stressors.

Although researchers had once hoped to differentiate antecedents from the effects of violence; in practice, that has become impossible. Partly this is because human processes are often reciprocal, partly because there are intergenerational effects, and partly because of how we define the factors. With regard to the latter, the focus has been on measurable behavior or states (e.g., hyperactivity, depression) and not on the function of behavior in interpersonal processes. Because these conditions overlap greatly across different types of violence and even across violence and substance abuse, a simple listing is given here, with the symptoms listed in approximate developmental order starting with those that appear in infancy to those most common in adolescence. Children exposed to violence have both immediate and long-term effects, and these include difficult temperament; weight, eating, and sleep disorders; separation anxiety; failure to comply; impulsive behavior; defiance, interpersonal conflict; externalizing behavior; aggression; conduct disorders; hyperactivity; attentional problems; learning difficulties; internalizing disorders; depression; fear; anxiety; health problems; limited social and interpersonal problem solving skills; social isolation and rejection; limited empathy; mood problems; obsessive-compulsive disorder; delinquency; and eating disorders (Crittenden, 1998a; Kolko, 1996; Margolin, 1998). A particular finding is that both abused children and their parents show distortions of attachment, often expressed in atypical patterns (e.g., Barnett, Ganiban, & Cicchetti, 1999; Cicchetti & Barnett, 1991; Crittenden, 1985a, 1985b, 1999; Seefeldt, 1997; Wekerle & Wolfe, 1998). Among parents, family violence is associated with authoritarian and inconsistent child management strategies, stressful life events, hostile or explosive personality, abuse during childhood, interpersonal or psychiatric disorder, and substance abuse (Famularo, Stone, Barnum, & Wharton, 1986; Kelley, 1992; Murphy, et al., 1991; Whipple & Webster-Stratton, 1991).

Sexual abuse has generally been treated as different from other forms of violence. In particular, researchers have noted various forms of atypical sexualized behavior as being among the developmental effects of sexual abuse. However, almost all forms of serious deviance involve some form of atypical sexual behavior, and research directed toward other forms of relationship violence has not systematically assessed sexual behavior. Thus, concluding that atypical sexualized behavior is a distinguishing feature of sexual abuse may be premature. In addition, as with substance abuse, the field of sexual abuse is less fully developed than that of child and marital abuse. Nevertheless, some of the most recent work is quite sophisticated in terms of design and theory. Developmental effects have been noted, such that the effects of sexual abuse can be tied somewhat to the age at which the abuse was experienced (Trickett & Putnam, 1998). Sexual abuse in early childhood affects physiological functioning in the form of psychosomatic complaints and physical disorders tied to sexual organs, such as enuresis (Trickett & Putnam, 1998). Inappropriate sexual behavior including display and masturbation may occur. In the school years, problems include enuresis, inappropriate sexual behavior, both internalizing (especially depression) and externalizing (aggression and conduct problems) behavior, short-term dissociation, poor peer relationships, poor academic performance (but not lower grades or test scores), and attention deficit hyperactivity disorder (ADHD). Nonetheless, school-aged sexually abused children do not display higher anxiety, posttraumatic stress disorder (PTSD), or somatic complaints. For adolescents, in some cases, the intensity of symptomatic behavior increases, for example, to suicidal and self-injurious behavior, delinquency, and running away. In addition, immune system functioning may be impaired. By adulthood, in severe cases, there is evidence of substance abuse, personality disorder (especially antisocial personality), hippocampal damage, and, in women, affective and anxiety disorders, and poor adjustment in social and intimate relationships that is sometimes displayed in revictimization (e.g., rape, battering). Nevertheless, knowledge about the causes and effects of sexual abuse is limited by the small numbers of subjects in most studies, the potentially skewed methods for obtaining subjects, and the limited range of variables assessed; in particular, measures of basic functioning, as opposed to self-report measures or clinical and diagnostic checklists are needed.

These findings for sexual abuse are intriguing for both the developmental perspective that is offered and for the focus on sexual and neurophysiological functioning. Developmentally, a transformation of behaviors typical of young children into similar behaviors typical of older children, adolescents, and adults can be discerned. For example, hyperactivity and conduct problems in preschoolers become conduct disorder in school-aged children, delinquency in adolescence, and antisocial personality disorder in adulthood. This pattern of age-related transformations is theoretically expectable, but has yet to be tested empirically to determine which conditions are associated with maintenance of the pathway (or escalation of severity) and which are indicative of a peaking of severity at younger ages or even a reversion to a less maladaptive pathway. This serves as a useful reminder that sexual behavior should be assessed for all at-risk children. Similarly, changes in neurophysiological functioning may be general to experiences of self-threatening danger. Studies of physically abused children that show neurophysiological effects (e.g., Pollak, Cicchetti, Klorman, & Brumaghim, 1997) suggest the importance of including such measures in studies of all types of disorders.

Nevertheless, it is clear that there is wide variation in the effects of family violence upon children. There is some evidence that differences in children's age, chronicity of exposure, and closeness (both physically and psychologically) to the victim affect outcomes to children (Garbarino et al., 1992; Martinez & Richters, 1993). Further, although some children seem free of symptoms of maladjustment, accounting for this is problematic because some psychological effects may be overlooked and because the protective factors seem quite general (i.e., support within the family, support outside the family, and protective child attributes) (Garmezy, 1983), and are precisely the factors most disrupted by family violence.

Theories of Relationship Violence.   The current perspective emphasizes universal principles that affect humans at different organizational levels (e.g., culture, community, family, dyad, and individual) differentially as a function of development, and across the full range of adaptive and maladaptive functioning (Belsky, 1980; Bronfenbrenner, 1979; Emery & Laumann-Billings, 1998; Garbarino, 1977). This systemic perspective emphasizes the bidirectionality of effects, multiple pathways to similar outcomes, and varied outcomes from similar initial conditions. Further, at all levels, interpersonal processes constitute the mechanism whereby environmental conditions affect individuals. Finally, the models emphasize the impact of developmental processes on the effects of similar experiences and the transformations in behavioral displays of disorder that occur as children mature. Put another way, complexity and inclusiveness are at the heart of current models of developmental psychopathology. This creates new problems. Where older, more simplistic approaches failed to account for much of the variation, thereby creating a void of understanding, the current approach provides such a wealth of detail and relations among factors that it threatens to obscure understanding.

☐ Coping Strategies and a Dynamic-Maturational Model of Strategic Behavior

The reviews of research on substance abuse and interpersonal violence make two things very clear: (1) people who abuse substances or one another grow up and live in chronically stressful circumstances, and (2) once their use of potentially addictive substances and interpersonal aggression has reached levels that can be labeled abusive, they are not coping adequately with these circumstances. Of interest here is the process by which the challenge of stressful circumstances, which should elicit adaptive coping strategies, has been transformed into the failure to cope that is indicated by the term abuse.

A Dynamic-Maturational Model of Self-Protective Strategies

A useful model should both reduce the number of unique variables to be accounted for and, concurrently, reflect the complexity of developmental pathways through which environmental conditions interact with interpersonal variables and intrapersonal characteristics to yield individual differences in strategies for resolving problems. The dynamic-maturational model proposed here is an integrative expansion of the Bowlby-Ainsworth attachment theory with social-ecological theory and information processing theory from the cognitive neurosciences and cognitive psychology.

Attachment theory provides two useful components: the notions of function and developmental pathways (from Bowlby) and the notions of functional equivalence of disparate behaviors and patterns of behavior that function strategically (from Ainsworth) (Bowlby, 1979; Ainsworth, 1979). Specifically, Bowlby focused on the function of attachment to protect children from danger; this is relevant to both the dangerous conditions associated with substance and person abuse and also the lack of protection offered by parents. Bowlby also referred to developmental pathways that have direction, but could change direction during development; thus permitting both predictability and variation in outcome. Ainsworth recognized that sets of behaviors could serve the same function, for example, reaching, crying, and shouting all function to keep parents nearby; this permits the clustering of many individual variables that researchers have used and that vary from person to person. If all serve the same function, a meta-variable can represent the set. Finally, Ainsworth's three basic infant patterns of attachment (ABC; Ainsworth, Blehar, Waters, & Wall, 1978) describe a set of strategies for eliciting parental protection. The cognitive neurosciences contribute the notion of rapid precortical processing of stimuli based on their (a) temporal order and (b) intensity. The former can be related to Ainsworth's Type A strategy of doing what will yield predictable outcomes and the latter to her Type C strategy of heightening affect, with Type B using both forms of information (Crittenden, 1999). Cognitive psychology contributes information regarding the organization of memory systems that can explain the process by which the ABC patterns are elaborated after infancy. Finally, social ecological theory nests these intrapersonal and dyadic processes in the context of families, communities, and cultures.

Strategies for Eliciting Protection in Infancy.   Parent-infant interaction fosters transformation of innate reflexes into three context-adapted patterns of behavior that function to maximize infants' access to parental protection and comfort (Ainsworth, 1979). Infants whose distress is followed temporally by parental attention and affectively by comfort organize using a Type B strategy (see Figure 3.1) of direct communication of needs and desires. If, however, the parents respond to infant distress in an angry, punitive man-

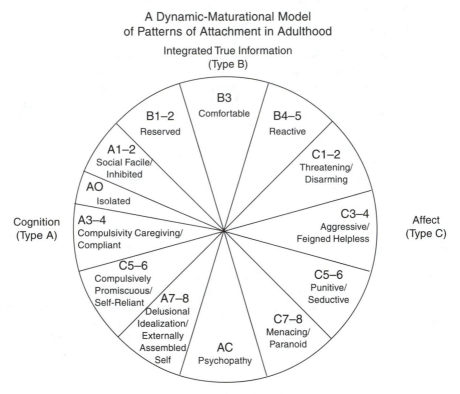

FIGURE 3.1. A dynamic-maturational model of self-protective strategies in adolescence and adulthood. Printed with permission from Patricia M. Crittenden. Numerous descriptive labels have been applied to the A, B, and C patterns. We chose not to use any of these in aggreement with Bowlby (1979) who advised Ainsworth (1979) to use nondescriptive notation until she knew the psychological meaning of the patterns (Ainsworth, 1979). We feel that this meaning is still unclear and that labels would be both premature and misleading. For example, the infant Type A pattern is commonly known as 'avoidant.' However, avoidance typifies both Type A infants and Type C individuals at older ages; thus, the term 'avoidant' becomes misleading. In addition, as we have come to understand the patterns more fully, it appears that each pattern confers benefits and also carries drawbacks; a single descriptive label can only refer to one of these and, therefore, is misleading. For example, Type A individuals are 'inhibited' with regard to affect, but they also are 'independent.' Which is the better label? Type B is 'secure,' but also 'naive' with regard to danger; for this reason we prefer 'balanced' for Type B. In the end, however, we choose not to use labels and to retain the alpha-numeric notational style recommended by Bowlby and adopted by Ainsworth.

ner, infants learn to inhibit the display of distress (probable Type A). Such infants learn that predictions based on temporal order yield the greatest safety and reduce discomfort with their caregivers; the corresponding strategy (A1-2) consists of doing what the parents reinforce and inhibiting the display of negative affect. The most complex situation is when the parents' response does not fit the infants' arousal synchronously in time or intensity, or both. Temporally, the parent responds either when there is no distress (i.e., too soon, or too late) or when the infants' increasing distress has already initiated a self-maintaining feedback loop of arousal. In intensity, the parent is either too little aroused (i.e., apparently uncaring and unperturbed) or too aroused, thus, distressing the infant. Moreover, the parent's behavior is unpredictable to the infant. In this context, infants experience complex combinations of feelings that create the incompatible dispositions to seek the parent for comfort, to avoid the parent fearfully, or to attack the parent angrily (probable Type C). Some of these babies are difficult to soothe and care for whereas others are placid and yielding, expressing little volition of their own. These three patterns form the core of three basic strategies for regulating parental behavior. By far the most complex is the Type C pattern for coping with unpredictable and dissynchronous conditions. Although each pattern differentiates with development into several substrategies, Type C has the most and the most complex array of subpatterns.

New Self-Protective Strategies in the Preschool Years.   At the end of the second year of life, a period of rapid neurological change yields new abilities including perspective taking, production of affective displays that do not match internal affective states (i.e., false affect), organization of behavior around changing contingencies, and strategic alternation of exaggerated angry and coy affect (i.e., distorted affect). The compulsive Type A substrategies involve children taking the parents' perspective and organizing their behavior to please the parent, through compulsive caregiving (using false positive affect and inhibition of negative affect) of withdrawn or neglectful parents (A3) or compulsive compliance (using inhibition of all affect except fear) with the demands of hostile and abusive caregivers (A4). Such children are quieter and more pleasing to adults than other children; their strategies reduce the probability of their being maltreated.

The coercive strategy involves splitting the negative affective states of anger, fear, and desire for comfort so as to display only anger (C1/3) or only fear and desire for comfort (C2/4), exaggerating the display of one while inhibiting the display of the other, and alternating the displays, contingent upon the behavior of the caregiver. This creates an unresolvable struggle for dominance between parent and child in which distorted nonverbal, affective communication is used to regulate parents' unpredictable and dissynchronous behavior. Aggressively coercive (C3) children use a variety of functionally equivalent behaviors to elicit attention including intense demands, provocation, and aggression. Passively helpless (C4) children use the display of apparent vulnerability and inability to protect themselves from victimization and elicit caregiving. All struggle anxiously to get attention which, when received, is still not well attuned to their needs. Moreover, by distorting their behavior, children using the Type C3-4 subpatterns mislead parents about their actual needs and feelings. Nevertheless, these subpatterns improve children's ability to elicit protection and comfort from relatively insensitive or unresponsive and unpredictable parents. The first 4–6 years of life are a period of increasing refinement of strategy to developmental context as maturation makes new response patterns possible. The extreme patterns both increase parental protectiveness and also create risks of dysfunction.

The School Years: Variability and Integration or Rigidity and Distortion.   During the school years, children in safe and supportive environments establish additional attachment relationships, for example, with grandparents and teachers. This facilitates the construction of new strategies, each suited to certain circumstances or relationships, that can be integrated into a self that is internally coherent while, nevertheless, varying strategically from one occasion or relationship to another. Children with less attentive, responsive, and predictable parents become more rigid and more extreme as they elaborate their strategies to both elicit more attention and also permit expression of anger through aggression while minimizing punitive consequences. Some behaviors attract attention while also expressing anger—for example, hyperactivity, aggression, and criminal activity. Deception and coy seductive behavior function to limit discovery and punishment. Such children integrate deception of others regarding their intentions into a punitive/seductive form of coercion (C5-6) that is used to blackmail or seduce others. This strategy typifies coercive relationships from bully-victim pairs, to gang activity, to couple violence, all of which have been associated with substance abuse and interpersonal violence.

Adolescence and Adulthood: Sexuality and Integration.   Following the second major period of neurological maturational, puberty, adolescents begin to integrate emerging reproductive strategies into their attachment strategies for selecting and regulating relationships. In addition, the transition from an egocentric, protection-seeking form of relationship to a reciprocal exchange of perspective-taking, protection, and comfort develops in couple relationships. When adolescents use extreme strategies (A3-4, C3-6), they are unlikely to function well either with peers or in intimate relationships. The outcome is isolation or conflict, both of which are painful. Some adolescents seek contact in gangs, whereas others form intensely conflicted love relationships (C5-6); others remain isolated (A5-6). The risk of both substance abuse (to please peers, ease social anxiety, and numb loneliness) and interpersonal violence (to coerce lovers to be attentive, caring, and faithful) is increased. Further, because these adolescents lack experience with mental integration, they are poorly prepared to inhibit action; in the context of sexuality, this may lead to early childbirth. Successful parenting requires substantial awareness of one's own motivations, competence at regulating behavior, and flexibility of strategy (Crittenden, Lang, Claussen, & Partridge, 2000) which is precisely what these young adults are least prepared to do.

☐ Substance Abuse and Relationship Violence in a Strategic Framework

Combined with current knowledge of mental functioning, the expanded ABC patterns have substantial implications for understanding (1) strategies for coping with threat and danger, (2) the relation between the neurobiological representation that underlies behavior (and is affected greatly by drugs and somewhat by violence) and the behavior itself, and (3) conditions that result in failed strategies. The second is possibly the greatest challenge, being least directly accessible and potentially most enduring. We offer here an integration in which we state theoretically derived hypotheses supported by evidence. What becomes especially clear, however, is that a linear approach to causal reasoning is insufficient to account for the ways in which substance abuse and interpersonal violence are related to each other or to strategies for self-protection.

Strategies Associated with Substance Abuse and Interpersonal Violence

The expanded ABC strategies fit the findings on the precursors and correlates of substance and person abuse quite well. The advantages of interpreting symptoms as part of organized strategies are that (1) the functional equivalence of diverse behaviors can be discerned, (2) the relation between exposure to danger and symptoms is clarified, (3) otherwise maladaptive behavior is reframed as coping with threat under restrictive conditions, and (4) the causal and maintaining conditions that require change are highlighted.

Tying Behavior, Strategies, and Development to Substance Abuse. The most commonly observed cluster of developmental precursors of substance abuse in children fits the Type C subpatterns well. The primary causal condition is relatively inattentive, unpredictable, and, in some cases, unprotective parenting. As young children, later substance abusers show behavior that fits the extreme C3-4 patterns (i.e., conduct disorder, hyperactivity, inattention, and risk taking). These function to focus children on parental availability or, by creating the need for attention, on safety by challenging others' safety (through aggression) or requiring rescue (through incompetence). Because children with unpredictable parents have less than usual influence on parental behavior, they go to great lengths to obtain some minimal control over their own safety and comfort. When low parent competence is combined with extreme child behavior, it is not surprising that these children are frequently physically or sexually abused or neglected. This, of course, increases children's anxiety and need for protection and, in some cases, leads to an escalation of the coercion. By the late school years and adolescence, the youths who are at greatest risk for later drug use have escalated to antisocial and delinquent behavior, behaviors that are consistent with the punitive and deceptive C5-6 strategy.

Compulsive A individuals also might be attracted to psychoactive substances as a way to reduce anxiety or to induce euphoria, although the data on early precursors are less indicative of this process. The association of dismissing attachment to adolescent substance abuse (Rosenstein & Horowitz, 1996) may point to such a connection. Certainly Type A5-6 individuals are candidates for being "quiet" drunks who drink alone until they are in a stupor that neither harms others nor comes to public attention.

The Strategic Function of Drug Use and Abuse. The strategic functions of drugs for adolescents would include social and biochemical functions. Substance use for social purposes would facilitate acceptance and feeling at ease in the complexity of social situations; in this case, whatever substance others were using would be the drug of choice. This may or not be a suitable drug for each individual, and dosages would, of course, be poorly regulated. Substance use as self-medication for uncomfortable affective states is easy to conceptualize, but possibly difficult to apply effectively in the real world. For example, alcohol as a CNS depressant might be expected to have several effects: (1) reducing anxiety and awareness of loneliness and stressors, (2) increasing depression and low self-esteem, and (3) reducing inhibitions. Reducing inhibitions would elicit relatively harmless socially inappropriate behavior in most users, but, when used in combination with a personality disorder (i.e., a C5 strategy) could release intense negative emotions, interpersonal conflict, and a pattern of testing personal control. Sedative-hypnotic opiates would be expected to calm and soothe excessive arousal by blunting emotions such as (1) anger and aggressive behavior and (2) various forms of anxiety, somatic distress, and panic disorder. CNS stimulants (cocaine, amphetamines) might (1) reduce depression, anergia, and low self-esteem, (2) exacerbate antisocial attention deficit disorder, conduct disorder, personality disorder, and bipolar/cyclothymic disorder, and (3) heighten emotions like anger that give a sense of control. The problems, however, are that individuals may not select the most appropriate drug, consider side effects, or regulate the dosage properly. In addition, these substances are addictive, thus, making their use very dangerous. Finally, although at times the substance use may achieve the desired effect, it would do nothing to actually relieve the underlying problem. This is potentially the most devastating effect of substance use and abuse.

Tying Behavior and Strategies to Interpersonal Violence.   The findings regarding the effects of violence on developmental pathways and the organization of self-protective strategies are more complete. Stress of all kinds is associated with interpersonal violence. Moreover, the various sorts of violence are related. As compared to substance abuse, family violence is more often associated with hostile, aggressive, and defiant patterns of behavior. That is, it fits the patterns described as C3 and C5. The passive forms of the strategies are far less often described. The descriptors associated with the compulsive Type A patterns are reported less often, especially after the preschool years. This may reflect either a change in older children's adaptation to violence and threat of violence or that the much less disruptive Type A behavior reduces both parental abuse and professional's attention as compared to Type C behavior. Certainly in infancy, Type A is the dominant pattern and, in the preschool years, compulsive A3-4 and A/C combinations are typical of most maltreated children. Strategically, it is easy to understand the advantage of the compulsive A strategies to abused and neglected children, but what is the advantage of acting out and attracting the attention of unpredictable parents? Use of this strategy gains attention at the risk of eliciting parental aggression. It seems likely that the strategy should be associated with use of drugs that reduce one's perception of vulnerability.

Neurobiology and Behavior

Although this topic seems far removed from the issue of developmental pathways leading to substance and person abuse, it is, in fact, central. The brain is the interface between the self and the external world. Anything that affects how the brain functions is relevant to adaptation. Substance and person abuse are both outcomes of certain kinds of inputs (i.e., the risk factors that generate strategies and affect developmental pathways) and also they themselves change brain functioning. It is quite obvious that drugs and alcohol affect brain functioning by inhibiting certain kinds of processing and facilitating others, by changing perception, and by changing processing times. Some drugs catapult the individual into action prior to cortical processing, whereas others slow functioning to the point that the individual does not respond even to critically important stimuli. Substances that heighten perception can create an excessive perception of threat and danger, thereby increasing the probability of affect-based strategies regulating behavior. Substances that depress perception or heighten pleasure reduce the probability that actual dangers will be perceived, thereby, decreasing self-protective behavior and increasing lethargy. The exact effects depend upon the chemical effects on the brain of particular substances and the dosage and frequency with which these substances are used.

Violence also affects brain function. It elicits rapid, precortical, self-protective behavior of a Type A sort in cases of temporally predictable threat and of a Type C sort in cases of unpredictability and affective arousal. In both cases, repeated use of the strategy strengthens these precortical pathways, thus, increasing the probability that future threat will elicit the same behavioral strategy and that it will do so with increasing rapidity. This also reduces the experience that developing Type A and C children have with the process of cortical integration. The brain, in other words, adapts to the prior experience in ways that affect future functioning. These conjectures are supported by research on the mental functioning of abusive parents in which differences in cognitive functioning were attributable to (1) lower intelligence (i.e., slower processing through fewer portions of the brain) and (2) depression and anxiety—which themselves are probably both causes and outcomes of violence (Nayak & Milner, 1998). Both the conditions that elicit substance and person abuse and these conditions themselves change brain functioning and this, in turn, is reflected in behavior. This increases the probability that the individual will behave in inappropriate and even pathological ways. In addition, if the individual is a parent, it increases the probability that his or her children will be raised in an environment characterized by unpredictability and inadequate protection and comfort.

When mind-altering substances are used in relatively low dosages, these effects are mild and relatively predictable. In higher dosages and as the addictive effect of the substance powerfully influences behavior, the motivating effects may no longer function predictably. That is, in high dosages and under conditions of chemical addiction, mind-altering substances interfere with the strategic organization of behavior. We hypothesize that conditions that increase the probability of the use of extreme problem solving strategies will carry increased risk for both substance and person abuse, and that the highest risk of co-occurrence of these problems will be when extreme strategies are employed in a dangerous developmental context. Further, because extreme strategies and substance and person abuse increase the danger and complexity of relationships, the possibility that functioning will become nonstrategic increases.

When Strategies Fail to Function

A failed strategy is one that is either insufficiently organized to yield any goal or an organized strategy used inappropriately, such that it fails to achieve the individual's goal, without being modified on the basis of feedback. One of the problems with using drugs or violence to regulate behavior in relationships is that, in addition to the desired effects that may, in fact, be achieved, both have side effects that can nullify the effect of the strategy. That is, substances do ease social discomfort, reduce anxiety, increase feelings of pleasure, reduce inhibition of feelings, and so forth. But, at the same time, they modify perception, have after-effects that are often the opposite of the desired effect, and reduce cortical processing of information. The latter may be important because without cortical processing, perception cannot be precise, alternative responses cannot be compared, probable outcomes cannot be foreseen, and complex solutions cannot be constructed. Instead, processing is limited to precortical pathways that necessarily exclude some potentially relevant information and, by operating rapidly, both maximize the potential for erroneous assumptions and appear impulsive. Under such conditions, behavior reflects past responses to threat and is not well adapted to current conditions. Finally, at sufficiently high levels, intake of psychoactive substances results in an inability to function strategically at all.

Similarly, violence in relationships has mixed effects. Violence does cause other people to attend to the violent person, to stop doing whatever elicited the violence, and to show respect or fear of the violent person. But it also reduces the openness of communication between individuals, thus, increasing the risk of unresolvable differences. In addition, it generates fear and anger that can motivate revenge in the recipient of the violence. Further, there is often the paradoxical effect that violence ties the aggressor and victim together in a mutually dependent relationship that both escalates in stressfulness and feels, to each party, essential to retain. This is true regardless of whether one of the parties is a child.

The Need to Test Hypotheses Drawn from the Dynamic-Maturational Model.   Considering the priority given to the ABC attachment strategies in this chapter, it would be helpful to have direct assessments of attachment applied to substance abusers and those who commit relationship violence. Unfortunately, most of the studies that have used the attachment paradigm have used the nonexpanded Ainsworth model (Ainsworth et al., 1978) and, even then, have reduced the results to Type B versus Types A and C combined. These studies have consistently found that drug use is associated with anxious attachment, but because the great majority of individuals using the anxious strategies are neither substance abusers nor at risk for psychopathology, more precise assessment is needed. The dynamic-maturational model is more precise. Moreover, there are associated assessment procedures that have been applied to child abuse (for example, the CARE-Index [Crittenden, 1998b], Strange Situation [Ainsworth et al., 1978], Preschool Assessment of Attachment [Crittenden, 1995], and Adult Attachment Interview [George, Kaplan, & Main, 1985]), but the model and assessments have not been applied to spousal or substance abusing populations.

Nevertheless, the primary advantage of the dynamic-maturational model and assessments may be the articulation of testable hypotheses. When parents use highly systematic and predictable violence, under explicitly stated, rigidly adhered to conditions and combined with cool affect or when parents' unprotective behavior could be regulated by children's caregiving or compliance, we would predict that the child would be at risk for maltreatment and would develop an A3-4 organization. When parents had limited predictability and ability to comfort young infants, we would predict risk for both C3-4 organization and, later, interpersonal aggression and substance abuse. When preschool-aged children adopted the A3-4 and, especially, C3-4 patterns, we would have a more restricted and specific hypothesis of risk with the greatest risk being to those children whose parents used violence in impulsive ways or who set few limits on child behavior. In the school years, use of the C5-6 patterns, particularly in neighborhoods or communities with substantial danger and many troubled children, would focus attention even more precisely on a group of youth at risk. In adolescence, intense social isolation (A5-6) would suggest risk for private sorts of substance abuse and possibly promiscuity, with its risk of violence. Antisocial patterns combined with sexuality (C5-6) would suggest risk for more disruptive forms of substance abuse as well as couple violence and, later, parental abuse of children. As a consequence, such problems might well recur in families across generations. When entire cultures are exposed to predictable forms or danger, we would expect high rates of Type A and its concomitant risks of social isolation, depression, and alcoholism. When the danger is unpredictable, the risks would be of Type C strategies, family violence and disruption, varied forms of substance abuse and addiction, and higher than usual rates of conduct, learning, and personality disorders. This process might explain the differential rates of substance and person abuse in different countries.

☐ Conclusion

This chapter has reviewed the literature on substance abuse and interpersonal violence as it affects children's risk for developing these disorders in adulthood. The perspective offered combined a developmental and maturational approach with an understanding of self-protective strategies drawn from attachment theory and combined with a social eco-logical perspective and principles from the cognitive neurosciences. The outcome is a dy-namic-maturation perspective on self-protection and risk for dysfunction (Crittenden, 2000). A particular advantage of this approach is that children and the adults that they become are viewed as attempting to solve life problems through the construction of self-protective strategies. Some of these strategies, however, carry risk of maladaptation under certain conditions. Awareness of which risks are associated with which conditions at what developmental phase can direct both research and intervention. The result has been a set of hypotheses about developmental pathways that contain risk for various forms of sub-stance and person abuse. These hypotheses require empirical testing but could focus fu-ture work in more precise directions.

☐ References

Ainsworth, M. D. S. (1979). Infant-mother attachment. *American Psychologist, 34*(10), 932–937.

Ainsworth, M. D. S., Blehar, M. C., Waters, E., & Wall, S. (1978). *Patterns of attachment: A psychologi-cal study of the strange situation.* Hillsdale, NJ: Erlbaum Associates.

American Psychiatric Association. (1994). *Diagnostic and statistical manual of mental disorders* (4th ed.). Washington, DC: American Psychiatric Association.

Ammerman, R. T., Ott, P. J., Tarter, R. E., & Blackson, T. C. (1999). Critical issues in prevention of substance abuse. In R. T. Ammerman, P. J. Ott, & R. E. Tarter (Eds.), *Prevention and societal impact of drug and alcohol abuse* (pp. 3–20). Mahwah, NJ: Lawrence Erlbaum.

Andrews, J. A., Hops, H., Ary, D., Tildesley, E., & Harris, J. (1993). Parental influence on early ado-lescent substance use: Specific and nonspecific effects. *Journal of Early Adolescence, 13*, 285–310.

Aseltine, R. H., Gore, S., & Colten, M. E. (1998). The co-occurrence of depression and substance abuse in late adolescence. *Development and Psychopathology, 10*(3), 549–570.

Azar, S. T. (1991). Models of child abuse: A meta-theoretical analysis. *Criminal Justice and Behavior, 18*, 30–46.

Ball, S. A., Carroll K. M., & Rounsaville, B. J. (1994). Sensation seeking, substance abuse, and psycho-pathology in treatment-seeking and community cocaine abusers. *Journal of Consulting and Clini-cal Psychology, 62*(5), 1053–1057.

Barnett, D., Ganiban, J., & Cicchetti, D. (1999). Maltreatment, negative expressivity, and the devel-opment of Type D attachments from 12 to 24 months of age. *Monographs of the Society for Re-search in Child Development, 64*(3), 97–118.

Baumrind, D. (1991). The influence of parenting style on adolescent competence and substance use. *Journal of Early Adolescence, 11*, 56–95.

Beeghly, M., & Tronick, E. (1994). Effects of prenatal exposure to cocaine in early infancy: Toxic effects on the process of mutual regulation. *Infant Mental Health, 15*, 158–175.

Bell, C. C., & Jenkins, E. J. (1993). Community violence and children on Chicago's southside. In D. Reiss, J. E. Richters, M. Radke-Yarrow, & D. Scharff (Eds.), *Violence and children* (pp. 46–54). New York: Guilford.

Belsky, J. (1980). Child maltreatment: An ecological integration. *American Psychologist, 35*, 320–335

Belsky, J. (1993). Etiology of child maltreatment: A developmental-ecological analysis. *Psychological Bulletin, 114*, 413–434.

Bernstein, V. J., & Hans, S. L. (1994). Predicting the developmental outcome of two-year-old children born exposed to methadone: Impact of social-environmental risk factors. *Journal of Clinical Child Psychology, 23*(4), 349–359.

Bernstein, V., Jeremy, R. J., Hans, S., & Marcus, J. (1994). A longitudinal study of offspring born to methadone-maintained women: II. Dyadic interaction and infant behavior at four months. *Ameri-can Journal of Drug and Alcohol Abuse, 10*, 161–193.

Blackwell, P., Kirkhart, K., Schmitt, D., & Kaiser, M. (1998). Cocaine/polydrug affected dyads: Impli-cations for infant cognitive development and mother-infant interaction during the first six post-natal months. *Journal of Applied Developmental Psychology, 19*(2), 235–248.

Bowlby, J. (1979) *Attachment and loss: Attachment*. New York: Basic.

Bronfenbrenner, U. (1979). *The experimental ecology of human development*. Cambridge, MA. Harvard University Press.

Brook, J., Whiteman, M., Cohen, P., Shapiro, J., & Balka, E. (1995). Longitudinally predicting late adolescent and young adult drug use: Childhood and adolescent precursors. *Journal of the American Academy of Child Adolescent Psychiatry, 34*, 1230–1238.

Brook, J., Whiteman, M., Finch, S., & Cohen, P. (1996). Young adult drug use and delinquency: Childhood antecedents and adolescent mediators. *Journal of the American Academy of Child and Adolescent Psychiatry, 35*(12), 1584–1592.

Burns, K., Chethik, L., Burns, W. J., & Clark, R. (1991). Dyadic disturbances in cocaine abusing mothers and their infants. *Journal of Clinical Psychology, 47*, 316–319.

Campbell, B. K., & Stark, M. J. (1990). Psychopathology and personality characteristics in different forms of substance abuse. *International Journal of the Addictions, 25*(12), 1467–1474.

Caspi, A., Moffitt, T. E., Newman, D. L., & Silva, P. A. (1998). Behavioral observations at age 3 years predict adult psychiatric disorders: Longitudinal evidence from a birth cohort. In M. E. Hertzig & E. A. Farber (Eds.), *Annual progress in child psychiatry and child development*: 1997 (pp. 319–331). Bristol, PA: Brunner/Mazel.

Caudill, B. D., Hoffman, J. A., Hubbard, R. L., Flynn, P. M., & Luckey, J. W. (1994). Parental history of substance abuse as a risk factor in predicting crack smokers' substance use, illegal activities, and psychiatry status. *American Journal of Alcohol Abuse, 20*(3), 341–354.

Chaffin, M., Kelleher, K., & Hollenberg, J. (1996). Onset of physical abuse and neglect: Psychiatric, substance abuse, and social risk factors from prospective community data. *Child Abuse and Neglect, 20*, 191–203.

Cicchetti, D., & Barnett, D. (1991). Attachment organization in maltreated preschoolers. *Development and Psychopathology, 3*(4), 397–411.

Cicchetti, D., & Rogosch, F. A. (1999). Psychopathology as a risk for adolescent substance use disorders: A developmental psychopathology perspective. *Journal of Clinical Child Psychology, 28*(3), 335–365.

Clark, D. B., Lesnick, L., & Hegedus A. M, (1997). Traumas and other adverse life events in adolescents with alcohol abuse and dependence. *Journal of the American Academy of Child and Adolescent Psychiatry, 36*(12), 1744–1751.

Claussen, A. H., & Anderson, W. (1997). *Attachment in children prenatally exposed to cocaine: Disorganization and the emergence of new subpatterns of attachment*. Paper presented at the 63rd Biennial Meeting of the Society for Research in Child Development, Indianapolis, IN.

Craig, R. J., & Olson, R. E. (1990). MCMI comparisons of cocaine abusers and heroin addicts. *Journal of Clinical Psychology, 46*(2), 230–237.

Crittenden, P. M. (1985a). Maltreated infants: Vulnerability and resilience. *Journal of Child Psychology and Psychiatry and Allied Disciplines, 26*(1), 85–96.

Crittenden, P. M. (1985b). Social networks, quality of child rearing, and child development. *Child Development, 56*(5), 1299–1313.

Crittenden, P. M. (1995). *The preschool assessment of attachment, PAA*. Miami, FL: Unpublished manual.

Crittenden, P. M. (1996). Research on maltreating families: Implications for intervention. In J. Briere, L. Berliner, & T. Reid (Eds.), *APSAC Handbook on Child Maltreatment* (pp. 158–174). Thousand Oaks, CA: Sage.

Crittenden, P. M. (1998a). Dangerous behavior and dangerous contexts: A thirty-five year perspective on research on the developmental effects of child physical abuse. In P. Trickett (Ed.), *Violence to children* (pp. 11–38). Washington, DC: American Psychological Association.

Crittenden, P. M. (1998b). *CARE-Index Manual* (3rd revision). Miami, FL: Unpublished manual.

Crittenden, P. M. (1999). Danger and development: The organization of self-protective strategies. In J. I. Vondra & D. Barnett (Eds.), *Atypical attachment in infancy and early childhood among children at developmental risk. Monographs of the Society for Research on Child Development, 164*, (3, serial no. 258), 145–171.

Crittenden, P. M. (2000). A dynamic-maturational exploration of the meaning of security and adaptation: Empirical, cultural, and theoretical considerations. In P. M. Crittenden & A. H. Claussen

(Eds.), *The organization of attachment relationships: Maturation, culture, and context* (pp. 358–384). New York: Cambridge University Press.

Crittenden, P. M., & Ainsworth, M. D. S. (1989). Child maltreatment and attachment theory. In D. Cicchetti & V. Carlson (Eds.), *Child maltreatment: Theory and research on the causes and consequences of child abuse and neglect* (pp. 432–463). New York: Cambridge University Press.

Crittenden, P. M., Lang, C., Claussen, A. H., & Partridge, M. F. (2000). Relations among mothers' procedural, semantic, and episodic internal representational models of parenting. In P. M. Crittenden & A. H. Claussen (Eds.), *The organization of attachment relationships: Maturation, culture, and context* (pp. 214–234). New York: Cambridge University Press.

Dobkin, P. L., Tremblay, R. E., Masse, L. C., & Vitaro, F. (1995). Individual and peer characteristics in predicting boys' early onset of substance abuse: A seven-year longitudinal study. *Child Development, 66*, 1198–1214.

Dobkin, P. L., Tremblay, R. E., & Sacchitelle, C. (1997). Predicting boy's early-onset substance abuse from father's alcoholism, son's disruptiveness, and mother's parenting behavior. *Journal of Consulting and Clinical Psychology, 65*(1), 86–92.

Doweiko, H. E. (1999). *Concepts of chemical dependency* (4th ed.). Pacific Grove, CA: Brooks-Cole.

Eiden, R. D., & Leonard, K. E. (1996). Paternal alcohol use and the mother-infant relationship. *Development and Psychopathology, 8*(2), 307–323.

Emery, R., & Laumann-Billings, L. (1998). An overview of the nature, causes, and consequences of abusive family relationships: Toward differentiating maltreatment and violence. *American Psychologist, 53*, 121–135.

Famularo, R. A., Stone, K., Barnum, R., & Wharton, R. (1986). Alcoholism and severe child maltreatment. *American Journal of Orthopsychiatry, 56*, 481–485.

Friedman, A. S., Bransfield, S. A., Tomko, L. A., & Katz, S. (1991). Early childhood and maternal antecedents to drug use. *Journal of Drug Education, 21*(4), 313–331.

Garbarino, J. (1977). The human ecology of child maltreatment: A conceptual model for research. *Journal of Marriage and the Family, 39*, 721–736.

Garbarino, J., Dubrow, N., Kostelny, K., & Pardo, C. (1992). *Children in danger.* San Francisco: Jossey-Bass.

Garmezy, N. (1983). Stressors of childhood. In N. Garmezy & M. Rutter (Eds.), *Stress, coping, and development in children* (pp. 43–84). New York: McGraw-Hill.

Garmezy, N., & Rutter, M. (1985). Acute reactions to stress. In M. Rutter & L. Hersov (Eds.), *Child and adolescent psychiatry: Modern approaches* (2nd ed., pp. 152–176). Oxford, England: Blackwell.

George, C., Kaplan, N., & Main, M. (1985). *An adult attachment interview.* Unpublished manuscript, University of California at Berkeley.

Goodman, G., Hans, S. L., & Cox, S. M. (1999). Attachment behavior and its antecedents in offspring born to methadone-maintained women. *Journal of Clinical Child Psychology, 28*(1), 58–69.

Hagan, J. C., & Myers, B. J. (1997). Mother-toddler play interaction: A contrast of substance-exposed and nonexposed children. *Infant Mental Health Journal, 18*(1), 40–57.

Hawkins, J. D., Catalano, R. F., & Miller, J. Y. (1992). Risk and protective factors for alcohol and other drug problems in adolescence and early adulthood: Implications for substance abuse prevention. *Psychological Bulletin, 112*(1), 64–105.

Hill, H. M., & Madhere, S. (1996). *Exposure to community violence and African- American children: A multi-dimensional model.* Unpublished manuscript, Howard University, Washington, DC.

Hoffmann, J. P. (1998). Parental substance use disorder, mediating variables and adolescent drug use: A non-recursive model. *Addiction, 93*(9), 1351–1364.

Horn, J. L., & Trickett, P. K. (1998). Community violence and child development: A review of research. In P. K. Trickett & C. J. Schellenbach (Eds.), *Violence against children in the family and community* (pp. 103–138). Washington, DC: American Psychological Association.

Hughes, H. M., Parkinson, D., & Vargo, M. (1989). Witnessing spouse abuse and experiencing physical abuse: A "double whammy"? *Journal of Family Violence, 4*, 197–210.

Jaeger, E., Hahn, N. B., & Weinraub, M. (2000). Attachment in adult daughters of alcoholic fathers. *Addiction, 95*(2), 267–276.

Jantzen, K., Ball, S. A., Leventhal, J. M., & Schottenfeld, R. S. (1998). Types of abuse and cocaine use in pregnant women. *Journal of Substance Abuse Treatment, 15*(4), 319–323.

Johnson, J. L., & Leff, M. (1999). Children of substance abusers: Overview of research findings. *Pediatrics, 103*(5 Pt. 2), 1085–1099.

Kelley, S. J. (1992). Parenting stress and child maltreatment in drug-exposed children. *Child Abuse and Neglect, 16*, 317–328.

Kelley, S. J. (1998). Stress and coping behaviors of substance-abusing mothers. *Journal of the Society of Pediatric Nurses, 3*(3), 103–110.

Kolko, D. J. (1996). Child physical abuse. In J. Briere, L. Berliner, J. A. Bulkey, C. Jenny, & T. Reid (Eds.), *The APSAC Handbook on Child Maltreatment* (pp. 21–50). Thousand Oaks, CA: Sage.

Kushner, M. G., Sher, K. J., & Erickson, D. J. (1999). Prospective analysis of the relation between DSM-III anxiety disorders and alcohol use disorders. *American Journal of Psychiatry, 156*(5), 723–732.

Langeland, W., & Hartgers, C. (1998). Child sexual and physical abuse and alcoholism: A review. *Journal of Studies on Alcohol, 59*(3), 336–348.

Lejoyeux, M., Feuche, N., Loi, S., Solomon, J., & Ades, J. (1999). Study of impulse-control disorders among alcohol-dependent patients. *Journal of Clinical Psychiatry, 60*(5), 302–305.

Margolin, G. (1998). Effects of domestic violence on children. In P. K. Trickett & C. J. Schellenbach (Eds.), *Violence against children in the family and community* (pp. 57–102). Washington, DC: American Psychological Association.

Martin, C., Earleywine, M., Blackson, T., Vanyukov, M., Moss, H., & Tarter, R. E. (1994). Aggressivity, inattention, hyperactivity, and impulsivity in boys at high and low risk for substance abuse. *Journal of Abnormal Child Psychology, 22*, 177–201.

Martinez, P., & Richters, J. E. (1993). The NIMH Community Violence Project: II. Children's distress symptoms associated with violence exposure. In D. Reiss, J. E. Richters, M. Radke-Yarrow, & D. Scharff (Eds.), *Violence and children* (pp. 22–35). New York: Guilford.

Masse, L. C., & Tremblay, R. E. (1997). Behavior of boys in kindergarten and the onset of substance use during adolescence. *Archives of General Psychiatry, 54*(1), 62–68.

May, L. C., & Bernstein, M. C. (1995). Developmental dilemmas for cocaine-abusing parents and their children. In M. Lewis & M. Bendersky (Eds.), *Mothers, babies and cocaine: The role of toxins in development* (pp. 251–272). Hillsdale, NJ: Lawrence Erlbaum.

May, L. C., Feldman R., Granger, R. H., Haynes, O. M., Bernstein, M. H., & Schottenfeld, R. (1997). The effects of polydrug use with and without cocaine on mother-infant interaction at 3 and 6 months. *Infant Behavior and Development, 20*(4), 489–502.

McCloskey, L. A., Figueredo, A. J., & Koss, M. P. (1995). The effects of systemic family violence on children's mental health. *Child Development, 66*(5), 1239–1261.

Miller, N. S., & Giannini, A. J. (1990). The disease model of addiction: A biopsychiatrist's view. *Journal of Psychoactive Drugs, 22*(1), 83–85.

Mirin S. M., Weiss, R. D., Griffin, M. L., & Michael, J. L. (1991). Psychopathology in drug abusers and their families. *Comprehensive Psychiatry, 32*(1), 36–51.

Murphy, J. M., Jellinek, M., Quinn, D., Smith, G., Poitrast, F. G., & Goshko, M. (1991). Substance abuse and serious child maltreatment: Prevalence, risk, and outcome in a court sample. *Child Abuse and Neglect, 15*, 197–211.

Nayak, M. B., & Milner, J. S. (1998). Neuropsychological functioning: Comparison of mothers at high- and low-risk for child physical abuse. *Child Abuse and Neglect, 22*(7), 687–703.

Newcomb, M. D., Bentler, P. M., & Fahy, B. (1987). Cocaine use and psychopathology: Associations among young adults. *International Journal of the Addictions, 22*(12), 1167–1188.

O'Connor, M. J., Sigman, M., & Brill, N. (1987). Disorganization of attachment in relation to maternal alcohol consumption. *Journal of Consulting and Clinical Psychology, 55*(6), 831–836.

O'Connor, M. J., Sigman, M. D., & Kasari, C. (1992). Attachment behavior of infants exposed prenatally to alcohol: Mediating effects of infant affect and mother-infant interaction. *Development and Psychopathology, 4*(2), 243–256.

Pfefferbaum, B., & Wood, P. B. (1994). Self-report study of impulsive and delinquent behavior in college students. *Journal of Adolescent Health, 15*(4), 295–302.

Platt, J. J., & Husband, S. D. (1993). An overview of problem-solving and social skills approaches in substance abuse treatment. *Psychotherapy, 30*(2), 276–283.

Pollak, S. D., Cicchetti, D., Klorman, R., & Brumaghim, J. T. (1997). Cognitive brain event-related potentials and emotion processing in maltreated children. *Child Development, 68*(5), 773–787.

Rhodes, T., & Quirk, A. (1998). Drug users' sexual relationships and the social organization of risk: The sexual relationship as a site of risk management. *Social Science and Medicine, 46*(2), 157–169.

Risser, D., Bonsch, A., & Schneider, B. (1996). Family background of drug-related deaths: A descriptive study based on interviews with relatives of deceased drug users. *Journal of Forensic Science, 41*(6), 960–962.

Rodning, C., Beckwith, L., & Howard, J. (1992). Quality of attachment and home environments in children prenatally exposed to PCP and cocaine. *Development and Psychopathology, 3*, 351–366.

Rosenbaum, A., & O'Leary, K. D. (1981). Children: The unintended victims of marital violence. *American Journal of Orthopsychiatry, 51*, 692–699.

Rosenstein, D. S., & Horowitz, H. A. (1996). Adolescent attachment and psychopathology. *Journal of Consulting and Clinical Psychology, 64*(2), 244–253.

Rounsaville, B. J., Kranzler, H. R., Ball, S., Tennen, H., Poling, J., & Triffleman, E. (1998). Personality disorders in substance abusers: relation to substance use. *Journal of Nervous and Mental Disorders, 186*(2), 87–95.

Schuckit, M. A. (1999). New findings on the genetics of alcoholism. *JAMA: Journal of the American Medical Association, 281*(20), 1875–1876.

Seefeldt, L. (1997). *Models of parenting in maltreating and non-maltreating mothers.* Unpublished doctoral dissertation, University of Wisconsin—Milwaukee. Milwaukee, WI.

Shedler, J. S., & Block, J. (1990). Adolescent drug use and psychological health. *American Psychologist, 45*, 612–630.

Shiffman, S., & Wills, T. A. (1985). *Coping and substance abuse.* Orlando, FL: Academic.

Singer, L., Arent, R., Parkas, K., Minces, S., Huang, J., & Yamashita, T. (1997). Relationship of prenatal cocaine exposure and maternal postpartum psychological distress to child development outcome. *Development and Psychopathology, 9*, 473–489.

Skodol, A. E., Oldham, J. M., & Gallagher, P. E. (1999). Axis II comorbidity of substance use disorders among patients referred for treatment of personality disorders. *American Journal of Psychiatry, 156*(5), 733–738.

Smyth, N. J., & Washousky, R. C. (1995). The coping styles of alcoholics with Axis II disorders. *Journal of Substance Abuse, 7*(4), 425–435.

Spaccarelli, S., Sandler, I. N., & Roosa, M. (1994). History of spouse violence against mother: Correlated risks and unique effects in child mental health. *Journal of Family Violence, 9*, 79–98.

Swaim, R .C. (1991). Childhood risk factors and adolescent drug and alcohol abuse. *Educational Psychology Review, 3*(4), 363–398.

Trickett, P. K., & Putnam, F. W. (1998). Developmental consequences of child sexual abuse. In P. K. Trickett & C. J. Schellenbach (Eds.), *Violence against children in the family and community* (pp. 39–56). Washington, DC: American Psychological Association.

Warner, L. A., Kessler, R. C., Hughes, M., Anthony, J. C., & Nelson, C. B. (1995). Prevalence and correlates of drug use and dependence in the United States. *Archives of General Psychiatry, 51*, 219–229.

Weinberg, N. Z., & Glantz, M. (1999). Child psychopathology risk factors for drug abuse: An overview. *Journal of Clinical Child Psychology, 28*(3), 290–297.

Wekerle, C., Wolfe, D. A. (1998). The role of child maltreatment and attachment style in adolescent relationship violence. *Development and Psychopathology, 10*(3), 571–586.

Whipple, E. E., & Webster-Stratton, C. (1991). The role of parental stress in physically abusive families. *Child Abuse and Neglect, 15*, 279–291.

Wills, T. A., Vaccaro, D., & McNamara, G. (1992). The role of life events, family support, and competence in adolescent substance use: A test of vulnerability and protective factors. *American Journal of Community Psychology, 20*(3), 349–374.

CHAPTER 4

Gordon L. Flett
Paul L. Hewitt

Personality Factors and Substance Abuse in Relationship Violence and Child Abuse: A Review and Theoretical Analysis

It is sometimes suggested that anyone can be aggressive and violent when confronted with a powerful and threatening situation. However, the fact remains that even in situations that could elicit a violent response, some individuals are violent and aggressive while others are not. There is little doubt that personality factors play a key role when violence and abuse occur; a growing body of research has examined the role of personality factors and shown that certain dispositional factors in perpetrators increase the likelihood of violence.

The purpose of this chapter is to selectively review existing research and theory on the role of personality factors in domestic violence and child abuse, with a particular focus on the associations among personality, substance abuse, and mistreatment of significant others. The chapter begins with an overview of various models and conceptualizations that focus on the role of personality factors in relationship violence. Next, research on the role of personality factors in relationship violence is reviewed, with the caveat that most of the research has focused on domestic violence, and relatively few investigations have examined the role of personality factors and substance abuse in child maltreatment. The review concludes with an integrative model that seeks to apply a diathesis-stress and coping approach to domestic violence and child maltreatment.

The current chapter was supported in part by a grant from the Social Sciences and Humanities Research Council and a sabbatical leave grant awarded to the first author from the Faculty of Arts at York University. The authors thank Hayley Flett for her technical assistance.

☐ Models and Conceptualizations of the Role of Personality

Personality factors are important to consider when examining the link between substance abuse and violence in intimate relationships for a variety of reasons. First, as alluded to at the beginning of this chapter, personality factors may account for the fact that individuals faced with similar situations often react quite differently, and only certain individuals engage in aggressive and violent behavior when under the influence of drugs.

Second, consideration of the factors associated with the development of certain personality traits may help explain why certain individuals engage in inappropriate behavior toward significant others after excessive drinking. Authors such as Dutton (1995) have concluded that there is an obvious link between alcohol use and violence, but one does not cause the other. Dutton (1995) observed that when it comes to alcohol use and violence, "Both are traced back to an earlier aspect of the self. One's personality is formed much sooner than one learns to use alcohol and hit" (p. 54). This observation suggests that personality factors that exist early in life may be responsible for violence and the link with substance abuse, and explanations should focus on the developmental origins of the personality factors.

Third, if it is possible to identify certain personality factors that predict who is most likely to be abusive and violent, preventive programs can be designed and implemented before the violence and abuse actually occur. That is, an early (i.e., in adolescence, when personality may be more amenable to change) focus on personality factors can be used to identify those individuals who are most likely to be violent and have substance abuse problems.

Finally, once it is recognized that certain personality factors play a key role, then treatment interventions can be modified and tailored to fit the needs of individuals with certain personality structures. Saunders (1996) has shown the potential usefulness of matching the type of intervention with a perpetrator's personality characteristics. The need to examine the fit between personality characteristics and types of treatment is implicit when considering evidence indicating that men with certain personality disorders (i.e., borderline, antisocial, and avoidant personalities) have higher levels of posttreatment recidivism in terms of levels of posttreatment spouse abuse (see Dutton, Bodnarchuk, Kropp, Hart, & Ogloff, 1997). The need for these interventions to include an explicit focus on substance abuse is indicated by research suggesting that "recidivists" have not only higher levels of narcissism, but also higher levels of substance abuse both before and after treatment (Hamberger & Hastings, 1990).

The Broad Scope of Personality Factors

One premise of the current chapter is that there are many different ways to define personality and much is to be gained in this area by examining various conceptualizations of personality. Most of this analysis focuses on a general trait approach to the study of personality. The trait approach is based on the view that people differ on a set of underlying, hypothetical dimensions, and these dimensions represent stable dispositions that are present early in life and generalize across a variety of situations. Previous authors who have reviewed the link between alcohol and personality without focusing primarily on violence (e.g., Sher, Trull, Bartholow, & Vieth, 1999; Sutker & Allain, 1988; Tarter, 1988) have mostly discussed personality traits as the appropriate unit of analysis. However, it is both possible and advisable to take a broad approach to the study of personality and go beyond traits by studying other aspects such as personality states, personality needs, personality capabilities, and styles of expression. Some research on personality, substance abuse, and violence has examined the role of personality needs, such as dominance and power, and this research is reviewed in a subsequent section of this chapter. There also have been some attempts to examine individual differences in capabilities, in terms of interpersonal skills; however, the main focus has been on personality traits. The need to adopt a broad approach to the study of personality is an issue that applies not only to this area, but to other areas as well, including depression (see Flett, Hewitt, Endler, & Bagby, 1995).

An analysis of personality *capabilities* illustrates the potential usefulness of considering other forms of individual differences as a means of more fully understanding the links among personality, substance abuse, and violence. Previously, Wallace (1966) stated that certain personality characteristics can be regarded not only as traits, but also as abilities or capabilities. The concept of capability incorporates the distinction between a person's typical tendencies in a domain (i.e., traits) versus their maximum possible response in this domain (i.e., capability). Whereas the trait approach focuses on how an individual *usually* behaves, the capability approach focuses on the *potential* to express certain behaviors in given situations. Paulhus and Martin (1987, 1988) incorporated this distinction into their research on interpersonal characteristics and showed that capability and trait ratings were relatively orthogonal, and both capability and trait ratings predicted levels of psychological distress.

The relevance of personality capabilities to violence is evident when considering individual differences in agreeableness. It is important to distinguish the individual who is usually agreeable and lacks the capacity to be disagreeable, from the individual who is usually agreeable but has a "dark side" and can respond with aggression when provoked. Basic research is needed in order to evaluate how spouse batterers and child abusers view their typical personality characteristics and how they are capable of behaving.

Distal Versus Proximal Personality Factors

When personality factors are included in conceptual models that examine the link between alcohol use and marital aggression, for example, personality traits tend to be regarded as distal or background factors that are considered along with more proximal influences such as acute alcohol effects, situational cues, and transient states (see Leonard, 1999). However, it should be noted from the outset that personality factors may play a more proximal role if a broad approach is taken when conceptualizing personality; that is, personality may play a more proximal role if both personality traits and personality states that fluctuate according to situational factors are considered. Also, personality factors may have a more proximal influence to the extent that the stable coping dispositions that have been identified (see Hewitt & Flett, 1996) are involved in how individuals under the influence of drugs and alcohol appraise and respond to situations that involve actual or possible interpersonal conflict.

Of course, the issue of whether a personality construct operates as a distal or proximal factor will depend on the personality factor in question, and how personality is defined. Although personality factors are usually viewed as distal influences, certain factors can have a more immediate impact. For instance, when considering individual differences in attachment style, Holtzworth-Munroe and Stuart (1994) included attachment to other individuals as the first proximal variable in their model of marital violence. Impulsivity is another personality construct that is included as a proximal correlate, along with maladaptive social skills and hostile attitudes toward women.

Regardless of whether personality factors are distal or proximal, there are many ways that personality factors can combine with other factors to contribute to the link between substance abuse and relationship violence. There are several possible models of the associations among personality factors, substance abuse, and physical and psychological abuse. These models can be modified to focus on traitlike, chronic substance abuse, and the more immediate impact of substance use in specific situations.

Four models are outlined in Figure 4.1. The additive model shown in Figure 4.1 involves the notion that although personality factors and levels of drinking and substance abuse may be related, they make independent contributions to the prediction of violence and aggression.

The mediational model shown in Figure 4,1 is based on the premise that personality factors are linked with substance abuse which, in turn, predicts violence and aggression. The usefulness of a mediational approach was shown by Leonard and Senchak (1996) who reported that a history of family violence in the husband is mediated by trait hostility and gender identity which have both a direct link with aggression, and an indirect link that involves the mediational role played by the husband's alcohol use. Stuart's (1998) research with 50 maritally violent and 36 nonviolent men showed that substance abuse mediated the link between impulsivity and psychological abuse.

A third possibility depicted in Figure 4.1 is the moderator model; this model is based on the hypothesis that personality factors interact with levels of drinking and substance abuse to predict levels of violence and aggression. That is, violence and aggression reflect a joint combination of a particular personality orientation and the presence of excessive drinking and substance abuse. For example, a study by Heyman, O'Leary, and Jouriles (1995) (described in more detail in a subsequent section of this chapter) found some evidence

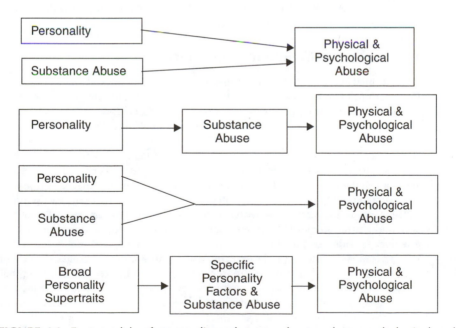

FIGURE 4.1. Four models of personality, substance abuse and use, and physical and psychological abuse: An additive model (top), a mediational model (second), a moderator model (third), and a supertrait model (bottom).

indicating that trait aggression interacts with level of alcohol consumption to predict subsequent levels of marital aggression.

A fourth possibility shown in Figure 4.1 is that specific facets of personality and excessive drinking or substance abuse are involved to various degrees in the prediction of violence, aggression, and other forms of abuse, but they reflect the effects of a superordinate personality construct. That is, there are broad personality supertraits that are included in frameworks, such as the five-factor model of personality, and it is these broad personality dispositions that account for incidents of violence, aggression, and abuse. At present, there have been almost no empirical attempts to examine how the trait dimensions associated with the five dimensions (i.e., extraversion, agreeableness, openness, neuroticism, and conscientiousness) contribute to the link between substance abuse and relationship violence. The sole exception is a study by Buss (1991) who examined the association between personality and measures of conflict and upset in 214 women and men in their first year of marriage. Buss found that low levels of agreeableness and low levels of emotional stability in both men and women were associated with a host of complaints, but only these characteristics in men predicted alcohol abuse and physical and verbal abuse. In addition, low intellect in men was associated with alcohol abuse and physical and verbal abuse.

Unfortunately, the Buss (1991) study appears to be the only one that has examined the five-factor personality model and levels of alcohol abuse and abusiveness toward intimates. However, a number of other studies have examined the link between the five-factor model and various forms of substance abuse. For example, Ball and Schottenfeld (1997) examined the five-factor model in a sample of 92 women addicted to cocaine. They completed the Zuckerman-Kuhlman five-factor measure (Zuckerman, Kuhlman, Thornquist, & Kiers, 1991) and found that neuroticism, impulsive sensation-seeking, and aggression-hostility predicted various subscales of the Addiction Severity Index (McLellan, Luborsky, Woody, & O'Brien, 1980). Overall, neuroticism was the most powerful predictor of a variety of forms of maladjustment, including measures of personal distress.

Dimensional Versus Categorical Approaches

The models outlined above are based on a dimensional view of personality factors in keeping with the definition of personality traits. That is, the focus is on individual differences that differ along a continuum that varies in levels (low, medium, and high). According to this approach, personality disorder occurs when an individual has extreme scores on maladaptive traits.

An alternative approach is to focus on personality types. Personality types are discrete categories that differ qualitatively in kind rather than in degree. Personality types are categories that can involve a constellation of personality characteristics that are present in an all-or-none fashion. One benefit of the categorical approach is that personality types can involve multiple characteristics that cluster together to increase the risk of violence, aggression, and abuse. Studies that examine personality traits from a dimensional perspective seldom consider the possibility that the presence of many personality factors, as opposed to a personality factor in isolation, combine to substantially increase the risk of violence or abuse. The need for such an approach is indicated by research showing that spousal abuse and child abuse are associated with the presence of multiple risk factors, including personality factors (see Brown, Cohen, Johnson, & Salzinger, 1998; Leonard & Senchak, 1996).

This observation notwithstanding, it is important to emphasize that comparative research in this area has not tested whether a dimensional or a categorical approach is most appropriate. General research on personality traits is limited but tends to support a dimensional approach (see Livesley, Schroeder, Jackson, & Jang, 1994). A research investigation by Trull, Widiger, and Guthrie (1990) tested the continuity issue with respect to borderline personality features and concluded that a dimensional approach is most appropriate. This study is especially noteworthy given that borderline personality characteristics are regarded as playing a key role in domestic violence and substance abuse (see Dutton, 1995).

The continuity issue is important to keep in mind when considering the next section on types of batterers. Although there is clear evidence of heterogeneity and different kinds of batterers, and personality factors play an important role in differentiating these types, it may still be the case that a dimensional approach is more appropriate. Indeed, in their most recent work, Holtzworth-Munroe and associates indicate that their ongoing project on types of batterers will eventually involve an empirical test of the continuity issue (see Holtzworth-Munroe, Meehan, Herron, & Stuart, 1999). The possibility that a dimensional approach provides a better fit to the data is suggested not only by the research findings in other fields that favor continuity (see Flett, Vredenburg, & Krames, 1997), but also by specific findings showing that assaultive men have high levels of alcohol use, and that increases in levels of alcohol use predict with increasing accuracy the extent to which these men fit the description of the abusive personality (see Dutton, 1995).

☐ Typologies of Batterers and Child Abusers

A growing number of empirical investigations have considered whether it is possible to identify different types of batterers, and personality characteristics have been included as key factors. A complete review of these investigations is beyond the scope of this chapter, so the primary focus here will be on those frameworks that have included a focus on individual differences in substance abuse.

Several studies by Hamberger and Hastings (Hamberger & Hastings, 1989, 1991) are among those most frequently cited in this area. These investigators have completed a number of studies in which they administered the Millon Clinical Multiaxial Inventory (MCMI; Millon, 1983) to various groups of men: Cluster analyses are then used to examine types of batterers. Hamberger and Hastings (1991) conducted one of the more relevant studies for our purposes, because it compared 38 alcoholic male batterers, 61 nonalcoholic batterers, 28 community-identified martially violent males, and 64 male nonviolent controls. Analyses of the MCMI responses showed that alcoholic and nonalcoholic batterers have higher borderline characteristics and, in general, alcoholic batterers had highest MCMI elevations. On measures of family-of-origin pathology and disruption, only alcoholic batterers differed from nonbatterers in terms of experienced and witnessed abuse victimization.

Gondolf (1988) relied on reports from abused women seeking shelter to derive a typology of spouse abusers. The variables in this analysis included demographic factors, levels of physical and verbal abuse, the husband's general use of violence, history of arrest, and substance abuse. Unfortunately, this study did not include an explicit focus on personality variables, but the study is still worth noting because of the specific findings involving substance abuse. Three clusters were identified. The cluster with the lowest level of abuse was described as typical batterers. These men were the most likely to be apologetic and to engage in relatively less spousal blame. These men were relatively less likely to have arrest records and a history of violence outside the home. This cluster was quite different from the other two clusters, which involved men described as either sociopathic or antisocial.

These men engaged in more severe forms of abuse, including child abuse. However, the groups differed in that the sociopathic group had higher levels of substance abuse and previous arrests for violence outside the home than the other two groups.

A secondary analysis of these data by Gondolf and Fisher (1988) examined heterogeneity within the first group of typical batterers (characterized by lower levels of violence compared to the other two groups). Gondolf and Fisher made an important distinction between chronic typical batterers and sporadic typical batterers and found that the chronic batterers not only engaged in abuse on a more regular basis, they also had a relatively higher level of alcohol problems.

Saunders (1992) reported the results of another cluster analysis that was conducted on self-report data from 165 men receiving treatment for marital violence. The cluster analysis was performed on self-report data on a variety of measures, including levels of generalized and marital violence, depression, and alcohol use during violent incidents. Three clusters were obtained and then group comparisons were conducted on several other variables. A group identified as family-only aggressors had relatively high levels of marital satisfaction and low levels of depression and anger. Alcohol use was acknowledged as playing a role in approximately half of the family violence incidents. A second group identified as emotionally volatile aggressors reported high levels of psychological abuse, along with marital problems, depression, anger, and jealousy. However, alcohol use was not identified as a key factor. In contrast, the role of alcohol and substance abuse was clearly evident for the third group of men who were identified as generally violent aggressors. These men engaged in the most severe violence both inside and outside the home. Violent episodes were usually linked with alcohol use and several of these men had a history of being arrested for drunk driving.

Holtzworth-Munroe and Stuart (1994) reviewed the available literature and proposed an influential model of marital violence based on the notion that there are three identifiable subtypes of batterers. According to their framework, there are key differences among batterers in terms of the severity of marital violence, the generality of violence (i.e., specific to the spouse or also expressed toward others), and the presence of certain personality disorder features and associated levels of psychopathology. Importantly, their analysis of personality disorder features and psychopathology included explicit predictions about individual differences in levels of alcohol and drug abuse. Each subtype is described briefly below.

The *family-only batterer* is characterized by relatively low levels of marital violence and violence outside the home. These men are characterized by low levels of criminal behavior. Personality disorders are generally seen as absent with the possible exception of excessive dependency. These men are also characterized by low to moderate levels of depression, moderate levels of anger, and low to moderate alcohol and drug abuse.

The *dysphoric/borderline batterer* is characterized by low to moderate extrafamilial violence but moderate to high levels of marital violence, including psychological and sexual abuse. These men are seen as having a borderline or schizoid personality, high levels of anger and depression, and moderate alcohol and drug abuse.

Finally, the generally *violent/antisocial batterer* is portrayed as an individual who is relatively indiscriminant in the use of violence. Men with this description have moderate to high levels of marital violence, psychological abuse, and sexual abuse, but this is accompanied by extremely high levels of extrafamilial violence and criminal behavior. The predominant personality characteristic here focuses on antisocial traits and psychopathy. These men are distinguished from dysphoric/borderline batterers by relatively low levels of depression and moderate levels of anger, but high levels of alcohol and drug abuse.

It was noted earlier that the Holtzworth-Munroe and Stuart (1994) framework includes attachment styles and impulsivity as proximal correlates of marital violence. In addition, Holtzworth-Munroe and Stuart (1994) suggest that genetic, biological factors also play a key role as distal factors in the form of an impulsive and irritable temperament. A hostile, irritable orientation is further promoted by negative family experiences during childhood (e.g., being the target of abuse, experiencing severe discipline, and witnessing parental violence).

There is little doubt that this model has already had a significant impact on the field as researchers test the predictions put forth by Holtzworth-Munroe and Stuart (1994). For instance, Rothschild, Dimson, Storaasli, and Clapp (1997) provided an analysis of the MCMI-II (Millon, 1987) scores of 183 veterans entering treatment for domestic violence. A cluster analysis of MCMI-II factors scores yielded three clusters described as subclinical narcissism, narcissistic personality disorder, and high general psychopathology with substance dependence. This third group had substantially high levels of alcohol dependence and drug dependence, relative to the other two groups, and elevated scores on the passive-aggressive, avoidant, borderline, antisocial, and schizoid personality scales. They also had elevated scores on the measure of dysthymic disorder.

Rothschild et al. (1997) summarized their results by suggesting that there were general similarities with the typology proposed by Holtzworth-Monroe and Stuart (1994). However, they noted that the proposed dysphoric/borderline type was similar to their high general psychopathology/substance dependence type in that these types are characterized by the highest levels of psychological distress; however, the general psychopathology group identified by Rothschild et al. (1997) was the one in their study characterized by the highest levels of substance abuse and antisocial tendencies, which are characteristics that Holtzworth-Munroe and Stuart (1994) ascribe to their generally violent/antisocial type. Rothschild et al. suggested appropriately that these differences may reflect the differences between veteran and nonveteran samples.

Previously, Hamberger, Lohr, Bonge, and Tolin (1996) tested the Holtzworth-Munroe and Stuart (1994) typology in a clinical sample of 833 men who were identified as abusive. A cluster analysis of MCMI responses yielded three distinct clusters identified as nonpathological (i.e., no significant elevations on the MCMI), antisocial, and passive-aggressive-dependent groups. The third cluster identified as the passive-aggressive-dependent group was obtained instead of the dsyphoric/borderline group postulated by Holtzworth-Munroe and Stuart (1994). The group of nonpathological men had the lowest levels of violence. Additional results indicated that the antisocial men were the most generally violent and had the most police contacts, while the passive-aggressive-dependent group had the highest frequency of violence. Overall, Hamberger et al. (1996) concluded that there was general support for the proposed typology.

Tweed and Dutton (1998) reported the results of a cluster analysis conducted on the MCMI-II responses of batterers. They identified two groups of batterers. The first group resembled the generally violent/antisocial type in many respects, while the second group represented the dysphoric/borderline type. However, it should be noted that the two types did not differ on antisocial personality characteristics despite the fact that the generally violent/antisocial group had engaged in more severe forms of violence. However, the dysphoric/borderline group did have higher scores on measures of borderline personality organization.

More recently, Holtzworth-Munroe, Meehan, Herron, and Stuart (1999) reported the preliminary results of a comprehensive investigation designed to test the accuracy of the typology proposed by Holtzworth-Munroe and Stuart (1994). They recruited 63 maritally violent men and their spouses, as well as two nonviolent husband comparison groups (maritally distressed and nondistressed). Holtzworth et al. only reported the results for the various groups of violent men and did not report the results for the control group because the complete findings will be described in subsequent work. Both the husbands and wives in this study completed an extensive battery of measures over a number of sessions in the laboratory. Importantly, husbands and wives were tested in separate rooms, and wives were asked to assess numerous aspects of their husbands' behavior and personal characteristics.

In addition to the measures of violence and aggression, the men in this study completed the MCMI-III (Millon, 1987), the Short Michigan Alcoholism Screening Test (SMAST) (Selzer, Vinokor, & van Rodjen, 1975), the Drug Abuse Screening Test (DAST) (Skinner, 1982), and an index assessing the quantity and frequency of alcohol use in the past year. Wives also evaluated their husbands' levels of alcohol and drug use by completing these measures. Additional measures that were completed by the husbands include the hostility subscale of the Buss-Perry Aggression Questionnaire (Buss & Perry, 1992), the Spielberger Trait Anger Inventory (Spielberger, 1988), the revised Hare Psychopathy Checklist, a criminality questionnaire (Hare, 1991), and measures of spouse-specific dependency, rejection sensitivity, attachment style, and impulsivity.

The preliminary results reported by Holtzworth-Munroe et al. (1999) provide general support for the model proposed by Holtzworth-Munroe and Stuart (1994). Cluster analyses confirmed the presence of the three proposed types (i.e., family-only battering, borderline/dysphoric batterers, and generally violent/antisocial batterers), with the caveat that only five men thus far are in the category described as generally violent/antisocial batterers. Also, Holtzworth-Munroe and colleagues have identified a fourth group of men they describe as comprising the low-level antisocial group. These men have relatively low levels of dysphoria and lower levels of marital violence similar to the family-only group; however, they are distinguished by elevated scores on the antisocial scale and engage in general violence outside the home.

Holtzworth-Munroe et al. (1999) reported a number of findings that pertain to our focus on substance use and abuse and personality factors. Consistent with earlier predictions, group comparisons revealed that the group of generally violent/antisocial men had significantly higher levels of alcohol and drug use. The men in the dysphoric and low-level antisocial groups had higher scores on the SMAST and DAST when compared with the family-only group, but the only group difference that emerged here involved the higher level of husbands' drug use reported by the wives of men in the dysphoric group.

Analyses of the personality measures suggested that the highest levels of trait anger were evident among men in the generally violent/antisocial and dysphoric groups. Spousal reports indicated that the generally violent/antisocial group was higher on impulsivity, as assessed by the Barratt Impulsivity Scale (Barrett, 1965). There were no significant differences in rejection sensitivity. However, the dysphoric group had the highest levels of jealousy.

Finally, the most recent study conducted thus far on types of batterers was reported by Waltz, Babcock, Jacobson, and Gottman (2000). This study was unique in that it was based on individuals recruited from the community and it identified types of batterers via a sophisticated statistical procedure known as a mixture analysis that is more sophisticated than a cluster analysis in several respects (see Waltz et al., 2000). The mixture analysis was conducted on MCMI-II responses as well as measures of frequency of violence (according to spousal reports) and general violence. The analysis yielded three groups of batterers: (1) generally violent; (2) pathological (i.e. dysphoric/borderline); and (3) family-only. These three groups of men were compared with a fourth group of men (nonviolent men with marital discord) on a variety of measures. Comparsions showed that the generally violent group had higher levels of marital and general violence, relative to the pathological and family-only batterers. Surprisingly, the three batterer groups did not differ in levels of dysthymia, which is not in keeping with descriptions of dysphoric/borderline batterers. However, there were group differences in antisocial and borderline personality characteristics. The pathological group had higher scores than the generally violent group on the antisocial measure, and the generally violent group, in turn, had higher scores than the family-only group. Analyses of borderline tendencies showed that the pathological and generally violent group had higher scores than the family-only group; also, the pathological group had higher scores than the generally violent group, but this difference was not significant. Analyses of the MCMI-II alcohol and drug dependence scales showed that the generally violent and pathological groups both had higher scores than the family-only and nonviolent groups. It should be noted that a variety of other measures were included in this study, including behavioral measures and attachment style measures. The results for attachment style are discussed in a subsequent section of this chapter.

In their discussion of these results, Waltz et al. (2000) observed that their findings involving the measures of personality disorder are not in keeping with some key respects of the predictions put forth by Holtzworth-Munroe and Stuart (1994). Specifically, Waltz et al. found that the pathological group, rather than the generally violent group, had elevated scores on the MCMI-II subscales of antisocial, aggressive-sadistic, and narcissistic personality disorder. They suggested that the failure to support the personality predictions may reflect the continuing tendency to rely on versions of the MCMI instead of other personality measures. Clearly, an important goal for future research is to employ multiple measures when it is feasible to do so.

Most research on subtypes has focused on aspects of spouse abuse, and there is relatively little research on different types of child abusers and associated personality factors. One notable exception is a study conducted by Francis, Hughes, and Hitz (1992). They investigated the responses to the Sixteen Personality Factor Questionnaire (16-PF; Cattell, Eber, & Tatsuoka, 1982) provided by 82 adults (37 women, 45 men) who were confirmed perpetrators of child abuse. The cluster analysis revealed the presence of five identifiable types of child abusers and a pattern of findings that are not at all inconsistent with the results obtained in studies of spouse abusers. That is, Francis et al. (1992) found one group with no apparent personality dysfunction; three groups that could be described as having dysphoric features, including a group that were isolated, withdrawn, suspicious, tense, and apprehensive; and a third group of child abusers who were described as compulsive, bold, dominant, and assertive. The group of abusive parents who were described as isolated and withdrawn were described as substantially more disturbed in terms of their psychological and emotional functioning. A previous analysis of personality profiles by Sloan and Meier (1983) also demonstrated the heterogeneity is evident among child abusers. They reported that more favorable prognoses were associated with rigid-compulsive versus hostile-aggressive, passive-dependent personality types. They also noted a relatively high incidence of fathers characterized by hostile-aggressive personalities and mothers characterized by passive-dependent personalities. Unfortunately, the role of substance abuse was not an explicit focus in either of these studies.

☐ The Borderline Male and the Abusive Personality

The existence of a group of men with borderline personality features has emerged in several studies that have utilized cluster analyses to examine batterer subtypes. The borderline personality was first described in detail by Gunderson (1984). Borderline characteristics are present when an individual has a fragile and unstable sense of self along with deep fears of being abandoned, a history of intense but unstable interpersonal relationships, interpersonal sensitivity, demandingness, impulsivity, and a tendency to respond with intense anger that borders on rage when disappointed by other people. Borderline personality characteristics are associated with a dispositional tendency to experience intense emotions (Flett & Hewitt, 1995). Parenthetically, high affect intensity is also associated with alcohol abuse (Flett & Hewitt, 1995).

The presence of a personality dominated by borderline characteristics is an important aspect of the theory of batterers advanced by Dutton (1994, 1995, 1999). His analysis of etiological factors has focused on three main characteristics—borderline personality organization, anger, and the chronic experience of traumatic symptoms. In addition, Dutton (1995, 1999) has suggested that batterers are characterized by an anxious and angry attachment style instead of the secure attachment style that is linked with interpersonal and personal adjustment. The importance of all of these characteristics has been confirmed in a series of research investigations by Dutton and his colleagues (e.g., Dutton & Starzomski, 1993).

Three characteristics identified by Dutton (i.e., anger, insecure attachment, and power and control needs) have been evaluated in a number of investigations by other researchers. Research findings involving these personality constructs are described below.

Trait Anger, Hostility, and Antisocial Personality

Beasley and Stoltenberg (1992) compared the personality features of 35 male nonbatterers and 49 male batterers. Participants completed the MCMI-I, the Narcissism Personality Inventory (NPI) (Raskin & Terry, 1988), and the state and trait versions of Spielberger's State-Trait Anger Inventory (Spielberger, 1988). Examination of the MCMI-I scores indicated that batterers had significantly higher scores on the subscale measures of narcissism, antisocial, schizotypal, borderline, and aggressive-sadistic personality, with scores on the aggressive-sadistic subscale indicating the presence of clinically significant dysfunction. The batterers also had higher levels of state and trait anger. Surprisingly, although there were group differences in narcissism as assessed by the MCMI-I, analyses of the NPI scores indicated that there were no significant differences. These findings illustrate the point made earlier about using multiple measures when assessing certain personality characteristics.

The role of trait hostility and trait aggressiveness has been investigated in research on drinking and marital aggression (e.g., Leonard & Blane, 1992; Margolin, John, & Foo, 1998). For instance, Leonard and Blane (1992) conducted an examination of alcohol use and hostility in 320 23-year-old men. They found that 7% of the men in this study reported that they hit their partners only when they themselves were drinking, while another 3% of the men reported hitting their partners when drinking and when sober. Analysis of personality scores indicated that alcohol use, trait hostility, and marital adjustment interacted to predict aggression. Specifically, they found that for men with elevated levels of trait hostility, there was a stronger association between drinking and aggression, compared to men with relatively low levels of hostility. Men with low levels of hostility were more likely to aggress against their partners when there was a high level of marital discord.

Leonard and Senchak (1996) formulated a mediational model of marital violence that included personality factors (i.e., hostility and gender identity), husband alcohol use, and marital conflict styles as mediators of aggression expressed by the husband to the wife. A sample of 541 couples took part in a three-year prospective study that included a premarital assessment period and a subsequent interview when the first anniversary was reached.

The premarital time period included an assessment of personality factors and premarital aggression.

Hostility was assessed with the Spielberger Trait Anger Scale (Spielberger, 1988), while gender identity was assessed with measures of masculinity and femininity. The results involving personality factors showed that significant personality measures included hostility in husbands and wives and the husband's gender identity, with higher femininity being associated with reduced marital aggression. However, the link between personality factors and marital aggression expressed by husbands was mediated by the husbands' level of alcohol use and marital conflict styles. Overall, the results suggest that personality factors may play an important role in mediational models of relationship violence. However, Leonard and Senchak (1996) observed that their model accounted for only 29% of the variance in marital aggression when premarital levels of aggression were not included in the model, and they suggested the need to explore other factors that may improve the prediction of marital aggression.

Heyman et al. (1995) questioned the results of the Leonard and Blane (1992) study on the grounds that aggression was assessed with only two items. This was because the Leonard and Blane research was not designed to focus primarily on the link between alcohol and aggression. Heyman et al. conducted a longitudinal investigation that involved a more comprehensive assessment of aggression, including reports from husbands and wives. The participants in this research were 272 couples who were asked to participate at four timepoints (1 month prior to marriage and 6, 18, and 30 months after being married). Personality traits were assessed by the Personality Research Form-Version E (PRF; Jackson, 1974). The PRF was designed to assess the psychological needs described by Henry Murray (Murray, 1938). Participants in the Heyman et al. study completed several PRF subscales, including abasement, aggression, autonomy, dependence, dominance, and immaturity, but only the results for trait aggression were reported. Overall, the authors found that alcohol consumption was a relatively weak predictor of marital outcomes, including the level of aggression that was reported. However, they did find that levels of alcohol consumption interacted with trait aggression to predict levels of aggression reported at 18 months of marriage. Most importantly, comparisons of the predictive utility of measures of alcohol consumption and personality showed that trait aggression was a much more robust predictor of levels of aggression. However, Heyman et al. found that neither alcohol consumption nor trait aggression predicted husband-to-wife aggression measured at 30 months of marriage. This changing pattern of findings highlights the need for multiple assessments at various timepoints. Regarding the role of alcohol consumption, Heyman et al. suggested that the role of alcohol consumption in marital violence may have been underestimated, but they did not examine the immediate effects of alcohol consumption in specific conflict situations.

O'Leary, Malone, and Tyree (1994) conducted a prospective study that did not assess alcohol consumption, but it did include various measures of personality as possible correlates of physical aggression and psychological aggression (e.g., verbal hostility and passive-aggressive behavior). The personality variables included in this study were the PRF subscale measures of defendence (i.e., defensiveness), impulsivity, and aggression. All three personality factors were predictors of psychological aggression in men and women, and aggression predicted physical aggression in the relationship for both men and women, but these associations were relatively small in magnitude (respective rs of .18 and .20).

Brown, Werk, Caplan, and Seraganian (1999) investigated the personality characteristics of 53 men receiving treatment for domestic violence. The sample was divided into 33 men who met DSM-III-R (American Psychiatric Association, 1989) criteria for psychoactive substance abuse or dependence disorder at the time of assessment and 20 men who did not meet diagnostic criteria at the time of assessment. However, it should be noted that 92.5% of the sample met criteria for a lifetime diagnosis of either abuse or dependence. Individual difference measures that were completed included the 16 PF and the Symptom Checklist-90-Revised (SCL-90-R) (Derogatis, 1983). Comparisons of the two groups showed that they differed in SCL-90-R hostility scores with the group characterized by violence and substance abuse having higher hostility scores than the group characterized solely by violence. Analyses of 16 PF scores indicated that the men characterized by violence and drug abuse also had higher levels of frustration, apprehensiveness, and suspiciousness. A related investigation by Brown, Werk, Caplan, Shields, and Seraganian (1998) found that men in substance abuse treatment who had higher levels of violence were also high in hostility and interpersonal sensitivity.

Miller, Smyth, and Mudar (1999) recruited mothers from a variety of clinical and community sites in order to examine the link between punitiveness toward their child and the presence of alcohol and drug problems. The measures in this study included the Conflict Tactics Scale (Strauss, 1979), the Parental Punitiveness Scale (Epstein & Komorita, 1965), and the Child Abuse Potential Inventory (Milner, 1986). Miller et al. found that women with current or past alcohol and drug problems were high in punitiveness. They also found that a measure of hostility predicted punitiveness, and hostility moderated links between alcohol and drug problems and punitiveness.

Downs, Smyth, and Miller (1996) reviewed existing evidence on the overall role of antisocial personality disorder in alcohol problems and wife battering, and they proposed that an antisocial personality disorder not only contributes to the link between alcohol abuse and partner violence, it also mediates the link between childhood violence and subsequent alcohol abuse as an adult. They also reviewed some developmental evidence suggesting that antisocial tendencies precede alcohol abuse. Magdol, Moffitt, Caspi, and Silva (1998) also have conducted a long-term developmental investigation of the antecedents of partner abuse, and they found that a history of early behavior problems in childhood was a consistent predictor of levels of partner abuse measured at the age of 21. These data suggest that an antisocial, aggressive personality style that develops throughout childhood is a dispositional risk factor that contributes to the link between violence and substance abuse. This personality style likely develops as a function of temperament factors and negative social experiences involving the witnessing and actual experience of abuse and neglect during childhood (see Bernstein, Stein, & Handlesman, 1998; Feldman, 1997).

Attachment Style Theory

The classic work of Bowlby (1973) has alerted researchers to the importance of individual differences in attachment style as key factors in the development of various forms of dysfunction. In their seminal work, Ainsworth, Blehar, Waters, and Wall (1978) observed infants with three different attachment styles (i.e, secure, anxious/ambivalent, and avoidant) in the Strange Situation. Ainsworth et al. (1978) suggested that infants will develop a secure attachment style if they experience consistent, responsive, and warm treatment from adult caregivers. In contrast, an insecure form of attachment emerges in response to inconsistent and harsh treatment from caregivers.

The developmental research on attachment styles and separation anxiety in infants has important implications for the study of individual differences in adults. Consistent with observations that "attachment behavior is held to characterize human beings from the cradle to the grave" (Bowlby, 1977, p. 203), extensive research over the past two decades on attachment styles in adults has shown that there are meaningful individual differences in adult attachment styles, with some adults characterized by a secure attachment style and other adults characterized by insecure forms of attachment and associated relationship problems (Bartholomew & Horowitz, 1991; Hazan & Shaver, 1987). Bowlby (1980) has suggested that early experiences with caregivers become incorporated into the internal working models that are central to the cognitive processes of adults. These internal working models may take the form of relational schemas (Baldwin, 1992).

The link between adult attachment styles and relationship violence has been noted by a number of theorists including Holtzworth-Munroe and Stuart (1994) and Dutton (1995). Holtzworth-Munroe and Stuart (1994) predicted that family oriented batterers would be characterized by either a secure attachment style or a preoccupied, anxious attachment style, while dysphoric/borderline batterers would have a preoccupied attachment style, and generally violent/antisocial batterers would have a dismissive attachment style. According to Bartholomew and Horowitz (1991), preoccupied attachment reflects a negative cognitive-affective model of the self and positive model of significant others, while dismissive attachment reflects a positive model of the self and negative model of significant others. In contrast, a fearful attachment style reflects negative models of the self and others, and secure attachment involves positive models of both the self and others. Research on attachment styles in perpetrators has focused on the link with relationship violence without also measuring substance abuse, with the exception of the Holtzworth-Munroe et al. (1999) study and the Waltz et al. (2000) study. However, these studies were not designed explicitly to examine the interrelations among substance abuse, attachment, and violence.

Dutton, Saunders, Starzomski, and Bartholomew (1994) examined the link between attachment style and abusive tendencies in abusive men and their spouses. Dutton et al. (1994) found that men with preoccupied and fearful attachment styles engaged in greater psychological and physical abuse, according to spousal reports. Tweed and Dutton (1998) compared their two types of batterers and found that the impulsive type (i.e., borderline/dysphoric batterers) exhibited fearful attachment, while the instrumental (i.e., generally violent/antisocial batterers) were highly dismissive in their attachment style. These findings contrast with the results of a study by Pistole and Tarrant (1993) that did not find any evidence of insecure attachment style among 62 convicted male batterers.

Holtzworth-Munroe et al. (1999) compared attachment styles in their preliminary report of the tendencies exhibited by family only, dysphoric, low level antisocial, and generally/violent batterers. Group differences were found on all four continuous measures of secure, dismissive, fearful, and preoccupied attachment, but the pattern of findings was not in keeping with predictions made by Holtzworth-Munroe and Stuart (1994). Rather than having a dismissive attachment style, the generally violent/antisocial group had the highest levels of fearful and preoccupied attachment. However, these results are limited because they were based on a group consisting of only five men; comparisons with nonviolent men will be reported at the completion of this study.

Waltz et al. (2000) compared the three batterer groups in their study (i.e., generally violent, pathological, and family only) and the group of nonviolent men in troubled marriages on two attachment scales. Consistent with Holtzworth-Munroe and Stuart (1994), they found that generally violent men were dismissive and avoidant, while pathological men had a preoccupied and ambivalent attachment style along with high levels of jealousy. The family only batterers and nonviolent men were quite similar on many measures, including the attachment style measures, but the family only batterers did have a form of attachment known as compulsive care-seeking, which is a feature of an anxious-ambivalent attachment style.

Bookwala and Zdaniuk (1998) compared the attachment styles of 26 men and 59 women in reciprocally-aggressive dating relationships with the attachment styles of men and women in nonaggressive relationships. Participants rated their levels of attachment style according to the four Bartholomew and Horowitz (1991) categories. Participants completed a modified Conflict Tactics Scale (CTS) and the Inventory of Interpersonal Problems (Horowitz, Rosenberg, Baer, Ureno, & Villasenor, 1988). Bartholomew and Horowitz found that men and women in reciprocally-aggressive relationships had higher levels of preoccupied and fearful-avoidant attachment styles and more interpersonal problems. The strongest link involved aggressive tendencies and preoccupied attachment, and this association held even after controlling for variance attributable to interpersonal problems.

Further evidence of a link between attachment styles and aggressive tendencies was provided in a recent study by Kesner and McKenry (1998) who studied 149 heterosexual couples who were married or cohabiting for at least seven years. Participants completed a variety of measures including the CTS, the Life Experiences Survey (Sarason, Johnson, & Siegle, 1978), and indices of secure and insecure attachment. Kesner and McKenry reported that higher levels of male violence were associated with the relative absence of a secure attachment style among men ($r = .19$) and with higher levels of life stress ($r = .26$). A logistic regression analysis showed that more violent men were characterized jointly by a relative absence of secure attachment and higher levels of fearful-avoidant attachment.

Roberts and Noller (1998) examined the associations among attachment style and violence in 181 couples recruited from the community and from psychology classes. They completed measures of attachment style, communication patterns, dyadic adjustment, and levels of physical violence. The results showed that both men and women reported using violence against their partner if they had an attachment style characterized by anxiety over possible abandonment (i.e., preoccupied). Partner characteristics also were important; women reported higher levels of violence against their partners if their partners were anxious about abandonment. Tests of interaction effects further illustrated the importance of jointly considering the personality characteristics of both members of the dyad because violence was more likely from individuals who feared abandonment and who had partners who were avoidant and uncomfortable with closeness. One important caveat about this study is that overall levels of physical violence were relatively low, and this may reflect the nature of the sample (i.e., community and student volunteers).

Numerous studies also have assessed the link between attachment style and hostile responses to conflict. Direct examinations of the experience of anger are consistent with the view that attachment styles may play a role in hostility and the expression of aggression. For instance, Mikulincer (1998) conducted a series of studies examining attachment styles and adaptive versus maladaptive responses to anger. Individuals with an ambivalent attachment style had higher levels of anger-in (i.e., anger directed at the self) and had reduced levels of anger control, relative to individuals with a secure attachment style. Individuals with an avoidant attachment style were characterized by high hostility and low awareness of the physiological indicators of anger.

Moncher (1996) used the same measure of attachment style developed by Brennan and Shaver (1995) to examine the link between attachment style and child abuse potential in 48 single mothers. They completed a variety of measures that included the Child Abuse Potential Inventory (Milner, 1986). Comparisons of the attachment style groups confirmed that avoidant and ambivalent attachment styles were associated with higher levels of child abuse potential, relative to the secure attachment style. Of course, it must be reiterated that these findings apply to *potential* child abuse and may not be entirely generalizable to *actual* child abuse.

As noted above, very little research has examined attachment, violence, and alcoholism/addiction within the same research, and this type of study is clearly needed. However, indirect evidence of the association among these factors is provided by research on stalkers who seem to be characterized by pathological forms of attachment that reflect an angry, obsessive preoccupation with a former love object (see Meloy, 1998). These studies are worth noting because many of the people who engage in stalking behavior of previous intimates also have a history of substance abuse or substance dependence (see Burgess et al., 1997; Meloy & Gothard, 1995; Mullen, Pathe, Purcell, & Stuart, 1999).

Overall, the bulk of available evidence suggests that an insecure attachment style does indeed appear to play an important role in relationship violence, and substance use has a disinhibiting effect. However, the role of related constructs, such as dependency is less obvious. Murphy, Meyer, and O'Leary (1994) compared levels of dependency and other personality factors in a sample of 24 male spouse abusers who had requested treatment for spouse abuse, 24 men in troubled marriages without violence, and 24 happily married men without a history of violence. Participants completed the Interpersonal Dependency Inventory (Rosenberg, 1965), the Rosenberg Self-Esteem Scale (Hirschfeld et al., 1977), and measures of jealousy and spouse-specific forms of dependency. The group of spouse abusers had higher overall levels of general dependency and spouse-specific dependency than the other two groups. The spouse abuse group also had lower self-esteem, but the groups did not differ in levels of jealousy. Holtzworth-Munroe et al. (1999) included a measure of spouse-specific dependency as part of their investigation of the batterer typology. Their initial analyses indicate that the dysphoric group had the highest levels of spouse-specific dependency and interpersonal jealousy, relative to their other two groups.

There is some doubt about the potential importance of dependency in light of findings reported by Hart, Dutton, and Newlove (1993). These investigators conducted an investigation of the prevalence of personality disorders in a sample of 85 men participating in wife assault treatment groups. Personality disorders were assessed via self-report scores on the MCMI-II and clinical judgments stemming from the Personality Disorder Examination (Loranger, Susman, Oldham, & Russakoff, 1987), a semi-structured interview. One surprising finding that emerged from this study is that very few men were identified as suffering from a dependent personality disorder.

When evaluating the limited research conducted thus far on dependency, it is important to keep in mind that different conceptualizations of dependency have emerged in recent years. Research has established that the dependency construct is exceedingly complex, and it is important to distinguish maladaptive dependency from healthier forms of dependency that reflect positive forms of communion (see Blatt, Zohar, Quinlan, Zuroff, & Mongrain, 1995). In future research, it may be important to adopt a more fine-grained analysis that involves separate analyses of adaptive and maladaptive forms of dependency.

Psychological Need For Control and Power

It was noted in an earlier segment of this chapter that most research in this area has adopted a trait approach. The main exception is research that has taken a motivational focus by examining psychological needs. Research on spousal violence has focused individual differences in psychological needs for control, power, and dominance. Representative research is described below.

An excessive need for control is a factor that has been identified in dating relationships, marital relationships, and relationships that have dissolved. For instance, Tjaden and Thoeness (1997) examined stalking in response to love relationships that went sour and found that the most common motivation for the stalking behavior was the desire to maintain control over the stalking victims. Follingstad, Bradley, Laughlin, and Burke (1999) investigated the correlates of the reported use of violence in relationships in 617 college students. Numerous variables were assessed in this study, including individual differences in jealousy, anger, control, daily stress, levels of substance abuse, anger, irrational beliefs, and communication skills. It was found that the most salient variable that distinguished those who did use physical violence was the level of effort used in order to control one's partner. Other significant factors include substance abuse, the outward expression of anger, daily stress, poor communication skills, and irrational beliefs. Higher frequencies of force were predicted jointly by the need to control the partner and a willingness to express anger. The severity of force was predicted solely by the need to control the partner. That is, the need for control was stronger than the extent of substance abuse.

Hamberger, Lohr, Bonge, and Tolin (1997) examined the stated motives for domestic violence expressed by 215 male and 66 female court-referred perpetrators. The desire to control others, anger expression, and coercive communication were among the more common motives reported.

The need for control is closely linked with the need for power. Mason and Blankenship (1987) conducted a study with male and female undergraduates in which they examined the associations among measures of need for power, need for affiliation, activity inhibition, life stress, and levels of physical abuse and psychological abuse. All participants were either married, cohabiting, engaged, or in dating relationships. Mason and Blankenship found that a high need for power in men was associated with being more physically abusive toward partners, but this association was not detected for women. Abusive behaviors by women were predicted by a pattern of individual differences involving high need for affiliation, low activity inhibition, and high levels of stress. Overall, there was a tendency for more abuse to occur among couples with higher levels of commitment, as determined by the length and status of the relationship.

Dutton and Strachan (1987) compared responses to the Thematic Apperception Test (TAT) (Morgan & Murray, 1935) provided by men with a history of spousal assault, men in discordant marriages without a history of spousal assault, and happily married control participants. The TAT responses were scored in terms of need for power imagery and it was found that the groups of assaultive men and men in conflicted marriages were higher in their need for power compared to the control group.

Importantly, the need for power also has been associated directly with higher levels of aggressiveness and the need for power also is a motive for drinking (McClelland, 1975; McClelland, Davis, Kallin, & Wanner, 1972; Winter, 1973). A need for power may be associated with a desire to be aggressive, but these desires are not necessarily expressed by everyone due to social inhibitions. For example, Boyatiz (1973) reported that a high need for power was associated with a self-reported desire to act aggressively in a variety of ways (e.g., yell at someone in traffic, insulting a store clerk), but it was not associated with actual acts of aggressive behavior.

Individual differences in the willingness to express or inhibit aggressive impulses was incorporated into McClelland's (1975) description of the "conquistador motive pattern." This pattern is characterized by a high need for power, a low need for affiliation, and low levels of activity inhibition (i.e., controlling the expression of urges). Men characterized by this pattern tend to drink more often and fight more often than men without this personality pattern. Women with this personality pattern get into more interpersonal disputes and express their tendencies in more indirect ways (e.g., breaking objects and slamming doors).

☐ Personality, Stress, and Coping Model

A preliminary model of the associations among personality factors, stress, coping, and physical and psychological abuse is presented in Figure 4.2. Our model is preliminary in the sense that many of the hypotheses that stem from this model have not been subjected to systematic empirical investigation; at present, it should be regarded as a heuristic framework that can guide future research.

Whereas previous authors have focused on types of spouse batterers and child abusers, this model begins with the identification of several personality constructs that are believed to be dimensional in nature. Clearly, the model does not identify all of the personality factors of potential importance. In fact, it is plausible that there are several other personality constructs that can be meaningfully explored in terms of the links with stress and coping factors.

Before describing the personality factors in more detail, a comment about the role of substance use and abuse in this model is in order. The importance of substance use is reflected in two ways. First, the model includes a focus on chronic substance abuse as a mediator of the effects of personality factors. This is in keeping with some of the mediational effects identified in earlier segments of this chapter. In addition, the role of substance use is reflected in the coping component of this proposed model, in accordance with the acknowledged role of substance use as a form of avoidance coping (see Wills & Herky, 1996).

The three personality constructs included in the model (i.e., psychopathy, perfectionistic overcontrol, and hostile depression) have been selected on the basis of past descriptions of spouse batterers and child abusers and on the basis of the authors recent work on two of these constructs. These personality dimensions are now described in more detail.

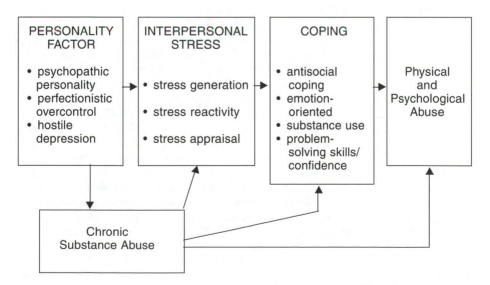

FIGURE 4.2. Theoretical model of personality, stress, and coping features in perpetrators of physical and psychological abuse in intimate relationships.

Psychopathy

Psychopathy is a personality orientation and behavioral style that has often been identified in studies of batterers. Antisocial, psychopathic characteristics also have been identified in child abusers (Bland & Orn, 1986; Dinwiddie & Bucholz, 1993). The nature of psychopathy will only be described briefly. Readers interested in further information are referred to a recent review by Huss and Langhinrichsen-Rohling (2000) of the nature and implications of psychopathy in batterers.

Psychopathy is evident in those individuals who have been described as highly antisocial, cold-hearted, and without any apparent remorse. Abusive and antisocial behaviors are nonspecific and may involve criminal behaviors in or outside the home. While some batterers experience increased heart rate activity during a marital conflict, psychopathic batterers actually experience decreases in heart rate activity in a manner that is in keeping with sadistic, antisocial individuals (see Gottman et al., 1995). Much of the empirical associations among personality characteristics and violent and nonviolent criminal behavior in individuals with a diagnosed substance use disorder (see Hernandez-Avila et al., 2000) can likely be attributed to stable individual differences in psychopathy and antisocial features. Spouse and child abuse is a reflection of a broader, pervasive pattern of antisocial behavior that occurs inside and outside the home.

Perfectionistic Overcontrol and Abusiveness

Perfectionistic overcontrol is a second personality orientation that is implicated in spouse and child abuse. Although research has not directly tested the link between perfectionism and either spouse abuse or child abuse, several lines of investigation combine to suggest the potential importance of this personality construct. The link between perfectionism and abuse becomes more evident when perfectionism is considered from a multidimensional perspective. Hewitt and Flett (1991) have shown that there are personal and interpersonal aspects of perfectionism. The Multidimensional Perfectionism Scale (Hewitt & Flett, 1991) was created to assess not only perfectionism in terms of the personal need to meet personal standards (i.e., self-oriented perfectionism), but also in terms of the importance of other people meeting expectations (i.e., other-oriented perfectionism). A third dimension assesses perfectionism in terms of the perception that others are demanding perfection from the self (i.e., socially prescribed perfectionism). Theoretically, extreme levels of other-oriented perfectionism and socially prescribed perfectionism should play a role in spouse abuse and child abuse. These factors are now described in more detail.

The other-oriented perfectionist is an individual who has exceedingly high standards for other people and who views the attainment of these standards as quite important. Whereas failures to attain personal standards of perfection are associated with feelings of self-criticism and self-punishment, the other-oriented perfectionist who perceives that others are not meeting expectations responds with other-directed blame and hostility (see Hewitt & Flett, 1991). Other-oriented perfectionism is associated with such attributes as authoritarianism, dominance, a need for control, and narcissism. Interpersonal circumplex analyses of other-oriented perfectionism in men and women have shown that this perfectionism dimension is associated with an exceedingly hostile interpersonal style (see Flynn, Hewitt, Broughton, & Flett, 1998; Hill, Zrull, & Turlington, 1997). Extreme forms of other-oriented perfectionism along with a perceived discrepancy between these extrapunitive standards and the behaviors of significant others could set the stage for the possibility of spouse abuse and child abuse.

Socially prescribed perfectionism is a dimension that "entails people's beliefs or perceptions that significant others have unrealistic standards for them, evaluate them stringently, and exert pressure on them to be perfect" (Hewitt & Flett, 1991, p. 457). Research has shown that individuals with high levels of socially prescribed perfectionism are resentful individuals characterized by high levels of anger (Hewitt & Flett, 1991), frustration reactivity (Flett, Hewitt, Blankstein, & Koledin, 1991), and the frequent occurrence of negative social interactions (Flett, Hewitt, Garshowitz, & Martin, 1997). Interpersonal circumplex analyses indicate that socially prescribed perfectionists also have a hostile interpersonal style (Flynn et al., 1998; Hill et al., 1997). Presumably, some socially prescribed perfectionists will respond to perceived frustrations by engaging impulsively in various forms of abusive behaviors.

Although research has not directly explored the link between these interpersonal perfectionism dimensions and abusive tendencies, several findings suggest that these factors may play a key role. Clearly, it is beyond the scope of this chapter to describe all of these findings in detail. However, one set of findings deserves mention because it shows how perfectionism overlaps with several personality characteristics identified in the cluster analyses of different types of batterers. Hewitt and Flett (1991; Study 5) examined the link between dimensions of perfectionism and the MCMI in a sample of psychiatric patients. This study showed that socially prescribed perfectionism was associated with alcohol abuse as well as borderline and passive-aggressive personality features. Other research has confirmed a link between socially prescribed perfectionism and borderline personality disorder diagnoses (Hewitt, Flett, & Turnbull-Donovan, 1994). These findings raise the possibility that the link between borderline features and spouse abuse stems, in part, from a sense that others are imposing unrealistic expectations on the self.

Hewitt and Flett (1991) found that other-oriented perfectionism was associated with drug abuse and MCMI measures of antisocial, narcissistic, and histrionic personality features. There was a positive association with alcohol abuse that approached but did not reach conventional levels of statistical significance. Overall, these findings are in keeping with the view that other-oriented perfectionism is an extrapunitive orientation that involves antisocial attempts to control others.

Dutton (1995) described a subtype of overcontrolled spouse abusers with perfectionistic tendencies. Specifically, he observed that "Wives of these men describe them as being meticulous, perfectionistic, and domineering" (Dutton, 1995, p. 29). These men have high scores on measures of dominance, social isolation of spouses, and emotional abusiveness. They are further described as individuals who seem compliant and have a strong desire to please their therapists.

Dutton (1995) also regards perfectionism as an element of the borderline personality organization involved in spouse abuse and noted that:

> Borderlines blame their partners when things go wrong in intimate relationships. And things are always going wrong, because they set impossibly high standards and double-binds for others. As their tension mounts, their need for perfect control in an imperfect world generates inevitable failure. People are fallible. One man would inspect the house after his wife did the chores, running his finger under the refrigerator, looking for dust. Eventually, he found some. Then a two-hour harangue would ensue in which he screamed at her about her lousy housekeeping. This personality profile creates an environment in which relationship conflict and abuse are inevitable. (Dutton, 1995, p. 146).

This description is in keeping with the description given of narcissistic abusers by Rothschild et al. (1997). They described narcissistic abusers as "individuals who have a rigid schema for how things should be. When reality does not conform to this schema, individuals with this profile are then likely to become enraged and violent" (p. 271). Indeed, an analysis of thoughts articulated after being angered showed that maritally violent men are especially likely to demean others and place absolute demands on them in a manner that suggests the presence of other-oriented perfectionism (Eckhart, Barbour, & Davison, 1998).

The importance of other-oriented perfectionism was highlighted in a recent interview that we had with a woman who had endured physical abuse from her husband for many years. When asked about her husband's perfectionism, this woman said:

> Perfectionism played a big part in the abuse I experienced. I had to be the perfect wife and I would get hit when I did not meet my husband's expectations. One time when I didn't answer the phone fast enough for his liking, he grabbed me by my hair, picked me up, and threw me across the room and against the wall. Another time I was cut and severely injured when he pulled me through a door in a fit of rage. And this usually occurred when he felt that I was not meeting his standards. I had to keep the house looking perfect and act the role of the perfect wife. The real irony is that he often said that the only mistake that *he* ever made was marrying me.

This account suggests that other-oriented perfectionism in the batterer may contribute to a sense of socially prescribed perfectionism in his abused mate.

At present, research has not investigated the link between spouse abuse and the interpersonal perfectionism dimensions identified by Hewitt and Flett (1991). However, at a general level, the role of perfectionism in spouse abuse was examined in research by Lohr, Hamberger, and Bonge (1988) on types of abusers. A sample of 188 men attending a domestic violence program were administered a number of measures including the MCMI and the Irrational Beliefs Test (IBT) (Jones, 1969). The IBT includes subscales that assess general perfectionism and high self-expectations. Cluster analyses yielded three types of men, including two types with perfectionistic tendencies. One cluster of men had the highest scores on the IBT perfectionism subscale. These men were described as narcissists who demanded perfection from their spouses. According to Lohr et al., these men:

> typically exhibit *a highly* self-centered and greatly inflated sense of importance and entitlement in their marital relationships. These individuals have "special knowledge" to the solutions of problems and "pronounce" to their spouses what the ultimate answer happens to be to any problem that arises. They become abusive when their partner fails to pay appropriate homage by accepting and agreeing with the self-evident truths which they have proclaimed. Indeed, the violence of these individuals . . . is not so much driven by dysphoria or anger as it is a method of "correction" or "motivation" to get their spouse to "do the right thing" (p. 183).

Unfortunately, when it comes to other-oriented perfectionism, the "right thing" is defined in terms of unrealistic absolutes that are bound to yield disappointment and conflict.

Lohr et al. (1988) described another cluster of spouse abusers who were distressed by their own imperfections and apparent inability to meet their own high self-expectations. These men had a number of characteristics associated with socially prescribed perfectionism, including a high need for social approval and a tendency to avoid problems and experience a sense of helplessness when change was required. According to Lohr et al., the pressure to be perfect is a key factor and they noted that:

> This person's expectations of himself as a person, a man and a spouse/partner probably exceed his capabilities. He demands perfection of himself and perfect loyalty from his partner. Since neither individual can possibly meet such expectations, he fears losing her respect and undying admiration as well as his own self-respect. He then catastrophically interprets himself as a "louse," who will never succeed in any such relationship. He also punishes his wife for failing to rescue him from his "lousiness" (p. 282).

Spouse abusers who fit this description seem to be suffering from fragile self-esteem. This contrasts with the characteristics of the narcissistic perfectionists who are fault-finders, recognizing imperfection in others, but not necessarily in themselves.

Various individuals can be the target of these impossibly high standards since perfectionism is a trait that generalizes across situations and circumstances; perfectionism is a factor that should be evident in various forms of childhood abuse. Indirect evidence is provided by research suggesting a link between child abuse and the presence of unrealistically high parental expectancies (see Azar, Robinson, Hekimian, & Twentyman, 1984; Azar & Rohrbeck, 1986; Klevens, Bayon, & Sierra, 2000).

Behavioral research on perfectionistic parenting behavior also has identified a pattern that can become abusive if taken to the extreme. Hyson, Hirsh-Pasek, Rescorla, Cone, and Martell-Boinske (1991) interviewed 90 mothers of preschoolers. They also observed the mothers' directive, controlling, perfectionistic, and critical behavior during two tasks requiring interaction between the mothers and their child. Cluster analyses of the ratings revealed an identifiable subset of 29 mothers who exhibited high frequencies of criticism, directiveness, control, and perfectionistic behaviors. Hyson et al. concluded that these mothers were most likely to put unwarranted pressure on their children, which is consistent with the anecdotal evidence we presented earlier. A broader analysis of perfectionism in parents and their children can be found in Flett, Hewitt, Oliver, and Macdonald (in press).

The Hostile, Depressive Personality

While other-oriented perfectionism can be conceptualized as a hostile, proactive form of overcontrol, it is more appropriate to regard socially prescribed perfectionism as a reactive personality dimension that involves both a tendency to experience resentment and hostility due to perceived mistreatment, as well as a sense of dejection due to feelings of hopelessness and helplessness stemming from the inability to please others with impossibly high standards. Socially prescribed perfectionism can be regarded as one of the facets of the hostile depression that is identified in Figure 4.2 as the third personality dimension associated with the perpetration of physical and psychological abuse. Specifically, it is posited that there is a personality orientation that is characterized by hostile depression. Individuals with this orientation have high levels of interpersonal sensitivity and respond with anger and hostility when they perceive various forms of mistreatment by others.

Extensive research on spouse abuse and child abuse has consistently pointed to the key role played by depression. One of the more well-known studies was conducted by Maiuro, Cahn, Vitaliano, Wagner, and Zegree (1988). This study examined convicted spouse batterers and identified a group of distressed spouse abusers characterized by elevated levels of hostility and depression. Another study by Barrera, Palmer, Brown, and Kalaher (1994) involved the administration of the Jackson Basic Personality Inventory (Jackson, 1989) to 86 court involved and 42 noncourt involved wife abusers. Analyses of Jackson Basic Personality Inventory scores showed that both groups had elevated levels of depression, anxiety, alienation, hypochondriasis, and impulse expression, relative to established norms.

Hostility and depression are often linked inextricably with substance abuse. For instance, a recent study by Eiden and Leonard (2000) did not examine abusiveness per se, but it did show the links among paternal alcoholism, antisocial tendencies, and aggravation with 12-month-old infants in 101 control families and 115 families with alcoholic fathers. Eiden and Leonard found that alcoholism was associated with greater aggravation with the infant and, importantly for our purposes, both depression and antisocial tendencies in fathers mediated the link between alcoholism and aggravation. A mediational model also predicted maternal aggravation with the infant; that is, alcoholism in fathers was linked with maternal aggravation via the mediating effects of maternal depression and antisocial tendencies.

The current model takes the associations among depression, hostility, and substance abuse a step further by suggesting that hostile depression is a stable component of personality in some individuals. This hostile, depressive personality will be associated with a variety of negative interpersonal outcomes and interactions, including the possibility of abusiveness, especially when substance use and abuse is involved.

Although depression is a consistent predictor of abusive tendencies, it is obviously the case that not all depressed individuals are abusive, and only a subset of depressives are characterized by the types of hostility associated with abusiveness toward family members. Research on general negative affectivity tends to focus on the link between depression and anxiety and much less attention is given to the consistent association between depression and hostility. However, cluster analyses seeking to identify depressive subtypes have often identified a hostile form of depression that could be involved in child or spouse abuse (e.g., Blashfield & Morey, 1979; Paykel, 1971). The link between hostility and depression was illustrated clearly in a study conducted by Hokanson and Butler (1992). A cluster analysis of depressed students identified "friendly" depressives with high levels of dependency and "aggressive" depressives who were autocratic, exploitive, and distrustful of others. Longitudinal analyses showed that both types of depressive students were rejected by their roommates, with the aggressive depressives becoming more socially isolated.

One obvious challenge when studying depression and abusiveness is to establish that the hostile, depressive tendencies existed prior to the acts of abuse because it could be that depression is simply a response to the consequences of being identified as a spouse or child abuser. Evidence that depression existed prior to the abusiveness comes from research designed to tap temperament styles believed to be present at birth and from longitudinal research.

Regarding depression as an aspect of temperament, Ammerman, Kolko, Kirisci, Blackson, and Dawes (1999) compared the characteristics of parents with a current substance use disorder or previous diagnosis of substance use disorder with parents without a history of substance use disorder. Participants completed the Child Abuse Potential Inventory (CAPI) (Milner, 1986), Tellegen's Multidimensional Personality Questionnaire (MPQ) (Tellegen, 1982), and the Child Behavior Checklist (Achenbach & Edelbrock, 1983). The MPQ provides scores for 11 subscales and three higher order factors representing trait negative affectivity, trait positive affectivity, and constraint. It should be noted that positive and negative affectivity as measured by the MPQ can be regarded as aspects of temperament with a significant genetic component (see Clark & Watson, 1999; Finkel & McGue, 1997).

As expected, mothers and fathers with a current diagnosis of substance use disorder or a past history of disorder had substantially higher scores on the measure of child abuse potential. Regression analyses showed that trait positive affectivity and negative affectivity (i.e., low positive affect, high negative affect) both predicted unique variance in child abuse potential scores for both mothers and fathers. These data point to a link between trait affect and child abuse, with the obvious caveat that the findings of the study are limited to child abuse potential scores and not actual child abuse.

Kotch, Browne, Dufort, Winsor, and Catellier (1999) conducted a longitudinal investigation of maternal predictors of child abuse and neglect. The study was conducted with mothers of at-risk infants who were interviewed shortly after having given birth. Reports of child abuse and neglect were obtained every six months for the next four years. A higher incidence of maltreatment was experienced by children who had mothers characterized by higher levels of depression, alcohol consumption, and psychosomatic symptoms, as well as having more than one dependent child in the home, and a history of being separated from their own mothers prior to age 14.

Another prospective study of child abuse and neglect (Christensen, Brayden, Dietrich, McLaughlin, & Sherrod, 1994) did not involve an assessment of depression per se, but it did involve measures of various facets of self-esteem; low self-esteem is a key symptom of depression. Low self-esteem is believed to be a contributing factor in child abuse (see Wolfe, 1987, for a review), though a number of studies have found only weak evidence of a link between low self-esteem and child abuse (see Christensen et al., 1994). Self-concept variables in the Christensen et al. study were assessed during the pregnancy period and state records were reviewed for incidents of child abuse and neglect. A total of 29 mothers engaged in either child abuse or neglect (or both). Comparisons with nonabusing mothers found that neglectful mothers had neurotic symptoms and had relatively lower scores on measures of overall self-esteem, moral self-worth, personal adequacy, social adequacy, and self-worth in family relationships. Physically abusive mothers were found to have relatively low scores on a measure of self-worth. Given that low self-esteem was more relevant to neglect than abuse, it is possible that measures associated with low self-esteem such as depression also have a stronger link with neglect.

Finally, Magdol, Moffitt, Caspi, and Silva (1998) found in their prospective study that depression in adolescents was a significant predictor of subsequent partner violence, and that the results differed for males and female perpetrators. Much stronger associations were found for men between partner violence and such factors as depression, violence toward strangers, polydrug use, and the presence of antisocial personality characteristics.

Depression Versus Egotism in Abusiveness

It should be noted that the inclusion of a personality dimension involving depression in this preliminary model of abusiveness is at variance with recent claims made by Baumeister and associates (see Baumeister, Bushman, & Campbell, 2000; Baumeister, Smart, & Boden, 1996; Bushman & Baumeister, 1998). They examined self-concept factors in aggression and violence and found evidence consistent with the position that narcissism and high self-esteem are associated with the expression of aggression, but low self-esteem is not associated with the expression of aggression. They suggest that research should focus primarily on egotism because several factors mitigate against a link between aggressiveness and low self-esteem. According to Baumeister et al. (2000), low self-esteem people are unlikely to aggress because they are:

> uncertain and confused about themselves, oriented toward avoiding risk and potential loss, shy, modest, emotionally labile (and having tendencies toward depression and anxiety), submitting readily to other people's influence, and lacking confidence in themselves (p. 26).

Clearly, narcissistic forms of egotism play a role in certain forms of aggression and abusiveness, and this may indeed be the dominant orientation in the university student samples studied by Baumeister and Bushman and their associates (Baumeister et al., 2000). However, the extensive research on different types of batterers and child abusers that was cited earlier shows that it is possible to identify a subset of individuals who are depressed, anxious, and angry. These individuals have a negative view of themselves and other people and they are likely to blame themselves and others when interpersonal problems are experienced.

☐ Stress Factors

The three personality constructs included in the preliminary model shown in Figure 4.2 should be regarded as risk factors associated with potential abusiveness that may or may not develop into actual abusiveness. The mediational model depicted in Figure 4.2 is based on the premise that these personality factors are associated with abuse potential, and the potential for abuse is much more likely to be realized if the individual experiences personally meaningful interpersonal stressors and responds with a maladaptive coping orientation. This model is generally consistent with the framework put forth by Bolger and Zuckerman (1995) who acknowledged that personality factors are involved both in the amount of exposure to stressors and in differences in stress reactivity (i.e., coping choice and coping effectiveness). The potential significance of stress and coping factors is now examined.

Recent research on different types of stressors has shown that the experience of negative social events can have a profound impact in terms of levels of psychological distress (for a review, see Flett, Hewett, Gershowitz, & Martin, 1997). Although there is a wide range of interpersonal stressors of possible relevance here, events that are interpreted as involving a sense of personal humiliation may serve as the catalysts for spouse abuse. Recently, Jennings and Murphy (2000) presented the argument that the domestic violence perpetrated by males has its roots in a sensitivity to humiliation. Humiliation is defined by Jennings and Murphy as the social version of shame, and it arises in males in response to alienation, an absence of effective male bonds, and rigid sex role socialization. Jennings and Murphy (2000) concluded that "humiliation is a powerful mechanism for shaping behaviors and attitudes; it pervades the same-sex relations of boyhood groups, male rites of passage, and even adult intimate relations" (p. 28).

Research is only beginning to examine the role of individual differences in perceived or actual humiliations, but existing studies have shown that the possibility of being humiliated is a significant source of distress (Hartling & Luchetta, 1999) and a sense of being humiliated is a factor that predicts aggression in dating relationships (Foo & Margolin, 1995). Moreover, high levels of defendence (i.e., a readiness to defend the self and be easily offended) in husbands predicts aggression towards wives (O'Leary et al., 1994). Humiliations that involve a sense of gender role identity may be particularly important; Copenhaver, Lash, and Eisler (2000) conducted a study of 163 inpatients in a substance abuse treatment program and found that men high in gender role stress (i.e., who experiencing difficulty coping with aspects of the traditional male role) were more likely to report being verbally and physically aggressive toward their partner relative to those men who reported low levels of gender role stress. Whereas perceived humiliation is likely to play a key role in abuse of intimate partners, child abuse is more likely to occur in response to chronic forms of general stress (Egeland, Breitenbucher, & Rosenberg, 1980), including parenting and child-related stressors (Chan, 1994), especially if negative events are seen as intentional misdeeds on the part of the child.

As can be seen in Figure 4.2, the preliminary model also includes the notion that personality orientations play a potentially important role in stress generation. This concept is derived from recent research in the depression field which suggests that negative social interactions may be a byproduct of core interpersonal needs that actually produce interpersonal problems or losses for the individual. In this instance, a tendency to treat people with hostility will elicit hostile reactions, which may culminate eventually in acts of abusiveness.

Another key aspect of stress is the stress appraisal process. A key aspect of stress appraisal that is relevant to abusiveness is the tendency to attribute negative intepersonal outcomes to the personal characteristics of one's partner (in the case of spouse abusers) or the characteristics of children (in the case of adults engaging in physical child abuse). This tendency to blame others has been referred to as the hostile attribution bias and extensive research has shown that this attributional bias plays a central role in acts of spousal violence (Eckhardt & Dye, 2000; Holtzworth-Munroe, Bates, Smutzler, & Sandin, 1997) and physical child abuse (Milner & Chilamkurti, 1991).

Finally, a caveat involving stress should be noted. As seen in Figure 4.2, the model includes the premise that chronic substance abuse leads to interpersonal stress. This is in keeping with extensive evidence that shows that substance abuse in violent and aggressive men is associated with a variety of interpersonal stressors involving marital problems (Leonard & Roberts, 1998). While this is certainly the case, Leonard and Roberts have cautioned appropriately that marital problems also can exacerbate problem drinking.

Coping Factors

As can be seen in Figure 4.2, a maladaptive coping orientation and poor problem-solving skills are important in the model that has been proposed. Specifically, it is suggested that the likelihood of physical and psychological abuse is increased substantially if the individual has an emotion-oriented and aggressive style of responding to interpersonal stressors and has poor problem-solving skills. Deficits in problem-solving include poor skills and a negative orientation toward problem-solving that promotes a sense of coping inefficacy. The tendency to respond to stress and feelings of negative emotions by drinking alcohol or taking drugs (i.e. drinking in order to cope) is well-documented (see Cooper, Frone, Russell, & Mudar, 1995), and is included in the model as a proximal coping factor that may contribute to subsequent acts of physical and psychological abuse.

The role of coping mechanisms in child abuse was illustrated by Cantos, Neale, O'Leary, and Gaines (1997). They compared the coping tendencies of 17 mothers who had physically abused their children and 16 mothers without a history of child abuse who nevertheless had children with behavioral problems involving poor conduct. Coping was assessed in three ways. First, mothers reported three stressful events and how they responded to these events. Various coping responses were then coded by raters (i.e., emotion-focused coping, effective problem-focused coping, and ineffective problem-focused coping). In addition, the mothers completed a structured coping inventory that provided measures of emotion-oriented, problem-oriented, and avoidance-oriented coping. Finally, the mothers completed a measure of problem-solving confidence. Analyses of self-reports showed that the abusive mothers had higher levels of emotion-oriented and avoidance-oriented coping, and lower levels of problem-oriented coping, especially in more stressful situations. They also had lower levels of confidence in their problem-solving ability. Analyses of ratings showed that the abusive mothers were rated as having higher levels of emotion-oriented coping and lower levels of effective problem-focused coping. This is in keeping with earlier reports of problem-solving deficits (see Azar et al., 1984).

The tendency to respond to interpersonal conflict with angry, aggressive forms of coping is an important element of the proposed model. Hobfoll and associates (see Hobfoll, Dunahoo, Ben-Porath, & Monnier, 1994) have criticized most existing coping measures on the grounds that they are too individualistic and do not contain enough content that is interpersonal in nature. Specifically, Hobfoll et al. have suggested the need to include a coping dimension that ranges from prosocial responses to stressful situations and life problems at one end of the continuum versus antisocial responses at the other end of the continuum. The definition of antisocial coping is coping behavior that is harmful to those in the social environment. Research in a variety of contexts has confirmed that there are meaningful individual differences in antisocial and aggressive coping, with men having higher levels of antisocial coping and women having higher levels of prosocial coping (Dunahoo, Monnier, Hobfoll, Hulsizer, & Johnson, 1998; Monnier, Stone, Hobfoll, & Johnson, 1998). Some research has shown that antisocial coping is linked with substance use (Blechman, Lowell, & Garrett, 1999). Also, Wills and Hirky (1996) have reviewed several studies with adolescents that show that anger coping responses are associated with higher levels of substance abuse.

Hobfoll and associates (1994) measure antisocial characteristics with subscale measures of antisocial action and aggressive action. The antisocial action subscale includes items such as "counterattack and catch others off-guard" and "look out for your best interests even if it means hurting others that are involved." The aggressive action subscale includes items such as "mount an all-out attack; be aggressive" and "move aggressively; often if you get another off-guard, things will work out to your advantage."

Individual differences in coping responses are important to include in models seeking to account for the associations among personality, substance abuse, and violence in intimate relationships because coping and stress factors may help explain why all individuals who are high in substance abuse do not engage in violence. Still, after examining the scale items shown above, some readers may respond to the proposed link between an aggressive coping style and a tendency to be more abusive by suggesting that the proposed association is too circular to be meaningful and that any empirical link simply reflects item overlap in the coping and abuse measures. It is for this reason that prospective research on antisocial and aggressive coping styles is vitally important. It is important to show that measures of hostile coping measure subsequent acts of violence and abuse that occur in response to perceived or actual stressors. It also is important to examine how levels of antisocial versus prosocial coping may vary according to the different types of abusers that have been identified.

☐ Conclusion

This chapter began with an overview of the various ways that personality may contribute to the link between substance abuse and violence in intimate relationships and this was followed by a selective review of relevant investigations. It should be evident from the current chapter that a considerable volume of research has examined the role of personality factors in perpetrators of spouse abuse, and a subset of studies in this area has included a focus on the role of substance use and abuse. Unfortunately, fewer studies have examined the role of personality factor in the perpetration of child abuse. Nevertheless, several investigations have shown that personality factors are vitally important and much is to be gained from an expanded approach that considers a wider range of individual difference factors, such as personality capabilities. If a broad approach to the study of personality is not conducted, it is conceivable that the predictive usefulness of personality variables will be underestimated.

The current review was limited in that it was not possible to conduct an extensive review of the effects of other personality factors (e.g., gender roles, locus of control, impulsivity) due to space limitations nor was it possible to provide a critical evaluation of significant methodological concerns. Also, given the paucity of relevant research at present, no attempt was made to examine the complex interplay of personality factors at the dyadic level. An important goal for future research is to examine the role of personality variables from a family perspective and conduct an extended analysis that includes, but goes beyond, a focus on the perpetrators of spouse abuse and child abuse.

This chapter concluded with a description of a proposed model that incorporates personality, stress, and coping factors. Hopefully, this preliminary model will prove to be useful as a heuristic framework that guides future research on this important topic. Longitudinal research is needed in order to assess the extent to which personality, stress, and coping factors are able to predict the frequency, intensity, and persistence of spouse abuse and child abuse. If this model does indeed prove to be useful, it will have important implications at the applied level. Although it may be difficult to change a personality structure that is deeply ingrained and has been present for many years, it should be less difficult to ameliorate maladaptive coping tendencies and stress appraisal processes. However, it is important to remain cognizant of the significant role played by those personality factors that set the stage for spouse abuse and child abuse.

☐ References

Achenbach, T., & Edelbrock, C. (1983). *Manual for the child behavior checklist and revised child behavior profile.* Burlington, VT: Author.

Ainsworth, M. D., Blehar, M. C., Waters, E., & Wall, S. (1978). *Patterns of attachment: A psychological study of the strange situation.* Hillsdale, NJ: Erlbaum.

American Psychiatric Association. (1987). *Diagnostic and statistical manual of mental disorder* (rev. 3rd ed.). Washington, DC: Author.

Ammerman, R. T., Kolko, D. J., Kirisci, L., Blackson, T. C., & Dawes, M. A. (1999). Child abuse potential in parents with histories of substance use disorder. *Child Abuse and Neglect, 23,* 1225–1238.

Azar, S. T., Robinson, R. R., Hekemian, E., & Twentyman, C. T. (1984). Unrealistic expectations and problem-solving ability in maltreating and comparison mothers. *Journal of Consulting and Clinical Psychology, 52,* 687–691.

Azar, S. T., & Rohrbeck, C. A. (1986). Child abuse and unrealistic expectations: Further validation of the parent opinion questionnaire. *Journal of Consulting and Clinical Psychology, 54,* 867–868.

Baldwin, M. W. (1992). Relational schemas and the processing of social information. *Psychological Bulletin, 112,* 461–484.

Ball, S. A., & Schottenfeld, R. S. (1997). A five-factor model of personality and addiction, psychiatric, and AIDS risk severity in pregnant and postpartum cocaine misusers. *Substance Use and Misuse, 32,* 25–41.

Barratt E. S. (1965). Factor analysis of some psychometric measures of impulsiveness and anxiety. *Psychological Reports, 16,* 547–554.

Barrera, M., Palmer, S., Brown, R. & Kalaher, S. (1994). Characteristics of court-involved men and non-court-involved men who abuse their wives. *Journal of Family Violence, 9,* 333–345.

Bartholomew, K., & Horowitz, L. M. (1991). Attachment styles among young adults: A test of a four-category model. *Journal of Personality and Social Psychology, 61,* 226–244.

Baumeister, R. F., Bushman, B. J., & Campbell, W. K. (2000). Self-esteem, narcissism, and aggression: Does violence result from low self-esteem or from threatened egotism? *Current Directions in Psychological Science, 9,* 26–29.

Baumeister, R. F., Smart, L., & Boden, J. (1996). Relation of threatened egotism to violence and aggression: The dark side of high self-esteem. *Psychological Review, 103,* 5–33.

Beasley, R., & Stoltenberg, C. D. (1992). Personality characteristics of male spouse abusers. *Professional Psychology: Research and Practice, 23,* 310–317.

Bernstein, D. P., Stein, J. A., & Handlesman, L. (1998). Predicting personality pathology among adult patients with substance use disorders: Effects of childhood maltreatment. *Addictive Behaviors, 23,* 855–868.

Bland, R. C., & Orn, H. (1986). Psychiatric disorders, spouse abuse, and child abuse. *Acta Psychiatrica Belgica, 86,* 444–449.

Blashfield, R. K., & Morey, L. C. (1979). The classification of depression through cluster analysis. *Comprehensive Psychiatry, 20,* 516–527.

Blatt, S. J., Zohar, A. H., Quinlan, D. M., Zuroff, D. C., & Mongrain, M. (1995). Subscales within the dependency factor of the Depressive Experiences Questionnaire. *Journal of Personality Assessment, 64,* 319–339.

Blechman, E. A., Lowell, E. S., & Garrett, J. (1999). Prosocial coping and substance abuse during pregnancy. *Addictive Behaviors, 24,* 99–109.

Bolger, N., & Zuckerman, A. (1995). A framework for studying personality in the stress process. *Journal of Personality and Social Psychology, 69,* 890–902.

Bookwala, J., & Zdaniuk, B. (1998). Adult attachment styles and aggressive behavior within dating relationships. *Journal of Social and Personal Relationships, 15,* 175-190.

Bowlby, J. (1973). *Attachment and loss. Vol. 2:* Separation, anxiety, and anger. London: Hogarth.

Bowlby, J. (1977). The making and breaking of affectional bonds: I: Aetiology and psychopathology in the light of attachment theory. *British Journal of Psychiatry, 130,* 201–210.

Bowlby, J. (1980). *Attachment and loss. Vol. 3: Loss, sadness, and depression.* New York: Basic.

Boyatiz, R. E. (1973). Affiliation motivation. In D. C. McClelland & R. C. Steele (Eds.), *Human motivation: A book of readings* (pp. 252–276). Morristown, NJ: General Learning.

Brennan, K. A., & Shaver, P. R. (1995). Dimensions of adult attachment, affect regulation, and romantic relationship functioning. *Personality and Social Psychology Bulletin, 21,* 267–283.

Brown, J., Cohen, P., Johnson, J. G., & Salzinger, S. (1998). A longitudinal analysis of risk factors for child maltreatment: Findings of a 17-year prospective study of officially recorded and self-recorded child abuse and neglect. *Child Abuse and Neglect, 22,* 1065–1078.

Brown, T. G., Werk, A., Caplan, T., & Seraganian, P. (1999). Violent substance abusers in domestic violent treatment. *Violence and Victims, 14,* 179–190.

Brown, T. G., Werk, A., Caplan, T., Shields, N., & Seraganian, P. (1998). The incidence and characteristics of violent men in substance abuse treatment. *Addictive Behaviors, 23,* 573–586.

Burgess, A. W., Baker, T., Greening, D., Hartman, C. R., Burgess, A. G., Douglas, J. E., & Halloran, R. (1997). Stalking behaviors within domestic violence. *Journal of Family Violence, 12,* 389–403.

Bushman, R., & Baumeister, R. F. (1998). Threatened egotism, narcissism, self-esteem, and direct and displaced aggression: Does self-love or self-hate lead to violence? *Journal of Personality and Social Psychology, 75,* 219–229.

Buss, A. H., & Perry, M. (1992). The Aggressive Questionnaire. *Journal of Personality and Social Psychology, 63,* 452–459.

Buss, D. M. (1991). Conflict in married couples: Personality predictors of anger and upset. *Journal of Personality, 59,* 663–688.

Cantos, A. L., Neale, J. M., O'Leary, K. D., & Gaines, R. W. (1997). Assessment of coping strategies of child abusing mothers. *Child Abuse and Neglect, 21,* 631–636.

Cattell, R. B., Eber, H. W., & Tatsuoka, M. M. (1982). *Handbook for the Sixteen Personality Factor Questionnaire (16 P-F).* Los Angeles, CA: Western Psychological.

Chan, Y. C. (1994). Parenting stress and social support of mothers who physically abuse their children in Hong Kong. *Child Abuse and Neglect, 18,* 261–269.

Christensen, M. J., Brayden, R. M., Dietrich, M. S. McLauglin, F. J., & Sherrod, K. B. (1994). The prospective assessment of self-concept in neglectful and physically abusive low income mothers. *Child Abuse and Neglect, 18,* 225–232.

Clark, L. A., & Watson, D. (1999). Temperament: A new paradigm for trait psychology. In L. A. Pervin & O. P. John (Eds.), *Handbook of personality: Theory and research* (pp. 399–423). New York: Guilford.

Cooper, M. L., Frone, M. R., Russell, M., & Mudar, P. (1995). Drinking to regulate positive and negative emotions: A motivational model of alcohol use. *Journal of Personality and Social Psychology, 69,* 990–1005.

Copenhaver, M. M., Lash, S. J., & Eisler, R. M. (2000). Masculine gender-role stress, anger, and male intimate abusiveness: Implications for men's relationships. *Sex Roles, 42,* 405–414.

DeRogatis, L. R. (1983). *Manual for the SCL-90-R.* Towson, MD: Clinical Psychometric Research.

Dinwiddie, S. H., & Bucholz, K. K. (1993). Psychiatric diagnoses of self-reported child abusers. *Child Abuse and Neglect, 17,* 465–476.

Downs, W. R., Smyth, N. J., & Miller, B. A. (1996). The relationship between childhood violence and alcohol problems among men who batter: An empirical review and synthesis. *Aggression and Violent Behavior, 1,* 327–344.

Dunahoo, C. L., Monnier, J., Hobfoll, S. E., Hulsizer, M. R., & Johnson, R. (1998). Even the Long Ranger had Tonto: There's more than rugged individualism in coping. *Anxiety, Stress, and Coping, 11,* 137–165.

Dutton, D. G. (1994). The origin and structure of the abusive personality. *Journal of Personality Disorders, 8,* 181–191.

Dutton, D. G. (1995). *The batterer: A psychological profile.* New York: Basic.

Dutton, D. G. (1999). Traumatic origins of intimate rage. *Aggression and Violent Behavior, 4,* 431–447.

Dutton, D. G., Bodnarchuk, M., Kropp, R., Hart, S. D., & Ogloff, J. P. (1997). Client personality disorders affecting wife assault post-treatment recidivism. *Violence and Victims, 12,* 37–50.

Dutton, D. G., Saunders, K., Starzomski, A., & Bartholomew, K. (1994). Intimacy-anger and insecure attachment as precursors of abuse in intimate relationships. *Journal of Applied Social Psychology, 24,* 1367–1386.

Dutton, D. G., & Starzomski, A. J. (1993). Borderline personality in perpetrators of physical and psychological abuse. *Violence and Victims, 8,* 327–337.

Dutton, D. G., & Strachan, C. E. (1987). Motivational needs for power and spouse-specific assertiveness in assaultive and nonassaultive men. *Violence and Victims, 2,* 145–156.

Eckhardt, C. I., Barbour, K. A., & Davison, G. C. (1998). Articulated thoughts of martially violent and nonviolent men during anger arousal. *Journal of Consulting and Clinical Psychology, 66,* 259–269.

Eckhardt, C. I., & Dye, M. L. (2000). The cognitive characteristics of maritally violent men: Theory and evidence. *Cognitive Therapy and Research, 24,* 139–158.

Egeland, B., Breitenbucher, M., & Rosenberg, D. (1980). Prospective study of the significance of life stress in the etiology of child abuse. *Journal of Consulting and Clinical Psychology, 48,* 195–205.

Eiden, R. D., & Leonard, K. E. (2000). Paternal alcoholism, parental psychopathology, and aggravation with infants. *Journal of Substance Abuse, 11,* 17–29.

Epstein, R., & Komorita, S. S. (1965). The development of a scale of parental punitiveness toward aggression. *Child Development, 36,* 129–142.

Feldman, C. M. (1997). Childhood precursors of adult interpartner violence. *Clinical Psychology: Science and Practice, 4,* 307–334.

Finkel, D., & McGue, M. (1997). Sex differences and nonadditivity in heritability of the Multidimensional Personality Questionnaire Scales. *Journal of Personality and Social Psychology, 72,* 929–938.

Flett, G. L., & Hewitt, P. L. (1995). Criterion validity and psychometric properties of the Affect Intensity Measure in a psychiatric sample. *Personality and Individual Differences, 19,* 589–591.

Flett, G. L., Hewitt, P. L., Blankstein, K., & Koledin, S. (1991). Dimensions of perfectionism and irrational thinking. *Journal of Rational-Emotive and Cognitive Behavior Therapy, 9,* 185–201.

Flett, G. L., Hewitt, P. L., Endler, N. S., & Bagby, M. R. (1995). Conceptualization and assessment of personality factors in depression. *European Journal of Personality, 9,* 309–350.

Flett, G. L., Hewitt, P. L., Garshowitz, M., & Martin, T. R. (1997). Personality, negative social interactions, and depressive symptoms. *Canadian Journal of Behavioural Science, 29,* 28–37.

Flett, G. L., Hewitt, P. L., Oliver, J. M., & Macdonald, S. (in press). Perfectionism in children and their parents: A developmental analysis. In G. L. Flett & P. L. Hewitt (Eds.), *Perfectionism: Theory, research, and treatment.* Washington, DC: American Psychological Association Press.

Flett, G. L., Vredenburg, K., & Krames, L. (1997). The continuity of depression in clinical and nonclinical samples. *Psychological Bulletin, 121,* 395–416.

Flynn, C. A., Hewitt, P. L., Broughton, R., & Flett, G. L. (1998, August). *Mapping perfectionism onto the interpersonal circumplex.* Paper presented at the annual meeting of the American Psychological Association, San Francisco, CA.

Follingstad, D. R., Bradley, R. G., Laughlin, J. E., & Burke, L. (1999). Risk factors and correlates of dating violence: The relevance of examining frequency and severity levels in a college sample. *Victims and Violence, 14,* 365–381.

Foo, L., & Margolin, G. (1995). A multivariate investigation of dating aggression. *Journal of Family Violence, 10,* 351–377.

Francis, C. R., Hughes, H. M., & Hitz, L. (1992). Physically abusive parents and the 16-PF: A preliminary psychological typology. *Child Abuse and Neglect, 16,* 673–691.

Gondolf, E. W. (1988). Who are these guys? Toward a behavioral typology of batterers. *Violence and Victims, 3,* 187–203.

Gondolf, E. W., & Fisher, E. R. (1988). *Battered women as survivors: An alternative to treating learned helplessness.* Lexington, MA: Lexington.

Gottman, J., Jacobson, N. S., Rushe, R. H., Short, J. W., La Taillade, J. J., & Waltz, J. (1995). The relationship between heart rate reactivity, emotionally aggressive behavior and generalized violence in batterers. *Journal of Family Psychology, 9,* 1–41.

Gunderson, J. G. (1984). *Borderline personality disorder.* Washington, DC: American Psychiatric Press.

Hamberger, K. L., & Hastings, J. E. (1989). Counseling male spouse abusers: Characteristics of treatment completers and dropouts. *Violence and Victims, 4,* 275–286.

Hamberger, L. K., & Hastings, J. E. (1990). Recidivism following spouse abuse abatement counseling: Treatment program implications. *Violence and Victims, 5,* 157–170.

Hamberger, L. K., & Hastings, J. E. (1991). Personality correlates of men who batter and nonviolent men: Some continuities and discontinuities. *Journal of Family Violence, 6,* 131–147.

Hamberger, L. K., Lohr, J. M., Bonge, D., & Tolin, D. F. (1996). A large sample empirical typology of male spouse abusers and its relationship to dimensions of abuse. *Violence and Victims, 11,* 277–292.

Hamberger, K. L., Lohr, J. M., Bonge, D., & Tolin, D. F. (1997). An empirical classification of motivations for domestic violence. *Violence Against Women, 3,* 401–423.

Hare, R. D. (1991). The Hare Psychopathy Checklist–Revised. Toronto, Ontario: Multi-Health Systems Inc.

Hart, S., Dutton, D. G., & Newlove, T. (1993). The prevalence of personality disorder among wife assaulters. *Journal of Personality Disorders, 7,* 329–341.

Hartling, L. M., & Luchetta, T. (1999). Humiliation: Assessing the impact of derision, degradation, and debasement. *Journal of Primary Prevention, 19,* 259–278.

Hazan, C., & Shaver, P. (1987). Romantic love conceptualized as an attachment process. *Journal of Personality and Social Psychology, 52,* 511–524.

Hernandez-Avila, C. A., Burleson, J. A., Poling, J., Tennen, H., Rounsaville, B. J., & Kranzler, H. R. (2000). Personality and substance use disorders as predictors of criminality. *Comprehensive Psychiatry, 41,* 276–283.

Hewitt, P. L., & Flett, G. L. (1991). Perfectionism in the self and social contexts: Conceptualization, assessment, and association with psychopathology. *Journal of Personality and Social Psychology, 60,* 456–470.

Hewitt, P. L., & Flett, G. L. (1996). Personality traits and the coping process. In M. Zeidner and N. S. Endler (Eds.), *Handbook of coping: Theory, research, and applications* (pp. 410–433). New York: Wiley.

Hewitt, P. L., Flett, G. L., & Turnbull-Donovan, W. (1994). Borderline personality disorder: An investigation with the Multidimensional Perfectionism Scale. *European Journal of Psychological Assessment, 10,* 28–33.

Heyman, R. E., O'Leary, K. D., & Jouriles, E. N. (1995). Alcohol and aggressive personality styles: Potentiators of serious physical aggression against wives? *Journal of Family Psychology, 9,* 44–57.

Hill, R. W., Zrull, M. C., & Turlington, S. (1997). Perfectionism and interpersonal problems. *Journal of Personality Assessment, 69,* 81–103.

Hirschfield, R. M., Klerman, G. L., Gough, H. G., Barrett, J., Korchin, S. J., & Chodoff, P. (1977). A measure of interpersonal dependency. *Journal of Personality Assessment, 41,* 610–618.

Hobfoll, S. E., Dunahoo, C. L., Ben-Porath, Y., & Monnier, J. (1994). Gender and coping: The dual axis model of coping. *American Journal of Community Psychology, 22,* 49–82.

Hokanson, J. G., & Butler, A. C. (1992). Cluster analysis of depressed college students' social behaviors. *Journal of Personality and Social Psychology, 62,* 273–280.

Holtzworth-Munroe, A., Bates, L., Smutzler, N., & Sandin, E. (1997). A brief review of the research on husband violence: I. Maritally violent versus nonviolent men. *Aggression and Violent Behavior, 2,* 65–99.

Holtzworth-Munroe, A., Meehan, J. C., Herron, K., & Stuart, G. L. (1999). A typology of male batterers:

An initial examination. In X. B. Arriaga & S. Oskamp (Eds.), *Violence in intimate relationships* (pp. 45–72). Thousand Oaks, CA: Sage.

Holtzworth-Munroe, A., & Stuart, G. L. (1994). Typologies of male batterers: Three subtypes and the differences among them. *Psychological Bulletin, 116,* 476–497.

Horowitz, L. M., Rosenberg, S. E., Baer, B. A., Ureno, A., & Villasenor, V. S. (1988). The Inventory of Interpoersonal Problems: Psychometric properties and clinical applications. *Journal of Consulting and Clinical Psychology, 56,* 885–892.

Huss, M. T., & Langhinrichsen-Rohling, J. (2000). Identification of the psychopathic batterer: The clinical, legal, and policy implications. *Aggression and Violent Behavior, 5,* 403–422.

Hyson, M. C., Hirsh-Pasek, K., Rescorla, L., Cone, J., & Martell-Boinske, L. (1991). Ingredients of parental "pressure" in early childhood. *Journal of Applied Developmental Psychology, 12,* 347–365.

Jackson, D. N. (1974). *Personality research form manual.* Goshen, NY: Research Psychologists.

Jackson, D. N. (1969). *Basic personality inventory manual.* Port Huron, MI: Sigma Assessment Systems.

Jennings, J. L., & Murphy, C. M. (2000). Male-male dimensions of male-female battering: A new look at domestic violence. *Psychology of Men and Masculinity, 1,* 21–29.

Jones, R. G. (1969). *The irrational beliefs test.* Wichita, KS: Test Systems, Inc.

Kesner, J. E., & McKenry, P. C. (1998). The role of childhood attachment factors in predicting male violence toward female intimates. *Journal of Family Violence, 13,* 417–432.

Klevens, J., Bayon, M. C., & Sierra, M. (2000). Risk factors and context of men who physically abuse in Bogota, Columbia. *Child Abuse and Neglect, 24,* 323–332.

Kotch, J. B., Browne, D. C., Dufort, V., Winsor, J., & Catellier, D. (1999). Predicting child maltreatment in the first 4 years of life from characteristics assessed in the neonatal period. *Child Abuse and Neglect, 23,* 305–319.

Leonard, K. E. (1999). Alcohol use and husband marital aggression among newlywed couples. In X. B. Arriaga & S. Oskamp (Eds.), *Violence in intimate relationships* (pp. 113–135). Thousand Oaks, CA: Sage.

Leonard, K. E., & Blane, H. T. (1992). Alcohol and marital aggression in a national sample of young men. *Journal of Interpersonal Violence, 7,* 19–30.

Leonard, K. E., & Roberts, L. J. (1998). Marital aggression, quality, and stability in the first year of marriage: Findings from the Buffalo newlywed study. In T. N. Bradbury (Ed.), *The developmental course of marital dysfunction* (pp. 44–73). Cambridge, England: Cambridge University Press.

Leonard, K. E., & Senchak, M. (1996). Prospective prediction of husband marital aggression within newlywed couples. *Journal of Abnormal Psychology, 105,* 369–380.

Livesley, W. J., Schroeder, M. L., Jackson, D. N., & Jang, K. L. (1994). Categorical distinctions in the study of personality disorder: Implications for classification. *Journal of Abnormal Psychology, 103,* 6–17.

Lohr, J. M., Hamberger, L. K., & Bonge, D. (1988). The nature of irrational beliefs in different personality clusters of spouse abusers. *Journal of Rational-Emotive and Cognitive-Behavior Therapy, 6,* 273–285.

Loranger, A. W., Susman, V. L., Oldham, J. M., & Russakoff, L. M. (1987). The personality disorder examination: A preliminary report. *Journal of Personality Disorders, 1,* 1–13.

Magdol, L., Moffitt, T. E., Caspi, A., & Silva, P. A. (1998). Developmental antecedents of partner abuse: A prospective-longitudinal study. *Journal of Abnormal Psychology, 107,* 375–389.

Maiuro, R. D., Cahn, T. S., Vitaliano, P. P., Wagner, B. C., & Zegree, J. B. (1988). Anger, hostility, and depression in domestically violent versus generally assaultive men and nonviolent control subjects. *Journal of Consulting and Clinical Psychology, 56,* 17–23.

Margolin, G., John, R. S., & Foo, L. (1998). Interactive and unique risk factors for husbands' emotional and physical abuse of their wives. *Journal of Family Violence, 13,* 315–327.

Mason, A., & Blankenship, V. (1987). Power and affiliation motivation, stress, and abuse in intimate relationships. *Journal of Personality and Social Psychology, 52,* 203–210.

McLellan, A. T., Luborsky, L., Woody, G. E., & O'Brien, C. P. (1980). An improved diagnostic instrument for substance abuse patients: The addiction severity index. *Journal of Nervous and Mental Disease, 168,* 26–33.

McClelland, D. C. (1975). *Power: The inner experience*. New York: Irvington.

McClelland, D. C., Davis, W. N., Kalin, R., & Wanner, E. (1972). *The drinking man*. New York: Irvington.

Meloy, J. R. (1998). *The psychology of stalking: Clinical and forensic perspectives*. San Diego, CA: Academic.

Meloy, J. R., & Gothard, S. (1995). Demographic and clinical comparison of obsessional followers and offenders with mental disorders. *American Journal of Psychiatry, 152*, 258–263.

Mikulincer, M. (1998). Adult attachment style and individual differences in functional versus dysfunctional experiences of anger. *Journal of Personality and Social Psychology, 74*, 513–524.

Miller, B. A., Smyth, N. J., & Mudar, P. S. (1999). Mothers' alcohol and other drug problems and their punitiveness toward their children. *Journal of Studies on Alcohol, 60*, 632–642.

Millon, T. (1983). *Millon Clinical Multiaxial Inventory*. Minneapolis: Interpretive Scoring Systems.

Millon, T. (1987). Manual for the MCMI-II (2nd ed.). Minneapolis: National Computer Systems.

Milner, J. S. (1986). *The Child Abuse Potential Manual* (2nd ed.). Webster, NC: Psyctec.

Milner, J. S., & Chilamkurti, C. (1991). Physical child abuse perpetrator characteristics: A review of the literature. *Journal of Interpersonal Violence, 6*, 345–366.

Moncher, F. J. (1996). The relationship of maternal adult attachment style and risk of physical child abuse. *Journal of Interpersonal Violence, 11*, 335–350.

Monnier, J., Stone, B. K., Hobfoll, S. E., & Johnson, J. R. (1998). How antisocial and prosocial coping influence the support processes among men and women in the U.S. postal service. *Sex Roles, 39*, 1–20.

Morgan, C. D., & Murray, H. A. (1935). A method for investigating fantasies: The thematic apperception test. *Archives of Neurology and Psychiatry, 34*, 289–306.

Mullen, P. E., Pathe, M., Purcell, R., & Stuart, G. W. (1999). Study of stalkers. *American Journal of Psychiatry, 156*, 1244–1249.

Murphy, C. M., Meyer, S-L., & O'Leary, K. D. (1994). Dependency characteristics of partner assaultive men. *Journal of Abnormal Psychology, 103*, 729–735.

Murray, H. A. (1938). *Explorations in personality*. New York: Oxford University Press.

O'Leary, K. D., Malone, J., & Tyree, A. (1994). Physical aggression in early marriage: Pre-relationship and relationship effects. *Journal of Consulting and Clinical Psychology, 62*, 594–602.

Paulhus, D. L., & Martin, C. L. (1987). The structure of personality capabilities. *Journal of Personality and Social Psychology, 52*, 354–365.

Paulhus, D. L., & Martin, C. L. (1988). Functional flexibility: A new conception of interpersonal flexibility. *Journal of Personality and Social Psychology, 55*, 88–101.

Paykel, E. S. (1971). Classification of depressed patients: A cluster analysis derived grouping. *British Journal of Psychiatry, 118*, 203–210.

Pistole, M. C., & Tarrant, N. (1993). Attachment style and aggression in male batterers. *Family Therapy, 20*, 165–173.

Raskin, R., & Terry, H. (1988). A principal components analysis of the narcissistic personality inventory and further evidence of its construct validity. *Journal of Personality and Social Psychology, 54*, 890–902.

Roberts, N., & Noller, P. (1998). The associations between adult attachment and couple violence: The role of communication patterns and relationship satisfaction. In J. A. Simpson & W. S. Rholes (Eds.), *Attachment theory and close relationships* (pp. 317–350). New York: Guilford.

Rosenberg, M. (1965). *Society and the adolescent self-image*. Princeton, NJ: Princeton University Press.

Rothschild, B., Dimson, C., Storaasil, R., & Clapp, L. (1997). Personality profiles of veterans entering treatment for domestic violence. *Journal of Family Violence, 12*, 259–273.

Sarason, I. G., Johnson, J. H., & Siegle, J. M. (1978). Assessing the impact of life changes: Development of the life experiences survey. *Journal of Consulting and Clinical Psychology, 46*, 932–946.

Saunders, D. G. (1992). A typology of men who batter women: Three types derived from cluster analyses. *American Journal of Orthopsychiatry, 62*, 264–275.

Saunders, D. G. (1996). Feminist-cognitive-behavioral and process-psychodynamic treatments for men who batter: Interaction of abuser traits and treatment models. *Violence and Victims, 11*, 393–414.

Selzer, M. L., Vinokur, A., & van Rooijen, L. (1975), A self-administered short Michigan Alcohol Screening Test (SMAST). *Journal of Studies on Alcohol, 36*, 117–126.

Sher, K. J., Trull, T. J., Bartholow, B. D., & Vieth, A. (1999). Personality and alcoholism: Issues, methods, and etiological processes. In K. E. Leonard & H. T. Blane (Eds.), *Psychological theories of drinking and alcoholism* (pp. 54–105). New York: Guilford.

Skinner, H. A. (1982). The Drug Abuse Screening Test. *Addictive Behaviors, 7,* 363–371.

Sloan, M. P., & Meier, J. H. (1983). Typology for parents of abused children. *Child Abuse and Neglect, 7,* 443–450.

Spielberger, C. D. (1988). *Manual for the trait-state anger expression inventory* (research edition). Odessa, FL: Psychological Assessment Resources.

Strauss, M. A. (1979). Measuring intrafamily conflict and violence: The conflict tactics (CT) scale. *Journal of Marriage and the Family, 41,* 75–88.

Stuart, G. L. (1998). Impulsivity as a predictor of marital violence: Testing a mediational model (Doctoral dissertation, Indiana University, 1998). *Dissertation Abstracts International, 59* (2-B), 0889.

Sutker, P. B., & Allain, A. N., Jr. (1988). Issues in personality conceptualizations of addictive behaviors. *Journal of Consulting and Clinical Psychology, 56,* 172–182.

Tarter, R. E. (1988). Are there inherited behavioral traits that predispose to substance abuse? *Journal of Consulting and Clinical Psychology, 56,* 189–196.

Tellegen, L. A. (1982). *Brief Manual for the Differential Personality Questionnaire (Multidimensional Personality Questionnaire).* Unpublished manuscript. Minneapolis, MN: University of Minnesota.

Tjaden, P., & Thoenness, N. (1997). *Stalking in America: Findings from the National Violence Against Women Survey.* Denver, CO: Center For Policy Research.

Trull, T. J., Widiger, T. A., & Guthrie, P. (1990). Categorical versus dimensional status of borderline personality disorder. *Journal of Abnormal Psychology, 99,* 40–48.

Tweed, R. G., & Dutton, D. G. (1998). A comparison of impulsive and instrumental subgroups of batterers. *Violence and Victims, 13,* 217–230.

Wallace, J. (1966). An abilities conception of personality: Some implications for personality measurement. *American Psychologist, 21,* 132–138.

Waltz, J., Babcock, J. C., Jacobson, N. S., & Gottman, J. M. (2000). Testing a typology of batterers. *Journal of Consulting and Clinical Psychology, 68,* 658–669.

Wills, T. A., & Hirky, A. E. (1996). Coping and substance abuse: A theoretical model and review of the evidence. In M. Zeidner and N. S. Endler (Eds.), *Handbook of coping: Theory, research, and applications* (pp. 279–302). New York: Wiley.

Winter, D. G. (1973) *The power motive.* New York: Free Press.

Wolfe, D. A. (1987). *Child abuse: Implications for child development and psychopathology.* Newbury Park, CA: Sage.

Zuckerman, M., Kuhlman, D. M., Thornquist, M., & Kiers, H. (1991). Five (or three) robust questionnaire scale factors of personality without culture. *Personality and Individual Differences, 23,* 929–941.

CHAPTER

Sherry H. Stewart
Anne L. Israeli

Substance Abuse and Co-Occurring Psychiatric Disorders in Victims of Intimate Violence

There is a well-documented relation between exposure to familial violence (e.g., childhood sexual and physical abuse, and partner-to-partner violence) and increased rates of substance use disorders in the victims of such violent exposure. Research also suggests significant associations between such intimate violence exposure and a variety of psychiatric disorders (e.g., depression, posttraumatic stress disorder [PTSD], and sexual dysfunction) among victims. In the present chapter, we explore the possible roles that these psychological sequelae might play in the well-documented relation between violence exposure and substance disorders in victims.

We first examine the mental health correlates of exposure to familial childhood physical and sexual abuse, including both psychiatric disorders as well as substance-related disorders. We include studies conducted with adults using long-term retrospective methodologies, with adolescents conducted closer in time to the childhood violence exposure, and the few existing prospective, longitudinal studies. Studies concerning the mental health correlates of partner-to-partner violence ("spousal battery"), including both psychiatric and chemical use disorders, are reviewed next. We explore specific mechanisms that may explain the higher rates of both certain psychiatric disorders and of substance-related disorders among victims of domestic violence, and review evidence regarding comorbidity and potential functional relations. We have chosen to focus on the three specific sets of psychiatric disorders (i.e., depression, PTSD, and sexual dysfunction) that have received the most research attention. We include coverage of symptoms of these disorders (e.g., suicidal ideation as a symptom of major depressive disorder; American Psychiatric Association [APA], 1994), as few studies have examined psychiatric disorders, per se, among victims of intimate violence. Finally, we provide a methodological critique of studies to

This work was supported, in part, by grants from the Alcoholic Beverage Medical Research Foundation (ABMRF) and the Social Sciences and Humanities Research Council of Canada (SSHRC), awarded to the first author. The second author was supported by a SSHRC Graduate Fellowship, and a New Brunswick Women's Doctoral Scholarship.

date, and propose suggestions for future research to clarify the mechanisms involved and their therapeutic implications.

☐ Theoretical Perspectives—Trauma Theories

We begin with a review of a number of theoretical perspectives that may prove relevant to understanding the comorbidity of certain psychiatric disorders with substance-related disorders among victims of domestic violence. Collectively, we refer to these various perspectives as trauma theories in that they all view psychiatric sequelae in intimate violence victims as being consequences of psychological reactions to a traumatic experience. The DSM-IV (APA, 1994) defines a traumatic event as a situation involving threatened or actual serious injury or death, or a threat to the physical integrity of the self or others, where the individual's response involves extreme fear, helplessness, or horror. Exposure to domestic violence (e.g., sexual or physical abuse in childhood, or partner-to-partner violence in adulthood) can clearly serve as a traumatic event (March, 1993).

Stewart and her colleagues (Stewart, 1996, 1997; Stewart, Conrod, Pihl, & Dongier, 1999; Stewart, Pihl, Conrod, & Dongier, 1998) have suggested a self-medication model to account for the common comorbidity between PTSD and substance-related disorders across various traumas. As applied to victims of familial violence, this model suggests that the traumatic nature of childhood physical or sexual abuse increases susceptibility to the development of clinically-significant PTSD symptoms in childhood and adolescence, or delayed onset PTSD in adulthood (cf. Kovach, 1986). Similarly, for victims of partner-to-partner physical violence, the traumatic nature of the violence exposure increases the battered spouse's susceptibility to PTSD. The presence of frequent and severe PTSD symptoms then increases the victim's susceptibility to the development of substance disorders, where substances are used in an attempt to reduce or control the behavioral, affective, cognitive, or physiological symptoms of PTSD. In operant conditioning terminology, victims are said to learn to drink or to use drugs for their "negatively-reinforcing" (e.g., tension-reducing, intrusive memory-dampening) effects (see Stewart, 1996, 1997).

Miller and Downs (1995) have developed a theory involving low self-esteem to explain the comorbidity of depression and substance use disorders among both adolescent and adult samples of intimate violence victims. They suggest that childhood sexual and physical abuse lead to self-devaluation and a loss of self-esteem among victimized children and adolescents. This self-derogation occurs when the emotional impact of the traumatic abusive events overwhelms the coping abilities of the young victim, leading to depressive symptoms or disorders. Substance abuse is then said to serve a self-medicating function for victims, in their attempts to cope with the resultant depression (Miller, Maguin, & Downs, 1997). This self-esteem model may also be applicable to understanding the elevated rates of both sexual dysfunction and substance use disorders in women who experienced sexual violence as children. Specifically, experiences of sexual abuse during childhood may undermine the development of appropriate levels of sexual self-esteem, which in turn may contribute to the development of sexual dysfunction. Victims may then abuse substances in attempts to self-medicate for sexual dysfunction (Covington & Kohen, 1984).

Janoff-Bulman and Thomas (1989) have developed a similar theory regarding the role of self-blame among victims of various types of trauma, including incest and spousal battery, that might explain the common comorbidity of depression and substance abuse in victims of intimate violence exposure. These theorists argue that there are two distinct types of self-blame: behavioral self-blame and characterological self-blame. The former type of attribution involves blaming a modifiable factor, and thus is seen as an adaptive response to victimization. Characterological self-blame, on the other hand, involves blaming more enduring qualities of the self. This latter type of self-blame is viewed as maladaptive, resulting in decreased self-esteem, which in turn can contribute to symptoms of depression (e.g., suicidality) and substance abuse among victims (Janoff-Bulman & Thomas, 1989).

Self-blame theory may also be applicable to understanding comorbid PTSD and substance related disorders in victims of domestic violence. Janoff-Bulman and Thomas (1989) argue that characterological self-blame attributions following a trauma can lead to increases in certain types of PTSD symptoms such as repetitive, intrusive thoughts about the trauma. In fact, Wolfe, Gentile, Michienzi, Sas, and Wolfe (1991) found that sexual abuse victims' attributions of self-blame and guilt (e.g., "I was to blame for what happened;" "I feel guilty about what happened") were positively related to intrusive thoughts ("I have dreams or nightmares about what happened"). Moreover, Wolfe, Sas, and Wekerle (1994) showed that, among child victims of sexual abuse, the victims' self-reported levels of guilt about the abuse served as a significant predictor of degree of PTSD symptoms over and above other relevant factors, including abuse severity. By contributing to increased PTSD symptoms, (characterological) self-blame may indirectly contribute to comorbid substance abuse if victims subsequently attempt to self-medicate the resultant PTSD symptoms through alcohol or drug use (cf. Stewart, 1996).

The study of vulnerability to depression in the context of social rank theory may also be applicable to understanding the high rates of both depression and substance abuse observed in victims of spousal abuse. Social rank theory asserts that how individuals respond to interpersonal threats involving real or perceived losses in rank may contribute to the experience of depression (e.g., Gilbert, 1992; Santor, Pringle, & Israeli, 2000). For example, in order to preserve her own life and the lives of her children, a battered woman may not retaliate against her violent partner but may choose to submit and accept his abusive behavior toward her. Submitting to a more dominant or aggressive other (e.g., an abusive partner who relies on violence to achieve status) may represent a social strategy aimed at maintaining interpersonal relatedness and reducing the probability of subsequent attacks. Unfortunately, over time, prolonged submissiveness may further promote feelings of helplessness and worthlessness in the victim and may predispose her to major depressive episodes (Gilbert, 1992). A battered wife may deal with such painful emotions by using alcohol and other substances to self-medicate.

Briere and Runtz (1993) present a classical conditioning model to explain the association between childhood sexual abuse and adult sexual dysfunction. Specifically, sexual stimuli present during the anxiety-provoking abuse experiences in childhood may come to elicit a conditioned anxiety response later on—even in objectively nonthreatening sexual situations (cf. Meiselman, 1978). In the case of physical abuse, physical touching could similarly come to elicit a conditioned anxiety response during later adult sexual encounters, due to repeated pairing of physical touch with anxiety-provoking physical abuse experiences in childhood. Alcohol, as a central nervous system depressant, can serve to depress higher brain functions that inhibit sexual behavior by reducing anxiety and fear (see Kaplan, 1974). Thus, women with sexual dysfunction secondary to childhood abuse may learn to use alcohol (or other depressant drugs) to reduce anxiety and fear and permit more "normal" sexual activity.

Most of these theories explicitly acknowledge the influence of trauma characteristics, such as severity and chronicity of the trauma exposure, in contributing to resultant psychopathology. For example, Terr (1991) has distinguished between the typical psychological effects of a single traumatic event and those of prolonged, repeated traumas, such as commonly endured by victims of domestic violence (see also Stewart, 1996). For example, the latter type of trauma is more likely than the former to be associated with emotional numbing PTSD symptoms in children (Terr, 1991). According to Janoff-Bulman and Thomas (1989), victimizations that occur repeatedly (e.g., battering or incest) are more likely than single, discrete-event types of trauma to change adaptive behavioral self-blame attributions to more global and maladaptive characterological attributions. As applied to the understanding of comorbid psychiatric and substance abuse disorders in domestic violence victims, more severe or chronic forms of intimate violence exposure might be most likely to result in comorbidity (cf. Stewart, 1996).

In the following sections, research pertaining to comorbid psychiatric and substance abuse disorders in victims of intimate violence is reviewed. We return to each of the above theoretical perspectives at relevant points throughout the chapter to explore mechanisms that may be responsible for observed comorbidity in victims.

☐ Substance Abuse and Psychiatric Disorders in Victims of Parent-To-Child Violence

Depression

Studies of the psychiatric correlates of both childhood sexual abuse and childhood physical abuse, including corporal punishment of children by parents or observation of parent-to-parent violence, have demonstrated that depressive symptoms (e.g., low self-esteem, suicidal ideation, negative mood, agitation, sleep difficulties) and depressive disorders are common sequelae in adult samples of victims (Malinosky-Rummell & Hansen, 1993; Polusny & Follette, 1995; Silvern et al., 1995; Straus & Kaufman Kantor, 1994). These data point to depression as a comorbid psychiatric disorder that might mediate or explain the relation between childhood intimate victimization and subsequent substance abuse.

Duncan, Saunders, Kilpatrick, Hanson, and Resnick (1996) screened a national sample of 4,009 adult women for a history of serious physical assault in childhood and for certain psychiatric disorders (e.g. major depressive disorder and substance abuse) in adulthood. Physical assault was stringently defined (i.e., episodes in which the victim was attacked with a weapon, or where the perpetrator's intent was to seriously injure or kill). Approximately 2.6% of the sample reported having experienced serious physical violence in childhood, with fathers and stepfathers identified as the most frequent perpetrators. Depression was measured with the Structured Clinical Interview for DSM-III-R (SCID; Spitzer, Williams, & Gibbon, 1986) and alcohol and drug abuse with an author-compiled set of interview questions (e.g., substance use contributing to difficulties with family, friends, or work). Compared to women who reported no histories of physical assault, childhood physical assault victims were twice as likely to meet criteria for lifetime major depressive disorder, and four times more likely to meet criteria for current major depressive disorder. Victims were also more likely to report alcohol- and drug-related problems.

Mullen, Martin, Anderson, Romans, and Herbison (1996) examined the longer-term impact of sexual, physical, and emotional abuse in childhood on a range of mental health problems in adulthood in a community sample of 497 women. Sexual abuse was defined stringently to include childhood exposure to abuse involving actual penetration and/or any genital contact on at least ten occasions. The Present State Examination (PSE; Wing, Nixon, Mann, & Leff, 1977) was used to examine psychiatric disorders, and the World Health Organization (WHO) alcohol questionnaire (Saunders, Aasland, & Grant, 1987) was administered to examine excessive drinking (i.e., consuming 14 or more standard units of alcohol per week). These researchers also employed a self-esteem questionnaire. About 22% of the sample reported histories of some form of abuse in childhood which was associated with increased rates of depression and suicidality on the PSE, as well as decreased self-esteem. Only participants with histories of childhood sexual abuse displayed increased excessive drinking. Since sexual abuse was defined quite stringently, the observed association of childhood sexual abuse with excessive drinking may reflect an association with abuse severity and/or chronicity rather than sexual abuse, per se. Furthermore, the observed relations between childhood abuse and adult psychiatric and substance abuse outcomes remained after controlling for general family dysfunction.

Turner and Lloyd (1995) examined the prevalence of lifetime traumas and their relations to psychological distress and to specific psychiatric disorders in adulthood. The study involved interviews with a random community sample of 1,393 adults. Psychological distress was assessed with the Center for Epidemiological Studies Depression scale (CES-D; Radloff, 1977). Specific psychiatric disorders were assessed with the Composite International Diagnostic Interview (CIDI; WHO, 1990). Participants were assessed for exposure to a variety of traumatic events throughout the life span including sexual abuse, physical abuse, and witnessing violence. Some, but not all, of the questions were particular to familial violence. Trauma exposure predicted the lifetime occurrence of both substance use disorders and depression, even after controlling for parental psychopathology. Moreover, trauma exposure predated the development of both depression and substance use disorders in the majority of cases.

McCauley et al. (1997) examined the prevalence of physical and sexual abuse histories in a sample of 1,931 women presenting to primary care practices. Of the women surveyed, 424 (22%) reported histories of physical or sexual abuse in childhood. Abused women obtained higher scores on the depression subscale of the 22-item version of the Symptom Checklist (SCL-22; Derogatis, 1975) than women denying childhood abuse histories. Abused women were more likely to have attempted suicide, to be currently abusing drugs, and to have a history of alcohol abuse, relative to nonabused controls. These effects persisted in those women who had only been abused as children (but not as adults) suggesting a truly long-term impact of childhood abuse. A dose response relation was found: women abused both as children and adults showed the highest levels of psychiatric symptoms.

A study by Wilsnack, Vogeltanz, Klassen, and Harris (1997) examined relations between childhood sexual abuse and psychiatric and substance abuse symptoms in adulthood among a nationally representative sample of 1,099 American women. Women who reported abusive sexual experiences before 18 years of age were compared to women without histories of childhood sexual abuse. Sexual abuse was defined broadly to include unwanted touching or fondling, genital contact, penetration, or any combination of these. Depression was assessed with the Diagnostic Interview Schedule (DIS; Robins, Helzer, Croughan, & Ratcliff, 1981), and women were queried about a variety of aspects of their alcohol and drug use behavior. Above and beyond demographic factors, childhood sexual abuse was associated with increased recent alcohol use, intoxication, drinking problems, and alcohol dependence symptoms, as well as lifetime use of both prescribed and illicit drugs. Childhood sexual abuse also was associated with a greater likelihood of having experienced at least one episode of clinically significant depression. It was suggested that increased substance abuse in the women with sexual abuse histories might represent an attempt to cope with depression secondary to the sexual abuse (cf. Miller & Downs, 1995).

The studies reviewed above suggest that a childhood history of violent victimization by intimates is associated with increased rates of both substance-related disorders and depressive disorders (or depressive symptoms) in adulthood. Nonetheless, all of these studies have been conducted with adults, using long-term retrospective self-report methods which may be subject to memory errors or other biases (Stewart, 1996). Studies with adolescents can, to some degree, overcome the limitations inherent in retrospective self-reports by examining the participants' reports of exposure to familial violence closer in time to event occurrence (Stewart, 1996).

Like findings with adults, studies of the effects of childhood sexual abuse and physical abuse have found elevated levels of depression and suicidality among child and adolescent victims of both genders of these forms of intimate violence in clinical and nonclinical samples (see Edwall & Hoffmann, 1988; Kendall-Tackett, Meyer Williams, & Finkelhor, 1993; Malinosky-Rummell & Hansen, 1993). However, relatively few studies have simultaneously examined relations between childhood exposure to familial violence and both emotional and substance use disorders in adolescents.

Kaplan et al. (1998) investigated whether exposure to physical violence in childhood accounts for adolescent psychopathology over and above other risk factors. Participants were 99 adolescents recruited from child protective services with documented histories of physical abuse and a sample of 99 controls who were matched with the physical abuse group on age, gender, race, and socioeconomic status. Adolescent participants and their parents were assessed for a variety of forms of psychopathology using the Schedule for Affective Disorders and Schizophrenia for Children (Kiddie-SADS; Orvaschel, Puig-Antich, Chambers, Tabrizi, & Johnson, 1982), and the SCID (Spitzer et al., 1986) for parents. After accounting for traditional risk factors (e.g., parental substance abuse, parental depression), physical abuse contributed significantly in predicting adolescents' lifetime drug abuse diagnoses, and lifetime and current diagnoses of depression and cigarette smoking.

Similar to findings in adult samples, both increased depression and increased substance use disorders are correlates of exposure to intimate violence among adolescents. These findings are consistent with both Miller and Downs' (1995) self-esteem model and with Janoff-Bulman and Thomas' (1989) self-blame model. Other aspects of these models have been tested in a rather piecemeal fashion, however. For example, a study by Morrow (1991) examined the relations between attributions given by 84 female adolescent incest victims for their abuse experiences and levels of both self-esteem and depression. Participants completed Rosenberg's (1965) Self-Esteem Scale and the Beck Depression Inventory (BDI; Beck & Steer, 1987). Results revealed that girls were significantly more depressed and displayed lowered self-esteem if they attributed the incest as having been due to something about the self (internal attribution) as opposed to some reason external to the self (external attribution). Thus, consistent with Miller and Downs' model, self-derogation (i.e., self-blame about childhood victimization) is related to lowered self-esteem and increased depression among victims. This study did not separate internal (self-blame) attributions into behavioral or characterological self-blame, however, and thus was unable to test predictions derived from Janoff-Bulman and Thomas' self-blame model.

Cavaiola and Schiff (1989) administered a measure of self-esteem to 145 physically and sexually abused, chemically dependent adolescents and to two comparison groups matched for age, race, and socioeconomic status: 58 nonabused chemically dependent adolescents and 59 nonabused, nonchemically dependent adolescents. The abused, chemically dependent group displayed lower self-esteem compared to the two control groups, providing some preliminary support for the predictions of Miller and Downs' (1995) and Janoff-Bulman and Thomas' (1989) models regarding relations among childhood victimization, lowered self-esteem, and drug misuse.

Results have not always been consistent, however. For example, Hussey and Singer (1993) compared a group of sexually abused adolescent psychiatric inpatients with a control group of nonabused inpatients on measures of self-esteem, depression, and substance abuse. The two groups were matched on demographics and psychiatric diagnoses. Depression levels were assessed with the BDI (Beck & Steer, 1987) and self-esteem with

Rosenberg's (1965) scale. The abused group scored significantly higher than controls on a variety of measures of substance abuse including recent drunkenness and frequency of drug use. However, the two groups did not differ in depression or self-esteem. The a priori matching on psychiatric diagnoses (e.g., rates of major depression diagnoses were controlled across the two groups) may have been responsible for the failure to observe increased BDI scores and decreased self-esteem among the sexually abused adolescents. However, the study does show that increased substance abuse can occur among abuse victims in the absence of increased dysphoric mood or lowered self-esteem.

Dembo et al. (1987) tested a portion of Miller and Downs' (1995) model in a cross-sectional analysis of data from a sample of 145 male and female adolescents in a juvenile detention facility. Detainees reported on their histories of physical and sexual abuse (including, but not limited to, familial abuse), levels of self-esteem (i.e., scores on Rosenberg's [1965] scale), and frequency of use of a variety of illicit drugs. Results suggested that, among both genders, sexual victimization had primarily a direct effect on illicit drug use. Physical abuse, in contrast, had both direct and indirect effects on illicit drug use where the indirect effect was mediated by decreased self-esteem. These cross-sectional findings provide support for Miller and Downs' (1995) model in suggesting that low self-esteem may at least partly explain the relation between childhood victimization and substance abuse in adolescents.

A later study by Dembo et al. (1990) used longitudinal methodology to test the hypothesis that physical abuse and sexual abuse would predict high-risk adolescents' future alcohol or drug abuse both directly and indirectly through increased psychological distress. Participants were 305 juvenile detainees, each of whom was interviewed at two time points: on intake into the detention center, and at a 10–15 month follow-up. Childhood physical and sexual abuse were assessed as described previously (i.e., Dembo et al., 1987). Psychological distress was assessed using the total score on the 90-item version of the Symptom Checklist—Revised (SCL-90-R; Derogatis, 1975), a well-established measure of psychological distress that includes assessment of symptoms of a wide range of psychiatric disorders including depression and anxiety. Three separate models were tested—one each for levels of use of alcohol, marijuana/hashish, and cocaine, respectively. For alcohol, results supported the mediating role of psychological distress in explaining relations over time between childhood sexual and physical abuse with alcohol use. This mediating role of psychological distress was evident even after accounting for levels of alcohol use prior to the initial interview. Results were generally similar for marijuana/hashish use and cocaine use over time. Psychological distress served as a mediator of the relations between physical abuse and both marijuana/hashish and cocaine use levels during the follow up interval. These relations held across gender. Moreover, in the case of all three drugs, reciprocal relations were seen between psychological distress and drug use at the follow-up such that increased psychological distress predicted increased drug use, which in turn predicted increased distress.

These findings support the potential mediating role of psychological distress in explaining the association between childhood victimization and substance use over time. However, the nature of these relations appears to be complex. Specific relations vary somewhat across drugs and types of abuse experiences, and likely involve reciprocal causality. Unfortunately, Dembo et al. (1990) did not examine which forms of psychological distress (e.g., depression versus anxiety) proved the best mediators. Nonetheless, the findings are largely consistent with Miller and Downs' (1995) model in supporting relations between childhood exposure to violence, subsequent depression (or at least general emotional distress), and increased later drug use.

Deykin, Buka, and Zeena (1992) examined the prevalence and correlates of depression in 223 adolescents undergoing treatment for a substance use disorder. Depression diagnoses were evaluated using the DIS (Robins et al., 1981). About 24% of the sample met full criteria for major depressive disorder (n = 54)—a rate that is approximately three times that reported for nonreferred groups of a similar age. Participants with physical abuse histories were significantly more likely to be diagnosed with comorbid depression than those without (odds ratios = 5.6 for females and 1.5 for males). However, the increased odds of comorbid depression associated with sexual abuse histories were not statistically significant for either gender. The authors then examined relative order of onset of the depression versus substance use disorder in the comorbid cases. Depression was more likely to precede than follow substance abuse or dependence in females. The opposite pattern was observed among males: Depression was most likely to follow substance use disorder onset. This observed gender difference in relative order of onset of these two disorders is consistent with other epidemiological findings on the comorbidity of major depression and substance disorders (see review by Miller et al., 1997). Moreover, those comorbid patients where the depression occurred first were more likely to report a history of abuse than were those where the substance use disorder occurred first. Deykin et al.'s (1992) finding that depression tended to emerge prior to substance abuse in comorbid females is consistent with the results of a longitudinal study by Calam, Horne, Glasgow, and Cox (1998) of 144 sexually abused children and adolescents (73% female) with court- or professionally-documented abuse histories. Calam et al. (1998) found depressive symptoms (e.g., sleep disturbance, dysphoric affect) emerged prior to substance abuse symptoms over their 2-year follow-up.

Taken together, the results of these studies with adolescents and adults alike suggest that exposure to familial violence in childhood is associated not only with drinking problems and drug abuse, but also with depression. Although few of the studies reviewed above have directly examined comorbidity of depression and substance use disorders in victims of childhood domestic violence, we do know from the general epidemiological literature that mood disorders and substance use disorders are frequently co-occurring conditions (see Merikangas et al., 1998). Some tentative conclusions can be reached from the few studies that did examine inter-relations among childhood victimization, mood disorder, and substance use disorders. First, depression appears to emerge prior to substance abuse among victims (Calam et al., 1998; Deykin et al., 1992). Second, depression (or at least psychological distress) and lowered self-esteem appear to partially mediate the relation between childhood victimization and subsequent alcohol or drug use (Dembo et al., 1987, 1990). Such findings are consistent with a self-medication model, where traumatic familial victimization in childhood contributes to lowered self-esteem and increased depression, which victims attempt to cope with through alcohol or drug abuse (cf. Miller & Downs, 1995). The role of characterological self-blame (Janoff-Bulman & Thomas, 1989) in explaining comorbid depression and substance use disorders in victims of childhood familial violence is deserving of further research attention.

However, even if self-medication for low self-esteem and depression is found to apply to the initiation of substance misuse among victims of childhood familial violence, the possibility of a vicious cycle between these two forms of behavioral pathology developing over the longer-term should be considered. For example, Raimo and Schuckit (1998) have reviewed evidence that chronic alcohol abuse can cause severe depressive episodes. Thus, although substance abuse among childhood violence victims may be initiated in an attempt to cope with depression, in the longer term their substance abuse may actually worsen the depressive symptoms.

Posttraumatic Stress Disorder

Posttraumatic stress disorder is an anxiety disorder that can develop following exposure to a trauma (APA, 1994). DSM-IV PTSD symptoms include intrusions (e.g., nightmares), avoidance/numbing (e.g., avoiding trauma reminders), and arousal (e.g., increased startle). Along with depression, PTSD is one of the more common psychiatric disorder correlates of childhood sexual abuse and parent-to-child physical violence (Briere & Runtz, 1993; Kendall-Tackett et al., 1993; Malinosky-Rummell & Hansen, 1993; Polusny & Follette, 1995). For example, Boney-McCoy and Finkelhor (1995) found a significant association between the presence of childhood sexual abuse and parent-to-child physical violence with increased PTSD symptoms in both males and females. Saunders, Villeponteaux, Lipovsky, Kilpatrick, and Veronen (1992) found that 64% of sexually abused children were likely to develop PTSD during their lifetime.

In addition to depression and substance abuse, Duncan et al. (1996) assessed rates of PTSD using the National Women's Study PTSD Module (NWS-PTSD; Resnick, Kilpatrick, Dansky, Saunders, & Best, 1993). Women with severe childhood physical violence histories were five times more likely to meet criteria for lifetime PTSD, and ten times more likely to meet criteria for current PTSD at the time of the interview. Moreover, victims were more likely than nonvictims to have experienced alcohol and drug-related problems.

Studies of individuals seeking treatment for a substance use disorder consistently report not only high rates of childhood sexual and physical victimization, but high rates of comorbid PTSD as well (e.g., Brady, Killeen, Saladin, Dansky, & Becker, 1994; Dansky, Saladin, Brady, Kilpatrick, & Resnick, 1995; Fullilove et al., 1993; Kovach, 1986). According to a review by Najavits, Weiss, and Shaw (1997), women substance abusers, in particular, show high rates of comorbid PTSD and substance use disorders, most commonly deriving from a history of repetitive childhood physical or sexual violence. For example, among 55 adult female inpatients with an alcohol or drug use disorder, Brady et al. (1994) found that 40% reported histories of childhood sexual or physical abuse, with 55% meeting SCID (Spitzer et al., 1986) criteria for lifetime PTSD. Those substance abusers with comorbid PTSD were more likely to be victims of sexual and physical abuse, particularly in childhood, than women with substance use disorder only (Brady et al., 1994). Rates of childhood exposure to interpersonal violence and of PTSD diagnoses in the Brady et al. study are much elevated compared with base rates among women in the general population (Resnick et al., 1993).

Ouimette, Wolfe, and Chrestman (1996) compared three nontreatment-seeking groups of American women who had served in the Vietnam war to clarify characteristics associated with comorbid PTSD and alcohol use disorders in women. The three groups were comorbid PTSD and alcohol abuse ($n = 12$), PTSD only ($n = 13$), and controls (no PTSD, no alcohol abuse; $n = 22$). Participants completed self-report questionnaires and structured interviews including Keane, Caddell, and Taylor's (1988) self-report measure of PTSD symptoms, and the Michigan Alcoholism Screening Test (MAST; Selzer, 1971). MAST scores were significantly correlated with degree of sexual abuse in childhood, and with levels of PTSD symptoms. The comorbid group reported a greater severity of PTSD symptoms than the other two groups, more sexual abuse as children (cf., Brady et al., 1994), and more adult sexual assault. It was suggested that cumulative effects of chronic trauma exposure across the lifetime (particularly sexual victimization) may be important in accounting for comorbid PTSD and alcohol abuse in women (cf. Terr, 1991).

Epstein, Saunders, Kilpatrick, and Resnick (1998) examined the relations between childhood sexual abuse, PTSD symptoms, and alcohol problems in adult women. Participants were a random nonclinical sample of 2,994 adult women who were interviewed about childhood sexual abuse history, and lifetime PTSD and alcohol abuse symptoms. The definition of childhood sexual abuse was conservative, including only instances involving penetration that had occurred prior to 18 years of age. Sexual abuse included, but was not limited to, victimization perpetrated by family members. PTSD was assessed using the NWS-PTSD Module (Resnick et al., 1993). Alcohol abuse was assessed using seven questions pertaining to the DSM-IV (APA, 1994) criteria. A history of childhood sexual abuse was associated with a doubling of the number of alcohol abuse symptoms experienced in adulthood. Alcohol abuse was greater in sexual abuse victims who developed PTSD symptoms. Path analysis demonstrated significant pathways connecting childhood sexual abuse to PTSD symptoms and PTSD symptoms to alcohol abuse. Consistent with Stewart's (1996) PTSD self-medication model, the association between childhood sexual abuse and adult alcohol abuse was completely mediated by PTSD symptoms. The authors suggested that PTSD might be an important variable affecting alcohol abuse patterns in women who were victims of sexual abuse in childhood.

Bissonnette et al. (1997) examined the relations between childhood familial abuse, PTSD symptoms, and alcohol consumption patterns in young adults. Participants were a sample of 379 undergraduates (144 males; 235 females) who completed self-report questionnaires about childhood exposure to familial violence, current PTSD symptoms, and current alcohol use patterns (i.e., weekly consumption, drinking to cope). Childhood maltreatment was assessed using a 40-item instrument that encompassed witnessing violence between parents or step-parents, emotional or physical abuse by an adult, or sexual abuse experiences, with occurrence before 18 years of age. Current PTSD symptoms were assessed using the Trauma Symptom Checklist-40 (TSC-40; Elliott & Briere, 1992). Childhood physical or emotional abuse predicted increased PTSD symptoms among both males and females, and childhood sexual abuse contributed to increased PTSD symptoms in women only. Nonetheless, the alcohol consumption patterns of those experiencing greater (versus lesser) levels of PTSD symptoms failed to differ significantly. The findings fail to support the hypothesis from Stewart's (1996) self-medication model that PTSD symptoms should mediate the relation between childhood familial violence exposure and increased drinking in young adults.

However, consistent with the PTSD self-medication model predictions (Stewart, 1996), students in the Bissonnette et al. (1997) study who reported greater levels of PTSD symptoms did report more coping-related drinking. In fact, other research suggests that alcohol consumption motivated by desires to cope with (i.e., avoid or reduce) negative emotional states is a strong predictor of alcohol-related problems over and above consumption levels alone (Cooper, Russell, Skinner, & Windle, 1992). Consistent with a PTSD self-medication model of substance abuse in familial violence victims, several studies indicate greater self-reports of drinking or drug use to cope among childhood abuse victims relative to controls with no abuse histories (e.g., Hussey & Singer, 1993). Future studies could employ validated measures of substance use motives (e.g., Stewart, Zeitlin, & Samoluk, 1996) to address the degree to which coping-motivated drinking or drug use explains the relation between PTSD symptoms and substance use disorders among familial violence victims.

Relatively few studies have simultaneously examined childhood exposure to intrafamilial violence, PTSD, and substance use disorder rates in adolescent samples. Clark and Jacob (1992) examined comorbid psychiatric diagnoses in a clinical sample of adolescents with DSM-III-R (APA, 1987) alcohol abuse and dependence. Twenty-seven percent of the adolescents with alcoholism were diagnosed with PTSD; 88% of those with comorbid PTSD and alcoholism diagnoses reported histories of sexual or physical abuse. Moreover, in the large majority of the comorbid cases, the anxiety disorder developed prior to the alcohol use disorder, and participants perceived that the anxiety disorder was causally linked to the development of the alcohol abuse problem. Therefore, Clark and Jacob's (1992) data on chronological patterns, and on patients' perceptions of associations, are consistent with the notion that PTSD secondary to childhood violence may be causally related to alcohol abuse (cf. Stewart, 1996).

Kilpatrick et al. (2000) tested the hypothesis that exposure to interpersonal violence (i.e., sexual assault, physical assault, corporal punishment, and witnessed violence) increases risk of alcohol, marijuana, and hard drug abuse and dependence among adolescents. Their study also tested the hypothesis emerging from the PTSD self-medication model (Stewart, 1996) that PTSD would further increase risk of substance abuse or dependence. A national household probability sample of 4,023 adolescents was interviewed. The interviews focused on personal substance abuse and dependence (defined according to DSM-IV [APA, 1994] criteria for alcohol, marijuana, and other hard drugs), victimization experiences (including intimate violence exposure), familial substance use and abuse, and PTSD symptoms (assessed with the NWS-PTSD Module; Resnick et al., 1993). In multivariate analyses, exposure to interpersonal violence increased risk for substance abuse and dependence for all three types of substances, over and above demographics and family history of substance use and abuse. Partially consistent with the PTSD self-medication model, PTSD further increased risk for drug disorders in the cases of marijuana and hard drugs, but not alcohol.

Stewart, Conrod, Samoluk, Pihl, and Dongier (2000) reasoned that if alcohol use serves a negatively-reinforcing function among traumatized individuals with PTSD (Stewart, 1996), the heavy drinking behavior of those substance abusers with PTSD should be relatively situation-specific. In other words, drinking behavior should be more frequent in contexts that have been previously associated with alcohol's tension-reducing effects. To test this situational-specificity hypothesis, Stewart et al. (2000) administered a lifetime measure of trauma exposure and measures of PTSD symptom severity and situation-specific drinking to a community-recruited sample of 294 adult women substance abusers. DSM-IV (APA, 1994) PTSD symptoms were assessed with the PTSD Symptom Self-Report Scale (PSS-SR; Foa, Riggs, Dancu, & Rothbaum, 1993). Situation-specific heavy drinking in "negative," "positive," and "temptation" situations was assessed with the 42-item Inventory of Drinking Situations (IDS-42; Annis, Graham, & Davis, 1987). Self-reported rates of trauma exposure were high for several events (e.g., 42% reported histories of physical violence and 47% reported histories of sexual victimization, including many instances of familial violence), and 63% of the sample met criteria for a DSM-IV diagnosis of PTSD based on PSS-SR responses. Consistent with the situational-specificity hypothesis, PTSD symptoms were significantly positively correlated with frequency of heavy drinking in negative situations (i.e., unpleasant emotions, physical discomfort, or conflict with others), but unrelated to frequency of heavy drinking in positive and temptation situations.

An additional finding of the Stewart et al. (2000) study pertained to the role of anxiety sensitivity (fear of anxiety-related sensations; Peterson & Reiss, 1992). Anxiety sensitivity is a cognitive, individual difference variable that is elevated in PTSD (Taylor, Koch, & McNally, 1992), and is a risk factor for substance abuse (see Stewart, Samoluk, & MacDonald, 1999). In fact, anxiety sensitivity levels are higher in PTSD than in all other anxiety disorders except panic disorder (Taylor et al., 1992). It has been suggested that anxiety sensitivity may represent a premorbid vulnerability factor for the development of PTSD following exposure to a traumatic event, such as domestic violence, since people with high anxiety sensitivity should be more likely to develop conditioned fear reactions (e.g., increased startle) to trauma cues. In turn, the experience of anxiety-related PTSD symptoms may increase anxiety sensitivity levels (Taylor et al., 1992). Stewart et al. (2000) found that anxiety sensitivity mediated the observed associations between PTSD symptoms and situation-specific heavy drinking in negative contexts. In other words, female substance abusers with more frequent PTSD symptoms drink heavily in certain negative situations (e.g., contexts involving physical discomfort) at least partly because they are highly fearful of anxiety symptoms (Stewart et al., 1999). The potential mediating role of other important psychological factors, such as self-blame and guilt (Janoff-Bulman & Thomas, 1989; Wolfe et al., 1994), in contributing to comorbid PTSD and substance related disorders in victims of familial violence exposure remain to be investigated empirically.

The studies reviewed in this section suggest that both elevated rates of substance-related disorders and elevated rates of PTSD are common correlates of exposure to familial violence in childhood. Few of these studies have directly assessed the issue of comorbidity between PTSD and substance-related disorders in victims of familial violence. However, we do know from the general epidemiological literature that these two forms of behavioral pathology commonly co-occur among victims of many different types of trauma (e.g., combat, disaster, rape; see Stewart, 1996). The few studies reviewed herein that directly examined relations among exposure to familial violence in childhood, PTSD, and substance abuse and dependence suggest some tentative conclusions. First, PTSD appears to precede the development of alcohol use disorders in comorbid cases with a history of childhood intimate violence exposure (e.g., Clark & Jacob, 1992). Second, PTSD symptoms may mediate between childhood victimization exposure and substance misuse in adulthood (Epstein et al., 1998). Finally, PTSD appears to contribute to adolescent drug abuse and dependence over and above other relevant factors including childhood victimization, per se (Kilpatrick et al., 2000). These findings are all consistent with predictions of the PTSD self-medication model (e.g., Stewart, 1996). However, even if self-medication for PTSD symptoms is found to apply to the initiation of substance misuse among victims of childhood familial violence, the possibility of a vicious cycle between these two forms of behavioral pathology developing over the longer-term should be considered. For example, Stewart (1996) has reviewed evidence that chronic alcohol abuse might lead to an intensification of certain types of PTSD symptoms (e.g., heightened startle) over time. Thus, although alcohol abuse among childhood violence victims may be initiated in an attempt to cope with aversive PTSD symptoms, in the longer term their alcohol abuse may actually worsen their anxiety and arousal symptoms.

Sexual Dysfunction

Sexual dysfunction is another long-term correlate of childhood sexual abuse in adults. In particular, sexual dysfunctions involving pain and avoidance of intercourse (e.g., vaginismus) have been associated with a history of traumatic sexual experiences (Sultan & Chambless, 1988). Very few studies on the adult correlates of childhood sexual abuse have simultaneously examined both sexual dysfunctions and substance use disorders in the same study. Mullen et al. (1994) examined women's sexual problems as a function of childhood abuse histories. In addition to demonstrating an association between childhood sexual abuse and excessive drinking (cf. Mullen et al., 1996), Mullen et al. (1994) showed relations between sexual abuse in childhood and adult sexual problems on the PSE (Wing et al., 1977). These relations persisted after controlling for general family dysfunction. Similarly, Wilsnack et al. (1997) found that childhood sexual abuse was not only significantly associated with increased alcohol and drug use and misuse among adult women, but also with greater rates of sexual pain disorder assessed using Kaplan's (1974) criteria. Wilsnack et al. (1997) suggested that increased substance abuse in the women with sexual abuse histories might represent an attempt to cope with sexual distress (cf. Briere & Runtz, 1993) secondary to the childhood sexual abuse.

A study by Covington and Kohen (1984) examined rates of sexual and physical abuse and sexual dysfunction in 35 alcoholic women as compared to a matched sample of 35 nonalcoholic female controls. With respect to the assessment of sexual dysfunction, women were first asked if they had experienced any of a set of six sexual difficulties (e.g., lack of sexual arousal/pleasure, painful intercourse, vaginismus). The alcoholic women reported significantly more of these sexual dysfunctions than the nonalcoholic women. Three of these items were then combined to assess general sexual dysfunction as it has usually been defined clinically (i.e., lack of sexual interest, lack of sexual arousal/pleasure, or lack of lubrication). The alcoholic women reported significantly more general sexual dysfunction on this latter measure (i.e., 85% of the alcoholic women versus 59% of the controls). Sexual dysfunction among the alcoholic women could not be attributed to their problem drinking alone, since 79% reported having developed sexual dysfunction prior to the onset of their alcoholism (cf. Skorina & Kovach, 1986).

Women in the Covington and Kohen (1984) study also reported on their lifetime histories of physical and sexual abuse. More of the alcoholic women reported histories of abuse than controls. The group difference was statistically significant in the case of sexual abuse (74% versus 50% of the alcoholic women versus nonalcoholic controls, respectively), but not in the case of physical abuse (52% versus 34%, respectively). The forms of sexual abuse experienced by the alcoholic women were more severe in nature (e.g., higher rates of childhood incest), occurred over a longer period of time, and began at an earlier age, relative to the sexual abuse experiences of those women in the nonalcoholic control group. In addition, the alcoholic women were significantly more likely to experience chronic physical abuse (i.e., abuse at least once a month for a year or more from the same perpetrator). Although data were not obtained on the age at which alcohol abuse began relative to the age at which abuse experiences occurred, the early ages reported by alcoholic women for their abuse experiences are highly suggestive that sexual and physical abuse preceded the development of alcohol problems in most cases. Unfortunately, Covington and Kohen (1984) failed to examine relations between sexual or physical abuse and the development of sexual dysfunction in alcoholic women compared to controls to test the hypothesis of self-medication for sexual dysfunction secondary to sexual or physical abuse in alcoholic women. Consistent with the self-medication notion, alcoholic women reported using alcohol more often with sexual activity than did controls.

Few studies have addressed the degree to which decreased self-esteem (cf. Miller & Downs, 1995) may be applicable to understanding the elevated rates of both sexual dysfunction and substance use disorders in women victimized as children. One study by Finkelhor (1984) is relevant to this issue. He showed that 121 young adult women with sexual abuse histories scored significantly lower than 685 nonvictim controls on a measure of sexual self-esteem. Further research is needed to clarify the role of low sexual self-esteem in the development of comorbid sexual dysfunction and substance use disorders in childhood sexual abuse victims.

Even if alcohol is misused among women with familial violence histories to acutely self-medicate for sexual dysfunction, the longer-term effects of chronic alcohol abuse on women's sexual functioning also must be considered. Much research indicates serious sexual dysfunction among women alcoholics (see Covington & Kohen, 1984). There are a variety of physiological mechanisms by which chronic heavy drinking could produce impaired sexual functioning in women (see Covington & Kohen). Although studies by Covington and Kohen and Skorina and Kovach (1986) suggest that sexual dysfunction precedes alcohol abuse in the majority of cases of alcoholic women with familial violence histories, the possibility of a vicious cycle exists. Chronic heavy drinking to self-medicate for sexual dysfunction secondary to childhood abuse could lead to a worsening of sexual dysfunction over time, thereby contributing to further attempts at self-medication through escalated drinking.

☐ Substance Abuse and Psychiatric Disorders in Victims of Partner-to-Partner Violence

Like forms of familial violence directed toward children, there appear to be relations between exposure to spousal violence (i.e., partner-to-partner violence) and both psychiatric and substance-related disorders in victims. Although research examining the relationship among spousal violence exposure and psychiatric disorder and substance use disorder comorbidity is in its infancy, we review the existing literature with the aim of delineating possible mechanisms by which these phenomena are interrelated. The studies reviewed in this section focus on adult women who are currently in violent relationships, or who have previously experienced domestic violence. We also consider research that has included women who have been dually victimized by spouses or partners and in the family of origin (i.e., childhood sexual or physical abuse) to examine possible cumulative effects of chronic exposure to violence across the lifetime.

Depression

Studies that have examined women exposed to spousal violence demonstrate not only high rates of substance abuse among victims, but also high rates of depression, suicidality, and low self-esteem (e.g., Campbell, Poland, Waller, & Ager, 1992; McCauley, Kern, Kolodner, Derogatis, & Bass, 1998). For example, a community-based survey of 1,952 female patients from the offices of general practitioners revealed that 5% reported experiencing spousal battery in the previous year (McCauley et al., 1995). Women completed measures of psychological distress (i.e., the SCL-22; Derogatis, 1975) and of substance abuse. The victims of recent spousal violence had higher levels of self-reported depression and suicidality on the SCL-22, and were more likely to be abusing drugs or alcohol, compared to women who had not recently experienced domestic violence. Later, McCauley et al. (1998) categorized women by the severity of recent physical violence exposure (i.e., high severity, low severity, or no violence exposure). Low severity violence cases were women who had been pushed or grabbed or had someone threaten to hurt them or someone they loved in the year prior to the survey. High severity violence cases had been hit, slapped, kicked, burned, choked, or threatened or hurt with a weapon. Women who had been exposed to violence as children were excluded. Self-reported depression on the SCL-22 (Derogatis, 1975) increased with increasing severity of violence exposure, providing evidence for a dose-response relation between the severity of recent violence exposure and the degree of depressive symptoms. Moreover, women with any current violence exposure were more likely to report alcohol or drug abuse problems.

Campbell et al. (1992) interviewed 488 postpartum women to retrospectively examine correlates of spousal battering during pregnancy. Questions included alcohol and drug use, violence experiences, and symptoms of depression. Seven percent of the women reported having been assaulted by partners during pregnancy. Battered women reported increases in both depression and use of alcohol and drugs. The experience of being battered by a partner during pregnancy was associated with a greater severity of this constellation of emotional and substance use symptoms compared to the experience of spousal battery prior to pregnancy only, or the experience of being physically assaulted by someone other than a partner.

These findings of increased depression and substance abuse in victims of partner-to-partner violence are consistent with predictions deriving from social rank theory (e.g., Gilbert, 1992; Santor, Pringle, & Israeli, 2000). Moreover, other studies similarly indicate that battered women present with symptoms of dysphoric affect, hopelessness, passivity, pessimism about the future, and self-criticism (Walker, 1977) which may reflect depressive symptoms relating to prolonged submission within an abusive relationship. However, studies have yet to directly test predictions derived from social rank theory regarding relations between spousal violence exposure and mood and substance use disorders in victims. Social rank theory would predict that only submissive responses to spousal violence should be related to increases in depressive symptoms over time, among victims. If substance abuse is indeed a form of self-medication for depression secondary to spousal violence, then substance-related disorders should be seen most often in women demonstrating submissive responses to partner violence—specifically those experiencing high levels of depressive symptoms.

Posttraumatic Stress Disorder

In addition to substance abuse and depression, PTSD is another psychiatric disorder that may commonly present in women exposed to partner-to-partner physical violence. Astin, Ogland-Hand, Coleman, and Foy (1995) compared PTSD prevalence rates in 50 battered women to 37 maritally distressed women who had not experienced spousal violence. Exposure to spousal battery was assessed using the Conflict Tactics Scale (CTS; Straus, 1979), and PTSD rates with the SCID (Spitzer et al., 1986). Battered women displayed significantly higher rates of PTSD than controls (i.e., 58% versus 19%). However, women with PTSD in the Astin et al. (1995) study were also more likely to have a history of childhood sexual abuse victimization, and a greater frequency of lifetime trauma exposure. These results suggest that the frequency of previous violent victimization is associated with the development of PTSD symptoms, beyond that which might be accounted for by current victimization experiences alone. Astin et al. suggested that cumulative violence exposure might be more likely to precipitate severe psychiatric symptoms, such as PTSD symptoms, in victims. It could be speculated that cumulative violence exposure across the life span (childhood abuse to spousal battery in adulthood) might also be related to an increased probability of drinking or drug use to cope with PTSD symptoms (cf. Ouimette et al., 1996). Unfortunately, Astin et al. did not assess substance use or abuse among battered women versus controls.

A recent study by Dansky, Byrne, and Brady (1999) simultaneously assessed exposure to intimate violence and rates of PTSD in a mixed gender sample of 91 patients seeking treatment for cocaine dependence. Assessment of physical assault included patient self-reports of exposure to aggravated assault with a weapon, aggravated assault without a weapon, and simple assault. Relationship of the perpetrator to the victim was also assessed to allow separation of intimate violence exposure from other forms of physical assault. PTSD was assessed using the NWS-PTSD Module (Resnick et al., 1993). Overall, about 86% of the cocaine dependent patients reported lifetime histories of at least one prior physical assault. About 46% of these individuals reported physical assault by an intimate partner, and half of the assault victims also met lifetime criteria for PTSD on structured interview. Victims assaulted by an intimate partner were more likely to meet criteria for comorbid PTSD than were victims assaulted by a nonintimate partner. This perpetrator effect was observed across genders. However, women were more likely than men to report having been physically assaulted by an intimate partner, and also were more likely to meet criteria for PTSD. The authors suggested that careful assessment of intimate violence exposure is essential among substance abusers given its high prevalence, and its strong association with comorbid PTSD.

One limitation of these studies on the psychiatric and substance disorder correlates of spousal violence is that the temporal order between violence exposure and substance abuse has not been directly examined. As a result, it is unclear whether substance abuse was a precipitant or a consequence of victimization. Although it has been suggested that substance abuse by women may provoke beatings by a partner, much research demonstrates that postviolence drinking is more common than drinking prior to or during an assault (see Kaufman Kantor & Asdigian, 1997). For example, in a 2-year longitudinal study of relations between violent assault and substance use or abuse in women, Kilpatrick et al. (1997) showed that after a new violent assault, the odds of both alcohol abuse and drug use were significantly increased. These increased odds were observed even among women with no previous substance abuse or assault history. Thus, it is plausible that victims of spousal battery may use alcohol and other drugs as a means of coping with the psychological impact of victimization by a partner. This self-medication may represent an attempt to cope with posttraumatic depression (Campbell et al., 1992; McCauley et al., 1995, 1998) or PTSD (Astin et al., 1995; Dansky et al., 1999) secondary to the spousal violence exposure.

It also is plausible that substance abuse among victims of spousal violence is related to either the experiencing of childhood violence victimization or the cumulative effects of both childhood and spousal violence victimization (Astin et al., 1995). Indeed, surveys indicate that victims of spousal violence are more likely than controls to have suffered abuse in childhood (see Kaufman Kantor & Asdigian, 1997). Childhood victimization may set the stage for the development of low self-esteem and psychological distress (e.g., depression or PTSD) which, in turn, may lead to the development of a substance use disorder (cf. Miller & Downs, 1995). Thus, self-medication models of substance abuse in spousal battery victims must consider the possible cumulative effects of a lifetime history of familial violence (childhood maltreatment to spousal battery) in which these women's negative self-perceptions and characterological self-blame attributions (Janoff-Bulman & Thomas, 1989) are reinforced over the life span.

☐ Conceptual and Methodological Issues

The body of research, to date, demonstrates that there are links between familial violence victimization and both the development of psychiatric disorders (depression, PTSD, and sexual dysfunction) and the development of substance use disorders. The pathways between these phenomena are undoubtedly complex and as a result, for the large part, have not been adequately tested. To date, what is known about the relationship between familial violence victimization and comorbid psychiatric and substance use disorders is largely based on the long-term retrospective reports of adults obtained in cross-sectional, correlational designs. Therefore, the accurate determination of relative order of onset and causality may be compromised. Prospective, longitudinal studies of abuse victims as compared to matched controls, are the theoretically most preferable methodology for examining causality with respect to childhood exposure to domestic violence and subsequent psychiatric and substance use disorder consequences. Further, the reliance on clinical samples raises the issue of Berkson's Bias (i.e., individuals with more than one mental health problem may be more likely to seek treatment) (Stewart, 1996) which can yield overestimates of rates of comorbid psychiatric and substance use disorders in familial violence victims (see Stewart, 1996). Difficulties in disentangling these intricate relationships are due to several additional conceptual and methodological issues that need to be addressed to improve upon existing research.

Assessment of Comorbidity and Functional Relations

Although most of the studies reviewed herein demonstrate that both certain psychiatric disorders and substance-related disorders are extremely common among victims of many different forms of familial violence exposure, few have examined psychiatric disorder and substance use disorder comorbidity per se. Thus, further research is required on the issue of whether various psychiatric disorders and substance use disorders are co-occurring correlates of domestic violence exposure among victims.

Even among studies that have directly examined the issue of comorbidity of psychiatric disorders and substance use disorders among victims of domestic violence, few have examined potential functional relations between these forms of behavioral pathology in victims. For example, few studies have examined whether psychiatric sequelae of familial violence might mediate the domestic violence–substance abuse relationship in victims, as is predicted in self-medication models (e.g., Miller & Downs, 1995; Stewart, 1996). Even fewer studies have examined whether substance abuse in victims of domestic violence might intensify or worsen symptoms of a co-occurring psychiatric disorder in the longer-term. To examine functional relations, Stewart (1996) proposes establishing relative order of onset and gradient of effect (i.e., as levels of symptoms of one disorder increase, so should levels of symptoms of the other disorder), and examining patients' perceptions of functional associations between symptoms of their two disorders. Lab-based experimental methods also can be employed to test predictions of the self-medication and alcohol or drug-induced psychiatric disorder symptom enhancement explanations of the comorbidity of psychiatric disorder and substance use disorders in victims. If victims of intimate violence with comorbid PTSD and substance abuse are indeed attempting to self-medicate their PTSD symptoms through substance use (cf. Stewart, 1996), exposure to reminders of their violent victimization should lead to increased self-reported drug cravings or increased substance intake in the lab (see Stewart et al., 1998).

Assessment Issues

Our current knowledge regarding the relations between familial violence exposure and comorbid psychiatric and substance use disorders in victims is limited by a lack of attention to distinctions between general psychological distress, specific symptoms of psychiatric disorders, and rates of psychiatric disorders, per se. Indeed, validated structured interviews that cover the spectrum of relevant DSM-IV (APA, 1994) disorders have only been employed occasionally, compromising our ability to make conclusions about comorbidity between disorders (i.e., syndromes involving specific sets of psychological symptoms). For example, many studies have measured symptoms of depression (e.g., low self-esteem, suicidal ideation, dysphoric mood, sleep difficulties) but have neglected to assess rates of major depressive disorder among victims of domestic violence. In an interview, researchers can gather details that might otherwise be missed in a self-report questionnaire, and can establish DSM-IV (APA, 1994) diagnoses. In fact, the use of symptom questionnaires without corroborating structured clinical interviews may lead to a high false positive rate of psychiatric diagnosis (e.g., Coyne, 1994). In comparison to structured interviews where the purpose is in establishing the presence or absence of a disorder, validated questionnaires can be useful in quantifying levels of psychiatric and substance disorder symptoms.

Thus, researchers investigating relations between psychiatric and substance use disorders in familial violence victims should incorporate both validated structured interviews and self-report questionnaires in their research protocols.

Third Variable Issues

Studies have often failed to consider possible third variable explanations for the relations between domestic violence exposure and psychiatric disorders and substance use disorders in victims. A tendency to confound general family environment problems with familial violence exposure exists in this research area (see Rind, Tromovitch, & Bauserman, 1998). In fact, domestic violence quite reliably occurs within the context of general family dysfunction and socioeconomic disadvantage. Moreover, family background characteristics (e.g., socioeconomic status of family of origin, general family dysfunction, family history of mental illness and substance abuse) themselves may contribute to the development of psychiatric symptoms and substance use disorders (see Miller & Downs, 1995). For example, several researchers note the importance of controlling for family history of substance abuse. Parental substance abuse is associated with increased rates of abuse of children (Hernandez, 1992) and of partner-to-partner violence (Kaufman Kantor & Asdigian, 1997), and with the development of substance abuse and other mental health disorders in the offspring (e.g., Sher, Walitzer, Wood, & Brent, 1991). These important third variable risk factors must be accounted for when examining whether domestic violence is causally related to comorbid psychiatric disorder and substance use disorders in victims.

Specificity of Overlap of Substance Use Disorders with Particular Psychiatric Disorders

In this chapter, we have reviewed evidence that certain psychiatric disorders may frequently co-occur with substance use disorders among victims of intimate violence (i.e., depression, PTSD, and sexual dysfunctions). We have treated these three sets of psychiatric disorders as if they represent distinct mental health correlates of domestic violence victimization. However, these disorders share certain overlapping features. For example, in terms of sexual dysfunction, lack of sexual interest is a symptom of major depression, and sexual avoidance can be a symptom of PTSD in individuals with a sexual trauma history (APA, 1994). Depression and PTSD also share some overlapping symptoms (e.g., loss of interest in activities, sleep disturbance, concentration impairment; APA, 1994). Based on the available evidence, it is difficult to ascertain whether these forms of psychiatric disorder represent distinct or shared correlates of intimate violence exposure. However, recent research by Conrod, Pihl, Stewart, and Dongier (2000) suggests that depression and PTSD may indeed represent distinct subtypes of comorbidity among substance abusing women with high rates of familial violence exposure. Specifically, distinct subtypes of substance abusing women were identified including an anxiety sensitive subtype and a hopeless subtype. The anxiety sensitive subtype was characterized by high scores on a measure of anxiety sensitivity and on a self-report measure of PTSD symptoms. The hopeless subtype evidenced low self-esteem, and high levels of depressive cognitions. The validity of these two subtypes was indicated by differing patterns of psychiatric comorbidity and drug dependence diagnoses. The anxiety sensitive subtype evidenced elevated rates of anxiety disorders and anxiolytic drug dependence whereas the hopeless subtype evidence elevated rates of depressive disorders and opioid analgesic drug dependence. Future research should include simultaneous assessment of a variety of psychiatric disorders in substance abusers to further investigate whether the various psychiatric disorders discussed herein represent distinct or shared correlates of victimization in substance abusers.

Nature of the Violence Exposure

Many studies fail to report on the relation of the perpetrator to the victim, obscuring relations potentially unique to exposure to familial versus extrafamilial violence. However, most of the victimization of children occurs at the hands of relatives (Finkelhor & Dziuba-Leatherman, 1994), making studies of childhood sexual abuse or physical abuse in general, highly relevant to the understanding of the effects of exposure to familial victimization experiences in particular. Nonetheless, familial forms of victimization may have particularly severe adverse effects because of the dependency status of the victim to the perpetrator (Finkelhor & Dziuba-Leatherman, 1994) and because the victimization occurs within the context of a relationship that should be nurturing rather than exploitive (Briere & Runtz, 1993). Moreover, familial violence is more likely to involve multiple victimization episodes, relative to extrafamilial violence experiences (see Briere & Runtz, 1993). These characteristics suggest that familial violence exposure might be expected to contribute to greater severity of psychiatric or substance abuse outcomes (cf. Janoff-Bulman & Thomas, 1989; Terr, 1991). Recent evidence does support this contention as it pertains to history of physical assault by intimate versus nonintimate perpetrators (Dansky et al., 1999).

Individual Differences

Many existing studies have failed to consider potentially important individual difference factors (e.g., age of the victim at time of violence exposure, victim gender). Researchers now believe that there are developmental aspects of risk pertaining to the victim's age and level of development when the abuse experiences occurred. The development of an addiction or a mental health problem following familial violence exposure may depend to some degree on the victim's physical, cognitive, and emotional development at the time of the abuse (Miller et al., 1997). Therefore, researchers need to document the age and developmental stage of research participants at the time(s) of victimization. Moreover, there may be gender differences in mental health responses to familial victimization experiences. For example, Miller et al. (1997) have suggested that posttraumatic depression may be a mediating factor in the development of substance abuse more often in female than in male victims of familial violence. Similarly, Najavits et al. (1997) have argued that PTSD may mediate the development of comorbid substance use disorders more often in female victims of childhood abuse.

☐ Conclusions and Clinical Implications

The research reviewed in this chapter suggests that victims of many different forms of familial violence present with elevated levels of not only substance use disorders, but also certain psychiatric disorders including depression, PTSD, and sexual dysfunction. Although little research has focused on the comorbidity of substance use disorders and these psychiatric disorders among victims of familial violence, we do know from the general epidemiological literature that addictive disorders co-occur with depression, PTSD, and sexual dysfunction at rates that far exceed chance levels. Future research should focus on clarifying the possible functional relations between familial violence exposure, substance use disorders, and these co-occurring psychiatric disorders by assessing relative order of onset, gradient of effect, and patient perceptions of associations, as well as through the use of experimental, lab-based methodologies. Such research would help clarify whether substance use represents an attempt at self-medication for psychiatric disorder symptoms and whether substance abuse intensifies symptoms of these psychiatric disorders in the longer term among familial violence victims.

These findings have several implications for clinical practice. We first review the implications for clinical assessment and then the treatment implications. The established relations between familial violence exposure, substance use disorders, and psychiatric disorders imply that clinicians working with addicted clients should be careful to assess not only for a history of intimate violence exposure, but also for the presence of depression, PTSD, and sexual dysfunction. Similarly, clinicians should be careful to assess not only for a history of familial violence exposure, but also for the presence of substance use disorders among patients presenting with depression, PTSD, or sexual dysfunction. Moreover, given the demonstrated mediating roles of self-derogation, low self-esteem, and high anxiety sensitivity (e.g., Dembo et al., 1987; Stewart et al., 2000) in explaining relations between domestic violence exposure and psychiatric and substance disorder comorbidity, we suggest that assessment include measurement of these constructs in victims. In terms of treating victims of familial violence who present with comorbid substance use disorders and psychiatric disorders, it remains unclear which disorder to tackle first, or whether a combined, simultaneous treatment approach is preferable. However, given evidence of possible reciprocal relations between these two forms of behavioral pathology, where one disorder serves to maintain the other, most agree that a simultaneous treatment approach is preferable (see Stewart, 1996). Integrated treatment packages that simultaneously address the violence history, the psychiatric disorder, and the addictive disorder are beginning to emerge (see Dansky et al., 1995; Najavits, Weiss, & Liese, 1996). Comparative outcome studies are required to determine which techniques, applied at which stage in therapy, are most effective in treating familial violence victims with comorbid psychiatric disorders and substance use disorders. Additional research is necessary to evaluate suggestions that mediating variables such as self-blame and guilt, low self-esteem, and increased anxiety sensitivity be included in the foci of these integrated treatment packages (cf. Stewart et al., 2000). For example, to the degree that characterological self-blame and guilt (Janoff-Bulman & Thomas, 1989) for abuse experiences is a potential mediator of comorbid substance use disorders with depression and PTSD, integrated treatments may wish to target such maladaptive self-concepts. Finally, if exposure to familial violence is causally related to the development of comorbid psychiatric and substance use disorders, preventative interventions that effectively reduce the incidence of familial violence also should have an impact in reducing rates of these costly and serious forms of co-occurring behavioral pathology.

☐ References

American Psychiatric Association. (1987). *Diagnostic and statistical manual of mental disorders* (3rd ed. Rev.). Washington, DC: Author.

American Psychiatric Association. (1994). *Diagnostic and statistical manual of mental disorders* (4th ed.). Washington, DC: Author.

Annis, H. M., Graham, J. M., & Davis, C. S. (1987). *Inventory of drinking situations (IDS) user's guide.* Toronto, Canada: Addiction Research Foundation.

Astin, M. C., Ogland-Hand, S. M., Coleman, E. M., & Foy, D. W. (1995). Posttraumatic stress disorder and childhood abuse in battered women: Comparisons with maritally distressed women. *Journal of Consulting and Clinical Psychology, 63,* 308–312.

Beck, A. T., & Steer, R. A. (1987). *The Beck Depression Inventory manual.* Toronto, Canada: The Psychological Corporation.

Bissonnette, M., Wall, A-M., Wekerle, C., McKee, S. A., Hinson, R. E., & Tsianos, D. (1997). Is a posttraumatic stress disorder (PTSD) mediational model a valid framework for understanding undergraduate drinking behavior? [Summary]. *Alcoholism: Clinical and Experimental Research, 21,* 54A.

Boney-McCoy, S., & Finkelhor, D. (1995). Psychosocial sequelae of violent victimization in a national youth sample. *Journal of Consulting and Clinical Psychology, 63,* 726–736.

Brady, K. T., Killeen, T., Saladin, M., Dansky, B. S., & Becker, S. (1994). Comorbid substance abuse and PTSD: Characteristics of women in treatment. *The American Journal on Addictions, 3,* 160–164.

Briere, J., & Runtz, M. (1993). Childhood sexual abuse: Long-term sequelae and implications for psychological assessment. *Journal of Interpersonal Violence, 8,* 312–333.

Calam, R., Horne, L., Glasgow, D., & Cox, A. (1998). Psychological disturbance and child sexual abuse: A follow-up study. *Child Abuse and Neglect, 22,* 901–913.

Campbell, J. C., Poland, M. L., Waller, J. B., & Ager, J. (1992). Correlates of battering during pregnancy. *Research in Nursing and Health, 15,* 219–226.

Cavaiola, A. A., & Schiff, M. (1989). Self-esteem in abused chemically dependent adolescents. *Child Abuse and Neglect, 13,* 327–334.

Clark, D. B., & Jacob, R. G. (1992). Anxiety disorders in 30 adolescents with alcohol abuse and dependence [Summary]. *Alcoholism: Clinical and Experimental Research, 16,* 371.

Conrod, P. J., Pihl, R. O., Stewart, S. H., & Dongier, M. (2000). Validation of a system of classifying female substance abusers on the basis of personality and motivational risk factors for substance abuse. *Psychology of Addictive Behaviors, 14,* 243–256.

Cooper, M. L., Russell, M., Skinner, J. B., & Windle, M. (1992). Development and validation of a three-dimensional measure of drinking motives. *Psychological Assessment, 4,* 123–132.

Covington, S. S., & Kohen, J. (1984). Women, alcohol, and sexuality. *Advances in Alcohol and Substance Abuse, 4,* 41–56.

Coyne, J. C. (1994). Self-reported distress: Analog or ersatz depression? *Psychological Bulletin, 116,* 29–45.

Dansky, B. S., Byrne, C. A., & Brady, K. T. (1999). Intimate violence and post-traumatic stress disorder among individuals with cocaine dependence. *American Journal of Drug and Alcohol Abuse, 25,* 257–268.

Dansky, B. S., Saladin, M. E., Brady, K. T., Kilpatrick, D. G., & Resnick, H. S. (1995). Prevalence of victimization and posttraumatic stress disorder among women with substance use disorders: Comparison of telephone and in-person assessment samples. *The International Journal of the Addictions, 30,* 1079–1099.

Dembo, R., Dertke, M., la Voie, L., Borders, S., Washburn, M., & Schmeidler, J. (1987). Physical abuse, sexual victimization and illict drug use: A structural analysis among high-risk adolescents. *Journal of Adolescence, 10,* 13–34.

Dembo, R., Williams, L., la Voie, L., Schmeidler, J., Kern, J., Getreu, A., Berry, E., Genung, L., & Wish, E. D. (1990). A longitudinal study of the relationships among alcohol use, marijuana/hashish use, cocaine use, and emotional/psychological functioning problems in a cohort of high-risk youths. *The International Journal of the Addictions, 25,* 1341–1382.

Derogatis, L. R. (1975). *SCL-90-R: Administration, scoring and procedures manual—II for the revised version and other instruments of the psychopathology rating scale series.* Towson, MD: Clinical Psychometric Research.

Deykin, E. Y., Buka, S. L., & Zeena, T. H. (1992). Depressive illness among chemically dependent adolescents. *American Journal of Psychiatry, 149,* 1341–1347.

Duncan, R. D., Saunders, B. E., Kilpatrick, D. G., Hanson, R. F., & Resnick, H. S. (1996). Childhood physical assault as a risk factor for PTSD, depression, and substance abuse: Findings from a national survey. *American Journal of Orthopsychiatry, 66,* 437–448.

Edwall, G. E., & Hoffmann, N. G. (1988). Correlates of incest reported by adolescent girls in treatment for substance abuse. In Walker, L. E. A. (Ed.), *Handbook on sexual abuse of children: Assessment and treatment issues* (pp. 94–106). New York: Springer.

Elliott, D. M., & Briere, J. (1992). Sexual abuse trauma among professional women: Validating the Trauma Symptom Checklist-40 (TSC-40). *Child Abuse and Neglect, 16,* 391–398.

Epstein, J. N., Saunders, B. E., Kilpatrick, D. G., & Resnick, H. S. (1998). PTSD as a mediator between childhood rape and alcohol use in adult women. *Child Abuse and Neglect, 22,* 223–234.

Finkelhor, D. (1984). *Child sexual abuse: Theory and research.* New York: Free Press.

Finkelhor, D., & Dziuba-Leatherman, J. (1994). Victimization of children. *American Psychologist, 49,* 173–183.

First, M. B., Spitzer, R. L., Gibbon, M., & Williams, J. B. W. (1995). *Structured clinical interview for DSM-IV.* New York: Biometrics Research Department, New York Sate Psychiatric Institute.

Foa, E. B., Riggs, D. S., Dancu, C. B., & Rothbaum, B. O. (1993). Reliability and validity of a brief instrument for assessing posttraumatic stress disorder. *Journal of Traumatic Stress, 6,* 459–473.

Fullilove, M. R., Fullilove, R. E., III, Smith, M., Winkler, K., Michael, C., Panzer, P. G., & Wallace, R. (1993). Violence, trauma, and posttraumatic stress disorder among women drug users. *Journal of Traumatic Stress, 6,* 533-543.

Gilbert, P. (1992). *Depression: The evolution of powerlessness.* New York: Guilford.

Hernandez, J. T. (1992). Substance abuse among sexually abused adolescents and their families. *Journal of Adolescent Health, 13,* 658–662.

Hussey, D. L., & Singer, M. (1993). Psychological distress, problem behaviors, and family functioning of sexually abused adolescent inpatients. *Journal of the American Academy of Child and Adolescent Psychiatry, 32,* 954–961.

Janoff-Bulman, R., & Thomas, C. E. (1989). Toward an understanding of self-defeating responses following victimization. In R. C. Curtis (Ed.), *Self-defeating behaviors: Experimental research, clinical impressions, and practical implications* (pp. 215–234). New York: Plenum.

Kaplan, H. S. (1974). *The new sex therapy: Active treatment of sexual dysfunctions.* New York: Brunner-Mazel.

Kaplan, S. J., Pelcovitz, D., Salzinger, S., Weiner, M., Mandel, F. S., Lesser, M. L., & Labruna, V. E. (1998). Adolescent physical abuse: Risk for adolescent psychiatric disorders. *American Journal of Psychiatry, 155,* 954–959.

Kaufman Kantor, G., & Asdigian, N. (1997). When women are under the influence: Does drinking or drug use by women provoke beatings by men? In M. Galanter (Ed.), *Recent developments in alcoholism, Vol. 13: Alcoholism and violence* (pp. 315–336). New York: Plenum.

Keane, T. M., Caddell, J. M., & Taylor, K. L. (1988). Mississippi Scale for Combat-Related PTSD: Three studies in reliability and validity. *Journal of Consulting and Clinical Psychology, 56,* 85–90.

Kendall-Tackett, K. A., Meyer Williams, L., & Finkelhor, D. (1993). Impact of sexual abuse on children: A review and synthesis of recent empirical studies. *Psychological Bulletin, 113,* 164–180.

Kilpatrick, D. G., Acierno, R. E., Resnick, H. S., Saunders, B. E., & Best, C. L. (1997). A 2-year longitudinal analysis of the relationships between violent assault and substance use in women. *Journal of Consulting and Clinical Psychology, 65,* 834–847.

Kilpatrick, D. G., Acierno, R. E., Saunders, B. E., Resnick, H. S., Best, C. L., & Schnurr, P. P. (2000). Risk factors for adolescent substance abuse and dependence: Data from a national sample. *Journal of Consulting and Clinical Psychology, 60,* 19–30.

Kovach, J. A. (1986). Incest as a treatment issue for alcoholic women. *Alcoholism Treatment Quarterly, 3,* 1–15.

Malinosky-Rummell, R., & Hansen, D. J. (1993). Long-term consequences of childhood physical abuse. *Psychological Bulletin, 114,* 68–79.

March, J. S. (1993). What constitutes a stressor?: The "Criterion A" issue. In J. R. T. Davidson & E. B. Foa (Eds.), *Posttraumatic stress disorder: DSM-IV and beyond* (pp. 37–54). Washington, DC: American Psychiatric Press.

McCauley, J., Kern, D. E., Kolodner, K., Derogatis, L. R., & Bass, E. B. (1998). Relation of low severity violence to women's health. *Journal of General Internal Medicine, 13,* 687–691.

McCauley, J., Kern, D. E., Kolodner, K., Dill, L., Schroeder, A. F., DeChant, H. K., Ryden, J., Bass, E.

B., & Derogatis, L. R. (1995). The "battering syndrome": Prevalence and clinical characteristics of domestic violence in primary care internal medicine practices. *Annals of Internal Medicine, 123,* 737–746.

McCauley, J., Kern, D. E., Kolodner, K., Dill, L., Schroeder, A. F., DeChant, H. K., Ryden, J., Derogatis, L. R., & Bass, E. B. (1997). Clinical characteristics of women with a history of childhood abuse: Unhealed wounds. *Journal of the American Medical Association, 277,* 1362–1368.

Meiselman, K. C. (1978). *Incest: A psychological study of causes and effects with treatment recommendations.* San Francisco, CA: Jossey-Bass.

Merikangas, K. R., Mehta, R. L., Molnar, B. E., Walters, E. E., Swendsen, J. D., Aguilar-Gaziola, S., Bijl, R., Borges, G., Caraveo-Anduaga, J. J., Dewit, D. J., Kolody, B., Vega, W. A., Wittchen, H.-U., & Kessler, R. C. (1998). Comorbidity of substance use disorders with mood and anxiety disorders: Results of the international consortium in psychiatric epidemiology. *Addictive Behaviors, 23,* 893–907.

Miller, B. A., & Downs, W. R. (1995). Violent victimization among women with alcohol problems. In M. Galanter (Ed.), *Recent developments in alcoholism, Vol. 12: Women and alcoholism* (pp. 81–101). New York: Plenum.

Miller, B. A., Maguin, E., & Downs, W. R. (1997). Alcohol, drugs, and violence in children's lives. In M. Galanter (Ed.), *Recent Developments in Alcoholism, Vol. 13: Alcoholism and Violence* (pp. 357–385). New York: Plenum.

Morrow, K. B. (1991). Attributions of female adolescent incest victims regarding their molestation. *Child Abuse and Neglect, 15,* 477–483.

Mullen, P. E., Martin, J. L., Anderson, J. C., Romans, S. E., & Herbison, G. P. (1994). The effect of child sexual abuse on social, interpersonal and sexual function in adult life. *British Journal of Psychiatry, 165,* 35–47.

Mullen, P. E., Martin, J. L., Anderson, J. C., Romans, S. E., & Herbison, G. P. (1996). The long-term impact of the physical, emotional, and sexual abuse of children: A community study. *Child Abuse and Neglect, 20,* 7–21.

Najavits, L. M., Weiss, R. D., & Liese, B. S. (1996). Group cognitive-behavioral therapy for women with PTSD and substance use disorder. *Journal of Substance Abuse Treatment, 13,* 13–22.

Najavits, L. M., Weiss, R. D., & Shaw, S. R. (1997). The link between substance abuse and posttraumatic stress disorder in women: A research review. *The American Journal on Addictions, 6,* 273–283.

Orvaschel, H., Puig-Antich, J., Chambers, W., Tabrizi, M. A., & Johnson, R. (1982). Retrospective assessment of prepubertal major depression with the Kiddie-SADS-E. *Journal of the American Academy of Child and Adolescent Psychiatry, 21,* 392–397.

Ouimette, P. C., Wolfe, J., & Chrestman, K. R. (1996). Characteristics of posttraumatic stress disorder—alcohol abuse comorbidity in women. *Journal of Substance Abuse, 8,* 335–346.

Peterson, R. A., & Reiss, S. (1992). *Anxiety Sensitivity Index Manual* (2nd ed.). Worthington, OH: International Diagnostic Systems.

Polusny, M. A., & Follette, V. M. (1995). Long-term correlates of child sexual abuse: Theory and review of the empirical literature. *Applied and Preventive Psychology, 4,* 143–166.

Radloff, L. (1977). The CES-D Scale: A self-report depression scale for research in the general population. *Applied Psychological Measurement, 1,* 385–401.

Raimo, E. B., & Schuckit, M. A. (1998). Alcohol dependence and mood disorders. *Addictive Behaviors, 23,* 933–946.

Resnick, H. S., Kilpatrick, D. G., Dansky, B. S., Saunders, B. E., & Best, C. L. (1993). Prevalence of civilian trauma and posttraumatic stress disorder in a representative national sample of women. *Journal of Consulting and Clinical Psychology, 61,* 984–991.

Rind, B., Tromovitch, P., & Bauserman, R. (1998). A meta-analytic examination of assumed properties of child sexual abuse using college samples. *Psychological Bulletin, 124,* 22–53.

Robins, L. N., Helzer, J. H., Croughan, J., & Ratcliff, K. S. (1981). The National Institute of Mental Health Diagnostic Interview Schedule: Its history, characteristics, and validity. *Archives of General Psychiatry, 38,* 381–389.

Rosenberg, M. (1965). *Society and the adolescent self-image.* Princeton, NJ: Princeton University Press.

Santor, D. A., Pringle, J., & Israeli, A. L. (2000). Enhancing and disrupting cooperative behavior in couples: Effects of dependency and self-criticism following favorable and unfavorable performance feedback. *Cognitive Therapy and Research, 24,* 379–397.

Saunders, B. E., Villeponteaux, L. A., Lipovsky, J. A., Kilpatrick, D. G., & Veronen, L. J. (1992). Child sexual assault as a risk factor for mental disorders among women: A community survey. *Journal of Interpersonal Violence, 7,* 189–204.

Saunders, J. B., Aasland, O. G., & Grant, M. (1987). *The World Health Organization screening instrument for harmful and hazardous alcohol consumption.* Geneva, Switzerland: World Health Organization.

Selzer, M. (1971). The Michigan Alcoholism Screening Test: The quest for a new diagnostic instrument. *American Journal of Psychiatry, 127,* 1653–1658.

Sher, K. J., Walitzer, K. S., Wood, P. K., & Brent, E. E. (1991). Characteristics of children of alcoholics: Putative risk factors, substance use and abuse, and psychopathology. *Journal of Abnormal Psychology, 100,* 427–448.

Silvern, L., Karyl, J., Waelde, L., Hodges, W. F., Starek, J., Heidt, E., & Min, K. (1995). Retrospective reports of parental partner abuse: Relationships to depression, trauma symptoms, and self-esteem among college students. *Journal of Family Violence, 10,* 177–202.

Skorina, J. K., & Kovach, J. A. (1986). Treatment techniques for incest-related issues in alcoholic women. *Alcoholism Treatment Quarterly, 3,* 17–30.

Spitzer, R. L., Williams, J. B., & Gibbon, M. (1986). *Structured clinical interview for DSM-III-R.* New York: Biometrics Research Department, New York State Psychiatric Institute.

Stewart, S. H. (1996). Alcohol abuse in individuals exposed to trauma: A critical review. *Psychological Bulletin, 120,* 83–112.

Stewart, S. H. (1997). Trauma memory and alcohol abuse: Drinking to forget? In J. D. Read & D. S. Lindsay (Eds.), *Recollections of trauma: Scientific evidence and clinical practice* (pp. 461–467). New York: Plenum.

Stewart, S. H., Conrod, P. J., Pihl, R. O., & Dongier, M. (1999). Relationships between posttraumatic stress symptom dimensions and substance dependence in a community-recruited sample of substance-abusing women. *Psychology of Addictive Behaviors, 13,* 78–88.

Stewart, S. H., Conrod, P. J., Samoluk, S. B., Pihl, R. O., & Dongier, M. (2000). Posttraumatic stress disorder symptoms and situation-specific drinking in women substance abusers. *Alcoholism Treatment Quarterly, 18,* 31–47.

Stewart, S. H., Pihl, R. O., Conrod, P. J., & Dongier, M. (1998). Functional relationships among trauma, PTSD, and substance-related disorders. *Addictive Behaviors, 23,* 797–812.

Stewart, S. H., Samoluk, S. B., & MacDonald, A. B. (1999). Anxiety sensitivity and substance use and abuse. In S. Taylor (Ed.), *Anxiety sensitivity: Theory, research, and treatment of the fear of anxiety* (pp. 287–319). Mahwah, NJ: Erlbaum.

Stewart, S. H., Zeitlin, S. B., & Samoluk, S. B. (1996). Examination of a three-dimensional drinking motives questionnaire in a young adult university student sample. *Behavior Research and Therapy, 34,* 61–71.

Straus, M. A. (1979). Measuring intra-familial conflict and violence: The conflict tactics (CT) scales. *Journal of Marriage and the Family, 41,* 75–87.

Straus, M. A., & Kaufman Kantor, G. (1994). Corporal punishment of adolescents by parents: A risk factor in the epidemiology of depression, suicide, alcohol abuse, child abuse, and wife beating. *Adolescence, 29,* 543–561.

Sultan, F. E., & Chambless, D. L. (1988). Sexual functioning. In E. A. Blechman & K. D. Brownell (Eds.), *Handbook of behavioral medicine for women* (pp. 92–102). Elmsford, NY: Pergamon,

Taylor, S., Koch, W. J., & McNally, R. J. (1992). How does anxiety sensitivity vary across the anxiety disorders? *Journal of Anxiety Disorders, 6,* 249–259.

Terr, L. C. (1991). Childhood traumas: An outline and overview. *American Journal of Psychiatry, 148,* 10–20.

Turner, R. J., & Lloyd, D. A. (1995). Lifetime traumas and mental health: The significance of cumulative adversity. *Journal of Health and Social Behavior, 36,* 360–376.

Walker, L. E. (1977). Battered women and learned helplessness. *Victimology, 2,* 525–534.

Wilsnack, S. C., Vogeltanz, N. D., Klassen, A. D., & Harris, T. R. (1997). Childhood sexual abuse and women's substance abuse: National survey findings. *Journal of Studies on Alcohol, 58,* 264–271.

Wing, J. K., Nixon, J. M., Mann, S. A., & Leff, J. P. (1977). Reliability of the PSE used in a population study. *Psychological Medicine, 7,* 505–516.

Wolfe, D. A., Sas, L., & Wekerle, C. (1994). Factors associated with the development of posttraumatic stress disorder among child victims of sexual abuse. *Child Abuse and Neglect, 18,* 37–50.

Wolfe, V. V., Gentile, C., Michienzi, T., Sas, L., & Wolfe, D. A. (1991). The Children's Impact of Traumatic Events Scale: A measure of post-sexual-abuse PTSD symptoms. *Behavioral Assessment, 13,* 359–383.

World Health Organization. (1990). *Composite International Diagnostic Interview (CIDI).* Geneva, Switzerland: Author.

Anne-Marie Wall
Sherry McKee

Cognitive Social Learning Models of Substance Use[1] and Intimate Violence

Except for elementary reflexes, people are not equipped with inborn repertoires of behavior. They must learn them (Bandura, 1973, p. 16).

Social learning theory (SLT) is a broad-based, multifactorial theoretical framework that has been advanced to account for the origin, expression, and maintenance of vastly divergent and differentially complex human behaviors, including substance use and intimate violence (i.e., partner-to-partner and parent-to-child). As a general theoretical framework, considerable research has accumulated in support of SLT (for reviews, see Bandura, 1969, 1977, 1986). While this model has been a dominant one within the field of alcohol addiction, its application to intimate violence, particularly with respect to its co-occurrence with substance use, is very much in its infancy. For example, while SLT-derived investigations on alcohol use have examined several critical constructs and multifactoral models have been developed and well validated, the majority of investigations within the intimate violence literature have focused on modeling influences in one's family of origin. Despite the addiction-intimate violence overlap (see Wekerle & Wall, this volume), only in the last decade have investigators more increasingly considered the complex relationship that likely exists between substance use and relationship violence within a SLT framework.

The present chapter is not intended to be an exhaustive review of findings from SLT-derived investigations that have been carried out independently within the fields of addiction and family violence (for reviews, see Abrams & Niaura, 1987; Maisto, Carey, & Bradizza, 1999; O'Leary, 1988). Rather, its purpose is to trace the evolution of this theoretical framework and, in so doing, critically appraise the manner in which SLT has been applied to substance use, intimate violence, and their overlap. By examining the current state of the literature and identifying conceptual and empirical gaps, this chapter is also intended to

---

[1]In keeping with SLT, the terms substance use and alcohol use are used throughout this chapter to refer to the spectrum of consumption patterns along a continuum ranging from nonproblematic to problematic.

This work was funded in part by the Alcoholic Beverage Medical Research Foundation, the Social Sciences and Humanities Research Council of Canada (A.-M. Wall), and the Canadian Institutes of Health Research (A.-M. Wall).

123

provide direction for future SLT-based research in this area. Constrained by the existing literature, this chapter will focus exclusively on SLT explanations of alcohol, rather than alternative drugs of abuse, and its relationship to intimate violence. More specifically, since the application of SLT to parent-to-child abuse and to victims of adult intimate violence is sorely lacking, this chapter will concentrate on the overlap between alcohol use and the perpetration of partner-to-partner violence.

The chapter begins with a discussion of SLT and how it has been applied to alcohol use and intimate violence. In this first section, a general overview of SLT is presented in order to articulate its innovative approach to understanding human behavior. Next, commonalities and points of departure concerning the application of SLT to drinking behavior and intimate violence are reviewed. This is followed by a synopsis of multifactorial models that have considered the co-occurrence of these behaviors. The next major section reviews investigations that have examined the role of specific SLT constructs that are postulated to be critical determinants of alcohol use and intimate violence. Following this, findings from the limited number of SLT multivariate investigations that have considered the link between alcohol use and relationship violence are discussed. The chapter concludes with a commentary concerning the current state of the literature and suggestions for future research.

☐ Social Learning Theory: Theoretical Foundations and its Application to Alcohol Use and Intimate Violence

Social Learning Theory as a General Model of Human Behavior

As a general model of human behavior, SLT emerged as an innovative approach that integrated traditional models of learning (i.e., operant and classical conditioning) and cognitive psychology, while simultaneously assigning paramount importance to the social context in which specific behaviors are learned. Although many prominent researchers (e.g., Dollard & Miller, 1950; Mischel, 1973; Patterson, 1982; Rotter, 1954) are considered major proponents of SLT, Bandura's exposition of the model is generally regarded as the most influential (Abrams & Niaura, 1987; Maisto et al., 1999; O'Leary, 1988). Specifically, Bandura's conceptualization of how social learning principles influence the origin, expression, and maintenance of behavior offered alternative views of human nature and psychopathology that deviated substantially from radical behavioral and drive-reduction models that dominated psychology prior to the 1970s. Consequently, the following general overview of SLT has been gleaned largely from Bandura's extensive writings. As a comprehensive review of Bandura's theorizing is beyond the scope of this chapter, we have chosen to focus on theoretical principles, critical constructs, and underlying mechanisms that, in our opinion, are central to SLT.

Since Bandura's (1969) exposition of SLT, empirical work has resulted in significant elaboration of the model and, consequently, some conceptual shifts. Specifically, subsequent articulation of SLT (Bandura, 1977, 1986) focused more extensively on individual, as opposed to environmental, influences and emphasized the role of cognitive processes (Abrams & Niaura, 1987; Maisto et al., 1999; O'Leary, 1988). Despite the evolution of SLT, its view of human nature has remained largely unaltered. The following fundamental principles, from our perspective, collectively distinguish SLT from alternative theoretical frameworks.

• Human beings are active, rather than passive, agents. In contrast to drive-reduction models of human functioning, SLT rejects the notion that behavior is motivated exclusively by internal, intrapsychic (e.g., personality traits and unconscious impulses), or biological mechanisms. Diverging from radical behavioral approaches, SLT also refutes the idea that behavior is controlled solely by external, environmental contingencies.

- Predisposing biological and genetic factors influence trajectories of social learning, but the acquisition, expression, and maintenance of specific behaviors is the result of one's idiosyncratic direct and indirect learning histories.
- Human functioning is adaptive and flexible since behavior is highly situation-specific.
- As a result of individuals' cognitive capabilities, behavior is conceptualized as being volitional and goal-directed, with outcome and efficacy expectancies figuring prominently.
- Maladaptive behaviors reflect the ways in which an individual has learned to cope with environmental or self-imposed demands, rather than an underlying pathological or disease state.
- All forms of human behavior (both adaptive and maladaptive) are subject to the same principles of learning and cognition that reflect a dynamic, reciprocal interplay between personal, environmental, and behavioral determinants.

A fuller appreciation of SLT's view of human nature is evident when one considers the following core elements of the model and the specific underlying learning mechanisms that have been proposed (for previous discussions of these critical constructs and principles, see Abrams & Niaura, 1987; Maisto et al., 1999; O'Leary, 1988).

Observational Learning.   Observational learning or modeling is one of the cornerstones of SLT as it illustrates unquestionably how social agents and cognitive capabilities influence learning. Contrary to traditional learning models, Bandura (1969, 1977, 1986) presented considerable evidence that a myriad of behaviors can be learned in the absence of direct experience (i.e., reinforcing or punishing behavioral outcomes), arguing quite convincingly that individuals have the capability to learn simply through observing others. To date, observational learning continues to be regarded as the most efficient means through which specific behavioral repertoires are initially acquired. In addition to influencing the initial acquisition of behavior, modeling is postulated to exert the following influences on previously acquired behaviors: it can either weaken or strengthen processes that inhibit performance (disinhibition and inhibition, respectively), or, alternatively, models can serve as discriminative, social stimuli that facilitate the enactment of behavior not performed previously because of insufficient inducements.

According to SLT, modeling influences function "principally through their informative function" (Bandura, 1977, p. 24). Four sequential processes purportedly govern observational learning. *Attentional processes* are necessary as observational learning is contingent on the degree to which the modeled behavior is initially attended to by the observer. In order for individuals to profit from modeling, *retention processes* are required for information to be initially stored in and subsequently activated from memory. *Motor reproduction processes* refer to requisite abilities individuals must possess in order to translate cognitive, symbolic representations into behavior. Finally, *motivational processes* are critical to whether behaviors acquired via observational learning will actually be performed. According to SLT, the probability that a specific behavior will be exhibited is determined primarily by the perceived functional value of the modeled behavior; behaviors acquired via observational learning are more likely to be performed when the perceived outcomes are viewed as being effective, positive, or highly valued. Elaborating on his early thinking concerning the underlying mechanisms of observational learning, Bandura (1986) presented a multiprocess analysis that further identified a number of subprocesses, related to the modeled behavior's (e.g., saliency and functional value), the observer's (e.g., perceptual, cognitive, and motor capabilities, arousal level, incentive preferences), and the model's (e.g., status, competence, and power, as well as perceived similarity) characteristics that could potentially impact on motivational processes. According to Bandura (1977), however, "the functional value of modeled behavior overrides the influence of either model or observer characteristics" (pp. 89–90).

Stimulus Control of Behavior.   In contrast to trait explanations of behavior, SLT refutes the notion that behavioral tendencies are manifestations of an underlying personality structure that is invariant across situations; rather, behavior is conceptualized as being highly situation-specific, largely as a consequence of differential reinforcing experiences. While Bandura concurred with proponents of traditional learning models that direct reinforcing and punishing experiences were important determinants of behavior, he viewed this as a rudimentary, trial and error form of learning. He contended that direct learning experiences functioned principally as a means of regulating, rather than creating, novel behavioral repertoires. More important, in his view, was the informative and motivational functions that direct learning experiences provided. Specifically, Bandura maintained that direct learning provided individuals with opportunities that allowed them to gauge the appropriateness and functional value of enacting a particular behavior in a given situation. In a similar vein, SLT purports that modeled behaviors are differentially reinforced depending upon the target to whom the behavior is expressed and the setting in which it is enacted. This association between varying environmental settings and observed differential reinforcement is thought similarly to serve an adaptive function as it allows individuals to identify stimulus conditions under which the modeled behavior is appropriate (Bandura, 1969). In this respect, SLT regards behavior, acquired via both direct and indirect learning, as being under anticipatory, cognitive control.

The Role of Cognition.   According to Bandura, "learning is largely an information-processing activity in which information about the structure of behavior and about environmental events is transformed into symbolic representations that serve as guides for action" (1986, p. 51). In addition to their potential for vicarious learning, individuals are thought to possess symbolizing, forethought, self-regulatory, and self-reflective capabilities. Symbolizing capabilities refer to individuals' ability to use symbols in order to convert transient experiences into cognitive representations that guide future decision-making. As opposed to learning by trial and error, individuals are, in essence, considered capable of generating hypotheses concerning adaptive behavioral options. Bandura argued, however, that individuals do not always engage in objective, rational behavior as faulty decision-making can occur as a result of deficient or underdeveloped reasoning skills, inadequate information, or misperceptions of cues. Forethought capabilities refer to SLT's view that most of human behavior is regulated by anticipatory thinking (expectations concerning consequences of future actions, goal-setting behavior, etc.). In this regard, behavior is conceptualized as being decidedly volitional and goal-directed. In fact, Bandura (1986) argues that cognitive representations of future events, rather than existing environmental conditions, exert a causal influence on behavior. SLT also views self-regulatory capabilities (i.e., the motivational influence of internal standards and self-evaluative processes) as being critical determinants of behavior. Finally, individuals' self-reflective capabilities, or meta-cognitive abilities, allow for the acquisition of general knowledge about themselves, others, and the environment. Collectively, these cognitive capabilities allow individuals to cope with ever-changing, complex environmental demands.

An essential feature of all these cognitive capabilities is the role that outcome and efficacy expectancies play in mediating behavior. An *outcome expectancy* is defined as an individual's belief that a given behavior will lead to specific outcomes, whereas an *efficacy expectancy* (self-efficacy) refers to one's confidence that he or she can successfully enact the behavior necessary in order to realize anticipated outcomes (Bandura, 1977). Both outcome and efficacy expectancies, which can be acquired through either direct or indirect learning, are considered to be highly situation-specific and critical to the expression of both adaptive and maladaptive behaviors. Relative to outcome expectancies, however, self-efficacy is postulated to be a more important determinant of individuals' coping strategies (i.e., whether a coping response will be initiated, how much effort will be expended, and one's willingness to persist when confronted with obstacles, real or perceived). Given the purported relationship between self-efficacy and coping, Bandura (1986, 1997, 1999) argues that the success of behavioral change strategies is contingent on creating and strengthening an individual's sense of self-efficacy.

Reciprocal Determinism.   Prior to the 1970s, dominant models of behavior ascribed to one-sided determinism. Specifically, radical behavioral approaches viewed behavior as being exclusively under environmental control, whereas theoretical frameworks emphasizing personal determinism regarded dispositional tendencies (e.g., traits, instincts, drives, etc.) as underlying causal mechanisms (Bandura, 1986). In his original SLT formulation, Bandura argued for reciprocal determinism, namely that the relationship between the environment and behavior was characterized by a continuous, reciprocal interaction. His more contemporary view of human functioning, social cognitive theory (Bandura, 1986), is based upon triadic reciprocality such that "behavior, cognitive and other personal factors, and environmental influences all operate interactively as determinants of each other" (p. 23). This complex and dynamic view of human nature is further evidenced by the fact that, while the development and activation of these three components is hypothesized to be highly interdependent, their relative influence is thought to vary across behaviors, individuals, and conditions (Bandura, 1986).

In summary, SLT is a multifactorial theoretical framework that integrates how basic principles of learning and cognition, as well as social influences, contribute to the development of adaptive and maladaptive behaviors. As discussed by Maisto et al. (1999) SLT affords a more dynamic and optimistic view of human functioning than that offered by alternative, one-sided deterministic models. While SLT's view of human nature has not been modified significantly since its original formulation, theorizing within this general framework has become more elaborate, with an increased emphasis on cognitive capabilities. Specifically, contemporary SLT argues that individuals' outcome and self-efficacy expectancies are important determinants of the environment-behavior relationship. Despite the heuristic value SLT has served in generating a large volume of research, we agree with Maisto et al. (1999) that this model "encompasses a broad range of constructs but does not specify well how these constructs may combine, or how they may mediate or moderate each other to determine the development and maintenance of behavior" (p. 112). Given the breadth and complexity of SLT, some investigators have criticized that this model lacks parsimony and, as such, have argued for the development of micro theories (e.g., see, O'Leary, 1988; Riggs & O'Leary, 1989).

Applications of SLT to Alcohol Use and Intimate Violence: Commonalities and Points of Departure

In reviewing the alcohol and family violence literatures, it would appear that, because researchers have focused on different aspects of SLT in order to understand deviance and substance abuse, it is most appropriate to refer to social learning as a "set of theories"

(Curran, White, & Hansell, 1997, p. 1379). Prior to summarizing the results of SLT-derived investigations that have examined the contributions of specific SLT constructs to alcohol use, intimate violence, and their overlap, it is important to consider how these behaviors have been conceptualized within this broad theoretical framework. In tracing the evolution of thinking that has occurred with respect to SLT formulations derived separately for alcohol use and intimate violence, common theoretical positions and points of departure are highlighted.

Applications of SLT to Alcohol Use.   In his original SLT formulation, Bandura (1969) refuted the notion of an alcoholic personality, arguing instead that a more fruitful approach to understanding alcoholism would involve the identification of specific learning contingencies and reinforcement mechanisms that govern the development of differential drinking patterns. According to Bandura, the initiation of drinking behavior typically occurs under nonstressful conditions as individuals attempt to emulate models within their broader societal and cultural contexts. Once drinking is initiated, observational learning (i.e., modeling behavior exhibited by peers, family members, and individuals depicted in the media) is thought to play a critical role in transmitting societal and cultural norms concerning appropriate drinking practices. In spite of the evidence Bandura (1969) reviewed that supported the contribution of social and cultural modeling influences to differential consumption patterns, he argued that this was an insufficient explanation for the development of excessive drinking since, within a particular societal or cultural group, heterogeneity exists.

In understanding the progression from normative use of alcohol to problematic consumption patterns, Bandura (1969) acknowledged that alcohol, because of its depressant and anxiolytic pharmacological properties, was inherently positively reinforcing when consumed during periods of stress. In contrast to the initiation of drinking behavior, he hypothesized that habitual drinkers intermittently experience this type of positive reinforcement. Once this pattern of reinforcement is established, the volitional use of alcohol is postulated to increase under aversive and frustrating conditions. Additionally, individuals whose alcohol consumption is becoming progressively problematic typically benefit from social reinforcement obtained via their association with similarly imbibing counterparts. With chronic and excessive use of alcohol, negative reinforcement also is postulated to play a role since drinking is, in part, motivated by the desire to alleviate negative physiological withdrawal symptoms. While Bandura acknowledged that biological and genetic factors (e.g., increased sensitivity to alcohol's stress-dampening effects) increase one's propensity toward alcoholism, he argued that individuals exposed to parental models who exhibit excessive use of alcohol as a means of coping with stress or other undesirable conditions are particularly at risk. From this early SLT perspective, "alcoholics are people who have acquired, through differential reinforcement and modeling experiences, alcohol consumption as a widely generalized dominant response to aversive stimulation" (Bandura, 1969, p. 536). In this regard, Bandura's SLT formulation of alcoholism is a coping deficits model. Bandura's recent social-cognitive analysis of substance use has afforded perceived self-efficacy a central role in understanding change processes in alcohol and other drug-taking behavior (Bandura, 1997; 1999).

Bandura's theorizing has spurred considerable research within the alcohol addiction field. We concur with previous reviews (e.g., see Abrams & Niaura, 1987; Maisto et al., 1999) that Marlatt and Gordon's (1985) relapse-prevention model is the most representative SLT based model of alcohol use that has been developed since Bandura's original formulation. This multifactorial model conceptualizes drinking as a volitional, goal-directed behavior where differential consumption patterns are determined by individuals' idiosyncratic learning histories. Excessive use of alcohol is viewed as a maladaptive coping response that is invoked in specific situations previously associated with drinking. Within this general framework, individuals' expectancies about alcohol (i.e., both outcome and self-efficacy expectancies) figure prominently. Other investigators who have adopted a SLT-based, multivariate approach to understanding drinking behavior have incorporated similar constructs such as coping, outcome expectancies, and self-efficacy (e.g., see Cooper, Russell, & George, 1988; Cooper, Russell, Skinner, Frone, & Mudar, 1992; Evans & Dunn, 1995). Overall, there is a large body of research supporting the notion that SLT is a valid framework for understanding alcohol consumption patterns (Maisto et al., 1999).

Paralleling the evolution of SLT, theoretical models of alcohol use have, since the early 1980s, assigned increasing importance to the role of cognitive mechanisms (for a recent review, see Goldman, Del Boca, & Darkes, 1999). Conceptualized as a distinct model, alcohol expectancy theory, nonetheless, shares many overlapping features with SLT, particularly its contemporary formulations. This theoretical framework, for example, views alcohol consumption as a volitional, goal-directed behavior that is proximally determined by individuals' beliefs about the affective, behavioral, and cognitive outcomes of drinking (alcohol outcome expectancies [AOEs]). Consistent with SLT, considerable evidence has accumulated that the acquisition of specific AOEs is determined by one's direct (personal experience with the pharmacological effects of alcohol) and vicarious (modeling influences of parents, peers, and individuals portrayed in the media) learning experiences (for a recent review, see Maisto et al., 1999). As well, investigators have demonstrated, both cross-sectionally and longitudinally, that AOEs are important predictors of differential consumption patterns among individuals who lie at differing points along the alcohol use continuum. In keeping with contemporary SLT's emphasis on cognition (Bandura, 1986), researchers have recently emphasized the role of memory in understanding the AOE–drinking behavior relationship (Goldman et al., 1999).

Applications of SLT to Intimate Violence. Bandura's (1983) SLT analysis of intimate violence, although not specifically stated as such, falls under the general rubric of aggression which he defines generally as "behavior that results in personal injury and physical destruction. The injury may be physical, or it may involve psychological impairment through disparagement and abusive exercise of coercive power" (Bandura, 1983, p. 2). In contrast to the drive-reduction theories of aggression, SLT refutes the notion that frustration is a necessary and sufficient condition for the occurrence of aggressive behavior; rather, from a SLT perspective, aversive stimulation of any sort (including frustration) leads to a general state of emotional arousal that can facilitate the enactment of a multitude of behavioral responses, including aggression, depending on the types of responses an individual has learned to perform in an attempt to cope with stress. Within this framework, the functional value (i.e., anticipated consequences and perceived valences) of available behavioral responses is considered a critical determinant of whether aggression will be employed as a coping strategy, albeit a maladaptive one (Bandura, 1969, 1973). In keeping with a SLT explanation of alcoholism, then, aggression is conceptualized as a volitional, goal-directed behavior within a general coping deficits framework.

Similar to Bandura's (1969) theorizing concerning alcohol use, he argues that aggressive behavior is best understood in terms of learning contingencies and reinforcing mechanisms. According to SLT, aggression is initially acquired under nonfrustrating conditions in which the behavior is typically directed toward inanimate objects. This initial acquisition of aggressive behaviors is postulated to occur, within modern day society, as a result of observational learning originating from three primary sources: the family, an individual's subculture, and symbolic modeling via media influences (Bandura, 1969, 1973). Although one's family of origin is thought to exert a prominent impact on an individual's social development,

Bandura also emphasized the potential facilitative or counteractive impact of community subsystems in which one is surrounded, as well as one's exposure to media influences. Within a SLT framework, "responses to frustration frequently originate from observation of parental and other models who provide repeated examples of how to deal with thwarting events. Only when a person has learned aggression as a dominant response to emotional arousal will there be a high probability of his (her) reacting aggressively to frustration" (Bandura, 1969; pp. 383–384). In addition to learning that aggression is a dominant and acceptable response to frustration, Bandura (1973) argues that exposure to aggressive models influences observers' attitudes and values toward aggression and victims of violence.

Once acquired, aggressive behavior is purportedly brought under stimulus control with respect to environmental influences that both instigate and regulate the enactment of aggressive behavior (for a more complete discussion, see Bandura 1973, 1977, 1983, 1986). Within this general framework, one's idiosyncratic learning history is postulated to determine whether environmental conditions (e.g., responses to verbal challenges, status threats, thwarting of goal-directed behavior, etc.) will serve as instigatory cues for aggressive behavior. Specifically, as a result of one's own aggressive behavior towards specific targets in specific situations being differentially reinforced, individuals purportedly learn, through trial and error, the probable consequences of such actions. As a result of the informative and motivational value of direct learning, individuals are thought to aggress in "safe" contexts where the probability of reinforcement is expected to be high; in situations in which punishment is likely to ensue, aggressive behavior is less likely to occur. The enactment of previously acquired aggressive behaviors is also thought to be governed by vicarious learning. Importantly, SLT emphasizes the distinction between the acquisition of aggressive behaviors and factors that determine whether they will be enacted. Considerable evidence exists that one's motivation to behave aggressively is influenced by several factors including perceived similarity to the model, characteristics of the model, and the perceived functional value of observed outcomes, with the latter exerting a relatively more important influence (Bandura, 1973). Finally, Bandura stressed the role of self-regulatory mechanisms, namely self-generated anticipated consequences, that regulate aggressive behavior. While Bandura acknowledged that there are certain individuals for whom aggression is inherently reinforcing and, hence, ethical and moral standards of conduct do not serve as deterrents, for most individuals anticipated self-reproach typically exerts an inhibitory influence. In understanding how individuals violate their own moral and ethical standards concerning the expression of violence, Bandura (1973, 1983) emphasized the disinhibiting role of cognitions (e.g., justification for the aggressive act, minimizing or misinterpreting the consequences, blaming the victim, etc.).

Bandura's writings on aggression are extensive, but the issue of whether intimate violence is an unique form of violence does not appear to be given much attention within a SLT framework (but see O'Leary, 1988; Riggs & O'Leary, 1989). Given that "the frequency with which aggressive behavior is displayed, the specific forms that it takes, the situations in which it is expressed, and the targets that are selected for attack are strongly influenced by social experience" (Bandura, 1973; p. 378), the lack of attention paid specifically to intimate violence is somewhat surprising. To date, controversy still exists as to whether intimate violence is best conceptualized as a distinct form of aggression or whether it merely represents a specific subtype of general aggressive and criminal tendencies (e.g., see Flett & Hewitt, this volume; Hotaling, Straus, & Lincoln, 1990).

Despite Bandura's lack of specificity concerning the application of SLT to intimate forms of aggression, there has been some research within the family violence literature that has been derived from this theoretical framework, albeit in a somewhat limited fashion. For example, the vast majority of work has focused on partner-to-partner, as opposed to parent-to-child, abuse. Additionally, SLT-derived research on partner violence has tended to adopted a univariate, rather than multi-variate, approach (MacEwen & Barling, 1988), with the impact of modeling influences being the most frequently tested assumption (O'Leary, 1988). Specifically, consistent with Bandura's original theorizing concerning the impact of parental modeling on the acquisition of aggressive behaviors, it is generally argued that the intergenerational transmission of intimate violence is a result of vicarious learning that occurs in one's family of origin (e.g., see Hotaling et al., 1990; Kalmuss, 1984; Straus, 1980; Widom, 1989). Although less extensively investigated, it is similarly argued that exposure to parental violence (either direct or indirect) accounts for adult survivors' propensity toward revictimization (e.g, see Strauss, 1980). Following from Bandura's coping-deficits model of aggression, both domestic violence (e.g., see Holtzworth-Monroe et al., 1995) and child abuse (e.g., Azar, Robinson, Hekemian, & Twentyman, 1984; see Wolfe, 1985) are thought to occur, in part, at the hands of psychologically distressed individuals who have impoverished coping skills.

Within the intimate violence literature there have been some attempts to formulate distinct multi-variate SLT models of spousal (O'Leary, 1988; O'Leary & Arias, 1988) and dating (Riggs & O'Leary, 1989) aggression. To date, however, there have been few attempts to empirically validate these models. We agree with Cano, Avery-Leaf, Cascardi, and O'Leary (1998) that Riggs and O'Leary's (1989) background-situational model of courtship aggression is the most comprehensive one that has been proposed in the literature. This model is comprised of two interrelated components. The first component consists of background factors (i.e., exposure to aggressive partners, being the victim of parental aggression, acceptance of aggression as a response to conflict, and prior use of aggression) that purportedly increase an individual's propensity to establish aggressive behavior patterns across situations, particularly within romantic relationships. The second component is comprised of situational variables (e.g., stress, expected outcomes for dating violence, and marital conflict) that predict the circumstances under which high-risk individuals will act aggressively toward their dating partners. Within this theoretical framework, expectations concerning the outcomes of dating violence figure prominently, and represent the point of intersection between background and situational components. In keeping with SLT, the actual consequences of courtship aggression are thought to serve as a feedback mechanism. While the limited cross-sectional research that has been conducted on this model suggests that it is a valid framework for predicting dating aggression among college (Riggs & O'Leary, 1996; Riggs, O'Leary, & Breslin, 1990) and high school (Cano et al., 1998) students, the purported contribution of expected and actual outcomes of courtship aggression to dating violence was not investigated in these studies.

This apparent empirical lack of emphasis on cognition and reinforcement may, in part, reflect the fact that researchers have, historically, conceptualized intimate violence as a form of expressive, rather than instrumental, behavior (Hotaling, Strauss, & Lincoln, 1990). Overall, in contrast to the alcohol literature that has mirrored the evolution of SLT with its increased emphasis on cognitive and memory, the hypothesized potential contribution of cognitive processes to intimate violence has not been extensively discussed or empirically tested. Although social-cognitive theories of aggression that have been derived from SLT (for a more complete discussion see Eron, 1994) resonate with expectancy models of alcohol use, and aggressive, in comparison to nonaggressive, children hold more positive expectations concerning violent behavior (e.g., see Hall, Herzberger, Skowronski, 1998), scant research attention has been given to the role of violence expectancies specifically with respect to the perpetration of intimate violence. Consistent with the background-situational model (Riggs & O'Leary, 1989), other investigators have begun to conceptualize intimate violence as a volitional, goal-directed behavior, wherein both positive (gaining power and control) and negative (termination of an aversive stimulus such as uncooperative child or spouse) reinforcement are thought to influence the perpetration of abuse (e.g., see Follingstad, Wright, Lloyd, & Sebastian, 1991; Straus, 1994; Tedeschi & Felson, 1995; Wolfe, 1985), but research on how basic principles of learning and cognition influence the perpetration of intimate violence is sorely lacking. Given the extensive research demonstrating the predictive validity of AOEs (for a review, see Goldman et al., 1999), and to the extent that intimate violence is a goal-directed behavior, future investigations on cognition, reinforcement, and memory may prove fruitful in understanding individuals' motivations to engage in partner-to-partner or parent-to-child abuse.

Social Learning Formulations Concerning the Overlap Between Alcohol Use and Intimate Violence

As discussed previously, Bandura conceptualized alcohol abuse and aggression as distinct, maladaptive coping strategies that, depending on one's idiosyncratic learning, are enacted during stressful periods. He did, however, give some consideration to factors that might influence the co-occurrence of these problem behaviors. Specifically, Bandura argued that intoxication could exert a disinhibitory influence on aggressive behavior, owing either to alcohol's pharmacological properties that impair one's judgments concerning anticipated outcomes (Bandura, 1969, 1973, 1986), or to self-exonerating thought processes that arise as a result of one's expectation that alcohol causes and excuses aggression (Bandura, 1986). Similar expectancy explanations concerning the link between alcohol and aggression have been made by others (e.g., see Leonard & Senchak, 1993; Quigley & Leonard, 1999). Likely as a result of the limited available research at the time, a comprehensive, multifactorial account of the overlap between drinking behavior and aggression is notably absent from Bandura's writings. Within the last decade, however, SLT formulations concerning the link between alcohol use and partner-to-partner violence have become increasingly more comprehensive and complex. While an in-depth discussion of these models is beyond the scope of this chapter, it is important to highlight the theoretical similarities and distinctions that exist with respect to how investigators have conceptualized the link between alcohol use (in conjunction with other SLT variables) and the perpetration of intimate violence.

In terms of commonalities, the multivariate models (Foo & Margolin, 1995; Leonard, 1999; Leonard & Senchak, 1993, 1996; Mihalic & Elliott, 1997; O'Keefe, 1997; O'Leary, 1988; O'Leary & Arias, 1988; Riggs & O'Leary, 1989; Stith & Farley, 1993; Tontodonato & Crew, 1992) have not conceptualized problem drinking and intimate violence as comorbid, dysfunctional styles of coping that could potentially arise from individuals' idiosyncratic backgrounds. In contrast, the vast majority of models have focused exclusively on the perpetration of general patterns of physical partnership violence, with general consumption patterns exerting either a hypothesized direct or indirect impact. To date, researchers have not examined episodic partnership violence that occurs during periods of intoxication within a multivariate SLT framework. In an attempt to understand how SLT factors influence the acquisition and expression of intimate violence, investigators have typically conceptualized model constructs as either distal or proximal variables. Distal variables are generally viewed as individual difference or contextual variables that allow for the discrimination between individuals who have (and do not have) the propensity to aggress against an intimate partner. In contrast, proximal variables are situational, personal, or dyadic factors that predict when or under what specific conditions partnership violence occurs (for a more complete discussion, see Leonard, 1999; O'Leary & Arias, 1988; Riggs & O'Leary, 1989). In keeping with the critical importance SLT ascribes to observational learning that occurs within the family context, exposure to violence in one's family of origin has been consistently incorporated into existing models as a risk factor for the adult perpetration of intimate violence. Differences exist, though, with respect to how exposure to violence has been hypothesized to impact on one's social development.

Despite these common features, there are some conceptual distinctions, particularly with respect to how one's idiosyncratic learning history is postulated to influence the development of differential consumption patterns, whether alcohol use is thought to directly influence the perpetration of intimate violence, and how drinking is thought to be interrelated to other model constructs. These conceptual variations are likely due, in part, to the lack of specificity that exists concerning how SLT constructs interrelate and function as mediators and moderators of behavior (Maisto et al., 1999). With respect to factors that influence the development of differential consumption patterns, some investigators view drinking behavior as being directly influenced by exposure to violence in one's family of origin (Mihalic & Elliott, 1997; Stith & Farley, 1993), others conceptualize drinking behavior as being indirectly associated with exposure to family violence, via personality tendencies (e.g., aggressive personality style, hostility) that are directly acquired (e.g., see Leonard & Senchak, 1993; O'Leary, 1988), and, in some instances, the antecedent conditions that give rise to differential consumption patterns have not been well articulated (O'Keefe, 1997). Discrepancies across models also exist as to whether general drinking patterns exert either a hypothesized indirect (Mihalic & Elliott, 1997; Leonard & Senchak, 1993; O'Leary, 1988; Stith & Farley, 1993) or direct (O'Keefe, 1997; Riggs & O'Leary, 1989; Stith & Farley, 1993; Tontodonato & Crew, 1992) influence on the perpetration of adult intimate violence. Finally, investigators have proposed that alcohol use is associated with other model components such as negative interpersonal interchanges (O'Leary, 1988), couple conflict style (Leonard & Senchak, 1993), approval of marital violence (Stith & Farley, 1993), and marital satisfaction and stress (Mihalic & Elliott, 1997) that more directly impact on the perpetration of intimate violence. Thus, although these models have been developed under the rubric of SLT, important conceptual differences exist.

While theorizing in this area from a SLT perspective has become increasingly more comprehensive, relatively little attention has been paid to the role of cognitive mechanisms. With the exception of Leonard and colleagues (e.g., see Leonard & Senchak, 1993; Quigley & Leonard, 1999) who have examined the contribution of AOEs (i.e., both with respect to one's expectation that alcohol causes aggression, as well as the belief that alcohol excuses aggression) to the perpetration of husband-to-wife physical abuse, beliefs about alcohol-related intimate violence have not been incorporated extensively into multivariate models. Moreover, although some researchers (O'Leary, 1988; Riggs & O'Leary, 1989) have articulated how individuals' beliefs about the functional value of intimate violence (i.e., anticipated outcomes, the valence associated with such aggressive acts, etc.) may influence the perpetration of such behavior, to date, these cognitive mechanisms have not been examined systematically within a multivariate SLT framework.

☐ Understanding how Social Learning Mechanisms Influence Alcohol Use and Intimate Violence: Critical Constructs and Hypothesized Mediating and Moderating Processes

Cognizant of the criticism that has been made against SLT models of deviance and substance abuse (Curran et al., 1997), the following section is a synthesis of empirical work that has investigated specific SLT constructs. Specifically, empirical work that has examined (1) family of origin as a critical context for observational learning, (2) the role of cognition, (3) coping, and (4) reciprocal determinism are reviewed. Our rationale for critically examining these constructs was threefold: SLT's fundamental view of human nature, the evolution of theorizing that has occurred within this general framework, and specific foci that have emerged within the alcohol and intimate violence literatures. This approach is intended to provide a theoretical and empirical context in order to critically appraise how SLT variables have been incorporated into multivariate investigations that have simultaneously considered alcohol use and intimate violence.

Family of Origin as a Critical Context for Observational Learning

As discussed above, observational learning is a cornerstone of SLT. Considerable evidence suggests that intimate violence and drinking behaviors are initially acquired through vicarious learning that occurs in one's family of origin, with the familial transmission of each behavior being estimated at 30% (Kaufman & Zigler, 1987; Schuckit, 1984). Notwithstanding biological (see Pihl & Hoaken, this volume), personality (see Flett & Hewitt, this volume), or other social (i.e., peer influences, see Pepler, Craig, Connolly, & Henderson, this volume) factors that may be involved in the intergenerational transmission of these behaviors, modeling of parental behaviors has received much attention. Based on vicarious learning, it stands to reason that offspring with a family history of alcoholism are a high-risk group for the development of problem drinking, but clearly some individuals with a family history of alcoholism develop nonabusive drinking patterns. Studies examining alcohol consumption in adult children of alcoholics, in comparison to adult children of nonalcoholics, have demonstrated all of the following: increased quantity in family history-positive participants (Kubicka, Kozeny, & Roth, 1990), no difference between those with and without a family history of alcoholism (Alterman, Searles, & Hall, 1989), and increased quantity and frequency in family history-negative participants (Alterman, Bridges, & Tarter, 1986). Studies examining the relationship between parental and offspring alcohol use have found evidence for the influence of parental drinking (Kandel & Andrews, 1987; Lau, Quadrel, & Hartman, 1990) which has been cross-validated in some studies (Webb & Baer, 1995), where other studies have failed to find support for parental influences on offspring use of alcohol (Kandel & Andrews, 1987). With respect to assessing the intergenerational hypothesis, exposure to abuse in one's family of origin (either indirect or direct) has been examined with respect to its impact on adult parternship and parent-to-child violence, however, results have been similarly mixed. Witnessing interparental aggression, for example, has been implicated as a risk factor for offspring partnership violence (e.g., see Doumas, Margolin, & John, 1994; Hotaling & Sugarman, 1986; Jankowski, Leitenberg, Henning, & Coffey, 1999; Kalmuss, 1984; Langhinrichsen-Rohling, Neidig, & Thorn, 1995), but other investigators have failed to find such a relationship, arguing against a modeling effect (e.g., see MacEwen & Barling, 1988; Marshall & Rose, 1988; Sigelman, Berry, & Wiles, 1984). Parent-to-child violence also has been linked to both offspring partner and parent-to-child violence, albeit equivocally so (Doumas et al., 1994; Hotaling & Sugarman, 1986; Kaufman & Zigler, 1987; Langhinrichsen-Rohling et al., 1995; MacEwen & Barling, 1988; Marshall & Rose, 1988; Sigelman et al., 1984; Widom, 1989).

Overall, results from both the alcohol and violence literatures are suggestive of a link between family of origin variables and offspring modeling behaviors, but results are far from conclusive. While it is recognized that offspring of parents who exhibit problematic drinking or aggressive behaviors are, in comparison to the general population, a high-risk group, it is also recognized that the majority of these offspring fail to model these behaviors (Dutton, 1999). The interplay between exposure, acquisition, and performance of these behaviors is not well understood and what is required is the identification of risk and protective factors that moderate the intergenerational transmission of alcohol use and abuse and intimate violence. In considering the impact of parental modeling of alcohol use or intimate violent exchanges, parental gender, offspring gender, quality of the relationship with the model, and the degree of exposure to the parental model have been identified as potential moderators. Each of these are considered in turn.

Interactions of Parental Model and Offspring Gender. With respect to the influence of modeling on both alcohol use and aggression, several investigators have suggested that it is important to consider gender (e.g., Avakame, 1998; Clayton & Lacy, 1982). In both the alcohol and intimate violence literatures, however, parental behaviors are typically aggregated and potential gender-specific effects on offspring behaviors have not been extensively examined. With regard to alcohol use, combined parental drinking or paternal drinking are usually examined, whereas maternal drinking is generally not considered. Studies that have examined the influence of gender on parental modeling of alcohol consumption typically find evidence of same-sex modeling (e.g., Clayton & Lacy, 1982), but this effect has been found to be moderated by offspring age (Johnson & Padina, 1991) and level of parental alcohol consumption (e.g., Harburg, Davis, & Caplan, 1982). Other studies have found no evidence that modeling of parental alcohol use varies as a function of gender (e.g., Weinberg, Dielman, Mandell, & Shope, 1994).

In examining the intergenerational transmission of intimate violence, some investigators have examined the singular or combined effects of gender of parental aggressor, gender of parental victim, and offspring gender. When examining partner violence, some studies have demonstrated a stronger modeling for exposure to family violence for male, in comparison to female, offspring (e.g., see O'Leary, Malone, & Tryee, 1994), however, apparent gender-specific modeling effects reported in the literature may be confounded by aggregating direct and indirect violent interchanges perpetrated by father and mother. Studies in which hypothesized same-sex modeling influences of violence in one's family of origin (either witnessing or direct) have been examined have yielded inconsistent support. While some studies have found same-sex modeling effects for the perpetration of adult partner violence (e.g., Jankowski et al., 1999), cross-gender and bidirectional parental modeling influences also have been reported for both offending (Avakame, 1998; Kalmuss, 1984; Langhinrichsen-Rohling et al., 1995) and victimization behaviors (Jankowski et al., 1999; Langhinrichsen-Rohling et al., 1995). In examining potential same-sex modeling influences concerning the impact of direct experiences of child abuse on adult partner and parent-to-child violence, investigators typically aggregate maternal and paternal perpetrated violent acts (e.g., Doumas et al., 1994; Sigelman et al., 1984), hence, the potential moderating effect of gender remains poorly understood. Recently, however, Avakame (1998) found same-sex modeling effects for father-, but not mother-, perpetrated physical punishment (i.e., defined as hitting or slapping) and adult physical abuse. In this study, non gender-specific modeling influences were observed, such that father-perpetrated physical punishment was associated with the perpetration of adult psychological abuse by both men and women.

Quality of Relationship with Parental Model. As highly valued models are more likely to be imitated, investigators have examined the quality of the relationship with a parental model as a potential moderator of modeling effects. Within the substance use and violence literatures, quality of the parent-child relationship has been operationalized as degree of identification (Brook, Whitman, Gordon, & Brook, 1986), quality of attachment (Foshee & Bauman, 1994), and level of parent-child conflict (Andrews, Hops, & Duncan, 1997). Degree of identification, however, most closely parallels SLT principles as it assumes that individuals who identify with a model have a desire to emulate his or her behavior. For both alcohol use (Andrews et al., 1997; McKee & Hinson, 1999) and intimate violence (MacEwen, 1994), quality of the parent-child relationship has been found to moderate the intergenerational transmission of these behaviors. For example, MacEwen (1994) found that male offspring who identified with violent fathers demonstrated greater levels of interpersonal violence than males who did not highly identify with violent fathers. Similar findings have been reported for alcohol use, but offspring age and gender have been found to further moderate these relationships (e.g., older boys model paternal alcohol use only if there is little father-son conflict; Andrews et al., 1997). Recently, McKee and Hinson (1999) found that identification with a nonalcohol abusing mother was a protective factor against modeling the drinking patterns of an alcohol abusing father. Overall, these results support a SLT explanation of behavior, but argue against a simple modeling effect since it appears that the quality of one's relationship with both parents, type of parental behaviors displayed (e.g., drinker, nondrinker, aggressor, victim), offspring gender, and offspring age are other important determinants to consider.

Exposure to parental models.   From SLT, it follows that the degree of exposure to parental models should influence vicarious learning by increasing the salience of the behavior, but, curiously, this has received little empirical attention. Research examining AOEs in individuals with a family history of alcoholism has, however, been based on the supposition that one's AOEs will be altered as a result of the salience of parental alcohol models (e.g., Brown, Creamer, & Stetson, 1987). With regards to modeling effects, researchers have suggested that individuals with a family history of alcoholism may be more susceptible to a drinking model. Experimental research has examined this issue in individuals with and without a family history for alcoholism in relation to their alcohol consumption in the presence of a drinking model. Chipperfield and Vogel-Sprott (1988) found that participants with a family history for alcoholism, in comparison to family history-negative individuals, were more susceptible to a drinking model. The degree of exposure to familial drinking models also mediates the influence of family risk on positive expectancy development (Brown, Tate, Vik, Hass, & Aarons, 1999). Unfortunately, in this latter study, the relationships among exposure to familial drinking models, positive AOEs, and drinking behavior was not assessed.

Within the violence literature, investigators have generally not considered whether the degree of exposure to or the severity of violence (witnessed or directly experienced) in one's family of origin influences the intergenerational transmission of intimate violence. In addition to being exposed to overall levels of parental problem drinking or aggressive behavior, the impact of these maladaptive behaviors on offspring may be an important factor. For example, if there is equal consumption by two fathers where one typically consumes in public drinking establishments while the other drinks primarily within the family home, it follows that there would be a greater impact of parental drinking behavior on offspring in the second scenario. It is likely that the level of parental alcohol consumption or severity of intimate violence and the impact of the parental model on children may not be completely interdependent and, thus, should be assessed separately.

The Role of Cognition

Outcome Expectancies.   As indicated above, research examining the contribution of AOEs to drinking behavior is consistent with a SLT framework (for a review, see Maisto et al., 1999). It is known, for example, that AOEs exist prior to initiation of alcohol consumption and that, as drinking experience increases, expectancies become more crystalized (Christiansen, Goldman, & Inn, 1982; Dunn & Goldman, 1996; Miller, Smith, & Goldman, 1990).Vicarious learning from both macro (e.g., culture, media) and micro (e.g., parents, peers) sources have been implicated in initial expectancy development (e.g., Ellis, Zucker, & Fitzgerald, 1997). In particular, several studies have focused on indices of parental alcohol consumption and parental AOEs as critical determinants of offspring AOEs (e.g., Brown et al., 1999; Johnson, Nagoshi, Danko, Honbo, & Chou, 1990; McKee & Hinson, 1999). Consistent with contemporary SLT formulations, AOEs also have been consistently shown to be proximal predictors of drinking behavior (for a review, see Goldman et al., 1999) and to partially mediate other distal influences (e.g., family history of alcoholism; Sher, Walitzer, Wood, & Brent, 1991).

In contrast to the extensive research that has been conducted concerning the antecedent conditions that influence the acquisition of specific AOEs and how these cognitive mechanisms influence drinking behavior, comparable work within the intimate violence literature is lacking. As is the case with drinking, a single violent encounter can have numerous anticipated outcomes that may be considered positive (e.g., regaining lost control, winning the argument, ending a negative interaction) or negative (e.g., refusal of partner to talk, termination of the relationship, arrest) in nature (Riggs & O'Leary, 1989). Our review of the literature revealed only two studies that have investigated the role of violence-related outcomes in the expression of intimate violence. Breslin, Riggs, O'Leary, and Arias (1990) examined the relationship between violence expectancies and the perpetration of physical violence among college dating partners. Consistent with an SLT explanation of aggression, these investigators found that aggressive dating partners held greater expectations that violence would lead to positive outcomes, whereas their nonaggressive counterparts endorsed stronger expectations that violence would lead to negative consequences. Similar findings have been reported more recently by Riggs and Caulfield (1997) who also found that individuals' intimate violence expectancies were significantly associated with the severity and frequency of self-reported perpetration of physical abuse. Breslin et al. (1990) examined whether perceived parental violence expectancies mediated the intergenerational transmission of intimate violence. Although no evidence for the hypothesized mediating effect of perceived parental violence expectancies was found, a more thorough test would have assessed whether participants' perceived parental violence expectancies influenced their own violence expectancies which, in turn, served a mediating function.

The expectation that alcohol results in an increased likelihood of aggression is a commonly held belief (e.g., Fromme, Stroot, & Kaplan, 1993; Rohsenow, 1983) that appears to vary as a function of gender and drinking status. Generally, men and heavy drinkers are more likely to expect that alcohol consumption will result in increases in aggressive behavior (e.g., Brown, Goldman, Inn, & Anderson, 1980), however, these results have been equivocal with some studies finding no evidence of gender differences (e.g., Rohsenow, 1983), while other studies have found that females report greater aggression expectancies (e.g., Lundahl, Davis, Adesso, & Lukas, 1997). Given that parents are important sources of information concerning the effects of alcohol, it is likely that children acquire expectancies concerning alcohol-related aggression within a familial context, particularly one in which problem drinking and intimate violence co-occur. This supposition receives support from a recent study that was carried out with adults undergoing treatment for alcohol dependence. Specifically, Wall, Wekerle, and Bissonnette (2000) found that treatment-seeking adults who were raised in alcoholic homes and who experienced high levels of child abuse (i.e., witnessing parental aggression, as well as direct physical, emotional, and sexual abuse), in comparison to their counterparts raised by nonalcoholic parents and who experienced low levels of maltreatment, were more likely to expect negative AOEs (i.e., cognitive-behavioral impairment, risk/aggression, negative self-perception) and alcohol-related power and courage. Additional research concerning the contribution of family of origin variables to the acquisition of specific AOEs is needed.

Outside of laboratory-based studies examining alcohol-related aggressive responding towards a stranger (e.g., Bjork & Dougherty, 1998), there have been a limited number of studies that have investigated the relationship between expectancies for alcohol-related aggression and intimate violence. Derman and George (1989) found that the relationship between individuals' self-reported frequency of alcohol consumption and their use of aggression to solve interpersonal disputes were greatest in males who held expectations that alcohol would increase the likelihood of aggression. Leonard and colleagues have examined the contribution of beliefs about alcohol-related aggression (i.e., expectations that alcohol both causes and excuses aggression) to the perpetration of husband-to-wife physical violence using both cross-sectional (Leonard & Senchack, 1993) and longitudinal (Quigley & Leonard, 1999) methodology. Overall, the results from these studies argue against a simple relationship between individuals' expectations for alcohol-related aggression and the perpetration of husband-to-wife violence. Specifically, Leonard and Senchak (1993) found that husband frequent heavy drinking was associated with premarital aggression only among men who believed that alcohol caused aggression. A complex relationship between husband heavy drinking, hostility, and tolerance for alcohol-related aggression also was observed such that, among low hostile men who strongly believed that alcohol excuses aggression, heavy alcohol use was associated with premarital aggression. Quigley and Leonard (1999) reported on the only prospective study that has examined whether similar alcohol-related expectancies for aggression, in concert with husband alcohol use and marital conflict styles, are associated with severe husband-to-wife aggression. While evidence was found that men's beliefs about both the causative and exonerating influence of alcohol, with respect to aggression, moderated the relationship between marital conflict style and the perpetration of husband-to-wife severe physical abuse, results were precisely opposite to what SLT would predict. As acknowledged by these investigators, individuals' general beliefs concerning alcohol-related aggression were assessed and, had the target of such beliefs been specified (i.e., marital partners), results may have differed. Additional work is needed in order to clarify the complex relationship that likely exists between individuals' expectations for alcohol-related aggression and the perpetration of adult partner violence.

Self-Efficacy Expectancies

Within the alcohol literature, self-efficacy has been conceptualized as the ability to refrain from drinking across a variety of high-risk situations (e.g., DiClemente, Carbonari, Montgomery, & Hughes, 1994). As such, self-efficacy has been typically assessed within clinical populations as a predictor of treatment outcome (McKay, Maisto, & O'Farrell, 1996), although other studies have demonstrated that self-efficacy predicts current drinking in nonclinical samples (e.g., Young, Oei, & Crook, 1991). Within the violence literature, there has been limited work concerning self-efficacy. Using vignettes likely to elicit aggressive responses towards peers (e.g., physical or verbal provocation, competition over resources, thwarting of personal goals), Perry, Perry, and Weiss (1986) found that aggressive children held greater self-efficacy expectancies with respect to engaging in aggressive behavior and reduced self-efficacy beliefs for inhibiting aggressive responses. To date, research has not examined self-efficacy beliefs related to intimate violence or one's ability to refrain from perpetrating intimate violence while under the influence of alcohol. As SLT holds that increasing self-efficacy beliefs for alternative behaviors is an important route for behavior change, it would seem important to understand the role of self-efficacy beliefs in alcohol-related intimate violence (Langhinrichsen-Rohling et al., 1995).

Coping

Both alcohol abuse and aggression are conceptualized, within a SLT framework, as behavioral repertoires that are invoked, depending on one's idiosyncratic learning history, in an attempt to cope with stress. Within the alcohol literature, the relationship between maladaptive coping and alcohol use has been well established. Deficits in active coping strategies have been consistently found to predict increased alcohol consumption and alcohol-related problems (Cooper et al., 1988; Cooper et al., 1992; Evans & Dunn, 1995). As well, many individuals undergoing treatment for alcohol dependence admittedly drink in an attempt to cope (Farber, Khavari, & Douglass, 1980). Although less extensively investigated, there is some evidence that the perpetration of physical violence in dating relationships is associated with escape-avoidant coping strategies among males (Carey & Mongeau, 1996). Among alcohol treatment-seeking adults, emotion-focused coping is associated with the perpetration of physical violence for both men and women, as well as emotional abuse inflicted by female partners (Wall & Wekerle, 1999).

In understanding antecedent conditions that, in part, influence individuals' reliance on alcohol and intimate violence as means of coping with stress, SLT would emphasize that one's family of origin functions as a critical context in which maladaptive coping mechanisms are learned. Indeed, it has been argued that exposure to parental models who rely on alcohol or who resort to violence in response to stressful circumstances may lead to the acquisition of general, maladaptive problem-solving and conflict resolution skills that could generalize beyond the family home and possibly persist into adulthood (Grych & Fincham, 1990). Evidence is accumulating that offspring of alcoholics (Clair & Genest, 1987; Hall, 1997), as well as victims of childhood sexual (Leitenberg, Greenwald, & Cado, 1992) and physical (Flannery, Singer, Williams, & Castro, 1998) abuse tend to employ maladaptive coping strategies. Among alcohol treatment-seeking men (but not women), the relationship between being raised in a dysfunctional family environment (i.e., characterized by parental alcoholism and various forms of childhood maltreatment) and self-reported perpetration of intimate violence appears to be moderated by the degree to which they engage in avoidant coping (Wall & Wekerle, 1999).

Reciprocal Determinism

As an alternative to one-sided deterministic theoretical approaches, SLT emphasizes the dynamic, reciprocal relationship between behavior, cognitive and other personal factors, and environmental influences over time (Bandura, 1986). Of all the core theoretical assumptions of SLT, triadic reciprocal determinism has received the least research attention within both the alcohol and intimate violence literatures. Undoubtedly, this is due largely to the fact that investigations of this sort require longitudinal, rather than cross-sectional, designs. There have, however, been a limited number of studies conducted within the alcohol literature that have specifically examined the reciprocal relationship between AOEs and drinking behavior. Based on the principle of reciprocal determinism, one would expect a bidirectional relationship between AOEs and alcohol consumption; AOEs are conceptualized as being prospective, proximal predictors of drinking which, in turn, serves to strengthen one's beliefs about alcohol. Research concerning the reciprocal relationship between AOEs and drinking behavior has yielded equivocal results. Specifically, while evidence in support of this SLT principle has been observed with adolescents (Bauman, Fisher, Bryan, & Chenoweth, 1985; Smith, Goldman, Greenbaum, & Christiansen, 1995) and young adults (Sher, Wood, Wood, & Raskin, 1996) over relatively short time intervals (i.e., one year periods), such bidirectional relationships are not evident when longer prospective periods are considered (e.g., see Sher et al., 1996; Stacy, Newcomb, & Bentler, 1991). To date, longitudinal investigations concerning the reciprocal relationship between individuals' expectancies regarding intimate violence (i.e., either partner-to-partner or parent-to-child) and the perpetration of such behaviors are nonexistent.

Summary of SLT-Derived Univariate Investigations on Alcohol Use and Intimate Violence

In considering the empirical work that has focused on specific SLT constructs and principles reviewed, it can be generally concluded that the alcohol, in comparison to the intimate violence, literature is more advanced. Overall, we concur with Maisto et al. (1999) that a substantial body of work has accumulated in support of a SLT explanation of drinking behavior and echo their call for future, longitudinal studies on reciprocal determinism, one of the defining principles of SLT. In understanding how individuals' distal, idiosyncratic learning histories (e.g., exposure to parental drinking models) influence differential consumption patterns, additional research that adopts a more complex view of modeling influences that flows directly from SLT (e.g., identification with parental models, degree of exposure, etc.) also is warranted. While SLT appears to hold great promise as a theoretical framework for understanding the perpetration of intimate violence, the application of this model to partner, and to a much greater extent child, abuse has been extremely limited. To date, the vast majority of SLT-derived investigations on intimate violence have focused almost exclusively on the family of origin as a critical context for modeling influences, predominantly examining a simple modeling effect. It is quite likely that additional factors (e.g., gender, relationship with one's parental models, degree of exposure to the model, etc.) might moderate the intergenerational transmission of intimate violence. There has also been a paucity of research conducted concerning the role of cognitions (i.e., outcome expectancies concerning the perpetration of intimate violence and self-efficacy beliefs), coping, and reciprocal determinism. In short, much more SLT-derived empirical work within the intimate violence literature is needed.

☐ Empirical Validations of SLT as a Multivariate Framework for Understanding the Co-occurrence of Alcohol Use and Intimate Violence

Moving from the existing research that has adopted a univariate approach to understanding alcohol use and intimate violence to SLT-derived, multivariate investigations that have considered the coexistence of these two behaviors, some general conclusions can be drawn. First and foremost, it would appear that relatively fewer investigations of this latter type have been conducted. Indeed, in our review of the literature, we were only able to identify six published studies that examined the relationship between alcohol use and abuse and intimate violence explicitly within a multivariate SLT framework (Foo & Margolin, 1995; Leonard & Senchak, 1996; Mihalic & Elliott, 1997; O'Keefe, 1997; Stith & Farley, 1993; Tontodonato & Crew, 1992). Of the limited work that has been conducted, gaps exist with respect to the type of intimate violence assessed. For example, researchers have typically focused on the perpetration of moderate-to-severe physical partnership violence, consequently giving little attention to other forms of abuse or how SLT applies to victimization experiences (but see, Mihalic & Elliott, 1997). Moreover, despite O'Leary's (1988) call for the need to develop a multivariate SLT model of child abuse, it would appear that empirical tests of such a formulation remain to be done. As a result, the existing literature is limited, both with respect to the sheer volume of work that has been conducted and to the range of intimate violence behaviors that have been examined.

As stated previously, existing multivariate studies have not conceptualized alcohol use and intimate violence as comorbid problem behaviors that might be expressed as a result of one's idiosyncratic learning history. In contrast, general alcohol and, less commonly, drug use patterns are included among a host of other distal and proximal predictor variables. While additional model constructs flow naturally from the existing univariate studies (e.g., family of origin as a critical context for modeling, stress), other SLT variables that have been shown to be important predictors of these problem behaviors (e.g., factors that moderate parental modeling influences, maladaptive coping, etc.) have not been incorporated. Contrary to contemporary SLT formulations, notably absent from most of these multivariate investigations are cognitive variables (i.e., expectations concerning alcohol-related aggression, anticipated outcomes of intimate violence) that might influence the perpetration of partner-to-partner violence. This latter observation may, once again, reflect the fact that intimate violence has not historically been viewed as a form of instrumental behavior. It is not surprising, then, that investigators have not examined the potential reciprocal relationships between cognitive mechanisms and the perpetration of intimate violence. Moreover, relatively little attention has been paid to antecedent conditions that influence the development of differential consumption patterns (e.g., exposure to alcoholic parents). In this latter regard, the extensive literature on SLT on alcohol use has not been well integrated into existing multivariate models.

Comparisons across these multivariate studies are hampered as a result of conceptual variations in SLT frameworks that have guided these investigations (i.e., specific constructs included, hypothesized direct and indirect paths). Once again, such conceptual variations may be related, in part, to the lack of specificity inherent in SLT's broad-based, multivariate framework. Indeed, it would appear that existing multivariate models have incorporated additional factors (e.g., personality variables, sex-role attitudes, humiliation, etc.) that, despite their predictive validity with respect to the perpetration of partnership violence, have not generally been given extensive consideration within a SLT framework. Alternatively, these conceptual differences might reflect the fact that some investigators have argued for the need for distinct multivariate models for marital (O'Leary, 1988), courtship (Riggs & O'Leary, 1989), and parent-to-child (O'Leary, 1988) abuse, owing to important relationship (e.g., length of relationship, degree of intimacy, power differential), situational (cohabitation, stressors unique to the relationship such as financial burdens), and individual difference (parenting skills) variables that differentiate these specific types of intimate relationships. Cross-study comparisons are also complicated as a result of methodological differences and varying data analytic strategies that have been employed. Consequently, the following synthesis of findings from this work will be limited to general conclusions.

Taken together, the existing research suggests that SLT is a promising theoretical framework for understanding the perpetration of intimate violence, with investigators reporting final models that account for 9.0%–54.0% of the variance in the perpetration of partner-to-partner physical abuse (16.0%–30.0% of victimization experiences; Mihalic & Elliott, 1997). Consistent with the view that one's family of origin is a critical context in which maladaptive behaviors are learned, the majority of studies have found that exposure to family violence is a significant risk factor for adult partner-to-partner violence. Importantly, however, results from these investigations generally argue against a simple modeling effect (but see, Foo & Margolin, 1995, and O'Keefe, 1997, for evidence of a direct pathway for witnessing violence for male college students); rather, these studies have provided evidence that exposure to violence in one's family of origin has a direct impact on attitudes toward violence, personality tendencies, and conflict resolution strategies. Specifically, these studies suggest that exposure to violence in one's family of origin is directly associated with other individual difference variables such as hostility (Leonard & Senchak, 1996), approval of marital violence (Stith & Farley, 1993), attitudes towards violence (Stith & Farley, 1993), sex-role attitudes and beliefs (Leonard & Senchak, 1996; Stith & Farley, 1993), marital conflict styles (Leonard & Senchak, 1996), and marital satisfaction (Mihalic & Elliott, 1997) that, in turn, are more proximal predictors of adult partnership violence. When gender differences have been examined, it would appear that the relative importance of specific distal and proximal risk factors varies for male and female perpetrators (Foo & Margolin, 1995; Mihalic & Elliott, 1997; O'Keefe, 1997; Tontodonato & Crew, 1992) and victims (Mihalic & Elliott, 1997) of partner physical abuse. Finally, the contribution of alcohol and drug use patterns to the perpetration of partner-to-partner violence remains equivocal with direct (Leonard & Senchak, 1996; O'Keefe, 1997; Tontodanto & Crew, 1992 for drug, but not alcohol, use), indirect (Stith & Farley, 1993), and nonsignificant (Foo & Margolin, 1995; Mihalic & Elliott, 1997) paths being reported.

☐ Conclusions and Directions for Future Research

As a general theoretical framework, SLT's innovative approach to understanding human behavior deviated radically from traditional behavioral and drive-reduction models that dominated psychology prior to the 1970s. Although SLT's view of human nature has, over time, remained largely unaltered, this model has become increasingly more complex, with a decided movement toward emphasizing the role of cognitive mechanisms. Despite the considerable amount of evidence that has accumulated in support of an SLT explanation of behavior, we concur with Maisto et al. (1999) that the interrelations between the myriad of constructs that have been proposed in contemporary SLT models, and how they might mediate or moderate behavior, have not been well articulated. Although the heuristic value of SLT has long been recognized, some investigators have, nonetheless, criticized its broad-based, multifactorial approach as lacking parsimony, arguing, instead, for the need for micro theories (e.g., see O'Leary, 1988; Riggs & O'Leary, 1989). It is perhaps for these reasons that research on deviancy and substance abuse has, characteristically, focused on different aspects of this model, thus leading to the conclusion that social learning is best described as a collection of theories (Curran et al., 1997). Notwithstanding these general concerns, our review of the literature suggests that SLT is a valid theoretical framework for understanding alcohol use, and that it holds great promise with respect to elucidating factors involved in the perpetration of intimate violence and the co-occurrence of these behaviors. As we have suggested throughout this chapter, however, additional empirical work is needed, particularly with respect to understanding intimate violence and how it overlaps with alcohol use. Prior to providing some suggestions for future research in this area, some general conclusions concerning the current state of the literature are warranted.

As stated at the outset of this chapter, the application of SLT to understanding how substance use is associated with intimate violence has been limited to alcohol, rather than alternative drugs of abuse. With respect to SLT investigations that have been conducted on intimate violence, researchers have focused primarily on one form of intimate violence—specifically the perpetration of moderate-to-severe physical abuse by men against their female partners. To date, limited empirical work has been conducted with respect to women's perpetration of partnership violence and other forms of abuse that occur within adult, intimate relationships. Furthermore, the application of SLT to victimization experiences of partner violence and the perpetration of child abuse has been virtually nonexistent. In comparing how SLT has been applied to alcohol use and intimate violence, it is clear that work within the alcohol addiction field has been more extensive. In addition to the multivariate, SLT-derived formulations that have been developed in the alcohol literature (e.g., Marlatt & Gordon, 1985), univariate investigations have, collectively, more comprehensively examined model constructs and theoretical principles that, in our view, are central to the model. In contrast, the intimate violence literature has been characterized predominantly by univariate studies that have almost exclusively focused on the intergenerational transmission hypothesis, predominantly investigating simple modeling effects emanating from exposure to violence in one's family of origin. The limited number of multivariate SLT studies that have simultaneously considered these two problem behaviors suggest that this model is, indeed, a valid approach. Unfortunately, varying conceptual and methodological approaches that have been adopted across these latter investigations have not resulted in a clear picture of how alcohol use, in conjunction with other SLT distal and proximal variables, contributes to intimate violence.

From a conceptual standpoint, SLT would argue for the relative superiority of multivariate, rather than univariate, approaches to understanding behavior. Clearly, however, theoretically sound univariate investigations play a vital role in model-building strategies as they afford the identification of critical constructs that bear a strong empirical relationship with the phenomenon under study. In reviewing the univariate investigations that have examined specific SLT constructs and principles that, in our opinion, are central to this model, additional gaps appear to exist. Following from Bandura's writings on observational learning, and the empirical work that has been conducted on alcohol use and adult partner violence, it would appear that parental figures exert a strong influence, but that a simple modeling effect does not exist. In understanding the intergenerational transmission of both drinking behavior and intimate violence, research directed at elucidating moderator variables (e.g., gender, quality of parent-child relationship, parental identification, degree of exposure) appears warranted. As well, given the apparent overlap between parental alcoholism and multiple forms of child abuse that tend to co-occur (see Wekerle & Wall, this volume), it seems important that the singular and combined influences of such maladaptive modeling behaviors within one's family of origin be assessed. In keeping with an SLT explanation of behavior, cognitive processes (i.e., AOEs, self-efficacy expectations) and coping have received consistent and strong empirical support within the alcohol literature, but the relevance of these critical SLT constructs to various forms of intimate violence awaits future empirical validation. Finally, although some studies on reciprocal determinism—specifically with respect to the dynamic interplay between drinking behavior and AOEs—have been conducted, evidence for this defining feature of SLT remains equivocal. To date, comparable studies within the intimate violence literature have not been carried out. Research designed to address these gaps in the literature would further advance SLT as a valid framework for understanding alcohol use and intimate violence. Equally important, it would elucidate factors that bear a strong empirical association with these behaviors.

Ultimately, however, the validity of SLT as a theoretical framework for understanding substance use, intimate violence, and, in particular, their co-occurrence is contingent on further empirical work that adopts a multivariate framework. With respect to understanding the overlap between substance use and intimate violence, a number of general suggestions are in order. Given that SLT maintains that individuals are more likely to aggress towards persons in safe contexts in which the probability of reinforcement is high and the likelihood of punishment is low, we agree with previous authors (e.g., O'Leary, 1988) that family violence should be considered a distinct form of aggression. Moreover, in light of variations in relationship (e.g., degree of intimacy, power differential), situational (e.g., stressors unique to the relationship such as financial burdens), and individual (e.g., parenting skills) variables that distinguish specific types of intimate relationships, we support previous investigators' contentions (O'Leary, 1988; Riggs & O'Leary, 1989) that distinct SLT models for spousal and courtship violence, as well as for child abuse need to be developed, arguing additionally for a specific model for victims of adult partnership violence. Based on the existing multivariate investigations that have examined the overlap between alcohol use and intimate violence, attention to gender differences is also needed.

In our view, the distinction between distal and proximal variables that has been made by investigators who have simultaneously considered alcohol use and intimate violence is a useful heuristic approach. Following from SLT's emphasis on the family of origin as a critical context in which many behaviors are initially learned and, based on the existing literature, we contend that it is important to include family of origin factors (i.e., presence of parental alcoholism and various forms of child maltreatment) in any multivariate theoretical framework. In addition to existing individual difference variables (e.g, hostility, sex-role attitudes, conflict resolution styles, etc.) that have been found to either moderate or mediate the influence of dysfunctional parental modeling behaviors on both alcohol use and intimate violence, the predictive validity of multivariate models may be enhanced by including additional factors found to be associated with differential consumption patterns (e.g., AOEs, coping). Pending the outcome of further univariate investigations concerning the role of expectancies in the perpetration of intimate violence, preliminary evidence (Breslin et al., 1990; Riggs & Caulfield, 1997) suggests that the inclusion of such variables as proximal predictors is warranted. Indeed, we echo O'Leary's (1988) contention that "with the exception of assessing attitudes toward violence, there have been very few research investigations that have used variables that flow directly from the cognitive elements of social learning theory. It is in this context, however, that social learning theory has its greatest potential" (p. 51). Subsequent prospective work directed at understanding the hypothesized bidirectional relationship between violence-related expectancies and intimate violence (for a more complete discussion, see Riggs & O'Leary, 1989) would serve as a rigorous test of the principle of reciprocal determinism.

To conclude, we would be remiss in not commenting on the complexity of SLT constructs and the likely multiple pathways that influence the co-occurrence of alcohol use and intimate violence. For individuals who experience either or both of these behaviors, subgroup heterogenity undoubtedly exists. For example, for some individuals, intimate violence may be the end result of a particular idiosyncratic learning history, with alcohol use exerting either a direct or indirect influence (e.g., individuals exposed to interparental aggression may acquire particular dispositional tendencies, such as hostility, and dysfunctional ways of resolving conflicts that, consequently, increase the likelihood of emulating such behavior in adult relationships, particularly if they engage in excessive drinking). For another subgroup of individuals, both alcohol use and intimate violence may be comorbid maladaptive ways of coping that emanate from particular idiosyncratic learning histories (e.g., exposure to both parental alcoholism and intimate violence in one's family of origin that gives rise to general maladaptive coping styles that, in turn, lead to the co-expression of problem drinking and intimate violence). While the existing research suggests that SLT is a promising theoretical framework for understanding the complexity of distal and proximal variables that influence these two prevalent, and often co-occuring, behaviors, in many respects, the application of this model is very much in its infancy. Significantly more empirical work is required in order to further advance SLT as a valid theoretical approach to understanding how substance use, and intimate violence overlap.

☐ References

Abrams, D. B., & Niaura, R. S. (1987). Social learning theory. In H. T. Blane & K. E. Leonard (Eds.), *Psychological theories of drinking and alcoholism* (pp. 131–178). New York: Guilford.

Alterman, A., Bridges, K., & Tarter, R. (1986). The influence of both drinking and familial risk statuses on cognitive functioning in social drinkers. *Alcoholism: Clinical and Experimental Research*, 10, 449–451

Alterman, A. I., Searles, J. S., & Hall, J. G. (1989). Failure to find differences in drinking behavior as a function of familial risk for alcoholism: A replication. *Journal of Abnormal Psychology, 98*, 50–53.

Andrews, J. A., Hops, H., & Duncan, S. C. (1997). Adolescent modeling of parent substance use: The moderating effect of the relationship with the parent. *Journal of Family Psychology, 11,* 259–270.

Avakame, E. F. (1998). Intergenerational transmission of violence, self-control, and conjugal violence: A comparative analysis of physical violence and psychological aggression. *Violence and Victims, 13,* 301–316.

Azar, S. T., Robinson, R. R., Hekemian, E., & Twentyman, C. T. (1984). Unrealistic expectations and problem-solving ability in maltreating and comparison mothers. *Journal of Consulting and Clinical Psychology, 52,* 687–691.

Bandura, A. (1969). *Principles of behavior modification.* New York: Holt, Rinehart, & Winston.

Bandura, A. (1973). *Aggression: A social learning analysis.* Englewood Cliffs, NJ: Prentice-Hall.

Bandura, A. (1977). *Social learning theory.* Englewood Cliffs, NJ: Prentice-Hall.

Bandura, A. (1983). Psychological mechanisms of aggression. In R. G. Green & E. I. Donnerstein (Eds.), *Aggression: Theoretical and empirical reviews* (pp. 1–35), New York: Academic.

Bandura, A. (1986). *Social foundations of thought and action: A social cognitive theory.* Englewood Cliffs, NJ: Prentice-Hall.

Bandura, A. (1997). *Self-efficacy: The exercise of control.* New York: W. H. Freeman.

Bandura, A. (1999). A sociocognitive analysis of substance abuse: An agentic perspective. *Psychological Science, 10,* 214–217.

Bauman, K., Fisher, L., Bryan, E. & Chenoweth, R. (1985). Relationship between subjective expected utility and behavior: A longitudinal study of adolescent drinking behavior. *Journal of Studies on Alcohol, 46,* 32–38.

Bjork, J. M., & Dougherty, D. M. (1998). Differences in alcohol expectancy between aggressive and nonaggressive social drinkers. *Alcoholism, Clinical and Experimental Research, 22,* 1943–1950.

Breslin, F. C., Riggs, D. S., O'Leary, K. D., & Arias, I. (1990). Family precursors: Expected and actual consequences of dating aggression. *Journal of Interpersonal Violence, 5,* 247–258.

Brook, J. S., Whitman, M., Gordon, A. S., & Brook, D. W. (1986). Father-daughter identification and its impact on her personality and drug use. *Developmental Psychology, 22,* 743–748.

Brown, S., Goldman, M., Inn, A., & Anderson, L. (1980). Expectancies of reinforcement from alcohol: Their domain and relation to drinking patterns. *Journal of Consulting and Clinical Psychology, 48,* 419–426.

Brown, S., Creamer, V. A., & Stetson, B. A. (1987). Adolescent alcohol expectancies in relation to personal and parental drinking patterns. *Journal of Abnormal Psychology, 96,* 117–121.

Brown, S. A., Tate, S. R., Vik, P. W., Haas, A. L., & Aarons, G. A. (1999). Modeling of alcohol use mediates the effect of family history of alcoholism on adolescent alcohol expectancies. *Experimental and Clinical Psychopharmacology, 7,* 20–27.

Cano, A., Avery-Leaf, S., Cascardi, M., & O'Leary, K. D. (1998). Dating violence in two high school samples: Discriminating variables. *The Journal of Primary Prevention, 18,* 431–446.

Carey, C. M., & Mongeau, P. A. (1996). Communication and violence in courtship relationships. In D. D. Cahn, & S. A. Lloyd (Eds.), *Family violence from a communication perspective* (pp. 127–150). Thousand Oaks, CA: Sage.

Chipperfield, B., & Vogel-Sprott, M. (1988). Family history of problem drinking among young male social drinkers: Modeling effects on alcohol consumption. *Journal of Abnormal Psychology, 97,* 423–428.

Christiansen, B. A., Goldman, M. S., & Inn, A. (1982). The development of alcohol-related expectancies in adolescents: Separating pharmacological from social learning influences. *Journal of Consulting and Clinical Psychology, 50,* 336–344.

Clair, D., & Genest, M. (1987). Variables associated with the adjustment of offspring of alcoholic fathers. *Journal of Studies on Alcohol, 48,* 345–355.

Clayton, R. R., & Lacy, W. B. (1982). Interpersonal influences on male drug use and drug use intentions. *International Journal of the Addictions, 17,* 655–666.

Cooper, M. L., Russell, M., & George, W. H. (1988). Coping, expectancies, and alcohol abuse: A test of social-learning formulations. *Journal of Abnormal Psychology, 97,* 218–230.

Cooper, M. L., Russell, M., Skinner, J. B., Frone, M. R., & Mudar, P. (1992). Stress and alcohol use: Moderating effects of gender, coping, and alcohol expectancies. *Journal of Abnormal Psychology, 101,* 139–152.

Curran, G. M., White, R. H., & Hansell, S. (1997). Predicting problem drinking: A test of an interactive social learning model. *Alcoholism: Clinical and Experimental Research, 121,* 1379–1390.

Derman, K. H., & George, W. H. (1989). Alcohol expectancy and the relationship between drinking and physical aggression. *The Journal of Psychology, 123,* 153–161.

Diclemente, C. C., Carbonari, J. P., Montgomery, R. P. G., & Hughes, S. O. (1994). The alcohol abstinence self-efficacy scale. *Journal of Studies on Alcohol, 55,* 141–148.

Dollard, J., & Miller, N. E. (1950). *Personality and psychotherapy.* New York: McGraw-Hill.

Doumas, D., Margolin, G., & John, R. S. (1994). The intergenerational transmission of aggression across three generations. *Journal of Family Violence, 9,* 157–175.

Dunn, M. E., & Goldman, M. S. (1996). Empirical modeling of an alcohol expectancy memory network in elementary school children as a function of grade. *Experimental and Clinical Psychopharmacology, 4,* 209–217.

Dutton, D. G. (1999). Limitations of social learning models in explaining intimate aggression. In. X. B. Arriaga & S. Oskamp (Eds.), *Violence in intimate relationships* (pp. 73–87). Thousand Oaks, CA: Sage.

Ellis, D. A., Zucker, R. A., & Fitzgerald, H. E. (1997). The role of familial influences in development and risk. *Alcohol Health and Research World, 21,* 218–240.

Eron, L. D. (1994). Theories of aggression: From drives to cognitions. In L. R. Huesmann (Ed.), *Aggressive behavior: Current perspectives* (pp. 3–9). New York: Plenum.

Evans, D. M., & Dunn, N. J. (1995). Alcohol expectancies, coping responses, and self-efficacy judgements: A replication and extension of Cooper et al.'s 1998 study in a college sample. *Journal of Studies on Alcohol, 56,* 186–193.

Farber, P. D., Khavari, K. A., & Douglass, F. M., IV (1980). A factor analytic study of reasons for drinking: Empirical validation of positive and negative reinforcement dimensions. *Journal of Consulting and Clinical Psychology, 48,* 780–781.

Flannery, D. J., Singer, M., Williams, L., & Castro, P. (1998). Adolescent violence exposure and victimization at home: Coping and psychological trauma symptoms. *International Review of Victimology, 6,* 29–48.

Follingstad, D. W., Wright, S., Lloyd, S., & Sebastian, J. A. (1991). Sex differences in motivations and effects in dating violence. *Family Relations, 40,* 51–57.

Foo, L., & Margolin, G. (1995). A multivariate investigation of dating aggression. *Journal of Family Violence, 10,* 351–377.

Foshee, V., & Bauman, K. E. (1994). Parental attachment and adolescent cigarette smoking initiation. *Journal of Adolescent Research, 9,* 88–104.

Fromme, K., Stroot, E., & Kaplan, D. (1993). Comprehensive effects of alcohol: Developmental and psychometric assessment of a new expectancy questionnaire. *Psychological Assessment, 5,* 19–26.

Goldman, M. S., Del Boca, F. K., & Darkes, J. (1999). Alcohol expectancy theory: The application of cognitive neuroscience. In K. E. Leonard & H. T. Blane (Eds.), *Psychological theories of drinking and alcoholism* (2nd ed.) (pp. 203–246). New York: Guilford.

Grych, J. H., & Fincham, F. D. (1990). Marital conflict and children's adjustment: A cognitive-contextual framework. *Psychological Bulletin, 108,* 267–290.

Hall, A. E. (1997). Coping resources and self-perceived well-being of college students who report a parental drinking problem. *American Journal of College Health, 45,* 159–164.

Hall, J. A., Herzberger, S. D., & Skowronski, K. J. (1998). Outcome expectancies and outcome values as predictors of children's aggression. *Aggressive Behavior, 24,* 439–454.

Harburg, E., Davis, E. R., & Caplan, R. (1982). Parent and offspring alcohol use: Imitative and aversive transmission. *Journal of Studies on Alcohol, 43,* 497–516.

Holtzworth-Munroe, A., Markman, H., O'Leary, K. D., Neidig, P., Leber, D., Heyman, R. E., Hulbert, D., & Smutzler, N. (1995). The need for marital violence prevention efforts: A behavioral-cognitive secondary prevention program for engaged and newly married couples. *Applied and Preventive Psychology, 4,* 77–88.

Hotaling, G., Straus, M. A., & Lincoln, A. J. (1990). Intrafamily violence and crime outside the family. In M. A. Straus & R. J. Gelles (Eds.), *Physical violence in American families: Risk factors and adaptations to violence in 8,145 families* (pp. 431–466). New Brunswick, NJ: Transaction.

Hotaling, G., & Sugarman, D. (1986). An analysis of risk markers in husband to wife violence: The current state of knowledge. *Violence and Victims, 1,* 101–124.

Jankowski, M. K., Leitenberg, H., Henning, K., & Coffey, P. (1999). Intergenerational transmission of dating aggression as a function of witnessing only same sex parents vs. opposite sex parents vs. both parents as perpetrators of domestic violence. *Journal of Family Violence, 14,* 267–279.

Johnson, R., Nagoshi, C., Danko, G., Honbo, K., & Chou, L. (1990). Familial transmission of alcohol use norms and expectancies and reported alcohol use. *Alcoholism: Clinical and Experimental Research, 14,* 216–220.

Johnson, V., & Padina, R. J. (1991). Effects of the family environment on adolescent substance use, delinquency, and coping styles. *American Journal of Drug and Alcohol Abuse, 17,* 71–88.

Kalmuss, D. (1984). The intergenerational transmission of marital aggression. *Journal of Marriage and the Family, 16,* 11–19.

Kandel, D. B., & Andrews, K. (1987). Processes of adolescent socialization by parents and peers. *International Journal of the Addictions, 22,* 319–342.

Kaufman, J., & Zigler, E. (1987). Do abused children become abusive parents? *American Journal of Orthopsychiatry, 57,* 186–192.

Kubicka, L., Kozeny, J., & Roth, Z. (1990). Alcohol abuse and its psychosocial correlates in sons of alcoholics as young men in the general population of Prague. *Journal of Studies on Alcoholism, 51,* 49–58.

Langhinrichsen-Rohling, J., Neidig, P., & Thorn, G. (1995) Violent marriages: Gender differences in levels of current violence and past abuse. *Journal of Family Violence, 10,* 159–176.

Lau, R. R., Quadrel, M. J., & Hartman, K. A. (1990). Development and change of young adults' preventative health beliefs and behavior: Influence from parents and peers. *Journal of Health and Social Behavior, 31,* 240–259.

Leitenberg, H., Greenwald, E., & Cado, S. (1992). A retrospective study of long-term methods of coping with having been sexually abused during childhood. *Child abuse and neglect, 16,* 399–407.

Leonard, K. E. (1999). Alcohol use and husband marital aggression among newlywed couples. In X. B. Arriaga & S. Oskamp (Eds.), *Violence in intimate relationships* (pp. 113–135). Thousand Oaks, CA: Sage.

Leonard, K. E., & Senchak, M. (1993). Alcohol and premarital aggression among newlywed couples. *Journal of Studies on Alcohol 11*(Supp.), 96–108.

Leonard, K. E., & Senchak, M. (1996). Prospective prediction of husband marital aggression within newlywed couples. *Journal of Abnormal Psychology, 105,* 369–380.

Lundahl, L. H., Davis, T. M., Adesso, V. J., & Lukas, S. E. (1997). Alcohol expectancies: Effects of gender, age, and family history of alcoholism. *Addictive Behaviors, 22,* 115–125.

MacEwen, K. (1994). Refining the intergenerational transmission hypothesis. *Journal of Interpersonal Violence, 9,* 350–365.

MacEwen, K. E., & Barling, J. (1988). Multiple stressors, violence in the origin, and marital aggression: A longitudinal investigation. *Journal of Family Violence, 3,* 73–87.

Maisto, S. A., Carey, K. B., & Bradizza, C. M. (1999). Social learning theory. In H. T. Blane & K. E. Leonard (Eds.), *Psychological theories of drinking and alcoholism* (2nd ed.) (pp. 106–163). New York: Guilford.

Marshall, L. L., & Rose, P. (1988). Family of origin and courtship violence. *Journal of Counseling and Development, 66.* 414–418.

McKay, J. R., Maisto, S. A., & O'Farrell, T. J. (1996). Alcoholics' perceptions of factors in the onset and termination of relapses and the maintenance of abstinence: Results from a 30 month follow-up. *Psychology of Addictive Behaviors, 10,* 167–180.

McKee, S. A., & Hinson, R. E. (1999). If your father drinks then you had better like your mother: Maternal buffering effects involved in parental identification and paternal alcohol use, *Alcoholism: Clinical and Experimental Research, 23,* 118a.

Marlatt, G. A., & Gordon, J. R. (1985). *Relapse prevention.* New York: Guildford.

Mihalic, S. W., & Elliott, D. (1997). A social learning theory model of marital violence. *Journal of Family Violence, 12,* 21–47.

Miller, P., Smith, G., & Goldman, M. (1990). Emergence of alcohol expectancies in childhood: A possible critical period, *Journal of Studies on Alcohol, 51,* 343–349.

Mischel, W. (1973). Toward a cognitive social learning reconceptualization of personality. *Psychological Review, 80,* 252–283.

O'Keefe, M. (1997). Predictors of dating violence among high school students. *Journal of Interpersonal Violence, 12,* 546–568.

O'Leary, K. D. (1988). Physical aggression between spouses: A social learning perspective. In V. B. Van Hasselt, R. L. Morrison, A. S. Bellack, & M. Hersen (Eds.), *Handbook of family violence* (pp. 31–56). New York: Plenum.

O'Leary, K. D., & Arias, I. (1988). Prevalence, correlates, and development of spouse abuse. In V. De, P. Ray, & R. J. McMahon (Eds.), *Social learning and system approaches to marriage and the family* (pp. 104–127). New York: Brunner/Mazel.

O'Leary, K. D., Malone, J., & Tryee, A. (1994). Physical aggression in early marriage: Prerelationship and relationship effects. *Journal of Consulting and Clinical Psychology, 62,* 594–602.

Patterson, G. R. (1982). *A social learning approach (Vol. 3): Coercive family processes.* Eugene, OR: Castalia.

Perry, D. G., Perry, L. C., & Weiss, R. J. (1986). Cognitive social learning mediatros of aggression. *Child Development, 61,* 1310–1325.

Quigley, B. M., & Leonard, K. E. (1999). Husband alcohol expectancies, drinking, and marital-conflict styles as predictors of severe marital violence among newlywed couples. *Psychology of Addictive Behaviors, 13,* 49–59.

Riggs, D. S., & Caulfield, M. B. (1997). Expected consequences of male violence against their female dating partners. *Journal of Interpersonal Violence, 12,* 229–240.

Riggs, D. S., & O'Leary, K. D. (1989). A theoretical model of courtship aggression. In M. A. Pirog-Good & J. E. Stets (Eds.), *Violence in dating relationships* (pp. 53–71). New York: Praeger.

Riggs, D., O'Leary, K. D., & Breslin, F. C. (1990). Multiple correlates of physical aggression in dating couples. *Journal of Interpersonal Violence, 5,* 61–73.

Riggs, D., & O'Leary, K. D. (1996). Aggression between heterosexual dating partners: An examiniation of a causal model of courtship aggression. *Journal of Intrpersonal Violence, 11,* 519–540.

Rohsenow, D. J. (1983). Drinking habits and expectancies about alcohol's effects for self versus others. *Journal of Consulting and Clinical Psychology, 51,* 752–756.

Rotter, J. B. (1954). *Social learning theory and clinical psychology.* Englewood Cliffs, NJ: Prentice-Hall.

Schuckit, M. (1984). Prospective markers for alcoholism. In D. Goodwin, K. Van Dusen & S. Mednick (Eds.), *Longitudinal research in alcoholism.* Boston: Kluwer.

Sher, K. J, Walitzer, K. S., Wood, P. K., & Brent, E. E. (1991). Characteristics of children of alcoholics: Putative risk factors, substance use and abuse, and psychopathology. *Journal of Abnormal Psychology, 100,* 427–448.

Sher, K. J., Wood, M. D., Wood, P. K., & Raskin, G. (1996). Alcohol outcome expectancies and alcohol use: A latent variable cross-lagged panel design. *Journal of Abnormal Psychology, 105,* 561–574.

Sigelman, C. K., Berry, C. J., & Wiles, K. A. (1984). Violence in college students' dating relationships. *Journal of Applied Social Psychology, 5*, 530–548.

Smith, G., Goldman, M. S., Greenbaum, P. E., & Christiansen, B. A. (1995). Expectancy for social facilitation from drinking: The divergent paths of high-expectancy and low-expectancy adolescents. *Journal of Abnormal Psychology, 104*, 32–40.

Stacy, A. W., Newcomb, M. D., & Bentler, P. M. (1991). Cognitive motivation and drug use: A 9-year longitudinal study. *Journal of Abnormal Psychology, 100*, 867–873.

Stith, S. M., & Farley, S. C. (1993). A predictive model of male spousal violence. *Journal of Family Violence, 8*, 183–201.

Straus, M. A. (1980). Wife beating: How common and why? In M. A. Straus & G. T. Hotaling (Eds.), *The social causes of husband wife violence* (pp. 23–38). Minneapolis, MN: University of Minnesota Press.

Straus, M. A. (1994). *Beating the devil out of them.* New York: Lexington Books.

Tedeschi, J. T., & Felson, R. B. (1995). *Violence, aggression, and coercive actions.* Washington, DC: American Psychological Association.

Tontodonato, P., & Crew, B. K. (1992). Dating violence, social learning theory, and gender: A multivariate analysis. *Violence and Victims, 1*, 3–14.

Wall, A-M., & Wekerle, C. (1999, November). Childhood and adult experiences of substance abuse and intimate violence: Does coping style play a role? Paper presented at the annual meeting of the Association for the Advancement of Behaviour Therapy, Toronto, Ontario.

Wall, A-M., Wekerle, C., & Bissonnette, M. (2000). Childhood maltreatment, parental alcoholism, and beliefs about alcohol: Subgroup variation among alcohol-dependent adults. *Alcoholcism, 18*, 49–60.

Webb, J. A., & Baer, P. E. (1995). Influence of family disharmony and parental alcohol use on adolescent social skills, self-efficacy, and alcohol use. *Addictive Behaviors, 20*, 127–135.

Weinberg, N. Z., Dielman, T. E., Mandell, W., & Shope, J. T. (1994). Parental drinking and gender factors in the prediction of early adolescent alcohol use. *International Journal of the Addictions, 29*, 89–104.

Widom, C. S. (1989). Does violence beget violence ? A critical examination of the literature. *Psychological Bulletin, 106*, 3–28.

Wolfe, D. A. (1985). Child abusive parents: An empirical review and analysis. *Psychological Bulletin, 97*, 462–482.

Young, R. M., Oei, T. P., & Crook, G. M. (1991). Development of a drinking self-efficacy questionnaire. *Journal of Psychopathology & Behavioral Assessment, 13*, 1–15.

PART II

RELATIONSHIP VIOLENCE AND ADDICTION ACROSS THE LIFESPAN

7 Bullying, Sexual Harassment, Dating Violence, and Substance Use among Adolescents
Debra J. Pepler, Wendy M. Craig, Jennifer Connolly, and Kathryn Henderson

8 Sexual Assault and Relationship Violence among College Students: Examining the Role of Alcohol and Other Drugs
Mark D. Wood and Kenneth J. Sher

9 Alcohol and Substance Abuse in Marital Violence and Child Maltreatment
Kenneth E. Leonard

10 Substance Abuse and Interpersonal Violence in Older Adults
Mandra L. Rasmussen Hall and Victoria M. Follette

Debra J. Pepler
Wendy M. Craig
Jennifer Connolly
Kathryn Henderson

Bullying, Sexual Harassment, Dating Violence, and Substance Use among Adolescents

The central theme of this book relates to the overlap between relationship violence and substance use. As Wekerle and Wall (this volume) indicate, there is a strong link between substance use and violence in close relationships. Parents' abuse of their children and adults' abuse of an intimate partner both are associated with patterns of substance abuse. In this chapter we provide a developmental perspective on the association between relationship violence and substance use by examining the links between aggressive behaviors and substance use in early adolescence. We start by considering the scope of the overlapping problems of adolescent aggression and substance use, followed by a consideration of theoretical frameworks and empirical data on these problems, drawing upon findings from our own research program. We conclude by discussing implications and directions for future research.

☐ Overview of Our Research Program

The data for this chapter are drawn from our ongoing study of four cohorts of students initially enrolled in Grades 5 through 8 at seven elementary schools in a large Canadian city. For the present analyses, data were examined at one point in time in which we surveyed 922 students (462 boys and 460 girls) during the winter academic term. The mean age of the sample was 12.7 years ($SD = 0.88$). Two hundred and forty two children were in grade 6 (117 boys and 125 girls), 257 in grade 7 (123 boys and 134 girls), and 423 in grade 8 (222 boys and 201 girls). The children in the sample came primarily from middle-class backgrounds and were living with two parents (77%). All participants completed a questionnaire package that included measures of aggression and substance use.

Against the background of research in the field, we examine our own data from early

This research was funded by the Ontario Mental Health Foundation. We are indebted to the students, parents, and teachers who participated in this research.

adolescents to assess the individual characteristic of aggressive behavior and boys' and girls' susceptibility to peer pressure as key factors in understanding the early roots of the overlap between relationship violence and substance use. The three central questions for this chapter are: (1) What are the developmental (grade and gender) patterns of substance use?; (2) How do different forms of aggression relate to alcohol and drug use?; and (3) Does susceptibility to peer pressure relate to the likelihood that early adolescents will engage in alcohol and/or drug use?

☐ Scope of the Overlapping Problem of Adolescent Aggression and Substance Use

When assessing the nature of problem behaviors such as aggression and substance use in early adolescence, it is important to consider both the developmental features of adolescence and the patterns of behavior that have been established prior to adolescence. Early adolescence is a period of substantial developmental change. The major physical changes associated with pubertal development are accompanied by psychological and social changes. For example, in early adolescence, there is an increase in sexual awareness and a move into mixed-sex peer groups (Connolly, Pepler, Craig, & Taradash, in press). In our program of research, we are examining whether and how the form and context of aggression begin to change in early adolescence. We hypothesize that although aggressive children may continue to use physical aggression in early adolescence, they also diversify to more subtle forms of verbal aggression and sexual harassment. Furthermore, we are concerned that the aggressive styles children establish in same-sex peer interactions may transfer to different contexts, such as romantic relationships, forming the earliest roots of dating and other forms of relationship violence. To date, there is very little research on peer-to-peer violence and substance use in early adolescence.

Some children are at greater risk than others for moving along the aggressive pathway from childhood to adolescence. These same children may be at risk for experimenting early with substance use. Individual characteristics play an important role in determining the developmental course in early adolescence. Youth who enter adolescence with established patterns of aggressive behavior are particularly vulnerable to maladaptive outcomes, including both relationship violence and substance use (Cairns & Cairns, 1994, Farrington, 1991; Huesmann, Eron, Lefkowitz, & Walder, 1984). Furthermore, the extent to which adolescents engage in aggressive behavior increases the likelihood that they will also engage in other forms of deviant behavior such as substance use (Loeber, Farrington, Stouthamer-Loeber, & Van Kammen, 1998).

In examining the links between aggression and substance use, it is important to consider gender differences in both aggression and substance use. Boys' physical aggression has been identified as a primary predictor of later problems (Nagin & Tremblay, 1999). Less is known, however, about girls' aggression and whether girls who are aggressive are at risk for the same antisocial outcomes as boys. In their longitudinal research, Cairns and his colleagues (Cairns & Cairns, 1994; Cairns, Cairns, Neckerman, Ferguson, & Gariepy, 1989) were among the first researchers to elucidate gender differences in forms of aggressive expression. They describe boys' conflicts from childhood through adulthood as characterized by direct confrontation and physical aggression. In contrast, girls' conflicts tend to involve verbal and social aggression, such as rumor spreading, social ostracism, and group alienation. Cairns and Cairns (1994) found that when girls did report conflicts involving physical aggression, they were more likely to be with boys than with girls. In this chapter, we consider three forms of boys' and girls' aggression that are salient during early adolescence and may be relevant to relationship violence in later life: bullying, dating aggression, and sexual harassment. We hypothesize that children who engage in these forms of aggression are at a higher risk for substance use than those who do not engage in these forms of aggression, given the generalization of antisocial behavior from one form to another (Loeber, et al., 1998).

Substance Use

As with other forms of antisocial behavior, there is a predictable developmental trajectory in substance use, with early alcohol use serving as a gateway to use of more serious substances. For example, Loeber and his colleagues (1998) found that substance use generally starts with alcohol use (beer and wine, followed by liquor). The use of alcohol is followed by the use of marijuana and other illegal substances such as crack and heroin (Loeber et al., 1998). Research indicates that fewer girls engage in substance use, particularly drugs, compared to boys (Abdelrahman, Rodriguez, Ryan, French, & Weinbaum, 1998; Duncan, Duncan, & Hops, 1994). Our concern is that there may be a group of girls who engage in aggression and substance use who may be at particular risk for troubled relationships later in life.

For our analyses of alcohol and drug use, we developed indices using confirmatory factor analyses of four items from the Self-Report Early Delinquency Scale (Moffitt & Silva, 1988), and one item from the Youth Self-Report Questionnaire (Achenbach & Edelbrock, 1991). We had originally intended to develop a single combined alcohol and drug use index, but the analyses supported the superiority of a two-factor model. Three items were summed to produce an alcohol use index: getting drunk on alcoholic drinks; buying or drinking alcoholic drinks (beer, wine) in bars or any other public place; and stealing beer or wine from a shop, your parents' home, or other places. Two items were summed to produce a drug use index: smoking pot or marijuana or hash, and using alcohol or drugs for nonmedical purposes. The alcohol and drug use data were dichotomized into categories of having used and not having used.

In our study of early adolescents, there were main effects for gender and grade in reported alcohol use. Figure 7.1 illustrates the developmental trends in reported alcohol use. Similar to other studies, boys reported more alcohol use than did girls. Additionally, older children reported greater alcohol use than did younger children. Large national surveys

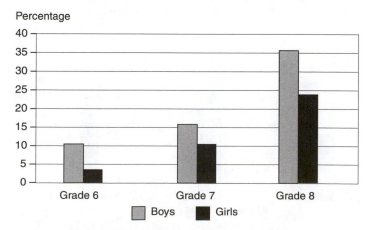

FIGURE 7.1. Prevalence of alcohol use.

have found that gender differences in alcohol use decrease with age. Among grade 12 students, there are no differences between boys' and girls' lifetime use; however, boys engaged in more problem drinking, such as binge drinking (Windle, 1999). In our study, the gender and grade effects for drug use were similar to those for alcohol use. The developmental trends in the prevalence of reported drug use are depicted in Figure 7.2. There was a main effect for gender: Boys acknowledged greater drug use than girls. As expected, older children were more likely to report having used drugs than younger children.

In examining the link between substance use and aggression in our study, we assessed the relative risks of engaging in alcohol and drug use for both boys and girls who report being aggressive with their peers. We now examine the links between antisocial behavior and substance use.

☐ Theoretical Framework for Considering the Overlap between Aggression and Substance Use

In considering the links between aggression and substance use early in the developmental trajectory, we can draw from two overriding themes that have guided the work on adolescent violence and substance use. First, there has been a focus on the individual characteristic of antisocial behavior as an important predictor of later relationship violence. Second, there has been an emphasis on considering adolescents' problem behaviors against the background of the sociocultural context of development during this period. The peer group is a central system in adolescence that may influence the development of both substance use and aggression problems. Similar to the processes related to delinquency, there may be substantial exposure to substance use and strong positive reinforcement for participating in substance use within deviant peer groups (White, Bates, & Johnson, 1991; Windle, 1999). Although research is not conclusive at this point, it is likely that the link between aggression and substance use in early adolescence can be best understood with a consideration of multiple, and perhaps reciprocal, influences (Wagner, 1996).

☐ Aggressive Behavior as a Risk for Substance Use

When children are aggressive, they are at risk for a variety of problems as they develop through adolescence and into adulthood. Longitudinal research reveals that children who

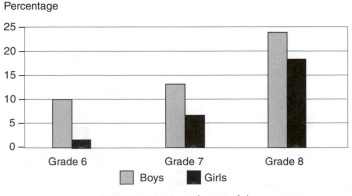

FIGURE 7.2. Prevalence of drug use.

are aggressive in elementary school are at risk of continuing their aggressive behavior patterns throughout their lives (Farrington, 1991; Huesmann et al., 1984). Their aggression often emerges in close relationships in the form of child abuse or marital violence. Longitudinal studies also indicate that aggressive behavior in childhood predicts movement into other forms of antisocial behavior, such as substance use. Therefore, from the time of early adolescence when experimentation with substance use begins, the link between relationship violence and substance use may already be germinating due to the common individual characteristic of antisocial behavior (White & Hansell, 1998). In other words, boys and girls who are experiencing problems of emotional and behavioral regulation in the conduct domain may be those who also will be undercontrolled in their early move into substance use (Windle, 1999). Another individual characteristic of interest in examining the convergence of the links between aggression and substance use is gender. Within this chapter, we examine the associations between aggressive behaviors and substance use for both boys and girls.

Aggressive Behaviors

Numerous longitudinal studies highlight the link between aggressive behaviors in childhood and substance use (White, 1997; White, Loeber, Stouthamer-Loeber, & Farrington, 1999). The dominant perspective in understanding this link is that both aggressive behaviors and substance use are part of a general antisocial behavior problem profile (Jessor & Jessor, 1977; Loeber et al., 1998; Patterson, Reid, & Dishion, 1992). A recent developmental analysis revealed that during adolescence, the longitudinal relationships between substance use and violence were found to be reciprocal (White et al., 1999). The risk factors associated with antisocial behavior problems are often similar across a range of behaviors. Loeber and his colleagues (1998) found that the risk factors for substance use were generally (but not completely) a subset of the risk factors for delinquency. In support of the perspective that problem behaviors generalize with development, longitudinal research has shown substantial continuity in problem behaviors from childhood to early adulthood. For example, Cairns and Cairns (1994) found that aggression in childhood was a significant predictor of substance use, as well as a range of other antisocial behaviors in early adulthood. In their study, about half of the children who identified as highly aggressive in childhood were maladjusted as adults. These young men and women were plagued by multiple problems including substance use, school dropout, teen parenthood, and criminal convictions. Therefore, from a developmental perspective, we are concerned that early adolescents who engage in aggressive behaviors will be at risk for engaging in substance use and will be on a path to many more significant problems in the future.

☐ Forms of Aggressive Behavior

To provide a developmental perspective on the early links between aggression and substance use, we draw from our longitudinal research program on aggression and victimization in early adolescence. Our current research program emerged from our earlier work on bullying in elementary school (Atlas & Pepler, 1998; Craig & Pepler, 1997; Craig, Pepler, & Atlas, 2000; Pepler, Craig, Zeigler, & Charach, 1995). As we observed bullying among elementary school children, we developed many questions and concerns about the long-term implications of bullying others or being bullied. Bullying is the assertion of power through aggression. Our current research program is based on the assumption that as children grow older, the form of bullying changes and the context of bullying expands (e.g., to romantic relationships). We contend that the combined use of power and aggression found in playground bullying is a key component of sexual harassment, gang attacks, date violence, criminal assault, marital violence, child abuse, workplace harassment, and elder abuse. In our study of adolescents, we have measured many aspects of bullying and antisocial behavior in order to track the development of problems such as sexual harassment, dating aggression, and other deviant behaviors. It is within the context of this study that we are able to consider the earliest links between relationship violence and substance use.

Against the backdrop of this book, we consider three forms of early adolescents' aggression in relation to substance use: bullying, dating aggression, and sexual harassment. We created dichotomous versions of the three aggression variables. Students were classified as bullies if they indicated that they had bullied over the previous six weeks, but had not been victimized. Students were classified as having engaged in dating aggression if they acknowledged using physical, verbal, or social aggression with their romantic partner. Similarly, students were classified as having engaged in sexual harassment if they reported using any form of verbal or physical harassment with a same- or opposite-sex peer. Table 7.1 provides a summary of the distribution of children who reported engaging in the various forms of aggression and substance use. To examine the association between the three forms of aggression and the two types of substance use, we first conducted six 2 × 2 chi-square analyses for boys and girls separately. Using a Bonferroni correction, the significance levels for these associations were set to .008. The associations of the three forms of aggression with substance use are explored in the following sections.

Bullying

Bullying is interpersonal aggression in which the bully always has more power than the victim. A critical feature of bullying is that it is repeated over time. When bullies are repeatedly successful in attacking their victims and causing distress, the power differential in their relationship becomes increasingly consolidated (Pepler, Craig, & O'Connell, 1999). Through these experiences, bullies learn to express and establish interpersonal power through aggression. We are concerned that this lesson will carry forward in many other forms of abuse throughout the lifespan (Pepler, Craig, & Connolly, 1997). If this is the case, then the associations of bullying and early substance use might provide some insights into the later links between relationship violence and substance abuse.

TABLE 7.1. Distribution of children by type of aggression and substance use

		Boys				Girls			
		Alcohol		Drugs		Alcohol		Drugs	
		Yes	No	Yes	No	Yes	No	Yes	No
Bullying	Yes	77	113	64	126	34	81	30	85
	No	34	238	17	255	27	318	17	328
Dating Aggression	Yes	22	17	21	18	18	21	14	25
	No	72	138	46	164	24	137	19	142
Sexual Harassment	Yes	75	90	60	105	30	72	24	78
	No	36	261	21	276	31	327	23	335

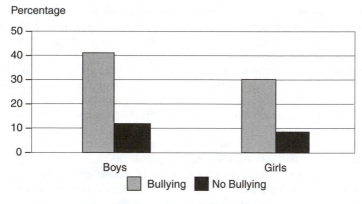

FIGURE 7.3. Bullying and alcohol use.

As Figure 7.3 illustrates, bullying was significantly associated with alcohol use for both boys, $\chi^2(1) = 48.14$, $p < .001$ and girls, $\chi^2(1) = 35.44$, $p < .001$. The odds ratios ([OR] i.e., the ratio of conditional odds) indicate that both boys (OR = 4.76) and girls (OR = 4.94) who bullied others were almost five times more likely to report alcohol use than boys and girls who did not report bullying. As Figure 7.4 illustrates, a similarly strong association was found between bullying and drug use for boys, $\chi^2(1) = 58.23$, $p < .001$ and for girls, $\chi^2(1) = 42.10$, $p < .001$. The odds ratios indicate that both boys (OR = 7.61) and girls (OR = 6.77) who bullied were about seven times more likely to report drug use than boys and girls who did not report bullying.

Dating Aggression

We were concerned that aggression within a dating relationship may also be linked to substance abuse. Within our current research, we have hypothesized that the behavioral style that characterizes bullying within the peer group (combined power and aggression) may transfer to the context of romantic relationships. We expected that the changing contexts for aggression reflect the general shift from same-sex peer groups to mixed-sex

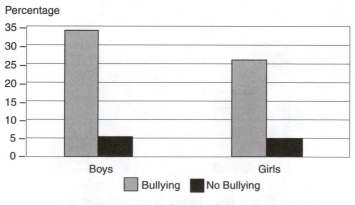

FIGURE 7.4. Bullying and drug use.

peer groups in early adolescence. Our preliminary data indicate that young adolescents who bully others are more likely to be involved in a romantic relationship and more likely to report verbal and physical aggression in these romantic relationships compared to boys and girls who do not bully (Connolly et al., 2000). If dating relationships provide a context in which bullies can experience their power and dominance, interactions in these relationships may lay the foundation for later relationship violence. Therefore, the early associations between this form of aggression and substance use may be relevant in understanding the later links between relationship violence and substance abuse. Although this link has been understudied in early adolescence, Wekerle, Hawkins, and Wolfe (2001) found that relationship aggression (both to and from the partner) was a significant predictor of drug use for females in mid-adolescence (ages 14–16).

Data on dating aggression exist only for a subset of our sample because only some of the participants had dating experience at the time of data collection. When including dating variables, therefore, the sample comprised 449 children. The gender by grade level breakdown is as follows: 123 junior boys, 126 senior boys, 101 junior girls, and 99 senior girls. The questions on dating aggression included physical, verbal, and social forms of aggression directed at a romantic partner.

In assessing the association between dating aggression and alcohol use, we found a significant relation for girls, $\chi^2(1) = 18.48$, $p < .001$ and a trend for boys, $\chi^2(1) = 6.85$, $p = .009$. Figure 7.5 illustrates the overlap between dating aggression and alcohol use. The odds ratios indicate that if they reported dating aggression, girls (OR = 4.77) were about five times more likely and boys (OR = 2.48) were about two and a half times more likely to use alcohol compared to girls and boys who did not report being aggressive with their dating partner. As illustrated in Figure 7.6, there was an association between dating aggression and drug use for boys, $\chi^2(1) = 17.06$, $p < .001$ as well as for girls, $\chi^2(1) = 12.26$, $p < .001$. The odds ratios indicate that both boys (OR = 4.16) and girls (OR = 4.00) who engaged in dating aggression were four times more likely to report using drugs than those students who were not aggressive with their dating partners.

Sexual Harassment

The final form of aggression in early adolescence that we have considered is sexual harassment. Since emerging sexuality in early adolescence is a highly sensitive developmental

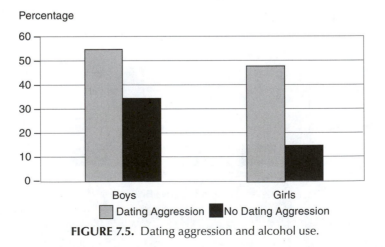

FIGURE 7.5. Dating aggression and alcohol use.

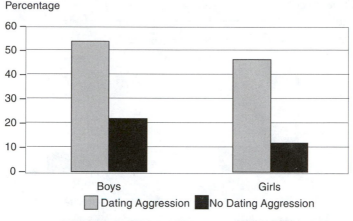

FIGURE 7.6. Dating aggression and drug use.

issue, there is considerable potential for aggressive students to assert their power by targeting others' vulnerabilities around sexual issues. Over 80% of high school youth report having experienced sexual harassment from peers (American Association of University Women [AAUW], 1993). Our preliminary data indicate that by early adolescence, as the peer group becomes increasingly blended along gender lines, sexual harassment emerges (McMaster, Connolly, Pepler, & Craig, 1999). Given that sexual harassment is a form of aggression that emerges in early adolescence, we examined the link between this form of interpersonal aggression and substance use.

The association between sexual harassment and alcohol use was significant for both boys, $\chi^2(1) = 64.57$, $p < .001$ and girls, $\chi^2(1) = 29.72$, $p < .001$. The overlap between sexual harassment and alcohol use is illustrated in Figure 7.7. The odds ratios indicate that girls (OR = 4.47) and boys (OR = 5.93) who acknowledged sexually harassing others were between four and six times more likely to use alcohol than those who did not sexually harass their peers. Finally, as illustrated in Figure 7.8, the associations between aggression and drug use also were evident in the sexual harassment data for both boys, $\chi^2(1) = 62.95$, $p < .001$ and girls, $\chi^2(1) = 25.32$, $p < .001$. The odds ratios indicate that, if they acknowledged

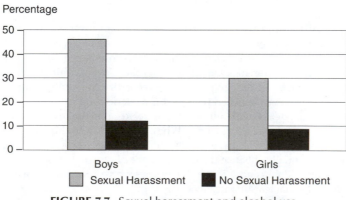

FIGURE 7.7. Sexual harassment and alcohol use.

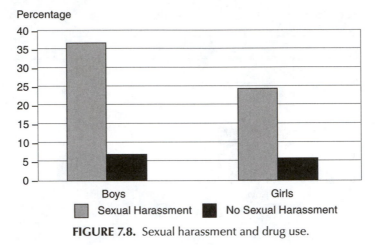

Percentage

FIGURE 7.8. Sexual harassment and drug use.

sexual harassment, boys (OR = 7.13) were seven times more likely to use drugs, and girls (OR = 4.42) were over four times more likely to use drugs than those students who did not sexually harass their peers.

When these data are considered together, there appears to be considerable overlap between various forms of aggressive behavior and substance use. Our data are similar to those of Loeber and his colleagues (1998): We find the extent to which early adolescents engage in aggressive behavior increases the likelihood that they also will engage in substance use. The patterns of association between the three forms of aggression and substance use are remarkably similar for boys and girls. From a developmental perspective, these data collected in early adolescence suggest that the overlap between relationship violence and substance use emerges in the earliest phases of substance use. Furthermore, the individual characteristic of aggressive behavior is salient in accounting for the likelihood of substance use. Boys and girls who show signs of aggressive behavior in their interactions with peers are much more likely to have experimented with alcohol and drugs compared to their nonaggressive peers. In the next section, we consider the potential influence of peers in promoting substance use.

☐ Peer Influences in Substance Use

The ecological theoretical perspective further informs our investigation of the potential link between aggression and substance use (Bronfenbrenner, 1979). When studying the development of both aggressive behavior and substance use, it is important to consider not only individual characteristics, but also influential factors within children's social environments. From a theoretical perspective, we recognize the multiple influences in development: The confluence between relationship violence and substance use is likely related not only to characteristics of individual adolescents, but also to other systemic factors, such as family, peer, and media influences (White et al., 1991). In this chapter, we focus on peer influences in the link between aggression and substance use because dynamics within the peer group potentially enhance the development of both antisocial behavior and substance use in early adolescence. These dynamics involve processes of association with deviant peers and social learning influences within these peer groups.

As children approach adolescence, peers become increasingly important and influen-

tial in their lives. In this developmental phase, peer groups become tightly organized social structures with internal norms and codes of behavior (Brown, 1990). In nonaggressive
adolescent groups, the internal group norms and codes become less tolerant of antisocial
behavior. Given this trend, aggressive children may find themselves increasingly isolated
from mainstream peer groups, leading them to drift into deviant peer groups where aggression continues to be reinforced (Cairns & Cairns, 1994). Deviant peer groups provide
a training ground for many forms of antisocial behavior. In these groups, adolescents are
often validated for their use of power and aggression, diversify in their repertoire of aggressive behaviors, and are provided with opportunities to engage in specific delinquent
behaviors such as substance use and gang involvement (Thornberry & Krohn, 1997).

Kandel (1973) was among the first researchers to note the association between adolescent substance use and peers' substance use. Since then, numerous studies have pointed
to the role of deviant peers in providing salient models and reinforcing substance use and
other delinquent behaviors (e.g., Dishion, Capaldi, Spracklen, & Li, 1995; Dishion & Loeber,
1985; Dishion, McCord, & Poulin, 1999; Elliott, Huizinga, & Ageton, 1985; Warr, 1993).
During the late elementary school years, students' conformity with peers' antisocial behaviors
is at its highest (Berndt, 1979). Therefore, we hypothesized that an adolescent's susceptibility
to these deviant peer influences is predictive of substance use in early adolescence.

We conducted regression analyses to examine the extent to which susceptibility to peer
pressure predicted alcohol and drug use, above and beyond the relation with the aggression scores. Since only a subset of the students had romantic partners and reported on
dating aggression, the regressions were run with all of the participants using the scores of
bullying and sexual harassment to predict alcohol and drug use. In all models, we controlled for the effects of gender, age, and socioeconomic status by entering these variables
in an initial block. In the second block, we entered the aggression scores followed by
susceptibility to peer influence scores. Preliminary analyses indicated that interaction terms
(i.e., gender × aggression, age × aggression, etc.) had very little predictive power, and so
these terms were not entered into the models. The exception was the age × peer influence
interaction term, which proved consistently predictive across a number of models; thus, it
was entered in a fourth block in each regression model. The data for the regressions are
presented in Table 7.2.

**TABLE 7.2. Prediction of alcohol and drug use by bullying and sexual harassment and
susceptibility to peer influence**

Predictors	Alcohol Use				Drug Use			
	b	S.E. b	β	ΔR^2	b	S.E. b	β	ΔR^2
Step 1								
Gender	−0.12	0.04	−.09**		−0.07	0.03	−.09**	
Age	0.32	0.05	.23**		0.15	0.03	.17**	
SES	0.00	0.00	.05	.07**	0.00	0.00	.06	.04**
Step 2								
Bullying	0.42	0.04	.31**		0.30	0.03	.34**	
Sex Harassment	0.05	0.00	.30**	.27**	0.04	0.00	.35**	.31**
Step 3								
Peer Orientation	0.11	0.02	.21**	.04**	0.07	0.01	.20**	.03**
Step 4								
Peer Orientation by Age	0.11	0.02	2.80**	.02**	0.05	0.01	1.94**	.01**

*$p < .05$ **$p < .01$

The regression equation for alcohol was significant, accounting for 40.2% of the variance in reported alcohol use. As expected, given the overlap discussed earlier, bullying and sexual harassment were both significant predictors of alcohol use by the early adolescents. Above and beyond aggression, students' reports of being susceptible to peer influence and the interaction of age with susceptibility to peer influence also were significant predictors of alcohol use. With increasing age, susceptibility to peer influence became a stronger predictor of alcohol use.

We conducted a similar series of regression analyses for students' reports of drug use. As with alcohol use, the regression equation using aggression variables and susceptibility to peer pressure was significant and predicted 39.8% of the variance in reported drug use. Similar to the prediction of alcohol use, bullying and sexual harassment were both significant predictors of drug use by early adolescents. Above and beyond aggression, students' reports of being susceptible to peer influence and the interaction of age with susceptibility to peer influence also were significant predictors of drug use. With increasing age, susceptibility to peer influence became a stronger predictor of alcohol use.

In summary, our data suggest that early adolescents' susceptibility to negative peer influences helps explain the variation in substance use, above and beyond the strong relationship between aggression and alcohol and drug use. These data are consistent with those of many others who cite peer influence in early adolescence as an important process that draws children to substance use (e.g., Dishion et al., 1995; Thornberry & Krohn, 1997).

☐ Theoretical Implications and Future Directions

The association between relationship violence and substance use has been well established in studies of college students and adults. In trying to understand this association, a critical question is whether individuals with a tendency to be aggressive also use substances or whether those who use substances become aggressive in close relationships. For this chapter, we have drawn from a developmental perspective to examine the association between interpersonal aggression and substance use with a sample of early adolescents. Although we cannot establish directionality with concurrent assessments of aggression and substance use, we can examine whether this association is present in the earliest stages of substance use. In studying the development of problem behaviors, current theory and empirical findings direct the focus to characteristics of individual children and to the social influences in their lives. Therefore, we have assessed the individual characteristics of aggressive behavior problems as a risk factor for movement into substance use. In addition, we have examined susceptibility to peer influence as a social process in early adolescence that may elucidate risks for substance use.

To examine whether individual patterns of aggressive behaviors are associated with substance use, we chose to focus on three forms of aggression that are developmentally salient in early adolescence and are presumed to lay the foundation for subsequent relationship violence in adulthood. The first form of aggression was bullying—interpersonal aggression in which the bully uses a position of power to attack his or her victim. We believe that the lessons learned about expressing and establishing interpersonal power in childhood bullying pave the way to many forms of relationship violence in adulthood. The combined use of power and aggression is a characteristic of marital violence, child abuse, and elder abuse. Our analyses indicated that both boys and girls who reported bullying others were at significant risk for substance use before entering high school. For every one boy or girl who did not report bullying but used alcohol, there were approximately five boys and girls who reported both bullying and using alcohol. The risks for drug use associated with bullying were even higher than those for alcohol. For every boy and girl who did not bully, but reported using drugs, there were almost eight boys and seven girls who bullied and reported that they used drugs. The association between bullying and substance use also was reflected in the regression analyses. Bullying was a significant predictor of both drug and alcohol use. These data indicate that both boys and girls who use their positions of power to bully others in late elementary school are already much more likely than their nonbullying peers to report that they have experience using alcohol and drugs.

The second form of aggression we examined was dating aggression. In the context of this book, in which the links between intimate violence and substance use are being explored, we examined the possibility of these being associated in the very earliest stages of romantic relationships. We asked early adolescents who had a romantic partner whether they had used physical, verbal, or social aggression with their partner. As with bullying, we found a strong association between reporting aggression in romantic relationships and reporting substance use. For the boys, there was a trend in the association of dating aggression with alcohol use; for the girls, this association was significant. For each boy who did not report dating aggression and used alcohol, there were more than twice as many boys who were aggressive in their dating relationships and used substances. The risk for girls was higher: Girls who reported dating aggression were almost five times more likely to acknowledge alcohol use than those who were not aggressive with their romantic partners.

Similar patterns were found in the associations between boys' and girls' dating aggression and drug use. Boys and girls who reported being aggressive in their dating relationships were approximately four times more likely to report drug use than boys and girls who did not report being aggressive in their dating relationship. Therefore, when we examine aggressive interactions in the early romantic relationships of young people, the association between aggression and substance use is clearly evident. Given the stability of antisocial behavior problems (Cairns & Cairns, 1994; Farrington, 1991; Huesmann et al., 1984), we can postulate that these children who are being aggressive with their dating partner and using substances prior to high school are at high risk to become young men and women who are aggressive in their intimate relationships and use substances in late adolescence and adulthood.

The final form of aggression that we examined in relation to substance use was sexual harassment. This form of aggressive behavior is salient during early adolescence when emerging sexuality is a key issue. From a developmental perspective, we recognize that sexual harassment is a form of bullying that arises during early adolescence. Sexual harassment combines power and aggression: Students who sexually harass their peers derive power from the knowledge of another's vulnerability around sexual issues and use this power as a vehicle for aggression. We found a strong association between sexual harassment and both forms of substance use. For every one girl and boy who did not sexually harass but reported alcohol use, there were about five girls and six boys who reported that they sexually harassed others and used alcohol. Similar patterns were found for drug use. For every one boy or girl who did not sexually harass others and yet used drugs, there were approximately seven boys and four girls who sexually harassed others and used drugs.

These results highlight the link between interpersonal aggression and substance use very early in the developmental trajectory. The individual characteristic of aggressive behavior appears to be an important factor in understanding the move into substance use. Those children who are aggressive in late elementary school are much more likely to report substance use than their nonaggressive peers. In the present analyses, there were no gender differences in the strength of associations: The risk of being aggressive for engaging in substance use was similarly strong for boys and girls.

From a theoretical perspective, we recognize the multiple influences in development. In these analyses, therefore, we looked beyond individual factors to consider the potential influence of peers on substance use. There is a large body of research linking peer influence to both deviant behavior and substance use in adolescence (e.g., Cairns & Cairns, 1994; Handel, 1973). In our analyses, children's reports of susceptibility to peer influence were significant predictors of their substance use above and beyond their aggressive behavior. In other words, the more that students indicated they would be negatively influenced by peers, the more likely it was that they reported using alcohol and drugs. At this point with concurrent correlational data, we cannot infer that susceptibility to negative peer influences causes young adolescents to use alcohol and drugs. We do know, however, from other analyses of our data, that the aggressive students in our sample reported being more susceptible to peer pressure than their nonaggressive peers (Pepler, Kent, Smith, Craig, & Connolly, 1999). The present regression analyses indicate that the combined effect of being aggressive and susceptible to peer pressure accounts for a substantial proportion of the variance in early adolescents' alcohol and drug use.

These analyses of the link between aggression and substance use in early adolescence highlight the need for longitudinal research that assesses the behavior of individual adolescents and also the behavior of their peers. With a prospective design, we could identify not only the risk factors associated with aggression and substance use, but also the unfolding patterns in both the transformation of aggression and the intensification of substance use from adolescence into adulthood. Such longitudinal research might elucidate the gateway and pathways in both substance use and relationship violence. With data from peers, we could assess the extent to which substance use among close friends and peers in the network predicts increases in adolescents' substance use. Family factors related to the development of both relationship violence and substance use in adolescence also are important domains for future research.

The analyses in the present chapter highlight important directions for prevention and early intervention to address the overlap in substance use and relationship violence. Prevention programs should highlight the skills and social cognitions that are essential to support positive relationships at the time that romantic relationships are beginning to form. Our data suggest that if prevention programs are not introduced until high school, many youth will have well-established antisocial behavior patterns and will already be involved in substance use. It is clear from our analyses that young adolescents who are aggressive with their peers are at increasing risk for substance use with each passing year. Identifying these youth and providing the necessary supports to them and their families would be the logical first step in averting their move to serious substance use and relationship violence. The data on susceptibility to peer pressure suggest that both prevention and intervention efforts need to take into account the potential for deviant peer processes. Prevention efforts can promote a supportive peer community and the skills required to withstand peer pressure. Interventions with aggressive youth must avoid aggregating these youth as the opportunity to engage in substance use and antisocial behavior is often enhanced in deviant peer groups (Dishion et al., 1999). Finally, the data from the present analyses highlight the relevance of a developmental perspective to understanding and addressing major social concerns, such as family violence. We have shown that the association between relationship aggression and substance use emerges early in development—before high school when a small number of students are starting to experiment with alcohol and other substances. It is in these early stages that risky behaviors are likely to be most amenable to intervention. By identifying and supporting children who are already relying on aggression to establish power in relationships, we may be able to help them deviate from the maladaptive pathway of relationship violence and substance use.

☐ References

Achenbach, T., & Edelbrock, C. (1991). *Manual for the Youth Self-Report and Profile.* Burlington VT: University of Vermont Department of Psychiatry.

Abdelrahman, A., Rodriguez, G., Ryan, J., French, J., & Weinbaum, D. (1998). The epidemiology of substance use among middle school students: The impact of school, familial, community, and individual risk factors. *Journal of Child and Adolescent Substance Abuse, 8,* 55–75.

American Association of University Women. (1993). *Hostile hallways. The AAUW survey on sexual harassment in America's school.* Washington, DC: American Association of University Women Educational Foundation.

Atlas, R., & Pepler, D.J. (1998). Observations of bullying in the classroom. *American Journal of Educational Research, 92,* 86–99.

Berndt, T. J. (1979). Developmental changes in conformity to peers and parents. *Developmental Psychology, 15,* 608–616.

Bronfenbrenner, U. (1979). The ecology of human development. Cambridge, MA: Harvard University Press.

Brown, B. B. (1990). Peer groups and peer cultures. In S. S. Feldman & G. R. Elliott (Eds.), *At the Threshold: The developing adolescent* (pp.171–196). Cambridge, MA: Harvard University Press.

Cairns, R. B., & Cairns, B. D. (1994). *Lifelines and risk: Pathways of youth in our time.* Cambridge, MA: Cambridge University Press.

Cairns, R. B., Cairns, B. D., Neckerman, H. J., Ferguson, L. L., & Gariepy, J. (1989). Growth aggression: 1. Childhood to early adolescence. *Developmental Psychology, 25,* 320–330.

Connolly, J., Pepler, D. J., Craig, W. M., & Taradash, A. (2000). Rating experiences in early adolescence. *Journal of Child Maltreatment, 5,* 299–310.

Craig, W., & Pepler, D. (1997). Observations of bullying and victimization in the schoolyard. *Canadian Journal of School Psychology, 2,* 41–60.

Craig, W., Pepler, D., & Atlas, R. (2000). Observations of bullying in the playground and in the classroom. *School Psychology International, 21,* 22–36.

Dishion, T., Capaldi, D., Spracklen, K., & Li, F. (1995). Peer ecology of male adolescent drug use. *Development and Psychopathology, 7,* 803–824.

Dishion, T., & Loeber, R. (1985). Male adolescent marijuana and alcohol use: The role of parents and peers revisited. *American Journal of Drug and Alcohol Abuse, 11,* 11–25.

Dishion, T., McCord, J., & Poulin, F. (1999) When interventions harm: Peer grops and problem behavior. *American Psychologist, 54,* 755–765.

Duncan, T., Duncan, S., & Hops, H. (1994). The effects of family cohesiveness and peer encouragement on the development of adolescent alcohol use: A cohort-sequential approach to the analysis of longitudinal data. *Journal of Studies on Alcohol, 55,* 588–599.

Elliott, D. S., Huizinga, D., & Ageton, S. (1985). *Explaining delinquency and drug use.* Beverly Hills, CA: Sage.

Farrington, D. P. (1991). Childhood aggression and adult violence: Early precursors and later life outcomes. In D. Pepler & K. Rubin (Eds.), *The development and treatment of childhood aggression.* Hillsdale, NJ: Erlbaum.

Huesmann, L. R., Eron, L. D., Lefkowitz, M. M., & Walder, L. O. (1984). Stability of aggression over time and generations. *Developmental Psychology, 20,* 1120–1134.

Jessor, R., & Jessor, S. L. (1977). *Problem behavior and psychosocial development.* New York: Academic Press.

Kandel, D. (1973). Adolescent marihuana use: Role of parents and peers. *Science, 181,* 1067–1070.

Loeber, R., Farrington, D. P., Stouthamer-Loeber, M., Van Kammen, W. (1998) Multiple risk factors for multiproblem boys: Co-occurrence of delinquency, substance use, attention deficit, conduct problems, physical aggression, covert behavior, depressed mood, and shy/withdrawn behavior.

In R. Jessor (Ed.) *New perspectives on adolescent risk behavior*. Cambridge, MA: Cambridge University Press.

McMaster, L., Connolly, J., Pepler, D., & Craig, W. (1999). Peer-to-peer sexual harassment among early adolescents: A developmental perspective. Manuscript submitted for publication.

Moffit, T. E., & Silva, P. A. (1988). Self-reported delinquency: Results from an instrument for New Zealand. *Australian and New Zealand Journal of Criminology, 21*, 227–240.

Nagin, D., & Tremblay, R. (1999). Trajectories of boys' physical aggression, opposition, and hyperactivity on the path to physically violent and nonviolent juvenile delinquency. *Child Development, 70*, 1181–1196.

Patterson, G. R., Reid, J. B., & Dishion, T. J. (1992). *Antisocial Boys*. Eugene, OR: Castilia Publishing.

Pepler, D., Craig, W., & Connolly, J. (1997). *Bullying and victimization: The problems and solutions for school-aged children*. Fact Sheet Prepared for the National Crime Prevention Council of Canada. Ottawa, Ontario: Government of Canada.

Pepler, D. J., Craig, W., & O'Connell, P. (1999). Understanding bullying from a dynamic systems perspective. In A. Slater & D. Muir (Eds.), *Developmental psychology: An advanced reader* (pp. 440–451). Malden, MA: Blackwell.

Pepler, D. J., Craig, W., Ziegler, S., & Charach, A. (1995). An evaluation of an anti-bullying intervention in Toronto schools. *Canadian Journal of Community Mental Health, 13*, 95–110.

Pepler, D., Kent, D., Smith, C., Craig, W., & Connolly, J. (1999, April). Aggressive girls in early adolescence: Risk in Relationships? Paper presented at the meetings of the Society for Research in Child Development, Albuquerque, NM.

Thornberry, T., & Krohn, M. (1997). Peers, drug use, and delinquency. In D. M. Stoff, J. Breiling, & J. Maser (Eds.), *Handbook of antisocial behavior*. New York: Wiley.

Wagner, E. F. (1996). Substance use and violent behavior in adolescence. *Aggression and Violent Behavior, 1*, 375–387.

Warr, M. (1993). Parents, peers, and delinquency. *Social Forces, 72*, 247–264.

Wekerle, C., Hawkins, D. L., & Wolfe, D. A. (2001). *Adolescent substance use: The contribution of childhood maltreatment and violence in teen partnerships*. Manuscript submitted for publication.

White, H. R. (1997). Alcohol, illicit drugs, and violence. In D. Stoff, J. Brieling, & J. Maser (Eds.), *Handbook of antisocial behavior* (pp. 511–523). New York: Wiley.

White, H. R., Bates, M., & Johnson, V. (1991). Learning to drink: Familial, peer, and media influences. In D. J. Pittman, H. R. White, H. R. et al. *Society, culture, and drinking patterns reexamined* (pp. 177–197). New Brunswick, NJ: Rutgers Center of Alcohol Studies.

White, H. R., & Hansell, S. (1998). Acute and long-term effects of drug use on aggression from adolescence into adulthood. *Journal of Drug Issues, 28*, 837–858.

White, H. R., Loeber, R., Stouthamer-Loeber, M., & Farrington, D. (1999). Developmental associations between substance use and violence. *Development and Psychopathology, 11*, 785–803.

Windle, M. (1999). *Alcohol use among adolescents: Developmental and clinical psychology and psychiatry*. Thousand Oaks, CA: Sage.

8

CHAPTER

Mark D. Wood
Kenneth J. Sher

Sexual Assault and Relationship Violence among College Students: Examining the Role of Alcohol and Other Drugs

The college years are a uniquely challenging developmental period. For most, entry into college is a watershed ontogenetic event—the initial, sustained foray into adult roles where individuals, for the first time, are largely unsupervised by parents or other adult authorities. Perhaps then, it should not be surprising that problems like substance abuse and violent behavior are comparatively frequent occurrences among college students. Indeed, epidemiological data indicate that alcohol and illicit drug use peak between the ages of 18 and 24 (Chen & Kandel, 1995), with college students demonstrating roughly comparable levels of illicit drug use and slightly higher levels of heavy drinking than their noncollege attending age peers (Johnson, O'Malley, & Bachman, 1999). Likewise, sexual assault and relationship violence are most prevalent in late adolescence and young adulthood (Federal Bureau of Investigation, 1997; Leonard & Senchak, 1993; Rogers, 1994) and, as detailed in this chapter, occur with relative frequency during the college years. Despite the comparatively high base rates for both substance use and violence among college students, research examining the overlap between these two behaviors in this population is limited both in scope and methodology. These shortcomings limit the ability to draw strong inferences regarding both the actual overlap between substance abuse and violence, as well as the underlying nature of the relations.

Given this initial caveat, this chapter has four major foci. First, we briefly review the overall prevalence of substance abuse, sexual assault, and relationship violence among college students and describe current knowledge regarding the extent of overlap among these phenomena in this population. Because alcohol is by far the drug of choice among college students (as in the larger society), and since there is a preponderance of research

This work was supported in part by a grant from the Alcoholic Beverage Medical Research Foundation and grant R29 AA12241 from the National Institute on Alcohol Abuse and Alcoholism to Mark D. Wood and grant R37 AA7231 from the National Institute on Alcohol Abuse and Alcoholism to Kenneth J. Sher.

169

on relations between alcohol and violent behavior, greater emphasis is placed on alcohol than other drugs. Additional emphasis is placed on examining definitional, sampling, and other methodological issues that hamper the ability to draw strong inferences regarding the substance use–violence relation. Second, we examine potential conceptual and theoretical explanations about how alcohol and other drugs may influence and exacerbate sexual assault and relationship violence. This section attempts to integrate specific explanations for the role of substance use and abuse in violence between intimates and acquaintances (e.g., Abbey, 1991, 2000) with more general models of substance use and violence and aggression (e.g., Taylor & Chermack, 1993; Taylor & Leonard, 1983), as well as with relevant recent theorizing on the effects of alcohol (and presumably other drugs) on cognitive processes (e.g., Steele & Josephs, 1990). Third, we briefly review recent efforts to reduce violent victimization on college campuses. This section critically examines the extent to which campus violence prevention efforts currently address alcohol and other drug abuse issues and makes recommendations for program planners and administrators. The chapter concludes with a brief discussion of unresolved issues and consequent research priorities.

☐ Prevalence and Incidence of Substance Abuse, Sexual Assault, and Relationship Violence Among College Students

Prevalence of Substance Use and Abuse Among College Students

Three ongoing epidemiological studies yield the best data currently available on substance use, abuse, and substance-related consequences among college students. These include: (1) the Harvard College Alcohol Study (CAS; Wechsler, Davenport, Dowdall, Moeykens, & Castillo, 1994; Wechsler, Dowdall, Maenner, Gledhill-Hoyt, & Lee, 1998; Wechsler, Lee, Kuo, & Lee, 2000); (2) the Monitoring the Future Study (MTF; Johnson et al., 1999); and (3) The Core Survey (Core Institute, 2000; Presley, Meilman, & Cashin, 1996). Generally, the data are quite consistent across the three studies. For example, the prevalence of heavy episodic drinking in the past two weeks was 44% in the most recent CAS study, as compared to 41.7% and 38.9% in the Core and MTF studies, respectively (Core Institute, 2000; Johnston et al., 1999).[1] Likewise, 35.9% of MTF college student respondents reported marijuana use in the past year, with similar prevalence levels (31.3%) observed in the Core Survey. College men report slightly higher levels of illicit drug use than college women (30 day prevalence = 23.1 versus 17.6%), and substantially higher levels of weekly drinking (6.8 versus 2.8 drinks per week) and heavy episodic drinking (51.5% versus 30.9%) (Johnston et al., 1999; Presley et al., 1996). College men are more than three times more likely to report having taken advantage of someone sexually as a result of alcohol or other drug use (10.3% versus 3.1%), and report a slightly lower prevalence of being taken advantage of sexually than do college women (10.6% versus 12.0%) (Presley et al., 1996).

The MTF study is particularly useful for examining differences in substance use between college students and their noncollege attending age peers. For illicit drug use, the most recent data indicate that the prevalence of most substance use is somewhat lower among college students than among their noncollege attending age peers. College students report slightly higher annual prevalence rates for marijuana use than age peers (35.9%

---

[1]The CAS adjusts the definition of heavy episodic drinking based on gender (five or more drinks in a row for men, four or more drinks in a row for women), while the MTF and Core surveys do not.

versus 32.9%), but slightly lower 30-day prevalence rates (18.6% versus 19.1). With respect to alcohol use, college students report slightly higher levels of heavy episodic drinking (38.9% versus 35.0%), but slightly lower levels of daily drinking (3.9% versus 5.5%). Interestingly, in contrast to recent media depictions, heavy episodic drinking among college students has actually decreased by 6.5% from its peak at 45.4% in 1984, although these decreases are less pronounced than those observed among those not attending college.

Among the three national databases, the Core Survey is unique in that it includes items assessing drug-related violence. Presley, Meilman, Cashin, and Leichliter (1997) report that 5% of Core respondents reported forced sexual touching and 4% reported unwanted sexual intercourse during the past year. Seventy-nine percent of students reporting unwanted sexual intercourse indicated that they were under the influence of alcohol or other drugs when the incident occurred, while 71% reported being under the influence when they experienced forced sexual touching. Additionally, individuals engaging in heavy episodic drinking were 2.3 times more likely to have experienced forced sexual touching and 2.7 times more likely to be the victims of unwanted sexual intercourse than students not engaging in heavy episodic drinking.

In summary, these three databases provide a fairly comprehensive picture of the prevalence of alcohol and other drug use among U.S. college students. In conjunction with longitudinal (e.g., Chen & Kandel, 1995) and population-based epidemiological data (e.g., Midanik & Clark, 1994), they indicate that alcohol and most other drug use are higher among young adults (as compared to other age cohorts), but that there are few differences in drug use between college students and their noncollege attending age peers. The modest difference in the prevalence of heavy episodic drinking among college attending and noncollege attending young adults is an exception to these overall patterns. These studies, while providing valuable data on substance use, are extremely limited in their assessment of substance-related violence perpetration and victimization. Accordingly, we turn next to a review of studies focusing on the prevalence of sexual victimization of college students prior to presenting a discussion of what is known about the extent and nature of the overlap between substance use and relationship or acquaintance violence.

Overview of Sexual Assault and Relationship Violence Among College Students

Over two decades of intensive research has suggested alarmingly high prevalence and incidence rates of sexual assault and relationship violence, with particularly high rates of victimization observed among college-aged women (Fisher, Sloan, Cullen, & Lu, 1998). Estimated rates of the incidence and prevalence of sexual assault vary widely, in large part due to the source of the data (e.g., government-conducted research, population studies) and because of definitional differences across studies. Generally speaking, lower prevalence rates are observed in studies that use one or two questions to assess sexual assault and in those that explicitly label behaviors as "rape" or "sexual assault" (Abbey, 2000). Largely for these methodological reasons, prevalence rates from population studies have been the matter of some debate (e.g., see Belknap, Fisher, & Cullen, 1999; Gilbert, 1991, 1993; Roiphe, 1993).

In this chapter we focus on two forms of victimization: sexual assault and relationship or courtship violence. Sexual assault refers to a range of coerced or forced sexual acts including touching, kissing, intercourse, and vaginal, oral, and anal penetration. Rape represents the extreme end of this continuum and is defined, consistent with Abbey (2000), to include behaviors involving "some type of penetration due to force or threat of force; a lack of consent; or inability to provide consent due to age, intoxication, or mental status"

(p. 2). Here we focus primarily, but not exclusively, on male-to-female sexual assault, as research indicates that between 90%–95% of sexual assault victims are women (Bureau of Justice, 1995; Scarce, 1997). Consistent with Belknap and Erez (1995), we use the term relationship or "courtship" violence to refer to the experience of nonsexual physical violence within the context of a dating relationship.

Sexual assault can be placed on a continuum according to the amount of coercion or force employed. Coercion may include attempts at bargaining, ignoring indications that intimacy is not desired, threats, or manipulation through the use of intoxicating substances. Force denotes the use of physical violence, such as pushing or holding a victim against his or her will and may also include the use of a weapon. While sexual assault is certainly not unique to college students, college students are in the age groups that appear to be at greatest risk for acquaintance rape and sexual assault. Specifically, as noted by Koss, Gidycz, and Wisniewski (1987), the 16–19 and 20–24 age ranges are the two highest risk groups for rape, with victimization rates approximately four times higher than the average for all women (see Fisher et al., 1998 for similar conclusions). Also germane to college student populations, 45% of alleged sexual assailants are under age 25 (Koss et al., 1987).

Prevalence and Incidence of Sexual Assault Among College Students

The most methodologically sound and widely cited research on the prevalence of sexual assault has been conducted by Koss and colleagues (Koss et al., 1987). In response to concerns about the methodology utilized in government-based research (e.g., Uniform Crime Reports [Federal Bureau of Investigation, 1986], National Crime Survey [Bureau of Justice Statistics, 1984]), Koss et al. (1987) sampled 6,159 U.S. college students at 32 institutions of higher learning in an attempt to accurately represent the U.S. higher education student population. Although some regions of the country were overrepresented, the sample was largely consistent with national enrollment data.[2] The study utilized the Sexual Experiences Survey (SES; Koss & Oros, 1982), which represents a substantial improvement in the measurement of sexual assault in that it includes ten behaviorally specific questions regarding the use of verbal coercion and force to engage in unwanted sexual touching, oral sex, anal sex, penetration by objects other than a penis, or sexual intercourse (defined as penetration of a woman's vagina by a man's penis). Overall, 53.7% of college women reported experiencing some form of sexual assault since the age of 14. Sexual assault was further classified into the following four categories (weighted prevalence in parentheses): sexual contact, defined as experiencing coerced or forced sexual touching, (14.4%); sexual coercion, defined as sexual intercourse coerced by argument, pressure, or position of authority (11.9%), attempted rape, defined as attempted (but not completed) intercourse by threat or use of force or drugs (12.1%); and rape, defined as forced sexual intercourse, oral or anal sex, or insertion of object other than the penis (15.4%). Eighty-four percent of respondents reporting rape or attempted rape indicated that they knew the assailant, and 57% of the assaults occurred on dates (Koss, 1988). Even though the behaviors assessed by the SES were not explicitly labeled as assault or rape, disparities exist between the rates of sexual assault experienced by women as compared to the perpetration levels reported by men. For example, while 15.4% of women reported being raped at least once since the age of 14, only 4.4% of male respondents reported engaging in behaviors meeting the criteria for rape. A number of potential reasons for this discrepancy exist, including: (1) perpetration of a number of rapes by extremely violent men; (2)

---

[2]Sample weighting was used to control regional disproportion when calculating prevalence data.

victimization by individuals not attending higher education institutions; (3) underreporting of illegal behaviors by men; and (4) misinterpretation of women's non-consent by men.

In terms of the incidence of sexual assault, Koss and colleagues (1987) found that approximately 6.5% of women reported being raped in the past year. Victimization rates were calculated in accordance with FBI definitions of rape, and were found to be 10–15 times greater than the rates reported for 16–19 year olds in the National Crime Survey (Bureau of Justice Statistics, 1984). These results provide strong support for the contention that government-based statistics severely underestimate the incidence of rape (Koss et al., 1987).

More recently, DeKeseredy and a colleague (DeKeseredy & Kelly, 1993) used a slightly modified version of the SES to examine the prevalence of sexual assault in a national sample of Canadian college women. This study found that 28% of Canadian college women reported being sexually assaulted in the past year, with 45% reporting that they had been sexually assaulted since leaving high school. As previously noted, the findings of Koss and colleagues (1987) have been challenged (Gilbert, 1991, 1993; Roiphe, 1993). However, similar prevalence rates were observed in DeKeseredy and Kelly's national sample, and in a number of smaller studies (Abbey, Ross, McDuffie, & McAuslan, 1996a; Copenhaver & Grauerholz, 1991; Kalof, 1993; Mills & Granoff, 1992; Muehlenhard & Linton, 1987; Neal & Mangis, 1995; Ward, Chapman, Colin, White, & Williams, 1991). Taken together, the existing data strongly support the prevalence levels observed by Koss and colleagues.

In one of the few prospective studies investigating sexual assault, Himelein (1995) surveyed women at freshmen orientation and again 32 months later. At follow-up, 29% of respondents reported some level of sexual assault since the beginning of college and 8% reported experiencing rape during this period.

Several studies have investigated prevalence rates as a function of individual and environmental factors. Koss et al. (1987) noted significant but modest differences in sexual assault victimization across ethnic categories, with rape reported by 16% of White women, 12% of Hispanic women, 10% of Black women, 7% of Asian women, and 40% of Native American women.[3] Considering this and other studies, Abbey (2000) concluded that rates of sexual assault appear to be generally comparable across races. Koss et al. (1987) also found higher rates of victimization among women at private and major universities as compared to religious institutions and slightly higher rates of sexual victimization in the Great Lakes and Plains states as compared to other regions. Copenhaver and Grauerholz (1991), examining the prevalence of sexual victimization among sorority women using the SES, found that 83% of respondents had experienced some form of sexual assault during college, with 17% reporting incidents that legally constituted rape. The modal location for the rapes were fraternity houses (41%), followed by apartments (21%) and cars (7%). More recently, Fisher et al. (1998) compared rates of sexual victimization at on- and off-campus locales, and found the on-campus sexual assault rate to be 1.4 times higher than the off-campus rate.

Relatively few studies have focused on the sexual victimization of men. Prevalence rates in these studies have ranged from 5.3% to 20.7% (Larimer, Lydum, Anderson, & Turner, 1999; Lott, Reilly, & Howard, 1982; Struckman-Johnson & Struckman-Johnson, 1994). The experience of sexual assault appears to be less psychologically traumatic to men (at least when perpetrated by women). Struckman-Johnson and Struckman-Johnson (1994) suggest that while men may not desire sexual contact in a given situation, because the outcome is "sex role congruent" (e.g., intercourse was experienced), negative reactions are mitigated. In any case, while research in this area generally suggests that men are

---

[2]Cell sizes for Asian and Native American women were quite small (i.e., 79 and 20, respectively).

victimized less frequently than women, the data also underscore the importance of study-ing victimization in men as well as women.

Prevalence and Incidence of Relationship Violence Among College Students

Relationship or "courtship" violence has been studied somewhat less frequently than sexual assault in college student populations. Nonetheless, because most studies that have exam-ined this type of violence among nonmarried individuals have used college student samples, there is a sufficient body of literature from which to draw conclusions on prevalence and incidence. Generally, the literature indicates that relationship violence, defined here as the experience of nonsexual physical violence within the context of a dating relationship, is a relatively common occurrence among college students. As would be expected, inci-dence and prevalence rates are greatly increased when threats are included in the operationalization of relationship violence and are further increased when verbal aggres-sion is included. Although the majority of studies have used either the Conflicts Tactics Scale (CTS; Straus, 1979) or subsets of items from this scale, accurate determination of prevalence rates and comparisons across studies are still complicated due to variability in sampling, methodology, and data analyses. The CTS was designed to measure the occur-rence of verbal aggression and physical violence, including pushing and shoving, beating up a partner, and the use of a weapon by one partner against another. The scale can be broken down into subscales (verbal aggression, physical aggression) and further subcategorized (e.g., minor physical aggression, major physical aggression). The CTS has been criticized by several researchers for its inability to account for the context, conse-quences, and motives of relationship violence (Bograd, 1990; DeKeseredy & Kelly, 1993; Dobash, Dobash, Wilson, & Daly, 1992; Jackson, 1999).

Sugarman and Hotaling (1989), comparing results from 21 studies of relationship vio-lence, found that college samples produced higher average prevalence rates for *either* ex-pressed or sustained violence (*M* = 31.9%, *n* = 17) than studies surveying high school stu-dents (*M* = 22.3%, *n* = 4). These authors also examined prevalence rates for expressed and sustained violence separately by gender, observing slightly higher lifetime prevalence of dating violence victimization among women (*M* = 36.2%) than men (*M* = 33.3%). In the studies reviewed by Sugarman and Hotaling, a higher proportion of women (*M* = 39.3%) than men (*M* = 32.9%) report having inflicted violence in a dating relationship. Overall, a great deal of variability in prevalence rates was observed across the studies, with lifetime dating violence prevalence rates in college student studies ranging from a low of 16.7% to a high of 66%. Likely conceptual and methodological contributors to this heterogeneity include variations in sampling procedures (e.g., random versus convenience), regions of the country sampled, and individual difference characteristics of the samples (e.g., gen-der, ethnicity).

Stets and Straus (1989) compared relationship violence among married (*n* = 5005), cohabiting (*n* = 237), and dating couples (*n* = 526). The dating sample was a probability sample of college students, while the other two groups came from the National Violence Survey (Straus & Gelles, 1986). Overall, this study found that cohabiting couples were much more likely to experience some form of relationship violence in the past year (35%) than either dating (20%) or married (15%) couples and that the level of severe violence was typically highest among cohabiting couples. When analyses controlled for age, the level of violent behavior was lower among the dating sample than that observed in the married sample. Stets and Straus also observed that female only violence comprised a larger pro-portion of the violence among dating couples (39%) as compared to cohabiting (27%)

and married (29%) couples. They also noted that male only violence was least common among dating couples as compared to cohabitating and married couples.

Dating violence also has been examined in national college samples from the U.S. and Canada. White and Koss (1991) examined courtship violence in a subset of respondents (*n* = 4707) from the national college sample from Koss et al. (1987).[4] Respondents indicated both how often they had perpetrated and experienced each of the violent behaviors described by the CTS during the last school year. Past year incidence for physical violence perpetration was approximately 37% for men and 35% for women. For physical violence victimization, 39% of the men and 32% of women reported experiencing physical violence from a member of the opposite sex during the past year. The typical mode of violent behavior was "pushing/shoving/grabbing" or "threats to hit or throw something." DeKeseredy and Kelley (1993) observed somewhat lower incidence and prevalence levels of dating violence in their national study of Canadian college students. Nearly 14% of male respondents reported physical abuse of a dating partner in the past year, with 22% of women reporting physical violence victimization during that period. The discrepancy between men and women's reports was more pronounced in the prevalence data, with 17.8% of men reporting the use of physical violence in a dating relationship since leaving high school and nearly twice as many women (35%) reporting victimization.

In addition to the investigation of gender differences described above, a few studies have gone beyond basic descriptions of incidence and prevalence and investigated variability in dating violence as a function of other sociodemographic (e.g., ethnicity, age, socioeconomic status [SES], geographic region) and contextual and situational (e.g., alcohol use, length of relationship, locations, pattern of violence initiation) factors. With the exception of alcohol use, which is covered in subsequent sections of the chapter, existing data on these factors are briefly summarized next.

In contrast to the data reviewed earlier on sexual assault, there is little consistent evidence that men more commonly perpetrate nonsexual violence in dating relationships than do women. In fact, as previously noted, most of the studies reviewed by Sugarman and Hotaling (1989), as well as in the study conducted by Stets & Straus (1989), found the proportion of self-reported dating violence to be higher among women than men. (See also and Jackson [1999] and Goodyear-Smith and Laidlaw [1999] for similar conclusions with reference to the general population.) Studies that have examined gender differences in the perpetration of severe physical violence are mixed as well. Makepeace (1983) and Lane and Gwartney-Gibbs (1985) found that men were from two to four times more likely than women to inflict severe violence against dating partners, while Arias, Samios, and O'Leary (1987) and Stets and Straus (1989) found no gender differences on violence severity. There is some evidence to suggest that women are significantly more likely than men to sustain injury as a result of courtship violence (Makepeace, 1984, 1986). Several explanations for the lack of gender differences in the prevalence rates for dating violence have been offered. These include: (1) underreporting by men due to the stigmatizing nature of violence perpetration against women; (2) socialization of men to avoid physical violence with women; and (3) enhanced power by women in dating relationships as opposed to other relationships with men (Sugarman & Hotaling, 1989).

There is little evidence for variability in dating violence as a function of either ethnicity or age. However, the ability to detect ethnic differences is severely limited due to the large

---

[4]In this study, respondents were asked to respond to CTS items by indicating "things that might have been done when you had a conflict or a disagreement with a member of the opposite sex" (White and Koss, 1991, p. 249). Thus, the context of violence was not limited to a dating relationship or dating situation.

proportion of White respondents in most studies (Carlson, 1996; Jackson, 1999). Likewise, age differences are inherently limited to a narrow range in college student samples, although, as previously noted, higher rates of dating violence have been observed in college samples as compared to studies with high school students. Existing data do suggest that there are SES differences in dating violence, with significantly higher rates observed at extreme (low and high) ends of the family income spectrum (Makepeace, 1987; Sugarman & Hotaling, 1989), although null findings also have been reported (White & Koss, 1991). Based on findings from earlier studies suggesting much higher rates of relationship violence in the Southern U.S., White and Koss (1991) investigated regional differences in courtship violence in Koss' national sample of college students. In this study, findings of regional variability were limited to men and the pattern varied somewhat from that reported by Sugarman and Hotaling (1989). For men, there were markedly higher rates of violence perpetration and victimization in the Great Lakes regions, followed by the Southeast, with the lowest levels of physical aggression in the Plain States and Far West regions.

In terms of contextual and situational factors, courtship violence is most likely to occur on weekends and in the great majority of cases in private settings—most often a residence or a vehicle (Sugarman & Hotaling, 1989). Consistent with the marital violence literature, there is evidence that multiple occurrences of dating violence are common within and across relationships (Roscoe & Benaske, 1985). While evidence is once again equivocal, it appears that dating violence is more likely to occur in more serious as opposed to casual dating relationships (Cate et al., 1982; Henton et al., 1983; Plass & Gessner, 1983; Rosco & Benaske, 1985; Roscoe & Kelsey, 1986; Sigelman, Berry, & Wiles, 1984). With respect to attributions of why dating violence occurred, there are interesting patterns in the data. Overwhelmingly, neither men nor women are likely to label themselves as instigators of violence, but when participants are asked to indicate whether they see themselves as victims or aggressors, clear gender differences emerge. Specifically, men are significantly more likely to label themselves as aggressors, while women are two to three times more likely to label themselves as victims (Sugarman & Hotaling, 1989).

In sum, while the studies reviewed above clearly indicate that dating violence is a prevalent phenomenon among college students, beyond the widely variable basic prevalence and incidence levels, the available data are quite limited. The findings of equal or greater dating violence perpetration among women are somewhat counterintuitive and suggest a much different pattern than that of the sexual assault literature. In part because of a lack of focus and in part because of contradictory findings, there are few consistent findings regarding variability in dating violence as a function of sociodemographic and contextual factors.

The preceding review brings several methodological issues to the fore. Namely, even if the CTS accurately reflects the level of violence victimization and perpetration among college students, it is not informative regarding why violence occurred (e.g., dominance, retaliation), whether it was symmetrical (both partners) or asymmetrical (one partner only), and what the outcomes of the acts were (e.g., injury, psychological trauma). These are fundamental questions that should be addressed in future research with men and women. Additionally, most research on this topic is conducted in predominantly White samples of convenience, or by mail surveys with response rates that limit generalizability (Jackson, 1999; Sugarman & Hotaling, 1989). Moreover, to date, intimate violence research has predominantly focused on heterosexual dating violence, although an emerging literature suggests that relationship violence is comparably high (and possibly higher) among lesbian and gay couples (Burke & Follingstad, 1999; Waldner-Haugrud, Gratch, & Magruder, 1997). Prospective studies are needed to identify the correlates and consequences of relationship violence, as are methodologically rigorous studies that go beyond simple counts of violence and better explicate patterns, motives, and consequences of violent behavior in a more diverse array of populations (e.g., minorities, lesbians, and gays).

☐ Relations Among Substance Use, Sexual Assault, and Relationship Violence

Violence researchers and prevention professionals have often pointed to a link between alcohol use and abuse and both sexual assault and relationship violence. In this section we examine what is known about the extent of the overlap between substance use, particularly alcohol consumption, and these violent behaviors among college students. More importantly, we focus on what is known (and not known) about the nature of these relations. Our discussion is largely constrained by methodological issues that limit the ability to draw strong inferences about the role of alcohol (and other drugs) in sexual assault and relationship violence. The major methodological limitations are imposed by the phenomena under investigation. For the obvious ethical reasons, sexual assault and relationship violence can only be studied in correlational designs or in experimental analogues with proxy dependent measures. As detailed below, additional methodological weaknesses, most typically related to the assessment of substance use patterns, sexual assault and relationship violence, as well as factors affecting the reliability and validity of findings, (e.g., potentially biased retrospective recall, convenience samples, poor survey response rates, measures with unknown psychometric properties) place additional limits on our understanding of the substance use–violence relation. It should be noted that when substance use and sexual assault or relationship violence are considered together, the potential biasing effects of these methodological limitations are likely to be further magnified.

Substance Use and Sexual Assault Among College Students

Over the past two decades, an increasing amount of research has examined the extent to which alcohol and other drugs are associated with sexual assault. Nonetheless, definitive answers to such seemingly simple questions as those about the overall prevalence of alcohol or drug use in sexual assault events are complicated by a range of factors. With respect to assessment of drug use, these include important considerations such as the substance or substances in question, whether typical use or preassault use is being assessed, whether the amount of preassault use is measured at all, and, if so, whether the amount differs from typical use (both for the individual in question and the population more generally). For sexual assault, critical considerations include the context and severity of the assault, characteristics of the perpetrator (e.g., stranger, acquaintance, boyfriend), and whether the assault is premeditated or opportunistic in nature.

Studies examining typical alcohol use by both victims and perpetrators of sexual assault have observed that both are positively associated with sexual assault (Abbey, Ross, McDuffie, & McAuslan, 1996a; Koss & Dinero, 1989; Larimer et al., 1999; Tyler, Hoyt, & Whitbeck, 1998; Ullman, Karabatsos, & Koss, 1999). Nonetheless, typical alcohol use is only a fairly weak predictor of sexual assault and is decidedly less informative than assessment of alcohol or other drug use immediately prior to assault (Roizen, 1993).

For perpetrators of sexual assault, preassault alcohol or drug use prevalence rates range from 44% to 79%, whereas for victims they range from 30% to 71% (Abbey et al., 1996a; Copenhaver & Grauerholz, 1991; Harrington & Leitenberg, 1994; Koss, 1988; Muehlenhard

& Linton, 1987; Presley, Leichliter, & Meilman, 1998). In a recent review of the literature, Abbey (2000) concluded that alcohol use occurred prior to at least half of sexual assaults involving college students. Beyond questions about whether alcohol or other drugs were consumed at all prior to the event, very few studies have queried respondents about their level of drinking, and none have done so in sufficient detail as to permit examination of dose-assault relations.

Muehlenhard and Linton (1987) included items assessing alcohol and drug use for respondents' most recent date and on a date when sexual aggression occurred (ranging from unwanted kissing to rape). Respondents' drug use was then categorized as light or heavy.[5] When overall drug use was considered, for both men and women, drug use was slightly less prevalent for dates on which sexual assault occurred as compared to the most recent date. However, heavy drug use by women was four times more likely on dates involving sexual assault as compared to most recent dates, and nearly two times more likely on dates involving sexual assault by men.

Ullman et al. (1999), using data from the National Survey of College Women (Koss et al., 1987), assessed general alcohol abuse propensity (frequency of intoxication) and preassault drinking among perpetrators and victims of sexual assault. Both victim and perpetrator preassault alcohol use was significantly related to greater sexual victimization severity. Additionally, alcohol abuse propensity predicted victimization, although not as strongly as preassault drinking. Notably, this study also examined interaction effects among preassault alcohol use by both victim and perpetrator, assault characteristics, and victim and offender behaviors. In contrast to expectations, aggression by perpetrators was more strongly associated with sexual assault severity in incidents without preassault alcohol use. As noted by Ullman et al. (1999), this pattern of results is not consistent with the notion of alcohol's disinhibiting effects on an offender's aggressive behavior.

With respect to associations between illicit drug use and sexual assault among college students, it appears that, overwhelmingly, when other drug use occurs it typically does so in conjunction with alcohol use (Muehlenhard & Linton, 1987; Testa & Livingston, 1999; Ullman et al., 1999). In fact, our review of the literature revealed no study examining both alcohol and other drug use that found sufficient cases of illicit drug use without alcohol use to enable separate analyses of associations between illicit drug use and sexual victimization. Recently, there has been increased attention to the use of substances like flunitrazepam (Rohypnol), gamma-hydroxybutyate (GHB), and ketamine in predatory sexual aggression. Although data specific to the prevalence of these drugs in conjunction with sexual assault in college student populations are lacking, a recent study by ElSohly and Salamone (1999) examined 1179 urine samples from victims of alleged sexual assault where drug use was suspected. Samples were solicited from law enforcement agencies, emergency rooms, and rape crisis centers in 49 states, Puerto Rico, and the District of Columbia. Each sample was tested by immunoassay for amphetamines, barbiturates, benzodiazepines, cocaine metabolites, cannabinoids, methaqualone, opiates, phencyclidine, propoxyphene, Rohypnol metabolites, and GHB. Overall, 60% (711) of the samples tested positive for at least one substance, with ethanol being the most frequent (451), followed by cannabinoids (218), cocaine metabolites (97), and benzodiazepines (97). Forty-eight samples (6.8%) of the positive samples had measurable levels of GHB. Moreover, 35% of the drug-positive samples contained multiple drugs, and nearly 20 different substances were identified from the samples. These data indicate the need for university student

---

[5]Light drug use included respondents who indicated that they used alcohol or drugs and felt either totally sober or a little tipsy or buzzed. Heavy drug use included respondents who indicated that they had used alcohol or drugs and felt either moderately or extremely intoxicated.

health services, as well as other treatment providers, to screen for a range of illicit drugs, including GHB, which is not typically tested in normal toxicology screens.

Substance Use and Relationship Violence Among College Students

It should be noted at the outset that rigorous examinations of the role of alcohol and other drugs in dating violence are even rarer than in the area of college student sexual assault. Earlier studies of dating violence found that drug and alcohol use, or disagreements about drinking, were frequently cited as perceived causes of dating violence (Cate et al., 1982; Makepeace, 1981). Sugarman and Hotaling (1989), in their review of over 40 studies of dating violence, concluded that alcohol use, although the second most frequently cited reason for dating violence, was far less frequently mentioned than the primary perceived cause—jealousy. They also noted that attributions of alcohol use as a precipitating factor for dating violence occurred much less often than for marital violence. In a rare early attempt to actually quantify alcohol consumption, Matthews (1984) found that more than half of those reporting dating violence in his study indicated that neither they nor their partners had been drinking prior to the violent episode. Based on these findings, most researchers in the area concluded that alcohol was not an important risk factor for dating violence (Brodbelt, 1983; Laner, 1983; Makepeace, 1981; Sugarman & Hotaling, 1989).

In contrast to this predominant view, some researchers have argued that alcohol use is an important determinant of dating violence (e.g., Riggs & O'Leary, 1989). Consistent with this notion, in an important methodological advance, Stets and Henderson (1991), in a national study of dating violence among 18–30-year-old women, assessed typical (past-year quantity and frequency) and proximal (either or both individuals three hours before or after the event) alcohol use. Typical drinking by either men or women was not associated with dating violence, but analyses revealed that drinking before an incident was positively and significantly associated with the use and receipt of physical violence. These positive findings sparked renewed interest in examining the role of alcohol in dating violence among college students. Nicholson et al. (1998) examined relations between alcohol and nonsexual violence among two cohorts of college students surveyed in 1994 and 1996. Although the authors concluded that there was a "clear association of alcohol use with non-sexual violence" (p. 47), in fact, the data do not support this assertion. For men in both cohorts, alcohol use, assessed with a single dichotomous item, was equally likely *not* to be present in violent incidents, whereas for women the data were mixed. Specifically, alcohol was involved in 60% of nonviolent acts reported in the first cohort, with a significant *decrease* in alcohol involvement (50%) observed in the second cohort. Thus, in three of four relevant comparisons, alcohol use was not demonstrated to be present more frequently in nonsexual violent incidents. Follingstad, Bradley, Laughlin, and Burke (1999), using a sample of incoming college freshmen, compared those who had never used physical violence in a dating relationship with those who reported one or more incidents of dating violence on a range of putative risk factors. Multivariate analysis of variance, with follow-up univariate analyses, indicated that substance abuse (assessed by two items on alcohol quantity/frequency and eight items on alcohol-related consequences) was significantly more likely among those who had expressed violence in a dating context as compared to individuals not reporting the use of dating violence. The effect size for the substance abuse–violence perpetration relation, although moderate in strength ($d = .36$), was much less than that observed for the strongest correlate, the use of control strategies in a romantic relationship ($d = .72$). Substance abuse was not associated with either frequency or severity of violence perpetration in this sample. More recently, Shook, Gerrity, Jurich, and

Segrist (2000) examined relations between both typical alcohol use and alcohol use in proximity to violent incidents. Typical alcohol use was measured by items assessing quantity and frequency. Drinking in proximity to violence was assessed by having participants indicate, for each item of the Conflict Tactics Scale, whether or not "either or both dating partners were drinking alcohol up to 3 hours before or 3 hours after the most recent abusive incident" (Shook et al., 2000, p. 7). Multiple regression analyses, examining relations between typical and proximal alcohol use (as well as several other predictor variables) and physical violence were conducted separately by gender. For women, but not men, proximal alcohol use was significantly associated with the expression of physical violence. For men, in contrast to expectations, typical alcohol use demonstrated significant, *negative* associations with perpetrating physical violence.

In summary, any gap between conclusions drawn about the role of alcohol in dating violence from earlier studies with those conducted more recently is likely more illusory than real. As noted, earlier reviewers of the literature (e.g., Sugarman & Hotaling, 1989) did not view alcohol use as a major determinant of dating violence. This conclusion, while largely based on reports of perceived causes of dating violence or, infrequently, upon examination of relations between typical or proximal drinking patterns and courtship violence, is not clearly refuted by more recent research. Although improvements with respect to the measurement of typical and proximal alcohol use have been demonstrated in some of the more recent studies, existing data with college student samples suggest that the relationship between typical alcohol use (independent of consequences) and dating violence is nonexistent, whereas relations between proximal alcohol use and dating violence are modest. To be sure, existing data are far too sparse to draw definitive conclusions with regard to the role of alcohol in dating violence among college students. Likewise, most of the methodological criticisms (e.g., assessment, sampling) raised earlier that obfuscate understanding of the true prevalence of substance use and abuse-related sexual assault cases are even more applicable to the dating violence literature.

For both the sexual assault and dating violence literatures, it is becoming increasingly recognized that relations between alcohol use and violent behaviors are complex, and that alcohol (and other drug) use are best viewed as operating in combination with a range of other individual and situational factors. Accordingly, next we review models (with reference to supporting data whenever possible) that incorporate substance use with other factors of etiologic relevance for the understanding of sexual assault and relationship violence.

☐ Potential Explanations for Relations Among Substance Use, Sexual Assault, and Relationship Violence

Although there is little question of a relation between alcohol use and sexual aggression, resolving the nature of the relation is an extremely complex undertaking. Consider the following points:

1. Even if it can be shown that heavier drinkers and drug users are more likely to perpetrate intimate violence, the substance use could be temporally unrelated with such violence. That is, it is possible that the violence takes place under conditions of both intoxication and sobriety and, in the extreme, may be equally likely to occur during periods of sobriety. Thus, the relation could be due to dispositional (i.e., time invariant) third variables such as common personality determinants.

2. Even if it can be shown that drinking tends to precede or co-occur with violence, this does not mean that the alcohol is causing the violence. For example, it is possible that the true causal mechanisms are embedded in the situational contexts in which substance use typically occurs but are not specific to substance use. For example, it could be that the social settings for drinking and violence are the same and that a statistical relation is due to temporally specific third variables (i.e., common context and settings).
3. Even if third variables such as common dispositions and settings can be ruled out, alcohol consumption might still not be causally related. It could be that an association exists because an individual intends to become violent and elects to consume alcohol or other drugs because it will provide justification for his or her behavior or permit him or her to feel more confident in acting violently.
4. Even if premeditation of violence prior to substance use can be ruled out, it is possible that violent behavior does not stem from substance use per se but rather from expectancies one holds about how people "under the influence" act.
5. Even if expectancy effects can be ruled out and a causal role for drug effects can be established, it does not mean that all or most individuals would react violently when intoxicated. That is, there might be important moderators at the person level (e.g., trait aggression, impulsive personality traits) or in the environment (e.g., provocative behaviors) that are necessary conditions for substance-related violence.
6. Even if the parameters necessary for causing violence can be specified, this still does not necessarily "explain" why violence occurs. That is, there might be a number of mechanisms that mediate the effect of alcohol on behavior.

None of the above possibilities are mutually exclusive and there are reasons to believe that each of these mechanisms (e.g., common third variables at the person and situational level, expectancy effects that are active prior to and during a violent encounter, moderation and mediation) are important explanatory concepts. Moreover, in considering the effects of alcohol and other drugs on intimate violence, one must consider not only the issue of the drinking of the perpetrator but also the drinking of the victim. Thus it may be necessary to consider additional factors. For example, it could be that:

7. Substance use on the part of the victim could serve as a provoking agent to the perpetrator. For example, partner drinking could be viewed as signaling sexual availability or defiance either symbolically or by leading to directly provocative behavior (e.g., sexual flirtation or aggressive behavior).
8. Drug or alcohol consuming victims may have impaired abilities to recognize increasing levels of danger, engage in behaviors to defuse the situation, or to mount effective escape strategies.

While a discussion of these issues requires attention to several distinct research literatures and lies outside the scope of this chapter, we feel that the issues raised above are useful for delineating the complexity of research in this area. Although basic research on alcohol and aggression has generated a spate of causal theories (see Chermack & Giancola, 1997) that differ both in the constructs employed and the emphases placed on different mechanisms, most contemporary theories of alcohol-related aggression place a major emphasis on the role of alcohol in disrupting cognitive processing (Hull, 1981; Sayette, 1993; Steele & Josephs, 1990; Taylor & Leonard, 1983). It has been noted that Steele and Josephs' (1990) theory of alcohol myopia is "perhaps the most influential cognitive theory of alcohol's effects on social behavior to appear in recent years" (Sayette, 1999, p. 255).

According to Steele and Josephs, alcohol exerts both its prized and dangerous effects by narrowing attentional focus to those cues that are most salient. From this perspective, alcohol can result in increased aggression by either reducing the ability to attend to inhibitory cues (that are often distal and not particularly salient) or by increasing the focus on instigating cues (that are often immediate and highly salient). Although at least one review has challenged the ability of the alcohol myopia theory to account for the data accumulated to date (Ito, Miller, & Pollock, 1996), it remains the single most compelling perspective and is largely consistent at a conceptual level with other theories that posit that alcohol's effects are mediated via disruptions in information processing or higher cognitive processing. It also provides a useful framework for conceptualizing how some individuals might interpret cues as suggesting sexual interest on the part of a date or acquaintance.

Alcohol and Sexual Aggression

Experimental research has amply demonstrated that alcohol appears to have the ability to result in increased aggression in some people under some circumstances (Bushman & Cooper, 1990; Ito et al., 1996; Taylor & Chermack, 1993). However, as noted at the outset of this section, the relation between alcohol use and sexual aggression likely involves a number of interpersonal processes, and a full consideration of how alcohol might lead to forced or coerced sex requires that the alcohol–sexual aggression relation be contextualized with respect to a wide range of variables. In addition to general mechanisms relating alcohol consumption to aggression described by aggression theorists, Abbey (1991, 2000) has outlined a number of ways that alcohol consumption on the part of the perpetrator or the victim can increase the likelihood of sexual aggression taking place.

Central to various forms of sexual aggression is the possibility that men misinterpret various verbal and nonverbal cues as indicative of sexual interest. Abbey (1991, 2000) presents considerable data showing that even nonintoxicated men frequently misperceive women's behaviors and dress as suggesting sexual interest whereas women do not. Superimposed upon this cognitive bias towards men misperceiving flirtatiousness or even friendliness as sexual interest are gender-based stereotypes (promoted by the popular culture) that women are supposed to be reluctant to initiate sexual contacts or reciprocate sexual advances initially, even when they are desired, and that men are to be persistent in the face of initial rebuffs. Thus, to some men, women's resistance to sexual overtures are viewed as token and as something to be overcome. Many victims of date rape who had been drinking had consented to lower levels of sexual intimacy earlier in the encounter (Harrington & Leitenberg, 1994; Koss et al., 1987) and perhaps the perpetrator believed that willingness to engage in kissing or petting is a more valid indicator of interest than verbal assertions to the contrary. Given alcohol's ability to narrow attentional focus, it is reasonable to hypothesize that these perceptual and response biases are accentuated when the perpetrator has been drinking (Steele & Josephs, 1990).

Drinking on the part of the victim could serve to increase the perception of sexual interest. First, the mere act of drinking alcoholic beverages is viewed by some men as indicating sexual willingness and promiscuity (George, Gournic, & McAfee, 1988), and the act of drinking on a date appears to personalize the stereotype; that is, it may suggest that the woman is interested in having sex with her date (Goodchilds & Zellman, 1984). Moreover, to the extent that alcohol consumption results in cognitive impairment, the woman may be less likely to accurately appraise the danger in the situation (e.g., Testa & Livingston, 1999). Even if the situation is accurately perceived, it is still possible that alcohol intoxication could lead to a failure to engage in effective verbal or nonverbal behavior that would signal clearer intentions to not have sex. Similarly, alcohol, and presumably other drugs, could impair the victim's ability to resist or escape from an impending or actual assault (e.g., Abbey, Ross, McDuffie, & McAuslan, 1996b).

The discussion so far has tended to focus on situational variables that by themselves or in conjunction with alcohol could tend to increase the likelihood of sexual aggression. However, it is clear that sexual intercourse is a premeditated goal of many dating situations and men may drink in order to enhance their own feelings of power or sexuality (Crowe & George, 1989) and may attempt to get their date drunk in the belief that she will be more willing to have sex (or less able to resist sexual advances) (Himelein, Vogel, & Wachowiak, 1994; Mandoki & Burkhart, 1989; Martin & Hummer, 1989; Testa & Livingston, 1999). Finally, at least one vignette study suggests that should rape occur, alcohol intoxication may be viewed as mitigating responsibility for a male perpetrator, while increasing it for a female victim (Richardson & Campbell, 1982).

Consideration of the characteristics of victims of sexual assault suggests additional contributors to alcohol-related sexual aggression. For example, Abbey (2000) notes that alcohol-related sexual assaults appears to be more common in women who are victims of childhood sexual abuse, are heavy drinkers, and who have had frequent sexual relationships. Abbey (2000) interprets these findings as suggesting women who are likely to be victims of sexual assault are those who put themselves in high-risk situations more frequently. It also is possible that men whose intimacies are rejected by heavy drinking, promiscuous women experience more anger toward these dates because such rejection is viewed as particularly damning. That is, rejection of sexual advances by a woman initially perceived as particularly indiscriminate about sexual partners could motivate more aggressive reactions by the perpetrator if it is internalized as a harsh, personal rejection.

The foregoing analysis suggests that human sexual encounters are extremely complex situations that reflect the values and expectancies that the participants bring to it and that unfold as a dyadic transactional process. Individuals have strong beliefs about the effects of alcohol on their own sexuality and the sexuality of others (Abbey, McAuslan, Ross, & Zawacki, 1999; Crowe & George, 1989). Their own and their dates' alcohol consumption are powerful occasion setters that can reflect or be discrepant with their own motivational states. As a sexual encounter progresses, alcohol consumption can result in enhancement of gender biases concerning the degree of sexual interest which, when coupled with increased tendencies toward aggression, can lead to coercive sexual behavior. If the woman is alcohol or drug impaired, she might be less likely to recognize the emerging risk in the situation or be less capable of engaging in behaviors most likely to successfully curtail an escalating bout of sexual force or coercion.

Alcohol and Dating Violence

Dating violence, like sexual aggression, is undoubtedly a multidetermined phenomenon that can only be understood in the context of a number of interacting historical and situational factors and as an escalating, transactional, dyadic process. Although there has been relatively little theoretical work on the role of alcohol in dating violence, the literature on alcohol in marital violence is considerably larger and most likely highly relevant given that there is an association between courtship violence and marital violence and that the predictors of violence towards one's partner are similar during courtship and the early stages of marriage (Leonard & Senchak, 1996). This is not to say that there might not be important unique aspects of dating violence in contrast to other forms of intimate partner violence (Riggs & O'Leary, 1989) and that, compared to marital violence, dating violence may be less related to alcohol involvement (Sugarman & Hotaling, 1989).

The relation between alcohol use and dating violence is not well established, and the research literature has yet to fully characterize the extent of the problem and the degree of moderation by ethnicity and other important population-level variables (Cunradi, Caetano, Clark, & Schafer, 1999). Collegiate environments differ on a number of dimensions (e.g., same sex versus coeducational, religious versus nonreligious, public versus private, two- versus four-year degrees offered, residential versus nonresidential) that are related to the types of students they attract as well as expectations on conduct (with respect to drinking, dating, and violence). This variability makes the inconsistent findings that do exist even more difficult to interpret.

Given that the extent to which alcohol plays a causal role in dating violence is not clear and that relevant data are sparse and inconsistent, consideration of mechanisms of alcohol-related dating violence is premature. Nevertheless, it is useful to briefly consider models of dating violence since they can serve as preliminary, organizing schemes for conceptualizing the accumulating findings.

Riggs and O'Leary (1989) present a model of intimate partner violence that is specifically tailored to the dating situation. Among other things, these authors note that there are important differences between both the nature of violence in dating couples (e.g., a high prevalence of female aggressing towards male partners) in comparison to marital couples (where violence is primarily directed from husband to wife). Riggs and O'Leary (1989) also note that, unlike marital relations that are characterized by legal, financial, and moral commitments, dating relationships typically present fewer or less intense forms of these commitments and, thus, are easier to terminate. Moreover, many dating partners view their relationship as temporary and not necessarily leading to long-term commitment. It is perhaps not surprising then that more serious dating relationships are more similar to marital relationships and are the types of dating relationships that are most likely to experience physical aggression.

Similar to models of marital violence (Leonard, 1993, see Leonard, this volume), Riggs and O'Leary (1989) make a distinction between more distal (contextual) variables and more proximal (situational) variables; the former set of variables provide general guidance as to the prediction of who is prone to violence, and the latter set of variables specify under what conditions violence is likely to occur in vulnerable couples. Perhaps not surprisingly, both the distal variables and the proximal variables are described similarly across the two models. However, it seems likely that one of the major domains of situational variables, relationship problems, could differ in nature between dating and married couples. For example, it is possible that certain types of problems such as jealousy and sexual conflicts may be more salient in dating couples than in those who are married.

In sum, this model provides numerous hypotheses to be tested concerning the role of alcohol and other drugs in dating violence among college students. More data are needed to help identify the extent of the problem (i.e., does alcohol use, either chronically or situationally, play a causal role and, if so, how are these effects mediated). Moreover, given the apparent multidetermined nature of dating violence, it also seems likely that any alcohol effects that do exist are probably heavily moderated by other factors.

☐ Policy and Prevention Implications

In reviewing the epidemiology of alcohol and violence, Roizen (1993) lamented the fact that judicial and health professionals need to make judgments about the role of alcohol in violent behaviors at a time when we actually know very little about the nature of these relations. Unfortunately, this rather grim assessment is no less applicable to the situations that many college administrators and health professionals find themselves in with respect to alcohol, other drugs, and violent behaviors among college students. However, it is important to note that the inability to make causal inferences about relations among alcohol (and other drugs) and sexual assault and relationship violence in no way precludes inclusion of alcohol- and drug-related information in preventive interventions. For example, policy and prevention efforts can and should focus on the prevalence of alcohol-related sexual assault, increase students' awareness of the likely mechanisms by which alcohol may increase risk for sexual assault or violence (e.g., disrupted cognitive processing), and make it clear that intoxication neither mitigates responsibility on the part of the perpetrator nor suggests culpability on the part of the victim.

Administration and Institutional Responses

There are a number of ways that college administrators can evaluate the sufficiency of resources being devoted to issues of sexual assault and relationship violence among college students. Of primary importance is the need to collect reliable and valid prevalence and incidence data on sexual assault and partner violence. Such needs assessments should be repeated on a regular basis so that baseline data can be compared against data collected in subsequent years in order to evaluate trends and help evaluate the effectiveness of ongoing policy and prevention initiatives. The inclusion of faculty and graduate students with interests in these areas can help to capitalize on research methodology skills that may not be present among prevention staff. Administration officials can actively encourage these interdepartmental collaborative efforts by increasing incentives for both staff (e.g., provision of graduate assistantships) and faculty (increased weighting of university service in the tenure and promotion process). Moreover, research by Meilman and Haygood-Jackson (1996) suggested that review and refinement of existing policies and procedures to ensure that they are "victim friendly" can produce a dramatic increase in reported sexual assaults. Likewise, university counseling centers can improve their responsiveness to issues of sexual assault and relationship violence by including items addressing these incidents on intake assessments. Existing alcohol and drug policies, as well as those under consideration, should also be evaluated to determine whether they are having intended (or unintended) effects. For example, recent research by Ruback, Menard, Outlaw, and Shaffer (1999) found that both men and women were less likely to recommend reporting sexual assault to the police when an underage victim was reportedly drinking. These findings suggest that efforts to increase awareness that reports of sexual assault or dating violence to campus police will not result in adjudication of victims are needed. Policies related to alcohol and drug use, sexual assault, and dating violence should be clearly delineated and disseminated in ways that ensure familiarity among students, staff, and faculty. At a minimum, such policy statements should include: (1) definitions of sexual harassment, sexual assault, and dating violence; (2) identification of who is responsible for handling formal complaints (e.g., police, grievance board) as well as for the provision of victim services (e.g., student health services, university counseling, women's center); and (3) the consequences for those violating violence policies (Belknap & Erez, 1995).

Implications for Preventive Interventions

As noted by Abbey (2000), the consistent association between pre-assault alcohol use and sexual assault makes it imperative that campus substance abuse and violence prevention professionals coordinate their prevention and intervention efforts. While many sexual assault prevention programs incorporate discussions of alcohol, the typical focus is not commensurate with the observed frequency of alcohol-related sexual assault. Similarly, based on earlier reviews of the dating violence literature that suggested that alcohol use was not a risk factor for dating violence, prevention efforts in this area may be even less likely to address alcohol or other drug use. Additionally, evaluations of the efficacy of dating violence prevention efforts are nonexistent (Abbey, 2000; Belnap & Erez, 1995; Nicholson et al., 1998).

Despite the paucity of empirically validated violence prevention programs, there are a number of clear implications from the alcohol literature for prevention professionals working on campuses. As noted earlier (see also Abbey, 2000), the predominant theories invoked to explain alcohol's role in sexual assault relate to disruptions in cognitive processing (e.g., Steele & Josephs, 1990) and expectations of alcohol's effects on aggression and sexual behaviors (Crowe & George, 1989; Hull & Bond, 1986). As Abbey (2000) noted, if alcohol myopia explanations are correct, preventive interventions that increase the salience of the consequences of sexual assault may decrease alcohol-related sexual assault because inhibiting information may remain accessible even under conditions of intoxication. Likewise, the prevention implications stemming from expectancy theory are twofold (Abbey, 2000). First, expectancy challenge approaches (e.g., Darkes & Goldman, 1993, 1998) that focus on altering alcohol expectancies related to sexuality and increasing awareness of negative consequences, although as yet untested with respect to sexual victimization, may prove efficacious. Second, students can be made aware that intoxication does not reduce responsibility for sexual assault or dating violence.

Campus violence prevention efforts also need to recognize the likelihood that alcohol and other drugs moderate relations between other known risk factors and violence victimization. For example, prevention efforts need to make women more aware that alcohol will impair their ability to competently implement the types of strategies (e.g., early risk appraisal, assertive verbal and physical resistance) that are associated with successful avoidance of victimization (Abbey, 1991; Levine-MacCombie & Koss, 1986; Muehlenhard & Linton, 1987). Prevention efforts with men should focus on increasing awareness of their tendency to misinterpret friendly interaction as sexual interest (Abbey, 1991) and to avoid stereotypes associated with the sexual promiscuity of drinking women (George et al., 1988). Finally, preventive interventions that address communication skills among both men and women are needed to assist in clarifying sexual interest and intent and in resolving conflict in dating relations before it escalates to physical violence.

☐ Unresolved Issues and Future Research Priorities

As the preceding review demonstrates, there are a great many unresolved methodological and theoretical issues with respect to the role of alcohol (and other drugs) in collegiate sexual assault and relationship violence. In the final section of this chapter, we briefly focus on what we believe to be the most critical research priorities within college student populations. In doing so, it is our contention that a range of complementary quantitative and qualitative approaches are necessary to achieve substantive advancements in this area.

Fundamental among the unresolved research issues is the need for refined measurement of both relationship violence and substance abuse, as well as greater attention to obtaining representative samples. From a measurement standpoint, increased attention to obtaining information on the context in which intimate violent occurs (e.g., motives, symmetry) and on the psychological and physical effects of the acts is needed. While some studies (e.g., Shook et al., 2000; Stets & Henderson, 1991) have included measures of both typical and proximal alcohol use, a more refined measurement of preassault alcohol use is needed to better determine specific relations among quantity of use, frequency of use, and partner violence. Despite the more frequent inclusion of some measure of alcohol use in studies of college student sexual assault, the need for more fine-grained alcohol use assessment applies equally to research in this area. At a minimum, assessment of alcohol use should include: typical and event-related quantity and frequency; the time period in which drinks were consumed; whether and how event-related use differed from typical use (e.g., time drinking, amount); subjective intoxication; and whether other drugs were consumed in conjunction with alcohol. Based on the findings of ElSohly and Salamone (1999), increased attention to a range of other drugs appears to be warranted. More detailed questions will enable more complex hypotheses-testing regarding relations among level of substance abuse and risk and severity of sexual assault or relationship violence. Researchers also need to be cognizant of methods that can improve the quality of self-report information, such as computer-administered surveys (e.g., Turner et al., 1998). With respect to sampling, decreased reliance on samples of convenience is necessary to enhance the generalizability of findings to the entire college population.

Prospective studies also are needed with initial assessments that take place, ideally, prior to matriculation and include more diverse populations (e.g., ethnically, culturally, sexually heterogeneous) than have been typically studied. Such research is critical for a host of reasons. For example, prospective research can definitively characterize risk for sexual assault and relationship violence during college and identify factors associated with revictimization (Roscoe & Benaske, 1985; Testa & Livingston, 2000). Prospective designs, although still correlational and therefore incapable of resolving causality, are more informative than cross-sectional studies with respect to the nature of associations (e.g., delineating whether substance abuse typically precedes intimate violence, occurs as a result of it, or if reciprocal, risk-exacerbating relations exist). Perhaps most critical to conceptual advancements in this area of investigation are prospective studies that: (1) begin to explicate the processes by which alcohol and drugs may influence sexual assault and relationship violence; and (2) test hypotheses regarding the ways in which substance use might moderate relations between both distal and proximal risk factors and intimate violence. For example, alcohol expectancies, particularly those related to sexual facilitation and aggression, have been hypothesized as important mediators of relations between alcohol consumption and sexual aggression (Abbey, 1991), but prospective examinations with explicit mediational analyses (e.g., Baron & Kenny, 1986) have yet to be conducted. Likewise, models of marital (Leonard, 1993) and dating (Riggs & O'Leary, 1989) violence posit that factors such as trait hostility or acceptance of violence interact with event-related alcohol use to increase the risk of intimate violence. Our review, however, failed to locate a single study of dating violence with college students that tested the type of interaction effects hypothesized in these models. It should be noted that, although these types of mediational and moderational analyses can be conducted in cross-sectional research, prospective studies, which allow for control of baseline associations, are a more powerful, and hence preferable, methodological approach.

Laboratory (i.e., experimental) studies also are needed to provide critical tests of hypothesized associations among alcohol, other drugs, and violent behavior (e.g., Abbey, 1991; Steele & Josephs, 1990). Only through random assignment to drug or no-drug conditions can causal inferences regarding the role of drugs in sexual assault and relationship violence be made. Consequently, additional research developing and validating proxy measures of sexual assault and relationship violence and investigating them in conjunction with drug use is sorely needed. Previous research by Abbey (e.g., Abbey, 1982; Abbey & Melby, 1986) and others (e.g., Hall & Hirschman, 1994; Hammock & Richardson, 1997; Richardson & Campbell, 1982) would be informative for those embarking on such efforts.

Qualitative studies investigating the role of alcohol and other drugs in sexual assault and, particularly, dating violence, also are needed. Toward this end, Testa and Livingston (1999), in a recent study of sexual assault which combined qualitative and quantitative data, examined alcohol's role in four categories of assault: date, relationship/previous claim, unsuspecting, and set-up. They found that alcohol use by both victims and perpetrators was more common in date and set-up situations as compared to those categorized as unsuspecting or relationship-related. Abbey (2000) notes several key questions that should be addressed by future qualitative research. These include questions about opportunistic assault (e.g., targeting a drinking woman); differences in sexual assaults as a function of level of relationship (i.e., casual versus steady); cue misperception by both men and women; and alcohol-related sexual aggression. In the area of dating violence, qualitative research is needed to better contextualize how alcohol use by either or both individuals may be intertwined with motives (e.g., control, jealousy), patterns of instigation, symmetry, and severity of partner violence.

The prevalence and seriousness of sexual aggression and dating violence mandate that we not be complacent while we wait for research to provide a detailed understanding of the individual, situational, and dynamic factors involved in both sexual aggression and dating violence, and the role that alcohol plays in these problems. Clearly, alcohol is frequently present in situations resulting in sexual aggression, and it may play a causal role, but it is neither a necessary nor a sufficient ingredient in the mix that culminates in forced sex. Because of this, research on the causes and prevention of sexual aggression needs to consider alcohol as just one part of a confluence of factors. In the case of dating violence, the role of alcohol is even less clear and we need to be cautious in assuming more than is justifiable on the basis of current data.

Still, it has been well established in prevention science that effective interventions can often be mounted on the basis of less-than-complete knowledge of causal mechanisms, and this undoubtedly applies to the prevention of both coercive sex and violence in dating relationships. It is our belief that the most effective approaches to reducing alcohol-related sexual aggression and dating violence will involve both interventions that seek to prevent high levels of alcohol consumption from occurring on campus (e.g., through alcohol control policies, campus environments that discourage intoxication, sanctions for alcohol-related violations that are consistently enforced, prevention programs for high risk drinkers) and that target sexual aggression (e.g., rape prevention training, heterosocial skills training, assertion training, clear policies that promote reporting and establish consequences for coercive sexual behavior) and dating violence (e.g., anger management, assertion training, couples therapy) specifically. We also believe that by dually targeting alcohol intoxication and intimate violence as separate but related problems we might be more likely to affect a change than by attending to either problem in isolation. We base this recommendation on the extensive data showing correlations between frequency of binge drinking in students and a host of alcohol-related problems (Wechsler et al., 2000) coupled with the realization that existing prevention approaches appear to be limited in their effectiveness and that both perpetrators and victims can be sober at the time of the offense.

In closing, we note that while sexual assault and dating violence among college students are somewhat distinct with respect to their epidemiology, apparent motives, and interpersonal dynamics, the extent to which these types of violence represent overlapping versus distinct phenomenon has yet to be addressed. What they do have in common beyond their harmful effects on the victims is that they are problems that arise at a time of life when dating and developing intimate relationships are primary developmental challenges that are occurring in an increasingly autonomous environment. From a developmental perspective, both can be viewed as maladaptive responses to these challenges and, if not resolved, can lead to continuing problems in romantic relationships in later years.

☐ References

Abbey, A. (1982). Sex differences in attributions for friendly behavior: Do males misperceive females' friendliness? *Journal of Personality and Social Psychology, 42,* 830–838.

Abbey, A. (1991). Acquaintance rape and alcohol consumption on college campuses: How are they linked? *Journal of American College Health, 39,* 165–169.

Abbey, A. (2000, April). *Alcohol-related sexual assault: A common problem among college students.* Paper prepared for the National Institute of Alcohol Abuse and Alcoholism's Advisory Panel on College Student Drinking, Washington, DC.

Abbey, A., McAuslan, P., Ross, L. T., & Zawacki, T. (1999). Alcohol expectancies regarding sex, aggression, and sexual vulnerability: Reliability and validity assessment. *Psychology of Addictive Behaviors, 13,* 174–182.

Abbey, A., & Melby, C. (1986). The effects of nonverbal cues on gender differences in perceptions of sexual intent. *Sex Roles, 5/6,* 283–298.

Abbey, A., Ross, L. T., McDuffie, D., & McAuslan, P. (1996a). Alcohol and dating risk factors for sexual assault among college women. *Psychology of Women Quarterly, 20,* 147–169.

Abbey, A., Ross, L. T., McDuffie, D., & McAuslan, P. (1996b). Alcohol, misperception, and sexual assault: How and why they are linked? In D. M. Buss & N. Malamuth (Eds.), *Sex, power, conflict: Evolutionary and feminist perspectives* (pp. 138–161). New York: Oxford University Press.

Arias, I., Samios, M., & O'Leary, K. D. (1987). Prevalence and correlates of physical aggression during courtship. *Journal of Interpersonal Violence, 2,* 82–90.

Baron, R. M., & Kenny, D. A. (1986). The moderator-mediator variable distinction in social psychological research: Conceptual, strategic, and statistical considerations. *Journal of Personality and Social Psychology, 56,* 1173–1182.

Belknap, J., & Erez, E. (1995). The victimization of women on college campuses: Courtship violence, date rape, and sexual harassment. In B. S. Fisher & J. J. Sloan (Eds.), *Campus crime: Legal, social, and policy perspectives* (pp. 156–178). Springfield, IL: Charles I. Thomas.

Belknap, J., Fisher, B. S., & Cullen, F. T. (1999). The development of a comprehensive measure of the sexual victimization of college women. *Violence Against Women, 5,* 185–214.

Bograd, M. (1990). Why we need gender to understand human violence. *Journal of Interpersonal Violence, 5,* 132–135.

Brodbelt, S. (1983). College dating and aggression. *College Student Journal, 17,* 283–286.

Bureau of Justice. (1995). *Criminal victimization in the United States.* Washington, DC: U.S. Department of Justice.

Burke, L. K., & Follingstead, D. R. (1999). Violence in lesbian and gay relationships: Theory, prevalence, and correlational factors. *Clinical Psychology Review, 19,* 487–512.

Bushman, B. J., & Cooper, H. M. (1990). Effects of alcohol on aggression: An integrative research review. *Psychological Bulletin, 107,* 341–354.

Carlson, B. (1996). Dating violence: Students beliefs about consequences. *Journal of Interpersonal Violence, 11,* 3–18.

Cate, R. M., Henton, J. M., Koval, J., Christopher, F. S., & Lloyd, S. (1982). Pre-marital abuse: A social psychological perspective. *Journal of Family Issues, 3,* 79–90.

Chen, K., & Kandel, D. B. (1995). The natural history of drug use from adolescence to the mid-thirties in a general population sample. *American Journal of Public Health, 85,* 41–47.

Chermack, S. T., & Giancola, P. R. (1997). The relation between alcohol and aggression: An integrated biopsychosocial perspective. *Clinical Psychology Review,17,* 621–649.

Copenhaver, S., & Grauerholz, E. (1991). Sexual victimization among sorority women: Exploring the link between sexual violence and institutional practices. *Sex Roles, 24,* 31–41.

Core Institute. (2000). Recent statistics on alcohol and other drug use on American college campuses [On-line]. Available: http://www.siu.edu/departments/coreinst/public_html/recent.html.

Crowe, L. C., & George, W. H. (1989). Alcohol and human sexuality: Review and integration. *Psychological Bulletin, 105*, 374–386.

Cunradi, C. B., Caetano, R., Clark, C. L., & Schafer, J. (1999). Alcohol-related problems and intimate partner violence among white, black, and Hispanic couples in the U.S. *Alcoholism: Clinical & Experimental Research, 23*, 1492–1501.

Darkes, J., & Goldman, M. S. (1993). Expectancy challenge and drinking reduction: Experimental evidence for a mediational process. *Journal of Consulting and Clinical Psychology, 61*, 344–353.

Darkes, J., & Goldman, M. S. (1998). Expectancy challenge and drinking reduction: Process and structure in the alcohol expectancy network. *Experimental and Clinical Psychopharmacology, 6*, 64–76.

DeKeserey, W. S., & Kelly, K. (1993). The incidence and prevalence of woman abuse in Canadian university and college dating relationships. *Canadian Journal of Sociology, 18*, 137–159.

Dobash, P., Dobash, R., Wilson, M., & Daly, M. (1992). The myth of sexual symmetry in marital violence. *Social Problems, 39*, 73–91.

ElSohly, M. A., & Salamone, S. J. (1999). Prevalence of drugs used in cases of alleged sexual assault. *Journal of Analytic Toxicology, 23*, 141–146.

Federal Bureau of Investigation. (1986). *Crime in the United States: Uniform Crime Reports.* Washington, DC: U.S. Department of Justice.

Federal Bureau of Investigation. (1997). *Uniform Crime Reports.* Washington, DC: U.S. Department of Justice.

Fisher, B. S., Sloan, J. J., Cullen, F. T., & Lu, C. (1998). Crime in the ivory tower: The level and sources of student victimization. *Criminology, 36*, 671–710.

Follingstad, D. R., Bradley, R. G., Laughlin, J. E., & Burke, L. (1999). Risk factors and correlates of dating violence: The relevance of examining frequency and severity levels in a college sample. *Violence and Victims, 14*, 365–380.

George, W. H., Gournic, S. J., & McAfee, M. P. (1988). Perception of post drinking female sexuality: Effects of gender, beverage, choice, and drinking payment. *Journal of Applied Social Psychology, 18*, 1295–1317.

Gilbert, N. (1991). The phantom epidemic of sexual assault. *The Public Interest, 103*, 54–65.

Gilbert, N. (1993). The wrong response to rape. *The Wall Street Journal,* June 29, p. 10.

Goodchilds, J. D., & Zellman, G. L. (1984). Sexual signaling and sexual aggression in adolescent relationship. In N. Malamuth & E. Donnerstein (Eds.), *Pornography and sexual aggression* (pp. 233–243). Orlando, FL: Academic.

Goodyear-Smith, F. A., & Laidlaw, T. (1999). Aggressive acts and assaults in intimate relationships: Toward an understanding of the literature. *Behavioral Sciences and the Law, 17*, 285–304.

Hall, G. C. N., & Hirschman, R. (1994). The relationship between men's sexual aggression inside and outside the laboratory. *Journal of Consulting and Clinical Psychology, 62*, 375–380.

Hammock, G. S., & Richardson, D. R. (1997). Perceptions of rape: The influence of closeness of relationship, intoxication, and sex of participant. *Violence and Victims, 12*, 237–246.

Harrington, N. T., & Leitenberg, H. (1994). Relationship between alcohol consumption and victim behaviors immediately preceding sexual aggression by an acquaintance. *Violence and Victims, 9*, 315–324.

Henton, J., Cate, R., Koval, J., Lloyd, S., & Christopher, S. (1983). Romance and violence in dating relationships. *Journal of Family Issues, 4*, 467–482.

Himelein, M. J. (1995). Risk factors for sexual victimization in dating: A longitudinal study of college women. *Psychology of Women Quarterly, 19*, 31–48.

Himelein, M. J., Vogel, R. E., & Wachowiak, D. G. (1994). Nonconsensual sexual experiences in precollege women: Prevalence and risk factors. *Journal of Counseling and Development, 72*, 411–415.

Hull, J. G. (1981). A self-awareness model of the causes and effects of alcohol consumption. *Journal of Abnormal Psychology, 90*, 586–600.

Hull, J.G., & Bond, C. F. (1986). Social and behavioral consequences of alcohol consumption and expectancy: A meta-analysis. *Psychological Bulletin, 99*, 347–360.

Ito, T. A., Miller, N., & Pollock, V. E. (1996). Alcohol and aggression: A meta-analysis on the moderating effects of inhibitory cues, triggering events, and self-focused attention. *Psychological Bulletin, 120*, 60–82.

Jackson, S. M. (1999). Issues in the dating violence research: A review of the literature. *Aggression and Violent Behavior, 4,* 233–247.

Johnston, L. D., O'Malley, P. M., & Bachman, J. G. (1999). *National survey results on drug use from the Monitoring the Future Study, 1975–1994. Vol. II: College students and young adults.* Rockville, MD: National Institute on Drug Abuse. NIH Publication No. 99-4661.

Kalof, L. (1993). Rape-supportive attitudes and sexual victimization experiences of sorority and nonsorority women. *Sex Roles, 29,* 767–780.

Koss, M. P. (1988). Hidden rape: Sexual aggression and victimization in a national sample of students in higher education. In A. W. Burgess (Ed.), *Rape and sexual assault, Vol. 2* (pp. 3–25). New York: Garland.

Koss, M. P., & Dinero, T. E. (1989). Discriminant analysis of risk factors for sexual victimization among a national sample of college women. *Journal of Consulting and Clinical Psychology, 57,* 242–250.

Koss, M. P., Gidycz, C. A., & Wisniewski, N. (1987). The scope of rape: Incidence and prevalence of sexual aggression and victimization in a national sample of higher education students. *Journal of Consulting and Clinical Psychology, 55,* 162–170.

Koss, M. P., & Oros, C. J. (1982). Sexual Experiences Survey: Reliability and validity. *Journal of Consulting and Clinical Psychology, 53,* 422–423.

Lane, K. E., & Gwartney-Gibbs, P. A. (1985). Violence in the context of dating and sex. *Journal of Family Issues, 6,* 45–59.

Laner, M. R. (1983). Courtship abuse and aggression: Contextual aspects. *Sociological Spectrum, 3,* 69–83.

Larimer, M. E., Lydum, A. R., Anderson, B. K., & Turner, A. P. (1999). Male and female recipients of unwanted sexual contact in a college student sample: Prevalence rates, alcohol use, and depression symptoms. *Sex Roles, 40,* 295–308.

Leonard, K. E. (1993). Drinking patterns and intoxication in marital violence: Review, critique, and future directions for research. In S. Martin (Ed.), *Alcohol and interpersonal violence: Fostering multidisciplinary perspectives* (pp. 253–280). NIAAA Research Monograph 24. Rockville, MD. Department of Health and Human Services.

Leonard, K. E., & Senchak, M. (1993). Alcohol and premarital aggression among newlywed couples. *Journal of Studies on Alcohol* 54(Suppl. 11,), 96–108.

Leonard, K. E., & Senchak, M. (1996). Prospective prediction of husband marital aggression within newlywed couples. *Journal of Abnormal Psychology, 105,,* 369–380.

Levine-MacCombie, J., & Koss, M. P. (1986). Acquaintance rape: Effective avoidance strategies. *Psychology of Women Quarterly, 10,* 311–320.

Lott, B., Reilly, M. E., & Howard, D. R. (1982). Sexual assault and harassment: A campus community case study. *Signs: Journal of Women in Culture and Society, 8,* 296–319.

Makepeace, J. M. (1981). Courtship violence among college students. *Family Relations, 30,* 97–102.

Makepeace, J. M. (1983). Life events, stress and courtship violence. *Family Relations, 32,* 102–109.

Makepeace, J. M. (1984, August). The severity of courtship violence injuries and individual precautionary measures. Paper presented at the Second National Family Violence Research Conference, University of New Hampshire, Durham, NH.

Makepeace, J. M. (1986). Gender differences in courtship violence victimization. *Family Relations, 35,* 383–388.

Makepeace, J. M. (1987). Social factors and victim offender differences in courtship violence. *Family Relations, 36,* 87–91.

Mandoki, C. A., & Burkhart, B. R. (1989). Sexual victimization: Is there a vicious cycle? *Violence and Victims, 4,* 179–190.

Martin, P. Y., & Hummer, R. A. (1989). Fraternities and rape on campus. *Gender and Society, 3,* 457–473.

Matthews, W. J. (1984). Violence in college couples. *College Student Journal, 18,* 150–158.

Meilman, P. W., & Haygood-Jackson, D. (1996). Data on sexual assault from the first 2 years of a comprehensive campus prevention program. *Journal of American College Health, 44,* 157–165.

Midanik, L. T., & Clark, W. B. (1994). Demographic distribution of US drinking patterns in 1990: Descriptions and trends from 1984. *Journal of Studies on Alcohol, 56,* 395–402.

Mills, C. S., & Granoff, B. J. (1992). Date and acquaintance rape among a sample of college students. *Social Work, 37,* 504–509.

Muehlenhard, C. L., & Linton, M. A. (1987). Date rape and sexual aggression in dating situations: Incidence and risk factors. *Journal of Consulting and Clinical Psychology, 34,* 186–196.

Neal, C. J., & Mangis, M. W. (1995). Unwanted sexual experiences among Christian college women: Saying no on the inside. *Journal of Psychology and Theology, 23,* 171–179.

Nicholson, M. E., Maney, D. W., Blair, K., Wambold, P. M., Mahoney, B. S., & Yuan, J. (1998). *Journal of Alcohol and Drug Education, 43,* 34–52.

Plass, M. S., & Gessner, J. C. (1983). Violence in courtship relations: A Southern example. *Free Inquiry into Creative Sociology, 11,* 198–202.

Presley, C. A., Leichliter, J. S., & Meilman, P. W. (1998). *Alcohol and drugs on American college campuses: A report to college presidents.* Carbondale, IL: Southern Illinois University.

Presley, C. A., Meilman, P. W., & Cashin, J. R. (1996, October). *Alcohol and drugs on American college campuses: Use, consequences, and perceptions of the campus environment.* Carbondale IL: Southern Illinois University.

Presley, C. A., Meilman, P. W., Cashin, J. R., & Leichliter, J. S. (1997). *Alcohol and drugs on American college campuses: Issues of violence and harassment.* Carbondale, IL: Southern Illinois University.

Richardson, D., & Campbell, J. L. (1982). Alcohol and rape: The effect of alcohol on attribution of blame for rape. *Personality and Social Psychology Bulletin, 8,* 468–476.

Riggs, D. S., & O'Leary, K. D. (1989). A theoretical model of courtship aggression. In M. A. Pirog-Good, & J. E. Stets (Eds.), *Violence in dating relationships: Emerging social issues* (pp. 53–71). New York: Praeger.

Rogers, K. (1994). Wife assault: The findings of a national survey. *Juristat Service Bulletin, 14,* 1–22.

Roiphe, K. (1993). *The morning after: Sex, fear, and feminism on campus.* Boston: Little, Brown.

Roizen, J. (1993). Issues in the epidemiology of alcohol and violence. In S. E. Martin (Ed.), *Alcohol and interpersonal violence: Fostering multidisciplinary perspectives* (pp. 3–36). National Institute on Alcohol Abuse and Alcoholism Monograph No. 24, Rockville, MD: National Institutes of Health. (NIH Publication No. 93-3496)

Roscoe, B., & Benaske, N. (1985). Courtship violence experienced by abused wives: Similarities in patterns of abuse. *Family Relations, 34,* 419–424.

Roscoe, B., & Kelsey, T. (1986). Dating violence among high school students. *Psychology, 23,* 53–59.

Ruback, R. B., Menard, K. S., Outlaw, M. C., & Shaffer, J. N. (1999). Normative advice to campus crime victims: Effects of gender, age, and alcohol. *Violence and Victims, 14,* 381–396.

Sayette, M. A. (1993). An appraisal-disruption model of alcohol's effects on stress responses in social drinkers. *Psychological Bulletin, 114,* 459–476.

Sayatte, M. A. (1999). Cognitive theory and research. In K. E. Leonard & H. T. Blane (Eds.). *Psychological theories of drinking and alcoholism* (pp. 247–291). New York: Guilford.

Scarce, M. (1997). Same-sex rape of male college students. *Journal of American College Health, 45,* 171–173.

Shook, N. J., Gerrity, D. A., Jurich, J., & Segrist, A. E. (2000). Courtship violence among college students: A comparison of verbally and physically abusive couples. *Journal of Family Violence, 15,* 1–22.

Sigelman, C. K., Berry, C. J., & Wiles, K. A. (1984). Violence in college students dating relationships. *Journal of Applied Social Psychology, 5–6,* 530–548.

Steele, C. M., & Josephs, R. A. (1990). Alcohol myopia: Its prized and dangerous effects. *American Psychologist, 45,* 921–933.

Stets, J. E., & Henderson, D. A. (1991). Contextual factors surrounding conflict resolution while dating: Results from a national study. *Family Relations, 40,* 29–36.

Stets, J. E., & Straus, M. A. (1989). The marriage license as hitting license: A comparison of assaults in dating, cohabitating, and married couples. In M. Pirog-Good & J. Stets (Eds.), *Violence in dating relationships* (pp 33–52). New York: Prager.

Straus, M. A. (1979). Measuring intrafamily conflict and violence: The Conflict Tactics Scales. *Journal of Marriage and the Family, 41,* 75–88.

Straus, M. A., & Gelles, R. J. (1986). Societal changes and change in family violence from 1975 to 1985 as revealed by two national surveys. *Journal of Marriage and the Family, 48,* 465–479.

Struckman-Johnson, C., & Struckman-Johnson, D. (1994). Men pressured and forced into sexual experience. *Archives of Sexual Behavior, 23,* 93–114.

Sugarman, D. B., & Hotaling, G. T. (1989). Dating violence: Prevalence, context, and risk markers. In M. Pirog-Good & J. Stets (Eds.), *Violence in dating relationships* (pp. 3–32). New York: Prager.

Taylor, S. P., & Chermack, S. T. (1993). Alcohol, drugs and human physical aggression. *Journal of Studies on Alcohol, 11*(Suppl.), 78–88.

Taylor, S. P., & Leonard, K. E. (1983). Alcohol and human aggression. In R. Geen & E. Donnerstein (Eds.), *Aggression: Theoretical and methodological issues* (pp. 77–101). New York: Academic.

Testa, M., & Livingston, J. A. (1999). Qualitative analysis of women's experiences of sexual aggression. *Psychology of Women Quarterly, 23,* 573–587.

Testa, M., & Livingston, J. A. (2000). Alcohol and sexual aggression: Reciprocal relations over time in a sample of high-risk women. *Journal of Interpersonal Violence, 15,* 413–427.

Turner, C. F., Ku, L., Rogers, S. M., Lindberg, L. D., Pleck, J. H., & Sonerstein, F. L. (1998). Adolescent sexual behavior, drug use, and violence: Increased reporting with computer survey technology. *Science, 280,* 867–873.

Tyler, K. A., Hoyt, D. R., & Whitbeck, L. B. (1998). Coercive sexual strategies. *Violence and Victims, 13,* 47–60.

Ullman, S. E., Karabatsos, G., & Koss, M. P. (1999). Alcohol and sexual assault in a national sample of college women. *Journal of Interpersonal Violence, 14,* 603–625.

Waldner-Haugrud, L. K., Gratch, L. V., & Magruder, B. (1997). Victimization and perpetration rates of violence in gay and lesbian relationships: Gender issues explored. *Violence and Victims, 12,* 173–184.

Ward, S. K., Chapman, K., Cohn, E., White, S., & Williams, K. (1991). Acquaintance rape and the college social scene. *Family Relations, 40,* 65–71.

Wechsler, H., Davenport, A., Dowdall, G., Moeykens, B., & Castillo, S. (1994). Health and behavioral consequences of binge drinking in college. *Journal of the American Medical Association, 272*(21), 1672–1677.

Wechsler, H., Dowdall, G. W., Maenner, G., Gledhill-Hoyt, J., & Lee, H. (1998). Changes in binge drinking and related problems among American college students between 1993 and 1997: Results of the Harvard School of Public Health College Alcohol Study. *Journal of American College Health, 47,* 57–68.

Wechsler, H., Lee, J. E., Kuo, M., & Lee, H. (2000). College binge drinking in the 1990s: A continuing problem. *Journal of American College Health, 48,* 199–210.

White, J. W., & Koss, M. P. (1991). Courtship violence: Incidence in a national sample of higher education students. *Violence and Victims, 6,* 247–256.

9

CHAPTER

Kenneth E. Leonard

Alcohol and Substance Abuse in Marital Violence and Child Maltreatment

One of the key developmental contexts for exploring the relationship between substance use and abuse and relationship violence is the early adult years. Although adult status is legally conferred at age 18 in the U.S., the transition to adulthood is a gradual process spanning the late teens to middle twenties. The transition is marked by a number of key developmental events. These include the completion of formal education, initiation of stable employment and career paths, and the establishment of an independent domicile. From the perspective of family violence, two other transitional events are likely to occur, the development of an enduring intimate relationship, usually, but not always marked by a marriage ceremony, and the further development of this evolving family structure with the addition of children. Consequently, while there are other opportunities for violence, these two aspects of early adulthood establish a consistent opportunity for partner violence and for violence toward children. In the midst of this gradual transition to adulthood, young adults reach the age of legal consumption of alcohol. Obviously, the restraint of a legal drinking age is not entirely effective, and many individuals will have consumed alcohol regularly prior to this time. However, the release of the previous constraints is associated with high rates of alcohol consumption, episodic heavy drinking, and alcohol problems. Thus, this period involves multiple interpersonal stresses associated with one's role as a marital partner and as a parent, and it coincides with the official sanctioning of alcohol use and the developmental period marked by the highest rates of alcohol problems. While other substances also are used within this timeframe, the prevalence of alcohol use and the extant literature focus one's attention primarily on this substance. Consequently, understanding the relationship between substance use and family violence within this developmental epoch is of paramount importance.

This research was supported by grant R01-AA08128.

☐ Developmental Issues in Alcohol Use across the Early Adult Years

Epidemiological studies of drinking, drinking problems, and dependence highlight the third decade of life as the period of greatest overall risk for men. With respect to women, there is evidence of higher risk in this age range (Clark & Midanik, 1982), though there are contrary findings as well (Hilton, 1991). However, studies that examine the period of 18–30 years of age more closely tend to suggest that drinking and drinking problems increase from age 18 through the early 20s with gradual declines throughout the later 20s and into the early 30s (Bachman et al., 1997; Clark & Midanik, 1982). For example, Bachman et al. report rates of heavy drinking (five or more drinks in a row) of 49% for 18-year-old men, 55% for 21–22-year-old men, and 38% for 29–30-year-old men. The comparable percentages for women were 29%, 31%, and 15%.

It has been suggested that the age trends in heavy drinking may reflect two co-occurring processes: increasing freedom—reflected in establishing a separate domicile and reaching the legal age of drinking in the late teens to early 20s—and increased responsibility as reflected in beginning a career, getting married, and having children. In examining any one of these transitional events, there are at least three issues that are important to consider. First, there is considerable variability with respect to the age that an individual will experience any given event. Some individuals in their early 20s may still be in school and residing with their parents, while others may have a full time job, be married, and have a child. Second, while there are cultural expectations concerning the temporal occurrence of these events, it is clear that many individuals, perhaps most individuals, do not follow this temporal expectation precisely. Third, it is not uncommon for later life events to essentially reverse transitional events, as with divorce, unemployment, or returning to school or to a parent's home. However, these reversals are not likely to return the individual to a state comparable to the pretransitional state. As a consequence of these factors, it is sometime difficult to link changes in drinking to a specific transitional event.

From a general developmental perspective, the most thorough analysis of developmental transitions was conducted by Bachman et al. (1997). This study was based on the Monitoring the Future study which involved the assessment on national samples of high school seniors and periodic follow ups of subsamples of these seniors. The surveys assess sociodemographic variables, alcohol use, as well as the use of other substances, and the occurrence of a variety of posthigh school experiences. Analyses essentially compared respondents' substance use before and after a developmental transition, and contrasted this with temporal changes across a similar time period with respondents who did not experience the event. Moreover, differences in sociodemographic factors and the occurrence of the other developmental transitions were controlled for in the analyses. The authors interpreted the results in this way: "The increases in alcohol use between ages 18 and 22 resulted mainly from new freedoms in living arrangements . . . as well as the freedom to purchase alcohol at age 21. The reductions in alcohol use between age 22 and 32 largely reflect the impacts of new responsibilities associated with engagement, marriage, pregnancy, and parenthood" (p. 106). Moreover, these general conclusions held for both marijuana and cocaine use, and to some extent, cigarette use. While little research has systematically addressed the importance of most of these developmental transitions to alcohol or substance use, a considerable body of research focused on the transition to marriage strongly supports these analyses (Curran, Muthen, & Harford, 1998; Miller-Tutzauer, Leonard, & Windle, 1991). Although there has been considerably less research, there is evidence that the transition to parenthood is associated with a reduction in alcohol use (Chilcoat & Breslau, 1996; Labouvie, 1996), though there have been reports of increased problem drinking accompanying parenthood as well (Richman, Rospenda, & Kelley, 1995).

In describing the transition to marriage and parenthood, the focus has primarily been on individual changes across this transition. However, these transitions, and, in particular, the marital transition, entail the development and legitimization of an interdependent social context, which as applied to the issue of alcohol use has been labeled the "drinking partnership." The nature of this context is defined, in part, by the selection of one's spouse or assortative mating, and by the mutual influence exerted by the members of marital dyad on each other, and the influence of external pressures that are exerted on the couple as a unit (e.g. socializing opportunities, other life transitions, and unexpected life events). There is some evidence for each of these processes. For example, as part of a longitudinal study, Yamaguchi and Kandel (1993) assessed individuals about substance use during adolescence (age 15–16) and reassessed these individuals 13 years later. At the second assessment, the spouses were asked about their lifetime substance use, their past year use, and the onset of use of the drugs. The findings indicated a relationship between the substance use prior to marriage of respondents and their partner. However, this study could not provide definitive conclusions with respect to the other two processes. As part of a larger study, Labouvie (1996) analyzed data collected as part of the Rutgers Health and Human Development project, a longitudinal study also spanning 13 years. At the fourth assessment (age 28–31), married individuals reported on the current alcohol, cigarette, and drug use of their spouse. Of interest, the subjects' use at the third assessment (age 21–24) was predictive of their spouse's use at the fourth assessment, suggesting an assorting process. More recently, Leonard and Eiden (1999) assessed both husbands and wives after they applied for their marriage licenses and then reassessed both at the first anniversary. Using structural equation models, these authors found evidence for assortative mating and common external influence on drinking. The study also found evidence that husband drinking had a longitudinal impact on wife drinking. While more research is needed to definitely address the relative importance of these processes, the implications for understanding family violence are clear: Husbands and wives tend to manifest similar drinking patterns, these similarities are observed very early in marriage, and drinking by husbands and wives tends to change in similar ways over development.

Although not typically considered in this vein, it is important to consider the possibility of husband-wife similarity as being influenced by differential divorce patterns. For example, more positive marriages have been reported by couples who have comparable drinking frequencies than among other couples (Wilsnack & Wilsnack, 1990). Roberts and Leonard (1998) reported high marital satisfaction among couples with frequent drinking that occurred together and in the home. The lowest marital satisfaction was apparent among couples in which the husband was a heavy drinker, but the wife was a very light drinker or abstainer. Not only does this suggest that there may be a press for similarity within the relationship, but it raises the possibility that discrepant drinking couples may be more likely to divorce.

☐ Developmental Issues in Marital and Parental Violence

Although there is considerable longitudinal and cross-sectional research focused on the developmental aspects of alcohol and substance use, there is very little comparable research focused on either marital or parental violence. Similar to the age-related changes observed in drinking, age is strongly associated with the risk of marital aggression. Although annual prevalence rates of marital aggression are approximately 12% for the general population, rates among individuals under 30 and among individuals in the early years of marriage are substantially higher. For example, McLaughlin, Leonard, and Senchak (1992) evaluated husband-to-wife violence in the year prior to marriage and found rates of approximately 28% according to either husbands or wives' reports. Combining husband and wife report led to an estimated prevalence of 38%. Even given the similar life stage, rates of aggression varied with age. Among men between 18 and 21, aggression was reported by either husband or wife in 46% of the couples. In contrast, the rates for 22–25-year-old men and 26–29-year-old men were 36% and 30%, respectively. Similar findings have been reported by O'Leary et al. (1989). Further, rates continue to decline into the 30s and throughout the lifespan of individuals (Suiter, Pillemer, & Straus, 1990). Aside from this general relationship between age and marital violence, other developmental aspects have not been well studied. Similar to the literature with respect to drinking, it is not uncommon to find similarity with respect to husband aggression toward wife and wife aggression toward husband. For example, information provided in O'Leary et al. (1989) suggests that in about 18% of couples there had been husband-to-wife and wife-to-husband aggression prior to marriage. At 18 months, the rate of both being aggressive was about 19%, and at 30 months the rate was about 16%. Thus, between 30% and 40% of violent couples displayed both husband-to-wife and wife-to-husband aggression when, based on the overall rates of violence, between 22% and 32% would show bilateral violence by chance. It is difficult to determine what this similarity reflects. Some of it probably reflects wives responding with defensive aggressive actions to protect themselves from their husbands' aggression. However, it is possible that this data could reflect some assortative processes whereby men with an acceptance of marital violence are more likely to marry women who also accept marital violence. There is little direct evidence of such a process, though there is some evidence that young couples, both married and dating, manifest similarity with respect to antisocial behavior (Krueger, Moffitt, Caspi, Bleske, & Silva, 1998).

There has been some concern about the possibility that pregnancy represents a period of heightened risk for marital violence. Gelles (1990) has reported somewhat elevated rates of marital violence among pregnant women than among nonpregnant women, though his subsequent analyses suggested that this was the result of pregnant women simply being younger, on average, than nonpregnant women.

Although fairly uncommon, there has been some longitudinal research focused on changes in marital violence over several years. Three studies have targeted newlywed couples and followed them into the early years of marriage. O'Leary et al. (1989) assessed 272 couples recruited through newspaper ads and assessed them prior to marriage, 18 months postmarriage and 30 months postmarriage. Bradbury and Lawrence (1999) recruited couples by sending a recruitment letter to couples who had applied for a marriage license. Approximately 18% responded to this letter and the first 172 couples who met eligibility requirements (which included being childless) and who made their first appointment were enrolled in the study. The couples were initially assessed at six months postmarriage and were reassessed 18 months postmarriage. In our Buffalo Newlywed Study (cf. Leonard & Roberts, 1998), we recruited couples in person as the couples applied for their marriage license. Couples were assessed at the time of marriage with complete data being collected from 647 couples (or 77% of the recruited sample). These couples were then reassessed at their first and third anniversaries, with information regarding violence available for 78% of the sample at the third anniversary. Together, these three studies provide some basic information regarding developmental aspects of marital aggression.

First, the studies suggest that approximately one third to one quarter of couples will experience marital aggression in the first several years of marriage. For example, O'Leary et al. (1989) found that 31% of males reported engaging in aggressive acts against their partners prior to marriage. This figure dropped to 27% at 18 months and 25% at 30 months. Among women, the rates dropped from 44% prior to marriage to 36% at 18 months and 32% at 30 months. In the Bradbury and Lawrence (1999) study, these investigators reported on couple reports of both husband and wife aggression. At six months, 29% of the couples were aggressive, but this decreased to 23% at 18 months. Research from our longitudinal study of newlyweds provides some additional insight on the developmental aspects of marital aggression over the early years of marriage. Before marriage, the rate of any husband-to-wife aggression was 34%. At the time of the third anniversary, we assessed husband-to-wife aggression retrospectively for the first, second, and third years of marriage. [1] The rate of any husband aggression by either husband or wife report was 35% in the first year of marriage, 35% in the second year, and 37% in the third year. Although these studies differ in the eligibility requirements, sampling frame, and definition of marital aggression (i.e., husband and/or wife aggression, individual report versus couple report), it is difficult to completely reconcile the different figures. Consequently, whether marital aggression is stable or decreasing over the early years is not clear. However, it is clear that it is experienced at least once by a sizeable proportion of married individuals.

The data from these studies also suggest that, although there are roughly stable rates in marital aggression over the early years of marriage, there is less stability in aggression over this time than might be expected. That is, there appears to be a small group of individuals who are aggressive over all of the early years, but a more sizeable group that experiences the aggression more erratically. In the O'Leary et al. (1989) study, only 8% of the men and 17% of the women reported aggression at all three assessments, while approximately 50% of the men and 39% of the women reported no aggression at any of the three assessments. Hence, 42% of the men and 44% of the women reported inconsistent aggression. In our own study, only 13% of the couples reported husband-to-wife aggression premaritally and in the first, second, and third years of marriage. Another 14% reported aggression in three of the time periods, 18% in two of the time periods, and 13% in any one of the time periods. Only 41% reported no husband-to-wife aggression in any of the periods.

The studies suggest that if aggression is going to occur, it will occur sooner in the marriage rather than later. O'Leary et al. (1989) found that among men who engaged in aggression within the first 30 months of marriage, 66% did so prior to marriage, with an additional 22% doing so by the 18th month of the marriage. Only 12% of the aggressive men initiated aggression after the 18 month assessment. Similarly, only 9% of the women initiated aggression after the 18 month assessment. Similar to the O'Leary et al. (1989)

---

[1]Although we did have reports of Year 1 husband-to-wife aggression at the first anniversary, we chose to present the retrospective reports from the third anniversary to ensure comparability with the report on the second year of marriage. It is worth noting that 80% of the couples had comparable reports of first year aggression at the first and third anniversaries (83% of nonaggressive couples at the first anniversary reported no retrospective Year 1 aggression at the third anniversary, and 74% of aggressive couples at the first anniversary reported retrospective Year 1 aggression). Moreover, our prevalence and turnover estimates are not changed when the first anniversary data is used rather than the retrospective third anniversary data.

study, among men in our study, 55% of the men who would engage in aggression by the third anniversary did so prior to marriage, 26% began in the first year of marriage, 10% began in the second year of marriage, and 9% began in the third year.

Finally, these studies provide some insight on the cessation of marital aggression. In general, about 40%–50% of couples who display marital aggression very early in marriage will not display aggression in the following time period. For example, O'Leary et al. (1989) found that 49% of men who reported aggression premaritally did not report aggression 18 months into marriage. This figure was based on only the husband's report of his aggression. Desistance rates that were based on both husband and wife report would be somewhat lower. Bradbury and Lawrence (1999), who reported couple aggression irrespective of whether it involved husband or wife aggression, found that 24 of the 45 couples who were moderately or severely aggressive at 6 months were not aggressive at 18 months for a desistance rate of 53%. In our study, 39% of the premaritally aggressive men were not aggressive during the first year according to both husbands and wives. While desistance over a short duration is fairly high in early marriage, desistance rates drop dramatically if one extends the duration. For example, Quigley and Leonard (1996) reported only 25% of couples who were aggressive during the first year of marriage were not aggressive in either the second or third year of marriage.

Taken together, these studies suggest that most aggression in marriages has an early onset, often prior to or in the first year of marriage. Couples who do not display aggression during this time period appear unlikely to display aggression subsequently. In contrast, among couples who behave aggressively, it appears that most will display aggression at some time later in their marriage. Relatively few initially aggressive couples are consistently aggressive throughout the early years of marriage, though the degree of consistency is greater among individuals who have displayed severe levels of aggression. Finally, although there may be some decreases in marital aggression over the early years of marriage, the extent of these decrements is modest at best.

In addition to the developmental research directed specifically at marital violence, there is a considerable body of such research focused on marital functioning and marital conflict, two factors that are associated with, and may be causally related to, marital aggression. In general, this research indicates that marital satisfaction decreases and marital conflict increases shortly after marriage. For example, Huston and Houts (1998) report "declines in love, satisfaction, affection, and maintenance, coupled with increases in ambivalence and conflict (p. 131)" occur over the first two years of marriage. Kurdek's (1993) large scale study of newlyweds found reductions in marital satisfaction over the first six years of marriage, but the steepest drop occurred between the first assessment shortly after marriage to the second assessment in the middle of the second year of marriage. Lindahl, Clements, and Markman (1998) assessed couples shortly before marriage and followed them until, on average, past eight years of marriage. Similar to the other research, there were reductions in marital satisfaction until about three years after the first assessment. Ratings of problem intensities, withdrawal, and verbal aggression remained elevated throughout this time, with declines apparent at assessment 6 (approximately 6–7 years postmarriage). In short, the first several years of marriage appear to be marked by heightened conflict and reductions in marital satisfaction. As the marriage continues beyond five years, marital satisfaction appears to plateau and conflict begins to decline. It is important to recognize that these broad trends may mask significant temporal variability among couples. In addition, these findings characterize marriages that survive beyond the first several years, and obviously do not address the trajectory of marriages that terminate prior to the final assessment point.

Developmental aspects of child abuse represents a neglected research area. There is evidence to suggest that the age of the child is differentially related to different forms of abuse. For example, Finklehor and Dziuba-Leatherman (1994) report that homicides of children that are committed by family members occur disproportionately among the very young (birth through two years old) and very rarely beyond the age of four or five, a finding echoed in Child Maltreatment, 1997 (United States Department of Health and Human Services, 1999). Similarly, Herrmann and Martin (1988) found that children hospitalized for abuse were likely to be under the age of three. In contrast, research based on official reports to child protective services and other professional agencies (e.g. schools, police) finds that the lowest rates are apparent among children from birth to age two, with gradually increasing rates through ages 12 to 14 (Cappelleri, Eckenrode, & Powers, 1993). Data provided in Child Maltreatment, 1997 (USDHHS, 1999) suggests low rates of physical abuse among children from birth to age three and among children 16 and older. Epidemiologic research suggests the rates of physical punishment and severe assault are very high among children from age one to three. However, in contrast to the extreme abuse reflected in homicides and hospitalizations, the epidemiologic research does not find the dramatic reductions after this developmental stage, but rather modest gradual reductions until the adolescent years, when the rates decline markedly (Wauchope & Straus, 1990). The most reasonable explanation for these disparate findings is that physical abuse declines somewhat with age. However, the high level of fragility among infants and very young children renders them much more vulnerable to an extreme outcome if abuse occurs. The higher rates of official reports of abuse that are observed among older children may reflect the children's more extensive contact with people in a position to report abuse to the proper authorities.

There has been little research examining the impact of parental age on child abuse. Connelly and Straus (1992) have reported that the age of the mother at the time of the child's birth was related to abuse, although the age of the mother at the time of the interview was only marginally associated with abuse. Because the age of the mother would be associated with the age of the child, these analyses controlled for the age of the child, and also controlled for race, education, number of children, and being a single parent.

☐ Developmental Challenges and the Alcohol-Family Violence Relationship

Clearly, the developmental period of early adulthood entails a number of individual and interpersonal challenges. Perhaps it is the demands of these developmental challenges coupled with the conflict engendered by having to reconcile important and potentially discrepant values that is responsible for the high rates of marital aggression. Although the evidence regarding child abuse is less clear, there does seem to be an excess among parents in their twenties. In any event, these stresses, the inexperience of young adulthood, and the potentially frustrating experiences associated with raising a young child may be responsible for the heightened risk of child abuse during this developmental period. Whether these factors are causes or whether other factors are of importance is less critical for the present discussion than the observation that the factors that promote family violence are very common during this developmental period.

This observation is critical because most explanations of the role of alcohol in violent behavior implicitly or explicitly suggest that alcohol does not have a simple, straightforward effect on aggression. Carpenter and Armenti (1972), arguing against such a simple, direct notion of causation, state "What is more likely to be true is that alcohol modifies the expression of sexual or aggressive behavior if either or both are appropriate to a particular set of stimulating conditions" (p. 540). Pernanen (1976) discusses a broad range of potential explanations for the alcohol-violence relationship and suggests the potential importance of conditional models, arguing that factors that produce aggression, such as frustration or stress, "could interact with alcohol use to produce a higher probability of aggression in alcohol as opposed to nonalcohol situations" (p. 402). Subsequent models by Taylor and Leonard (1983) and Steele and Josephs (1990) also make this prediction. In short, most models of alcohol and violence suggest that alcohol facilitates aggression primarily in instances in which other factors, either within the person or in the situation, frame the situation as aggressive and provoke the aggressive incident. Given the overall prevalence of aggressive behaviors in the young adult period, alcohol-related aggression should be of particular prominence at this time.

The developmental perspective highlights early adulthood as a critical period, but it also raises some critical issues that arise in alcohol and family violence research that include subjects across the entire range of adult ages. In particular, given that the incidence of family violence and the extent of heavy drinking are substantially decreased in cohorts in their 30s and 40s, studies of general population samples may be characterized by restricted ranges on these two variables. As a consequence, to the extent that a sample is dominated by these somewhat older subjects, larger sample sizes would be required to observe a relationship. In addition, both heavy drinking and marital violence increase the likelihood of divorce. Consequently, there is a possibility that those couples in which alcohol and violence co-occurred might gradually decrease in prevalence in married populations. Such problems would, of course, be confined to general population and community studies, but would not be applicable to clinical samples. Clinical samples are confronted with other potential limitations. These limitations are primarily concerned with the differences between those who seek clinical services and those with similar problems who do not seek such services. For example, spouses of alcoholics often urge their husbands to seek treatment. If a past occurrence of violence inhibited the women from pressing this issue, rates of family violence in the clinical sample might underestimate the true extent of the problem. Although these problems do have important implications for clinical studies, these problems would seem to cross different developmental periods.

In the next section of this chapter, I review research concerning the relationship between alcohol and family violence, beginning with studies that span adulthood, and then focusing more specifically on studies of the developmental period of early adulthood, roughly age 18–35.

☐ The Alcohol-Marital Violence Relationship

Although there are occasional disconfirming reports, it seems clear that the drinking behavior of men is consistently and pervasively associated with marital violence. Epidemiologic studies have provided the strongest and most consistent support for this relationship. In particular, analyses of the 1975 and 1985 National Family Violence Surveys have found that drinking patterns in men were consistently related to marital violence (Coleman & Straus, 1983; Kaufman-Kantor & Straus, 1990). For example, Kaufman Kantor and Straus (1990) reported husband-to-wife violence rates of approximately 17–19% for high and binge drinkers in contrast to rates of 9–11% for low and low-moderate drinkers. This association held even after controlling for the husband's occupational status and his acceptance or rejection of "wife slapping" under some conditions. With over 2000 men in this study, this represents one of the largest, most comprehensive studies of the issue. Interestingly, other analyses of this data set that focused on frequency of drinking failed to find associations between drinking and overall couple violence (Suitor et al., 1990). The positive association in the Kaufman Kantor and Straus paper could be attributed to the use of the usual quantity of alcohol consumption in the derivation of the alcohol variable, although it also could be attributed to the exclusive focus on husband-to-wife violence.

In addition to the broad, nationally representative studies, more focused epidemiologic studies have linked patterns of alcohol use to marital violence. Leonard, Bromet, Parkinson, Day, and Ryan (1985) evaluated 352 married, blue collar workers and found that men with a current diagnosis of alcohol abuse or dependence had higher rates (50% and 39%, respectively) of marital aggression than men with no diagnosis (15%) or a past diagnosis of abuse (8%) or dependence (18%), suggesting the importance of current alcohol use. It is of interest that of the three criteria for an alcohol diagnosis (pathological pattern, social consequences, signs of dependence), only a pathological pattern of consumption was related to marital aggression. Moreover, the overall amount of alcohol consumed was not related to marital violence, leading to the suggestion that the pattern of consumption ("instances of very excessive consumption" [Leonard et al., 1985, p. 281]) was more important than the total consumption. This suggestion was later supported by Kaufman Kantor and Straus's observation of the high rates associated with binge drinking.

Surveys that have focused on different ethnic groups also have found support for the relationship between alcohol and marital violence. Kaufman Kantor (1997) reported on the 1992 National Alcohol and Family Violence Survey that involved approximately 1000 Anglo-Americans and 800 Hispanic Americans. Despite variations in the strength of the association, this study reported higher rates of violence among heavy drinkers in the Anglo population, and in the three largest Hispanic subgroups. This contrasts with the findings reported by Neff, Holamon, and Schluter (1995) who assessed Anglo, Mexican-American, and African-American men and women. The results of this study indicated a relationship between drinking and men's report of their violence to their partner, although this relationship was not significant after controlling for the respondent's report of the partner's drinking. Among women reporting on their husband's drinking and his violence, there was no association, but the very crude assessment of partner drinking may have easily obscured any relationship.

Studies of clinical samples have tended to support the association between alcohol use and marital violence. Julian and McKenry (1993) compared 42 violent men (mostly court referrals) with 50 nonviolent men recruited through newspaper ads. Based on scores on the Michigan Alcoholism Screening Test (MAST; Selzer, 1971), 57.5% of violent men were alcoholic while 42.5% of controls were alcoholic (MAST scores of 6 or more). This difference was significant at the bivariate level, but not in multivariate analyses. Stith and Farley (1993) assessed 44 men in treatment for male violence and 77 men in treatment for alcoholism. Combining these two samples, the frequency of severe violence correlated with scores on the MAST. In the final path model, the MAST score was related to the approval of marital violence, which, in turn, was related to severe violence. However, the MAST was not uniquely related to severe violence after controlling for the approval of marital violence. Barnett and Fagan (1993) compared 43 maritally violent, uncounseled men, 46 maritally violent counseled men, 42 nonviolent distressed men, and 50 nonviolent maritally satisfied men. Overall, the frequency of drinking did not distinguish the groups but the usual amount of beer and liquor and total quantity of drinking did.

Summarizing across these and other studies, most reviewers have concluded that there is an association between alcohol use and marital violence (Gelles, 1993; Hotaling & Sugarman, 1986; Tolman & Bennett, 1990). Most recently, Lipsey, Wilson, Cohen, and Derzon (1997) reported a weighted correlation of .22 across 34 studies of chronic alcohol use and domestic violence. While these authors suggest that this correlation could be inflated by uncontrolled confounding factors, this weighted correlation combined very diverse studies. For example, some studies focused on average level of use while others focused on binge use, lifetime alcohol problems, and alcoholism. Although significant findings have been reported with respect to several different measures of alcohol use, including the MAST, the average amount of alcohol consumed per day, and diagnostic criteria, there is a growing consensus that measures that assess frequent episodes of intoxication, and perhaps serious levels of intoxication, provide the strongest support for the alcohol-marital violence relationship. Several of the studies included in the analyses of Lipsey et al. (1997) involved child abuse and sexual abuse, while others involved spouse or partner abuse. Consequently, while their conclusions may be warranted with respect to a broad alcohol-violence relationship that occurs across these diverse alcohol variables, samples, and types of violence, strong relationships with respect to certain drinking patterns (frequent excessive drinking) and certain forms of violence (marital physical violence) could be easily masked. It is of interest that 11 of the 13 domestic violence studies that employed multivariate analyses reported an alcohol variable that was a significant independent predictor of violence.

In addition to the above issues most of these studies have focused on a rather broad developmental period, leading to the possibility that studies within more specific developmental periods might yield somewhat different results. There have been four longitudinal studies that have focused specifically on young couples, two of which evaluated long term predictors of marital violence (Magdol, Moffitt, Caspi, & Silva, 1998; Mihalic & Elliott, 1997) and two of which evaluated predictors over a shorter period of time (Heyman, O'Leary, & Jouriles, 1995; Leonard & Senchak, 1996).

The study by Magdol et al. (1998) was based on the Dunedin Multidisciplinary Health and Development study (Silva, 1990). The Dunedin study identified a complete cohort of infants born between April 1, 1972 and March 31, 1973 in Dunedin, New Zealand. These children were assessed at ages 3, 5, 7, 9, 11, 13, 15, 18, and 21. At age 21, approximately 435 males and 425 females who had been involved in a romantic or dating relationship in the past 12 months were interviewed with respect to aggression (both perpetration and victimization) involving that partner. Substance abuse was assessed at age 15 on the basis of buying alcohol underage, public intoxication, marijuana use, sniffing glue, and other drug use. Moreover, the construct was incorporated into a larger construct of problem behaviors that included difficult temperament at age 3–5, conduct problems at age 7–9, conduct problems and aggressive delinquency at age 15, and juvenile police contact. At the bivariate level, substance use at age 15 was associated with male and female perpetration and victimization. Although the unique impact of substance use was not reported, problem behaviors were uniquely related to partner aggression after controlling for socioeconomic resources, family relations, and educational achievements.

The Mihalic and Elliot (1997) study focused on 374 males and 423 females between the ages of 18 and 28 who were participants in the National Youth Survey (Elliott, Angeton, Huizinga, Knowles, & Cantor, 1983). Participants in this survey were initially interviewed in 1976 between age 11 and 17 (Wave 1), and were reinterviewed eight times in the ensuing 16 years. Mihalic and Elliott focused on married and cohabiting participants who answered a series of marital violence questions in 1983 (Wave 6), 1986 (Wave 7), or 1989 (Wave 8). In order to maintain an appropriate temporal ordering, they constructed a "problem alcohol" use measure that assessed the occurrence or nonoccurrence of problems in seven different areas, and summed this measure across Waves 2–5 (1977–1980). In addition, these investigators evaluated a number of other variables relevant to a social learning model of marital aggression, including marital satisfaction and stress, which were assessed at the same time point as the marital aggression measure. At the simple, bivariate level, problem alcohol use was longitudinally related to male and female acknowledgment of minor violence, and to female acknowledgment of severe violence. It also was related to male and female reports of minor victimization, and male reports of severe victimization. However, when examined multivariately in path analysis, problem alcohol use was not related to marital violence, nor was it related to either of two hypothesized mediators, marital satisfaction and stress.

In interpreting the findings from these two studies, several key issues are worth noting. First, the measure of problem alcohol preceded the measurement of marital violence by anywhere from three to nine years. Given the instability of drinking from adolescence to adulthood, participants who exhibited problem use in adolescence may or may not have exhibited any problem use in a time period more proximal to the measurement of marital violence. Similarly, some of the participants who were not exhibiting problem use in adolescence, may have developed problems subsequently. Second, given the temporally distal nature of the alcohol use variables, one would not necessarily think of these variables as reflecting causal processes whereby drinking patterns per se facilitated the occurrence of aggression. Instead, as conceptualized by Magdol et al. (1998), these variables would most likely be viewed as representing a more enduring facet of the individual, such as adolescent problem behavior (Donovan, Jessor, & Jessor, 1983).

The two other studies evaluated the impact of alcohol prior to marriage and early in marriage on subsequent marital aggression. Heyman, O'Leary, and Jouriles (1995) evaluated the association between alcohol and husband marital aggression in the sample of newlywed couples reported on by O'Leary et al. (1989). Utilizing the MAST to define problem and nonproblem drinkers, they reported a cross-sectional association between problem drinking and premarital aggression at premarriage and at six months into marriage. However, the association was not significant at 18 or 30 months. From a longitudinal perspective, these investigators reported a marginal relationship between premarital problem drinking and serious aggression at some point in the ensuing 2.5 years. Interestingly, they also reported that among premaritally aggressive men, problem drinkers were more likely to discontinue aggression (six out of 18 respondents, or 33%) than were nonproblem drinkers (five of 43 respondents, or 12%).

In contrast to these relatively weak findings, Leonard and Senchak (1996) conducted a very similar study and reported that the husband's premarital drinking pattern was a strong predictor of the extent of violence in the first year of marriage. This study involved assessments of 541 couples at the time of their marriage and at their 1 year anniversary. Utilizing the Alcohol Dependence Scale (ADS; Skinner & Allen, 1982) and average daily alcohol consumption as measures of drinking patterns, Leonard and Senchak (1996) evaluated the role of drinking patterns in a broad social learning model of marital aggression. In the context of this social learning model, verbally aggressive conflict styles, husband and wife hostility, gender identity, relationship power, and history of family violence were assessed, along with sociodemographic factors. Similar to the Mihalic and Elliott (1997) study, nearly every social learning construct was bivariately related to premarital aggression and to subsequent marital aggression. In the multivariate analyses, heavy alcohol consumption on the part of the husband was related to subsequent marital aggression after controlling for premarital aggression as well as the other social learning constructs. Heavy alcohol use by the wife also was related to husband aggression at the bivariate level, however it was unrelated to aggression when the other social learning variables were statistically controlled.

Recently, Quigley and Leonard (2000) extended these analyses to determine whether husband or wife drinking at the first anniversary were predictors of husband to wife violence in the second and third year of marriage. As with the earlier analyses, these analyses indicated that husband heavy alcohol use was predictive of later marital aggression. Interestingly, however, the predictive value was strongest among couples in which the wife was a light drinker. Thus, the couples' drinking pattern consisting of heavy husband alcohol use and light wife alcohol use was most associated with subsequent aggression.

There obviously remains a need for further prospective research, and the conclusions that we can draw at this point are somewhat tentative. First, alcohol variables are longitudinally predictive of relationship and marital aggression. Second, longitudinal studies that attempt to determine whether heavy drinking temporally precedes marital aggression in order to address issues of causality must be attentive to the time lag between the assessment of drinking and the occurrence of violence. It would be unreasonable to expect, for example, that drinking in early adulthood would predict marital aggression among elderly couples. The appropriate time lag is difficult to estimate, but it depends upon the hypothesized causal processes underlying the link between heavy drinking and marital violence. Given the changeable nature of adolescent and early adult drinking, time lags of one year or less seem optimal. Finally, the studies to date suggest that patterns of heavy drinking have both a distal association, through their relationship with adolescent deviance, and a more proximal association, possibly reflecting a causal effect, on marital and partner aggression.

Although the studies are supportive of a relationship between alcohol and marital violence, it is clear that many heavy drinkers are not violent, and than many violent individuals are not heavy drinkers. While this may simply speak to the confluence of other causal processes, it does raise the possibility that the relationship between alcohol and marital violence is stronger for some individuals or couples than for others. In other words, it seems reasonable to assume that other factors may moderate the relationship between alcohol and marital violence.

Moderators of the Alcohol-Marital Violence Association

There are several studies that have examined interactions involving alcohol variables and other constructs that might predict marital violence. In one of the early studies, Leonard and Blane (1992) assessed the relationship between heavy drinking (assessed by the ADS) and marital aggression among 320 men drawn from a nationally representative sample of young men. These men were participants in the High School and Beyond Study conducted by the National Opinion Research Center under the direction of the U.S. Department of Education (Sebring, Campbell, Glusberg, Spencer, & Singleton, 1987). The 320 men involved in this study were married or living together with a woman, and were part of a larger sample of men who were assessed with respect to alcohol use, personality, and other measures. Because the sampling strategy involved an initial cohort of high school sophomores, the age range of the men was very narrow, and they were about 23 years old at the time of the assessment. Overall 13% of these men acknowledged hitting their spouse either while drinking or while sober. After controlling for sociodemographic factors, marital satisfaction, hostility, negative affect, and self-consciousness, scores on the ADS were still significantly associated with marital aggression. In addition, there was a significant interaction involving the ADS, hostility (a composite involving anger, assaultiveness, resentment, and suspicion), and marital satisfaction. This interaction suggested that ADS scores were associated with marital aggression under all conditions except when the participant was low in hostility and high in marital satisfaction. In addition, an interaction between negative affect (a composite score involving anxiety, hopelessness, social avoidance and distress, fear of negative evaluation, suspicion, and resentment) and the ADS was observed. Similar to the other interaction, the ADS was more strongly associated with marital aggression among participants scoring high on negative affect.

In a more recent study, Margolin, John, and Foo (1998) assessed a volunteer sample of 175 men (recruited with their wives and children for a study of marital conflict's effects on children). The men in this sample were considerably older, with a mean age of 39.6, and had been married for at least 10 years. These investigators used the Impairment Index (Armor, Polich, & Stambul, 1976), which assesses difficulties relating to alcohol in the preceding month. In addition, they also assessed negative life events, marital satisfaction, abuse in the family of origin, attitudes condoning physical aggression, and hostility. In contrast to other research, alcohol impairment was not associated with husband abuse (physical and emotional). However, the authors note a restricted range with respect to the scores on alcohol impairment. They also report that alcohol impairment appeared to be associated with increased husband abuse among men with high negative life events and among men with low marital satisfaction.

In the Buffalo Newlywed Study (BNS), we have examined the possibility of moderators of the alcohol-marital aggression relationship both cross-sectionally (Leonard & Senchak, 1993), as well as longitudinally (Quigley & Leonard, 1999). In the cross-sectional analyses, we assessed 607 couples who participated in Wave 1 of the BNS. As part of a brief interview completed separately at the time they applied for their marriage license, husband and wife each reported on the frequency of two husband-to-wife aggression items, "push, grab, or shove" and "slap or hit." These four items were summed as part of a scale ($\alpha = .79$) of husband-to-wife aggression. In addition to reporting an association between husband heavy drinking (composite of ADS and frequency of heavy drinking/drunkenness) and husband aggression this study evaluated several potential moderators. First, the study tested whether husband and wife drinking interacted to predict aggression, and found no support for this interaction. Similar to the findings reported by Leonard and Blane (1992) and Margolin et al. (1998), there was a significant interaction involving alcohol and marital satisfaction, with alcohol being associated with premarital aggression only among less maritally satisfied men. In addition, this study found that alcohol was strongly related to premarital aggression among men who believed that alcohol increased feelings of power and aggression and among low hostile men who believed that alcohol excused aggression. These latter two findings are of potential interest because they support the possibility that alcohol is related to marital aggression because an individual who is aggressive while drinking is subject to less social sanction than an individual who is aggressive while sober. Of course, because this finding is based on cross-sectional analyses, it is plausible that individuals who have behaved aggressively toward their wife while drinking might adopt beliefs reflecting this experience. As a consequence, it is important to examine these moderation effects longitudinally.

Factors that moderate the longitudinal relationship between heavy drinking and marital violence were examined by Quigley and Leonard (1999). This analysis, which grew from the longitudinal study of Leonard and Senchak (1996), focused on the evaluation of moderation effects on the strongest substantive predictor of first year marital violence, verbally aggressive conflict styles. In addition to assessing the interaction of heavy drinking and conflict styles, this study evaluated whether the relationship between premarital heavy drinking and first year marital violence was moderated by beliefs that alcohol either caused or excused aggression. This study demonstrated that heavy drinking (high ADS scores and average daily consumption) predicted subsequent aggression only among couples high in verbally aggressive conflict styles. However, the belief that alcohol neither caused nor excused aggression moderated the longitudinal effect. In fact, men who believed that alcohol increased aggression were less likely to engage in severe marital aggression, and particularly unlikely in the presence of verbally aggressive conflict styles.

While there remains a fundamental need for further examination of potential moderators, the few studies to date that have reported moderation analyses are strikingly consistent. Alcohol is most strongly associated with marital aggression among individuals who, by virtue of hostility, verbal aggression, or marital dissatisfaction, are already at risk for marital aggression. Among individuals without these characteristics, alcohol does not appear to be related to aggression.

Acute Alcohol Effects in Marital Violence[2]

Although patterns of heavy alcohol consumption may be linked to the occurrence of marital aggression through a variety of distal processes, one of the key hypotheses is that the acute consumption of alcohol may facilitate the occurrence of marital aggression. There are numerous estimates of the extent to which alcohol consumption, either by the victim or by the assailant, preceded episodes of violence. Even though these estimates tend to be large, ranging from 40%–60% depending on the nature of the violence and the person reporting the violence, these estimates, by themselves, are not very informative regarding the potential causal role of alcohol on the occurrence of violence. They become informative when comparisons can be drawn to the presence of alcohol in control events. For example, Bard and Zacker (1974) compared police officers judgments of alcohol use in domestic calls involving and not involving an assault. Surprisingly, 21% of assaults were reported to involved alcohol use while 40% of the nonassaultive episodes involved alcohol, suggesting that alcohol use may have prevented violence. In contrast to these findings, more recent research has suggested that alcohol use is associated with either the occurrence or severity of domestic violence. In Pernanen's (1991) community survey, he asked a random community sample about their most recent victimization. Among instances of domestic aggression, 13% of victims of sober violence were injured while 26% of victims of intoxicated violence were injured. Although this difference was not significant, possibly due to a relatively small sample, it suggests that alcohol may increase the severity of aggressive episodes. Martin and Bachman (1997) also compared severe with less severe assaults. Utilizing data from the National Crime Victimization Survey for 1992 and 1993 (United States Department of Justice, 1993), these authors found a significant association between assailant alcohol use and severity in instances of intimate violence toward women; 54% of alcohol-involved assaults were severe (i.e., assault with injury), but only 43% of the sober assaults were severe. In our own research based on the BNS, Leonard and Quigley (1999) compared episodes of verbal aggression with episodes of physical aggression, and compared episodes of moderate aggression with episodes of severe aggression. The variable, husband drinking in the event, was statistically predictive of a physical episode occurring (in comparison to a verbal episode) by both husband and wife report, and after controlling for wife drinking. In contrast, wife drinking in the event was not predictive of a physical episode after controlling for husband drinking. In addition, these associations held after controlling for sociodemographic factors, personality, distal drinking patterns,

---

[2]In addition to the survey data discussed below, there is experimental evidence bearing on the impact of alcohol on physical aggression, based on studies examining the administration of noxious noises or shock, as well as studies examining alcohol and verbal behavior. The interested reader is referred to Leonard and Roberts (1998), Bushman (1997), and Lipsey et al. (1997).

and other event based information. Husband drinking in the event also was predictive of severe versus moderate aggression by husband report, but not by wife report. However, according to wife report, there was a marginal association between wife drinking and severe versus moderate drinking after controlling for husband drinking. This association appeared to reflect an enhanced likelihood of severe aggression when both husband and wife were drinking, because there were very few instances in which the wife was drinking but the husband was not (7% according to husband report, 3% according to wife report).

Summary of the Alcohol/Marital Violence Research

Research regarding the relationship between alcohol use and marital violence has grown in diversity and sophistication. It encompasses both large scale epidemiologic studies as well as smaller, more intensive clinical studies. Focusing on the early adult years, there is clearly an association between patterns of alcohol use and marital violence. Moreover, there is both a theoretical rationale as well as longitudinal, experimental, and event-based evidence in support of some causal contribution of alcohol on marital violence. In asserting this, it is important not to overstate this contribution. Neither alcohol abuse or dependence nor alcohol intoxication are necessary or sufficient causes of violence. Nonetheless, they appear to play an important facilitative role in marital violence, particularly among young married couples.

There is clearly more research needed to fully delineate the potential role of alcohol in marital violence. It is still the case that much of the research is conducted without a clear theoretical framework, leaving the literature with many studies continuing to document an association, but little work attempting to explain the relationship. Although broad epidemiological research is important, more focused investigations are required to be able to address potential explanations of the relationship. Although there has been important longitudinal research, this has been limited primarily to adolescence and early adulthood. Longitudinal and detailed event-based research is lacking with respect to other developmental periods or populations (except for some work on violence after alcoholism treatment by O'Farrell (O'Farrell & Murphy, 1995; O'Farrell, Van Hutton, & Murphy, 1999) and his colleagues). Future research needs to begin to fill these gaps.

☐ The Alcohol-Child Abuse and Child Neglect Relationship

The issue of whether alcohol use or alcoholism are causal factors in child abuse is complicated and poorly understood. There is certainly a widespread perception that these factors are strongly and pervasively associated. For example, the National Center on Addiction and Substance Abuse at Columbia (National Center on Addiction and Substance Abuse, 1998) surveyed a national sample of 915 professionals involved in the child welfare system (of the 3486 surveys that were sent out). Substance abuse was seen as causing or contributing to 50% or more of all the cases of child maltreatment by 80% of the sample. A substantial minority of the sample (40%) viewed it as being causal or contributory in 75% of the cases (National Center on Addiction and Substance Abuse, 1998).

Despite this perception of a powerful and pervasive causal association, the empirical support for an association is less clear. Reviews lamenting the lack of information date back more than 15 years. Orme and Rimmer (1981) reviewed the existing literature and concluded that despite the widespread belief that was held at the time, "the most striking finding that emerged from our study was that there was not adequate empirical data to support the association between alcoholism and child abuse (p. 285)." They also identified several key methodological problems in the literature including inadequate definitions of child abuse and alcoholism, confusion as to whether the issue was alcoholism or alcohol intoxication, and the overrepresentation of the poor and members of minority groups. Leonard and Jacob (1988) found little progress, noted similar methodological concerns, and argued that it was necessary to distinguish among the different forms of child maltreatment. Miller, Maguin, and Downs' (1997) more recent review reported that methodologically stronger research had begun to demonstrate significant associations between alcoholism and both physical and sexual abuse of children.

Cross-sectional research continues to suggest that alcohol and substance use are associated with different forms of maltreatment (e.g. Famularo, Kinscherff, & Fenton, 1992; Holmes & Robins, 1988; Murphy, Jellinek, Quinn, Smith, Poitrast, & Goshko, 1991; Whipple & Webster-Stratton, 1991). Two of the more informative deserve comment. Kelleher, Chaffin, Hollenberg, and Fischer (1994) utilized the Epidemilogical Catchment Area (ECA) sample to examine the issue of parental alcoholism and maltreatment. The results indicated that any alcohol disorder or any drug disorder was associated with an increased likelihood of abuse and neglect. Of particular importance, the authors also report that substance abuse (any alcohol or drug diagnosis) was still significantly associated with abuse and neglect after controlling for the number of people in the household, the availability of a confidant, depression, and antisocial personality. Miller, Smyth, and Mudar (1999) assessed 170 women recruited from alcoholic outpatient treatment programs, classes for drivers who had been convicted of driving under the influence, shelters from battered women, outpatient mental health treatment programs, and from a random sample of households. Current alcohol or other drug use was related to verbal aggression, moderate physical aggression on the Conflict Tactics Scale (CTS; Straus, 1979), and severe physical violence on the Parental Punitiveness Scale (PPS; a scale assessing parents' ratings of likelihood of severe disciplinary practices in response to hypothetical child misbehavior) (Epstein & Komorita, 1965). These relationships held for verbal and moderate physical aggression even when the mother's own child sexual abuse, experience of violence as child, and experience of severe violence from her partner were controlled. Alcohol and drug use continued to be related to verbal and moderate physical aggression, but not severe violence on the PPS after controlling for hostility. Perhaps the most critical finding of this study, however, was that it was primarily current alcohol or drug problems that predicted moderate and severe violence, but that past alcohol or drug problems were not significantly associated with these forms of violence.

There have been several cross-sectional studies that have specifically examined childhood sexual abuse. Most of these studies employ retrospective reports of child abuse from subjects in adulthood. For example, Maker, Kemmelmeier, and Peterson (1999) assessed 130 college students with respect to sexual abuse prior to age 16. Parent substance use, a scale that combined mother and father scores on the Short MAST (SMAST; Selzer, Vinokur, & Rooijen, 1975) and on 18 drug use items, was correlated with the occurrence of sexual abuse. However, the effect was explained by maternal and paternal sociopathy. Fleming, Mullen, and Bammer (1997) sent a postal questionnaire to 6000 women on the electoral rolls in Australia (where voting is compulsory). Of the 3958 (66%) women who returned the survey, 184 had alcohol problems and 910 served as controls. Childhood sexual abuse (defined as any sexual contact before age 12 with a person five or more years older and any unwanted or distressing contact occurring between age 12 and 16 with a person five or more years older) was acknowledged by 20% of the sample. Having an alcoholic father and an alcoholic mother were among the many factors significantly differentiating those with and without childhood sexual abuse. Separate multivariate analyses found that having an alcoholic father was uniquely associated with familial childhood sexual abuse, while having an alcoholic mother was uniquely associated with nonfamilial abuse. Vogeltanz, Wilsnack, Harris, Wilsnack, Wonderlich, and Kristjanson (1999) conducted a similar study with a national sample of women in the United States. Depending on the specific criteria used to define childhood sexual abuse (CSA), between 15.4% and 32% of women had experienced CSA. In general, father drinking associated with less risk of CSA, and mother drinking associated with greater risk. However, there was a significant interaction that suggested that "women who grew up with both biological parents were more likely to report CSA if their mothers drank but their fathers did not. Women with drinking fathers and abstaining mothers were more likely to report CSA if by age 16 their biological family was no longer intact" (p. 589). If one were to assume that biological families that were no longer intact were more likely to have experienced familial sexual abuse, these results would be very consistent with the findings of Fleming et al. (1997).

Finally, another similar design was employed by Fergusson, Lynskey, and Horwood (1996) in their study of a New Zealand birth cohort of 1265 children. The birth cohort was studied prospectively to the age of 16 years with assessments of parent drug use occurring when the cohort was 11 and assessments of parent alcoholism occurring when the cohort was 15. At age 18, retrospective reports of CSA were obtained. Of the cohort, 20.4% (17.3% of females and 3.4% of males) reported having experienced CSA before the age of 16. Multivariate analyses suggested that the risk of CSA was elevated among females, those exposed to high levels of marital conflict, those reporting low parental attachment, those reporting high levels of paternal overprotection, and those with parents who reported alcoholism or alcohol problems. Unlike the other two studies, the same variables predicted nonfamilial abuse as predicted abuse overall, however, these authors did not consider mother and father alcohol problems separately.

In addition to these cross-sectional reports, there have been three longitudinal studies that address the issue of alcoholism and child maltreatment. In the first of these, Chaffin, Kelleher, and Hollenberg (1996) reported a follow-up of their earlier cross-sectional analyses of the ECA study. Focusing on the approximately 7100 parents who did not report abuse or neglect at the first wave of the ECA study, 63 new instances of child abuse were identified in the second wave, one year later. In addition, 84 new instances of neglect were identified as were 4 instances of both abuse and neglect. Substance abuse disorders at the first wave occurred in 15.1% of the new child abuse cases, 21% of the new neglect cases, but in only 5.7% of the controls who did not report abuse or neglect at either wave. This difference remained significant after controlling for sociodemographic differences between the groups.

In the second study, Brown, Cohen, Johnson, and Salzinger (1998) evaluated 644 families as part of a larger random sample in upstate New York. The sample was originally recruited in 1975 when the children were between 1 and 10 years of age. At age 18, the children were interviewed with respect to physical abuse, neglect, and sexual abuse. In addition, the records of the New York State Central Registry for Child Abuse and Neglect were reviewed to determine if the family had been reported. Overall, 58 of the adult children reported some form of maltreatment (29 reported physical abuse, 18 reported sexual abuse, 16 reported neglect, and 5 reported some combination of these). From the registry, 46 of the families had reported and substantiated maltreatment (20 physical abuse, 7 sexual abuse, 37 neglect, and 18 a combination of these). There were 48 cases of self report of maltreatment that were not confirmed by records and 27 cases of registry maltreatment that were not self-reported. Registry and self-report information were combined such that a positive report of maltreatment by either report was coded as the presence of that form of maltreatment. Although specific information regarding alcohol problems was not reported separately, maternal and paternal sociopathy, which included alcohol problems, drug use, or police involvement, were both related to child neglect. Maternal sociopathy was predictive of both child sexual and physical abuse. It is worth noting that the sample was predominantly Caucasian and nonurban.

Kotch, Browne, Dufort, Winsor, and Catellier (1999) conducted in home evaluations of 708 mothers, most of whom were at high risk for problematic parenting (i.e. low birth weight baby, low maternal age [<14], birth defects, congenital abnormalities, or other significant medical or social problems) shortly after mothers and babies were discharged. Reports of child maltreatment were collected from the North Carolina Central Registry of Child Abuse and Neglect over the next four years. During this time, 172 were reported for maltreatment over the first four years of life, with nearly 50% (83) of these occurring in the first year. Of the 290 reports on these 172 children, 83% were for neglect, 9% for abuse, and 85% for both abuse and neglect. Stepwise logistic regression indicated that maternal alcohol use was significantly predictive of maltreatment after controlling for social well being, maternal depression, and education.

There is a growing literature on the role of alcohol and drug use in the re-report of maltreatment among individuals who have been reported for child maltreatment to child welfare agencies. Wolock and Magura (1996) followed up 239 child protective services cases that had been closed for a variety of reasons (judged to be isolated incident, less severe, situation resolved, family already receiving services, unsubstantiated). Re-reports of child abuse were more common among all substance use groups (44% alcohol only, 48% drugs only, 58% both alcohol and drugs) compared to families with no substance use (25%). In contrast, DePanfilis and Zuravin (1999) followed 446 families with substantiated neglect or physical abuse for five years after treatment. Mother factors, which included ratings of drug problems, alcohol problems, and problem solving deficits were not related to recurrence of abuse, though child factors, partner abuse, family stress, and social support were related. The strongest factor, however, was whether the child remained in the family or was placed out of the family for some time. The lack of a relationship between mother factors and recurrence of abuse was surprising and was attributed by the authors to potential measurement problems by the caseworkers. Some support for this explanation is provided by Wood (1997) who reported that alcohol or drug problems that contributed to the current incident could not be reliably rated from child protective service files.

Unlike the alcohol and marital violence area in which there has been some focused attention on developmental aspects of the relationship, very little research in this regard is apparent in the alcohol and child abuse area. Some information relevant to this issue can be gleaned the National Center on Child Abuse and Neglect's 1993 Report to Congress (United States Department of Health and Human Services, 1993) entitled "Study of Child Maltreatment in Alcohol Abusing Families." This report collected information on over 1200 substantiated cases reported to 35 different child protective agencies (involving approximately 1800 maltreated children). Utilizing these statistics and assuming a rate of alcohol abuse of 10%, this report estimated incidence rates for several different forms of child abuse for children in alcohol abusing and nonabusing families. Across every form of abuse, ranging from physical abuse to emotional neglect, the estimated rates of abuse were substantially higher among alcohol abusing families. While there are numerous problems with utilizing this data to support a causal relationship between alcohol abuse and child maltreatment, other comparisons between alcohol abusing and nonabusing cases are of interest. From a developmental perspective, the age distribution of child victims was fairly similar for alcohol abusing and nonalcohol abusing families. However, differences emerged with respect to preschool children (ages 1–4) which were more common among the alcohol abusing families, and early school aged children (ages 5–9), which were less common among alcohol abusing families. In addition, perpetrators that were suspected of alcohol abuse were more likely to be the biological father of the maltreated child, less likely to be the biological mother, and were more likely to be between the ages 30 and 49, rather than younger or older. This contrasts with the cases in which the caretaker was suspected of illicit drug use. In these cases, the perpetrator was more likely to be the biological mother and to be younger than 30. Because all of these comparisons included neglect, physical abuse, and other forms of abuse, the significance of these differences is difficult to discern. However, this represents the form of analysis that would be of some use in elucidating developmental time frames that are important for the occurrence of alcohol-related child maltreatment.

☐ Moderators of the Alcohol-Child Abuse/Child Neglect Relationship

Unlike the alcohol and marital violence literature in which there have been several efforts to identify factors that combine with alcohol to predict high levels of marital abuse, there have been few, if any, such studies focused on child abuse. Aside from the potential moderating effects of mother versus father, and possibly the age of the parent, there have been few reports of moderating effects. Miller et al.'s (1999) study of women from a variety of different community agencies found a significant interaction in the prediction of parental punitiveness. This interaction suggested that alcohol and other drug use was associated with higher verbal aggression and higher severe violence on the PPS among women who were low in hostility.

Acute Alcohol Effects Relevant to Child Abuse and Neglect

Unlike the marital violence literature in which the possibility of acute alcohol effects have been considered more extensively, there is considerably less research addressing whether acute alcohol use accompanies child abuse. MacMurray's (1979) archival study of 1645 cases of child abuse reported to the Alberta Registry for Child Abuse and Neglect found that 33% of the cases mentioned alcohol, and that in 83% of these instances, the suspect was reported to be intoxicated at the time of the abuse. This suggests that, at a minimum, 27% of all of the reported incidents involved intoxication (assuming a 0% intoxication rate for the 67% of cases in which alcohol was not mentioned). In the National Center on Child Abuse and Neglect's 1993 Report to Congress (United States Department of Health and Human Services, 1993), it was estimated that 17% of physical abuse cases involved perpetrators suspected of being under the influence of alcohol or drugs. The rate for sexual abuse was 9.6%, and the rate for emotional abuse was 11.9%. For neglect, the rate was very high, 68.8%.

As discussed with respect to the marital violence literature, the presence of intoxication in 17%–27% of physical abuse episodes does not specifically address whether alcohol had any causal influence on the occurrence of violence. The differential rate for physical abuse versus sexual or emotional abuse is more suggestive of an acute influence, but is by no means definitive. Coupled with experimental literature which suggests that the administration of alcohol can alter interactions with children (Pelham & Lang, 1993), one might conclude that some occurrences of child abuse may be precipitated by alcohol or substance use. However, the paucity of research specifically addressing this issue necessitates caution.

☐ Summary of the Alcohol-Child Abuse Relationship

There are several key points to consider with respect to the research regarding alcohol and child abuse. First, it is clear that both the cross-sectional and the small longitudinal literature indicate an association between parental alcoholism and child maltreatment. Second, many of the studies involve large samples, well defined variables of child maltreatment and alcoholism, and clear differentiation among the different types of abuse. Many of the studies are noteworthy by virtue of their attempt to go beyond simple associations. For example, Miller et al. (1999) took the additional step of differentiating recent from past alcohol and drug abuse. This is critical because it ensures that the child maltreatment and the parental alcoholism occurred within the same timeframe. These authors also controlled for a variety of potential confounds. Similarly, Chaffin et al. (1996) were able to link both an alcohol diagnosis as well as a drug diagnosis to abuse and neglect after controlling for other critical factors, including depression and antisocial personality. Fleming et al. (1997) and Vogeltanz et al. (1999) evaluated both maternal and paternal drinking and suggested somewhat different relationships of these factors to sexual abuse.

While there is clearly stronger evidence of an association between alcohol abuse (and drug abuse) and child maltreatment, and there is a steady progression in the methodological sophistication of the research, there are still many issues to address in this literature. The fundamental overriding issue, however, is the nearly universal absence of any theoretical processes underlying the relationship between alcohol abuse and child maltreatment. As noted earlier, such models have been proposed with respect to marital aggression and have served a useful purpose in identifying potential confounds, mediators, and moderators of the relationship. However, such models have not been proposed in the child maltreatment area.

In developing hypotheses as to why alcohol abuse and alcoholism is associated with child maltreatment, attention has to be directed at several different issues. First, investigators clearly recognize the importance of distinguishing among child neglect, child physical abuse, and child sexual abuse, suggesting the need for different models for these types of maltreatment. For example, the association between child neglect and parental alcoholism may be attributed simply to the difficulty of attending to children's needs if one is frequently drunk or recovering from drinking when taking care of the children. However, whether such a simple explanation would hold for sexual abuse is not clear. Similarly, in line with the theme of this book, there should be a consideration of the developmental factors associated with maltreatment. Child abuse among infants and young children most probably has a somewhat different etiology than child abuse among older children and adolescents. Second, there needs to be a clear specification regarding whether the mother or the father (or a surrogate father) had the alcohol problem, and which of the parents has been involved in abuse. It is interesting, for example, that there is some evidence that mother's drinking is related to nonfamilial sexual abuse, but that father's drinking is related to familial sexual abuse. This suggests that maternal alcoholism may play some role with respect to impaired protection of the child from outside influences (e.g., exposing the child to risky circumstances, lack of parental monitoring), while paternal alcoholism may play some role in facilitating the occurrence of sexual abuse (presuming that the father is the offender in many of the familial instances of sexual abuse). Third, there should be a clearer specification of the temporal parameters involved in both the alcoholism and the maltreatment. For example, studies that link lifetime alcoholism with lifetime child maltreatment do not clarify processes. Finally, the procedure of subsuming alcohol problems together with drug abuse and other psychiatric or social problems obscures any unique aspects of alcoholism and creates an implicit view of alcoholism as simply another form of psychopathology.

Finally, there is a need to examine alcohol abuse in the context of the joint occurrence of child abuse and marital violence. There has been some research examining the relationship between alcohol problems and child abuse potential controlling for relationship violence (Merrill, Hervig, & Milner, 1996). However, it is important to move beyond simply controlling for one form of violence in the study of another form of violence. For example, Appel and Holden (1998) delineate five different models for understanding the relationship between marital violence and child abuse, depending on the specific perpetrator(s), specific target(s), and the mutuality of aggression. At the simplest level, there is the single perpetrator model in which one person (presumably but not necessarily, the husband) is violent towards his spouse and child, but there is no violent behavior displayed by the spouse or the child. The most complicated model, family dysfunction, involves mutual aggression between husband and wife, father and child, and mother and child. Alcohol abuse in either husband or wife may be influential in the shaping of these models. Moreover, returning to the developmental theme of the chapter, the age of the child may also influence the shaping of these models.

☐ Concluding Comments

Although alcohol abuse and marital violence and child abuse has been a concern of research for approximately 25 years, the role of acute intoxication and chronic heavy consumption remains incompletely understood. This state of the literature reflects, in part, the uncritical acceptance of one of two diametrically opposed positions. One of these positions is that alcohol is not causally relevant, but is only an excuse for violence. The second position is that alcohol is a potent disinhibitor of aggressive and antisocial behaviors. The impact of both of these positions has been to minimize the research focus on alcohol use and abuse because alcohol's effects were seen as irrelevant or because alcohol's effects were seen as patently obvious. The research literature supports neither of these positions, but instead emphasizes that acute and chronic alcohol use play important roles in violence for certain people under certain circumstances. In this context, the relationship between alcohol and family violence may differ importantly across developmental epochs.

Research focusing on marital violence and child maltreatment has, with rare exceptions, neglected these developmental aspects of the violence. Although some research has examined age of the couple or age of the child, even this rather cursory approach to development has not been effectively integrated into models of violence. While it is clear that violent behavior has its roots in childhood, the developmental transitions to adolescence, early adulthood, and parenthood provide contextual shifts in which this behavior may be altered. The empirical and theoretical groundwork for examining these transitions are only now being established. As this basic foundation is elaborated, it will be important to integrate developmental frameworks for alcohol and substance use in order to fully understand the causal influence of alcohol use and abuse on marital and parental violence.

☐ References

Appel, A. E., & Holden, G. W. (1998). The co-occurrence of spouse and physical child abuse: A review and appraisal. *Journal of Family Psychology, 12*(4), 578–599.

Armor, D. J., Polich, J. M., & Stambul, H. B. (1976). *Alcoholism and treatment* (R-1739-NIAAA). Santa, Monica, CA: Rand.

Bachman, J. G., Wadsworth, K. N., O'Malley, P. M., Johnston, L. D., & Schulenberg, J. E. (1997). *Smoking, drinking, and drug use in young adulthood. The impacts of new freedoms and new responsibilities. Research monographs in adolescence.* Mahwah: Lawrence Earlbaum.

Bard, K. A., & Zacker, J. (1974). Assaultiveness and alcohol use in family disputes. *Criminology, 12*(3), 281–292.

Barnett, O. W., & Fagan, R. W. (1993). Alcohol use in male spouse abusers and their female partners. *Journal of Family Violence, 8*(1), 1–25.

Bradbury, T. N., & Lawrence, E. (1999). Physical aggression and the longitudinal course of newlywed marriage. In X. B. Arriga & S. Oskamp (Eds.), *Violence in intimate relationships* (pp. 181–202). Thousand Oaks, CA: Sage.

Browne, J., Cohen, P., Johnson, J. G., & Salzinger, S. (1998). A longitudinal analysis risk factors for child maltreatment: Findings of a 17 year prospective study of officially recorded and self-reported child abuse and neglect. *Child Abuse and Neglect, 22*(11), 1065–1078

Bushman, B. J. (1997). Effects of alcohol on human aggression: Validity of proposed explanations. In M. Galanter (Vol. Ed.), *Recent developments in alcoholism, Vol. 13, Alcohol and violence* (pp. 227–242). New York: Plenum Press.

Cappelleri, J. C., Eckenrode, J., & Powers, J. L. (1993). The epidemiology of child abuse: Findings from the second national incidence and prevalence study of child abuse and neglect. *American Journal of Public Health, 83*(11), 1622–1624.

Carpenter, J. A., & Armenti, N. P. (1972). Some effects of ethanol on human sexual and aggressive behavior. In B. Kissin & H. Begeoter (Eds.), *The biology of alcoholism: Physiology and behavior* (Vol. 2, pp. 509–542). New York: Plenum.

Chaffin, M., Kelleher, K., & Hollenberg, J. (1996). Onset of physical abuse and neglect: Psychiatric, substance abuse, and social risk factors from prospective community data. *Child Abuse & Neglect, 20*(3), 191–203.

Chilcoat, H. D., & Breslau, N. (1996). Alcohol disorders in young adulthood: Effects of transitions into adult roles. *Journal of Health and Social Behavior, 37*, 339–349.

Clark, W. B., & Midanik, L. (1982). Alcohol use and alcohol problems among U. S adults: Results of the 1979 National Survey. In National Institute on Alcohol Abuse and Alcoholism, *Alcohol and health monographn No. 1: Alcohol consumption and eelated problems* (pp. 3–52), DHHS Publication No. ADM 82-1190. Washington, DC: U.S. Government Printing Office.

Coleman, D. H., & Straus, M. A. (1983). Alcohol abuse and family violence In E. Gottheil, K. A. Druley, T. E. Skoloda & H. M. Waxman (Ed.), *Alcohol, drug abuse and aggression* (pp. 104–124). Springfield, IL: Charles C. Thomas.

Connelly, C. D., & Straus, M. A. (1992). Mother's age and risk for physical abuse. *Child Abuse and Neglect, 16*, 709–718.

Curran, P. J., Muthen, B. O., & Harford, T. C. (1998). Influence of changes in marital status on developmental trajectories of alcohol use in young adults. *Journal of Studies on Alcohol, 59*(6), 647–658.

DePanfilis, D., & Zuravin, S. J. (1999). Predicting child maltreatment recurrences during treatment. *Child Abuse and Neglect, 23*(8), 729–743.

Donovan, J. E., Jessor, R., & Jessor, J. (1983). Problem drinking in adolescence and young adulthood: A follow-up study. *Journal of Studies of Alcohol, 44,* 109–137.

Elliott, D. S., Ageton, S. S., Huizinga, D. H., Knowles, B. A., & Cantor, R. J. (1983). The prevalence and incidence of delinquent behavior: 1976–1980. The National Youth Survey (Report No. 26). Boulder, CO: Behavioral Research Institute.

Epstein, R., & Komorita, S. S. (1965). The development of a scale of parental punitiveness toward aggression. *Child Development, 36,* 129–142.

Famularo, R., Kinscherff, R., & Fenton, T. (1992) Parental substance abuse and the nature of child maltreatment. *Child Abuse and Neglect, 16,* 475–483.

Fergusson, D. M., Lynskey, M. T., Horwood, J. L. (1996). Childhood sexual abuse and psychiatric disorder in young adulthood: I: Prevalence of sexual abuse and factors associated with sexual abuse. *Journal of the American Academy of Child & Adolescent Psychiatry, 35*(10), 1355–1364.

Finkelhor, D., & Dzuiba-Leatherman, J. (1994). Victimization of children. *American Psychologist, 49*(3), 173–183.

Fleming, J., Mullen, P., & Bammer, G. (1997) A study of potential risk factors for sexual abuse in childhood. *Child Abuse and Neglect, 21*, 49–58.

Gelles, R. J. (1990). Violence and pregnancy: Are pregnant women at greater risk of abuse? In M. A. Straus & R. J. Gelles (Eds.), *Physical violence in American families: Risk factors and adaptions to violence in 8,145 families* (pp. 279–286). New Brunswick, NJ: Transaction.

Gelles, R. J. (1993). Alcohol and other drugs are associated with violence they are not its cause. In R. J. Gelles & D. R. Loseke (Eds.), *Current controversies on family violence* (pp. 182–208). Newbury Park, CA: Sage.

Herrmann, C. K.,& Martin, M. J. (1988). Factors associated with hospitalization in confirmed cases of physical child abuse. *Early Child Development and Care, 31*(1–4), 35–41.

Heyman, R. E., O'Leary, K. D., & Jouriles, E. N. (1995). Alcohol and aggressive personality styles: Potentiators of serious physical aggression against wives? *Journal of Family Psychology, 9*(1), 44–57.

Hilton, M. E. (1991). The demographic distribution of drinking patterns in 1984. In W. B. Clark & M. E. Hilton (Eds.), *Alcohol in America: Drinking practices and problems* (pp. 73–86). Albany, NY: State University of New York Press.

Holmes, S. J., & Robins, L. N. (1988) The role of parental disciplinary practices in the development of depression and alcoholism. *Psychiatry, 51*(1), 24–36.

Hotaling, G. T., & Sugarman, D. B. (1986). An analysis of risk markers in husband to wife violence: The current state of knowledge. *Violence and Victims, 1,* 101–124.

Huston, T. L., & Houts, R. M. (1998). The psychological infrastructure of courtship and marriage: The role of personality and compatibility in romantic relationship. In T. N. Bradbury (Ed.), *The developmental course of marital dysfunction* (pp. 114–151). New York: Cambridge University Press.

Julian, T. W., & McKenry, P. C. (1993). Mediators of male violence toward female intimates. *Journal of Family Violence, 8*(1), 39–56.

Kaufman-Kantor, G. (1997). Alcohol and spouse abuse: Ethnic differences. In M. Galanter (Vol. Ed.), *Recent developments in alcoholism, Vol. 13, Alcohol and violence* (pp. 57–75). New York: Plenum.

Kaufman-Kantor, G., & Straus, M. A. (1990). The "drunken bum" theory of wife beating. In M. A. Straus & R. J. Gelles (Eds.), *Physical violence in American families: Risk factors and adaptations to violence in 8,145 families* (pp. 203–224). New Brunswick, NJ: Transaction Publishers.

Kelleher, K., Chaffin, M., Hollenberg, J., & Fisher, E. (1994). Alcohol and drug disorders among physically abusive and neglectful parents in a community-based sample. *American Journal of Public Health, 84*(10), 1586–1590.

Kotch, J. B., Browne, D. C., Dufort, V., Winsor, J., & Catellier, D. (1999). Predicting child maltreatment in the first 4 years of life from characteristics assessed in the neonatal period. *Child Abuse and Neglect, 23*(4), 305–319.

Krueger, R. F., Moffitt, T. E., Caspi, A., Bleske, A., & Silva, P. A. (1998). Assortative mating for antisocial behavior: Developmental and methodological implications. *Behavior Genetics, 28*(3), 173–186.

Kurdek, L. A. (1993). Predicting marital dissolution: A 5-year prospective longitudinal study of newlywed couples. *Journal of Personality and Social Psychology, 64*(2), 221–242.

Labouvie, R. (1996). Maturing out of substance use: Selection and self-correction. *Journal of Drug Issues, 26*, 457–476.

Leonard, K. E., & Blane, H. T. (1992). Alcohol and marital aggression in a national sample of young men *Journal of Interpersonal Violence, 7,* 19–30.

Leonard, K. E., Bromet, E. J., Parkinson, D. K., Day, N. L., & Ryan, C. M. (1985). Patterns of alcohol use and physically aggressive behavior in men. *Journal of Studies on Alcohol, 46,* 279–282

Leonard, K. E., & Eiden, R. D. (1999). Husbands and wives drinking: Unilateral or bilateral influences among newlyweds in a general population sample. *Journal of Studies on Alcohol. 13*(Suppl.), 130–128.

Leonard, K. E. & Jacob, T. (1988). Alcohol, alcoholism, and family violence. In V. B. Van Hasselt, R. L. Morrison, A. S. Bellack, & M. Hersen (Eds.), *Handbook of family violence* (pp. 383–406). New York: Plenum.

Leonard, K. E., & Quigley, B. M. (1999). Drinking and marital aggression in newlyweds: An event based analysis of drinking and the occurrence of husband marital aggression. *Journal of Studies on Alcohol, 60*, 537–545.

Leonard, K. E. & Roberts, L. . (1998). The effects of alcohol on the marital interactions of aggressive and nonaggressive husbands and their wives. *Journal of Abnormal Psychology, 107*(4), 602–615.

Leonard, K. E., & Senchak, M. (1993). Alcohol and premarital aggression among newlywed couples. *Journal of Studies on Alcohol, 11*, 96–108.

Leonard, K. E., & Senchak, M. (1996). The prospective prediction of husband marital aggression among newlywed couples. *Journal of Abnormal Psychology, 105*(3), 369–380.

Lindahl, K., Clements, M., & Markman, H. (1998). The development of marriage: A 9-year perspective. In T. N. Bradbury (Ed.), *The developmental course of marital dysfunction* (pp. 205–236). New York: Cambridge University Press.

Lipsey, M. W., Wilson, D. B., Cohen, M. A., & Derzon, J. H. (1997). Is there a causal relationship between alcohol use and violence?: A synthesis of evidence. In M. Galanter (Vol. Ed.), *Recent developments in alcoholism, Vol. 13, Alcohol and violence* (pp. 245–282). New York: Plenum.

MacMurray, V. (1979). The effect and nature of alcohol abuse in cases of child neglect. *Victimology, 4*, 29–45.

Magdol, L., Moffitt, T., Caspi, A., & Silva, P. A. (1998). Developmental antecedents of partner abuse: A prospective-longitudinal study. *Journal of Abnormal Psychology, 107*(3), 375–389.

Maker, A. H., Kemmelmeier, M., & Peterson, C. (1999). Parental Sociopathy as a predictor of childhood sexual abuse. *Journal of Family Violence, 14*, 47–59.

Margolin, G., John, R. S., & Foo, L. (1998). Interactive and unique risk factors for husbands' emotional and physical abuse of their wives. *Journal of Family Violence, 13*(4), 315–344.

Martin, S. E., & Bachman, R. (1997). The relationship of alcohol to injury in assault cases. In M. Galanter (Ed.), *Recent Developments in Alcoholism, Vol 13: Alcohol & Violence* (pp. 41–56). New York: Plenum.

McLaughlin, I. G., Leonard, K. E., & Senchak, M. (1992). Prevalence and distribution of premarital aggression among couples applying for a marriage license. *Journal of Family Violence, 7*(4), 61–71.

Merrill, L. L., Hervig, L. K., & Milner, J. S. (1996). Childhood parenting experiences, intimate partner conflict resolution, and adult risk for child physical abuse. *Child Abuse & Neglect, 21*(11), 1049–1063.

Mihalic, S. W., & Elliott, D. (1997). A social learning theory model of marital violence. *Journal of Family Violence, 12*(1), 21–47.

Miller, B. A., Maguin, E., & Downs, W. R. (1997). Alcohol, drugs, and violence in children's lives. In M. Galanter (Vol. Ed.), *Recent developments in alcoholism, Vol. 13, Alcohol and violence* (pp. 357–386). New York: Plenum.

Miller, B. A., Smyth, N. J., & Mudar, P. J. (1999). Mothers' alcohol and other drug problems and their punitiveness toward their children. *Journal of Studies on Alcohol, 60*, 632–642.

Miller-Tutzauer, C., Leonard, K. E., & Windle, M. (1991). Marriage and alcohol use: A longitudinal study of maturing out. *Journal of Studies of Alcohol, 52*, 434–440.

Murphy, J. M., Jellinek, M., Quinn, D., Smith, G., Poitrast, F. G., & Goshko, M. (1991). Substance abuse and serious child mistreatment: Prevalence, risk, and outcome in a court sample. *Child Abuse and Neglect, 15*, 197–211.

National Center on Addiction and Substance Abuse (1988). No safe haven: Children of substance-abusing parents: Final report. New York: Columbia University.

Neff, J. A., Holamon, B., & Schluter, D. T. (1995). Spousal violence among Anglos, Blacks, and Mexican Americans: The role of demographic variables, psychosocial predictors, and alcohol consumption. *Journal of Family Violence, 10*(1), 1–21.

O'Farrell, T. J., & Murphy, C. M. (1995). Marital violence before and after alcoholism treatment. *Journal of Consulting and Clinical Psychology, 63*, 256–262.

O'Farrell, T. J., Van Hutton, V., & Murphy, C. M. (1999). Domestic violence before and after alcoholism treatment: A two-year longitudinal study. *Journal of Studies on Alcohol, 60*, 317–321.

O'Leary, K. D., Barling, J., Arias, I., Rosenbaum, A., Malone, J., & Tyree, A. (1989). Prevalence and stability of physical aggression between spouses: A longitudinal analysis. *Journal of Consulting and Clinical Psychology, 57*, 263–268.

Orme, T. C., & Rimmer, J. (1981). Alcoholism and child abuse. A review. *Journal of Studies on Alcohol, 42*(3), 273–287.

Pelham, W. E. & Lang, A. R. (1993). Parental alcohol consumption and deviant child behavior: Laboratory studies of reciprocal effects. *Clinical Psychology Review, 13*, 763–784.

Pernanen, K. (1976). Alcohol and crimes of violence. In B. Kissin & H. Begletier (Eds.), *The biology of alcoholism: Social aspects of alcoholism* (pp. 351–444). New York: Plenum.

Pernanen, K. (1991). *Alcohol in human violence.* New York: Guilford.

Quigley, B. M., & Leonard, K. E. (1996). Desistance of husband aggression in the early years of marriage. *Violence and Victims, 11*(4), 355–370.

Quigley, B. M., & Leonard, K. E. (1999). Husband alcohol expectancies, drinking, and marital-conflict styles as predictors of severe marital violence among newlywed couples. *Psychology of Addictive Behaviors, 13*(1), 49–59.

Quigley, B. M., & Leonard, K. E. (2000), Alcohol and the continuation of early marital aggression. *Alcoholism: Clinical and Experimental Research, 24*, 1003–1010.

Richman, J. A., Rospenda, K. M., & Kelley, M. A. (1995). Gender roles and alcohol abuse across the transition to parenthood. *Journal of Studies on Alcohol, 56*(5), 553–557.

Roberts, L. J., & Leonard, K. E. (1998). An empirical typology of drinking partnerships and their relationship to marital functioning and drinking consequences. *Journal of Marriage and the Family 60*(2), 515–526.

Sebring, P., Campbell, B., Glusberg, M., Spencer, B., & Singleton, M. (1987). *High school and beyond: 1980 sophomore cohort third follow-up (1986): Vol I. Data file user's manual.* Center for Education Statistics, U.S. Department of Education (Pub. No. 1987-194-138). Washington, DC: U.S. Government Printing Office.

Selzer, M. L. (1971). Michigan Alcoholism Screening Test: The quest for a new diagnostic instrument. *American Journal of Psychiatry, 127,* 1653–1658.

Selzer, M., Vinokur, A., & Rooijen, L. (1975). Self-administered Short Michigan Alcoholism Screening Test (Smast). *Journal of Studies on Alcohol, 36,* 117–126.

Silva, P. A. (1990). The Dunedin Multidisciplinary Health and Development Study: A fifteen-year lognitudinal study. *Paediatric and Perinatal Epidemiology, 4,* 96–127.

Skinner, H. A., & Allen, B. A. (1982). Alcohol dependence syndrome: Measurement and validation. *Journal of Abnormal Psychology, 91,* 199–209.

Steele, C. M., & Josephs, R. A. (1990). Alcohol myopia: Its prized and dangerous effects. *American Psychologist, 45,* 921–933.

Stith, S. M., & Farley, S. C. (1993). Predictive model of male spousal violence. *Journal of Family Violence, 8*(2), 183–201.

Straus, M. A. (1979). Measuring intrafamily conflict and violence: The Conflict Tactics (CT) Scales. *Journal of Marriage & the Family, 41,* 75–88.

Suiter, J. J., Pillemer, K., & & Straus, M. (1990). Marital violence in a life course perspective. In M. A. Straus & R. J. Gelles (Eds.), *Physical violence in American Families: Risk factors and adaptations to violence in 8,145 families,* (pp. 305–320). New Brunswick, NJ: Transaction.

Taylor, S. P., & Leonard, K. E. (1983). Alcohol and human physical aggression. In R. G. Geen & E. I. Donnerstein (Eds.), *Aggression: Theoretical and empirical reviews* (pp. 77–101). New York: Academic.

Tolman, R. M., & Bennett, L. W. (1990). A review of quantitative research on men who batter. *Journal of Interpersonal Violence, 5*(1), 87–118.

United States Department of Health and Human Services. (1999). *Child maltreatment 1997: Reports from the states to the national child abuse and neglect data system.* Washington, DC: United States Government Printing Office.

United States Department of Health and Human Services, The National Center on Child Abuse and Neglect. (1993). *Study of child maltreatment in alcohol abusing families: A report to congress.* Washington, DC: United States Government Printing Office.

United States Department of Justice: Bureau of Justice Statistics. (1993). *Criminal victimization in the United States, 1992* (NCJ145125). Washington, DC: United States Government Printing Office.

Vogeltanz, N. D., Wilsnack, S. C., Harris, T. R., Wilsnack, R. W., Wonderlich, S. A., & Kristjanson, A.

F. (1999). Prevalence and risk factors for childhood sexual abuse in women: National survey findings. *Child Abuse and Neglect, 23*, 579–592.

Wauchope, B. A., & Straus, M. A. (1990). Physical punishment and physical abuse of American children: Incidence rates by age, gender, and occupational class. In M. A. Straus & R. J. Gelles (Eds.), *Physical violence in American families risk factors and adaptions to violence in 8,145 families*, (pp.133–148). New Brunswick, NJ: Transaction Publishers.

Whipple, E. E., & Webster-Stratton, C. (1991). The role of parental stress in physically abusive families. *Child Abuse & Neglect, 15(3)*, 279–291.

Wilsnack, R. W., & Wilsnack, S. C. (1990, June). *Husbands and wives as drinking partners*. Paper presented at the 16th Annual Alcohol Epidemiology Symposium of the Kettil Bruun Society for Social and Epidemiological Research on Alcohol, Budapest, Hungary.

Wolock, I., & Magura, S. (1996). Parental substance abuse as a predictor of child maltreatment reports. *Child Abuse and Neglect, 20(12)*, 1183–1193

Wood, J. M. (1997) Risk predictors for Re-Abuse and Re-Neglect in a Predominantly Hispanic Population. *Child Abuse and Neglect, 21*, 379–389.

Yamaguchi, K., & Kandel, D. (1993). Marital homophily on illicit drug use among young adults: Assortative mating or marital influence. *Social Forces, 72(2)*, 505–528.

Mandra L. Rasmussen Hall
Victoria M. Follette

10
CHAPTER

Substance Abuse and Interpersonal Violence in Older Adults

By the year 2030, officials estimate that 25% of the population will be 60 or older (U.S. Department of Health and Human Services, 1990). Given that the number of older adults is growing so rapidly, it is essential to examine mental health issues in this population. According to prevalence estimates (e.g., Adams & Cox, 1997; Deitch, 1997), a significant number of older adults experience substance abuse problems and interpersonal violence. However, for older adults in particular, problems related to substance abuse or trauma experiences may be overlooked or misdiagnosed by health care professionals and service delivery agencies (e.g., Allers, Benjack, & Allers, 1992; DeHart & Hoffman, 1995; Finney, Moos, & Brennan, 1991; King, Van Hasselt, Segal, & Hersen, 1994). In addition, while researchers have begun to examine how substance abuse and exposure to interpersonal violence impact adults as they age, no research has assessed specifically the relationship between substance abuse and interpersonal violence in older adults. In order to successfully assess and treat this growing population, it is essential that we, as scientist-practitioners, fully understand how substance abuse and interpersonal violence function in the lives of older adults.

This chapter reviews the existing literature on substance abuse and interpersonal violence in older adults, emphasizing both the empirical and clinical observations regarding these two phenomena. We begin with a brief discussion of the definition of 'older adult' and an overview of the prevalence rates of substance abuse and interpersonal violence in this population. We then present the methodological challenges associated with assessing and studying these problems in older populations, and continue with a theoretical conceptualization of the link between substance abuse and interpersonal violence in older adults. Finally, we comment on the clinical and empirical implications of the literature to date, and suggest important avenues for future investigation and clinical work.

☐ Operational Definition of Older Adults

The group comprised of 'older adults' is defined differently in different organizations, government agencies, and fields of study. For example, the American Association of Retired Persons (AARP) includes adults 50 and older in its membership (AARP, 2000), while the U.S. Social Security Administration defines "full retirement age" as 65 years (U.S. Social Security Administration, 2000). The U.S. Census Bureau Population Estimates Program groups adults into two categories, 65 years and over and 85 years and over, in its "special age categories" section (U.S. Census Bureau, 2000). Gerontologists, on the other hand, define older adults more specifically using three different categories: early old age, which includes adults aged 65–74 years; middle old age, which includes adults aged 75–84 years; and advanced old age, which includes adults aged 85 and older (Fisher, Zeiss, & Carstensen, in press). In contrast, most research described in this chapter more broadly defines older adults using a cutoff age such as 55 or older, 60 or older, or 65 or older. The methodological issues related to such broad definitions of the older adult are addressed later in the chapter.

☐ Substance Abuse Prevalence

Alcohol

Prevalence estimates of heavy or problem drinking in older adults vary considerably, ranging from between 1–8% in population-based studies (e.g., Blazer, Crowell, & George, 1987; Meyers, Hingson, Mucatel, & Goldman, 1982; Molgaard, Nakamura, Stanford, Peddecord, & Morton, 1990), between 8–31% in retirement community samples (Adams, 1995; Alexander & Duff, 1988; Paganini-Hill, Ross, & Henderson, 1986), and between 4–26% in clinical samples (e.g., Adams, Magruder-Habib, Trued, & Broome, 1992; Buchsbaum, Buchanan, Lawton, & Schnoll, 1991; Curtis, Geller, Stokes, Levine, & Moore, 1989). In general, both longitudinal and cross-sectional studies have shown *lower* rates of alcohol use and misuse in older adults as compared to younger cohorts (see Adams & Cox, 1997). Across studies, older women in particular report the lowest levels of alcohol use and abuse compared to all other groups of men and women (Wilsnack, Vogeltanz, Diers, & Wilsnack, 1995). However, the prevalence estimates of alcohol use and misuse in older adults are large enough, particularly in clinical and retirement settings, to raise concern among researchers and health care providers about how to address this problem (Adams & Cox, 1997).

While alcohol abuse rates in older cohorts certainly include those individuals who have been abusing alcohol across their lifespans, some studies indicate that a significant number of older adults with alcohol use problems developed those problems in late-life (see Schutte, Brennan, & Moos, 1998). Studies examining clinical populations report wide ranges in the age of onset of problematic drinking behavior, estimating that between 11 and 88% of older individuals who report alcohol-related problems developed those problems after the age of 50 (e.g., Adams & Waskel, 1991; Atkinson, Turner, Kofoed, & Tolson, 1985; Brennan & Moos, 1991; Hurt, Finlayson, Morse, & Davis, 1988; Schonfeld & Dupree, 1991; Wiens, Mensutik, Miller, & Schmits, 1982; for a review, see Liberto & Oslin, 1997). Demographically, there are no differences between early-onset and late-onset problem drinkers, with the exception of gender. In a review of studies examining differences between these two groups, Liberto and Oslin (1997) found that women accounted for a greater proportion of the number of late-onset problem drinkers than early-onset problem drinkers.

Prescription Medication

Although they account for only 12% of the general population (U.S. Census Bureau, 2000), older adults consume the greatest proportion, 25–33%, of prescription medications distributed in the U.S. (U.S. General Accounting Office, 1987). In a review of studies examining prescription drug use by older adults (Finlayson, 1997), general findings indicate that benzodiazepine use increases with age, that older adults are more likely than younger adults to be prescribed increased dosages for longer periods of time, and that older women are more likely than older men to be prescribed benzodiazepine medication. While limited research has been conducted to investigate the prevalence of prescription medication *abuse*, the pattern of use among older adults suggested above is significant enough to warrant concern (Finlayson, 1997). Although some older adults may be seeking out prescription medication, health care providers may also be overprescribing some types of drugs in order to decrease patient complaints or demands for attention. This may be particularly true in nursing home settings where behavior problems exhibited by patients create stressful situations for health care staff, resulting in inappropriate use of psychoactive medication in some health care facilities (e.g., Beers et al., 1992).

Illicit Drugs

The majority of studies examining substance abuse in older adults focus on the use and abuse of alcohol and prescription medications. Although older adults' use of illicit substances such as heroin, marijuana, or cocaine appears to be uncommon, too little research has been conducted on illicit drug use by older adults to provide adequate prevalence estimates. Some researchers speculate that illicit drug addiction among older adults will increase as younger cohorts, who report higher rates of illicit drug use, age (Rosenberg, 1997). Given that the population of older adults is growing steadily, this speculation suggests the need for further empirical exploration of younger cohorts' illicit drug use over time if researchers and health care providers are to understand how to recognize and treat older adults with drug abuse problems.

☐ Interpersonal Violence Prevalence

Historical Reports

Traumatic stress researchers have estimated the lifetime prevalence of different types of interpersonal violence in the general adult population, including child sexual abuse, child physical abuse, adult sexual assault, and relationship violence (e.g., Duncan, Saunders, Kilpatrick, Hanson, & Resnick, 1996; Finkelhor, Hotaling, Lewis, & Smith, 1990; Housekamp & Foy, 1991; Koss, Heise, & Russo, 1994; Polusny & Follette, 1995). Unfortunately, there is little information about the prevalence of these types of interpersonal violence in either the histories or current experiences of older adults because many studies do not include older adults in their samples at all, or too few are included to make any significant statement about prevalence (Higgins & Follette, 1999).

In the few studies that have examined rates of interpersonal violence in the history of older adults, conclusions drawn are limited by small sample sizes, retrospective self-reports, and cross-sectional designs. For example, in a clinical sample of older women with panic disorder (Sheikh, Swales, Kravitz, Bail, & Taylor, 1994), 10 of 17 subjects reported experiencing child physical abuse, child sexual abuse, or both during their lifetimes. In a more recent study, Higgins and Follette (1999) found that 72% of a sample of women aged 60 and older reported experiencing either child physical abuse, child sexual abuse, adult rape, or domestic violence, or a combination of these types of interpersonal trauma, during their lifetimes. These rates of lifetime experience of interpersonal violence are similar to rates found in younger cohorts, however, further examination of the life experiences of older adults in the general population are necessary before firm conclusions can be drawn.

Contemporaneous Reports

Little is known about the prevalence of ongoing interpersonal violence among older adults. Wolkenstein & Sterman (1998) found that in two outpatient samples of women aged 55 and older, 67% and 42% of the women sampled reported experiencing domestic violence throughout their marriages. In the general population, prevalence estimates of domestic violence among older adults are emerging in studies examining various types of elder abuse. Although many people often think of elder abuse as harm committed by adult children who care for their aging parents (Vinton, 1992), some research indicates that elder abuse initiated by a spouse occurs more frequently than elder abuse committed by adult children (Pillemer & Finkelhor, 1989; Sengstock, 1991). Estimated rates of elder abuse in the older adult population fall between 4–5% (Lachs & Pillemer, 1995); however, this research is still in a preliminary phase of development. In a Boston survey of adults 65 and older (Pillemer & Finkelhor, 1988), 3% reported being victims of abuse or neglect by others, and 58% of the perpetrators named in the survey were the spouses of the victims. Pillemer & Finkelhor (1988) point out that this rate may be exaggerated given that more older adults live with their spouses than with their children or other relatives. However, these researchers found that of those respondents who lived with their spouses, 4.1% reported experiencing abuse from that person. This study also indicated that similar numbers of older men and women self-identified as victims of abuse, while more women than men were victims in reported cases.

Taken together, studies estimating the rates of substance abuse and interpersonal violence in older cohorts suggest that many older adults suffer from alcohol-related problems or have experienced or are currently experiencing some type of interpersonal trauma. While a few studies address the relationship between substance abuse and major life stressors (e.g., Brennan & Moos, 1990), no studies specifically examine the number of older adults who suffer from both substance use problems and interpersonal violence. However, it is clear from the existing research that these problems are significant enough to warrant further investigation. Many researchers have speculated about the relationship between substance abuse and interpersonal violence, and have conceptualized the nature of that relationship in different ways; however, no empirical studies clearly indicate specific links between these two phenomena in older adults. Before we propose one potentially useful theoretical conceptualization of this relationship, we address some important clinical and research considerations in studying these problems in older populations.

☐ Methodological Considerations

Methodological considerations play a significant role in any examination of the empirical literature on older adults; however, substance abuse and interpersonal violence may be particularly vulnerable to a wide variety of methodological issues when studied in older cohorts. While the literature on these problems in older adults provides information on rates of alcohol abuse and interpersonal violence, it offers little information about how these two problems are related. Additional research will certainly contribute to our understanding of these problems, but only as long as scientist-practitioners appreciate and address the complicated ways in which these phenomena are defined, measured, diagnosed, and studied in older adults. In order to ensure that future assessment and research of substance abuse and interpersonal violence yields useful information, we must fully understand the difficulties associated with studying these problems in older cohorts. In the following sections, we will discuss issues of categorization, definition, assessment, diagnosis, and research methodology related to the study of older adults. Most of our discussion will utilize the literature on alcohol use and abuse among older adults due to the limited existing research on prescription medication and illicit drug abuse and interpersonal violence in this population.

Categorization and Definition

Inconsistent definitions and categorizations in research studies on older adults can produce varying results and cloud interpretation of the literature. For example, the wide ranges in prevalence rates reported on alcohol abuse in older adults may be due, in part, to the way in which studies define alcohol use and misuse and categorize age groups of older adults. This problem is not only limited to the elderly. In the field of alcohol research, consensus has not been reached on how best to characterize alcohol consumption and define alcohol abuse. Across studies, alcoholism, alcohol abuse, alcohol dependence, heavy drinking, and problem drinking all refer to alcohol misuse and are often defined differently (Adams & Cox, 1997). In addition, researchers are often inconsistent in the way they define the age range of older adult populations. Some studies include adults in their sixties in the same sample as adults in their eighties and analyze them as one group, while other studies examine a narrower age range of older adults. Researchers, at times, define older adults as individuals over age 55, while others use the cutoff of 65 years of age. This makes interpretating findings across studies difficult. Additionally, the inclusion of adults 20 years apart from each other in the same age group assumes a similarity between these adults that limits investigation of how older adults may change over time in their later years (Adams & Cox, 1997; DeHart & Hoffman, 1995; see Fisher, Zeiss, & Carstensen, in press). For example, while we know little about the prevalence of substance abuse in older adults, we know even less about how substance abuse changes over time among different age groups of older adults. These inconsistencies in categorization and definition not only affect communication between researchers, but also make it difficult for practitioners to use research findings in their clinical practice.

Assessment and Diagnosis

Assessment and diagnosis of mental health problems in older adults can be complicated by several age-related factors and may affect the results obtained in research studies on older adults. For example, the lower prevalence rates for alcohol misuse among older adults compared to younger cohorts may be underestimated for several reasons. First, criteria used to determine alcohol abuse in older adults may be insensitive to signs and symptoms of alcohol abuse in aging populations. For example, the criteria used to determine alcohol abuse in a given study may affect the detection of alcohol misuse in some older adults. Although some older individuals consume less alcohol than their younger counterparts, they may experience the same physiological effects due to age-related changes in the body's absorption of alcohol (DeHart & Hoffman, 1995). Additionally, it may be that late-onset problem drinking is related to stable rates of consumption that do not become problematic until older adulthood, when older adults' bodies become less able to metabolize alcohol efficiently. In this case, older adults may respond with greater cognitive and physiological impairment despite the same level of alcohol consumption (Schutte, Brennan, & Moos, 1998). In general, researchers have suggested that both increased physiological vulnerability to alcohol and greater potential for interactions between alcohol and medications may result in older adults experiencing more problems associated with alcohol consumption even if the frequency and amount of their consumption has not changed from earlier years (Finney, Moos, & Brennan, 1991). Older adults who misuse alcohol may also be less likely to demonstrate typically observed drinking-related problems. Older adults who are retired, widowed, or no longer able to drive may not experience the work, marital, and driving under the influence problems usually seen in younger problem drinkers (Adams & Cox, 1997; DeHart & Hoffman, 1995; Finney, Moos, & Brennan, 1991).

Furthermore, older adults may underreport alcohol misuse, a problem exacerbated by the fact that alcohol abuse in this population can be overlooked by health care providers who are often poorly trained to consistently screen for alcohol use and misuse in older adults (see DeHart & Hoffman, 1995). As mentioned above, older adults with alcohol problems may not show the decreased occupational functioning frequently observed in younger problem drinkers. Some health care providers may also carry biases that alcohol abuse is not a significant problem among older adults because those individuals with substance abuse problems have died or recovered before reaching old age (Atkinson, 1990).

Symptoms of alcohol abuse may mimic the signs and symptoms of other illnesses, or may appear to be characteristics associated with the basic aging process, making assessment and diagnosis of alcohol abuse problems in older adults extremely difficult. Age-related physical or biological problems, such as major illness and balance and coordination problems, may show the same symptomology as alcohol or drug abuse. Symptoms of problem drinking may also mimic that of other psychological problems such as depression. Likewise, cognitive deficits such as memory loss or confusion might be indications of either a normal aging process or impairment related to alcohol misuse (King, Van Hasselt, Segal, & Hersen, 1994).

Similarly, behavior related to experiences of interpersonal violence also may be misdiagnosed in older adults. Symptoms such as forgetfulness or confusion related to intrusive memories or thoughts about a traumatic experience may be mischaracterized as signs of dementia (see Allers, Benjack, & Allers, 1992). For example, in a case study, McCartney and Severson (1997) point out the difficulty of separating posttraumatic stress disorder (PTSD) symptomology from characteristics of dementia in an older woman sexually assaulted by another nursing home resident. In addition, the same symptoms that might be labeled dementia could also be signs of substance abuse or misuse of prescription medication.

In sum, assessment and diagnosis of substance abuse and trauma symptoms in older adults are difficult given the myriad of age-related considerations involved. Criteria and assumptions used in assessment and diagnosis of mental health problems in younger adults are not necessarily appropriate for older cohorts and can significantly affect both research and treatment of this population. Given the complicated nature of assessing specific mental health problems in older adults, scientist-practitioners may need to adopt more idiographic approaches to assessment and diagnosis of older adults' behavior. One such approach is discussed later in the chapter.

Research

In addition to the issues described above, there are unique methodological difficulties in researching problems in older populations. For example, the true prevalence of alcohol abuse in older adults is difficult to determine for several reasons. Much of the epidemiological research on alcohol abuse in older adults is cross-sectional, and so it provides limited information about changes in drinking behavior as individuals age and only offers prevalence estimates for older cohorts at a single period in time. In this type of research, it is unclear how many members of the cohort stopped or started drinking with age or died as a result of alcohol-related problems. In the longitudinal studies that have been conducted, results can be attributed to *either* changes in age *or* differential environmental and social influences on drinking patterns for the given cohort.

The research design most often employed to examine variables in older adults, the cross-sectional design, has many limitations. This design allows the researcher to compare different age groups, yielding age differences that could be due to aging itself or due to cohort effects. In this type of design, it is impossible to know exactly how to interpret the results (Schaie & Willis, 1986). For example, the changes between rates of alcohol use for one cohort born in the 1920s and another cohort born in the 1950s might be due to changes in age, but might also be due to differences in the social environments of the two decades in which these cohorts were born. Cross-sectional designs used to determine prevalence rates of alcohol abuse in older adults are subject to additional problems. The overall lower rates of alcohol use and abuse observed in older compared to younger cohorts may be attributed to gender ratio and health status changes in older adult populations. For example, men have higher mortality rates than women at all ages (Adams & Cox, 1997), and cross-sectional data indicate that women of all ages are less likely than men to use and abuse alcohol (Fillmore et al., 1997). This means that as cohorts age, the female to male ratio increases, thus decreasing the rate of alcohol abuse seen in the oldest cohorts. While research conducted using the cross-sectional design provides some information about current cohorts of older adults, it contributes little to our understanding of how problems of interest change over time as adults age.

Another important difficulty in examining samples of older adults for specific characteristics is age-associated selection bias. For example, it is possible that a given sample of older adults may be more psychologically or physically healthy than deceased members of the same cohort. It could then be problematic to assume that particular dimensions of the problem decrease in old age when those who suffer from such problems may have died as a result of those very problems. This might be especially true for problems such as substance abuse that have a number of associated health problems (Fisher, Zeiss, & Carstensen, in press). Some individuals with alcohol abuse problems die or are institutionalized due to alcohol-related health complications, resulting in a decrease in the rate of alcohol abuse in older cohorts (see Adams & Cox, 1997). Also, as individuals age, many may stop consuming alcohol due to age-related illness or increased possibility of medication-alcohol interactions (Bristow & Clare, 1992).

Additionally, the measurement of particular problems in older adults contributes further to the difficulty in studying this population. Because most measures are normed on younger samples, the instruments' reliabilities, validities, and cutoff scores may be very different when used with older samples. For example, reliabilities of self-report measures in older cohorts may differ due to memory changes (Fisher, Zeiss, & Carstensen, in press). Given that older individuals may show increased sensitivity to the physiological effects of alcohol, cutoff scores may differ in alcohol abuse assessment of older adults while other instrument psychometrics remain the same (DeHart & Hoffman, 1997).

Scientist-practitioners must address these methodological considerations in order to improve the study and treatment of substance abuse and interpersonal violence in older adults. However, attending to these issues will not sufficiently address the limitations of existing research on these problems in aging adults. In order to better understand how substance abuse and interpersonal violence interact as adults age, theory-driven research and practice is an essential next step. The following discussion outlines one theoretical conceptualization of the relationship between substance abuse and interpersonal violence in older adults that may provide the theory-driven direction necessary for future research and practice.

☐ The Relationship between Substance Abuse and Interpersonal Violence

As discussed earlier, there are no empirical studies that specifically examine the relationship between substance abuse and interpersonal violence in older adults. However, many researchers have offered different explanations for the prevalence of substance abuse and interpersonal violence in older adult populations. These researchers also have suggested how both problems might be related. As scientist-practitioners, we believe theory is an important element in further understanding the relationship between these problems. In attempting to understand any phenomena, theoretical frameworks provide direction for both research and clinical practice. A good theory can offer a foundation from which to collect information or deliver treatment in such a way as to efficiently test the theory and further contribute to existing knowledge about the phenomena of interest. Without a theory from which to continue examining a given problem, we may never fully comprehend the nature of the problem. Thus, in order to better understand how substance abuse and interpersonal violence may be linked in older adults, and to help guide further research and clinical practice, we feel it is essential to organize researchers' speculations about the relationship between these problems in a theoretically coherent manner. In the following sections, we describe a particular theoretical framework within which the relationship between substance abuse and interpersonal violence in older adults can be usefully understood. We also provide examples from the literature that suggest support for this theory.

Theoretical Conceptualization

Given that the interaction of substance abuse and interpersonal violence is not well specified in the empirical literature, clinical scientists have generated many explanations for the relationship between these problems. Conceptualizations that have broad utility and applicability are essential in organizing and clarifying complex phenomena such as the relationship between substance abuse and violence in the elderly. A contextual behavioral approach is one useful way to understand these problems. The value of this perspective is that it allows us to examine individuals and problems in a broad sense, considering both historical and environmental factors. From our perspective, the interaction of the problems addressed in this chapter are best understood as an interactive whole, allowing us to fully consider the complex nature of the relationship between substance abuse and interpersonal violence in the context of an elderly population. Experiential avoidance (EA) has been recognized as one approach to understanding problems within a contextual framework (Hayes, Strosahl, & Wilson, 1999). While EA is not a new concept and has been identified as a process by clinicians from a number of theoretical perspectives (for a review and discussion, see Hayes, Wilson, Gifford, Follette, & Strosahl, 1996), the inclusion of this concept in a functional contextual analysis of problems is somewhat new.

The theory of EA (Hayes et al., 1996) is one way of functionally conceptualizing the link between substance abuse and interpersonal violence in older adults. EA is described as "the phenomenon that occurs when a person is unwilling to remain in contact with particular private experiences (e.g., bodily sensations, emotions, thoughts, memories, behavioral predispositions) and takes steps to alter the form or frequency of these events and the contexts that occasion them" (Hayes et al., 1996, p. 1154). The behavioral theory of EA can make sense of a number of diverse clinical phenomena observed in the elderly. While no one is protected from the many difficulties that are a part of every life, the elderly are particularly vulnerable to negative life events. The death of spouses, friends, and even children; the decline in physical health and cognitive abilities; and changes in role functioning can all contribute to feelings of sadness, loss, and pain. EA is a culturally supported way of dealing with these losses that are often of a fundamentally existential nature. The phenomena of avoidance can take many forms, including avoiding or suppressing negative thoughts or feelings. The theory of EA would suggest that behaviors such as substance abuse might function for some older adults as escape from painful thoughts, emotions, or bodily sensations related to stressors or past traumatic events. Similarly, violent behavior might also function to reduce distressing private experiences or environmental situations. The proposed function of both substance abuse and interpersonal violence in older adults, and the possible relationship between both phenomena, is discussed in the following sections with relevant support from the literature included throughout.

Substance Abuse as Avoidance

Many researchers have suggested that substance abuse problems may occur as a result of stressful events associated with age, such as loss of a partner, loss of role functioning, or isolation (Gomberg, 1997; Gurnack & Thomas, 1989; King, Van Hasselt, Segal, & Hersen, 1994). Mixed research results on early- and late-onset alcohol abuse offer two possible explanations of late-life problem drinking consistent with the theory of experiential avoidance. First, Brennan and Moos (1990), in a study examining differences between late-life problem and nonproblem drinkers (men and women age 55–65), found that late-life problem drinkers reported experiencing more stressors, including both acute negative events and chronic difficulties, and less social support than nonproblem drinkers. In addition, women with problem drinking reported experiencing more negative life events than did problem-drinking men. These results suggest that abuse of alcohol in late-life may function for some older adults as temporary escape from distressing thoughts and feelings associated with specific life stressors.

Somewhat different results were found in a more recent study that followed a group of nonproblem drinking older adults over a seven-year period (Schutte, Brennan, & Moos, 1998). Researchers found that those individuals who developed drinking problems (late-onset problem drinkers) over the course of the study were more likely than nonproblem drinkers at baseline assessment to report heavier alcohol consumption, greater use of avoidant coping strategies, and a history of responding to life stressors with increased alcohol consumption. Interestingly, life stressors measured at baseline did not predict late-onset problem drinking, suggesting that coping strategies play a greater role in the development of late-onset problem drinking than specific stressors (Schutte, Brennan, & Moos, 1998). These results suggest that those older adults who abuse alcohol in late-life may not be responding to specific age-related stressors per se, but instead may be continuing a pattern of behavior as they age that functions to alleviate painful thoughts and feelings about the difficulties in their life.

Researchers also have hypothesized that substance abuse may help some older adults reduce the frequency or unpleasantness of distressing interactions with their partners, ranging from general relationship discord, to sexual dysfunction, to domestic violence (Wilsnack, Vogeltanz, Diers, & Wilsnack, 1995). This suggestion is consistent with the theory of EA. Research investigating relationship variables in older adults have found that marital and couple distress is an issue in this population. Speer, Williams, West, and Dupree

(1991) found that marital problems were the third most frequent diagnosis for adults age 55 and over at an outpatient mental health services center. O'Farrell, Choquette, Cutter, and Birchler (1997) reported that couples were more dissatisfied with their frequency of intercourse and experienced impotence at a higher frequency the older the age of the husband. In addition, both alcoholic and conflicted couples in which the husband was older reported experiencing less frequent intercourse, with a greater age-related decline in frequency of intercourse among alcoholic than among conflicted couples. While this example does not specifically identify substance abuse as a response to relationship difficulties, it does suggest that some older couples experience sexual dysfunction in their intimate relationships, and that alcohol abuse by one partner may function to reduce the frequency of the couple's sexual intimacy. It also is possible that alcohol abuse might function for one partner to alleviate painful thoughts and feelings associated with the couple's sexual difficulties.

Still other researchers have proposed that substance abuse may serve as a way for some older adults to cope with stressors in their histories (Brennan & Moos, 1990; Hyer & Woods, 1998). EA is particularly appropriate for explaining this link. Some older adults may abuse alcohol to avoid or alleviate painful emotions or intrusive memories about past traumatic events such as interpersonal victimization. In younger cohorts, EA has been used to conceptualize the wide range of long-term problems associated with a history of interpersonal violence, such as PTSD and substance abuse (Polusny & Follette, 1995). However, little research has examined these issues longitudinally, and the long-term course of these problems is not known at this time.

A few studies do indicate that early experiences of interpersonal violence continue to impact some older adults. Researchers have suggested that the long-term effects of a history of interpersonal violence may persist for many years, possibly lasting into old age for some individuals (Allers, Benjack, & Allers, 1992; Browne & Finkelhor, 1986; Polusny & Follette, 1995; Resick, 1993; Walker, 1991). In a community sample of women aged 60 and older, Higgins and Follette (1999) found that women who reported histories of child sexual abuse, child physical abuse, relationship violence, or rape exhibited greater long-term psychological distress and reported more health problems and medication use than women with no interpersonal trauma history. These researchers also found that women who reported multiple types of interpersonal trauma showed higher levels of depression and general psychological distress than women who reported no trauma or only one type of traumatic experience during their lifetime. While the conclusions drawn from these findings are limited, they do suggest that women who report histories of interpersonal victimization may be at risk in later life of continued psychological distress, possibly including greater health problems and overuse of medications. If some women adopted EA as a way of coping with thoughts and feelings about their abuse histories as young adults, over time, this strategy could become negatively reinforced by the temporary reduction of distress. In old age, the decrease in environmental stimulation may make it more and more difficult for individuals to escape their private experiences. Substance use may then function for these older adults as a means of continued avoidance of their private experiences, particularly if substance use in general is perceived by these older adults as a more socially acceptable behavior than when they were younger.

Interpersonal Violence as Avoidance

Just as substance abuse may function as avoidance or escape for some older adults, interpersonal violence may function similarly, particularly violence such as late-onset spousal abuse and elder abuse. Some researchers have proposed that spousal abuse in older couples may reflect a history of domestic violence that has escalated over time (Pillemer & Finkelhor, 1988; Sengstock, 1991). However, other researchers have described the phenomenon of late-onset spousal abuse, violence possibly precipitated by a number of aging-related events such as changes in health status, financial strain, grief, substance abuse, medication misuse, relationship distress, and dementia (Deitch, 1997; Pillemer & Suitor, 1991; Ramsey-Klawsnick, 1993; Wolf, 1995). In addition, Sengstock (1991) suggests that marital rape in older couples might be related to the perpetrator's sexual dysfunction in later life, possibly precipitated by alcohol abuse, hypertension, or other health problems. The violent behavior of some older adults with dementia also may affect the abusive behavior of their partners and other caregivers (Penhale & Kingston, 1997).

In other words, according to the theory of EA, late-onset spousal abuse, including marital rape, may function for the perpetrator as an escape from private experiences about such stressors as loss of independence and sexual dysfunction, or may serve to reduce unpleasant behavior exhibited by a partner. The latter possibility is demonstrated in research examining caregiver behavior toward older adults with dementia. Coyne, Reichman, and Berbig (1993) surveyed caregivers who responded to a free dementia hotline and found that 33% reported being physically abused by the relative for whom they were caring, and 12% reported physically abusing the person under their care. A majority of those caregivers who reported being abused by their relative also reported being abusive. In addition, those caregivers who reported being abusive also reported caring for their relative for a longer period of time overall than those caregivers who did not report abusive behavior. This and other research suggests that violent and disruptive behavior exhibited by the person receiving care may be a risk factor for subsequent caregiver violence (see Penhale & Kingston, 1997), or that abuse may function for some caregivers to reduce feelings of stress by terminating violent behavior exhibited by older adults under their care.

☐ Clinical and Research Issues

Addressing substance abuse and trauma-related problems in older adults presents an array of complicated assessment, diagnosis, and treatment issues. Regardless of these complexities, we believe that clinicians can best assess these issues using a functional analysis of the problem, which includes situational and historical factors. Functional assessment of these problems for a given older adult can inform a clinician's treatment plan and guide treatment strategies in an efficient and testable manner. For older adults in particular, it is crucial to understand the context in which their behavior occurs. In some older cohorts, use of prescription medication as a coping strategy for stress or anxiety may be more socially acceptable than misuse of alcohol or illicit drugs. Some older adults may also be reluctant to report mental health problems, or may be hesitant to question a physician or pharmacist about appropriate use of a prescription. It is important that health care providers be aware of these contextual variables in order to effectively screen for problems such as this. In addition to patient-instigated overuse of medication, it is also critical that families and mental health professionals be sensitive to potential overuse of medications by health care providers as a chemical restraint to control behavior that might be better managed using environmental strategies. As discussed earlier, nursing home settings may be particularly vulnerable to inappropriate use of psychoactive medication.

While many researchers have focused on the lower rates of alcohol use and abuse reported in prevalence estimates in older adults as compared to younger cohorts, it is important not to overlook the higher rates reported in some studies of health care settings and retirement communities. Given that medical illness and death are often associated with life-long alcohol abuse, the higher rates of alcohol use and misuse observed in health care settings is not unexpected (see Friedmann et al., 1999). Higher rates in retirement communities, however, point to the need for further investigation of changes in drinking behavior among individuals who choose to live in communities designed specifically for healthy, aging adults. It is unclear what role alcohol consumption plays in the social environment of these communities, and how this environment might reinforce the drinking patterns of its members (Wilsnack, Vogeltanz, Diers, & Wilsnack, 1995). Individuals who already use or misuse alcohol may be more likely to choose retirement communities where their alcohol use patterns are supported socially. Alternatively, some retirement communities may organize social activities around alcohol use, possibly increasing rates of use and abuse in community residents.

The few studies that have assessed the prevalence of interpersonal violence in older adults indicate that a significant number of older adults suffer from spouse or elder abuse. Unfortunately, these older adults may not be receiving the assistance they need. For example, Vinton's (1992) examination of Florida battered women's shelters found that older battered women were poorly represented among the population of women served by these shelters, a serious concern given the large number of elderly residents living in Florida. Vinton (1992) also found that few shelters offered programming designed for older clients, and suggested ways in which domestic violence shelters might better meet the needs of older victims of domestic violence. For example, older battered women are often perceived by service providers as victims of elder abuse, and are, thus, often referred to different agencies, such as nursing homes and other elder care settings where they may not receive appropriate services. Moreover, issues related to violence are frequently not addressed at all with the elderly. In a study of community women who were 60 and older, many of them reported that they had never been asked about issues related to abuse and relationship problems (Higgins & Follette, 1999). At the time that study was proposed, some individuals on the institution's human subjects committee thought that asking elderly women such questions would be too upsetting and intrusive. The researchers countered with explanations of efforts to minimize risk that included a very clear informed consent form. Interestingly, the women who participated in the study reported feeling grateful to be able to share their experiences and validated by the interview process. One clinical implication of that research was the importance of including individuals from all age groups in research on interpersonal violence.

Given the cross-sectional nature of much of the research on aging adults, it is difficult to determine the trend of problems reported by adults across the lifespan. For example, it is unclear whether problems reported by younger trauma survivors will continue into later life, or whether these problems will decrease with age. It seems possible that younger adults, who were born in very different cohorts from those currently being studied, may continue to have higher rates of substance abuse and interpersonal violence as they age than older cohorts. In addition, the limited number of studies examining substance abuse and interpersonal violence in older adults have yielded mixed results, forcing researchers to speculate about the true prevalence of these problems in aging populations. Because even less research has investigated the relationship between substance abuse and interpersonal violence in older adults, researchers can only make assumptions about how these problems function together in older adults.

Despite the limitations of existing research in this area, studies have provided some direction for future investigation. Research described earlier in this chapter suggests that substance abuse and interpersonal violence are pervasive enough in older adult populations to warrant further examination. Research also suggests that substance abuse may function to help some older adults avoid facing relationship or health changes associated with aging or help these adults escape unwanted thoughts and feelings about their interpersonal trauma experiences. However, until more rigorous longitudinal research is conducted, we will never be able to understand exactly how substance abuse and interpersonal violence influence each other over time to affect older adults.

We suggest that further research on substance abuse and interpersonal violence in older adults address several important issues. First, if we are to better understand the relationship between interpersonal violence and substance abuse in our aging population, research must target a consistent measurement of reported problems in older adults. Research that categorizes older adults into one large age group, measures substance abuse inconsistently across studies, or uses criteria for defining substance abuse and interpersonal violence that has been normed on younger samples will contribute little to our understanding of these problems in older adults. Second, researchers must conduct longitudinal studies aimed at examining trends in reported problems across the lifespan so we can determine how these problems change as individuals age. Cross-sectional studies will not provide the comprehensive information necessary to predict substance abuse and interpersonal violence problems in aging adults. Third, studies designed to examine the relationship between substance abuse and interpersonal violence must be theory-driven in order to guide our further understanding of the link between these phenomena more efficiently. The theory of EA may be an appropriate conceptualization from which to carry on this research. The construct of EA is useful in that it can help practitioners understand the functional connection between behavior that is topographically very different. Finally, if we are to effectively assess and treat those older adults who suffer from substance abuse and interpersonal violence, research must examine those older adults who demonstrate resiliency in the face of life's stressors. Without understanding the course of psychological health or resilience, it is difficult to understand how to intervene and treat maladaptive coping strategies or psychological distress.

☐ Conclusion

Our suggested directions for further study will help researchers conduct investigations that not only inform clinicians about how to assess and treat our growing older adult population, but also influence how policy-makers, health care providers, and community leaders address these problems across the lifespan. Given that individuals aged 60 and older are fast becoming one of the largest age groups in the general population, it is crucial to better understand the problems that affect this group. Substance abuse and interpersonal violence, in particular, are serious problems that impact both the health of individuals who suffer from these problems and the larger community. These problems tax health care systems, government agencies, and other community service resources and influence treatment and policy decisions made by health care providers and politicians. If we can better understand how substance abuse and interpersonal violence influence each other across the lifespan, we may be able to prevent their impact on adults in late-life.

☐ References

Adams, S. L., & Waskel, S. A. (1991). Late onset of alcoholism among older midwestern men in treatment. *Psychological Reports, 68,* 432–434.

Adams, W. L. (1995). Potential for adverse drug-alcohol interactions in elderly retirement community residents. *Journal of the American Geriatrics Society, 43,* 1021–1025.

Adams, W. L., & Cox, N. S. (1997). Epidemiology of problem drinking among elderly people. In A. M. Gurnack (Ed.), *Older adults' misuse of alcohol, medicines, and other drugs: Research and practice issues* (pp. 1–23). New York: Spring.

Adams, W. L., Magruder-Habib, K., Trued, S., & Broome, H. L. (1992). Alcohol abuse in elderly emergency department patients. *Journal of the American Geriatrics Society, 40,* 1236–1240.

Alexander, F., & Duff, R. W. (1988). Social interaction and alcohol use in retirement communities. *The Gerontologist, 28,* 632-636.

Allers, C. T., Benjack, K. J., & Allers, N. T. (1992). Unresolved childhood sexual abuse: Are older adults affected? *Journal of Counseling and Development, 71,* 14–17.

American Association of Retired Persons. (2000). *AARP webplace* [On-line]. Available: http://www.aarp.org.

Atkinson, R. M. (1990). Aging and alcohol use disorders: Diagnostic issues in the elderly. *International Psychogeriatrics, 2,* 55–72.

Atkinson, R. M., Turner, J. A., Kofoed, L. L., & Tolson, R. L. (1985). Early versus late onset alcoholism in older persons: Preliminary findings. *Alcoholism: Clinical and Experimental Research, 9,* 513–515.

Beers, M. H., Ouslander, J. G., Fingold, S. F., Morgenstern, H., Reuben, D. B., Rogers, W., Zeffren, M. J., & Beck, J. C. (1992). Inappropriate medication prescribing in skilled-nursing facilities. *Annals of Internal Medicine, 117,* 684–689.

Blazer, D., Crowell, B. A., & George, L. K. (1987). Alcohol abuse and dependence in the rural South. *Archives of General Psychiatry, 44,* 736–740.

Brennan, P. L., & Moos, R. H. (1990). Life stressors, social resources, and late-life problem drinking. *Psychology and Aging, 5,* 491–501.

Brennan, P. L., & Moos, R. H. (1991). Functioning, life context, and help-seeking among late-onset problem drinkers: Comparisons with nonproblem and early-onset problem drinkers. *British Journal of Addiction, 86,* 1139–1150.

Bristow, M. F., & Clare, A. W. (1992). Prevalence and characteristics of at-risk drinkers among elderly acute medical inpatients. *British Journal of the Addictions, 87,* 291–294.

Browne, A., & Finkelhor, D. (1986). The impact of child sexual abuse: A review of the research. *Psychological Bulletin, 99,* 66–77.

Buchsbaum, D. G., Buchanan, R. G., Lawton, M. J., & Schnoll, S. H. (1991). Alcohol consumption patterns in a primary care population. *Alcohol and Alcoholism, 26,* 215–220.

Coyne, A., Reichman, W. E., & Berbig, L. J. (1993). The relationship between dementia and elder abuse. *American Journal of Psychiatry, 150,* 643–646.

Curtis, J. R., Geller, G., Stokes, E. J., Levine, D. M., & Moore, R. D. (1989). Characteristics, diagnosis, and treatment of alcoholism in elderly patients. *Journal of the American Geriatrics Society, 37,* 310–316.

DeHart, S. S., & Hoffman, N. G. (1995). Screening and diagnosis of "alcohol abuse and dependence" in older adults. *The International Journal of the Addictions, 30,* 1717–1747.

DeHart, S. S., & Hoffman, N. G. (1997). Screening and diagnosis: Alcohol use disorders in older adults. In A. M. Gurnack (Ed.), *Older adults' misuse of alcohol, medicines, and other drugs: Research and practice issues* (pp. 25–53). New York: Spring.

Deitch, I. (1997). When Golden Pond is tainted: Domestic violence and the elderly. In I. Deitch & C. W. Howell (Eds.), *Counseling the aging and their families* (pp. 87–101). Alexandria, VA: American Counseling Association.

Duncan, R. D., Saunders, B. E., Kilpatrick, D. G., Hanson, R. F., & Resnick, H. S. (1996). Childhood physical assault as a risk factor for PTSD, depression, and substance abuse: Findings from a national survey. *American Journal of Orthopsychiatry, 66,* 437–448.

Fillmore, K. M., Golding, J. M., Leino, E. V., Motoyoshi, M., Shoemaker, C., Terry, H., Ager, C. R., & Ferrer, H. P. (1997). Patterns and trends in women's and men's drinking. In R. W. Wilsnack & S. C. Wilsnack (Eds.), *Gender and alcohol: Individual and social perspectives* (pp. 21–47). New Brunswick, NJ: Rutgers Center of Alcohol Studies.

Finkelhor, D., Hotaling, G., Lewis, I. A., & Smith, C. (1990). Sexual abuse in a national survey of adult men and women: Prevalence, characteristics, and risk factors. *Child Abuse and Neglect, 14,* 19–28.

Finlayson, R. (1997). Misuse of prescription drugs. In A. M. Gurnack (Ed.), *Older adults' misuse of alcohol, medicines, and other drugs: Research and practice issues* (pp. 158–184). New York: Spring.

Finney, J. W., Moos, R. H., & Brennan, P. L. (1991). The Drinking Problems Index: A measure to assess alcohol-related problems among older adults. *Journal of Substance Abuse, 3,* 395–404.

Fisher, J. E., Zeiss, A. M., Carstensen, L. L. (in press). Psychopathology in the aged. In P. B. Sutker & H. E. Adams (Eds.), *Comprehensive handbook of psychopathology* (3rd ed.). New York: Plenum.

Friedmann, P. D., Jin, L., Karrison, T., Nerney, M., Hayley, D. C., Mulliken, R., Walter, J., Miller, A., & Chin, M. H. (1999). The effect of alcohol abuse on the health status of older adults seen in the emergency department. *American Journal of Drug and Alcohol Abuse, 25,* 529–542.

Gomberg, E. S. L. (1997). Alcohol abuse: Age and gender differences. In R. W. Wilsnack & S. C. Wilsnack (Eds.), *Gender and alcohol: Individual and social perspectives* (pp. 225–244). New Brunswick, NJ: Rutgers Center of Alcohol Studies.

Gurnack, A., & Thomas, J. (1989). Behavioral factors related to elderly alcohol abuse: Research and policy issues. *The International Journal of the Addictions, 24,* 641–654.

Hayes, S. C., Strosahl, K. D., & Wilson, K. G. (1999). *Acceptance and commitment therapy: An experiential approach to behavior change.* New York: Guilford.

Hayes, S. C., Wilson, K. G., Gifford, E. V., Follette, V. M., & Strosahl, K. (1996). Experiential avoidance and behavioral disorders: A functional dimensional approach to diagnosis and treatment. *Journal of Consulting and Clinical Psychology, 64,* 1152–1168.

Higgins, A. B., & Follette, V. M. (1999). *Coping with interpersonal trauma in later life: A study of older women.* Unpublished doctoral dissertation, University of Nevada, Reno, Nevada.

Housekamp, B., & Foy, D. (1991). The assessment of posttraumatic stress disorder in battered women. *Journal of Interpersonal Violence, 6,* 367–375.

Hurt, R. D., Finlayson, R. E., Morse, R. M., & Davis, L. J. (1988). Alcoholism in elderly persons: Medical aspects and prognosis of 216 inpatients. *Mayo Clinic Proceedings, 63,* 753–760.

Hyer, L., & Woods, M. G. (1998). Phenomenology and treatment of trauma in later life. In V. M. Follette, J. I. Ruzek, & F. R. Abueg (Eds.), *Cognitive-behavioral therapies for trauma* (pp. 383–414). New York: Guilford.

King, C. J., Van Hasselt, V. B., Segal, D. L., & Hersen, M. (1994). Diagnosis and assessment of substance abuse in older adults: Current strategies and issues. *Addictive Behaviors, 19,* 41–55.

Koss, M. P., Heise, L., & Russo, N. F. (1994). The global health burden of rape. *Psychology of Women Quarterly, 18,* 509–537.

Lachs, M. & Pillemer, K. (1995). Abuse and neglect of elderly persons. *New England Medical Journal, 332,* 437–443.

Liberto, J. G., & Oslin, D. W. (1997). Early versus late onset of alcoholism in the elderly. In A. M. Gurnack (Ed.), *Older adults' misuse of alcohol, medicines, and other drugs: Research and practice issues* (pp. 94–112). New York: Spring.

McCartney, J. R., & Severson, K. (1997). Sexual violence, posttraumatic stress disorder and dementia. *Journal of the American Geriatric Society, 45,* 76–78.

Meyers, A. R., Hingson, R., Mucatel, M., & Goldman, E. (1982). Social and psychological correlates of problem drinking in old age. *Journal of the American Geriatrics Society, 30,* 452–456.

Molgaard, C. A., Nakamura, C. M., Stanford, E. P., Peddecord, K. M., & Morton, D. J. (1990). Prevalence of alcohol consumption among older persons. *Journal of Community Health, 15,* 239–251.

O'Farrell, T. J., Choquette, K. A., Cutter, H. S. G., & Birchler, G. R. (1997). Sexual satisfaction and dysfunction in marriages of male alcoholics: Comparison with nonalcoholic maritally conflicted couples and nonconflicted couples. *Journal of Studies on Alcohol, 58,* 91–99.

Paganini-Hill, A., Ross, R. K., & Henderson, B. E. (1986). Prevalence of chronic disease and health practices in a retirement community. *Journal of Chronic Disease, 39,* 699–707.

Penhale, B., & Kingston, P. (1997). Elder abuse, mental health and later life: Steps towards an understanding. *Aging and Mental Health, 1,* 296–304.

Pillemer, K. A., & Finkelhor, D. (1988). The prevalence of elder abuse: A random sample survey. *Gerontologist, 28,* 51–57.

Pillemer, K. A., & Finkelhor, D. (1989). Causes of elder abuse: Caregivers' stress vs. problem relatives. *American Journal of Orthopsychiatry, 59,* 179–187.

Pillemer, K. A., & Suitor, J. (1991). Sharing residence with an adult child: A cause of psychological distress in the elderly? *American Journal of Orthopsychiatry, 61*, 144–148.

Polusny, M. A., & Follette, V. M. (1995). Long-term correlates of child sexual abuse: Theory and review of the empirical literature. *Applied & Preventive Psychology, 4*, 143–166.

Ramsey-Klawsnik, H. (1993). Interviewing elders for suspected sexual abuse: Guidelines and techniques. *Journal of Elder Abuse and Neglect, 5*, 5–19.

Resick, P. A. (1993). The psychological impact of rape. *Journal of Interpersonal Violence, 8*, 223–255.

Rosenberg, H. (1997). Use and abuse of illicit drugs among older people. In A. M. Gurnack (Ed.), *Older adults' misuse of alcohol, medicines, and other drugs: Research and practice issues* (pp. 206–227). New York: Spring.

Schaie, K. W., & Willis, S. L. (1986). *Adult development and aging* (2nd ed.). Boston: Little, Brown and Company.

Schonfeld, L., & Dupree, L. W. (1991). Antecedents of drinking for early- and late-onset elderly alcohol abusers. *Journal of Studies on Alcohol, 52*, 587–592.

Schutte, K., Brennan, P., & Moos, R. (1998). Predicting the development of late-life late-onset drinking problems: A 7-year prospective study. *Alcoholism: Clinical and Experimental Research, 22*, 1349–1358.

Sengstock, M. (1991). Sex and gender: Implications in cases of elder abuse. *Journal of Women and Aging, 3*, 25–43.

Sheikh, J. I., Swales, P. J., Kravitz, J., Bail, G., & Taylor, C. B. (1994). Childhood abuse history in older women with panic disorder. *American Journal of Geriatric Psychiatry, 2*, 75–77.

Speer, D. C., Williams, J., West, H., & Dupree, L. (1991). Older adult users of outpatient mental health services. *Community Mental Health Journal, 27*, 69–76.

U.S. Census Bureau. (2000). *Population estimates* [On-line]. Available: http://www.census.gov/population/www/estimates/popest.html.

U.S. Department of Health and Human Services (1990, January). *Seventh Special Report to the U.S. Congress on Alcohol and Health*. Public Health Service, Alcohol, Drug, and Mental Health Administration (ADAMHA), National Institute of Alcohol Abuse and Alcoholism, Rockville, MD.

U.S. General Accounting Office (1987). *Report to the Chairman, special committee on aging, U.S. Senate, medicare, prescription drug issues*. Washington, DC: Author.

U.S. Social Security Administration. (2000). *Social security questions* [On-line]. Available: http://ssa-custhelp.ssa.gov/cgi-bin/ssa.

Vinton, L. (1992). Battered women's shelters and older women: The Florida experience. *Journal of Family Violence, 7*, 63–72.

Walker, L. E. (1991). Posttraumatic stress disorder in women: Diagnosis and treatment of battered woman syndrome. *Psychotherapy, 28*, 21–29.

Wiens, A. N., Mensutik, C. E., Miller, S. I., & Schmits, R. E. (1982). Medical-behavioral treatment of the older alcoholic patient. *American Journal of Drug and Alcohol Abuse, 9*, 461–475.

Wilsnack, S. C., Vogeltanz, N. D., Diers, L. E., & Wilsnack, R. W. (1995). Drinking and problem drinking in older women. In T. Beresford & E. Gomberg (Eds.), *Alcohol and aging* (pp. 263–292). New York: Oxford University Press.

Wolf, R. S. (1995). A brief look at elder abuse and Alzheimer's disease. *National Center on Elder Abuse Exchange, 2*, 6–12.

Wolkenstein, B. H., & Sterman, L. (1998). Unmet needs of older women in a clinic population: The discovery of possible long-term sequelae of domestic violence. *Professional Psychology: Research and Practice, 29*, 341–348.

CLINICAL ISSUES IN INTERVENTION FOR INTIMATE VIOLENCE AND ADDICTION PROBLEMS

11   Violence and Alcohol: Cultural Issues
     and Barriers to Treatment
     John Schafer and Raul Caetano

12   Treating Dual Problems of Partner
     Violence and Substance Abuse
     William R. Downs and Brenda A. Miller

13   Treating the Addicted Male Batterer: Promising
     Directions for Dual-Focused Programming
     Caroline Easton and Rajita Sinha

14   Behavioral Couples Therapy for Alcoholism and
     Drug Abuse: Encountering the Problem
     of Domestic Violence
     Timothy J. O'Farrell and Christopher M. Murphy

15   Bridging the Gap: Prevention of Adolescent
     Risk Behaviors and Development of Healthy
     Nonviolent Dating Relationships
     Anna-Lee Pittman and David A. Wolfe

16 Conclusion: Clinical and Research Issues in Relationship Violence and Substance Abuse
Christine Wekerle and Anne-Marie Wall

CHAPTER 11

John Schafer
Raul Caetano

Violence and Alcohol: Cultural Issues and Barriers to Treatment

The stress associated with managing the complicated paperwork to file insurance claims for medical coverage is a grudgingly accepted chore for millions of residents in the United States. For millions of others without medical coverage, this often-frustrating task often leads nowhere. Health care has been a controversial issue in the United States during the past several decades, and it still holds the attention of a majority of the citizenship (De La Rosa, 1989). Access to health care in the U.S. is a function of many variables, including income, education, health insurance coverage, and ethnicity. In turn, these variables differ as a function of several moderating variables, including ethnic identification.

In this chapter, we briefly discuss the barriers associated with access to health insurance coverage and how this crucial gateway to health care is associated with alcohol consumption and intimate partner violence (IPV). It is not our intention to provide a comprehensive examination of the issues surrounding access to treatment for alcohol and intimate partner violence. Rather, we provide a focused introduction to new empirical data on a specific aspect of the barriers to treatment for intimate partner violence and alcoholism for ethnic Americans. There are certainly many other factors that act as barriers to health treatment in the United States, including geographical location, cultural issues not considered here, social stigmatization, attitudes toward health care as a privilege rather than a right, as well as others. We do not mean to minimize the complexity of the problems facing ethnic Americans in the U.S. struggling to gain access to competent health care. Our intention is, instead, to provide one particular stone to lie at the foundation that provides support for health care reform for ethnic residents of the United States.

This work was supported by a grant from the National Institute on Alcohol Abuse and Alcoholism (R37AA10199) to the Houston School of Public Health, University of Texas. Data collection also had the support of a National Alcohol Research Center grant (AA05595) from the National Institute on Alcohol Abuse and Alcoholism to the Alcohol Research Group, Public Health Institute, Berkeley, California.

☐ Access to Health Care for Ethnic Americans

While the projected population estimates by the U.S. Census Bureau of the ethnic break-down for 1995 characterizes the nation as predominantly White (72%; Black, 12%; Hispanic, 11%), projections for 2005 demonstrate that the White population will decrease (to 70%), the Hispanic population will increase (to 13%), and the Black population will increase slightly (up .2%). Black and Hispanic Americans represent the largest ethnic groups in the United States. Future projections suggest that this trend will continue. In 2005, Hispanics will be the largest minority group in the U.S., and by 2060, "minorities" will constitute the majority of the U.S. population, while Whites will account for only 49.6% of the population.

In the U.S., access to health care is, in large part, a function of ethnic identity; over one third of Hispanics in the U.S. have no health coverage, and over a fifth of Black Americans are uninsured. In contrast, only 15% of the U.S. White population is uninsured (March, 1998, CPS, U.S. Census Bureau). This disparity represents an ongoing trend that has not been reduced in the 11-year period charted in Figure 11.1. The overall slope for the U.S. population as a whole and Hispanic and White Americans separately is slightly positive from 1987 to 1997, suggesting that the number of uninsured Americans is increasing. A slight downward trend for Black Americans suggests that health care coverage is increasing slightly for this population. In any case, it is evident from Figure 11.1 that the gaps in health care coverage are not decreasing substantially.

The data from the U.S. Census Bureau are supported by findings from the Medical Expenditure Panel Survey (MEPS), a complex, multifaceted study conducted from 1995 to 1996 by the Agency for Health Care Planning and Research (AHPCR) as an addition to the National Health Interview Survey. The 1996 household component of this study found that 13% of White Americans are uninsured, and that 23% and 34% of Black and Hispanic Americans are uninsured, respectively. These figures closely match those of the U.S. Cen-

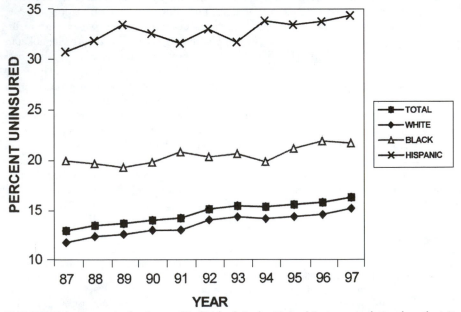

FIGURE 11.1. Percent of uninsured individuals in the United States population by ethnicity, 1987-1997 (U.S. Census Bureau, 1998).

sus Bureau estimates for the same period (+ 1.3%), again indicating a noticeable gap in health insurance coverage for ethnic Americans.

Kass, Weinick, and Monheit (1999) comprehensively explored the MEPS data on ethnic disparities in health care. In addition to the findings mentioned above, they reported that heads of Hispanic families cited more barriers to accessing health care compared to Black and White households, and that the primary barrier to health care mentioned by Hispanic family heads of household was cost. In addition, Kass et al. (1999) found that Hispanics were the most likely to report fair or poor health, followed by Black and then White Americans. These national data clearly paint a dismal picture: Hispanic and Black Americans are underinsured for health coverage and are more likely to report poor health than their White counterparts. In addition, economic factors are indicated as a potential barrier to health care coverage.

This situation led the Clinton Administration to establish a 34-member Advisory Commission on Consumer Protection and Quality in the Health Care Industry on March 26, 1997. This Commission produced a Consumer Bill of Rights and Responsibilities. The Commission's report contains an important statement about ethnic Americans' access to health care: "Discrimination on the basis of race, ethnicity, national origin, or religion in the provision of health care has also been well documented." The Clinton Administration reacted in part to the report by creating the Initiative to Eliminate Racial and Ethnic Disparities in Health as a result of a presidential address on February 21st, 1998. President Clinton committed the resources of the U.S. Department of Health and Human Services to eliminate the health care gaps experienced by ethnic Americans by the year 2010, a seemingly Herculean endeavor.

☐ Alcohol Treatment

Alcohol treatment service utilization has been increasing steadily in the U.S. population (Weisner & Greenfield, 1999; Weisner, Greenfield, & Room, 1995). Yet, by some accounts, the United States population is underserved in treatment for alcohol problems. A number of sources indicate that all ethnic subgroups receive less treatment than is needed (Grant et al., 1994; NIAAA, 1997), with Grant et al. stating that less than 10% of those in need of alcohol treatment actually receive it.

Alcohol problems cost the U.S. approximately $166 billion per year. One study has suggested that for every dollar of treatment invested, a savings of seven dollars is realized (Gerstein et al., 1994). A second study has estimated that the average economic benefit to society is three times larger than the average cost of a treatment episode (Center for Substance Abuse Treatment, 1999). Given the disparity between the numbers of Americans needing alcoholism treatment and those actually receiving it, an enormous economic incentive should thus drive greater access to alcoholism treatment. While Hispanic Americans have been identified as those most likely to seek help for alcohol problems, it is clear that, given the high proportion of individuals uninsured in this ethnic group, Hispanics face some of the greatest barriers to accessing health care services (Kaskutas, Weisner, & Caetano, 1997).

☐ Intimate Partner Violence

Intimate partner and family violence is a widespread health problem in the United States (e.g., Schafer, Caetano, & Clark, 1998; Sorenson, Upchurch, & Shen, 1996). Intimate partner violence is primarily a public health concern for women. One in three women will be assaulted by an intimate male partner during her lifetime (Browne, 1993). Male-to-female partner violence is more often repeated and is more likely to result in injury and death than female-to-male partner violence (Bachman & Saltzman, 1995; Craven, 1997; Dobash & Dobash, 1978; Sorenson, Upchurch, & Shen, 1996). One study, using data from 1994, found that 243,000 hospitalizations were due to intimate violence, and that women were approximately eight times more likely to be victims than men (Rand, 1997).

Unadjusted (crude) rates of intimate partner violence are known to be higher in Black and Hispanic couples compared to White couples (Caetano, Cunradi, Schafer, & Clark, 2000). Because these ethnic Americans also have greater difficulty in accessing health care, it can be inferred that access to treatment for intimate violence-related injuries and, possibly, less documented forms of abuse also is difficult for Black and Hispanic Americans. In addition, a national survey of partner abuse treatment programs suggests that where treatment is available, little effort is made to adapt treatment to the special needs of ethnic Americans (Williams & Becker, 1994).

☐ Analysis of the 1995 National Couples Study: Ethnicity, Alcohol, and Intimate Partner Violence

Existing data suggest a common link between alcoholism and intimate partner violence, with Maiden (1997) reporting comorbidity rates from 25%–80%. In this section, we describe results from data analyses that examine health care coverage and alcoholism treatment coverage for a nationally representative sample of married and cohabiting couples. This unique data set allows us to examine health care coverage as a function of the type of couple, a variable often ignored in similar analyses of national data sets on access to health care. We also are able to examine alcoholism treatment coverage in this data set. The data for these analyses come from a nine-year study funded by the National Institute on Alcohol Abuse and Alcoholism (R37AA10199). The general goal of this study is to examine the relationship between ethnic identification, alcohol consumption, and intimate partner violence in a nationally representative sample of married and cohabiting couples. Trained, experienced interviewers from the Institute for Survey Research at Temple University collected baseline data for a one-year period beginning in April of 1995. The data from the couples were collected as part of a larger survey designed as a multistage probability (cluster) sample of adults residing in the 48 contiguous United States. A response rate of 85% was obtained yielding a sample of 1635 couples; a "working sample" of 1599 couples is used for this study when homosexual ($n = 4$), invalid response patterns ($n = 11$), and couples with most or all of the violence data missing ($n = 21$) are excluded. For the present analyses, couples were grouped into one of four categories representing couple-level ethnic identification: couples in which both partners were (1) Black, (2) Hispanic, or (3) White and, mixed couples in which one member was Black, Hispanic, or White, and the other partner was of a different ethnicity (group 4). Nearly four out of five of the mixed couples had one Hispanic and one White partner. Using this grouping variable, 1540 couples were available for subsequent analyses.

Participants were privately interviewed face-to-face in their homes.[1] Participants re-

---

[1]It was logistically impossible to provide participants with local resource numbers. Instead, all participants were given the direct telephone number of the first author (a clinical psychologist) and several national crisis and other resource numbers. None of the 3,270 participants contacted the first author.

sponded to questions about demographic characteristics, alcohol consumption patterns, and the occurrence of 11 violent behaviors during the past year that they may have perpetrated against their partners, or that their partners may have perpetrated against them. The violence items were adapted from the Conflict Tactics Scale, Form R, and included the following: threw something; pushed, grabbed or shoved; slapped; kicked, bit, or hit; hit or tried to hit with something; beat up; choked; burned or scalded; forced sex; threatened with a knife or gun; and used a knife or gun (Straus & Gellies, 1990). Several questions were available on health insurance coverage including number of current policies the couple was insured under, type of plan, and whether alcoholism treatment was covered. A list of alcohol problems was asked of each respondent and a couple-level variable was formed based on these responses, coded 0 for no alcohol problems in either partner, 1 for alcohol problems reported for the female partner only, 2 for male partner only, and 3 for alcohol problems reported for both partners. A similar variable was created for intimate partner violence, with 0 coded for no reported violence, a 1 for any (see Schafer et al., 1998) reported female-to-male partner violence (FMPV) but no reported male-to-female partner violence (MFPV), a 2 for the reverse of 1, and a 3 for any reports of both FMPV and MFPV. For the combination of violence and alcohol problems, another couple-level variable was created that was coded 0 for none, 1 for the presence of any reported intimate partner violence but no reported alcohol problems in the couple, 2 for the reverse of 1, and 3 for reports of both violence and alcohol problems. A couple-level variable for acculturation in the Hispanic variables also was created and the frequencies of the couple matches are reported in Table 11.1. Further information on the acculturation variable is given in Caetano, Schafer, Clark, Cunradi, and Raspberry (2000). Total household income was used in the analysis, as were two variables representing census-tract poverty and education level. These latter two variables were coded dichotomously. The census tract poverty level indicator was coded 1 for census tracts where 20% or more of the population was living at or below the poverty index, and 0 otherwise. Similarly, census tracts where 25% or more of the adult population did not graduate from high school were coded 1. Frequencies for these variables and for other characteristics of the sample are presented in Table 11.1. About 82% of the couples were both White. Again, most couples of mixed ethnicity were constituted by a partner who was White and the other who was a Hispanic. Ninety percent of the couples were married and the median relationship length was 15 years. Median age was 42 years for female respondents and 45 years for male respondents. Over half of the respondents had a high school education or more.

Data from complex survey designs must be analyzed with great care. There are two principal concerns: (1) that the statistics are estimated appropriately for the target population by using weights, and (2) that the standard errors for the statistics are adjusted for the clustering effects of the multicluster sampling design. To give a simple illustration of the former, suppose that an estimate of intimate partner violence is based on a survey in which oversamples of Black and Hispanic respondents are obtained. If violence is higher in the oversampled respondents, then the violence estimate (say, a proportion) will be too high for the population as a whole if the proportion is computed based on the unweighted, pooled sample. If the oversamples are appropriately downweighted prior to estimating the proportion, however, the estimate will be appropriate for the population.

Weights were constructed for the present sample to adjust the sample for unequal probabilities of selection (e.g., the Black and Hispanic oversamples; differential recruitment strategy) and differential levels of nonresponse across demographic subgroups. In addition, a poststratification weight was calculated to adjust the sample to known population distributions on certain demographic variables (ethnicity of the household informant, metropolitan status, and region of the country). Weights were used in all statistical estimations in this chapter.

TABLE 11.1. Sample characteristics in the 1995 national couples study (weighted percentages)

Couple-Level Ethnicity	
Black (B)	6.9%
Hispanic (H)	7.2%
White (W)	81.7%
Mixed (M)	4.1%
Gender and Ethnic	
Composition of Mixed BHW Couples (unweighted)	
WW/MH	48.2%
WH/MW	30.4%
WW/MB	8.9%
WB/MH	5.4%
WH/MB	3.6%
WB/MW	3.6%
Couple-Level Alcohol Problems	
None	41.5%
Female Partner	7.6%
Male Partner	27.2%
Both	23.7%
Couple-Level Acculturation (Hispanic Couples Only)	
Both Low	35.2%
Both Medium	22.6%
Both High	8.2%
Low-Medium	20.8%
High-Medium	12.1%
High-Low	1.1%
Intimate Partner Violence	
None	79.0%
FMPV Only	7.6%
MFPV Only	3.3%
Both	10.1%
Alcohol Problems and Violence	
None	37.0%
Violence Only	4.5%
Alcohol Prob. Only	41.9%
Both	16.6%
Household Income	
< 4K–6K	3.2%
6001–10K	4.8%
10001–15K	6.2%
15001–20K	7.4%
20001–30K	16.7%
30001–40K	14.6%
40001–60K	24.1%
60001–80K	11.8%
80001–100K	6.0%
>100K	5.1%
Contextual Variables	
20% in Census Tract at Poverty:	15.4%
25% in Census Tract < High School:	40.2%

In addition to weighting procedures, which assist in producing accurate estimates of the desired statistics, clustering effects due to the multistage design of the study must be controlled. Individuals that are sampled from clustered geographic sampling units are more likely to be similar than a random sample from the entire target population (Lehtonen & Pahkinen, 1995; Wolter, 1985), a well-known phenomenon in the educational arena (Bryk & Raudenbush, 1992). To control for these clustering effects, analyses were conducted using the sample-reuse method known as balanced repeated replication. This method is implemented in the software WesVar Complex Samples 3.0 by Westat, Inc. (http://www.westat.com). WesVar was used to estimate corrected chi-square statistics for the cross-tabulations, and corrected standard errors and F-statistics for the regression models. Statistics that are cited below as statistically significant are significant at $p < .05$ using the corrected (generally, more stringent) standard error. Correct nonresponse and poststratification weights for each replicate sample were calculated.

Insurance and Alcoholism Treatment Coverage in the Pooled Sample of Couples

Overall, 10% of the couples reported that they were not covered by any medical or health insurance plans (Table 11.2). Two thirds of the couples reported coverage under one insurance plan, and nearly a quarter of the couples reported that they were covered by two or more health insurance plans. Almost a third of the couples reported that they were insured under a traditional insurance plan, while one fifth reported coverage under a health maintenance plan (HMO) and 14.5% reported coverage under a preferred provider organization (PPO). The most commonly reported combination of insurance coverage was a traditional insurance plan along with Medicare (8.1%). The remaining response pattern frequencies are displayed in Table 11.2.

When respondents were asked about coverage for alcoholism treatment under their current insurance plans, 43% said that alcoholism treatment was covered, while 11% stated that it was not. A significant proportion of the couples, the remaining 46%, did not know whether alcoholism treatment was covered under their current policy. No questions were asked concerning insurance treatment options or services for family violence.

TABLE 11.2. Weighted distribution of insurance coverage for the pooled sample of Black, Hispanic, White, and mixed couples

Insurance Coverage	%
A) None	10.5
B) Health Maintenance Organization (HMO)	18.9
C) Preferred Provider Organization (PPO)	14.5
D) Traditional insurance plan	30.6
E) Medicare	2.7
F) Medicaid and/or Medical Assistance	1.9
G) Federal Health Plans or the Veteran's Administration	1.3
H) Other	1.9
D + E	8.1
E + H	1.6
B + E	1.4
C + D	1.0
Other combinations	5.1

TABLE 11.3. Weighted distributions of couple ethnicity cross-tabulated with number of medical plans

Number of Insurance Plans	Ethnic Identification			
	Black (%)	Hispanic (%)	White (%)	Mixed (%)
0	17	41.1	6.4	16.9
1	65.1	51.8	68.2	76.9
2+	17.9	7.1	25.4	6.2
Total	100	100	100	100

In Table 11.3, the distribution of the number of insurance plans as a trichotomous variable is cross-tabulated with that of couple ethnicity. The corrected chi-square statistic for this table is statistically significant. Hispanic couples were much less likely, by a factor of 6.4, to report medical coverage than White couples, and also were less likely to report coverage than Black and Mixed couples by a factor of 2.4. Mixed couples were the least likely to be covered by two or more medical plans, followed by Hispanic couples, Black couples, and White couples.

Predictors of Health Insurance Coverage: The Role of Alcohol Problems, Intimate Partner Violence, Income, and Neighborhood Characteristics

In this section, we examine health insurance coverage in the full sample in relation to several other factors. Number of health plans was significantly associated with the couples' reports of alcohol problems (Table 11.4). Couples in which only the female partner reported alcohol problems were the most likely to report insurance coverage, while couples in which both partners reported alcohol problems were the least likely to report coverage. Couples with no reported alcohol problems were the most likely to report coverage under two or more plans—at 30.1%, nearly two and a half times that of couples in which both reported alcohol problems. Couples in which both reported alcohol problems were also significantly more likely to report that they knew that their health plan covered treatment for alcoholism (88.3%), as compared with couples reporting only alcohol problems (85.7%) or intimate partner violence (IPV) (74.3%), or couples reporting neither (71.5%).

Health insurance coverage also was significantly related to reported IPV. Couples that

TABLE 11.4. Weighted distributions of couple-level alcohol problems cross-tabulated with number of medical plans

Number of Insurance Plans	Alcohol Problems			
	None (%)	Female Partner (%)	Male Partner (%)	Both (%)
0	8.9	5.1	11.8	12
1	61	67.8	69.7	75.2
2+	30.1	27.1	18.5	12.8
Total	100	100	100	100

TABLE 11.5. Weighted distributions of intimate partner violence cross-tabulated with number of medical plans

Number of Insurance Plans	Intimate Partner Violence			
	None (%)	F → M (%)	M → F (%)	Both (%)
0	8	13.7	12	22.9
1	66.5	70.1	82	65
2+	25.5	16.2	6	12.1
Total	100	100	100	100

did not report any IPV were significantly more likely to report insurance coverage (92%) than couples reporting only female-to-male (86.3%) or male-to-female (88%) partner violence, or couples reporting both (77.1%). Couples without IPV were over four times more likely to be covered by two or more policies than couples where both types of violence were reported (Table 11.5). There was not a significant association between IPV and reported coverage for alcoholism treatment in the pooled sample.

Next, we examine the relationships among couples with no reported alcohol problems or IPV, couples reporting either alcohol problems or IPV *only*, and couples where both problems were reported to health insurance coverage (Table 11.6). Couples that did not report alcohol problems or IPV were the most likely to report coverage (92.3%), closely followed by couples that reported IPV but no alcohol problems (91.7%). Couples reporting any IPV, but no alcohol problems, were the least likely to be insured (80.9%). Nearly a third of the couples that did not report IPV or alcohol problems were insured under two or more plans (32.3%), a significantly higher proportion than among the other couples. Couples with insurance coverage and reporting alcohol problems alone were significantly more likely to report coverage for alcoholism treatment (87.6%) than couples reporting alcohol problems and IPV (77.7%), IPV alone (70.8%), or those couples that did not report alcohol problems or IPV (71.6%).

Health insurance coverage was significantly related in a linear fashion to total household income, with lower income related to lower coverage. Couples with less than $15,000 annual income ranged from 45.5%–68.2% reporting coverage, 85.6%–90.8% coverage for couples in the $15,000–$40,000 range, and 97.6%–99.4% coverage reported for couples with annual household income greater than $40,000 per year. A similar, significant relationship was observed between reported coverage for alcoholism treatment and household income.

TABLE 11.6. Weighted distributions of intimate partner violence and alcohol problems cross-tabulated with number of medical plans

Number of Insurance Plans	IPV + Alcohol Problems			
	None (%)	IPV Only (%)	Alcohol Problems Only (%)	Both (%)
0	7.7	19.1	8.3	17.6
1	60	69.1	72.3	69.5
2+	32.3	11.8	19.4	12.9
Total	100	100	100	100

IPV = Intimate Partner Violence

The number of reported medical plans also was related to the two contextual variables included in these analyses, the census tract poverty and education level indicators. Couples living in census tracts with 20% or more of the population living at or below the poverty index were nearly four times as likely to report no coverage (26.6%), as compared to couples living in census tracts with less than 20% of the population living in poverty (7.1%). Living in census tracts where 25% or more of the adult population did not report graduating from high school also was associated with a lower reported rate of medical coverage, 16.2% versus 6%, respectively. A similar pattern was observed for the relationship between these contextual variables and reported coverage for alcoholism treatment.

Health Insurance and Alcohol Treatment Coverage by Couple Ethnicity

In this section, we study the bivariate relationships between alcohol problems, intimate partner violence, and insurance coverage, separately, for each of the ethnic groups. In addition, we examine the partial relationships for all of the variables in regression equations, with the insurance coverage variables as the dependent variables. The dependent variable of health insurance coverage, coded to represent no, one, or two or more health insurance plans for the household was analyzed using ordinary least-squares (OLS) regression in the statistical package WesVar Complex Samples 3.0, described above. The variable representing coverage for alcoholism treatment coverage was analyzed in the same statistical program using logistic regression (Hosmer & Lemeshow, 1989). Simple direct entry was used for all of the regression models, and to conserve space, only those regression models and variables that are statistically significant are discussed.

Black Couples.   For the Black couples (n = 354), the variable representing the types and presence of IPV was not found to be related to either of the principal insurance variables. Alcohol problems were not related to the number of reported insurance plans, but were related to alcoholism treatment coverage. Alcoholism treatment coverage was much more likely among Black couples where only the female partner reported alcohol problems (71.4%), as compared with couples with no reported problems (30.2%), problems for the male partner only (60%), or couples where both reported alcohol problems (65.4%). These results are represented schematically in Table 11.7.

The variable representing the combinations of alcohol problems and violence in the Black couples was significantly related to both health insurance coverage and alcoholism treatment coverage. Couples reporting violence without any alcohol problems were the least likely to report coverage (72.4%) and also the least likely to report coverage for alcoholism treatment (19%), as compared to couples without reported violence or alcohol problems (86.1% and 32.4%, respectively), couples reporting alcohol problems without violence (89.3%, 65%), and couples reporting both (74.4% versus 60.6%).

Household income and the census tract poverty and education level indicators were all related to health insurance coverage among the Black couples; income and census tract poverty also were related to alcoholism treatment coverage. In general, income was positively related to health insurance coverage, so that lower income was associated with less coverage. Similarly, couples living in census tracts with higher poverty levels were significantly less likely to report health insurance coverage (73.1% versus 92.5%), as well as alcoholism treatment coverage (35.7% versus 64.3%) when compared to couples not living in these census tracts. In like fashion, couples living in census tracts with lower education levels were less likely to report health insurance coverage (78.8% vs. 91.5%) and alcoholism treatment coverage (43.2% vs. 58.9%) than those not living in these tracts.

TABLE 11.7. Variables identified as significantly related to health insurance coverage and alcoholism treatment coverage by ethnicity

| | Health Insurance Coverage | | | |
| | Couple-Level Ethnicity | | | |
Variables	Black	Hispanic	White	Mixed
Alcohol Problems			X Ŏ	
IPV			Ŏ	
Alcohol Problems + IPV	X	X	X	
Income	X Ŏ	X Ŏ	X	Ŏ
Census Tract Education	X	X		
Census Tract Poverty	X	X	X	
Acculturation	N A	X	NA	NA

| | Coverage for Alcohol Treatment | | | |
| | Couple-Level Ethnicity | | | |
Variables	Black	Hispanic	White	Mixed
Alcohol Problems IPV	X	X		
Alcohol Problems + IPV	X		X	
Income	Ŏ	X		
Census Tract Education			X	
Census Tract Poverty	X		X	
Acculturation	N A		NA	NA

Note: "**X**" means significant at p < .05 for the cross-tabulation or bivariate level, "Ŏ" similarly significant in the multivariate regression model.
IPV = Intimate Partner Violence

Among Black couples, the only variable that was uniquely associated with health insurance coverage and alcoholism treatment coverage, while controlling for the other variables examined here, was household income. Lower income was associated with less coverage, even when controlling for variables such as census tract poverty level.

Hispanic Couples. As with the Black couples, the variable representing the types and presence of IPV was not found to be related to either of the insurance variables for the Hispanic couples (n = 521) as well (Table 11.7). Also as before, alcohol problems were not related to the number of reported insurance plans, but were related to reported alcoholism treatment coverage. Hispanic couples where both (58.8%) reported alcohol problems or only the female partner (45.5%) were more likely to report alcoholism treatment coverage than couples where alcohol problems were reported for the male partner only (34.4%) or couples with no reported problems (21.2%).

The variable representing the combinations of alcohol problems and violence in the Hispanic couples was significantly related to health insurance coverage, but not to alcoholism treatment coverage. Couples reporting violence alone (67.7%) or alcohol problems alone (66.2%) were more likely to report coverage, as compared to couples without reported violence *or* alcohol problems (52.5%), and couples that did report violence and alcohol problems (52.1%).

Household income, the census tract poverty and education level indicators, and acculturation were all related to health insurance coverage among the Hispanic couples; income and acculturation were also related to alcoholism treatment coverage. Generally, income was positively related to health insurance coverage and alcoholism treatment coverage, so that higher income was associated with more coverage. Hispanic couples living in census tracts with higher poverty levels (52.4% vs. 67.7%) and lower education levels (54.5% vs. 71.4%) were significantly less likely to report health insurance coverage than couples who did not live in these tracts. A lower level of acculturation was identified as a risk factor associated with less coverage for the Hispanic couples. Couples where both were identified as low-acculturation were the least likely to be insured (39.6%). Low-medium (53.7%) and medium-medium matched couples (68.4%) were the next least likely to be insured, followed by high-low (83.3%) and high-high (90.7%) matched couples. A similar pattern was observed for the relationship between acculturation and alcoholism treatment coverage. Two variables were uniquely associated with health insurance coverage while controlling for the other variables: household income and acculturation. Lower income and less acculturation were associated with less coverage in the Hispanic couples.

White Couples. While the pattern of significant associations between the variables examined here and the health coverage variables were similar for the Black and Hispanic couples, a different pattern of relationships was observed for the White couples ($n = 552$) (Table 11.7). Alcohol problems were only related to health insurance coverage in the White couples. Couples with no reported alcohol problems (95.7%) and couples in which only the female partner reported alcohol problems (97.7%) had significantly higher rates of health insurance coverage compared to couples where only the male partner reported alcohol problems (92.9%) or both reported problems (89.6%). Unlike in the Black and Hispanic couples, alcohol problems were not related to alcoholism treatment coverage in the White couples.

The variable representing the combinations of alcohol problems and violence in the White couples was significantly related to both health insurance coverage and alcoholism treatment coverage. Couples that did not report any violence or alcohol problems were the most likely to report health insurance coverage (96.2%) and the least likely to report coverage for alcoholism treatment (32.8%), compared to White couples reporting violence without alcohol problems (90.5% versus 33.3%), couples reporting alcohol problems without violence (93.7% versus 49.1%), and couples reporting both (87.8% versus 47.9%).

Census tract poverty level was related to both health insurance coverage and alcoholism treatment coverage in the White couples, while household income was related to health insurance coverage alone and census tract education level was related to alcoholism treatment coverage alone. Couples living in census tracts with higher poverty levels were significantly less likely to report health insurance coverage (84.6% versus 94.6%) as well as alcoholism treatment coverage (23.3% versus 44%) than those not in these areas. As with the Black and Hispanic couples, household income was positively related to health insurance coverage in the White couples. Couples living in census tracts with lower education levels were less likely than those not in those areas to report alcoholism treatment coverage (35% versus 45.9%).

Among the White couples, the variables representing alcohol problems and violence separately were uniquely associated with health insurance coverage, while controlling for the other variables examined here. No other variables were identified as significant in the regression of the health insurance variable on the set of variables studied here, and the regression equation for alcoholism treatment coverage was not significant.

Mixed Ethnicity Couples. For couples where one partner was Black, Hispanic, or White, and the other partner was of a different ethnic background, few significant relationships emerged. This may be due in part to reduced power ($n = 113$) compared to the other ethnic groups examined here. One variable, income, was significantly and positively related to health insurance coverage in the regression equation for the Mixed couples.

☐ Summary and Conclusions

In comparing our findings on the percentage of uninsured couples in our study to the results of the Census Bureau and MEPS data for the same period, we find some interesting differences. First, the Black couples in the 1996 U.S. Census Bureau data and the 1996 MEPS data were found to have uninsured rates among individuals of 22% and 23%, respectively. In our data, we found that 17% of Black couples reported no health coverage. Similarly, the Census Bureau and the MEPS reported 14% and 13% (respectively) of White Americans as uninsured, while we found that only 6% of the White couples reported no health coverage. National data are not available for health insurance coverage for couples of mixed ethnicity. Finally, for Hispanics, the Census and MEPS data both produced estimates of this population's uninsurance rate at 34%, while we found that 41% of the Hispanic couples in our study reported no health coverage.

It would appear that marriage or cohabitation provides a protective factor for Black and White couples, in that higher rates of health coverage were found for the couples in our study, compared to the rates for individuals estimated by the Census Bureau and MEPS. This should not be a surprise given that samples of individuals who are married or cohabiting are older and more stable socioeconomically. However, Hispanic couples had considerably higher rates of uninsurance than individuals estimated by the Census and MEPS data. This disparity between our data and the Census and MEPS data is difficult to explain. Our sample is representative of Hispanic couples living in the continental United States. The MEPS data is also representative of the U.S., and the Census data additionally covers Hawaii and Alaska. We do not think that differential sample coverage could explain the difference in rates. It is possible that this difference results from a sample artifact, which is intrinsic to the nature of all samples and is an expression of sampling error.

In examining coverage for alcohol treatment, a high percentage of couples did not know whether they were covered for alcoholism treatment under their insurance plan. This is in spite of the fact that since the late 1980s most states had legislation mandating insurance coverage for alcoholism (Schmidt & Weisner, 1993). This lack of knowledge about coverage is probably reflective of the fact that these couples did not have any one in their family with an alcohol problem and did not have an alcohol problem of their own. In other words, being free of alcohol-related problems, they did not have to be concerned about coverage for alcohol treatment. Intimate partner violence was related to health insurance coverage. Couples who did not report any incidence of partner violence were more likely than other to be covered by health insurance. These relationships between intimate partner violence and health coverage disappeared in the regression analysis. In the regression equations for the Black, Hispanic, and Mixed couples, household income was the only variable significantly and uniquely associated with health insurance coverage. This is not surprising given that in many models of access to health care, income is a prominent individual level predictor of access to health care coverage and general care and substance abuse treatment (Aday, Begley, Lairson, & Slater, 1993; Gerstein & Harwood, 1990).

A different pattern of results was observed for the variables associated with alcoholism treatment coverage. For each of the ethnic groups, a unique pattern of associations was observed. Alcohol problems and income were significantly associated with alcoholism treatment coverage in the Hispanic couples, and no significant partial relationships with alcoholism treatment coverage were found in the regression equation. Alcohol problems and the variable representing the combination of IPV and alcohol problems, and census tract poverty level were found to be associated with alcoholism treatment coverage in the Black couples. However, only income was identified as having a unique, significant relationship with alcoholism treatment coverage, after controlling for the other variables in the regression. It is difficult to explain, however, why this effect was present only for Black couples.

While neighborhood variables were importantly associated with the insurance variables studied here, arguably the most important variable that emerged from these analyses was household income. Minority couples that have lower incomes are especially disadvantaged, above and beyond the effects of alcohol problems, IPV, and living in poor and undereducated neighborhoods. Black and Hispanic couples did not differ significantly in household income, but both groups had significantly lower incomes than White and Mixed couples, whose incomes were not significantly different from one another.

In conclusion, our analyses underscore a well-known factor regarding health care in the United States: Barriers to minority health care exist and are particularly prevalent among U.S. Hispanics. Income, not surprisingly, appears as the most important factor in determining health insurance coverage status. This is of considerable concern. Access to health care should not be based on income level, but should be seen as a right of individuals to lead not only healthy, but also fulfilling lives. The problem of lack of access to health care, like so many other health-related problems, affects ethnic minorities more so that the White majority population. Thus, those minority couples who are affected by alcohol problems, including alcohol-related intimate partner violence, will be less likely to find the appropriate care to solve their problems. This is particularly problematic because of the increased rate of intimate partner violence especially among Blacks in the U.S. The inequality in access to care described here is likely to further contribute to this disparity in intimate partner violence across ethnic groups.

☐ References

Aday, L. A., Begley, C. E., Lairson, D. R., & Slater, C. H. (1993). *Evaluating the medical care system: effectiveness, efficiency, and equity.* Ann Arbor: Health Administration Press.

Bachman R., & Saltzman, L. E. (1995). *Violence against women: Estimates from the redesigned survey (NCJ 154348).* Washington, DC: U.S. Department of Justice.

Browne, A. (1993). Violence against women by male partners. *American Psychologist, 48,* 1077–1087.

Bryk, A. S., & Raudenbush, S. W. (1992). *Hierarchical linear models: Applications and data analysis methods.* Thousand Oaks, CA: Sage.

Caetano, R., Cunradi, C. B., Schafer, J., & Clark, C. L. (2000) Intimate partner violence and drinking patterns among white, black and Hispanic couples in the U.S. *Journal of Substance Abuse, 11,* 123–138.

Caetano, R.C., Schafer, J., Clark, C.L., Cunradi, C.B., & Raspberry, K. (2000). Intimate partner violence, acculturation, and alcohol consumption among Hispanic couples in the United States. *Journal of Interpersonal Violence, 15,* 30–45.

Center for Substance Abuse Treatment (1999). *Benefits far exceed costs of substance abuse treatment.* NEDS Fact Sheet 24. Rockville, MD: Author.

Craven, D. (1997). *Sex differences in violent victimization.* Washington, DC: Bureau of Justice Statistics.

De La Rosa, M. (1989). Health care needs of Hispanic Americans and the responsiveness of the health care system. *Health and Social Work, 14,* 104–113.

Dobash, R. E., & Dobash R. P. (1978). Wives: The 'appropriate' victims of marital violence. *Victimology, 1,* 416–441.

Gerstein, D. R., & Harwood, H. J. (1990). *Treating drug problems: Vol. 1. A study of the evolution, effectiveness, and financing of public and private drug treatment systems*. Washington, DC: National Academy Press.

Gerstein, D. R., Johnson, R. A., Harwood, H. J., Fountain, D., Suter, N., & Malloy, K. (1994). *Evaluating recovery services: The California Drug and Alcohol Treatment Assessment (CALDATA)*. Publication No. ADP 94-629, Sacramento, CA: State of California Department of Alcohol and Drug Problems.

Grant, B. F., Harford, T. C., Dawson, D. A., Chou, P., Dufour, M., & Pickering, R. (1994). Prevalence of DSM-IV alcohol abuse and dependence; United States, 1992. *Alcohol Health and Research World, 18*(3), 243–248.

Hosmer, D. W., & Lemeshow, S. (1989). *Applied logistic regression*. New York: Wiley.

Kaskutas, L. A., Weisner, C., & Caetano, R. (1997). Predictors of help seeking among a longitudinal sample of the general public, 1984–1992. *Journal of Studies on Alcohol, 58*(2), 155–161.

Kass B. L., Weinick, R. M., & Monheit, A.C. (1999). *Racial and ethnic differences in health, 1996*. Rockville, MD: Agency for Health Care Policy and Research; 1999. MEPS Chartbook No. 2. AHCPR Pub. No. 99-0001.

Lehtonen, R., & Pahkinen, E. J. (1995). *Practical methods for design and analysis of complex surveys*. Chichester, England: Wiley.

Maiden, R. P. (1997). Alcohol dependence and domestic violence: Incidence and treatment implications. *Alcoholism Treatment Quarterly, 15*, 31–50.

NIAAA Subcommittee on Health Services Research, National Advisory Council on Alcohol Abuse and Alcoholism. (1997). *Improving the delivery of alcohol treatment and prevention services: Executive summary*. NIH Publication No. 4224. Bethesda, MD: National Institute on Alcohol Abuse and Alcoholism, National Institutes of Health, Department of Health and Human Services.

Rand, M. R. (1997). *Violence-related injuries treated in hospital emergency departments (NCJ-156921)*. Washington, DC: U.S. Department of Justice.

Schafer, J., Caetano, R., & Clark, C. (1998). Rates of intimate partner violence in the United States. *American Journal of Public Health, 88*, 1702–1704.

Schmidt, L., & Weisner, C. (1993). Developments in alcoholism treatment: a ten year review. In M. Galanter (Ed.), *Recent developments in alcoholism* (pp. 369–396). New York: Plenum.

Sorenson, S. B., Upchurch, D. M., & Shen, H. (1996). Violence and injury in marital arguments: Risk patterns and gender differences. *American Journal of Public Health, 86*(1), 35–40.

Straus, M. A., & Gelles, R. J. (1990). *Physical violence in American families: Risk factors and adaptations to violence in 8,175 families*. New Brunswick, NJ: Transaction Publishers.

Weisner, C., & Greenfield, T. (1999). *Continuing trends in entry to treatment for alcohol treatment in the U.S. general population: 1984–1995*. Berkeley, CA: Alcohol Research Group.

Weisner, C., Greenfield, T., & Room, R. (1995). Trends in the treatment of alcohol problems in the U.S. general population, 1979–1990. *American Journal of Public Health, 85*, 55–60.

Williams, O. J., & Becker, R. L. (1994). Domestic partner abuse treatment programs and cultural competence: The results of a national survey. *Violence and Victims, 9*, 287–296.

Wolter, K. M. (1985). *Introduction to variance estimation*. New York: Springer-Verlag.

CHAPTER 12

William R. Downs
Brenda A. Miller

Treating Dual Problems of Partner Violence and Substance Abuse

Providing treatment for men and women with alcohol or drug problems who are also either perpetrators or victims of violence is a growing concern for behavioral health care providers and family violence specialists (Miller & Downs, 2000; Miller, Wilsnack, & Cunradi, 2000). The association between substance abuse and men's perpetration of partner violence, and the association between substance abuse and women's victimization have been empirically demonstrated (see Wekerle & Wall, this volume). Among clients receiving services for partner violence, high levels of substance abuse problems have been identified. For example, approximately 60%–70% of men in Batterer's Educations Programs (BEP's) (Brown, Werk, Caplan, & Seraganian, 1999; Gorney, 1989) and 30%–40% of women in shelters for battered women (Downs, Patterson, Barten, Rindels, & McCrory, 1998; Downs et al., 1999) have been found to have substance abuse problems, mostly alcohol abuse. Among patients receiving clinical care for alcohol or drug problems, the levels of partner violence are quite high. For example, approximately 60%–70% of women in substance abuse treatment have been victimized by partner violence at least once in the past six months (Downs et al., 1998; Downs et al., 1999). Brown, Werk, Caplan, Shields, and Seraganian (1998) found that 57.6% of men in substance abuse treatment had perpetrated family violence in the past year, although this figure included both partner and child abuse.

Despite the overlap between substance abuse and partner violence, there have been different philosophies, treatment approaches, and perspectives that have made the bridging of services between these problems difficult. In this chapter, these differences are examined and potential directions for developing harmonious approaches are explored. Initially, definitional and conceptual issues are addressed. Treatment approaches for partner violence that include the feminist approach and the relationship counseling interventions are explored. Next, the efforts to date for combining these approaches are discussed. Finally, there is an exploration of how to merge these interventions in future program development.

Throughout this chapter, the term "substance abuse" is used in a generic and inclusive sense to refer to alcoholism, alcohol dependence, alcohol abuse, drug dependence, and drug abuse. Also, throughout this chapter, the term "relationship counseling" is used to refer generically to the set of interventions known as marital therapy, marital counseling, couples therapy, and couples counseling. Where appropriate, the specific term developed by researchers or clinicians to describe their intervention approach will be used. For example, the work of O'Farrell and Murphy (see O'Farrell & Murphy, this volume) is referred to as Behavioral Marital Therapy.

☐ Definitional Issues and Constructs Regarding Partner Violence

Defining Violence

There has been debate over the appropriate terminology to describe women's experiences of physical violence from partners, reflecting a larger discussion of whether violence between partners is mutual or primarily male-to-female. Terms such as "partner violence" or "domestic violence" may connote that violence between partners is mutual, thus deemphasizing the cultural and gendered aspects of the issue (Whalen, 1996), and obscuring male violence to women (Bograd, 1988; Schechter, 1982; Dobash & Dobash, 1979). Because of this concern, some feminists prefer the terms "wifebeating" or more generally "battered women," thus indicating that the primary problem is violence that men perpetrate on women (Whalen, 1996). The distinction between violence being mutual or primarily male-to-female has important implications for treatment. Mutual violence implies the need for relationship counseling; violence that is primarily male-to-female implies the need for interventions targeted toward ending men's violence and empowering women.

The term "battered women" connotes primarily severe violence against women. Less severe forms of physical violence and psychological abuse also are injurious to women (Rollstin & Kern, 1998). Further, there is the reality that for some relationships, violence is mutual, that is, perpetrated by both men and women, though not necessarily with equal consequences, duration, and meanings. Thus, in this chapter the term "partner violence" is used to refer to all acts of physical violence that women experience in their intimate relationships with partners. Likewise, the term "partner abuse" is used to refer to both physical and nonphysical acts intended to threaten, induce fear, control, or reduce self-esteem of women.

Objective and Subjective Definitions of Partner Violence

Objective definitions of partner violence would include such behavioral experiences as those found on the Conflict Tactics Scale or other indices such as the Abusive Behavior Inventory (Straus & Gelles, 1990; Shepard & Campbell, 1992), which identify acts such as hitting or slapping, beating up, and using a knife or gun on another person. While objective definitions of partner violence have merit, they also have several limitations. In using objective definitions of partner violence, some researchers may be treating women's violence against men as equivalent to men's violence against women; for example, her slapping of him is treated quantitatively as equivalent to his slapping of her. Second, in using objective definitions of partner violence, many researchers may be counting behaviors within a single episode, implicitly viewing partner violence as a series of discrete episodes. However, from the point of view of women, partner violence can be viewed as an ongoing pattern created by violent episodes connected to each other, as well as to incidences of psychological abuse that occur between violent episodes. Finally, in using only objective definitions of partner violence, some researchers may be missing the important point that women's perceptions and subjective experiences of violence are at least as important as an objective definition (Sleutel, 1998).

Women's subjective experiences of partner violence may be important for several reasons. First, the same violent behavior may vary subjectively across women, based on how much violence women have experienced earlier in their life, as well as how much violence they have experienced from their current partner. In addition, psychological abuse may have an impact on how a particular violent act is experienced. Further, the extent to which women are able to defend themselves, have alternatives to their current partner, and have support for leaving if they so decide are additional factors that might affect the impact of specific violent acts. Second, objective measures of violence have difficulties in assessing the effects of different combinations of violent acts that occur within a single episode. Further, women's experiences of these episodes may vary based on past experiences of abuse, as well as their ability to leave the relationship. Third, many women do not experience partner violence as a series of discrete episodes. Rather, these women are aware that violence is unpredictable and can occur at any time. Thus, for these women, partner violence creates a climate of fear, a climate in which they live on a daily basis with their partner (Herman, 1992).

There are additional factors that may affect women's experiences of partner violence. These include: women's economic dependence on their partner, level of investment in the relationship, and perception of the positive aspects of their partner. Women's perceptions of violence may vary as a function of psychological abuse. Threats against a woman's person or life, destruction of a woman's property or pets, and threats against children may increase the psychological impact of physical violence, just as physical violence may increase the impact of these acts of psychological abuse. Because of these factors, women's perceptions and self-definitions of abuse are at least as important as objective definitions. In a meta-analytic review, Weaver and Clum (1995) concluded that the effect of subjective factors of interpersonal violence (e.g., general appraisal, life threat, self-blame, perceived controllability) on women's psychological distress was about twice the magnitude as that for objective factors of interpersonal violence.

Changes in Definitions and Views of Partner Abuse over Time

Over the past 30 years, there have been profound changes in both the definitions and theories of partner abuse. Thirty years ago, partner violence was not yet widely recognized as a problem despite a long history of attempts to publicize, prevent, and reduce violence experienced by women from their husbands. During the 1970s, the second wave of feminism resulted in the beginning and growth of shelters for battered women, and the development of services for partner violence. Initially, wives victimized by husband violence were the predominant group receiving recognition and services. However, women not married but in partner relationships also began to be recognized as victims and in need of services for partner violence. Services for battered women thus began and initially grew as an outgrowth of a political movement to improve the lives of women. During the 1980s, partner violence was criminalized (Whalen, 1996).

Also, during the 1980s, marital rape began to be identified, defined, and recognized as a problem experienced by large numbers of women. As a result of extending the political debate on partner violence to marital rape, eventually rape within marriage also began to be criminalized (Healey, Smith, & O'Sullivan, 1998). Today, rape within marriage has been criminalized in all 50 states, and has increasingly been a topic for researchers (Whatley, 1993). As with nonsexual forms of partner violence, it has been more difficult to extend the definition of marital rape to include women in partner relationships who are not married. Recently, psychological abuse has also been recognized as having a negative impact on women (Dutton, Goodman, & Bennett, 1999; Rollstin & Kern, 1998). Further, stalking by partners or former partners has been identified and defined as a problem (Abrams & Robinson, 1998; Tjaden & Thoennes, 1998). Different forms of partner violence and abuse tend to co-occur. Meyer, Vivian, and O'Leary (1998) found that compared to nonabused and moderately physically abused wives, severely abused wives reported the highest rates of sexual coercion and threatened or forced sex, and that in a multivariate analysis, psychological aggression predicted husbands' sexual coercion, and severe physical violence predicted husbands' use of threatened or forced sex. Thus, since the initial focus on physical violence, conceptualizations of partner abuse grew to include these additional behaviors.

☐ Differential Philosophies and Conceptual Approaches for Addressing Partner Abuse

Partner violence theories and interventions also changed as abusive behaviors were criminalized. In some cases these theories are diametrically opposed to each other, and when applied to practice situations support mutually exclusive interventions with partner violence and abuse. Many of these controversies are yet to be resolved. In large part, the political debate of the 1970s and 1980s continues to define the parameters for interventions for partner violence and to underlie the philosophical differences between treatment modalities. The political movements of the 1970s and 1980s were necessary steps to gain public recognition, initiate the development of services, and commence research into the problem of partner violence. However, one result has been conceptualization of service goals based largely on feminist theories of partner abuse, and primarily on the more severe forms of partner violence. A breach has developed between those who believe that relationship counseling is appropriate for partner violence, and those who believe that relationship counseling is not only inappropriate but potentially harmful to women.

This breach has been most likely to occur between proponents of the feminist and classical family systems models. According to proponents of the feminist model, the concepts of codependence and enabling imply that the codependent partner may be viewed as partially responsible for the continuation of the substance abuse. There is concern that if women are viewed as contributing to addicted male partners' behavior, this will tacitly permit and condone men's use of violence against women. Thus, proponents of the feminist approach are concerned that women might be held partially responsible for the violence they experience from addicted male partners, and that women might accept this responsibility. Conversely, proponents of the classical family systems model are concerned that feminists minimize the contributions of women to relationship issues associated with addicted partners' substance abuse. Over time, substance abuse has harmed relationships between partners, which requires repair during recovery. According to proponents of the classical family systems model, strict adherence to the feminist approach places all responsibility for relationship repair on the addicted partner. This view limits the ability of relationship counselors to assist the couple in repairing their relationship.

Feminist Theories

According to the feminist approach, major factors that are related to partner abuse include patriarchal cultural norms that tolerate the existence of abuse (Dobash & Dobash, 1979), gender-based power differences that men exploit to control women (Dobash & Dobash, 1979; Pence & Paymar, 1993), and misogynistic sex role attitudes that allow men to rationalize violence and abuse against women (Downs, 1999). Examples of cultural norms that tolerate partner abuse are the lack of laws proscribing partner violence until the 1980s and marital rape until the 1990s, the failure of society to enforce systematically these laws once they were enacted, and the development of dual arrest policies. In dual arrest policies, both the male perpetrator and female victim of violence are arrested and, ironically, the victim's request for help from police results in her own prosecution (Downs, 1999). Furthermore, violence and abuse against women are rooted in a society in which men have greater access to economic resources, political power, and the criminal justice system than do women, and men use this greater access to maintain women in a lower status making women more vulnerable to violence and abuse (Dobash & Dobash, 1979; Dobash, Dobash, Wilson, & Daly, 1992; Pence & Paymar, 1993; Yllo, 1993). In addition, men use misogynistic views of women to justify verbal and psychological abuse of women, for example in peer relationships with verbalizations such as shared jokes that denigrate women (Downs, 1999). Proponents of feminist theories hold men responsible personally and legally for violence they perpetrate against women, viewing this violence as no different from a legal standpoint than extrafamilial assaults that are perpetrated against women (Pence & Shepard, 1999; Downs, 1999).

Appropriate interventions against partner violence and abuse, thus, are at societal, community, and individual levels. Societal level interventions for men include passing and enforcing laws that proscribe violence, and mandating referral of perpetrators to Batter's Education Programs based on the feminist model (e.g., Pence & Paymar, 1993). Societal level interventions for women include providing women with equal access to all types of societal resources that men enjoy, including economic, legal, and social resources. Community level interventions for women include providing adequate funding and support for shelters for battered women, and developing community coordinated responses to partner violence (Shepard, 1999). Appropriate interventions for women at the individual level include empowerment to maximize their capabilities for leaving the perpetrator. Individual level interventions for men who perpetrate partner violence include educational programs to enable men to replace controlling behaviors with behaviors based on equality in their relationships with female partners, and to replace misogynistic attitudes with egalitarian attitudes (Pence & Paymar, 1993).

In most cases, according to this model, relationship counseling should not be practiced. This perspective emerges from the view that relationships are altered by the violence, rather than violence being an outgrowth of relationships (Pence & Shepard, 1999). Furthermore, there are serious questions as to whether women, in terror of violence, can contribute equally or at all to the counseling process. McMahon and Pence (1996) have noted that violence must be responded to and terminated prior to treating the relationship. Furthermore, a victim of coercion needs a time period free from coercion, and presumably free from fear of abuse, in which to think and reflect prior to participation in couples treatment (McMahon & Pence, 1996).

Classical Family Systems Theories

Classical family systems theories are in diametric opposition to feminist theories on the issue of partner violence. A major assumption of classical family systems theories is that partner abuse results from dysfunctional family relationships (Healey et al., 1998). These dysfunctions include communication problems, unresolved relationship conflict within family relationships (Giles-Sims, 1983), and failure to set appropriate boundaries on partner's behaviors (Healey et al., 1998). Partner violence is viewed as an intrinsic part of the relationship; therefore, the unit of analysis is the relationship. Instead of focusing interventions separately on the two individuals in the relationship, classical family systems interventions focus on improving the relationship itself (Healey et al., 1998; Downs,

1999). Relationship counseling has the goals of increasing the communication, nonviolent conflict resolution, and interpersonal skills of both partners. According to classical family systems theories, resolving these issues will greatly assist in reducing violence between partners. Interventions based on classical family systems theories typically do not attempt to modify criminal justice sanctions, work at the societal level, or involve women in separate interventions for purposes of empowerment. These limitations are the source of many of the concerns regarding the use of relationship counseling in the area of partner violence.

A major reason for these concerns is that women's safety must be the predominant consideration in relationship counseling in cases where partner violence has occurred. Relationships must be examined in a context in which women are safe from violence or the threat of violence from partners. This examination must include the possible outcomes that one or both partners may decide to end the relationship permanently, or that women may decide to leave the relationship temporarily for reasons of safety. In addition, the view that partner abuse results from dysfunctional relationships does not prevent relationship counselors from holding men accountable for the violence they perpetrate on partners. Transactional patterns may or may not increase the likelihood of certain individual behaviors. However, the principle of individual choice has a clear role within classical family systems theories, especially as applied to the decision to use violence. Therefore, perpetrators are always held accountable for violence that they perpetrate.

Peterson and Calhoun (1995) stated that relationship counseling in the case of partner violence should be performed with caution and only after a number of conditions have been met. First, prior to the beginning of relationship counseling, the threat of abuse (including emotional abuse) must be greatly reduced from the precounseling level. With this threat remaining at a high level, women's contributions to counseling, and thus the effectiveness of counseling, is likely to be greatly reduced. Furthermore, to the extent that violence constrains women's contributions to counseling, women may accurately perceive counseling as having no useful purpose, further limiting its positive effects. Second, the violence must have been stopped for a time period greater than the previous longest time period without violence. The rationale for this second condition is that men frequently promise that violence has ended "this time" as a device to maintain women in their relationships and entice women into relationship counseling, only to resume that violence when men believe it necessary to control women's behavior.

With these first two conditions, Peterson and Calhoun (1995) are addressing cases in which violence and abuse have already constrained the actions of the women. Referral to a batterer's education program and an advocate for battered women are likely to be necessary to achieve a reduced threat of abuse and a period in which the male partner does not perpetrate violence. Therefore, relationship counselors must develop close working relationships with the local batterer's education program and shelter for battered women. These two programs will likely be able to assist in the assessment of the level of violence and abuse, and in the determination of cases in which relationship counseling will be possible. In this sense, it is important for relationship counselors to become part of what Pence and Shepard (1999) have called a coordinated community response to the partner violence.

A third condition is that both partners must agree to repair the relationship (Peterson & Calhoun, 1995). However, the first two conditions must be achieved for women to be capable of agreeing, free of constraint, to repair the relationship. In addition, the first two conditions must be achieved prior to the man agreeing to repair the relationship. The history of violence has led male partners to be essentially satisfied with their ability to use violence to control the women. Removing men's ability to resort to violence is, thus, an important step in motivating men to work toward equality, nonviolence, and justice in their relationships with women.

Intimate Justice Theory

Jory, Anderson, and Greer (1997) discussed a particular form of relationship counseling that may be applicable to the problem of partner violence. According to these authors, intimate justice theory is based on the principles of accountability, respect, and freedom. The authors define accountability as the ability of both partners to set limits on each other's behavior, and also to provide corrective feedback to the other partner's behavior. The principle of accountability is crucial to providing a context for equality in the absence of abuse or violence. The opposite of accountability is entitlement; men often believe they have the right to entitlement in relationships with women, and that women are subordinates to men. Counselors must confront this perceived right to entitlement. One method for confrontation might be to ask men questions such as "What if you changed into your partner?" followed by "If you did, how would you want your partner to act toward you?" and "Would you be happy with how your partner has acted toward you?" (Jory et al., 1997).

According to the principle of respect, the relationship counselor must confront the shield of hierarchy that men use to protect their perceived right to entitlement. This confrontation must include challenging the hierarchical language of power and the concept that respect is based on fear. According to this view, men have used violence and abuse to increase women's fear of men, thereby controlling women's actions, attitudes, and beliefs. Instead, the concept that respect is earned over time by such positive behaviors as intimacy, empathy, and nurturance is promoted. Once established, respect then forms the basis for a relationship based on these positive attributes as well as those of equality and justice.

The third principle, freedom, is defined as women being able to speak openly, unrestricted and not constrained by partners. To achieve this, counselors must constantly confront the violence and the consequent vulnerability of women (Jory et al., 1997). Once freedom has been established, it becomes possible to negotiate additional important dimensions such as equal rights and responsibilities and fairness in negotiation processes. Relationship counselors adhering to the paradigm of intimate justice theory explore the experiences with empowerment, disempowerment, and abuses of power that both partners may have experienced in their family of origin. These explorations are used in part to provide a context for understanding these same issues in the current relationship. Furthermore, relationship counselors adhering to this approach challenge internalized beliefs about violence and abuse, and confront disempowerment and abuses of power as they are displayed and practiced in the current relationship. Finally, relationship counselors provide a context for developing an awareness of the social context of justice and injustice.

Issues for Incorporating Relationship Counseling into Cases of Partner Violence

For partner violence, classical family systems theories have provided an academic and philosophical underpinning for relationship counseling. Many counselors treating addicted men and women use this intervention with couples in which the male partner has perpetrated partner violence on the female partner and, in fact, many clients request this intervention. However, both Shamai (1996) and Hansen (1993) have pointed out several concerns regarding the use of relationship counseling with couples in which there has been partner violence. Understanding these issues may lead to general guidelines for using relationship counseling appropriately with partner violence.

A primary concern is that many counselors limit their definition of the problem to the relationship itself, failing to extend their view to other issues that might be exacerbating the violence, causing it in the first place, or allowing it to continue (Shamai, 1996). These other issues may include lack of support services for women, a criminal justice system that tacitly allows violence to continue, or a failure of local batterer's education programs (BEP) to address the issue of partner violence. Extending the definition of the problem to include these other issues implies the need for additional systems to provide support for relationship counseling (Shamai, 1996). Therefore, in cases of partner violence, counselors must consider the need to involve the criminal justice system, BEP, or shelter for battered women in providing service to the couple. In assessing this need, counselors must consider at a minimum both the severity of violence and the fear toward their partner expressed by women.

Second, Shamai (1996) notes that the interactive nature of classical family systems theories as applied to relationship counseling limits attribution of individual responsibility for violent and abusive behaviors. Aldarondo and Straus (1994) also noted that relationship counseling is ill-equipped to deal with issues of coercion and violence. A major reason is that abusive behaviors are deemphasized in systemic formulations and, in particular, relationship counseling diffuses men's responsibility for violence that they have perpetrated. This criticism is at the very core of the different philosophies of partner violence from the points of view of the feminist models and classical family systems theories. In feminist models, violence is viewed as solely the responsibility of the perpetrator, and not part of an interactive system. Further, reducing men's responsibility for his violence, within systems formulations, implies that women need to work on stopping their own victimization. Therefore, it is incumbent on relationship counselors to hold the men accountable for violence they perpetrate against women. In particular, the threat of violence cannot be used to control or constrain partner's behavior. Furthermore, relationship counselors must clarify that all other forms of partner abuse, such as emotional abuse, are unacceptable (Shamai, 1996).

Third, many relationship counselors adhere to the principle of therapist neutrality, meaning that they view both partners as equally responsible for relationship issues. Ironically, it is this principle that precludes many therapists from holding male partners accountable for violence they perpetrate (Shamai, 1996), thereby tacitly tolerating or condoning violence. Based on the assumption of therapist neutrality, relationship counselors often ignore status and power differences between men and women, fail to see the need for cultural and social sanctions against violence, obscure the seriousness of violence, obscure the emotional and physical experience of violence, and functionally eliminate men's responsibility for violence (Hansen, 1993).

Therapist neutrality is a difficult concept as applied to cases in which partner violence has occurred, because of the likelihood of colluding with batterers and inadvertently supporting their denial that violence is a problem. Relationship counselors may inadvertently or implicitly collude with batterers even before the counseling begins. For example, relationship counselors typically begin work with the most flexible part of the family system, usually women (Hansen, 1993). That is, counselors often join with women to try to convince men of the need for relationship counseling, thereby placing the onus for initiating counseling on women. Men may interpret this dynamic as support for their belief that the primary problem in the relationship lies with women, because women are advocating for the counseling more than the men are. If men strongly resist relationship counseling, women may be better served by exploring alternatives to the present relationship.

Once the counseling is started, an important set of decisions is which issues counselors, women, and men choose to discuss. Women may be more likely than men to focus on how they can change their behavior to improve the relationship. However, the more time that is spent on discussing the need for women's behavior change, the more that counselors may fail to confront violence or hold men accountable for violence. In addition, men may interpret the time and energy spent on changes women can make as supporting their view that responsibility for the violence is shared between women and men, or that it lies with women entirely. In such cases, relationship counseling implicitly and inadvertently supports men's denial of their violence or of their responsibility for their violence. Clearly, then, techniques that are useful in nonviolent cases are not appropriate in cases of violence. Relationship counselors might help women more by discussing with men their role in creating an unsafe environment that destroys the relationship.

Fourth, relationship counselors and marital therapists often perceive violence as a symptom of family dysfunction rather than being a problem in and of itself (Shamai, 1996). According to Hansen (1993), relationship counselors who view violence as a symptom rather than a problem in its own right are likely to fail to assess the seriousness of the violence and, thus, minimize violence as a problem which requires an intervention. If so, then perpetrators enter counseling perceiving that their violence is not a problem. Failing to identify or assess violence then contributes to maintaining the power differential in the relationship (Shamai, 1996).

A fifth concern for relationship counseling with issues of partner violence is based on the possibility that violence has altered the relationship, or at least the woman's view of the relationship, beyond the capability of the couple to improve it. According to McCloskey and Fraser (1997), once battering and control have been established in a relationship it becomes difficult to reestablish a healthy relationship. Battering is a lifelong learned behavior pattern that has been instrumentally successful for batterers; they have used violence and abuse to force women to conform to their desires. Since perpetrators have moved in and out of periods of violence (Sleutel, 1998), it may take considerable convincing for women to accept that their partner is violence-free. This process is similar to that of substance abuse counselors who are working with family members of addicted men or women; family members have seen addicted men or women move in and out of periods of abstinence. That is, even under the best of circumstances, it may be difficult for women to accept that their partner will stop the violence and abuse that they have perpetrated. Family members may be reluctant, especially at first, to believe that this time will be a permanent period of nonviolence.

Furthermore, the climate of fear resulting from violence and abuse may have altered women's views of their partners and of their relationships. Even if women accept that their partners will, this time, stop perpetrating violence, there may still be the residual psychological effects from past experiences of violence. Several studies have shown that violence and abuse against women affect their mental health as well as their views regarding the relationship and their partner (e.g., Rollstin & Kern, 1998). Physically abused women enter relationship counseling with generally greater problems than do women who have not been physically abused or than the man in the relationship. Cascardi, O'Leary, Lawrence, and Schlee (1995) found that abused women seeking treatment for marital conflict reported significantly more fear and posttraumatic stress disorder (PTSD) than nonabused women in discordant relationships and community control women. Based on a literature review, Gauthier and Levendosky (1996) concluded that the impact, consequences, severity, likelihood of a severe injury, depression, anxiety, suicidal ideation, and substance abuse as a result from violence are greater for women than for men in relationships.

Based on the foregoing concerns, Jory et al. (1997) raised the possibility of iatrogenic harm resulting from relationship counseling. First, women might stay in the relationship when it would be preferable for them to leave. That is, unless counselors raise the possibility of options to the current relationship, with its violence and abuse, women might fail to see these options and choose to remain in an abusive relationship. In this sense, relationship counselors may inadvertently support the power and control issues of perpetrators, issues that are designed to limit women's options. For example, perpetrators may use the fact that they agreed to therapy as evidence of their commitment to change. Perpetrators may then use this implied commitment as a rationale for women to remain in the relationship. Second, perpetrators might learn therapeutic language that then can be used to rationalize their behavior both to themselves and their partners (Jory et al., 1997). For example, perpetrators might learn explanations for their violent or abusive behavior that then are used to evade responsibility for that behavior. For these reasons, relationship counseling may not be applicable and may be precisely the wrong intervention.

Issues Relevant to Considering the Use of Relationship Counseling

A large number of women who have experienced partner violence request relationship counseling as the preferred intervention. In particular, a majority of women seeking help for marital conflict, though not specifically for partner violence, have experienced violence in the relationship. For example, O'Leary, Vivian, and Malone (1992) surveyed 132 couples presenting for marital therapy and found that 56% of couples reported ongoing violence, and that 67% of couples reported at least one violent act in the past year. Using a modified Conflict Tactics Scale, Cascardi et al. (1995) reported that 65% to 70% of women seeking treatment for marital problems reported at least one act of physical victimization in the year before assessment. Also using a modified Conflict Tactics Scale, Cascardi, Langhinrichsen, and Vivian (1992) found that 71% of clinic couples (i.e., maritally discordant couples seeking psychological treatment) had experienced physical aggression in their marital relationship at least once during the past year. Approximately 86% of this violence included both husband-to-wife and wife-to-husband violence. Cascardi et al. (1995) also found that psychological aggression correlated with physical aggression and, thus, women entering relationship counseling are likely to have experienced psychological abuse as well as physical partner violence.

There are several possible reasons for failing to uncover partner violence in the field of relationship counseling. First, relationship counselors only rarely attempt to discover the existence of partner violence among their clients. Only a very small percentage of clinicians have attempted to assess or identify partner violence, and few clients take the initiative to self-report violence to counselors. Cascardi et al. (1995) found that only 3%–6% of marital counselors attempted to assess partner violence. Aldarondo and Straus (1994) also noted that very few therapists are actually aware of violence and abuse that is ongoing in the relationship.

Second, the women themselves may not be ready for interventions other than relationship counseling. McCloskey and Fraser (1997) cite Davies (1994) that services and options have been mostly geared toward helping women leave, and that women who stay may even be seen as impaired. According to Dutton and Golant (1995), many women victimized by partner violence are not ready for the relationship to be terminated. Rather these women are likely to perceive multiple issues with their partner, and desire relationship counseling to resolve these issues. These women may perceive violence as an issue of low priority and, thus, not be ready to invoke community resources, such as criminal justice systems or the use of a shelter to end the violence. Shamai (1996) also noted that a majority of women continue marriages or relationships even though they had experienced violence from partners. In fact, some couples are too afraid or ashamed to deal with violence and believe that relationship counseling has less negative connotations than accessing a shelter or batterer's education program (Shamai, 1996). Often, women do not leave the relationship until their sanity or their lives are repeatedly threatened, or until they no longer accept the justifications for violence (Shamai, 1996). Until many women have reached this point, they neither want their partners referred to a BEP nor want services for battered women. Relationship counseling, according to Dutton (1994), may be an alternative for these clients, at least initially.

Third, clients rarely initiate discussion on partner violence that has occurred. O'Leary et al. (1992) found that only 1.5 % of husbands and 6.0% of wives reported physical aggression as the presenting problem for marital therapy. Ehrensaft and Vivian (1996) surveyed 136 clinic couples and found the three top reasons that couples did not spontaneously report violence or identify it as a presenting problem were that clients (1) did not view violence as a problem, (2) perceived the violence as unstable or infrequent, and (3) considered the violence to be secondary or caused by other problems. Aldarondo and Straus (1994) also noted that clients may not divulge partner violence because they perceived the violence as tolerable, viewed violence as an acceptable form of conflict resolution (because clients have seen so much of it), or wanted to make a good impression on the therapist and would be ashamed by admitting the existence of violence. Ironically, women may fail to recognize themselves as victims of violence because their experiences of violence have become so common. Women may have experienced so much violence in their lives that their frame of reference is to view violence as typical for relationships. Therefore, it is incumbent upon counselors to ask women about the violence they have experienced in relationships, to do so when the male partner is not present, to explore specific violent acts women may have experienced (instead of a general inquiry about violence), and to ask the women if they have ever feared their partner.

The Distinction between Common Couple Violence and Patriarchal Terrorism

Some women who seek relationship counseling view their experiences of partner violence as less important than other problematic aspects of their relationship. This finding raises an important point. Perhaps there are qualitative differences in women's subjective experiences in cases where violence is low in severity and frequency, as compared to cases where violence is high in severity and frequency. Because of these differences, women who have experienced only low levels of violence may benefit more from relationship counseling than from interventions based on feminist models. Several researchers have, in fact, made a distinction between mild and severe violence (Straus & Gelles, 1990) or moderate and severe violence (e.g., Murphy & O'Farrell, 1994).

In a thoughtful article, Johnson (1995) discussed two different types of violence: "common couple" violence and "patriarchal terrorism." According to Johnson, common couple violence is similar to the "mild" violence studied in national victimization surveys. Common couple violence consists primarily of less severe physical violence, violence that is essentially mutual, and with fewer of the power and control issues defined by advocates such as Pence and Paymar (1993). Conversely, patriarchal terrorism is similar to the severe violence and abuse studied by feminist researchers and found largely in populations of battered women. Patriarchal terrorism is more severe physically, primarily initiated by the male partner, and is characterized by extensive use of power and control techniques as defined by advocates such as Pence and Paymar (1993). According to Johnson (1995), failure to distinguish between common couple violence and patriarchal terrorism might be the source of numerous disputes among researchers and practitioners in the area of partner violence.

Although not empirically established, the potential of two or more different types of partner violence may have important implications for interventions. In the case of common couple violence, for example, relationship counseling may be the generally preferred mode of treatment. Common couple violence may be one of numerous presenting problems brought to relationship counselors. Indeed, common couple violence may rank low among the priorities of both men and women. Women who have experienced only this type of violence from partners may still perceive equal power with partners. Further, neither partner may be sufficiently fearful to constrain their contributions to the counseling. That is, neither partner may have sufficient fear of the other partner's violence to take the possibility of that violence into account in responding to counselor's questions, carrying out homework assignments, confronting partners, or in general participating in the counseling.

Conversely, at the other end of the distribution, in the case of patriarchal terrorism, relationship counseling may be contraindicated. Violence and abuse may have been severe, even life-threatening. There may have been a lengthy history of partner violence and abuse, primarily by male partners with the goal of constraining female partners' behaviors. There may have been severe consequences, and women may fear for their lives. Certainly in their responses to therapist questions, or in anything they say during the counseling session, women must take into account the possibility that they could go beyond the bounds defined by male partners and that they are risking yet another violent episode. Furthermore, women's ability to carry out homework assignments is likely to be severely limited. Instead of relationship counseling, the preferred mode of intervention in these cases might be the work of trained advocates. Women who have experienced the more severe, asymmetrical, patriarchal, and coercive type of violence may benefit more from referral to a shelter or advocate for individualized services, instead of relationship counseling.

A key concept in assessing which form of intervention might be optimal could be the level of women's fear of her partner and the level of coercion used by her partner. Unfortunately, Cascardi et al. (1995) noted that neither fear nor coercion were typically assessed in samples of women seeking treatment for marital problems, despite the fact that coercion and dominance distinguish maritally distressed violent relationships from maritally distressed nonviolent relationships. Nevertheless, the existence of low levels of mutual partner violence, as well as research indicating that some women prefer relationship counseling, even when they have experienced partner violence, imply the need to develop forms of relationship counseling to address this problem. In addition, research showing that a high percentage of addicted men and women have either perpetrated or experienced partner violence indicates the need for relationship counseling that proactively addresses partner violence.

☐ Combining Treatment for Partner Violence and Substance Abuse

Family Systems Theories, Relationship Counseling, and Substance Abuse

The field of substance abuse has incorporated family therapy and relationship counseling into substance abuse treatment. O'Farrell and Feehan (1999) noted that there have been three theoretical perspectives in the alcoholism field: the family disease approach, family systems theory, and, more recently, the behavioral approach. Within the family disease model, substance abuse counselors focus directly on the individual family members themselves. There is not a focus on improving family relationships. Instead, counselors work with individual family members on the negative effects of the alcoholism on their behaviors, self-perceptions, and other individual issues. In the family systems approach, general systems theory is applied to the family. Unhealthy family relationships are assumed to be related to the drinking, thus the focus is on changing these. In addition, there are attempts to change dysfunctional roles (e.g., the enabler role) based on the belief that changing these will increase the likelihood of family members adjusting to and supporting the abstinent behavior of the addicted person. The family systems approach is similar to classical family systems theories discussed in the previous section. The behavioral approach has been the most recent development. In this approach, family members are taught procedures to support abstinence and work directly on interactional patterns that are related to drinking. In addition, the behavioral approach relies upon contracts between family members to support abstinence from both substance abuse and violence. As will be seen later, the behavioral approach has empirical support for its effectiveness in reducing partner violence over time with certain types of addicted men and women (O'Farrell, Van Hutton, & Murphy, 1999; O'Farrell & Fals-Stewart, 2000).

Thus, unlike the field of partner violence, there has been a tendency for the field of substance abuse treatment to view family involvement in treatment as integral to the recovery of addicted men and women. In fact, involvement in a relationship with a supportive spouse has been viewed as important both to the initial treatment and relapse prevention for the substance dependent person. Given the overlap between substance abuse and partner violence discussed elsewhere in this book, this means that substance abuse counselors are involving partners in relationship counseling in cases in which addicted male partners have perpetrated violence on female partners. Furthermore, the field of substance abuse treatment has not yet examined the impact of partner violence on relationship counseling with an addicted male partner. As discussed above, this use of relationship counseling as an adjunct to substance abuse treatment is precisely what women's advocates as well as the regulating boards of many states recommend not doing. These differences between the battered women's movement and substance abuse treatment are fundamental. However, these differences must be overcome if services to women and violent addicted men are to be developed.

Behavioral Couples Therapy

As reported previously, there is overlap between substance abuse and the perpetration of partner violence. Conjoint programs have the potential to reduce both partner violence and substance abuse. Horton and Johnson (1993) found that the most dramatic reports of change in abusive relationships derive from batterer's gaining control of an alcohol or drug problem. Saunders (1996) reported that alcohol use predicted failure to complete BEPs as well as recidivism in samples of men referred to intervention programs for male perpetrators of partner violence. However, there have been very few attempts to develop conjoint programs that simultaneously address both issues. An exception has been Behavioral Couples Therapy.

O'Farrell, Murphy, and their associates (e.g., O'Farrell & Murphy, 1995) conducted a number of studies examining the communication and other relationship difficulties of couples with a violent addicted partner. A major purpose of these studies was to develop, pilot, and refine a set of intervention strategies for couples with an addicted partner who might also be violent. In general, research has shown that couples in which one partner is alcoholic (Murphy & O'Farrell, 1996, 1997) or in which there has been partner violence

(Berns, Jacobson, & Gottman, 1999) have more communication problems than distressed couples in the absence of substance abuse or partner violence. However, the combination of both substance abuse and partner violence appears to exacerbate communication problems.

Maritally violent alcoholics have been found to display significantly higher levels of hostile and defensive communication than nonviolent alcoholics (Murphy & O'Farrell, 1996). Maritally violent alcoholics also were significantly less likely to have aversive exchanges when sober than when drinking (Murphy & O'Farrell, 1996). Murphy and O'Farrell (1997) examined couples with an alcoholic husband in sober interactions in lab situations. Within this sample, the authors found that aversive-defensive communication was significantly higher for couples with a physically aggressive husband than couples in which the husband was not physically aggressive. In sequential analyses these authors found that physically aggressive husbands had more negative reciprocity. Further, husbands' aggression may have instrumental effects on wives; that is, wives acquiesced more in the presence of aggression, which may have been the goal of husbands' aggression (Murphy & O'Farrell, 1997). Finally, gender differences in the results indicate that wives are more constructive problem solvers than are husbands, especially when husband-wife aggression is present.

Based on these results, O'Farrell, Murphy, and associates developed Behavioral Couples Therapy (BCT) which was designed specifically to address the marital interactions in which one member of the couple is addicted. In some cases, BCT is designed to deal also with cases in which partner violence may have occurred. The major goal during treatment is to assist the couple in changing alcohol-related interactional patterns. The major goals after treatment are to help the couple prevent relapse to abusive drinking and to deal with marital issues frequently encountered during long-term recovery (O'Farrell & Rotunda, 1997). Treatment frequently begins with the alcoholic member of the couple. During the first phase of treatment with the alcoholic, therapists must obtain the alcoholic's permission to contact the spouse. The alcoholic may fear both this contact and the outcome of subsequent treatment. In particular, the alcoholic may fear that the therapist will advise the partner to separate from the alcoholic, or that in any case an eventual outcome of treatment will be separation. Due in part to issues such as these, therapists must obtain the agreement of both members of the couple to commit to the assessment, stay together, not to threaten separation or divorce, and to refrain from bringing up the issues of separation or divorce in anger at home (O'Farrell & Rotunda, 1997).

Because of the overlap between partner violence and substance dependence, O'Farrell and colleagues recommend that the existence of partner violence also be addressed during the assessment phase of counseling. In addition, assessment periods are critical junctures to determine whether alcohol use is related to violence (O'Farrell & Rotunda, 1997). In particular, therapists need to determine whether partner violence occurs only or primarily when the violent spouse has been drinking (O'Farrell & Rotunda, 1997). Additional assessment issues include whether violence is more intense or severe during episodes of drinking. The latter is an important part of assessment since Sleutel (1998), in her review of qualitative research, noted that many women reported that while there was violence during both drinking and sober periods, violence was worse when the partner was drinking.

The sequencing of interventions is also critical: "once the alcohol abuser has decided to change his/her drinking and has begun successfully to control or abstain from his/her drinking, the therapist can focus on improving the couple's relationship" (O'Farrell & Rotunda, 1997, p. 569). Goals for improving the relationship include: (1) increasing positive feeling, goodwill, commitment to the relationship and (2) resolving conflicts, problems, and desires for change (O'Farrell & Rotunda, 1997). Techniques to achieve these goals include: (1) the therapist educating the couple in and modeling positive behaviors; (2) the couple practicing these positive behaviors under therapist supervision; (3) the couple completing homework assignments generally designed to transport positive behaviors to the home environment; and (4) reviews of homework with further practice (O'Farrell and Rotunda, 1997). Finally, the authors also have discussed relapse prevention, including techniques such as: (1) reviewing which therapeutic interventions have been most helpful, (2) anticipating high-risk situations for drinking, and (3) rehearsing and practicing what to do when a relapse occurs (O'Farrell & Rotunda, 1997).

O'Farrell, Murphy, and associates have conducted a number of evaluations regarding the effectiveness of BCT. O'Farrell and Murphy (1995) found that marital violence had decreased significantly one year after BCT and, further, that the extent of violence after BCT was related to alcoholics' drinking status. Remitted alcoholics no longer had elevated marital violence compared to matched controls; however, actively drinking alcoholics did have elevated levels of marital violence (O'Farrell & Murphy, 1995). For remitted alcoholics, partner violence was seriously elevated prior to BCT, but was reduced significantly to levels found among nonalcoholic couples after BCT. O'Farrell et al. (1999) found that these results were extended for later years; for the first two years after BCT, partner violence continued to be significantly reduced. In addition, the extent of marital violence was associated with the extent of drinking, and the frequency of violence was correlated with number of days drinking. Furthermore, remitted alcoholics no longer had elevated marital violence levels, compared with matched controls, while relapsed alcoholics did have elevated levels of violence. In a literature review, O'Farrell and Feehan (1999) provided results indicating that, for alcohol dependent persons, remission after individual alcoholism treatment combined with BCT was associated with improved family functioning in a number of areas. These areas included: reduced family stressors, improved marital adjustment, reduced partner violence and verbal conflict, reduced risk of separation and divorce, improvement in family processes related to cohesion, conflict, and caring, and reduced emotional distress in spouses.

Concerns with the Use of Behavioral Couples Therapy

BCT has been shown to have considerable potential to reduce both substance abuse and partner violence for addicted violent men. Nevertheless, based on discussions earlier in this chapter, there are several concerns regarding the use of BCT in relationships in which partner violence has occurred.

The first issue is deciding for which clients BCT is appropriate. Given that both members of the couple must endorse the goals of BCT and agree to participate fully in its process, BCT is likely to be inappropriate in cases of severe partner violence. Thus, as O'Farrell, Murphy, and associates (Murphy & O'Farrell, 1996) have consistently pointed out, the assessment phase of BCT is critical to determining its feasibility. The therapist must identify severity and frequency of partner violence, whether drinking contributes to partner violence, and whether the drinking partner is more dangerous when drinking. In addition, the therapist must identify and assess the woman's level of fear of partner—too great a level of fear would contraindicate the use of BCT.

The process of this assessment can be complex. BCT is heavily dependent on non- addicted partners. Their role in treatment is clearly defined, for example in regard to reducing and controlling alcohol availability in the home, improving couple reactions related to alcohol, the use of behavioral contracting concerning abstinence, and enforcement of contracting regarding addicted partner's use of Antabuse. Thus, a nonaddicted partner leaving the relationship is likely to be disruptive to the recovery of addicted partners. Conversely, it is unclear whether contracting can work in situations where there has been violence severe enough to constrain women, where their fear of the male partner is too great, or where they are not committed to maintaining the relationship.

A second and related issue concerns the agreement not to threaten separation or divorce. In fact, this portion of the BCT agreement might limit women in partner violence situations. Women might need these options to leave for safety reasons alone. Women also may need these options as leverage over partners in case they threaten to resume violence. As Jory et al. (1997) pointed out, an important principle is the ability to set limits and constrain partner's behavior, especially regarding violence and abuse. Murphy and O'Farrell (1996) recognize this need, referring to this issue in their discussion of timeouts in the case of one spouse being violent. In that case, nonviolent spouses have the option to leave temporarily. In general, the authors recommend the use of timeouts for conflict containment and to prevent a situation that might escalate to violence (O'Farrell & Rotunda, 1997).

Third, the use of BCT does not preclude the use of other approaches for addressing violence. For instance, according to the coordinated community response model (Pence & Shepard, 1999), the best intervention for partner violence involves practitioners from multiple fields (e.g., criminal justice, substance abuse) working together to reduce violence. In their model of Behavioral Couples Therapy, Epstein and McCrady (1998) stated that interventions at many levels were implied, including other social systems. For example, assessment of women's fear of partner might include their discussing this fear with an advocate from a shelter for battered women. In the case of timeout, the agreement between partners might also include the option for a safety plan developed with battered women's advocates. In this case, if violence or the threat of violence does occur, women would be able to leave temporarily and safely. In addition, it might be important for any no-separation agreement to be reexamined in light of violence or threat.

A fourth concern with BCT is that it includes interventions designed to decrease spousal behaviors that trigger or enable drinking. While these interventions are appropriate for assisting in recovery from substance abuse, there may be a need to articulate clearly that partner violence does not fall into the same treatment philosophy; otherwise, perpetrators may begin or continue to use female partner's behavior as a rationale for their violence. Given the history in which male partners have minimized their responsibility for violence by blaming it on what they believe to be women's shortcomings, it is critical that therapists consistently hold men accountable for violence. This criticism also highlights a core philosophical difference over whether there are behaviors by female partners that increase the likelihood of violence. Some therapists might view women's use of verbal abuse or failure to invoke the timeout agreements of BCT, in combination with their partner's lack of nonviolent alternatives to provide limits to her behavior, as resulting in situations that increase the likelihood of male partner's violence. However, we believe that the principle of individual responsibility for perpetration of violence has long been established and must be communicated to the couple during BCT or other forms of relationship counseling.

During individual work, it may still be helpful to assist female partners in identifying behaviors to which male partners have responded with violence, at the very least for reasons of maximizing their safety. This work will be important only for the prevention of violence, not for the cessation of violence after it has begun. Jacobson, Gottman, Gortner, Berns, & Shortt (1996) provided data that while husband violence did escalate in response both to wife violent and nonviolent behaviors, wive's behaviors had no effect on husbands once violence started. This intervention is complex since there is always the potential for female partners to misread it as providing rationales for male partner's use of violence. Therefore, it must be communicated to female partners that this work is to assist her in maximizing her safety, but that it will not necessarily prevent partner violence; in fact the responsibility for male partner's violence rests with him alone.

☐ Summary and Conclusions: Fitting the Services to the Needs of the Client

Ganley (1989) long ago made the point that there needs to be a decoupling of counseling format from theoretical assumptions regarding violence. For too long clinicians have imposed their favored interventions on clients without fully considering the desires of the clients themselves. Wileman and Wileman (1995) noted that women's powerlessness to effect change in their partner has been promoted in the literature, leading to an overreliance on legal remedies. Pence and Shepard (1999) and others have pointed out the dangers of clinicians (including relationship counselors) inadvertently colluding with the violent partner and contributing to violence continuing. Many women want their relationships to continue and do not want to use legal remedies although they want the violence to stop; others may want to leave but find this too difficult. According to Rhodes and McKenzie (1998), battered women's situations are unique; therefore, researchers and clinicians need to stop searching for a unitary theory that fits all battered women. Instead, researchers and clinicians must develop multiple theories and multiple interventions to better serve women who have experienced violence from their partners. Clinicians need to fit the services to the woman instead of fitting the woman to the services (McCloskey & Fraser, 1997).

Of paramount importance, interventions are needed for addicted men who perpetrate partner violence. Family therapy and relationship counseling have long been considered important components of treating addicted adults. In particular, the impact of substance abuse on family relationships has resulted in the view that family therapy is needed to repair this impact and improve family dynamics harmed by substance abuse. However, advocates in the area of partner violence have pointed out the harm that can result if family therapy or relationship counseling is used in cases in which the male partner has perpetrated violence. In particular, relationship counseling is considered contrary to state regulations for intervention with partner violence in over 20 states in the U.S. (Austin & Dankwort, 1999; Healey et al., 1998). Given the overlap between substance abuse and partner violence, these opposing views on relationship counseling place those working with addicted men and women in a quandary. Under what circumstances should relationship counseling be offered, or should it be offered at all?

Although there are no clear answers, there are some possible directions for future practice and research based on a complex triage system. Women assessed as having experienced common couple violence (Johnson, 1995), that is low levels of violence, who do not fear partners, and who are themselves ready to endorse the goals and process of relationship counseling free of constraint from partners, might benefit most from relationship counseling. In cases where addictions are combined with partner violence, BCT has been shown consistently to be the most successful intervention. However, based on the principle of coordinated community intervention, it is important for relationship counselors to include advocates for battered women as well as staff from BEP in the intervention process. These additional professionals can assist in the formation of safety plans, continued assessment of violence, and as supports for nonviolent alternatives.

Women who have experienced patriarchal terrorism (Johnson, 1995), that is high levels of violence, and who fear partners may not be ready or willing to endorse the goals and process of relationship counseling free of constraint from partners. In these cases, relationship counseling is likely to be inappropriate or even harmful. These women might instead benefit most from receiving services (i.e., services from advocates for battered women) with the goal of increasing empowerment and independence from partners, with the potential long-term goal of separating from partners. Additional needs of women who have experienced partner violence at this level may include employment, access to financial resources, child care, medical attention, social services, and safe housing (Sullivan & Bybee, 1999). In the case of these women also being addicted, the coordinated community response might include the provision of substance abuse treatment. In addition, in these cases male partners might benefit most from referral or mandate to a batterer's education program to reduce or end his use of patriarchal violence against women. In the case of perpetrators also being addicted, it may be necessary to provide joint treatment for substance abuse.

Many women have experienced partner violence that is in the middle of the distribution for partner violence. These women cannot easily be characterized as having been victimized by common couple violence or, alternatively, as having been victimized by patriarchal terrorism (Johnson, 1995). The assessment phase is especially important for these women. The assessment should be multimodal in that violence, fear, substance abuse, and women's readiness to endorse relationship counseling need to be examined; in addition, the assessment must involve professionals from multiple fields of services as part of a community coordinated response to violence. In these cases, relationship counselors, advocates for battered women, and workers in BEP must work together to provide the best services for women. These services may include relationship counseling or, alternatively, referral to advocates for battered women, and mandated referral to BEP for men; the decisions must be made on a case-by-case basis. Of utmost importance, however, is to listen closely to the women themselves. It is the women who are most able to describe what they want and how they want to proceed. Only then will we be able to fit the services to people's needs instead of fitting people to the services.

References

Abrams, K. M., & Robinson, G. E. (1998). Stalking. Part I: An overview of the problem. *Canadian Journal of Psychiatry, 43*, 473–476.

Aldarondo, E., & Straus, M. A. (1994). Screening for physical violence in couple therapy: Methodological, practical, and ethical considerations. *Family Process, 33*, 425–439.

Austin, J. B., & Dankwort, J. (1999). The impact of a batterer's program on battered women. *Violence Against Women, 5*(1), 25–42.

Berns, S. B., Jacobson, N. S., & Gottman, J. M. (1999). Demand-withdraw interaction in couples with a violent husband. *Journal of Consulting and Clinical Psychology, 67*(5), 666–674.

Bograd, M. (1988). Feminist perspectives on wife abuse: An introduction. In K. A. Yllo & M. Bograd (Eds.), *Feminist perspectives on wife abuse*. Newbury Park, CA: Sage.

Brown, T. G., Werk, A., Caplan, T., & Seraganian, P. (1999). Violent substance abusers in domestic violence treatment. *Violence and Victims, 14*(2), 179–190.

Brown, T. G., Werk, A., Caplan, T., Shields, N., & Seraganian, P. (1998). The incidence and characteristics of violent men in substance abuse treatment. *Addictive Behaviors, 23*(5), 573–586.

Cascardi, M., Langhinrichsen, J., & Vivian, D. (1992). Marital aggression: Impact, injury, and health correlates for husbands and wives. *Archives of Internal Medicine, 152*, 1178–1184.

Cascardi, M., O'Leary, K. D., Lawrence, E. E., & Schlee, K. A. (1995). Characteristics of women physically abused by their spouses and who seek treatment regarding marital conflict. *Journal of Consulting and Clinical Psychology, 63*(4), 616–623.

Davies, J. (1994). *Using safety planning as an approach to woman-defined advocacy.* Hartford, CT: Legal Aid Society of Hartford County.

Dobash, R. E., & Dobash, R. (1979). *Violence against wives: A case against the patriarchy.* New York: The Free Press.

Dobash, R. P., Dobash, R. E., Wilson, M., & Daly, M. (1992). The myth of sexual symmetry in marital violence. *Social Problems, 39*(1), 71–91.

Downs, W. R. (1999). The use of cognitive behavioural techniques in groups for male perpetrators of domestic violence: A framework for intervention. *Cogntive Behavioural Social Work Review, 20*(1), 2–35.

Downs, W. R., Patterson, A., Barten, S., Rindels, B., & McCrory, M. (November, 1998). *Partner violence, mental health, and substance abuse among two samples of women.* Paper presented at the Annual Meeting of the American Society of Criminology, Washington, DC.

Downs, W. R., Patterson, A., Barten, S., Spring, S., Crudo, S, & Lingenfelter, T. (November 1999). *Childhood violence and adulthood problems for women in a shelter for battered women.* Paper presented at the Annual Meeting of the American Society of Criminology, Toronto, Canada.

Dutton, D. G. (1994). Patriarchy and wife assault: The ecological fallacy. *Violence and Victims, 9*(2), 167–182.

Dutton, D. G., & Golant, S. K. (1995). *The batterer: A psychological profile.* New York: Basic.

Dutton, M. A., Goodman, L. A., & Bennett, L. (1999). Court-involved battered women's responses to violence: The role of psychological, physical, and sexual abuse. *Violence and Victims, 14*(1), 89–104.

Ehrensaft, M. K., & Vivian, D. (1996). Spouses' reasons for not reporting existing marital aggression as a marital problem. *Journal of Family Psychology, 10*(4), 443–453.

Epstein, E. E., & McCrady, B. S. (1998). Behavioral couples treatment of alcohol and drug use disorders: Current status and innovations. *Clinical Psychology Review, 18*(6), 689–711.

Ganley, A. L. (1989). Integrating feminist and social learning analyses of aggression: Creating multiple models for intervention with men who batter. In P. L. Caesar & L. K. Hamberger (Eds.), *Treating men who batter: Theory, practice, and programs* (pp. 196–235). New York: Springer.

Gauthier, L. M., & Levendosky, A. A. (1996). Assessment and treatment of couples with abusive male partners: Guidelines for therapists. *Domestic Violence and Couple's Therapy, 33*(3), 403–417.

Giles-Sims, J. (1983). *Wife-battering: A systems theory approach.* New York: Guilford.

Gorney, B. (1989). Domestic violence and chemical dependency: Dual problems, dual interventions. *Journal of Psychoactive Drugs, 21*(2), 229–238.

Hansen, M. (1993). Feminism and family therapy: A review of feminist critiques of approaches to family violence. In M. Hansen & M. Harway (Eds.), *Battering and family therapy* (pp. 69–81). Newbury Park, CA: Sage.

Healey, K., Smith, C., & O'Sullivan, C. (1998). Batterer intervention: Program approaches and criminal justice strategies. *Issues and Practices in Criminal Justice.* Washington, DC: U.S. Department of Justice, National Institute of Justice.

Herman, J. L. (1992). *Trauma and recovery.* New York: Basic.

Horton, A. L., & Johnson, B. L. (1993). Profile and strategies of women who have ended abuse. *Families in Society: The Journal of Contemporary Human Services,* (October), 481–492.

Jacobson, N. S., Gottman, J. M., Gortner, E., Berns, S., & Shortt, J. W. (1996). Psychological factors in the longitudinal course of battering: When do the couples split up? When does the abuse decrease? *Violence and Victims, 11*(4), 371–392.

Johnson, M. P. (1995). Patriarchal terrorism and common couple violence: Two forms of violence against women. *Journal of Marriage and the Family, 57,* 283–294.

Jory, B., Anderson, D., & Greer, C. (1997). Intimate justice: Confronting issues of accountability, respect, and freedom in treatment for abuse and violence. *Journal of Marital and Family Therapy, 23*(4), 399–419.

McCloskey, K. A., & Fraser, J. S. (1997). Using feminist MRI Brief Therapy during initial contact with victims of domestic violence. *Psychotherapy, 34*(4), 433–446.

McMahon, M., & Pence, E. (1996). Physical aggression in intimate relationships can be treated within a marital context under certain circumstances. *Journal of Interpersonal Violence, 11*(3), 452–455.

Meyer, S. L., Vivian, D., & O'Leary, K. D. (1998). Men's sexual aggression in marriage. *Violence Against Women, 4*(4), 415–435.

Miller, B. A., & Downs, W. R. (2000). Violence against women. In M. B. Goldman & M. C. Hatch (Eds.), *Women and Health* (pp. 529–540). San Diego, CA: Academic.

Miller, B. A., Wilsnack, S. C., & Cunradi, C. B. (2000). Family violence and victimization: Treatment issues for women with alcohol problems. *Alcoholism: Clinical and Experimental Research.*

Murphy, C. M., & O'Farrell, T. J. (1994). Factors associated with marital aggression in male alcoholics. *Journal of Family Psychology, 8*(3), 321–335.

Murphy, C. M., & O'Farrell, T. J. (1996). Marital violence among alcoholics. *Current Directions in Psychological Science, 5*(6), 183–186.

Murphy, C. M., & O'Farrell, T. J. (1997). Couple communication patterns of maritally aggressive and nonaggressive male alcoholics. *Journal of Studies on Alcohol* (January), 83–90.

O'Farrell, T. J., & Fals-Stewart, W. (2000). Behavioral couples therapy for alcoholism and drug abuse. *Journal of Substance Abuse Treatment, 18*(1), 51–54.

O'Farrell, T. J., & Feehan, M. (1999). Alcohol treatment and the family: Do family and individual treatments for alcoholics adults have preventive effects for children? *Journal of Studies on Alcohol* (Suppl. 13), 125–129.

O'Farrell, T. J., & Murphy, C. M. (1995). Marital violence before and after alcoholism treatment. *Journal of Consulting and Clinical Psychology, 63*(2), 256–262.

O'Farrell, T. J., & Rotunda, R. J. (1997). Couples interventions and alcohol abuse. In W. K. Halford, & H. J. Markman (Eds.), *Clinical handbook of marriage and couples interventions* (pp. 555–588). Chichester, England: Wiley.

O'Farrell, T. J., Van Hutton, V., & Murphy, C. M. (1999). Domestic violence before and after alcoholism treatment: A two-year longitudinal study. *Journal of Studies on Alcohol, 60*(3), 317–321.

O'Leary, K. D., Vivian, D., & Malone J. (1992). Assessment of physical aggression against women in marriage: The need for multimodal assessment. *Behavioral Assessment, 14,* 5–14.

Pence, E., & Paymar, M. (1993). *Education groups for men who batter: The Duluth model.* New York: Springer.

Pence, E. L., & Shepard, M. F. (1999). An introduction: Developing a coordinated community response. In M. F. Shepard, & E. L. Pence (Eds.), *Coordinating community responses to domestic violence* (pp. 3–23). Thousand Oaks, CA: Sage.

Peterson, L., & Calhoun, K. (1995). On advancing behavior analysis in the treatment and prevention of battering: Commentary on Myers. *Journal of Applied Behavior Analysis, 28,* 509–514.

Rhodes, N. R., & McKenzie, E. B. (1998). Why do battered women stay?: Three decades of research. *Aggression and Violent Behavior, 3*(4), 391–406.

Rollstin, A. O., & Kern, J. M. (1998). Correlates of battered women's psychological distress: Severity of abuse and duration of the postabuse period. *Psychological Reports, 82,* 387–394.

Saunders, D. G. (1996). Interventions for men who batter: Do we know what works? *In Session: Psychotherapy in Practice, 2*(3), 81–93.

Schechter, S. (1982). *Women and male violence: The visions and struggles of the battered women's movement.* Boston: South End.

Shamai, M. (1996). Couple therapy with battered women and abusive men. In J. L. Edleson & Z. C. Eisikovits (Eds.), *Future interventions with battered women and their families* (pp. 201–215). Thousand Oaks, CA: Sage.

Shepard, M. F. (1999). Advocacy for battered women: Implications for a coordinated community response. In M. F. Shepard, & E. L. Pence (Eds.), *Coordinating community responses to domestic violence* (pp. 115–125). Thousand Oaks, CA: Sage.

Shepard, M. F., & Campbell, J. A. (1992). The abusive behavior inventory: A measure of psychological and physical abuse. *Journal of Interpersonal Violence, 7*(3), 291–305.

Sleutel, M. R. (1998). Women's experiences of abuse: A review of qualitative research. *Issues in Mental Health Nursing, 19,* 525–539.

Straus, M. A., & Gelles, R. J. (1990). How violent are American families? Estimates from the National

Family Violence Resurvey and other studies. In M. Straus & R. Gelles (Eds.), *Physical violence in American families: Risk factors and adaptations to violence in 8,145 families* (pp. 95–112). New Brunswick, NJ: Transaction.

Sullivan, C. M., & Bybee, D. I. (1999). Reducing violence using community-based advocacy for women with abusive partners. *Journal of Consulting and Clinical Psychology, 67*(1), 43–53.

Tjaden, P., & Thoennes, N. (1998). *Stalking in America: Findings from the National Violence Against Women Survey*. Washington, DC: National Institute of Justice, U.S. Department of Justice.

Weaver, T. L., & Clum, G. A. (1995). Psychological distress associated with interpersonal violence: A meta-analysis. *Clinical Psychology Review, 15*(2), 115–140.

Whalen, M. (1996). *Counseling to end violence against women*. Thousand Oaks, CA: Sage.

Whatley, M. A. (1993). For better or worse: The case of marital rape. *Violence and Victims, 8*(1), 29–39.

Wileman, R., & Wileman, B. (1995). Towards balancing power in domestic violence relationships. *Australian and New Zealand Journal of Family Therapy, 16*(4), 165–176.

Yllo, K. A. (1993). Through a feminist lens: Gender, power, and violence. In. R. J. Gelles, & D. R. Loseke (Eds.), *Current Controversies on Family Violence* (pp. 47–62). Newbury Park, CA: Sage.

CHAPTER

Caroline Easton
Rajita Sinha

Treating the Addicted Male Batterer: Promising Directions for Dual-Focused Programming

Substance use and family violence problems commonly co-occur, and constitute a major public health issue that is being encountered throughout criminal justice and mental health systems. Rates of co-occurring substance abuse and domestic violence are high, ranging from 40%–92% across studies (Bennett & Lawson, 1994; Brookoff, O'Brien, Cook, Thompson, & Williams, 1997; Easton, Suzanne, & Sinha, 2000a, 2000b; Wekerle & Wall, this volume; Wilt & Olson, 1996). For example, Davidovich (1990) reported that 60% of batterers were intoxicated during their assault, and 70% were under the influence of both drugs and alcohol during their violent episode. A recent study by Brookoff et al. (1997) showed that 92% of assailants used alcohol or drugs on the day of the domestic violence assault, 44% had prior arrests for charges related to violence, and 72% had arrests related to substance use. Thus, the base rates for substance-related problems among batterers are quite high.

Further, studies suggest that substance use may be related to the severity of the domestic violence episode. Holtzworth-Munroe and Stuart (1994) found that alcohol and drug use was highest among a moderate to highly violent group of batterers. Also, Rivera and colleagues (1997) found that alcohol and illicit drug abuse was related to an increased risk of violent death in the home. In an attempt to understand the relationship between substance use and severity of violence, it becomes important to understand the type and amounts of substance being used. In a number of domestic violence cases, it has been noted that more than one substance is being abused among batterers. Severe physical violence has been associated with drug abuse and a dual problem with alcohol and drug abuse (Roberts, 1988). Miller (1990) reported that the combination of both alcohol and drug abuse was more predictive of domestic violence than alcohol alone.

It is important to thoroughly assess all the different substances being abused among batterers, both in combination and alone. A number of researchers have assessed whether

Portions of the work reported here were supported by a grant awarded to Caroline Easton by the Donaghue Foundation.

a particular type of substance triggers or exacerbates aggression. For example, research-ers have shown a specific association between alcohol and aggression (Badawy, 1998; Chermack & Giancola, 1997; Giancola & Zeichner, 1997; Hoaken, Giancola, & Pihl, 1998; Lee & Weinstein, 1997; Pihl & LeMarquand, 1998; van Erp & Miczerk, 1997) and that the consumption of an intoxicating dose of alcohol increases the likelihood of violent behav-ior (Pihl & Hoaken, this volume; Pihl & LeMarquand, 1998). Current literature findings indicate that alcohol leads to heightened aggression (Bushman, 1997; van Erp & Miczek, 1997) and violent crime (Zhang, Wieczorek, & Welte, 1997). Further, specific psychoactive drugs have also been associated with physical violence. For example, Tardiff and colleagues (1997) found that heroin and cocaine are linked to physical aggression. Most recently, withdrawal from chronic marijuana use has been shown to increase aggressive behavior (Kouri, Pope, & Lukas, 1999).

Despite this overlap between substance abuse and domestic violence, well-coordinated or integrated treatment services for both violence problems and substance abuse in batterers are rare. Presently, when batterers are arrested on violence charges, substance abuse is often not thoroughly assessed. When it is detected, individuals are sent to separate treat-ment agencies for substance abuse and domestic violence treatment, with little coordina-tion or communication between services (Bennett & Lawson, 1994).

It should be noted that a common theme throughout the various treatment facilities is that batterer treatment is forced: Court-mandated batterers account for the majority of clients attending battering programs. Further, any batterer intervention may be more prop-erly regarded as a public safety program, where the need is for on-going monitoring of abusive behavior and victim safety. Otherwise, such programs run the risk of engender-ing a "safe haven" for perpetrators (Healey, Smith, & O'Sullivan, 1998). This also raises an important issue about the batterer's level of motivation to change his behaviors with re-spect to internal (i.e., self-esteem, pride, etc.) versus external (i.e., avoiding legal fines, incarceration) motivators. For example, as noted above, perpetrators are usually court-mandated to treatment and, from our clinical experience, many of these individuals have clear external, but questionable internal, motivations for change. The growing literature on bringing about behavior change suggests that increasing internal motivation is more effective in facilitating behavior change (DiClemente, 1999; Miller, 1998; Prochaska, DiClemente, & Norcross, 1997). However, there is little empirical evidence that such mo-tivational approaches can help a perpetrator change their behavior (Daniels & Murphy, 1997; Easton et al., 2000a). There remains a dire need to understand who male batterers are in terms of not only their violence and legal histories, but also with regard to their psychiatric status, including substance abuse and dependence, within the context of what brings the batterer to treatment.

☐ Criminal Justice Issues Affecting Batterer Interventions

One of the main obstacles to understanding and preventing domestic violence is the lack of a uniform set of definitions. The mental health and legal professions, for example, have differing definitions of what constitutes domestic violence, who the participants are, and what kinds of services they need. Although there are many agencies and fields of study that specialize in domestic violence, the definitions that follow target the two major ser-vice professions—the legal and mental health professions.

Within the mental health profession, domestic violence is defined as the use of emo-tional, psychological, sexual, or physical force by one family member or intimate partner to control the other. Violence is verbal, emotional, and physical behaviors that invoke fear in or serve to control the victim. These include: property damage; maiming or killing pets; forced sex; and threats, slapping, punching, kicking, choking, burning, stabbing, shooting, and killing victims (Alpert, Cohen, & Sege, 1997).

The legal profession distinguishes family violence that is directed towards children and elders from domestic violence from violence that is directed toward the intimate partner (spouse, former spouse, partner, former partner) (Robinson, 1997). Unlike the mental health field, the legal profession does not recognize economic control or psychological abuse as a form of domestic abuse (Robinson, 1997). However, regardless of differences in the definitions of domestic violence between the mental health and legal professions, some common legal definitions for battering occur across states. For example, some legal definitions recognize harassment, assault and battery, kidnapping, breaking and entering, destruction of property, sexual assault, stalking, terrorism, or damage to property as forms of domestic violence (Healey et al., 1998). Other legal definitions describe intimate relationships as involving current or former spouses, boyfriends, or girlfriends.

The criminal acts in spouse abuse can include murder, rape, sexual assault, robbery, aggravated assault, and simple assault (Rennison & Welchans, 2000). Data from the Bureau of Justice Statistics (Rennison & Welchans, 2000) showed that 65% of all intimate partner violence against women was a simple assault, that is, an attack without a weapon that results with either no injury or minor injuries such as black eyes, bruises, cuts, scratches, or swelling. The data also showed that 16% of all intimate partner violence against women involved aggravated assault, 12% robbery, and 7% rape or sexual assault against women. In 1998, intimate partner homicides accounted for 11% of all murders nationwide. Of the persons murdered by intimate partners, 72% were women. Comparable rates have been found for police-reported data in Canada (e.g., 75% common assault; 14% assault with a weapon or causing bodily harm and aggravated assault; 7% criminal harassment or stalking; and 88% of spousal assault victims were women; Statistics Canada, 1999).

As discussed above, domestic violence is defined in a number of ways between and among professions. It should be noted that state laws covering domestic violence-related crimes vary considerably. It may be too much to expect all states to enact the same laws on domestic violence crimes. However, a standard definition for domestic violence-related behaviors and crimes should be implemented in both the mental health care and service professions, as it may help improve assessment and delivery of treatment. It has been shown that providing comprehensive, mandated training in domestic violence-related issues is effective in improving the mental health and legal professions' responses to domestic violence (Marwick, 1994; Robinson, 1997). Although more comprehensive training is needed among the mental health and legal professions, there are specific domestic violence policies and procedures that must be followed when there is an alleged domestic violence offense. In the United States, federal regulations have been established to prosecute the offenders and protect the victims.

☐ Domestic Violence Legislation

The Violence Against Women Act (VAWA), a United States civil rights statute, was passed in 1994 and is cited as Title IV of the Violent Crime Control and Law Enforcement Act (Public Law 103-322). This act was intended to promote a well-coordinated criminal justice system response to violent crimes against women, including domestic violence, sexual assault, and stalking. The VAWA was developed specifically to address and eradicate violence against women. In the past, violence against women, particularly abuse by partners or intimates, was ignored by the legal system. It has only been in the past two decades, largely because of the women's movement, that society has begun to condemn such behavior. In fact, over the past several years, domestic violence has moved from a private family matter to the center of public debate. However, the National Organization for Women (NOW) and the National Task Force on Violence Against Women noted many areas that needed further developing and funding requirements to help stop violence against women.

NOW and the National Task Force on Violence Against Women played an instrumental role in developing and backing a major expansion of the 1994 Violence Against Women Act (VAWA), which was introduced to Congress in 1998. The VAWA II was passed in 2000, and it is now known as the Victims of Trafficking and Violence Prevention Act of 2000. It is divided into two parts: (1) the Trafficking Victims Protection Act of 2000, and (2) the Violence Against Women Act of 2000. The Trafficking Protection Act of 2000 was developed in order to monitor and combat trafficking. Trafficking pertains to persons who are trafficked into the international sex trade. It involves sexual exploitation of persons related to prostitution, pornography, and sex tourism. The Violence Against Women Act of 2000 was developed in order to strengthen law enforcement as a method to reduce violence against women. This act also contains grants that encourage arrest policies, child abuse enforcement, efforts to stop rural domestic violence, and policies to strengthen services to victims of violence (i.e., legal assistance to victims, shelter services and transitional housing assistance, further development of a national domestic violence hotline, enhancing protections for older and disabled women from domestic violence and sexual assault). This act also contains funds to help limit the effects of violence on children, as well as educational and training initiatives to combat violence against women.

It is largely pursuant to the VAWA that the courts are allowed to implement and enforce protective orders that ensure the protection of the victim and the victim's family. This regulation, as it pertains to protective orders, is valid and enforceable in all 50 states, any territory or possession of the United States, the District of Columbia, the Commonwealth of Puerto Rico, and tribal lands (Connecticut General Statutes 46b-15, 1999). Although there may be subtle differences in state laws regarding the preliminary investigation procedures and sentencing requirements, it should be the responsibility of the clinicians and staff to familiarize themselves with their own state laws. This is important for a number of reasons. First, substance abuse treatment providers should be familiar with all federal, state, and local regulations when providing services to battered women and batterers. Second, treatment providers are obligated by law to report domestic violence, since it relates to suspected child abuse and neglect. Third, treatment providers must know the policies and procedures regarding confidentiality regulations when discussing information with courts, lawyers, or court officials without their client's permission. Fourth, it is important for providers to be familiar with domestic violence policies and procedures in order to be able to offer appropriate services and levels of care for individuals with domestic violence-related problems. Clinicians who familiarize themselves with domestic violence regulations within the context of treatment and the criminal justice system will help facilitate proper linkage between agencies.

☐ Diversion Programs and Conditions of Probation

The following section is provided to help readers understand how batterers surface within treatment agencies and how substance use is factored into the equation. It is fair to say that most batterers are not self-referred, but rather emerge within treatment facilities as a function of the legal system. Most courts offer presentencing programs, diversion programs, or probation. Most of these programs are structurally similar, proceeding from intake through assessment, victim contact, group treatment, and completion. However, most programs differ with regard to their theoretical approaches to domestic violence.

It is important to describe what presentencing or diversion programs are. A deferred prosecution agreement (DPA), sometimes known as a presentence suspension program, can occur if: (1) the charge is a misdemeanor, (2) there is no physical injury, or only a minor injury, (3) the defendant is a first time offender, (4) the defendant has no prior criminal record, (5) there was no use or threat of use of a weapon, and (6) and the defendant does not have a history of contact with law enforcement for domestic violence. There may be input from the victim as to the appropriateness of a deferred prosecution for the offender, or whether the defendant is likely to voluntarily engage in counseling. It should be noted that input from the victim is not necessarily a standard procedure. In the state of Connecticut, for example, if the victim drops the domestic violence charge, the state will pick up the case and continue to prosecute. At any rate, DPAs should be in writing and signed by the district attorney, staff, and the defendant (if applicable). The defendant admits, in writing, all elements of the crime charged, and agrees to participate in therapy or community programs.

This does not, however, necessarily specify whether the therapy is anger management alone, substance abuse treatment alone, or some combination of the two. If the arrest was specifically for domestic violence, offenders are often sent to anger management programs because substance abuse or dependency problems were not thoroughly assessed, if assessed at all. Likewise, if a substance abuser is arrested on a drug charge, domestic violence issues are not assessed and, therefore, it is likely that the offender receives only substance abuse treatment.

Most courts require an offender of domestic violence to receive anger management as a stipulation of their presentence agreement or a condition of their probation (for more serious offenders). However, substance abuse treatment is often neglected as a stipulation by the court. If a substance abuser is arrested on a drug charge and is stipulated to substance abuse treatment and assessment reveals that they are a perpetrator of domestic violence, anger management is not necessarily required as a function of their probation or diversion program. Most presentence diversion programs or divisions of probation will accept dual-focused programs and have, in our experience, voiced enthusiasm to the concept. It has been noted that batterers are barely motivated to attend one treatment program, let alone two separate programs (Colllins, Kroutil, Roland, & Moore-Gurrera, 1997; Easton et al., 2000a). From a practical and theoretical standpoint, dual-focused programs that treat both aggressive behaviors and substance use in an integrated way, acknowledging that negative mood states can trigger substance use, and that substance use can trigger aggression, appear to offer a promising treatment strategy for the future. Examples of such programs are described in the following section that discusses treatment models for batterers.

☐ Treatment Compliance and Treatment Outcome

The court or probation officer monitors compliance, and the district attorney resumes prosecution if the defendant fails to meet or comply with any condition of the DPA. Also, the court will dismiss, without prejudice, any charge that was subject to the agreement of the completion of the DPA, unless prosecution has been resumed. The courts often require some form of documentation by the treatment facilities that the batterers have completed the program. However, it should be noted that there is no gold standard to categorize treatment success for batterers. Based on clinical practice, generally, treatment facilities send letters stating that the batterer "successfully completed treatment." This may carry very different meanings. For example, successfully completing treatment can mean any of the following: had good attendance (9 out of 10 sessions), participated in group, victims reported that violence had stopped, the defendant/offender had abstained from substance use and violent behaviors, or no further arrests have been incurred. There is no standard, structured, or objective criteria required and, at present, research is lacking in this area of inquiry. Research evaluating batterer interventions, with special attention to the development of discharge criteria (Gondolf, 1995, 1997), has challenged the use of clinical judgment and other forms of treatment outcome criteria. Gondolf (1995) developed a 10-item set of discharge criteria: attendance (e.g., arrives at group on time, attends), nonviolence (e.g., has not abused partner, no threats), sobriety (e.g., no abuse of alcohol or drugs), acceptance (e.g., admits to violence), using techniques (e.g., takes steps to avoid violence), help-seeking (e.g., seeks information from others, open to referrals), process conscious (e.g., lets others speak one at a time), actively engaged (e.g., maintains eye contact, speaks with feelings), self-disclosure (e.g., reveals feelings about self), and uses sensitive language (e.g., respectful to partner, nonsexist language). Such recommendations for more systematic set of discharge criteria may be useful in batterer programs. There are, however, some limitations with presentencing, or diversion programs. These include:

1. *Lack of licensed/credentialled staff.* Designated agencies can be facilities that are provided within the criminal justice system or by mental health agencies. Either one of these systems can have staff that lack licenses and necessary credentials. Second, the staff often lack training in the very specialty areas that are being discussed, namely domestic violence and addiction.
2. *Court and mental health agencies have large caseloads.* Diversion programs and probation officers often have large caseloads, making it difficult to track and correspond with the treatment agencies. Likewise, clinicians at the treatment facilities often have increased caseloads, creating challenges for a timely consultation with court and probation officials.
3. *There is a lack of any standard or objective treatment outcome measure for domestic violence offenders.* Treatment outcome for batterers can be defined in a number of ways. For example, a batterer may successfully attend all of his 10 required sessions, but never participate in self-disclosure, be still drinking alcohol, and be aggressive at home, yet receive a letter stating he successfully completed anger management. Clearly, single criterion outcome or outcomes that do not reflect the batterer's pattern of responding may be problematic.
4. *Substance use is often not thoroughly assessed among domestic violence offenders.* Likewise, domestic violence is often not assessed among substance abusers. There should be a comprehensive psychiatric evaluation that assesses substance use, domestic violence issues, and any co-occurring psychiatric condition (depression, anxiety disorders, psychosis, personality disorders). This should be a requirement in order to match batterers to the appropriate level of care, targeting co-occurring disorders.
5. *There is no mandated dual track for substance using domestic violence offenders.* If an offender of domestic violence has a co-occurring substance dependency disorder, the offender may be referred to a substance abuse program, but it may or may not be a part of their DPA. When a batterer is assessed to determine whether substance abuse services are needed, this assessment is often done separately, as opposed to simultaneously assessing both anger management and substance dependency needs.

☐ Policies Regarding Substance Use at the Time of an Alleged Offense

Just as there are specific policies and laws regarding domestic violence offenses, some states have laws that pertain to the use of alcohol or drugs at the time of the alleged offense. It is important for treatment providers to be familiar with policies regarding substance abuse treatment for the same reasons that were listed in the policy and procedures section for domestic violence. For example, in the state of Connecticut, there is a specific statute (17a-694) that was established in 1990 to divert appropriate individuals away from the division of corrections to substance abuse treatment. When an individual commits an offense and is arrested, it is the judge's discretion to order a substance dependency evaluation. Such a court-ordered evaluation will occur if the court (either the defendant's lawyer, the judge, or the prosecuting attorney) suspects that the defendant has a problem with substances and that substance use was related to the offense committed.

In Connecticut, for example, this current statutory authority resides in Connecticut General Statutes (CGS 17a-694 to 17a-701). There are two specific evaluations: (1) Pretrial evaluations (suspension of prosecution) and (2) Postconviction evaluations (modification of sentencing). This statute requires that the following clinical findings be made: (1) the defendant was substance-dependent (meeting DSM-IV criteria [The American Psychiatric Association, 1994], as determined by a licensed social worker or psychologist) at the time of the alleged offense, (2) the defendant is in need of and will likely benefit from treatment, (3) the type of treatment, as well as the duration of care [there is no length of stay requirement in the Connecticut statute (17a-694)], location of care [which can be inpatient, intensive outpatient (5 days per week) or standard outpatient (1–3 days per week)], and (4) the level of treatment must be specified. In the case of the Postconviction evaluations, the findings must also include the relationship between substance dependency and the crime. After the defendant is evaluated by a licensed psychologist or social worker, a report is sent to the court. The judge presiding may or may not support a recommendation for treatment. In any case, there is a high co-occurrence for substance dependency issues and family violence but, at present, the Connecticut State Law treats substance-related offenses and domestic violence offenses as separate issues. Further investigation is needed regarding the relationship between integrated treatment programs for offenders with co-occurring substance dependency problems and how current legislation manages this dual problem. This Connecticut statute is very specific to substance dependency at the time of the alleged offense. This law was written as an attempt to divert substance users to treatment. It was not driven by research, but, rather, it was developed by a task force review of the system. As noted above, however, it would be extremely important to include programming that targets substance-using domestic violence offenders. A separate statute may be needed to mandate substance-using domestic violence offenders to the appropriate level of care. This would need to be properly evaluated by licensed staff who have a specialization in substance use and domestic violence areas.

☐ Treatment Models for Male Batterers

To date, there have been a limited number of treatment models that have been developed for male batterers, and even rarer is the batterer program that takes into account substance abuse. Two dual-focused programs are described here: (1) Dade County's Integrated Domestic Violence Model, and (2) The Substance Abuse Treatment Unit's Substance Abuse-Domestic Violence (SATU-SADV) Program.

Dade County's Integrated Domestic Violence Model (Goldkamp, Weiland, Collins, & White, 1996)

This program was a two phase project in which a specialized treatment was implemented with Dade County's Domestic Violence Court in Florida. It is based on the Duluth Psychoeducational Model (Pence & Paymer, 1993) in which aggression and anger directed at spouses are conceptualized as stemming from issues with power and control. The main task in counseling is, therefore, to alter the batterer's power-abusive interactional style towards a more egalitarian stance. This model, however, is limited to violence programming; substance use and abuse is not a target of this intervention model. In the Dade County Integrated Domestic Violence Model, misdemeanor divertees and probationers were ordered to treatment and randomly assigned to one of two conditions: (1) regular treatment process (n = 140) (which included batterer and substance abuse treatment in separate programs, as separate issues), or (2) a new integrated treatment program (n = 210) (which integrated batterer and substance abuse treatment) tailored to treat both co-occurring problems at one site, and to address these problems as interrelated.

The treatment experiment found three significant findings. Clients in the integrated treatment approach were more likely than those in the regular treatment process (i.e., separate batterer and substance abuse treatments) to begin treatment (i.e., to attend at least one session), stay in treatment for one month or more, and show a lower reoffense rate toward the same victim at a seven month follow-up. While these results speak to treatment adherence and potential benefits associated with an integrated program, it was limited to the extent that the theoretical framework was underarticulated and a thorough evaluation of comorbid psychopathology was not apparent. Furthermore, empirical support for the efficacy of interventions based on the Duluth Model remains elusive, despite 20 years of implementation (Hoff, 1999; Lee & Weinstein, 1997). Positively, however, this program followed the Drug Court Model, using urine toxicology screens to monitor substance use, with the judge and the courtroom having a more "hands on" involvement in the treatment process. For example, communication between treatment and judicial staff on the client's attendance and substance use occurred on an ongoing basis.

The Substance Abuse Treatment Unit's Substance Abuse-Domestic Violence Program (SATU-SADV Model): An Integrated Model of Treatment for Violence and Substance Abuse among Male Batterers

The SATU-SADV model targets and treats substance use and violence in an integrated way. Our model incorporates aspects of the Dade County's Integrated Domestic Violence Model program (Goldkamp, Weiland, Collins, & White, 1996). Specifically, the Duluth Model program serves as a basis for addressing violence-specific intervention targets (e.g., understanding and defining relationship violence). Additionally, a cognitive-behavioral coping skills approach (Kadden et al., 1995; Monti et al., 1990; Monti, Abrams, Kadden, & Cooney, 1989), that has been used to target substance abuse-related issues, serves as the theoretical framework and mode of intervention for our program. Cognitive-behavioral coping skills intervention models are grounded in social learning theory (for a discussion, see also Wall & McKee, this volume) and, accordingly, conceptualize alcohol consumption as a maladaptive means of coping. In such skills training programs, which typically consist of 12 sessions, there is a focus on ameliorating skill deficits, and identifying and coping with high-risk situations associated with relapse, including interpersonal difficulties and intrapersonal distress (e.g., negative mood states such as anger, agitation, depression, etc.). Additionally, interventions are designed to develop active behavioral and cognitive general coping strategies in order to circumvent the likelihood that individuals rely on alcohol as a means of coping with stress. Empirical support for a social learning theory conceptualization of alcohol abuse is well substantiated (for reviews, see Abrams & Niaura, 1987; Maisto, Carey, & Bradizza, 1999). Moreover, validated treatment manuals exist to support a standardized delivery of treatment that has been shown to be effective with alcohol-dependent and cocaine-dependent populations (Carroll, 1998; Carroll et al., 1998; Project MATCH Research Group, 1997). Given that most of our clients are alcohol-dependent, a cognitive-behavioral coping skills approach is particularly well suited for this population of batterers. Although grounded in social learning theory and modeled after cognitive-behavioral coping skill intervention approaches, our program differs in so far as both substance use and violent behaviors are targeted in each session, with a particular focus on engendering adaptive coping skills as adaptive alternatives to substance use and spouse-directed aggressive behaviors.

The following sections overview the SATU-SADV program. Specifically, the program's theoretical foundation and its general approach and format are presented. Next, treatment entry, compliance strategies, and termination procedures are described (for a condensed session by session summary of the SATU-SADV program, please refer to Table 13.1). Finally, preliminary evidence suggesting the promising nature of this dual program are presented.

General Overview of SATU-SADV Program.   As noted, we have adapted the Project MATCH manual (Project Match Research Group, 1997) to treat our population of batterers. Project MATCH was predicated on the notion that patient-treatment matching is an important determinant of outcome, such that improved efficacy would be evident when treatment targets patient-specific needs and characteristics. Following this rationale, we selected specific Project MATCH sessions that, in our view, suited characteristics of domestic violence offenders. These characteristics include: awareness of anger, managing anger, coping with negative mood states, problems with communication skills, problem solving skills, managing criticism, emergency planning, and family involvement. Across sessions, a variety of intervention strategies, including psychotherapy, reinforcing positive behavioral change, behavioral contracting, relapse prevention, and teaching healthy communication skills are employed for both substance use and violence. The program, which is carried out over 12 sessions, is an interactive group format. Sessions, lasting 1.5 hours, are conducted in a style that is consistent with behavioral training principles such that prosocial, nonaggressive, and drug-free behaviors are positively reinforced, with a view towards extinguishing antisocial, aggressive, and deviant verbal and nonverbal behaviors. Clients are given homework assignments which include practicing newly learned skills. Internal or external obstacles in carrying out homework assignments are assessed, and a behavioral analysis is conducted in order to generate solutions in overcoming such barriers.

Treatment Entry.   Batterers enter our treatment program either in response to a stipulation by the courts or by probation. One way to facilitate a smooth referral process and to increase linkages to the proper service settings when a domestic violence docket is involved or when a case is being considered for a DPA is to provide a comprehensive evaluation on the day their case is being decided. Our program completes such an evaluation, where collateral contacts (e.g., victim reports) are sought (given the typical underreporting of domestic violence activities by batterers). In this evaluation process, informed consents

(*text continues on page 290*)

TABLE 13.1. The substance abuse treatment unit's substance abuse-domestic violence program (SATU SADV model): An integrated model of treatment for violence and substance abuse among male batterers

Session Title	Goal of Treatment	Topic of Discussion	Specific Intervention
Introduction	Help client take responsibility for behaviors (substance use and violence) that led him to treatment	Understanding the link between substance use and violence	Clients introduce themselves, discuss their problem substance and their domestic violence charge. Self-disclosure and steps toward taking responsibility are reinforced
Awareness of Violent Behaviors & Substance Use	Identify clients' aggressive behaviors in their relationships	Understanding the types of violence (physical, verbal, psychological, property damage, and sexual) & the cycle of violence. Discussion of where substance use occurs in cycle of violence	Each group member is reinforced for taking responsibility and self-disclosing aggressive behaviors that they exhibited. Cycle of violence is illustrated
Coping with Cravings & Negative Mood States	Identify high risk situations and triggers that lead to substance use and/or aggressive behaviors. Promote self-efficacy	Coping with cravings and negative mood states (distracting activities, time outs, anger cool downs, supportive others)	Self-monitors are administered. Each group member completes a behavioral record of what their triggers for substance use and aggression were/are. Group discusses their records in session. Positive behaviors are reinforced in session
Managing Anger & Negative Mood States (Anxiety, Depression, Hostility)	Identify negative thoughts and feeling prior to substance use and aggressive urges; utilize alternative adaptive behaviors	Alternative coping behaviors to substitute for maladaptive behaviors (substance use and violent behaviors)	Each group member discusses what his thoughts, feeling, and physical sensations are prior to drug use and/or aggression. Alternative coping skills are provided and discussed
Communication Skills	Identify maladaptive communication styles and utilize assertive style and reflective listening skills	Discussion of assertive, aggressive, passive, and passive-aggressive styles of communicating	Role plays are performed for each communication style and each group member role plays an experience from their relationship

(Continued)

TABLE 13.1. Continued

Session Title	Goal of Treatment	Topic of Discussion	Specific Intervention
Family History of Substance Use & Violence: Repeat or Repair	Identify patterns of substance use and violent behaviors within one's family	Discussion of how group members can "repeat or repair" substance use or violence within their own families. Emphasis on positive behavior change and coping skills	Genograms (family map) are created for each group member with emphasis on family history of substance use, domestic violence, & communication styles
Effects of Substance Use & Violence on Children	Create an awareness of how substance use and violence affects client's own children	Effects of substance use and violence on children are highlighted with an emphasis on the fact that the children are at risk for mental health, substance use, and violent behavioral problems.	Hand-outs are distributed on maladaptive behaviors that children exhibit from the effects of substance use and violence. Members are reinforced for positive self-disclosure
Problem Solving Skills	Help clients recognize, identify, and cope with problems	Problem solving skills are introduced for both substance use and anger	Each group member discusses a current problem. Each member brainstorms alternative ways to solve the problem other than with substance use or violence
Managing Criticism	Help clients recognize the difference between constructive and destructive criticism	Develop skills to cope with criticism	Group members role play ways to respond to both constructive and destructive criticism. Positive responses are reinforced. Examples from their relationships are elicited and discussed.
Managing Stress	Identify stressors and utilize healthy coping skills	Coping with stress	Each group member discusses current stressors. Relaxation training is discussed and alternative coping skills (time outs, cools downs, pleasant activities) are provided
Emergency Planning: Lapse	Help clients develop a personal emergency plan to cope with a high risk situation or a lapse	Development of personal emergency plan	Each group member develops and discusses with the group their own personal emergency plan (leaving the situation, put off a decision or reaction, call supportive others, emergency list of numbers)

(Continued)

TABLE 13.1. Continued

Session Title	Goal of Treatment	Topic of Discussion	Specific Intervention
Promoting Positive Social Support Systems	Promote self-efficacy and reinforce skills acquired	Developing & continuing positive sober support networks networks	Each group member discusses what specifically they learned from group, a certificate of completion is administered, additional referrals & 12 step/AA/ NA/CA meeting schedules are administered.

*In addition to the weekly sessions, breathalyzers and supervised urine toxicology screens are obtained twice a week.

for sharing information are obtained from the batterer's partner and court documents. Also, supervised urine toxicology screens and breathalyzer assessments are conducted.

There is a growing body of literature indicating that personality factors, psychiatric problems, and a family history of trauma often co-occur among batterers. The co-occurring psychological problems most typically involve personality (Flett & Hewitt, this volume; Hamberger & Hastings, 1986; Hastings & Hamberger, 1988) and affective (Bersani, Chen, Pendelton, & Denton, 1992; Gondolf, 1985) disorders. Additionally, it has been shown that partner assaultive men are more likely to report childhood histories of trauma such as physical abuse (Flett & Hewitt, this volume; Murphy, Myer, & O'Leary, 1993). Further, research has shown that males who witnessed abuse as children are more likely to engage in partner abuse (Hastings & Hamberger, 1988; Hotaling & Sugarman, 1986). It is similarly well established that individuals with substance use disorders often have co-occurring psychopathology, such as depression, anxiety, and personality disorders (Caton, Gralnick, Bender, & Simon, 1989; Greenfield, Weiss, & Tohen, 1995; Ries & Ellingson, 1990). These additional mental health problems can further complicate and predispose individuals to family violence. For example, Keller (1996) found that alcohol and drug abuse, antisocial personality disorder, and depression are associated with increased risk of male violence in the home. Easton and colleagues (2000b) found that clients in substance abuse treatment with a history of physical violence had significantly more cocaine and alcohol-related problems, as well as depressive symptomatology. Given these findings, a thorough evaluation is needed in order to determine suitability and readiness for treatment.

In our program, a clinical diagnostic interview, assessing for comorbid Axis I and Axis II DSM-IV disorders (American Psychiatric Association, 1994), and the need for additional treatment referrals is completed. Our program is tailored to treat substance using domestic violence offenders without any major Axis I (mood disorders, anxiety disorders, psychosis) or Axis II (personality disorders, mental retardation) disorders. Clients are admitted to our program if they: (1) are not in need of detoxification or inpatient treatment, (2) do not have a major Axis I disorder (e.g., Psychotic or Bipolar Disorder), or (3) do not suffer from a major medical illness with complications. Our program is offered on a sliding fee scale that is determined by clients' income levels. Further, while participants in our studies pay fees for service, they are remunerated for their research participation.

As standard procedure in our program, clinicians obtain informed consent from the patient to talk with their significant others regarding the offender's substance use and domestic violence-related problems. Partners are administered the Revised Conflict Tactic Scale (CTS2; Straus, Hamby, Boney-McCoy, & Sugarman, 1996), which is a self-report instrument designed to assess specific types of partner violence. Using the Timeline Follow-Back (TFB) procedure (Sobell, Sobell, Leo, & Cancil, 1988), partners are administered a substance use timeline schedule in order to provide information about batterer's substance use. During this data collection victim treatment issues may arise, but our program does not provide direct services to victims. Rather, our standard practice is to provide women with numbers of appropriate treatment agencies. A caveat to obtaining information from batterer's partners is that batterers may be guarded about disclosing their partner contact information when restraining orders are in place. Also, batterers may be without a partner at the time of treatment entry. In our preliminary research, approximately 50% of the batterers who were arrested for physical assault and referred to treatment were residing with their partners (Easton et al., 2000a).

Encouraging Treatment Compliance.

The format of our program, as well as how it is overviewed to clients, was designed to engage individuals and, thus, increase compliance. In an effort to reduce the possibility that clients terminate their involvement, treatment goals are mutually determined. We also emphasize the relatively short-term nature of the program by using metaphoric language (e.g., running a mile versus a marathon) to support realistic goal-setting. From our experience and based on the existing literature (Miller, 1998), confrontational strategies are often countertherapeutic. Admittedly, in working with batterers, one must be mindful of the possibility that individuals may appear compliant so as to avoid further negative consequences (i.e., avoid incarceration, legal fines, etc.). It is important, however, to encourage offenders to be forthcoming in order to facilitate actual change. This is a difficult task to juggle when treatment facilities are so closely linked with their referral sources, and the offenders start viewing treatment as an arm of the court. Clearly, a confidential setting that facilitates disclosure seems a necessary condition in order to effect behavior change. Despite our ongoing efforts, we still encounter clients who are not motivated to change and also refuse treatment, despite being court-mandated. Although clients sign a release of information to obtain and exchange data with collaterals (the court) and we send our report to the court, they may have legal council that helps them avoid treatment noncompliance negative consequences.

Exit Criteria, Termination, and Referrals.

Our program requires the following three exit criteria: (1) completion of at least 10 sessions, (2) participation and self-disclosure during group sessions, and (3) abstinence from alcohol, drugs, and violence. In order to evaluate whether clients meet these criteria, their motivation to change is assessed via role play activities and homework assignments (i.e. reviewing daily self-monitoring records involving urges to either use substances or lose control). Weekly supervised urine toxicology screens, urine analyses, and collateral data collection regarding substance use and violence also are obtained. If all three criteria are met, a brief letter confirming this is forwarded to the court. Graduates of the problem are asked to share their treatment experiences and to discuss skills they have learned as a result. During these discussions, members give feedback to one another. At the cessation of the program, individuals receive graduation certificates and given a handout of additional referrals and intervention programs (e.g., couples treatment, family therapy, individual therapy, AA and NA 12-step support meetings, vocational services) available within the district or region they reside. All graduates are encouraged to continue treatment.

Assessing the Effectiveness of the SATU-SADV Program: Preliminary Data. Despite being in its early stage of development, preliminary data indicate that our program is a promising approach to treating alcohol-dependent, male batterers. Specifically, we have found that the SATU-SADV model effectively enhances participants' motivation for change, improves their treatment compliance, and decreases male batterers' anger and levels of alcohol consumption. For example, in one preliminary study (Easton et al., 2000a), we assessed the prevalence of substance abuse among male batterers and the impact of motivational enhancement techniques (MET; Miller, Zweben, DiClemente, & Rychtarik, 1995) on their motivation to change their co-occurring substance abuse. MET, which is designed to produce rapid, internally motivated change, is not intended to guide clients step-by-step throughout recovery. Rather, MET is based on a treatment strategy designed to mobilize the client's own resources. Typical elements of a session involve empathy, rolling with resistance, avoiding confrontation, reinforcing positive self-statements, pointing out discrepancies, and reinforcing self-efficacy. This study was conducted with male batterers attending a 10 session psychoeducational group that was modeled after the Duluth Program. At Week 9, during which substance abuse was the main topic of discussion, the MET intervention was implemented. The comparison group received a standard psychoeducational approach. Both groups were matched on all demographic, substance use, and legal characteristics. Not surprisingly, high rates of substance dependence (67%) and abuse (41%) were observed across both groups which had low, presession, motivation to change scores (the Readiness to Change Subscale of the SOCRATES; Miller & Tonigan, 1996). Following the session, however, the MET group demonstrated significantly elevated motivation to change scores. Unfortunately, not one member of the MET group signed up for a more thorough substance abuse evaluation or treatment when appointments were provided. Thus, while these male offenders did not actually take steps to change their substance use, the intervention was successful in facilitating thoughts and attitudes about behavior change. Behavior change may occur more readily if motivational techniques are incorporated as a standard procedure within each session of an integrated treatment model in conjunction with coping skills.

In a second study (Easton & Sinha, 2000), we examined treatment retention among court-referred, substance abusing domestic violence offenders attending the integrated treatment model versus standard substance abuse counseling. In this study, 29 male clients, with a domestic violence charge, were referred to outpatient substance abuse treatment. Sixteen of the clients were referred to the integrated SATU-SADV treatment group, while 13 received standard substance abuse counseling based on a 12-step support model. These groups did not differ with respect to age, education, racial composition, marital status, court referral status, depression scores (as assessed by the BDI; Beck, Ward, Mendelson, Mock, & Erdbaugh, 1971), alcohol-related problems (as assessed by the MAST; Selzer, 1971), primary drug of use, or drug toxicology screens. Results indicated that the offenders who participated in the integrated SATU-SADV treatment group attended significantly more sessions than those who received standard substance abuse counseling (13 versus 5 sessions for the integrated and standard programs, respectively). Additionally, participants in the integrated group demonstrated a decrease in self-report anger ratings, as well as the amount and frequency of alcohol use. Further investigation is ongoing to assess substance use and violence outcomes at 6 and 12 months posttreatment.

☐ Summary and Future Directions

Clearly, the prevalence of substance abuse among male batterers well exceeds that observed in the general population. While inroads have been made with respect to the enactment of legislation to promote a well-coordinated criminal justice system response to eradicate violence against women, and while there is growing awareness within the courts concerning the overlap between substance abuse and domestic violence, dual-focused programs for male batterers are rare. Preliminary data on the SATU-SADV program indicates that this is a promising approach for treating such dual problems. Such a novel approach, however, is very much in its infancy and much work remains to be done.

In terms of future directions, it would appear important to elucidate the essential ingredients (e.g., motivational interviewing, coping skills training, etc.) that facilitate change and reduce recidivism rates among substance-abusing domestic violence offenders. From a systemic perspective, it may be beneficial if both the victim and offender were willing to engage in separate treatment tracks that target both domestic violence and violence-related sequelae (e.g., PTSD symptomatology among victims) and substance use. Given that antidepressants that regulate serotonin levels in the brain have been shown to decrease anger and hostility levels (Van Praag, 1994), another future direction would be to explore when adjunctive pharmacotherapy could bolster the efficacy of dual-focused programs with offenders suffering from co-occurring depressive symptomatology. Future investigations of this nature may inform policy and procedures as they relate to the addiction–domestic violence treatment equation, namely validated treatment approaches that could be administered by trained professionals in a standardized manner.

☐ References

Abrams, D. B., & Niaura, R. S. (1987). Social learning theory. In H. T. Blane & K. E. Leonard (Eds.), *Psychological theories of drinking and alcoholism* (pp. 131–178). New York: Guilford.

Alpert, E. J., Cohen, S., & Sege, R. D. (1997). Family violence: An overview. *Academic Medicine*, 72(1 Suppl): S3–6.

American Psychiatric Association. (1994). *Diagnostic and statistical manual of mental disorders* (4th ed.). Washington, DC: Author.

Badawy, A. (1998). Alcohol, aggression and serotonin: Metabolic aspects. *Alcohol and Alcoholism, 33,* 66–72.

Beck, A., Ward, C., Mendelson, M., Mock, J., & Erdbaugh, J. (1971). An inventory for measuring depression. *Archives of General Psychiatry, 4,* 561–571.

Bennett, L., & Lawson, M. (1994). Barriers to cooperation between domestic-violence and substance-abuse programs. *Families in Society, 75,* 277–286.

Bersani, C., Chen, H., Pendelton, B., & Denton, R. (1992). Personality traits of convicted male batterers. *Journal of Family Violence, 7,* 123–134.

Brookoff, D., O'Brien, K., Cook, C., Thompson, T., & Williams, C. (1997). Characteristics of participants in domestic violence. Assessment at the scene of domestic assault. *Journal of the American Medical Association, 277,* 1369–1373.

Bushman, B. (1997). Effects of alcohol on human aggression. Validity of proposed explanations. *Recent Developments in Alcoholism, 13,* 227–243.

Carroll, K. (Ed.). (1998). *A cognitive-behavioral approach: Treating cocaine addiction.* NIH Publication 98-4308. Rockville, MD: National Institute on Drug Abuse.

Carroll, K. M., Connors, G. J., Cooney, N. L., DiClemente, C. C., Donovan, D. M., Longabaugh, R. L., Kadden, R. M., Rounsaville, B. J., Wirtz, P. W., & Zweben, A. (1998). Internal Validity of Project MATCH treatments: Discriminability and Integrity. *Journal of Consulting and Clinical Psychology, 66,* 290–303.

Caton, C., Gralnick, A., Bender, S., & Simon, R. (1989). Young chronic patients and substance abuse. *Hospital and Community Psychiatry, 40,* 1037–1040.

Chermack, S., & Giancola, P. (1997). The relation between alcohol and aggression: an integrated biopsychosocial conceptualization. *Clinical Psychology Review, 17,* 621–649.

Collins, J. J., Kroutil, L. A., Roland, E. J., & Moore-Gurrera, M. (1997). Issues in the linkage of alcohol and domestic violence services. *Recent Developments in Alcoholism, 13,* 387–405.

Connecticut General Statutes (CGS) (1999). 46b-15.

Connecticut General Statutes (CGS) (1999). 17a-694-17a-701.

Daniels, J. W., & Murphy, C. M. (1997). Stages and processes of change in batterers' treatment. *Cognitive and Behavioral Practice, 4*(1), 123–145.

Davidovich, J. (1990). Men who abuse their spouse: Social and psychological supports. *Journal of Offender Counseling and Service Rehabilitation, 15*, 27–44.

DiClemente, C.C. (1999). Motivation for change: Implications for substance abuse treatment. *Psychological Science, 10*(3), 209–213.

Easton, C., & Sinha, R. (2000, June 17–22). Are there differences in severity of substance use and violence among substance abusing domestic violence offenders? Paper presented at the College on Problems of Drug Dependence (CPDD) Annual Meeting, San Juan, Puerto Rico.

Easton, C., Suzanne, S., & Sinha, R. (2000a). Motivation to change substance use among offenders of domestic violence. *Journal of Substance Abuse Treatment, 19*, 1–5.

Easton, C., Suzanne, S., & Sinha, R. (2000b). Prevalence of family violence in clients entering substance abuse treatment. *Journal of Substance Abuse Treatment, 18*, 23–28.

Giancola, R., & Zeichner, A. (1997). The biphasic effects of alcohol on human physical aggression. *Journal of Abnormal Psychology, 106*, 598–607.

Goldkamp, J., Weiland, D., Collins, M., & White, M. (1996). The role of drug and alcohol abuse in domestic violence and its treatment: Dade county's domestic violence court experiment. *Research on Legal Interventions in Domestic Violence Cases*, 1–75.

Gondolf, E. (1985). Fighting for control: A clinical assessment of men who batter. *Social Casework, 66*, 48–54.

Gondolf, E. W. (1995). Discharge criteria for batterer programs. *Minnesota Center Against Violence and Abuse*, 1–12.

Gondolf, E. W. (1997). Multi-site evaluation of batterer intervention systems. A summary of findings for a 12-month follow-up. Report submitted to Centers for Disease Control (CDC), Atlanta, GA. Available: http://www.mincava.umn.edu/papers/gondolf/published.htm

Greenfield, S., Weiss, R., & Tohen, M. (1995). Substance abuse and the chronically mentally ill: A description of dual diagnosis treatment services in a psychiatric hospital. *Community Mental Health Journal, 3*, 265–277.

Hamberger, K., & Hastings, J. (1986). Personality correlates of men who abuse their partners: A cross validation study. *Journal of Family Violence, 1*, 323–341.

Hastings, J., & Hamberger, K. (1988). Personality correlates of spouse abusers: A controlled comparison. *Violence Victims, 3*, 31–48.

Healey, K., & Smith, C., & O'Sullivan, C. (1998). Batterer intervention: Program approaches and criminal justice strategies. *U.S. Department of Justice Office of Justice Programs, National Institute of Justice*, pp. 1–155. Available: http://www.ojp.usdoj.gov/nij/pubssum/168638.htm

Hoaken, P., Giancola, R., & Pihl, R. (1998). Executive cognitive functions as mediators of alcohol-related aggression. *Alcohol and Alcoholism, 33*, 47–54.

Hoff, B. H. (1999). What's wrong with the Duluth model? A report on men and domestic violence. *Battered Men—The Hidden Side of Domestic Violence and Gender Polarization in Domestic Violence Programs*, 1–6. Available: http://www.vix.com/menmag/batdulut.htm

Holtzworth-Munroe, A., & Stuart, G. (1994). Typologies of male batterers: Three subtypes and differences among them. *Psychological Bulletin, 116*, 476–497.

Hotaling, G., & Sugarman, D. (1986). An analysis of risk markers in husband to wife violence: The current state of knowledge. *Violence Victims, 1*, 101–124.

Kadden, R., Carroll, K., Donovan, D., Cooney, N., Monti, P., Abrams, D., Litt, M., & Reid, H. (1995). *Cognitive behavioral coping skills therapy manual. (Vol. 3 NIH publication No. 94-3724)*. Rockville, MD: National Institutes of Health.

Kadden, R. M., Carroll, K., Donovan, D., Cooney, N., Monti, P., Abrams, D., Litt, M., & Hester, R. (Eds.). (1992). *Cognitive-behavioral coping skills therapy manual: A clinical research cuide for therapists treating individuals with alcohol abuse and dependence*. Rockville, MD: National Institute of Alcohol Abuse and Alcoholism.

Keller, L. (1996). Invisible victims: Battered women in psychiatric and medical emergency rooms.

Bulletin Menniger Clinic, 60, 1–21.

Kouri, E., Pope, H., & Lukas, S. (1999). Changes in aggressive behavior during withdrawal from long-term marijuana use. *Psychopharmacology, 143,* 302–308.

Lee, W., & Weinstein, S. (1997). How far have we come? A critical review of the research on men who batter. *Recent Developments in Alcoholism, 13,* 337–56.

Maisto, S. A., Carey, K. B., & Bradizza, C. M. (1999). Social learning theory. In K. E. Leonard & H. T. Blane (Eds.), *Psychological theories of drinking and alcoholism* (2nd ed.) (pp. 106-163). New York: Guilford.

Marick, C. (1994). Health and justice professionals set goals to lessen domestic violence. *Journal of the American Medical Association, 271*(15), 1147–1148.

Miller, B. (1990). The interrelationships between alcohol and drugs and family violence. In L. Y. De La Rosa & B. Gropper (Eds.), *Drugs and violence: Causes, correlates, and consequences* (pp. 177–207). Rockville, MD: NIDA Research Monograph 103 U.S. Department of Health and Human Services, National Institute on Drug Abuse.

Miller, W. R. (1998). Enhancing motivation to change. In W. R. Miller & N. Heather (Eds.), *Treating addictive behaviors* (2nd ed.) *Applied clinical psychology* (pp.121–132). New York: Plenum.

Miller, W. R., & Tonigan, S. J. (1996). Assessing drinkers' motivation for change: The stages of change: The Stages of Change Readiness and Treatment Eagerness Scale (SOCRATES). *Psychology of Addictive Behaviors, 10,* 81–89.

Miller, W., Zweben, A., DiClemente, C., & Rychtarik, R. (1995). *Motivational Enhancement Therapy Manual. (Vol. 2 NIH Publication No. 94-3723), (2),* 94–3732,

Monti, P., Abrams, D., Binkoff, J., Zwick, W., Liepman, M., Nirenberg, T., & Rohsenow, D. (1990). Communication skills training, communication skills training with family and cognitive behavioral mood management training for alcoholics. *Journal of Studies on Alcohol, 51,* 263–270.

Monti, P., Abrams, D., Kadden, R., & Cooney, N. (1989). *Treating alcohol dependence: A coping skills training guide.* New York: Guilford.

Murphy, C., Myer, S., & O'Leary, D. (1993). Family of origin violence and millon clinical multiaxial inventory II. Psychopathology among partner assaultive men. *Violence Victims, 8,* 165–176.

O'Farrell, T., & Fals-Stewart, W. (2000). Behavioral Couples Therapy for Alcoholism and Drug Abuse. *The Behavior Therapist, 23,* 49–54.

Pence, E., & Paymer, M. (1993). *Education groups for men who batter: The Duluth model.* New York: Springer.

Pihl, R., & LeMarquand, D. (1998). Serotonin and aggression and the alcohol-aggression relationship. *Alcohol and Alcoholism, 33,* 55–65.

Prochaska, J. O., Diclemente, C. C., & Norcross, J. C. (1997). In search of how people change: Applications to addictive behaviors. In G. A. Marlatt & G. R. VandenBos (Eds.), *Addictive behaviors: Readings on etiology, prevention, and treatment* (pp. 671–696). Washington, DC: American Psychological Association.

Project Match Research Group. (1997). Matching alcoholism treatments to client heterogeneity: Project Match posttreatment drinking outcomes. *Journal of Studies on Alcohol, 58,* 7–25.

Rennison, C. M., & Welchans, S. (2000). Intimate partner violence. *Bureau of Justice statistics. A special report.* U.S. Department of Justice, Office of Justice Programs, May 2000, 1–11.

Ries, R., & Ellingson, T. (1990). A pilot assessment at one month of 17 dual diagnosis patients. *Hospital and Community Psychiatry, 41,* 1230–1233.

Rivera, F., Mueller, B., Somes, G., Mendoza, C., Rushforth, N., & Kellermann, A. (1997). Alcohol and illicit drug abuse and the risk of violent death in the home. *Journal of the American Medical Association, 278,* 569–75.

Roberts, A. (1988). Substance abuse among men who batter their mates: The dangerous mix. *Journal of Substance Abuse Treatment, 5,* 83–87.

Robinson, L. (1997). Domestic violence and stalking. The second annual report to Congress under the Violence Against Women Act. Violence Against Women Grants Office. Office of the Justice Programs, U.S. Department of Justice, pp. 1–10.

Selzer, M. (1971). The Michigan Alcohol Screening Test: The quest for a new diagnostic instrument. *American Journal of Psychiatry, 127,* 1653–1658.

Sobell, L. C. Sobell, M. B., Leo, G. I., & Cancil, A. (1988). Reliability of a timeline method: Assessing normal drinker reports of recent drinking and a comparative evaluation across several populations. *British Journal of Addiction, 83,* 393–402.

Statistics Canada (1999). *The Daily—Family violence: A statistical profile* [On-line]. Available: http://www.statcan.ca/Daily

Straus, M. A., Hamby, S. L., Boney-McCoy, S., & Sugarman, D. B. (1996). The Revised Conflict Tactics Scale (CTS2): Development and preliminary psychometric data. *Journal of Family Issues, 17*(3), 283–316.

Tardiff, K., Marzuk, P., Leon, A., Portera, L., & Weiner, C. (1997). Violence by patients admitted to a psychiatric hospital. *American Journal of Psychiatry, 154,* 88–93.

van Erp, A., & Miczek, K. (1997). Increased aggression after ethanol self-administration in male resident rats. *Psychopharmacology, 131,* 287–295.

Van Praag, H. M. (1994). 5-HT-related, anxiety-and/or aggression-driven depression. *International Clinical Psychopharmacology, 9*(Suppl. 1), 5–6.

Violence Against Women Act. (1994). *Title IV of the Violent Crime Control and Law Enforcement Act* (Public Law 103-322).

Violence Against Women Act. (2000). Federal Legislation and Regulations. [On-line]. Available: http://www.ojp.udsoj.gov/vawo/regulations.htm

Wilt, S., & Olson, S. (1996). Prevalence of domestic violence in the United States. *Journal of the American Medical Womens' Association, 51,* 77–82.

Zhang, L., Wieczorek, W., & Welte, J. (1997). The nexus between alcohol and violent crimes. *Alcoholism, Clinical and Experimental Research, 21,* 1264–1271.

CHAPTER

Timothy J. O'Farrell
Christopher M. Murphy

Behavioral Couples Therapy for Alcoholism and Drug Abuse: Encountering the Problem of Domestic Violence

Behavioral couples therapy for alcoholism and drug abuse (BCT; O'Farrell & Fals-Stewart, 2000) has encountered the problem of domestic violence. While BCT does not hold violent behavior as an a priori intervention target, it is a component of the BCT assessment strategy and, when present, is attended to in treatment. While designed for substance-abusing clients, we have found that BCT demonstrably reduces the frequency and intensity of male-to-female violence. This chapter describes and clarifies the role of BCT in treating partner violence among men seeking treatment for alcoholism and drug abuse, as well as discusses general clinical issues in intervention for intimate violence and addiction problems. We conclude with a plea for reliance on evidence rather than ideology to guide interventions for the combined problems of intimate violence and addiction so that best practices may be consonant with evidence-based therapy.

☐ Behavioral Couples Therapy for Alcoholism and Drug Abuse

Behavioral Couples Therapy (BCT) Treatment Methods

As described by O'Farrell and Fals-Stewart (2000), BCT works directly to increase relationship factors conducive to abstinence. A behavioral approach assumes that family members can reward abstinence and that alcoholic and drug abusing patients from happier, more cohesive relationships with better communication have a lower risk of relapse. The substance abusing patient and the spouse or cohabiting partner are seen together in BCT,

Preparation of this chapter was supported by grants to Timothy J. O'Farrell from the National Institute on Alcohol Abuse and Alcoholism (R01AA10356 and K02AA00234) and by the Department of Veterans Affairs.

typically for 15–20 outpatient couple sessions over 5–6 months. Generally, couples are married or cohabiting for at least a year, without current psychosis, and one member of the couple has a current problem with alcoholism or drug abuse. Most couples have children in the home. The couple starts BCT soon after the substance user seeks help.

BCT sees the substance abusing patient with the spouse to build support for sobriety. The therapist arranges a daily Sobriety Contract in which the patient states his or her intent not to drink or use drugs that day (in the tradition of one day at a time), and the spouse expresses support for the patient's efforts to stay abstinent. For alcoholic patients who are medically cleared and willing, daily Antabuse ingestion witnessed and verbally reinforced by the spouse also is part of the Sobriety Contract. The spouse records the performance of the daily contract on a calendar provided by the therapist. Both partners agree not to discuss past drinking or drug use or fears about future drinking or drug use at home to prevent substance-related conflicts that can trigger relapse. Instead the partners reserve these discussions for the therapy sessions.

At the start of each BCT couple session, the therapist reviews the Sobriety Contract calendar to see how well each spouse has done their part. If the Sobriety Contract includes 12-step meetings, for patients who agree to such meetings, or urine drug screens, which are a standard part of BCT if the patient had a drug problem when seeking help, these are marked on the calendar and reviewed. The calendar provides an ongoing record of progress that is rewarded verbally at each session. The couple performs the behaviors of their Sobriety Contract in each session to highlight its importance and to let the therapist observe how the couple does the contract.

Using a series of behavioral assignments, BCT increases positive feelings, shared activities, and constructive communication because these relationship factors are conducive to sobriety. Catch Your Partner Doing Something Nice has each spouse notice and acknowledge one pleasing behavior performed by their partner each day. In the Caring Day assignment, each person plans ahead to surprise their spouse with a day when they do something special to show their caring. Planning and doing Shared Rewarding Activities is important because research has shown that many substance abusers' families have stopped shared activities. These activities are associated with positive recovery outcomes (Moos, Finney & Cronkite, 1990). Each activity must involve both spouses, either by themselves or with their children or other adults, and can be at or away from home. Teaching Communication Skills can help the alcoholic or drug abusing patient and spouse deal with stressors in their relationship and in their lives, which may reduce the risk of relapse.

Relapse prevention is the final activity of BCT. At the end of weekly BCT sessions, each couple completes a Continuing Recovery Plan that is reviewed at quarterly follow-up visits for an additional two years.

Results from Outcome Studies of BCT

Randomized studies comparing BCT with individual-based treatment show a fairly consistent pattern of more abstinence and fewer substance-related problems, happier relationships, and lower risk of marital separation for alcoholic patients who received BCT than for patients who received only individual treatment. These results have been observed both for male alcoholic patients (Azrin, Sisson, Meyers, & Godley, 1982; Bowers & Al-Rehda, 1990; Hedberg & Campbell, 1974; Kelley & Fals-Stewart, 2000; McCrady, Stout, Noel, Abrams, & Nelson, 1991; O'Farrell, Cutter, Choquette, Floyd, & Bayog, 1992) and for male drug abusing patients (Fals-Stewart, Birchler, & O'Farrell, 1996; Fals-Stewart & O'Farrell, 1999; Fals-Stewart, O'Farrell, & Birchler, 2001; Kelley & Fals-Stewart, 2000). In addition, cost savings due to reduced hospitalizations and jailings after BCT are five times greater than the cost of delivering the BCT program for both alcoholic (O'Farrell, Choquette, Cutter, Floyd, et al., 1996; O'Farrell, Choquette, Cutter, Brown, et al., 1996) and drug abusing patients (Fals-Stewart, O'Farrell, & Birchler, 1997). Further, the BCT sobriety contract appears to be a non-coercive way to encourage compliance with pharmacotherapy for substance abusing patients (e.g., disulfiram, Azrin et al., 1982; O'Farrell, Allen, & Litten, 1995; naltrexone, Fals-Stewart & O'Farrell, 1999; HIV medications, Fals-Stewart, 1999) and to encourage commitment to recovery. Finally, for male alcoholic and drug abusing patients, BCT improves functioning of the couples' children, as indicated by maternal ratings on the Pediatric Symptom Checklist (Jellinek & Murphy, 1990), more than individual-based treatment does (Kelley & Fals-Stewart, 2000).

BCT and Partner Violence

An initial study (O'Farrell & Murphy, 1995; O'Farrell, Murphy, Neavins, & Van Hutton, 2000; O'Farrell, Van Hutton, & Murphy, 1999) examined partner violence in the year before and the two years after BCT for 88 married or cohabiting male alcoholic veterans, and used a demographically matched nonalcoholic comparison sample. Results showed that male-to-female violence in the year before BCT had a 64% prevalence rate, over five times greater than in the comparison sample. Violence was significantly reduced from pretreatment levels in the two years after BCT, but remained greater than in the comparison sample. The extent of violence after BCT was associated with the extent of the alcoholics' drinking. Frequency of posttreatment drinking was positively correlated with violence, and remitted alcoholics no longer had elevated domestic violence levels when compared with matched controls while relapsed alcoholics did. For example, in the first year after BCT, only 10% of remitted alcoholics, versus 43% of relapsed alcoholics, engaged in violence. Preliminary results from a second study with a larger, more varied sample ($N = 303$ male alcoholics and their partners) showed similar results (O'Farrell, Murphy, Hoover, Fals-Stewart, & Feehan, 2000). Finally, a randomized study of male drug abusing patients found that BCT was more effective than individual treatment in alleviating domestic violence (O'Neill, Freitas, & Fals-Stewart, 1999). Specifically, while nearly half of the couples reported male-to-female violence in the year before treatment, the number reporting violence in the year after treatment was significantly lower for BCT (17%), as compared to individual treatment (42%).

To summarize, two studies suggest that male-to-female partner violence among male alcoholics is reduced after BCT and returns to the level of violence experienced by couples without alcohol problems if the alcoholic patient stays nearly or completely abstinent. This should not be surprising because other aspects of marital, family, and psychosocial functioning improve after successful treatment of alcoholism (Moos, Finney, & Cronkite, 1990). Further, one study with drug abusing men shows greater reductions in partner violence after treatment for BCT than for individual-based drug abuse treatment. Therefore, although BCT was not designed to treat violence, recent evidence shows reductions in violence after BCT.

How Partner Violence is Handled in BCT with Alcoholic and Drug Abusing Patients

BCT therapists use a series of methods to deal with partner violence in couples seeking BCT for alcoholism and drug abuse problems. The first step is to assess for partner violence in every couple during the initial couple session and in a separate interviews with each member of the couple. The Conflict Tactics Scale (Straus, 1979), or a similar measure of partner aggression, is usually given to each member of the couple along with other assessment measures. Each spouse completes these questionnaires in private to avoid influence from the other spouse in answering sensitive questions.

The second step, for couples in which assessment questions reveal a history of partner violence, is to determine by questioning the male and female partner, usually separately and also together, about the extent of the current risk of lethal or physically injurious violence. The BCT therapist determines whether severe violence has ever occurred, how long ago the last incident was, and whether there have been recent threats of such violence. The circumstance of violent incidents are reviewed including whether the police were called, the couple separated, and the extent to which violence was perpetrated only by the male versus also by the female. The therapist also inquires whether either member of the couple, particularly the female victim, fears that such violence may occur in the near future. The presence or availability of weapons is also questioned. Finally, it is important to determine whether the violence occurred only or mostly when the substance abusing patient was under the influence of alcohol or drugs. If so, then the patient's willingness to use methods such as Antabuse or attend regular AA meetings to deal with the substance abuse may reduce some of the couple's and the therapist's concern about immediate risk of violence. If this second stage of assessment indicates that there is an active and acute risk for severe domestic violence that could cause serious injury or be potentially life-threatening, it is better to treat the substance abuser and the partner separately rather than together. This includes making a safety plan to prevent violence to the potential victim.

The third step—if the assessment indicates that there is *not* an active and acute risk for severe domestic violence that could cause serious injury or be potentially life-threatening— is to treat the couple together in BCT and address the violence in the therapy. Although partner violence is frequently detected among patients seeking substance abuse treatment, in our experience, most of this violence is not so severe that it precludes couples therapy. It is important to note here that violence is very common among couples without substance use problems seeking outpatient couples therapy, and similar criteria have been used to determine whether conjoint therapy is an acceptable treatment in that context (O'Leary, Heyman, & Neidig, 1999; O'Leary, Vivian, & Malone, 1992). As mentioned below, the BCT treatment was not designed explicitly to treat partner violence, but it became a pragmatic necessity to devise methods to address violence in BCT for couples with a history of such behavior.

The first such method was for BCT therapists to convey a norm of nonviolence in couple relationships. This included getting each member of the couple to commit not to threaten or use violence against their partner. A clear stance was taken that each person is responsible for controlling their own actions and behaviors. For example, therapists would not accept an attempt by the male member of the couple to blame the female partner for his getting verbally abusive or threatening. The BCT therapist reviewed at each session the couple's successes and challenges in keeping the nonviolence commitment. This included examining angry interchanges or other situations that occurred in the previous week that presented a risk for escalation to violence. A nonviolence commitment that was reviewed at each BCT session fit well with the other behavioral commitments that are reviewed at each BCT session.

The second method involved teaching couples alternative communication behaviors to the hostile and negative interaction patterns that may escalate to violence in some couples. As part of this communication skills training, a timeout agreement was presented as a useful procedure for containing conflict. In this procedure if either party gets uncomfortable that a discussion may be escalating, he or she says, "I'm getting uncomfortable. I want a five-minute timeout." Spouses go to separate rooms and use slow deep breathing to calm themselves. Afterward, the couple may restart the discussion if both desire it. If either partner requests a second time out, then the couple must stop the discussion.

Finally, a third method to prevent violence, which was associated with substance use in many couples, was to support abstinence from alcohol and drugs using the sobriety contract and other BCT methods already described. In the vast majority of cases, BCT therapists noted that these methods were successful at preventing partner violence while the couple was attending BCT sessions. Outcome data already described indicate that most couples continued without violence in the two years after BCT.

In addition, for couples with a history of partner violence, it was important for BCT therapists to be prepared to address the risk of violence if the substance abusing patient relapsed. Practical advice would be provided to the nonoffending spouse if relapse occurred in cases with a history of partner violence. The spouse would be encouraged not to engage in arguments or problem discussions when the substance abusing patient was under the influence of alcohol or drugs, to leave the situation if any warning signs of aggression were detected, to call the police if violence or threats of violence occurred and, if necessary, to use domestic violence shelter services in the local community. For cases that showed repeated violence while the couple was attending BCT sessions, separate treatment for each member of the couple was generally recommended and BCT was terminated.

Cautions and Clarifications about BCT and Partner Violence in Treating Substance Abusing Patients

There are a number of cautions and clarifications about BCT and partner violence in treating substance abusing patients. First, it is important to realize that BCT was not designed as a treatment method for partner violence. BCT is a couples-based treatment for alcoholism and drug abuse. We simply learned through our clinical experience treating couples and through our research that male patients seeking help for substance abuse problems are a high risk group for perpetrating partner violence, and that the violence should not be ignored.

Second, data currently available support the use of BCT for a specific subgroup of men with co-occurring problems of addiction and partner violence. BCT is recommended for married or cohabiting male substance abusing patients who have sought help for their substance abuse problem if there is not an acute high risk of severe, injurious, or lethal violence (as already described above). BCT is not recommended for substance abusing patients seeking help but not currently living with a partner. A dual-focused intervention program may be better suited to the substance-abusing, violent male who is not in a partner relationship as one means of prevention of future domestic violence. BCT has not been tested on batterer clinic male patients with substance abuse problems, and is therefore not currently recommended for this population.

Third, we do not know why partner violence is reduced after BCT. Several possible explanations exist. First, violence may be reduced because alcohol and drug use are reduced or eliminated. Second, violence may be reduced because one or both members of the couple learns constructive communication skills that prevent arguments from escalating to violence. Finally, a combination of these factors may explain the violence reduction associated with BCT.

Some results seem to support the importance of reduced substance use after BCT in reducing violence risk. For example, in one study for both the first and second year after BCT, violence was significantly reduced; further, the extent of violence and of clinically elevated verbal aggression levels were associated with the extent of the alcoholics' drinking (O'Farrell & Murphy, 1995; O'Farrell, et al., 1999; O'Farrell, Murphy, Neavins, & Van Hutton, 2000). Frequency of posttreatment drinking was positively correlated with frequency of violence and verbal aggression, and remitted alcoholics no longer had elevated violence and verbal aggression levels when compared with matched controls, while relapsed alcoholics did. These results were observed even after baseline violence levels were taken into account.

Several studies that show reduced violence and an association between substance use and continued violence after individual (not couple) treatment, also seem to support the importance of reduced substance use in reduced partner violence after treatment. One study of drug abusing men with comorbid alcohol problems found that partner violence was significantly reduced from the year before to the year after receiving individually-based substance abuse treatment (Fals-Stewart, 1998). This study showed the same pattern of results found with BCT. The greatest violence reductions occurred among patients who were remitted after treatment; and those remitted after treatment experienced similar levels of violence as did a nonalcoholic normative control group. Fals-Stewart (1998) also found that, in the year after individually-based treatment, the likelihood of male-to-female violence was 18 times higher on days when the man used alcohol or illicit drugs than on days when he did not. These findings and greater violence among relapsed than remitted patients remained significant and of similar magnitude when baseline violence levels were controlled. Finally, two other longitudinal studies of partner violence after individual alcoholism treatment reported high levels of violence before treatment that were significantly reduced in the year after treatment (Maiden, 1996; Stuart et al., 2000).

Other results suggest that couple relationship factors may be important in reduced violence after substance abuse treatment. For example, a randomized study of male drug abusing patients found that BCT was more effective than individual treatment in alleviating partner violence (O'Neill et al., 1999). A second study, which investigated differences between partner violent and nonviolent male alcoholic patients found that relationship distress and alcohol problem severity had independent associations with partner violence (Murphy, O'Farrell, Fals-Stewart, & Feehan, 2001). Further, relationship adjustment remained significantly associated with partner violence, whereas alcohol problem severity did not, after controlling for demographic variables and patient antisocial traits.

We have noted that BCT is contraindicated if there is an acute high risk of severe violence that is potentially injurious or lethal. However, once cases with acute risk of serious injury or death have been eliminated, it is not completely clear where to draw the line on the violence severity continuum when considering the use of BCT. For example, in two studies using the Conflict Tactics Scale (Straus, 1979) definition of severe violence (i.e., kicked, bit, or hit with fist; hit with something; beat up; threatened with knife or gun; used knife or gun), 20%–30% of male alcoholic patients entering and accepted for treatment into BCT have engaged in severe violence toward their female partner in the year before BCT (O'Farrell & Murphy, 1995; O'Farrell, Murphy, Hoover, et al., 2000; O'Farrell et al., 1999). Prevalence of severe violence is significantly reduced to 8%–12% in the two years after BCT in these studies, suggesting that some cases of severe violence can be helped by BCT.

Another issue in any form of couples' therapy is whether being in therapy has an impact on participants' perceptions regarding the integrity of the relationship and their decision-making regarding its possible dissolution, as well as how responsibility is construed. In BCT, participants do not need to have an open-ended commitment to maintaining the relationship. In fact, many couples enter BCT as a last chance to salvage their relationship; often the nonaddicted spouse has made it clear that if violence or serious substance use recurs, then the relationship is over. However, in our work on BCT, participants both need to be willing to work to see if the relationship can be improved and to agree to refrain from threatening separation or divorce in anger. Couples promise not to continue to make threats of separation or divorce in the heat of anger at home because such threats usually sabotage the couple's progress and can lead to heightened anger than can escalate to violence or substance use. However, they also agree to discuss serious thoughts they may have about possible separation or divorce during BCT sessions where they can get help from the therapist in dealing with this issue. In this regard, BCT therapists are careful to stress that the spouse's role of assisting the male substance abusing patient's recovery does not mean that the female partner is responsible for the male's substance use or violence.

☐ Evidence, Rather Than Ideology, Should Guide Interventions

The problem of domestic violence is too profound, both as public health and social issues, to be content with intervention approaches that sound good or look right based on some conceptual model, but that have no empirical support for their efficacy. Unfortunately, this has been the tradition regarding interventions in this field—many earnest appeals and opinions, very little data.

It is important in conceptualizing interventions for partner violence to distinguish between interventions that are inefficacious and interventions that are harmful. The limited available evidence suggests that many partner violence interventions, both legal and psychosocial, may be relatively inefficacious when examined relative to no-treatment control conditions (e.g., Dunford, 2000; Harrell, 1991), although combined legal and clinical interventions may have small, additive effects on outcome variables such as criminal recidivism (Murphy, Musser, & Maton, 1998; Syers & Edleson, 1992). To date, no intervention has been shown to have large, powerful effects in ending partner violence in controlled studies. Thus, the search for highly efficacious intervention approaches remains a major and urgent priority in the field.

With respect to the harmfulness of interventions, although a great many articles have warned of the harmfulness of couples interventions for partner violence, and many states explicitly forbid the use of couples interventions for court-mandated abusers, we know of no empirical evidence indicating that such interventions are, in fact, harmful. Two controlled trials have found couples interventions to be no less effective than the widely promoted gender-specific interventions for wives with a violent husband (Brannen & Rubin, 1996; O'Leary et al., 1999). O'Leary and colleagues (1999) further demonstrated that couples intervention did not produce greater attributions by women of self-blame for their partner's aggression relative to gender-specific treatment in women's groups, nor was there any evidence that the content of couples' sessions provoked abusive incidents. Brannen and Rubin (1996) found that couples treatment was somewhat more effective than gender-specific treatment for cases with co-occurring substance abuse and domestic violence. Finally, as noted above, O'Neil and colleagues (1999) found that BCT for drug abusers was more effective than individual treatment in alleviating domestic violence.

Another important concern involves the presumption that battered spouses are a homogenous population with regard to the goals of intervention, and the assumption that alternative victim services are efficacious. Even the best available victim advocacy interventions have somewhat discouraging outcomes as demonstrated by Sullivan and Bybee (1999). They found that a community-based advocacy program for battered women after they left a shelter had a substantial, significant impact on violent revictimization, as compared to treatment as usual with normal shelter services. Despite these significant findings, 76% of the battered women who received the intensive advocacy intervention reported that they were physically abused during a 24 month follow-up period (compared to 89% of the treatment-as-usual control group). Although the intervention significantly reduced violence exposure, the absolute levels of revictimization indicate that a high degree of long-term safety has not been achieved with either standard shelter services or the enhanced advocacy program.

Likewise, there is heterogeneity among batterers, with clinical observations suggesting a distinction between "normal couple violence" and "patriarchal terrorism," and the issue has been raised as to whether the latter group of "terrorist" individuals may not be appropriate for couple services (see Downs & Miller, this volume). Although such a distinction is appealing, and may eventually guide intervention, we know of no validated methods to distinguish between these suggested group of violence in couples, nor of any outcome research showing that these groups respond differentially to different treatment formats. The available data suggest that there is a severity continuum of partner violence, not necessarily discrete categories. Those on the high end of the continuum tend to have many complicating issues, including severe and frequent partner violence perpetration, antisocial personality characteristics, generalized violence, and affective instability (O'Leary, 1993). Not surprisingly, individuals with these characteristics have higher violence recidivism after batterer counseling, when compared to less severe cases (Dutton, Bonarchuk, Kropp, Hart, & Ogloff, 1997; Kropp & Hart, 2000; Murphy, Morrel, Elliott, & Neavins, 2000). Although it seems quite sensible to steer such severe cases away from couples interventions, there is no compelling reason to believe that they will respond more favorably to gender-specific interventions. As yet, there is no empirical basis upon which to recommend treatment matching for various forms of substance abuse treatment based on violence frequency or severity.

It is a popular misconception that intervention programs for domestic violence perpetrators exclusively handle severe cases. Even among those who are court-mandated to counseling, there is a wide range of case severity that can impact treatment outcome (Murphy et al., 2000). Some referrals have engaged exclusively in verbal abuse, phone harassment, or other nonviolent domestic-abuse related offenses and, by self and partner report, have perpetrated little if any physical violence. Others have engaged in repetitive, severe, injurious, and life-threatening partner violence. The entire continuum between these extremes is represented in abuser treatment programs, not just patriarchal terrorists. One small-scale study found that the prevalence and frequency rates of abusive behaviors were only slightly higher for a sample of men from a domestic violence treatment program when compared to a sample of married or cohabiting men from an alcohol treatment program (Stith, Crossman, & Bischof, 1991). Thus, the common perception that partner violence is vastly different in batterer treatment programs than in other contexts such as alcohol treatment needs to be carefully reexamined in further studies.

Not surprisingly, clinical experience and empirical research suggest that abusive men have much in common with nonabusive men in distressed relationships, and their differences are often a matter of degree rather than kind. This point is illustrated by serious problems that researchers face when they attempt to find men in distressed relationships who have absolutely no prior history of physical aggression toward the relationship partner (Holtzworth-Munroe, Waltz, Jacobson, & Monaco, 1992). The vast majority of individuals in distressed marriages have a history of physical partner aggression at some point in the relationship, although many have not engaged in recent physical aggression. Thus, partner violence is an important aspect of the continuum of relationship distress and dysfunction, and the violence itself falls along a continuum of frequency and severity.

Efforts to parse the continuum at discrete points may be arbitrary, yielding subgroups that vary with respect to other markers of relationship distress and interpersonal functioning, but that are not qualitatively distinct.

For this area of practice and inquiry to advance, scholars and practitioners may need to move beyond polemics to rededicate ourselves to determining what works to attain desired goals and outcomes. Broad consensus is available to support goals such as the cessation of all physical aggression in intimate relationships. There is no utility in assuming that any particular intervention is either helpful or harmful in the absence of supporting evidence. In the absence of empirical data, it may be risky to assume that any particular group of potential clients will, or will not, respond to any particular intervention. We need a moratorium on unbridled speculation and a new devotion to evidence-based practice in this arena. Will anything less truly serve the interests of individuals and families suffering under the burden of problems with domestic violence and addiction?

☐ References

Azrin, N. H., Sisson, R. W., Meyers, R., & Godley, M. (1982). Alcoholism treatment by Disulfiram and community reinforcement therapy. *Journal of Behavior Therapy and Experimental Psychiatry, 13,* 105–112.

Brannen, S. J., & Rubin, A. (1996). Comparing the effectiveness of gender-specific and couples groups in a court-mandated spouse abuse treatment program. *Research on Social Work Practice, 6,* 405–424.

Bowers, T. G., & Al-Rehda, M. R. (1990). A comparison of outcome with group/marital and standard/individual therapies with alcoholics. *Journal of Studies on Alcohol, 51,* 301–309.

Dunford, E. W. (2000). The San Diego Navy Experiment: An assessment of interventions for men who assault their wives. *Journal of Consulting and Clinical Psychology, 68,* 468–476.

Dutton, D. G., Bonarchuk, M., Kropp, R., Hart, S. D., & Ogloff, J. P. (1997). Client personality disorders affecting wife assault post-treatment recidivism. *Violence and Victims, 12,* 37–50.

Fals-Stewart, W. (1998, January). Domestic violence among male drug abusing patients and their female partners. In T. J. O'Farrell (Chair), *Family violence and substance abuse.* Paper presented at the International Conference on the Treatment of Addictive Behaviors, Santa Fe, New Mexico.

Fals-Stewart, W. (1999). *Behavioral couples therapy enhancement of HIV-medication compliance among HIV-infected male drug abusing patients.* Unpublished manuscript, Research Institute on Addictions, State University of New York at Buffalo.

Fals-Stewart, W., Birchler, G. R. & O'Farrell, T. J. (1996). Behavioral couples therapy for male substance-abusing patients: Effects on relationship adjustment and drug-using behavior. *Journal of Consulting and Clinical Psychology, 64,* 959–972.

Fals-Stewart, W., & O'Farrell, T. J. (1999). *Behavioral therapy enhancement of opioid antagonist treatment: Naltrexone with supervised administration using behavioral family counseling.* Unpublished manuscript, Research Institute on Addictions, State University of New York at Buffalo.

Fals-Stewart, W., O'Farrell, T. J., & Birchler. G. R. (1997). Behavioral couples therapy for male substance abusing patients: A cost outcomes analysis. *Journal of Consulting and Clinical Psychology, 65,* 789–802.

Fals-Stewart, W., O'Farrell, T. J., & Birchler, G. R. (2001). Behavioral couples therapy for male methadone maintenance patients: Effects on drug-using behavior and relationship adjustment. *Behavior Therapy, 32,* 391–441.

Harrell A. (1991). *Evaluation of court-ordered treatment for domestic violence offenders: Final report.* Washington, DC: The Urban Institute.

Hedberg, A.G., & Campbell, L. (1974). A comparison of four behavioral treatments of alcoholism. *Journal of Behavior Therapy and Experimental Psychiatry, 5,* 251–256.

Holtzworth-Munroe, A., Waltz, J., Jacobson, N. S., & Monaco, V. (1992). Recruiting nonviolent men as control subjects for research on marital violence: How easily can it be done? *Violence and Victims, 7,* 79–88.

Jellinek, M. S., & Murphy, J. M. (1990). The recognition of psychosocial disorders in pediatric office practice: The current status of the Pediatric Symptom Checklist. *Developmental and Behavioral Pediatrics, 11,* 273–278.

Kelley, M. L., & Fals-Stewart, W. (2000). Couples versus individual-based therapy for alcoholism and drug abuse: Effects on children's psychosocial functioning. Manuscript submitted for publication.

Kropp, P. R., & Hart, S. D. (2000). The Spousal Assault Risk Assessment (SARA) Guide: Reliability and validity in adult male offenders. *Law and Human Behavior, 24,* 101–118.

Maiden, R.P. (1996). The incidence of domestic violence among alcoholic EAP clients before and after treatment. *Employee Assistance Quarterly, 3,* 21–46.

McCrady, B., Stout, R., Noel, N., Abrams, D., & Nelson, H. (1991). Comparative effectiveness of three types of spouse involved alcohol treatment: Outcomes 18 months after treatment. *British Journal of Addiction, 86,* 1415–1424.

Murphy, C. M., Musser, P. H., & Maton, K. I. (1998). Coordinated community intervention for domestic abusers: Intervention system involvement and criminal recidivism. *Journal of Family Violence, 13,* 263–284.

Murphy, C. M., Morrel, T. M., Elliott, J. D., & Neavins. T. M. (2000). *Prognostic indicators in the treatment of domestic abuse perpetrators.* Manuscript under review.

Murphy, C. M., O'Farrell, T. J., Fals-Stewart, W., & Feehan, M. (2001). Correlates of physical partner assault among male alcoholic patients. *Journal of Consulting and Clinical Psychology, 69,* 528–546.

Moos, R. H., Finney, J. W., & Cronkite, R. C. (1990). *Alcoholism treatment: Context, process, and outcome.* New York: Oxford University Press.

O'Farrell, T. J., Allen, J. P., & Litten, R. Z. (1995). Disulfiram (Antabuse) contracts in treatment of alcoholism. In J. D. Blaine & L. Onken (Eds.), *Integrating behavior therapies with medications in the treatment of drug dependence* (NIDA Research Monograph 150, pp. 65–91). Washington DC: National Institute on Drug Abuse.

O'Farrell, T. J., Choquette, K. A., Cutter, H. S. G., Floyd, F. J., Bayog, R. D., Brown, E. D., Lowe, J., Chan, A., & Deneault, P. (1996). Cost-benefit and cost-effectiveness analyses of behavioral marital therapy as an addition to outpatient alcoholism treatment. *Journal of Substance Abuse, 8,* 145–166.

O'Farrell, T. J., Choquette, K. A., Cutter, H. S. G., Brown, E. D., Bayog, R., McCourt, W., Lowe, J., Chan, A., & Deneault, P. (1996). Cost-benefit and cost-effectiveness analyses of behavioral marital therapy with and without relapse prevention sessions for alcoholics and their spouses. *Behavior Therapy, 27,* 7–24.

O'Farrell, T. J., Cutter, H. S. G., Choquette, K. A., Floyd, F. J., & Bayog, R. D. (1992). Behavioral marital therapy for male alcoholics: Marital and drinking adjustment during the two years after treatment. *Behavior Therapy, 23,* 529–549.

O'Farrell, T. J., & Fals-Stewart, W. (2000). Behavioral couples therapy for alcoholism and drug abuse. *Journal of Substance Abuse Treatment, 18,* 51-54.

O'Farrell, T. J., & Murphy, C. M. (1995). Marital violence before and after alcoholism treatment. *Journal of Consulting and Clinical Psychology, 63,* 256–262.

O'Farrell, T. J., Murphy, C. M., Hoover, S., Fals-Stewart, W., & Feehan, M. (2000). *Domestic violence before and after alcoholism treatment: The role of treatment involvement and abstinence.* Proceedings of the 34th Annual Meeting of the Association for the Advancement of Behavior Therapy, New Orleans.

O'Farrell, T. J., Murphy, C. M., Neavins, T. M., & Van Hutton, V. (2000). Verbal aggression among male alcoholic patients and their wives in the year before and two years after alcoholism treatment. *Journal of Family Violence, 15,* 295–310.

O'Farrell, T. J., Van Hutton, V., & Murphy, C. M. (1999). Domestic violence after alcoholism treatment: A two-year longitudinal study. *Journal of Studies on Alcohol, 60,* 317–321.

O'Leary, K. D. (1993). Through a psychological lens: Personality traits, personality disorders, and levels of violence. In R. J. Gelles & D. R. Loseke (Eds.), *Current controversies on family violence* (pp. 7–29). New York: Plenum.

O'Leary, K. D., Heyman, R. E., & Neidig, P. H. (1999). Treatment of wife abuse: A comparison of gender-specific and conjoint approaches. *Behavior Therapy, 30,* 475–505.

O'Leary, K. D., Vivian, D., & Malone, J. (1992). Assessment of physical aggression against women in marriage: The need for multimodal assessment. *Behavioral Assessment, 14*, 5–14.

O'Neill, S., Freitas, T. T., & Fals-Stewart. W. (1999, November). *The effect of behavioral couples therapy on spousal violence among drug abusers*. Paper presented at the annual convention of the Association for the Advancement of Behavior Therapy, Toronto, Canada.

Stith, S. M., Crossman, R. K., & Bioshcof, G. P. (1991). Alcoholism and marital violence: A comparative study of men in alcohol treatment programs and batterer treatment programs. *Alcoholism Treatment Quarterly, 8*, 3–20.

Straus, M. A. (1979). Measuring intrafamily conflict and violence: The Conflict Tactics Scales. *Journal of Marriage and the Family, 41*, 75–88.

Stuart, G. L., Ramsey, S. E., Recupero, P. R., Farrell, L. E., Francione, C. L., Webster, B. A., & Brown, R. A. (2000, November). The relationship between treatment for substance abuse and marital violence: One-year follow-up. Paper presented at the annual convention of the Association for the Advancement of Behavior Therapy, New Orleans.

Sullivan, C. M., & Bybee, D. I. (1999). Reducing violence using community-based advocacy for women with abusive partners. *Journal of Consulting and Clinical Psychology, 67*, 43–53.

Syers, M. A., & Edleson, J. L. (1992). The combined effects of coordinated criminal justice intervention in woman abuse. *Journal of Interpersonal Violence, 7*, 490–502.

15
CHAPTER

Anna-Lee Pittman
David A. Wolfe

Bridging the Gap: Prevention of Adolescent Risk Behaviors and Development of Healthy Nonviolent Dating Relationships

During adolescence, friends and peers become far more influential than before, and intimate dating relationships become primary interests (Laursen & Williams, 1997). Along with these important developmental changes, however, come increased risks of pregnancy, sexually transmitted disease, and abuse by and toward dating partners (Leaper & Anderson, 1997). As well, alcohol and drug use and abuse enters the picture, which may contribute to the occurrence of the other risk behaviors (Milgram, 1993; National Center on Addiction and Substance Abuse, 1999). Although some of these developments are harmless, there is a growing awareness of the importance of education and prevention to increase teens' personal safety and responsibility.

In this chapter, we focus on risk behaviors that are detrimental to personal and intimate relationships among youth, specifically dating violence, alcohol abuse, early onset of sexual behavior, and unsafe sex practices. The age of onset and prevalence of each risk behavior varies, based on individual and community risk and protective factors (Roth & Brooks-Gunn, 2000), as well as ethnicity and gender. In addition, key components to successful prevention programs in the areas of dating violence and alcohol use are discussed, which provide examples of model programs. Our primary goal is to raise awareness of the overlap among many of these adolescent risk behaviors and risk factors—in particular, dating violence, alcohol use, and unsafe sex practices—with the intention of improving the delivery and breadth of education and prevention services.

☐ Adolescent Risk Behaviors: Description and Common Characteristics

Not surprisingly, prominent adolescent risk behaviors discussed in this chapter—alcohol and drug abuse, unsafe sexual behavior, and dating violence—share many of the same contributing risk factors, although to important and differing degrees. These include problems related to the family, such as family conflict and violence, poor relationship attachment, early and persistent behavior problems, as well as peer and academic problems, such as school failure, peer rejection, and exposure to community violence (Hawkins, Catalano, & Miller, 1992; Kilpatrick, Acierno, Saunders, Resnick, & Best, 2000; Malik, Sorenson, & Aneshensel, 1997; O'Keefe, 1997, 1998; Bensley, Spieker, Van Eenwyk, & Schoder, 1999; Wekerle, Hawkins, & Wolfe, 2001; Wekerle & Wolfe, 1998). In addition to the above, teen pregnancy, early sexual intercourse, and risky sexual behaviors are associated with early onset of puberty (Capaldi, Crosby, & Stoolmiller, 1996), truancy, and delinquency (Luster & Small, 1994; Moore, Miller, Sugland, Morrison, & Blumenthal, 1995; O'Hara, Parris, Fichtner, & Oster, 1998). In the absence of compensatory factors, such as education and social competence, these varied risk factors can contribute to or become risk behaviors (e.g., alcohol use is associated with teen pregnancy and violence).

A common family element found among teens who engage in these high risk behaviors is the amount of time spent without proper adult involvement or supervision (Canadian Council on Social Development, 1999; Dishion, Capaldi, Spracklen, & Li, 1995). Not surprisingly, children who grow up in caring and supportive homes are more likely to resist risky behaviors, while children who have grown up witnessing or experiencing alcohol abuse or violence in their homes, having poor family structure and insecure attachment-related experiences are more likely to be less resistant to these same risky, unhealthy behaviors.

A description of the age, gender, and ethnic identities of youth who engage in high risk behavior is provided by the Youth Risk Behavior Surveillance, which tracks data regarding many health risk behaviors for adolescents in the United States. Table 15.1 identifies selected results from this survey, conducted with over 15,000 youth in 1999. Black youth, for example, report significantly higher rates of sexual intercourse before age 13 than do Whites and Hispanics, while White youth report the highest levels of forced sexual intercourse. Black youth also report less alcohol consumption at last sexual intercourse and higher condom use than do White and Hispanic youth. Not surprisingly, males report more alcohol use before the age of 13 than females, across all ethnic groups. These data on prevalence of self-reported adolescent risk behaviors is descriptive only, and tell us little about the contextual factors contributing to such risk. We turn now to a closer look at some of the factors that may contribute to these risk behaviors.

Alcohol Use

Alcohol use among teenagers remains prevalent in today's society. A national probability sample of 4,023 adolescents between the ages of 12 and 17 found that 15% of the sample used alcohol, 10% used marijuana, and 2% reported hard drug use in the past year (Kilpatrick et al. 2000). Although some alcohol consumption among adolescents is considered normative, there is great concern for the number of teens who are exhibiting signs of alcohol abuse or dependence with 7% of the above sample meeting diagnostic criteria for alcohol, marijuana, or hard drug abuse or dependence. Trends in alcohol use reported in the Youth Risk Behavior Survey indicate that binge drinking (five or more drinks on one occasion during the 30 days prior to the survey) has shown little variation over the past several years, ranging from 31.3% in 1991 to 33.4% in 1997 to 31.5% in 1999 (Centers for Disease Control, 2000). Binge drinking continues to be a problem among youth and needs to be targeted specifically.

A survey of 1236 grade 9–13 Canadian high school students revealed that half of all students in the sample currently drank alcohol (Feldman, Harvey, Holowaty, & Shortt,

TABLE 15.1. Prevalence (% endorsement) of selected adolescent risk behaviors among high school students in the United States, February to May, 1999

Adolescent Risk Behaviors	Whites			Blacks			Hispanics		
	Females	Males	Total	Females	Males	Total	Females	Males	Total
Current Alcohol Use	82.3	81.8	82.0	75.8	73.8	74.8	84.8	82.2	83.4
Alcohol Use Before Age 13	25.2	34.1	29.9	26.5	44.3	35.2	30.7	39.7	35.1
Ever had Sexual Intercourse	44.8	45.4	45.1	66.9	75.7	71.2	45.5	62.9	54.1
Sexual Intercourse Before Age 13	3.5	7.5	5.5	11.4	29.9	20.5	4.4	14.2	9.2
Experienced Forced Sexual Intercourse	10.1	13.5	15.1	3.5	9.7	5.9	6.7	11.6	10.5
Condom Use at Last Sexual Intercourse of Those Reporting to be Sexually Active	47.6	63.0	55.0	64.5	75.3	70.0	43.0	6.1	55.2
Alcohol or Drug Use at Last Sexual Intercourse	21.5	33.7	27.4	9.3	26.6	18.1	14.4	30.0	22.5
Have Been or Gotten Someone Pregnant	5.8	3.0	4.3	14.1	12.7	13.4	6.2	6.6	6.4
Dating Violence (Physically Hurt by Partner on Purpose)	7.4	7.3	7.4	14.1	10.6	12.4	10.9	7.3	9.1

Data obtained from the 1999 Youth Risk Behavior Surveillance, Centers for Disease Control (June 9, 2000).

1999). Levels of alcohol consumption varied with 39% of the sample reporting to be moderate drinkers, 11% heavy drinkers, 22% abstaining, 24% had never tasted alcohol, and 5% chose not to respond to the question. Significantly more males than females were heavy drinkers. The Ontario Student Drug Use Survey reported higher prevalence rates with 58.8% of students reporting alcohol use in the past year in 1995 (Adlaf, Paglia, & Ivis, 1999; Adlaf, Paglia, Ivis, & Ialomiteanu, 2000) and 67.5% in 1999 (Ontario Student Drug Use Survey, 2000). More students are drinking on a weekly basis (19.7%), and 7.1% report frequent binge drinking (five or more drinks, five or more times, during the last four weeks).

Importantly, studies have found that alcohol use influenced the practice or involvement in a number of other high-risk behaviors (Feldman et al., 1999). Sexual activity, smoking, and drinking and driving were significantly related to heavy drinking. Another study examining trauma experiences among adolescents found that those who reported alcohol abuse or dependence were 6–12 times more likely to have a history of childhood physical abuse, and 18–21 times more likely to have a sexual abuse history (Clark, Lesnick, & Hegedus, 1997). The continued increase in alcohol consumption among teenagers is cause for concern, particularly as it relates to and influences other risk factors and behaviors.

Dating Relationships

Teens generally begin dating, either singly or in small groups, between 13 and 18 years of age, with a range of variability regarding frequency, level of intimacy, seriousness, and importance of these relationships. An illustration of dating, intimacy, and sexual experiences and expectations is provided by an in-depth survey conducted by the Kaiser Family Foundation and YM Magazine, involving 650 boys and girls ages 13–18 years (Henry J. Kaiser Family Foundation and YM Magazine, 1999). They discovered levels or stages of intimacy that developed by age of the youth; that is, intimacy progressed as the youth developed in age chronologically, not as the relationship progressed in length. Most 13–14-year-old teens (72%) reported that it is typical for dating couples their age to kiss, with 45% reporting that French kissing, petting (15%), and intercourse (4%) are expected. Adolescents 15–16 years of age expected an increased level of sexual activity, with 93% reporting kissing, and slightly higher rates of French kissing (71%), petting (48%), and intercourse (28%) as normative. Couples at this age typically spend more time alone together. Older teens (ages 17–18 years) have significantly more sexual experience, with 57% reporting petting to be typical and slightly more than half (52%) reporting intercourse to be typical of their dating relationships.

Just as intimacy becomes more involved and prevalent in older teens' relationships, so does the significance of the relationship. Although teens continue to value relationships with parents, siblings, other family members, and nonrelated adults, relationships with dating partners begin to gain in importance. Gender differences emerge in how relationships develop in significance and closeness during the adolescent years. A study of the network of relationships among younger adolescents found that dating partners were ranked 6th out of 7 in terms of support received (i.e., companionship, intimacy, instrumental help, affection, enhancement of worth, nurturance of the other, and reliable alliance). By midadolescence, dating partners were tied for second place with mothers and, in college, males rated their dating partner as the most supportive person in their network, while females gave equally high ratings to partners, same sex friends, siblings, and mothers (Furman & Buhrmester, 1992). A similar study comparing dating and nondating adolescents found older adolescents and males interacted more frequently with romantic dating partners, whereas younger adolescents and females divided their social interaction time among several relationships (Laursen & Williams, 1997). What is not clearly understood, however, is how these relationships emerge in early adolescence, and how these relationships transform over the course of adolescence (Furman & Wehner, 1997). Gender differences in expectations and closeness may lead to conflict and tension in dating relationships, if these expectations are not clearly understood or reciprocated.

Patterns for more high-risk youth (e.g., those involved in dropout prevention and alternative school programs) stand in contrast to these normative patterns. Of high-risk youth, 35% report being 13 years or younger at first intercourse, 33% were 14–15 years old, and 13% were 16 years or older (O'Hara et al., 1998). Moreover, the prevalence of sexual intercourse in the O'Hara study was 8 times higher than that reported in the Kaiser study. Again, we see that youth with other risk behaviors (such as alcohol abuse or school problems) are more likely to also engage in high-risk sexual behavior.

Violence in Dating Relationships.   Monitoring dating abuse and violence among adolescents is fairly new. Surveys of high school students report 36%–45% of students experience any form of violence in the relationship as a victim or perpetrator (Malik, Sorenson, & Aneshensel, 1997; Molidor & Tolman, 1998; O'Keefe & Treister, 1998). Recently, a measure of physical abuse in dating relationships has been added to the Youth Risk Behavior Survey. Intentional physical violence, including being hit, slapped, or physically hurt on purpose by a boyfriend or girlfriend, was reported by 8.8% of youth in the 1999 Youth Risk Behavior survey (Centers for Disease Control, 2000). This figure does not seem to match rates reported in other studies, however, the difference may be that it is only measuring what is considered to be intentional victimization, not perpetration.

A series of focus group studies with adolescent males and females ages 14–19 years regarding teen dating relationships revealed many disturbing attributions regarding harassment and abuse in dating relationships. Factors that caused violence as reported by the teens were grouped into individual, couple, and social levels (Lavoie, Robitaille, & Hebert, 2000). Individual factors attributed to the aggressor included jealousy, the boy's need for power, and alcohol and drug use. During focus group discussions, youth identified factors attributed to the victim including provocation by the girl, previous experience with violence, a victim personality type (i.e., one who is easily preyed upon), and a strong need for affiliation. Factors attributed to the couple included communication problems and sadomasochism. There was endorsement for consensual violent sex, meaning that a little force during intimacy was considered acceptable as long as both partners agreed. Although consensual, the youth did regard this as sometimes being problematic because partners have agreed to the violence, but may not be sure when one or the other has then crossed the line. Teens in this study frequently attributed blame for violence in the relationship to the victim.

Importantly, physical violence in a dating relationship has different ramifications for males and females. While there is a trend to believe that males and females are equally violent, there is evidence that females perpetrate more violence than males out of self-defense (Foshee, 1996). There are also differences in the severity of violence experienced, as well as the impact it has on the victim (Molidor & Tolman, 1998). A study of high school dating violence revealed that girls experienced significantly more severe physical violence than boys (Jackson, Cram, & Seymour, 2000). Females were more likely to be punched and to be forced into sexual activity, whereas males were more likely to be pinched, slapped, scratched, and kicked. The physical effects of the violence were more severe for females, with 48% reporting that it "hurt a lot" or caused bruises (29%). Males (56%) more frequently reported that it did not hurt at all. Reaction to the worst incident of violence in the relationship also was assessed. Males most frequently reported that they laughed (54%) in reaction to the situation, while females reported a number of other responses: crying (40%), running away (11%), and fighting back (36%); 12% reported that they obeyed their partner.

Sexual assault and forced sexual intercourse also occur at an alarming rate during adolescence (9–10% of first sexual intercourse experiences were forced). Males perpetrate more sexual dating violence than females, and females sustain more sexual violence than males (Foshee, 1996). A study of attitudes among adolescent females related to sexual victimization revealed that levels of self-efficacy predicted forced sexual activity (Walsh & Foshee, 1998).

Sexual Activity among Adolescents

Although there has been a decline in teen birth rates of 12% from 1991–1996 in the United States (U.S. Department of Health and Human Services, 1998), sexual activity among adolescents remains common, with approximately half (54.1% in 1991; 49.9% in 1999) of teens in the United States having sexual intercourse (Centers for Disease Control, 2000). Pregnancy rates among Black females remain higher than among White females, in spite of a greater decrease in teen pregnancies. Pregnancy rates among teens, while decreasing, remain higher in the United States than any other industrialized nation (Nitz, 1999). Safer sexual behaviors are showing some improvement in this trend with 58% of adolescents reporting using a condom at last sexual intercourse, and having fewer sexual partners (Centers for Disease Control, 2000). While more adolescents are using condoms for sex, fewer report having used the birth control pill at last sexual intercourse (20.8% in 1991; 16.2% in 1999) (Centers for Disease Control, 2000).

While it is easy to track female pregnancy rates, adolescent males are typically not researched or surveyed regarding their histories of fathering pregnancies. A study of urban African-American male youth regarding pregnancy history and other health-risk behaviors indicated that 24.2% reported a pregnancy history. These males were 14 times more likely to report three or more sex partners in the last year, more than five times as likely to report a sexually transmitted disease history, and more than three times as likely to test positive for drugs than males without a pregnancy history. Safe sex practices also seem to be of little concern to these males, as they were 2.5 times as likely to be inconsistent or nonusers of condoms during sexual intercourse (Guagliardo, Huang, & D'Angelo, 1999). Disturbingly, a study of youth in dropout prevention and alternative school programs assessed for risk of HIV/AIDS prevention found that use of alcohol and drugs and age of sexual initiation were significantly associated with a high risk profile for AIDS/HIV (O'Hara et al., 1998). Males (29%) were more likely than females (14%) to use alcohol and drugs before having sex and were more than likely to have had sex with two or more partners (males, 78%; females, 22%).

Early onset of sexual intercourse is cause for concern, particularly as it increases the likelihood of increased numbers of sexual partners and condom nonuse during the adolescent years (Shrier, Emans, Woods, & DuRant, 1996). Increased numbers of sexual intercourse partners has been correlated with risk behaviors such as unintended pregnancy, HIV/AIDS, and other sexually transmitted diseases. Connections between dating violence and alcohol use were found to be among the strongest predictors for an increased number of sexual intercourse partners for Black and White adolescent males and females (Valois, Oeltmann, Waller, & Hussey, 1999).

Younger dating youth who have older partners may be at greater risk of experiencing dating violence. Not including cases where physical force was threatened or used at first sexual intercourse, 34% of male partners of 11–12 year old females were five or more years older; 12% of male partners of 13–15 year old females were five or more years older; and 7% of male dating partners of 16–18 year olds were five years or more older (Leitenberg & Saltzman, 2000). Although the disparity in age range between the male and female partners seems to decrease as females get older, such disparity has important prevention implications.

Information about onset of sexual intercourse is available, but information is scarce about feelings regarding the experience, planning for the event, and discussion regarding birth control or safe sex practices before intercourse has occurred (Henry J. Kaiser Family Foundation and YM Magazine, 1999). Females tend to feel more pressure to participate in some form of sexual activity and are more concerned about what friends, peers, and the dating partner think of them. Motivation for initiation of sexual intercourse has not been significantly examined. Predictors for early initiation of sexual intercourse include a belief that they are more mature than their peers, early physical maturity, a tendency to use hard drugs, and a desire for earlier autonomy from parents (Rosenthal, Smith, & de Visser, 1999).

Research regarding individual risk factors and risk behaviors has been conducted primarily in isolation. Recently, research into how these many behaviors are related has begun to take place. Making the links between these factors and behaviors may have important consideration when designing prevention programs, as discussed below.

☐ Making the Links

The links between adolescent risk behaviors described above merit careful investigation. While it is understood that these behaviors do not usually occur in isolation, there seems to be no clear understanding of how they operate together, and what the ramifications might be for adolescent dating relationships. From the survey data presented earlier, we know that some adolescents begin drinking at an early age, and many begin to experience sexual intercourse at an early age. We also understand that there are serious health ramifications to these issues (i.e., potential for pregnancy, sexually transmitted diseases, alcohol and other drug dependence, and increased aggression). Typically, researchers have considered these ramifications in the context of the individual, yet attention needs to be drawn as well to the occurrence of these behaviors in peer and dating relationships, and the possible impact on individuals and relationships.

Linking Alcohol and Sexual Activity

A report written by the Center on Addiction and Substance Abuse used data from two prominent surveys in the United States: the 1997 Youth Risk Behavior Survey; and the 1995 National Longitudinal Study of Adolescent Health, regarding adolescent risk behaviors to develop a comprehensive and in-depth analysis of the connections among alcohol, drug use, and all aspects of sexual activity and violence (National Center on Addiction and Substance Abuse, 1999). Again, the links among dating violence and alcohol and sex are not explicit because data were not available to examine this issue. However, significant findings from this report reveal that teens who use alcohol and drugs are more likely to have sexual intercourse, initiate sexual intercourse at an earlier age, have multiple sex partners, and be at greater risk for sexually transmitted diseases and pregnancy. Early onset of drug use and number of years of sexual intercourse has been found to be associated with increased numbers of sex partners. In addition, students with more partners are more likely to be heavier drug users (Shrier et al., 1996). The Kaiser Family Foundation study found that almost two in ten (17%) teens, aged 13–18, who have had an intimate encounter, admit having done something sexual while under the influence of drugs or alcohol that they otherwise might not have done. One in three (32%) girls, 17–18 years of age, have had this experience.

Linking Alcohol and Intimate Violence

The links between alcohol use and marital aggression have been documented, but the same attention has not been shown to adolescent dating relationships. Only recently have questions regarding dating violence been added to the Youth Risk Behavior Survey (Centers for Disease Control, 2000). Substance abuse is frequently linked with sexual violence. Alcohol has been named the primary culprit for date rape on college campuses (National Center on Addiction and Substance Abuse, 1999). A study of college men and women found that 78% of undergraduate women experienced sexual aggression, and 57% of men reported being sexually aggressive. Dates that included sexual aggression were more likely to include heavy drinking or drug use, in comparison to the last date that did not include sexual aggression (Muehlenhard & Linton, 1987). Among high school students, experiencing dating violence has been identified as a salient risk factor for females for using alcohol or street drugs, and increases the odds 20-fold for alcohol and drug use (Wekerle, Hawkins, & Wolfe, 2001).

There is a move toward establishing a better understanding of the significance and links among adolescent risk behaviors. With this understanding will come a need to develop new prevention programs that deal with these risk behaviors in a broader sense, rather than in isolation. The state of prevention for adolescents is discussed below, including descriptions of model prevention programs for dating violence and alcohol use. Ideas for bridging the gap between the risk behaviors through comprehensive prevention programs are discussed.

☐ Adolescent Risk Behavior Prevention Programs: What Works?

Prevention programs developed over the past decade have been targeted specifically at adolescents for a number of risk behaviors: dating violence, alcohol abuse, drug abuse, pregnancy prevention, safe sex programs, and prevention of sexually transmitted diseases, to name a few. Literature reviews and program evaluation studies point to the conclusion that programs may be successful at providing information and delaying onset of the risk activity, but long-term prevention of the focused risk behavior is seldom achieved (for a comprehensive review of dating violence prevention programs see Wekerle & Wolfe, 1999; pregnancy prevention see Hughes & Sutton, 1996; Nitz, 1999; Thomas, 2000; programs to reduce sexual risk taking behavior see Kirby & Coyle, 1997; substance abuse prevention see Brounstein & Zweig, 2000). Evaluation of prevention programs in all of these areas has been limited due to methodological problems (Kirby & Coyle, 1997; Pittman, Wolfe, & Wekerle, 2000; Thomas, 2000), such as inadequate standardized measures, ambiguity of terms (e.g., defining dating relationships), lack of multiple informants and control groups, lack of trained facilitators, and long-term follow-up issues. Some programs are developed for universal prevention, while others are targeted at groups considered to be at greater risk based on presence of known risk factors.

Good prevention programs are derived from theory, input from youth, and practice.

There are several theories that have contributed to the creation of prevention programs for dating violence, substance abuse, and pregnancy or safe sex education. Social learning theory postulates that youth are vulnerable as a result of the social environment in which they are raised (Bandura, 1977). Negative family, peer, and community influences will contribute to risk for adapting to negative behaviors. Problem behavior theory relies on the belief that some youth may have a natural tendency for deviance or nonconformity and, therefore, may be more likely to engage in problem behaviors (Jessor, 1998; Jessor & Jessor, 1977). Adolescents may engage in alcohol consumption or early onset of sexual intercourse because they perceive it as a means to achieve a goal, that is, peer acceptance, or to cope with boredom, unhappiness, anxiety, or rejection (Botvin & Botvin, 1992).

Theory and model testing of problem behaviors in a recent study of early adolescents found support for a model that included specific factors related to aggression, drug use, and delinquent behaviors, and a higher order problem behavior factor (Farrell, Kung, White, & Valois, 2000). Life-skills training programs that have been developed based on problem behavior theory are built on the philosophy that targeting the underlying determinants (such as personal and social competence skills) will affect the factors that cause the risk behavior (Kim, Crutchfield, Williams, & Helper, 1998). Similarly, social bonding theory links healthy attachments to family and school as factors that protect youth from deviant behavior; unhealthy attachments are regarded as risk factors (Kim et al., 1998).

Instead of focusing on preventing something negative from happening to youth, some recent programs emphasize youth involvement and empowerment, which shifts the focus to promoting positive youth development. In this approach, youth are considered as assets and resources rather than problems or "targets." Prevention programs, such as the Youth Relationships Program (described below) have expanded the role of theory to include youth empowerment as a central theme in educating youth about positive, healthy relationships program and the avoidance of violence and abuse (Pittman, Wolfe, & Wekerle, 1998; Wolfe et al., 1996).

Several factors have been identified as being essential components of prevention programs among adolescents, regardless of the topic. The location of the program is often debated as to whether schools or other community service agencies are better. In the case of sexuality and education prevention programs, there is no question that these programs should be offered in schools; however, what programs should be taught remain a concern (Kirby & Coyle, 1997). Some groups favor teaching abstinence until marriage only, while others favor education regarding contraception and sexuality. Similarly, dating violence prevention programs have been offered in schools and in community service agencies with varying degrees of success. These programs may be most effective when embedded in a declared school context of "zero tolerance" for any type of school violence. The advantages of school-based programs include access to youth, space, and time, and staffing support. The disadvantages include concerns that truant youth, who may need the program most, are not available in the schools; disclosures of abuse in the classroom may not be handled well in a large classroom situation; a large group may not be a safe place to discuss personal beliefs and attitudes; and learning may be limited to only the school context of the individual's life (Kim et al., 1998; Wekerle & Wolfe, 1999).

These concerns not withstanding, the main advantage of community-based programs has been the development of community partnerships (U.S. Department of Health and Human Services, 1998). Although the advantages may not be inherently evident in the results of the prevention program itself (i.e., preventing something bad is hard to prove), such programs appear to reduce duplication of services, increase cooperation and efficiency among service providers, and help integrate services into the community. In turn, communities that have a "face"—a reputation for cooperative and active prevention—have significantly reduced the perceived and actual levels of violence, even in the poorest neighborhoods (Sampson & Morenoff, 1997).

Advocates of prevention programs favor sustained, long-term efforts in education to make prevention successful. Programs should be on-going from kindergarten to the final year of high school, and should be especially intensive just prior to the age of initiation of substance use or similar risk behaviors (Center for Addiction and Mental Health, 2000). Unfortunately, it seems that this does not transfer readily into practice. In the case of sexuality education in Canada, a report by the Council of Ministers of Education indicates that curriculum time in schools available for sexuality education has been reduced as health education becomes combined with physical and career education. Fewer public health nurses in schools also severely reduced the quality and availability of preventive sexual health education services to adolescents (Council of Ministers of Education of Canada, 1999).

Pregnancy prevention and sexuality education programs, while deemed extremely important in reducing teen pregnancy rates and incidence of sexually transmitted disease, are critically received by a number of groups and agencies when being implemented in communities (Vincent, Berne, Lammers, & Strack, 1999). Differing views regarding how to handle this issue conflict with effective program implementation. For example, some religious and moral beliefs dictate that youth should remain abstinent during adolescence, that parents are responsible for protecting their children from negative influences, and that education will positively influence knowledge, attitudes, and beliefs. Programs that focus on abstinence or pregnancy prevention have typically been delivered to females only. While females need to take responsibility for their choices and actions, males also need to be educated about the same issues in order to make responsible choices as well. Males who have unprotected sex are also at risk of becoming fathers and contracting sexually transmitted diseases (Pierre, Shrier, Emans, & DuRant, 1998).

Recent evaluations of pregnancy prevention programs and programs designed to reduce sexual risk taking behavior have drawn similar conclusions regarding the success and status of these programs (Brooks-Gunn & Paikoff, 1993; Kirby & Coyle, 1997; Nitz, 1999). The focus of prevention programs in the 1970s was to provide better health and child care to babies of adolescent mothers or to increase knowledge about sex and the risks and consequences of teenage pregnancy (Hughes & Sutton, 1996; Thomas, 2000). During the 1980s, due to concerns about rising teen birth rates, prevention programs focused on abstinence with the message "Just Say No" (Hughes & Sutton, 1996), including an emphasis on values, communication, and decision-making. Although headway has been made in pregnancy prevention programs in the 1990s, merely providing skills training, education, and knowledge has not been successful in reducing pregnancy rates among teens (Kirby & Coyle, 1997; Nitz, 1999).

Substance abuse prevention programs have typically been school-based and education focused (Botvin & Botvin, 1992; Gilvarry, 2000; Weinberg, Rahdert, Colliver, & Glantz, 1998). Evaluations of earlier programs have consistently found them to be ineffective (Botvin, Schinke, & Orlandi, 1995). One school-based intervention was able to show significant reductions in drug use enduring for six years after implementation of the program. The success of this program was attributed to teaching a combination of resistance and social competence skills, the proper implementation of the program, and sufficient length for program with at least two years of booster implementations (Botvin, Schinke, Epstein, Diaz, & Borvin, 1995).

The Center for Substance Abuse Prevention (Brounstein & Zweig, 2000) has identified six prevention strategies that can be used in combination to develop prevention programs that focus on risk and protective factors for substance abuse, including: information dissemination, prevention education, alternatives, problem identification and referral, community-based process, and environmental approaches. The Center for Substance Abuse Prevention has recently completed an analysis of substance abuse prevention programs that have been evaluated. Rigorous statistical criteria for evaluation were adopted, resulting in the definition of eight model programs which have adopted a combination of these prevention strategies, representing a number of age groups, as well as universal, selective, and indicated prevention for children and youth (for a complete review, see Brounstein & Zweig, 2000). Of these eight programs, only one included information regarding sex or health education, and one provided information and skills for violence and gang prevention and conflict resolution. Although these programs were successful in reducing risk factors and increasing protective factors, they did not demonstrate alcohol and drug use prevention.

Model Programs

Many programs have been identified as model programs due to their success in reducing targeted risk behaviors. The Center for the Study and Prevention of Violence in Colorado (Blueprints for Violence Prevention, 2000) has developed a program entitled "Blueprints for Violence Prevention." These Blueprint programs have been identified due to their success in meeting a scientific standard of program effectiveness and have the potential to provide an initial nucleus for a national violence prevention initiative. These blueprints describe the theoretical rationale, the core components of the program as implemented, the evaluation designs and results, and the practical experiences programs encountered while implementing at multiple sites. The Center for Substance Abuse Prevention also has defined best practice models that are replicable, include community involvement, and have a focus on reducing risk factors and enhancing protective factors.

Project Northland

One substance abuse prevention program identified as a model program by both these agencies, Project Northland, has been identified as a promising program in "Blueprints for Violence Prevention" and by the Center for Substance Abuse Prevention. Project Northland has been in existence in the state of Minnesota since 1991, and is a community-based research program developed to reduce adolescents' alcohol use. While still in the evaluation stages, this program has been adopted and successfully implemented in rural, lower middle-class and middle-class, communities throughout the United States. The success of the program lies in its comprehensive and long-term design (Blueprints for Violence Prevention, 2000).

The evaluation of the program has used random assignment and incorporated 24 school districts into the study. There have been two phases developed for the program. Phase I involved students from grades 6–8, and Phase II involved the same students when they were in grades 11–12. Prevention program strategies include social behavioral curricula, peer leadership activities, parent education and involvement, and community-wide attempts to change norms and practices regarding alcohol use among young teens. Phase I of the program relies extensively on the use of peer leaders based on the following objectives: (1) providing youth opportunities for involvement in the promotion of being alcohol-free, (2) training student volunteers to plan and promote alcohol-free activities for their peers, and (3) providing opportunities and support for alcohol-free recreational activities as an alternative to parties where alcohol is served (Komro, Perry, Veblen-Mortenson, Williams, & Roel, 1999). Phase I demonstrated effectiveness in lowering the rates of alcohol use among young adolescents (Bernstein-Lachter, Komro, Veblen-Mortenson, Perry,

& Williams, 1999), but was less effective in changing perceptions of access to alcohol and actual access to alcohol. At the end of eighth grade, after three years of involvement in the project, monthly drinking was 20% lower, and weekly drinking was 30% lower among students who received the intervention. Project Northland also was effective in changing peer influence regarding alcohol use, normative expectations about how many youth consume alcohol, and parent-child communication about the consequences of drinking (Williams, Perry, Farbakhsh, & Veblen-Mortenson, 1999). The greatest program effects were found among those students in 6th grade that had not yet begun drinking prior to the intervention, suggesting that primary prevention may be more effective.

Phase II of Project Northland began in 1996 and used the same cohort of students as was used in Phase I. These students were now in grades 11 and 12 of high school. Interventions in Phase II included organizing the community to take direct action and create community-level changes; parent education and involvement; print media to support community initiatives and to communicate healthy norms about underage drinking; a mock trial classroom curriculum for 11th grade students; and youth development involving high school students in youth action teams. Phase II program objectives included: increasing students' opportunities and motivation to participate in community activities that would influence policies and practices related to alcohol use and problems; increasing students' self-efficacy and social support to participate in these community activities; increasing students' knowledge about alcohol; and increasing positive recognition of teens in the community.

These objectives were carried out through the development of youth action teams. Youth were recruited from information sessions, similar group activities (i.e., Students Against Drunk Driving [SADD]) youth referral, and so forth. Youth action groups consisted of approximately five students per group and were assisted by an adult coordinator who received training regarding both stages of the project (Bernstein-Lachter, Komro, Veblen-Mortenson, Perry, & Williamson, 1999). In grades 11 and 12, community action projects were introduced to the students. Students were encouraged to develop projects that filled a prescribed list of criteria designed to guide students into designing action-oriented projects. The intent was to generate school or community level change in these action-oriented projects. The youth action teams proved to be quite productive in the majority of the 18 schools that participated in the project, completing a range of 2–24 projects per team, all designed to involve the entire school. Findings regarding Phase II are still forthcoming, but program evaluation by students indicated that they gained skills in teamwork, planning, and taking action, and that their confidence to stand up for reduced drinking increased. Project Northland has been successful in incorporating many of the aspects of successful prevention strategies into its programs. The success of this program may be attributed to the community involvement, presence in the community, longevity of the program, and the focus on developing protective factors and reducing risk behaviors.

The Youth Relationships Program

There are very few dating violence prevention programs, and even fewer that have been fully evaluated (Wekerle & Wolfe, 1999). Dating violence prevention programs also have been largely school-focused. Programs have targeted social skill development, awareness of violence in relationships, changing attitudes and beliefs regarding violence, awareness of gender differences, and challenging stereotypes. One program for dating violence prevention that incorporates many of the aspects of successful prevention strategies outlined for substance abuse prevention is the Youth Relationships Program.

The Youth Relationships Program is an 18-week dating violence prevention program targeted at adolescents aged 14–17 who are at-risk of relationship violence due to a history of witnessing marital violence or childhood maltreatment. This program draws from feminist and empowerment theory and social learning theory and has three main components: education and awareness, skill development, and social action (Pittman, Wolfe, & Wekerle, 1998; Wolfe et al., 1996; Wolfe, Wekerle, & Scott, 1996). Trained facilitators who are experienced with youth issues as well as woman abuse, and who are able to model egalitarian relationships, facilitate the program. The program is multifaceted, offering a number of different learning and education strategies including guest speakers, videos, role-plays, visits to community agencies, and a social action project.

The education component focuses on woman abuse, violence, sexual assault, and date rape. Information is presented through statistics, experiences of guest speakers (i.e., a survivor of woman abuse, and a former male batterer), and informational videos. Information regarding power and control and sexism also is presented. Youth are encouraged to explore social power, personal power, naming the violence, and the gendered state of interpersonal violence. Strategies for approaching interpersonal communication are developed and practiced through role-plays, exercises, and activities. Specific communication skills that are enhanced include active listening, empathy, and emotional expressiveness. As well, the knowledge and skills that males need to ensure consent in sexual relations and that females need to be clear, up-front, and safe are developed. The cultural and societal influences that contribute to the normalization of interpersonal dating violence including sexism, sex-role stereotypes, and gender role rigidity are examined. An exploration of how we choose dating partners and the perils, and positives of these choices, provides insights to youth as to how they may enter abusive or unhealthy relationships. Stereotypes regarding how men and women are expected to behave are explored through discussion and activities such as "Act Like a Man" and "Act Like a Lady." Help-seeking skills are developed in a proactive fashion at a time when crisis is not encountered, including how to find services in the phone book, how to make contact when help is needed, and so forth. Information regarding community social service agencies and programs is provided, and youth visit a community agency and report back to the group what they have learned. Empowerment is further developed through the creation of a social action project. Social action projects have included public service announcements, fund raising activities such as car washes and bake sales, and marches to support a local community service agency. In each activity, information is presented to the community regarding dating violence or woman abuse, its consequences, and how to avoid it. Empowerment is developed via opportunities to become facilitators either through the role of junior facilitator that is offered to alumnae of the program, or as exercise leaders. Youth may take home curriculum and develop a strategy for leading an exercise in the next session.

Results of a recent three-year evaluation of the YRP with youth at-risk of dating violence due to their histories of maltreatment found that youth receiving the program showed less physical abuse (perpetration) and were recipients of less threatening behavior and emotional abuse (victimization) over time (Wolfe, Wekerle, Scott, Straatman, & Grasley, 2001). Youth in the program also showed greater reduction in trauma-related symptoms. These findings, although preliminary, suggest this age group may represent a valuable window of opportunity for reducing the cycle of violence. The program was active and participatory, which teens enjoyed. This program is currently being modified for use at a more universal level in Grade 9 health classes.

Both the Youth Relationships Program and Project Northland possess many similar elements that have assisted in their success in preventing dating violence and alcohol use. The comprehensive and long-term sustainability of the program, as well as the inclusion of community, parents, and other stake holders in Project Northland has proven to be particularly successful. Empowerment strategies have shown to be making a difference in both programs as well (Bernstein Lachter et al., 1999; Grasley, Wolfe, & Wekerle, 1999). During its evaluation Project Northland has begun to realize that alcohol use prevention may have an effect on reducing subsequent violent behaviors (Komro, Williams, et al., 1999). While these programs are showing some moderate successes, there are still a number of gaps that can be addressed in these programs that will make them even more comprehensive and effective.

☐ Bridging the Gap

Unfortunately, there are no existing programs that address alcohol and dating violence prevention together. Although some alcohol abuse prevention programs do discuss or deal with aggression, it is usually in the context of community violence not intimate interpersonal violence. A review of prevention programs that focus on teenage sexual risk behavior indicated that they also were narrowly focused to one aspect of this behavior, that is, abstinence only, contraception programs, and HIV/AIDS awareness programs (Kirby & Coyle, 1997). It is time to begin linking these risk behaviors together in universal and targeted prevention efforts, focusing on the intimate and personal effects of these risk behaviors on teenage dating relationships. Adolescence provides an opportunity to enter into discussions regarding the impact, consequence, and prevalence of these behaviors and explore the perceived benefits and drawbacks of these risk behaviors. Prevention programs can offer an opportunity for youth and adults to engage in discussions regarding the motivators for initiating these behaviors and relevant information regarding short-term effects (Center for Addiction and Mental Health, 2000).

Prevention of specific risk behaviors requires community coordination and varied input. Parents, teachers, school officials, health care workers, and community workers need to be part of strategies to prevent risk behaviors (Cohall, Cohall, Bannister, & Northridge, 1999). Community organizations and resources have learned to work collaboratively on a number of issues, including violence, alcohol, drug use, and the prevention of pregnancy (U.S. Department of Health and Human Services, 1998). Collaboration and coordination helps to reduce costs and improve efficiency as well as build community. The growing research provides evidence that youth may possess a number of concurrent risk factors for any of the behaviors that are outlined in this chapter. There is overlap among the risk factors and behaviors and, therefore, prevention programs need to better consider the clustering of these components and develop programs that will address a number of these issues simultaneously (Saner & Ellickson, 1996).

However, intervention and prevention programs have been weak in helping youth to manage risk and anticipate risky situations in advance (Brooks-Gunn & Paikoff, 1993). Because all risks cannot be eliminated, youth need to learn how to manage them. Prevention programs that make youth aware of how they may be at increased risk in certain situations and provide skills to deal with or avoid the situation may be most promising.

Focus on the Positives

By their very nature, prevention programs focus on preventing the negative and may, in fact, forget to emphasize the positive. It may be very difficult for youth to be motivated or stay interested in programs that are continually sending out the same message, that alcohol, drugs, sex, and dating are dangerous. Studies show repeatedly that peers have the most influence in the lives of youth as they progress through adolescence (Sieving, Perry,

& Williams, 2000; Laursen & Williams, 1997). Instead of focusing on all the risk behaviors youth may be engaging in, a focus on skills to develop healthy dating and peer relationships offers a positive alternative. Many of these risk behaviors occur in the context of interpersonal relationships with peers or dating partners, therefore the focus of prevention should examine how to develop healthy relationships and the skills and knowledge to avoid risky behaviors in these relationships. In developing positive, healthy relationships among teens, we are able to focus on a number of prevention strategies that do not limit the program to only those who are currently engaging in or at risk for certain problem behaviors. All youth need to be able to develop healthy relationships; there is no ceiling on relationship functioning.

Keys to Healthy Relationships

Although there is an increasing desire for and movement toward gender equality in society, equality in intimate heterosexual relationships has not been as forthcoming. Issues of power and control can dominate these relationships. Research indicates that predictors of relationship satisfaction include self-disclosure and listening skills, as well as how couples are able to deal with conflict and disagreement (Leaper & Anderson, 1997). Communication skills—listening, responding, and sharing of feelings and emotions—are important assets in all relationships. Adolescent dating relationships provide the first opportunity to develop these skills in intimate relationships. Programs that provide exercises and activities that incorporate active listening and negotiation skills will assist the youth in many situations. Negotiating skills will benefit youth in their relationships, particularly dating relationships. When entering new relationships, youth need to learn how to discuss their hopes and expectations regarding the relationship. Often, assumptions made by partners regarding their relationship include the level of commitment, how much time will be spent together, and whether sexual activity will be a part of the relationship. Expectations regarding the use of alcohol and drugs are also seldom discussed and so we incorporate this topic in our program. Teaching communication and negotiation skills around the hopes and expectations of the relationship will assist in preventing dangerous assumptions from being made and, perhaps, prevent risky behaviors from developing.

Empowerment

Empowerment moves the emphasis of prevention from creating "problem-free youth" to developing "fully prepared youth" (Kim, Crutchfield, & Hepler, 1998). Empowerment builds on the risk factor approach, but expands the focus from the concept of prevention to promotion. A number of strategies have been developed to encourage empowerment in prevention programs. An awareness of negative behaviors and their consequences, as well as strategies that promote positive, healthy youth development contribute to the concept of empowerment.

Although information, skill development, and social action are important elements of prevention programs, teens need to be active participants in the process, not only through teen leadership, peer mentors, and so forth, but also through the process of self-exploration. Teens need to be given the opportunity to explore and develop their own goals and objectives for the course of action they want to take in their lives (Leventhal & Keeshan, 1993). Encouraging youth to set goals and objectives is usually found within the context of education and career aspirations. However, an opportunity to consider values and choices regarding healthy lifestyles should be just as important. Making choices and goal setting for issues such as onset of sexual intercourse, safe sex practices, alcohol and drug use, as well as choices regarding dating partners and dating relationships give youth an opportunity to explore how these choices and goals may influence other goals and aspirations, and hence have a greater impact on their decision-making and behavior. Youth need to understand that they always have choices, and that they can and do have control over many situations. A sense of helplessness can be avoided if teens have the knowledge and skills to know what their choices are and where to get help when necessary. An opportunity for self-exploration regarding morals and values, as well as long-term goals and expectations will provide a basis for conscious decision-making regarding healthy and unhealthy behaviors and relationships.

Help-seeking and information-seeking skills should be promoted in all prevention programs. Of benefit to youth are programs that teach about resources available in the community and how to access them. This also provides a vehicle for community-wide collaboration in the prevention program; agencies are made aware of the program and open their doors to the youth involved so they can learn more about their services. In addition, an opportunity to develop social action skills will be of benefit to youth. Standing up and making a difference through advocacy and fund raising for organizations and charities affirms choices and commitments made by youth to avoid risky behaviors.

Changing Norms

Making healthy choices regarding dating partners will assist in preventing abusive and unhealthy relationships from developing. Educating youth about what behaviors may cause an unhealthy relationship and learning how to choose partners based on qualities rather than stereotypes will assist in the prevention of abusive relationships. There is an overwhelming subtext in youth dating relationships regarding what is considered to be acceptable and normative behavior. Reasons youth report for having early sexual intercourse include: (1) being physically attracted to their partner, (2) being alone with their partner where "it just happened," (3) having friends who were having sex, (4) feeling grown-up, (5) feeling like they had to, and (6) either the youth or his or her partner being drunk or high (Rosenthal, Burklow, Lewis, Succop, & Biro, 1997). Acceptance of sexual coercion seems to become normalized early in teen dating relationships. It is believed by youth that some aggression or force regarding sexual interaction is common in teen dating relationships, without seemingly much consideration of the consequences to such mind set (Lavoie, Robitaille, & Hebert, 2000). Similarly, the consequences of teenage pregnancy do not seem to be well understood. Youth who perceive positive consequences of teenage pregnancy were at increased odds of engaging in sexual intercourse and unprotected sex (Unger, Molina, & Teran, 2000).

While youth may cognitively understand the choices they make regarding using drugs and alcohol, unprotected sex, and dating aggression, there is a sense of indestructibility among youth—"that will never happen to me." Putting these behaviors into the context of the relationship may provide a different impact perspective for youth (i.e., their relationship partner and the health of the relationship overall). Providing a forum and a context for dialogue about the ramifications for both themselves and their romantic partners of combining drinking and sex or drinking and anger, may provide new learning opportunities for youth.

Cultural Appropriateness

It is often hoped that a universal prevention program will address the needs of all youth in the community; however, this does not appear to be the case. Programs need to be tailored to the needs of the community it is addressing, with sensitivity to developmental issues (age, gender, pubertal status), as well as cultural differences. Cultural and ethnic issues influence youth behaviors and decision-making. For example, Latina women are more likely to perceive positive outcomes of teenage pregnancy (Unger, Molina, & Teran, 2000). Youth who live in rural settings are just as much at risk as those in suburban and urban areas (Stewart Fahs et al., 1999). While the needs of these youth will be the same, the issues will be somewhat different, and program implementation will need to adapt to client characteristics.

In conclusion, prevention programs need to be developed that consider the whole health and well being of adolescents, as opposed to being segmented by problem domains. Although some areas have not yet been adequately researched, such as the link between alcohol and adolescent interpersonal violence, research indicates that risk behaviors often develop and occur concurrently. At a time when youth are beginning to develop more autonomy from family and greater attachment to peers, guidance, information, and assistance with decision-making need to be offered. Since peers and dating partners become the central focus of teen lives, developing prevention skills that focus on these relationships provides a natural conduit for discussion and personalization to the youths' lives. Long-term, sustained prevention programs are needed. Programs that are offered on a continuing basis and are open to "repeat visitors," may have greater impact, especially since some youth may require longer time and more practice to develop skills or explore choices and make decisions. Greater flexibility and comprehensiveness is required in prevention to address the needs of the many versus the few.

☐ References

Adlaf, E. M., & Ivis, F. J. (1998). Recent findings from the Ontario Drug Use Survey. *Canadian Medical Association Journal, 159,* 451–454.

Adlaf, E. M., Paglia, A., & Ivis, F. J. (1999). *Drug use among Ontario students 1977–1999: Findings from the OSDUS.* Toronto, Ontario: Addiction Research Foundation. Available: http://www.camh.net/addiction/OSDUS99.

Adlaf, E. M., Paglia, A., Ivis, F. J., & Ialomiteanu, A. (2000). Nonmedical drug use among adolescent students: Highlights from the 1999 Ontario Student Drug Use Survey. *Canadian Medical Association Journal, 162,* 1677–1680.

Bandura, A. (1977). *Social learning theory.* Englewood Cliffs, NJ: Prentice Hall.

Bensley, L., Spieker, S. J., Van Eenwyk, J., & Schoder, J. (1999). Self-reported abuse history and adolescent problem behaviors. II. Alcohol and drug use. *Journal of Adolescent Health, 24,* 173–180.

Bernstein-Lachter, R., Komro, K. A., Veblen-Mortenson, S., Perry, C. L. & Williamson, C. L. (1999). High school students' efforts to reduce alcohol use in their communities: Project Northland's Youth Development component. *Journal of Health Education, 30*(6) 330–335, 342.

Blueprints for Violence Prevention. (2000). Project Northland: http://www.Colorado.EDU/cspv/blueprints/promise/projectnorthland.html

Botvin, G. J. & Botvin, E. M. (1992). Adolescent tobacco, alcohol, and drug abuse: Prevention strategies, empirical findings, and assessment issues. *Developmental and Behavioral Pediatrics, 13*(4) 290–301.

Botvin, G. J., Schinke, S., & Orlandi, M. A. (1995). School-based health promotion: Substance abuse and sexual behavior. *Applied & Preventive Psychology, 4,* 167–184.

Botvin, G. J., Schinke, S. P., Epstein, J. A., Diaz, T., & Botvin, E. M. (1995). Effectiveness of culturally focussed and generic skills training approaches to alcohol and drug abuse prevention among minority adolescents: Two-year follow-up. *Psychology of Addictive Behaviors, 9,* 183–194.

Brooks-Gunn, J., & Paikoff, R. L. (1993). "Sex is a gamble; Kissing is a game: Adolescent sexuality and health promotion. In S. G. Millstein, A. C. Petersen & E. O. Nightingale (Eds.), *Promoting the health of adolescents: New directions for the twenty-first century* (pp. 180–208). New York: Oxford University Press.

Brounstein, P. J., & Zweig, J. M. (2000). *Understanding substance abuse prevention. Toward the 21st century: A primer on effective programs.* Washington, DC: Substance Abuse and Mental Health Services Administration.

Canadian Council on Social Development. (1999). *The progress of Canada's children.* Ottawa: Canadian Council on Social Development.

Capaldi, D. M., Crosby, L., & Stoolmiller, M. (1996). Predicting the timing of first sexual intercourse for at-risk adolescent males. *Child Development, 67,* 344–359.

Centers for Disease Control. (June 9, 2000) Youth risk behavior surveillance—United States 1999. *Morbidity and Mortality Weekly Report, 49,* 1–96.

Centre for Addiction and Mental Health. (2000). *Alcohol and drug prevention programs for youth: What works?* Toronto: Author.

Clark, D. B., Lesnick, L., & Hegedus, A. M. (1997). Traumas and other life events in adolescents with alcohol use and dependence. *Journal of the American Academy of Child and Adolescent Psychiatry, 36*(12), 1744–1751.

Cohall, A., Cohall, R., Bannister, H., & Northridge, M. (1999). Love shouldn't hurt: Strategies for health care providers to address adolescent dating violence. *Journal of the American Woman's Medical Association, 54*(3), 144–148.

Council of Ministers of Education of Canada. (1999). *Schools, public health, sexuality and HIV: A status report.* Toronto: Author.

Dishion, T. J., Capaldi, D., Spracklen, K. M., & Li, F. (1995). Peer ecology of male adolescent drug use. *Development and Psychopathology, 7,* 803–824.

Farrell, A. D., Kung, E. M., White, K. S., & Valois, R. F. (2000). The structure of self-reported aggression, drug use and delinquent behaviors during early adolescence. *Journal of Clinical Child Psychology, 29*(2), 282–292.

Feldman, L., Harvey, B., Holowaty, P., & Shortt, L. (1999) Alcohol use beliefs and behaviors among high school students. *Journal of Adolescent Health, 24,* 48–58.

Foshee, V. A. (1996). Gender differences in adolescent dating abuse prevalence, types and injuries. *Health Education Research, 11*(3), 275–286.

Furman, W., & Buhrmester, D. (1992). Age and sex in perceptions of networks of personal relationships. *Child Development, 63,* 103–115.

Furman, W., & Wehner, E. (1997) Adolescent romantic relationships: A developmental perspective. *New Directions for Child Development, 78,* 21–36.

Gilvarry, E. (2000). Substance abuse in young people. *Journal of Child Psychology and Psychiatry, 41*(1), 55–80.

Grasley, C., Wolfe, D. A., & Wekerle, C. (1999). Empowering youth to end relationship violence. *Children's Services: Social Policy, Research, and Practice, 2*(4), 209–223.

Guagliardo, M. F., Huang, Z., & D'Angelo, L. J. (1999). Fathering Pregnancies: Marking health-risk behaviors in urban adolescents. *Journal of Adolescent Health, 24,* 10–15.

Hawkins, J. D., Catalano, R. F., & Miller, J. Y. (1992). Risk and protective factors for alcohol and other drug problems in adolescence and early adulthood: Implications for substance abuse prevention. *Psychological Bulletin, 112*(1), 64–105.

Henry J. Kaiser Family Foundation and YM Magazine. (1999). *1998 National Survey of Teens: Teens talk about dating, intimacy, and their sexual experiences.* Menlo Park, CA: Kaiser Family Foundation.

Hughes, R., & Sutton, D. (1996). *Adolescent pregnancy prevention: A practitioner's guide.* [On-line]. Available: http://www.hec.ohio-state.edu/famlife/prevent/guidea.htm

Jackson, S. M., Cram, F., & Seymour, F. W. (2000). Violence and sexual coercion in high school students' dating relationships. *Journal of Family Violence, 15,* 23–26.

Jessor, R. (Ed.) (1998). *New perspectives on adolescent risk behavior.* New York: Cambridge University Press.

Jessor, R., & Jessor, S. (1977). *Problem behavior and psycho-social development.* New York: Academic.

Kilpatrick, D. G., Acierno, R., Saunders, B., Resnick, H. S., & Best, C. L. (2000). Risk factors for adolescent substance abuse and dependence: Data from a national sample. *Journal of Consulting and Clinical Psychology, 68*(1), 19–30.

Kim, S., Crutchfield, C., & Hepler, N. (1998). Toward a new paradigm in substance abuse and other problem behavior prevention for youth: Youth development and empowerment approach. *Journal of Drug Education, 28*(1), 1–17.

Kirby, D., & Coyle, K. (1997). School-based programs to reduce sexual risk-taking behavior. *Children and Youth Services Review, 19*(5/6), 415–436.

Komro, K. A., Perry, C. L., Veblen-Mortenson, S., Williams, C. L., & Roel, J. P. (1999). Peer leadership in school and community use alcohol use prevention activities. *Journal of Health Education, 30*(4), 202–208.

Komro, K. A., Williams, C. L., Forster, J. L., Perry, C. L., Farbakhsh, K., & Stigler, M. (1999). The relationship between adolescent alcohol use and delinquent and violent behaviors. *Journal of Child & Adolescent Substance Abuse, 9*(2), 13–28.

Laursen, B., & Williams, V. (1997). Perceptions of interdependence and closeness in family and peer relationships among adolescents with and without romantic partners. *New Directions for Child Development, 78*, 3–20.

Lavoie, F., Robitaille, L., & Hebert, M. (2000). Teen dating relationships and aggression. *Violence against Women, 6*(1), 6–36.

Leaper, C., & Anderson, K. J. (1997). Gender development and heterosexual romantic relationships during adolescence. *New Directions for Child Development, 78*, 85–103.

Leitenberg, H., & Saltzman, H. (2000). A statewide survey of age at first intercourse for adolescent females and age of their male partners: Relation to other risk behaviors and statutory rape implications. *Archives of Sexual Behavior, 29*, 203–215.

Leventhal, H., & Keeshan, P. (1993). Promoting healthy alternatives to substance abuse. In S. G. Millstein, A. C. Petersen, & E. O. Nightingale (Eds.), *Promoting the health of adolescents: New directions for the twenty-first century*. New York: Oxford University Press.

Luster, T., & Small, S. A. (1994). Factors associated with sexual risk-taking behaviors among adolescents. *Journal of Marriage and the Family, 56*, 622–632.

Malik, S., Sorenson, S., & Aneshensel, C. (1997). Community and dating violence among adolescents: Perpetration and victimization. *Journal of Adolescent Health, 21*, 291–302.

Milgram, G. G. (1993). Adolescents, alcohol and aggression. *Journal on the Study of Alcohol, Supplement No. 11*, 53–61.

Molidor, C., & Tolman, R. M. (1998). Gender and contextual factors in adolescent dating violence. *Violence Against Women, 4*(2), 180–194.

Moore, K. A., Miller, B. C., Sugland, B. W., Morrison, D. R., & Blumenthal, C. (1995). *Beginning too soon: Adolescent sexual behavior, pregnancy, and parenthood*. Washington, DC: Child Trends.

Muehlenhard, C. L., & Linton, M. A. (1987) Date rape and sexual aggression in dating situations: Incidence and risk factors. *Journal of Counseling Psychology, 34*(2) 186–196.

National Center on Addiction and Substance Abuse. (1999). *Dangerous liaisons: Substance abuse and sex*. New York: Author.

Nitz, K. (1999). Adolescent pregnancy prevention: A review of interventions and programs. *Clinical Psychology Review, 19*(4), 457–471.

O'Hara, P., Parris, D., Fichtner, R. R., & Oster, R. (1998). Influence of alcohol and drug use on AIDS risk behavior among youth in dropout prevention. *Journal of Drug Education, 28*(2) 159–168.

O'Keefe, M. (1997). Predictors of dating violence among high school students. *Journal of Interpersonal Violence, 12*(4), 546–568.

O'Keefe, M. (1998). Factors mediating the link between witnessing interparental violence and dating violence. *Journal of Family Violence, 13*(1), 39–57.

O'Keefe, M., & Treister, L. (1998). Victims of dating violence among high school students: Are the predictors different for males and females? *Violence Against Women, 4*(2), 195–223.

Pierre, N., Shrier, L. A., Emans, S. J., & DuRant, R. H. (1998). Adolescent males involved in pregnancy: Associations of forced sexual contact and risk behaviors. *Journal of Adolescent Health, 23*(6), 364–369.

Pittman, A. L., Wolfe, D. A., & Wekerle, C. (1998). Prevention during adolescence: The Youth Relationships Project. In J. Lutzker (Ed.), *Handbook of child abuse research and treatment* (pp. 341–356). New York: Plenum.

Pittman, A. L., Wolfe, D. A., & Wekerle, C. (2000). Strategies for evaluating dating violence prevention programs. In S. Ward & D. Finkelhor (Eds.), *Program evaluation and family violence research* (pp. 217–238). Binghamton, NY: Haworth.

Rosenthal, S. L., Burklow, K. A., Lewis, L. M., Succop, P. A., & Biro, F. M. (1997). Heterosexual romantic relationships and sexual behaviors of young adolescent girls. *Journal of Adolescent Health, 21*, 238–243.

Rosenthal, D. A., Smith, A. M., & de Visser, R. (1999). Personal and social factors influencing age at first sexual intercourse. *Archives of Sexual Behavior, 28*(4), 319–333.

Roth, J., & Brooks-Gunn, J. (2000) What do adolescents need for healthy development? Implications for youth policy. *Social Policy Report, 14*(1), 3–19.

Sampson, R. J., & Morenoff, J. (1997). Ecological perspectives on the neighborhood context of urban poverty: Past and present. In J. Brooks-Gunn, G. J. Duncan, & J. L. Aber (Eds.), *Neighborhood poverty: Vol. 2. Policy implications in studying neighborhoods* (pp.1–22). New York: Russell Sage Foundation.

Saner, H., & Ellickson, P. (1996). Concurrent risk factors for adolescent violence. *Journal of Adolescent Health, 19*, 94–103.

Shrier, L. A., Emans, S. J., Woods, E. R., & DuRant, R. H. (1996). The association of sexual risk behaviors and problem drug behaviors in high school students. *Journal of Adolescent Health, 20*, 377–383.

Sieving, R. E., Perry, C., & Williams, C. (2000). Do friendships change behaviors, or do behaviors change friendships? Examining paths of influence in young adolescents' alcohol use. *Journal of Adolescent Health, 26*, 27–35.

Smith, J. P., & Williams, J. G. (1992). From abusive household to dating violence. *Journal of Family Violence, 2*, 153–165.

Stewart Fahs, P. S., Smith, B. E., Atav, A. S., Britten, M. X., Collins, M. S., Lake Morgan, L. C., & Spencer, G. A. (1999) Integrative research review of risk behaviors among adolescents in rural, suburban, and urban areas. *Journal of Adolescent Health, 24*, 230–243.

Thomas, M. (2000). Abstinence-based programs for prevention of adolescent pregnancies. *Journal of Adolescent Health, 26*, 5–17.

Unger, J. B., Molina, G. B., & Teran, L. (2000). Perceived consequences of teenage childbearing among adolescent girls in an urban sample. *Journal of Adolescent Health, 26*, 205–212.

U.S. Department of Health and Human Services. (1998). *A national strategy to prevent teen pregnancy: 1997–1998 annual report.* Washington, DC: Author.

Valois, R. F., Oeltmann, J. E., Waller, J., & Hussey, J. R. (1999). Relationship between number of sexual intercourse partners and selected health risk behaviors among public high school adolescents. *Journal of Adolescent Health, 25*(5), 328–335.

Vincent, M., Berne, L. A., Lammers, J. W., & Strack, R. (1999). Pregnancy prevention, sexuality education, and coping with opposing views. *Journal of Health Education, 30*(3), 142–149.

Walsh, J. F., & Foshee, V. (1998). Self-efficacy, self-determination and victim blaming as predictors of adolescent sexual victimization. *Health Education Research, 13*(1), 139–144.

Weinberg, N. Z., Rahdert, E., Colliver, J. D., & Glantz, M. D. (1998). Adolescent substance abuse: A review of the past 10 years. *Journal of the American Academy of Child and Adolescent Psychiatry, 37*(3), 252–261.

Wekerle, C., Hawkins, D. L., & Wolfe, D. A. (2001). Adolescent substance use: The contribution of child maltreatment and violence in teen partnerships. Manuscript under review.

Wekerle, C., & Wolfe, D. A. (1998). The role of child maltreatment and attachment style in adolescent relationship violence. *Development and Psychopathology, 10*, 571–586.

Wekerle, C., & Wolfe, D. A. (1999). Dating violence in mid-adolescence: Theory, significance, and emerging prevention initiatives. *Clinical Psychology Review, 19*(4), 435–456.

Williams, C. L., Perry, C. L., Farbakhsh, K., & Veblen-Mortenson, S. (1999). Project Northland: Comprehensive alcohol use prevention for young adolescents, their parents, schools, peers, and communities. *Journal of Studies on Alcohol* (Suppl. No. 13), 112–124.

Wolfe, D. A., Wekerele, C., Gough, R., Reitzel-Jaffe, D., Grasley, C., Pittman, A., Lefebvre, L., & Stumpf, J. (1996). *The Youth Relationships Manual: A group approach with adolescents for the prevention of woman abuse and the promotion of healthy relationships.* Thousand Oaks, CA: Sage.

Wolfe, D. A., Wekerle, C., & Scott, K. (1996). *Alternatives to violence: Empowering youth to develop healthy relationships.* Thousand Oaks, CA: Sage.

Wolfe, D. A., Wekerle, C., Scott, K., Straatman, A.-L., & Grasley, C. (2001). *Prevention in teen relationships: Interrupting the cycle of violence.* Manuscript under review.

16
CHAPTER

Christine Wekerle
Anne-Marie Wall

Conclusion: Clinical and Research Issues in Relationship Violence and Substance Abuse

"Damn kid!" The huge man jumped to his feet, spilling the bottle of whisky he kept by him night and day. "I'll teach you to talk back!" He threw the boy to the couch, pressing one knee on his chest. "Quit your crying! You baby!" The beating lasted long enough to knock the child unconscious. "There! Now you aren't so smart, are you!" The man walked back to the table. He cursed at the sight of the spilled whisky. "See what you made me do!" He went to the kitchen and retrieved a half bottle he had left over from last night. He poured himself a glass. "C'mon, you baby! Get up! Start cleaning up around here!" But my father was too drunk to realize I was still unconscious (Tyman, 1995, p. 7).

I was an alcoholic drinker from the start. I drank alone. When I was sixteen, I was told I was an alcoholic. . . . I only drank like my parents. . . . I drank not to feel, and then when that became intolerable, I'd drink to feel. I did that for thirteen years. . . . My gut feeling about my mother was that she had reached so far inside my body that there was nowhere to hide. . . . I had wanted contact with her—even if it was sexual contact ("Anna Stevens" as cited in Bass & Davis, 1994, pp.400–401).

Professional involvement in the field of family violence is not for the faint hearted. . . . the willful harming of one family member by another is a painful reminder of the darker side of our existence and understandably evokes intense emotions (Fincham, 2000, p.685).

There are a myriad of situations where relationship violence and addiction intersect: an addicted parent who is directly abusive to the child; the adult survivor of childhood maltreatment who is substance abusing; a child growing up with addicted parents where there is domestic violence; an addicted or battered parent who is short on the resources

We are grateful for the valuable assistance of Abby Goldstein. We acknowledge the support of research funding to both authors from the Canadian Institutes of Health Research and the Social Sciences and Humanities Research Council of Canada. The Alcoholic Beverage Medical Research Foundation (A.-M. Wall), and the Ontario Mental Health Foundation New Investigator Fellowship (C. Wekerle).

needed to protect the child from abuse from within or outside the family; and a perpetrator of partner violence with a substance abuse problem, be he a teen, a college student, a married adult, or an older adult, whose partner may or may not be substance-abusing and reciprocally violent. The breadth of the violence and addiction overlap seems staggering and, clearly, our most vulnerable citizens may bear a disproportionate weight of the adversity.

North American statistics are generally similar in pattern, and their dramatic impact stems not only from the harshness of the reality of the current state of affairs, but also from our realization that a lifetime of consequences remain to be seen and fully appreciated. For instance, the United States Administration for Children and Families (ACF) compiles statistics on babies abandoned by their birth parents. In 1991, 21,600 babies were abandoned in hospitals. This figure increased 43% to 30,800 in 1998, where a majority of these babies (65%) were drug-exposed. In 1998, the recorded average daily base hospital costs for these babies were $520, with an average length of stay of 32 days. This is set within the national context that shows increases in the number of children in foster care, as well as the number of abused and neglected children (ACF Press Room, U.S. Department of Health and Human Services [USDHHS], July 2000). To this selected figure on newborns, we must add the numbers of infants, children, and youth who, while in the care of their families, experienced physical, sexual, and emotional abuse and neglect, including witnessing domestic violence, where substance abuse was a co-occurring factor. For instance, one in four children in the U.S. are exposed at some time prior to age 18 to familial alcohol dependence, alcohol abuse or both (Grant, 2000). It has been suggested that substance-involved families comprise 50% or more of the total population of individuals involved in child protective services (CPS); specifically, illicit drug use (e.g., crack cocaine) has been advanced as underlying the increase in rates of child maltreatment cases observed from the 1980s to mid-1990s (e.g., National Incidence Studies [NIS]; Sedlak & Broadhurst, 1996).

Perhaps greater empirical weight can be applied to the problem of the overlap between addiction—including polysubstance abuse—and relationship violence—including domestic violence—in child welfare samples by an, as yet unconducted, epidemiological study, where child welfare families are an oversampled subpopulation of national survey respondents. The number of substance-involved, child welfare families must be substantial, given that the 1998 estimates of abused and neglected children reside at close to 1 million (ACF Press Room, USDHHS, July 2000). An on-going community survey effort would be important for a number of reasons: (1) the numbers of dual-problem families is likely greater than what can be determined from official reports; (2) there may be trends in drug use of parents over time; (3) family violence and addiction experiences often escape detection by formal systems; and (4) the continuum of the overlap in assessing families whose violence and addiction levels remain largely at subclinical thresholds should be evaluated. The extent of current addiction-violence overlap estimates would, however, seem to create a clear imperative for including standardized measures for parental/perpetrator acute and lifetime substance abuse—screening instruments at intake with follow-up interviews and collateral measures (e.g., urine toxicology, assessment of blood alcohol concentration levels)—to be included in the data-gathering protocol and official record keeping in child welfare. The converse also is true: in treatment programs for batterers and substance abusers who have dependents, abusive parenting, in addition to a history of child abuse and child welfare involvement, should form part of the assessment strategy at intake and across treatment.

Beyond the numbers of children affected, we must address the potential for increased subsequent health risks from a lifespan perspective. One large-scale survey (Felitti et al.,

1998) examining the impact of childhood adversity on adult health assessed seven categories of negative events: physical, sexual, and psychological abuse, mother-directed violence, substance abuse mental illness/suicidality, and ever imprisoned household member. These researchers found that, as compared to persons without childhood adversity, persons with four or more adverse child conditions showed a 4 to 12-fold increase in the risk for adult alcoholism, drug abuse, depression, and suicide attempt. Also, a 2 to 4-fold increase was noted with regard to smoking, poor self-rated health, sexually transmitted diseases, and having more than 50 sexual partners; a 1.4 to 1.6-fold increase was noted for physical inactivity and severe obesity. Finally, the number of adverse childhood experiences showed a graded relationship to the presence of adult diseases (i.e., heart, lung, liver disease, cancer, skeletal fractures). Beyond examining health outcomes from a cumulative perspective across the lifespan, as many authors in this volume emphasize, the addiction-violence overlap may be more fully understood by considering outcome over time with specific attention to periods of developmental transition and stage-salient developmental tasks.

As noted by Pihl and Hoaken (this volume), psychopathology outcomes have a significant genetic component and, in particular, the heritability of risk for both addiction and aggression is substantial. A recent study on the psychopathology outcomes associated with a history of child sexual abuse attempted to assess the relative contribution of biological and environmental factors. This co-twins study by Dinwiddie et al. (2000) was based on 1341 monozygotic (MZ; 940 female) and 776 dizygotic (DZ; 540 female) twin pairs who were obtained from the Australian National Health and Medical Research Council Twin Register. Participants were derived from two sources: (1) in 1980–1982 twins participated in a mail survey with a follow-up assessment in 1988–1989, and (2) twins who had participated in an alcohol challenge study in 1978–1979 were given a follow-up interview in 1992–1993. The foci of this report was the long-term sequelae of CSA (assessed with a single question: "Before age 18, were you ever forced into sexual activity, including intercourse?"). CSA was reported among 5.9% of women and 2.5% of men, with no MZ male twin pairs and only 1 DZ male twin pair both reporting CSA. The authors speculate that these low CSA rates may have been related to the use of the word "force" in the question, as similar rates were found in another Australian study on physically forced CSA, as compared to verbally coerced CSA. These authors found support for a shared familial influence for both the risk of victimization and subsequent psychopathology.

Specifically, the concordance rate for CSA was not significantly greater for female MZ than DZ twins, indicating either an important shared environmental risk of reported CSA or joint abuse of both twin sisters. Comparisons were made between twin pairs who both reported CSA history, twin pairs who were discordant for CSA, and nonabused twin pairs. Elevated rates among abused individuals were observed across many disorders for both genders (e.g., serious suicide attempt, major depression, panic disorder, conduct disorder, alcohol dependence), with lifetime rates of psychopathology being 2.47 times greater for women and 3.79 times greater for men. Estimating these rates for female twin pairs discordant for CSA, a trend was observed ($p = .06$) for increased alcohol dependence in the abused twin, as compared to their nonabused twin sibling. Further, abused twins were less likely to have children and they were more likely to report low income than their nonabused counterparts.

Dinwiddie et al. (2000), however, found important associations between parental alcoholism and CSA. Specifically, CSA was associated with paternal alcoholism and depression, as well as maternal depression, for both men and women. For women, CSA also was related to maternal alcoholism. In families where both twins were abused, 48.4% had at least one parent with a history of alcohol-related problems. In comparison to twin pairs in which neither twin reported CSA, significantly elevated odds for psychopathology (i.e., social phobia in women and conduct disorder in men) were observed among nonabused respondents whose co-twin reported CSA. An increased risk for alcohol dependence in women, but not men, was observed when either one or both twins reported CSA. Further, but with the exception of conduct problems in men, the pattern of increased risk to abused persons whose co-twin was also abused, compared to families where only one twin was abused, was found across all measures of psychopathology, including alcohol dependence. These results emerged even though birth cohort and a history of parental alcohol problems were statistically controlled. If a mental health economics analysis could be applied to these lifespan outcomes, the sheer cost to society would fixate policy planners to the addiction-violence problems that negatively impact children exposed to substance abuse and violence. The personal burden of suffering, though, remains incalculable.

Both the burden of suffering and the volume of persons embroiled in the violence and addiction equation create a challenge for service delivery and research that is not easy to approach or accommodate. When the problems of relationship violence and addiction overlap, they have the potential to overwhelm professionals from the frontline to the "ivory tower." The visceral weightiness emanating from violence and addiction experiences propels us toward multiple intervention pathways, including public awareness, early education, prevention, and treatment. To manage, professionals may acquire some desensitization and focus more on one domain, perhaps to the detriment of adequate attention to the other. Given the complexity of the overlap between addiction and violence, cross-training for all, as well as collaboration among specially-trained professionals, seems essential. Specifically, the areas of child maltreatment, adolescent dating violence, young adult courtship violence, and domestic violence, as they overlap with alcohol and other drug use and abuse, may be maximally addressed with a coordinated and collaborative effort across research, service, and governmental domains. The present volume represents one collaborative effort, which will ideally spark greater dialogue and support among professionals in the demanding fields of addiction and relationship violence.

☐ Moving from Research to Clinical Practice: The Conceptualization of an Urgent Public Health Issue

Substance abuse and relationship violence are encountered in every health arena—primary care, emergency rooms, specialized treatment facilities, welfare, education, child protection, criminal justice, faith-based practices, community outreach, and advocacy. The overlap between relationship violence (child maltreatment, partner violence) and substance abuse (alcohol and other drugs) is a real world phenomenon of significant proportion and, among multiproblem families, of substantial magnitude (Wekerle & Wall, this volume). Child abuse, woman abuse, and addictions individually represent serious public health issues, where priority can be indicated by the estimated costs of the negative impact on persons.

Given the absence of such figures for situations in which violence overlaps with substance abuse, it may be instructive to consider these problems as separate concerns, knowing that the overlap costs are buried within. For example, one Canadian study estimated the annual costs of woman abuse with respect to psychiatric interventions at over a half a billion dollars, based on hospital admissions, emergency care, and ambulatory/day clinics, with the total costs of woman abuse estimated at $1.54 billion/year (Day, 1995). United

States estimates of woman abuse have conservatively placed financial loss to the victim at about $150 million per year (Greenfield et al., 1998). These costs are situated in prevalence information on being a victim of domestic violence. A review of studies found, for example, that: (1) 1 in 4 women seeking emergency room (E.R.) care for any reason is a victim of violence, (2) 37% of female patients who are treated in the E.R. for violent injury have been victimized by their partner, (3) 1 in 6 pregnant women is abused during pregnancy, and (4) 1 in 4 women seen in primary care settings have been a victim of domestic violence at some time in her life; of these, 1 in 7 report abuse within the last 12 months (Eisenstat & Bancroft, 1999).

Within Canada and the U.S., the health care costs associated with alcohol and drug abuse are monumental. During 1992 in Canada, for example, it was estimated that there were 86,076 hospital admissions as a result of alcohol-related morbidity, accounting for approximately 1.2 million inpatient days (Single et al., 1996). Comparable estimates for illicit drugs were substantially lower (7,095 hospital admissions resulting in an approximated total of 59,000 days spent in hospital), but nonetheless notable. Direct health care costs to Canada for alcohol and illicit drug use were estimated at $1.3 billion and $88 million, respectively, with the total economic cost equalling 8.87 billion ($7.5 billion for alcohol use and $1.37 billion for illicit drug use). Statistics from the United States in 1992 show an even greater allocation of resources directed towards the treatment of alcohol and drug abuse (Harwood, Fountain, & Livermore, 1998). Specifically, in 1992, it was estimated that there were 524,000 discharges from hospital settings in which treatment was provided primarily for alcohol and drug abuse, resulting in approximately 4.2 million days of care (65% for an alcohol diagnosis). Direct health care costs to the United States in 1992 were $18.8 billion for alcohol problems and medical consequences of alcohol consumption, and $9.9 billion for drug problems (specialized services for the treatment of alcohol and drug problems cost 5.6 and 4.4 billion dollars, respectively). The overall economic cost to society from alcohol and drug abuse was $246 billion ($148 billion and $98 billion for alcohol and drug use, respectively). Based on both inflation and growth in the U.S. population, this report includes projections about the economic effects of alcohol and drug abuse that have been estimated for 1995. A 12.5% increase in total costs was estimated between 1992 and 1995; translated into dollars, the cost of alcohol abuse is placed at $166.5 billion and drug abuse at $109.8 billion. There is no question from an economic standpoint about the imperative to more fully understand and address the overlap in addiction and violence when the costs of these, individually, leave an unambiguous impression.

A prime concern for future research in the addiction-violence field is the continued effort toward theory building and theory testing. There are many ways to understand the overlap between addiction and violence. Across this volume, contributors articulate potential explanations that embrace the dyadic feature inherent in the addiction-violence overlap. For example, Wood and Sher (this volume) identify that while resolving the nature of the relationship is a complex endeavor, the demonstrated association between alcohol and violence may be due to third variables (e.g., common personality traits or common contextual variables). These authors go on to point out that, to the extent that third variable explanations can be ruled out, proximal influences such as beliefs concerning alcohol-related violence (e.g., expectations that alcohol leads to or excuses violence) may play a role. Further, if a causal relationship is possible, for example, ruling out such expectancy effects, there may be important moderators at the person or environmental level, or alternative mediational influences. The complexity of theorizing about the meaning of the overlap is heightened by the need to address these potential third mediator, and moderator variables that may be transformed in a dynamic fashion across development, and subject to differential degrees of sociocultural influences. As Leonard (this volume) highlights, systematic inquiry concerning the role of acute and chronic consumption in the expression of intimate violence and dynamic dyadic effects is critical and, at present, incompletely understood. Conceptual development remains the underpinning to a systematic program of inquiry into the meaning of the overlap among substance use, abuse, and relationship violence. Throughout this volume, several multifactorial theoretical models differentially emphasizing biological, cognitive, affective, personality, and sociocultural influences are discussed. To facilitate our understanding of the overlap, there remains a strong need for continued collaboration between "addiction" and "violence" researchers in a multidisciplinary fashion.

To take the example of child maltreatment, theory-building and testing are especially challenging since such a broad array of experiences—sexual abuse, physical abuse, physical neglect, emotional neglect, emotional abuse, witnessing domestic violence—are captured, and there is considerable variation within type and overlap among types. To illustrate the within variation issue, we can consider the area of child physical abuse. Physical abuse includes excessive corporal punishment that may be impulsive or explosive, experiences that may be less clearly discipline-related and more planfully sadistic (e.g., burning and scalding), and events that may be reactive to unyielding aversive child stimuli (e.g., crying bouts of young infants, as in the case of Shaken Baby Syndrome). While all the above can result in physical injury, they may originate from very different etiological bases. For instance, the Canadian Incidence Study (Trocme et al., 2001) found that physical abuse as the primary category of investigation occurred within a corrective context at an incidence rate of 4.55 per 1,000 children; physical abuse that did not appear intended as punishment occurred at a rate of 2.91 per 1,000 children; Shaken Baby Syndrome occurred at a rate of .09 per 1,000 children. Burns and scalds were noted in 2% of the primary physical abuse cases, and 11% of the primary neglect cases, suggesting a hypothesis of possible different causes. While parental substance abuse was evident in 40% of substantiated primary category physical abuse cases, 50% of substantiated primary neglect cases, and 68% of the substantiated cases with multiple abuse categories, whether parental substance abuse overlapped more with abusive discipline (as compared to the non-discipline related physical abuse, including acts of omission) was not a focus of this study. One might expect that alcohol-related behavioral disinhibition (see Pihl & Hoaken, this volume) may overlap more with excessive discipline (i.e., continuing corporal punishment to the point of bruising) or high parental reactivity (i.e., Shaken Baby Syndrome), than abuse that is inherently more effortfully sequential (e.g., scalding or burning the child). These are potentially important empirical questions that provide opportunities to test out various theoretical tennets and, ultimately, better inform intervention. In terms of special populations, there exists a particular need for more research with CPS samples. It is important to be in a position to compare these families to those maltreated children and youth who remain undetected in the community (thereby facilitating the detection, protection, and service delivery to such community families). In addition to potentially different processes underlying the different within type and forms of child maltreatment, there may be important contextual differences (e.g., socioeconomic disadvantage; Lipman, MacMillan, & Boyle, 2001; Wekerle & Wall, this volume) among maltreating families who are in and out of CPS.

The role of contextual stress continues to be an important future direction for research and practice in the overlap between violence and addiction (e.g., negative peer environment, see Pepler, Connolly, Craig, & Henderson, this volume; family dysfunctionality, see Stewart & Israeli, this volume). Social ecology (e.g., Bronfenbrenner, 1979) and, in particular, ecological models of child maltreatment (e.g., Cicchetti & Lynch, 1993; Garbarino,

1977; Garbarino, Dubrow, Kostelny, & Pardo, 1992) draw our attention to the exacerbating or buffering role of multilevel contextual factors, from the individual child and his or her family, to school and peers, neighborhood, community, and societal level factors. For example, Luthar and D'Avanzo (1999) found that suburban teens reported significantly higher levels of substance use, as indicated by a composite score of nicotine, alcohol, and marijuana use, than did inner city youth. Further, among suburban males only, substance use was associated with popularity with peers, but was associated with rejection by peers among females. While neither childhood maltreatment nor dating violence was a goal for this study, delinquency indices were considered. These were more strongly related to substance use scores among students from suburban as compared to inner city schools. Thus, this study found that the community context significantly interacted with youth symptom indices in predicting substance use.

Another important theory discussed in this volume is Bandura's social learning theory (e.g., Bandura, 1986). As Wall and McKee (this volume) point out, the application of social learning theory to the violence fields has been largely limited to univariate investigations. Within both the fields of addiction and family violence, however, potential moderators of observational learning (e.g., identification with the model, the perceived authority of the model, same versus opposite sex modeling, etc.) need to be more fully investigated. A main mediator in social learning theory are cognitions about expected consequences of behavior, and Wall and McKee (this volume) highlight the need for increased attention to violence outcome expectancies, given the utility and tradition of work in the area of alcohol outcome expectancies (e.g., see Goldman, Del Boca, & Darkes, 1999; Maisto, Carey, & Bradizza, 1999).

Executive functioning problems and aspects of information-processing have been similarly articulated in the substance abuse and violence fields (e.g., appraisal of stressors, see Flett & Hewitt, this volume; frontal lobe functioning, see Pihl & Hoaken, this volume). By way of example, the issue of selected attention to the detriment of adaptive interpersonal functioning has been highlighted in cognitive theories of alcohol-related behaviors, such as alcohol myopia (e.g., see Josesphs & Steele, 1990; Sayette, 1999; Wood & Sher, this volume). In a similar fashion, in the child abuse literature, a stress-induced narrowing of attention and a consequent biased processing of affectively negative information has been advanced (Dumas & Wekerle, 1995; Milner, 1993; Wahler & Dumas, 1989). As discussed by Wall and McKee (this volume), maladaptive coping strategies, such as avoidant coping, are hypothesized to be related to the expression of both addictive and intimate violent behaviors. In this volume, Rasmussen Hall and Follette highlight the construct of emotional avoidance as a conceptual bridge between relationship violence and substance abuse problems, which would be important to consider in future empirical work with dual-issue clients. Crittenden and Claussen (this volume) highlight the range of specific insecure attachment constellations, including those that involve an avoidant strategy, that are likely to be involved in individuals struggling with relationship violence, substance abuse, and their co-occurrence. Biased information processing, maladaptive coping, emotional avoidance, and attachment models represent important potential moderators and mediators of the violence and addiction relationship and, accordingly, may be important considerations for intervention.

For an integration of social ecology and information-processing with attachment theory (e.g., Ainsworth, 1979; Ainsworth, Blehar, Waters, & Wall, 1978; Bowlby, 1969/1982; 1972; 1980), readers are directed to the developmental psychopathology perspective presented by Crittenden and Claussen (this volume). As a guiding structure for moving research into clinical practice, this developmental psychopathology framework is important for its integrative, dynamic-maturational emphasis, including a search for processes supporting continuities and discontinuities in pathways across the lifespan, as well as consideration of common outcomes from diverse beginnings (equifinality) and diverse outcomes from similar initial constellations (multifinality). A developmental psychopathology approach has been employed in the study of substance use and abuse (e.g., Cicchetti & Luthar, 1999; Cicchetti & Rogosch, 1999) and violence (e.g., Cicchetti & Manly, in press). A developmental psychopathology framework would be of considerable value in directing future research on the overlap between addiction and violence.

As emphasized throughout this volume, such basic research on important moderators and mediators in the pathways toward a violence-addiction overlap forms the critical mass for moving efficaciously into intervention research. A search for best practices must be initiated from a clearly developed theoretical base. Yet, given the urgent public health issues that are represented in the overlap between addiction and relationship violence, intervention development must proceed simultaneously with our efforts to understand these joint phenomena better. Based on our current state of knowledge, we turn to the issue of how to prioritize our intervention research efforts.

☐ Clinical Issue 1: Identifying, Recognizing, and Referring

A conclusion that can be drawn in both the relationship violence and addiction fields is that the level of problems encountered has shown an increasing trend over time, at least in some domains and some populations. For instance, in reviewing official estimates of child physical abuse, Miller-Perrin and Perrin (1999) discuss that, while rates have increased in the last two decades (i.e., rates per 1,000 children: 3.1 in 1981; 4.9 in 1986; 9.1 in 1993), public awareness, mandatory reporting laws, 24-hour hotlines, and so forth also have increased. Given that the reporting rate is not evenly distributed across severity classification (i.e., the number of serious, but not mild cases changed over time), this suggests that increasing rates are not dominantly reflective of increasing encouragement to report. Trends beg a closer inspection of correlates and, as noted, this increase in child maltreatment reporting was postulated as parallelling parental illicit drug use (Sedlak & Broadhurst, 1996). In addition to trend analyses, a consideration of peaks also would be important. As Pittman and Wolfe (this volume) detail, teens abusing substances have multiple difficulties in other developmentally-timed ways, such as safe sex practices. A peak in risky behaviors during adolescence would argue more strongly for comprehensive prevention efforts as a potentially cost-effective means to stem the tide towards the more costly treatment services. Prevention also may proceed in a selected fashion, targeting those youth at greater risk (e.g., substance abusing and expectant teenagers).

Considering substance use and abuse, an examination of general trends and patterns of drug and alcohol use suggests a need to target specific drugs of choice and subgroups. For example, results from the 1999 National Household Survey on Drug Abuse (NHSDA) indicate that, among individuals in the general population aged 12 and older, rates of illicit drug use have remained generally stable to those observed during the 1990s. There were, however, some significant increases among particular age groups with respect to specific drugs (Office of Applied Studies, 2000). Specifically, among adults aged 18–25, there has been an increased trend since 1997 for marijuana use. While rates for current alcohol heavy use and binge drinking remained stable to rates observed during the 1990s, a comparison of collegiate and nonstudent individuals (aged 18–22) revealed that full-time college students had higher rates of binge drinking and heavy alcohol use. Indeed, among college students, binge drinking rates continue to be alarmingly high (Gliksman, Demers, Adlaf, Newton-Taylor, & Schmidt, 2000; Wechsler, Dowdall, Maenner, Gledhill-

Hoyt, & Lee, 1998; Wood & Sher, this volume). While there has been a decline in binge drinking among Caucasian students between 1993 and 1997, there has been a significant increase in this type of hazardous drinking behavior among Asian students (Wechsler et al., 1998).

With respect to adolescents, results from the 2000 Monitoring the Future Study (Johnston, O'Malley, & Bachman, 2001) have shown that, after one or two years of decline, illicit drug use (including marijuana, hallucinogens other than LSD, amphetamines, tranquilizers, barbiturates, and alcohol) among teenagers has remained steady, and rates of some specific drugs (e.g., inhalants, LSD, crystal methamphetamine, Rohypnol, crack cocaine) have decreased since their peak levels during the mid 1990s. Disturbingly, however, there was a significant increase in MDMA ("ecstasy") use among eighth, tenth, and twelfth grade students, as well as heroin use among twelfth grade students (Johnston, O'Malley, & Bachman, 2001). An examination of the Ontario Student Drug Use Survey (OSDUS), the longest ongoing study of adolescent drug use in Canada, reveals important differences in trends in drug and alcohol use between U.S. and Canadian youth (Adlaf, Paglia, & Ivis, 1999). Specifically, the 1999 cycle of this survey revealed that, after a lengthy period of decline during the 1980s, there has been a resurgence of adolescent drug use, showing significant increases across a variety of specific drug categories such as alcohol (including heavy consumption), cannabis, MDMA, PCP, hallucinogens, cocaine, as well as polysubstance use (four or more drugs).

Research examining rates of alcohol use and abuse and intimate violence across Hispanic, Black, and White couples in the United States has revealed that ethnic minorities may be at particularly high risk for alcohol abuse, intimate partner violence, and their co-occurrence. For example, Black and Hispanic men experience more alcohol-related problems in comparison to Caucasian males (Caetano & Clark, 1998; Curandi, Caetano, Clark, & Schafer, 1999). A longitudinal investigation on trends in alcohol-related problems across ethnic groups has revealed that, in 1995, the prevalence of Hispanic men reporting three or more alcohol-related problems was almost double that observed in 1984 (Caetano & Clark, 1998). Ethnic differences in intimate partner violence also exist, with Black and Hispanic couples being at particularly high risk for experiencing both male-to-female and female-to-male partner violence (MFPV and FMPV respectively) (Caetano, Cunradi, Clark, & Schafer, 2000; Curandi et al., 1999). Given the limited access members of these ethnic groups have to health care (see Schafer & Caetano, this volume), prevention efforts targeting these apparent high-risk groups seem especially important.

Variation across ethnic groups also appears to exist with respect to the overlap between alcohol use and abuse and the perpetration of intimate partner violence. After controlling for sociodemographic and psychosocial (e.g., childhood victimization experiences of physical abuse) variables, Cunradi et al. (1999) found that racial/ethnic group-specific, multivariate models revealed that female and male alcohol-related problems significantly predicted the perpetration of MFPV among Black, but not Hispanic or White, couples. Ethnic differences also were observed with respect to the perpetration of FMPV, with both male and female alcohol problems emerging as predictors among Black couples. While female alcohol problems predicted FMPV among White couples, neither partners' alcohol problems predicted FMPV among Hispanic couples.

In examining acute versus general alcohol consumption patterns as predictors of MFPV and FMPV among Black, White, and Hispanic couples, Caetano, Cunradi, et al. (2000) found that the relationship between intimate partner violence, alcohol consumption, and ethnicity is complex, showing variations across ethnic groups with respect to alcohol consumption patterns, as well as sociodemographic and psychosocial factors. Indeed, the complexity of ethnic differences concerning the overlap between alcohol use and abuse and intimate partner violence is highlighted by the finding that, among Hispanic couples, level of acculturation exerts a moderational influence (Caetano, Schafer, Clark, Cunradi, & Raspberry, 2000). Consequently, we concur with Caetano, Cunradi, et al.'s (2000) contention that future research attempts to predict intimate partner violence (IVP), particularly with respect to its co-occurrence with alcohol use and abuse, should be ethnically sensitive and include separate analyses for specific ethnic groups. In this regard, prevention and intervention efforts should similarly be guided by the apparent ethnic differences that exist with respect to the addiction-violence overlap. Moreover, as discussed by Cunradi et al. (1999), reducing the prevalence of intimate violence in these minority groups may have significant implications for children who witness such violent acts, thereby helping to "stem a constellation of psychiatric problems whose origins begin in childhood" (p. 1500). Despite these cross-cultural considerations, it is important to keep in mind that the victims of intimate violence, namely women and children, universally bear the burden of suffering (for a more detailed discussion of the needs of women and child victims of domestic violence, see Downs & Miller, this volume).

Another potential avenue for prioritizing service delivery may lie in empirical efforts to delineate more homogenous subgroups of individuals located within the problems of relationship violence and substance abuse. Such efforts may prove especially useful for reducing the higher cost of treatment, as it may facilitate client-treatment matching (see Flett & Hewitt, this volume), avoiding any pitfalls associated with a one size fits all approach to services (see Downs & Miller, this volume). As O'Farrell and Murphy (this volume) note, without empirical validation, the utility of such distinctions remains unknown. One area that has established fairly consistent research findings is batterer typologies (e.g., Holtzworth-Munroe, Rehman, & Herron, 2000). With regard to its utility, few efforts at assessing treatment retention and outcome variables by subgroup typologies exist. Although based on a small sample size, Langhinrichsen-Rohling, Huss, and Ramsey (2000) found subgroup differences in terms of salient correlates (e.g., perpetrator history of childhood abuse, substance-involved criminality), therapist-rated variables (e.g., estimated probability of being violence free six months posttreatment), and rates of treatment completion. These authors, however, acknowledge the need to consider whether different batterer treatments should be delivered to members in the different batterer subtypes. As such, the utility question remains. Any lack of demonstrated treatment-client matching may reside, though, in the lack of understanding of etiology than in the veridicality of identified subgroups. That is, the delivered intervention may not be targetting the essential mediating variables for particular subgroups. Thus, in investigating subtypes, we need to direct energies toward understanding how they are most probably formed and, importantly, how such constellations are maintained over time. Flowing from a clear identification of important mediators or moderators, intervention models may be developed from an empirical basis for the critical constructs that should be targets for change. As service providers, we are challenged to efficiently and effectively intervene. Prior to discussing intervention issues, we need to examine potential barriers to treatment.

☐ Clinical Issue 2: Barriers to Treatment—Help-Seeking Behavior, Access, Quality, and Diversity

Access to treatment encompasses not only physical availability and the existence of services, but also variables related to readiness for and attitudes towards services. First and foremost, psychological access to treatment is contingent on the client's acknowledgment that a problem exists. Within both the addiction (Baxter, Hinson, Wall, & McKee, 1998) and family violence (Kazarian & Kazarian, 1998; Kenny & McEachern, 2000; Malik & Lindahl, 1998) literatures, there is a growing awareness that an individual's appraisal that a particular behavior is maladaptive is influenced, in part, by his or her cultural beliefs and values. Although research on cross-cultural variations in the incidence and prevalence of substance abuse, intimate partner violence, and childhood maltreatment is still developing, cross-cultural differences in how these problems are defined may influence disclosure rates, help-seeking behavior, and so forth.

Acknowledging the methodological shortcomings that characterize research on cross-cultural variations in child sexual abuse (e.g., varying operational definitions, equating race with culture, as well as a failure to consider socioeconomic status and level of acculturation, etc.), Kenny and McEachern (2000) raise the possibility that variation in cultural beliefs and family values may influence the probability of disclosure, as well as how such disclosure is received among family members, and the consequent psychological difficulties that the victim experiences. In considering intimate partner violence, it has been suggested that cross-cultural differences with respect to values such as egalitarianism and interdependence may promote or inhibit power differentials within intimate relationships which, in turn, may differentially promote the expression of and tolerance for violent exchanges (e.g., see Downs & Miller, this volume; Flett & Hewitt, this volume). In a similar vein, results from the Cross-Cultural Applicability (CAR) study (Bennett, Janca, Grant, & Sartorius, 1993) indicate that, while "normal" and problem drinking are valid constructs across cultures, the defining conditions are culture-specific. As such, Baxter et al. (1998) argue that "in determining whether an individual is suffering from alcohol abuse or dependence, it is critical that drinking and alcohol-related behaviors be considered within the cultural context in which they occur" (p. 218).

Regarding the overlap between substance abuse and intimate violence, little is known about whether attributions of blame, responsibility, as well as tolerance for the co-occurrence of these problem behaviors varies cross-culturally. The classic work by MacAndrew and Edgerton (1969), however, demonstrated that "alcohol disinhibition," which may include alcohol-related violence (see Pihl & Hoaken, this volume), is interpreted, enacted, and manifested differentially across cultures, suggesting that important cross-cultural differences may exist. Acknowledging that heterogeneity exists within specific cultural groups and that other variables may exert an impact (e.g., geographic differences in value systems, varying levels of acculturation, SES, etc.), culture-specific determinations of "abusive" behaviors may well influence individuals' propensity to seek out available treatment services. Elucidating the requisite conditions that influence culture-specific behavioral decision-making concerning the need to seek treatment may assist policy makers and inform the development of primary prevention efforts, such as public awareness campaigns.

Beyond considering cross-cultural problem definition issues, there are cultural differences in access to treatment. As Schaefer and Caetano (this volume) point out, a substantial number of persons in the U.S., particularly members of minority groups, have limited insured health care coverage. As such, medical intervention is more likely to be sought when one's physical health is threatened dramatically. Survey studies suggest that broad insurance coverage for mental health is needed in order to gain access to treatment of sufficient duration and with mental health specialists; in one study, primary-care physicians were found to be twice as likely to provide services for mental health than specialists (Wang et al., 2000). There also appears to be inequalities in service as signalled by cultural differences. Wang et al. (2000) found that African-Americans were 10% as likely to receive what researchers deemed as adequate or evidence-based treatment (i.e., eight or more visits with a mental health specialist; psychopharmacological treatment with four follow-up visits with a physician), as were Caucasians. These authors interpreted this result as possibly reflecting a bias among service providers (e.g., premature termination of services) or a tendency for African-American clients to leave treatment more prematurely than other ethnic groups. Clearly, it is important to consider the cultural sensitivity of treatment as it relates to treatment adherence.

In addition to these cross-cultural considerations, individuals entangled in the addiction-violence equation present unique challenges that may impinge on their willingness to engage in treatment. If individuals with violence or substance-related problems have a mistrust of agencies or services, then any amount of insurance coverage would not prevent an underutilization of existing services. The following quotes from addicted mothers in the child welfare system provide a glimpse of some of the varied psychological obstacles to treatment.

> I was always looked at as self-sufficient. I don't like asking for help . . . SRS, treatment, all of it has always seemed to me like a weakness. It's hard to ask for help. It's hard to admit that I'm doing something wrong and not doing what I should be doing or I'm not perfect . . . Asking for help, to me it would be like I wasn't being a good mother (Participant K., as cited in Akin & Gregoire, 1997, p. 397)

> You can't make me do what you want me to do, and that's what they started doing. Telling me, like I was a child or something, that I got to do this. No, I don't have to do anything (Participant J., as cited in Akin & Gregoire, 1997, p. 400).

Peterson, Gable, and Saldana (1996) examined clients' resistance to discussing current substance abuse among mothers who were considered at-risk for maltreatment. In this study, clients were low income mothers of young children, over half of whom were unmarried and unemployed (59% Caucasian, 33% African-American, 8% other minority). These authors identified that lifetime, as opposed to current, substance abuse was a more readily tolerated domain of inquiry, and a positive endorsement was utilized as a basis for discussion about referral to substance abuse treatment. It is important to examine such psychological barriers to treatment when dual-focused interventions may be considered.

A growing area of empirical work concerns the study of how services are delivered. This is especially relevant when the same individual is part of many systems (e.g., within the United States, an individual may be involved with Medicaid, CPS, court-mandated batterer treatment programs, and substance abuse treatment, etc.). Such service utilization research efforts would also provide opportunities for both professionals and consumers/ clients to provide feedback to the service system. Qualitative research involving children and their families, care providers, and other stakeholders can provide depth to quantitative survey methods utilized in order to assess the benefits of various changes to the system of service delivery. We need to not only know what works for whom, but also what works best in what way. Mental health services research, where method of implementation is a variable under study, remains an important future direction and should be a parallel effort in any dual-focused program trial.

☐ Clinical Issue 3: State of Evidence on Interventions

Treatment Programs

In a review of the child abuse and neglect research between 1988 and 1998, Kaplan, Pelcovitz, and Labruna (1999) found a disheartening lack of empirical intervention work. They note the need for well-designed studies in order to assess current services utilization by maltreated children and the effectiveness of psychotherapeutic and psychopharmacological interventions for both maltreated children and their parents. Kaplan et al. make specific mention of the need to understand parent-directed intervention for mothers with affective or substance abuse disorders with regard to the prevention of child maltreatment. There is a substantial literature on how maternal depression intereferes with parenting, as well as the academic, social, and emotional risks to children of depressed mothers (for a discussion, see Cicchetti & Toth, 1998; Dawson, Ashman, & Carver, 2000). Efficacious parenting programs for depressed mothers show improved child outcomes for intervention families as compared to controls in both socioeconomically disadvantaged (e.g., Lyons-Ruth, Connell, Grunebaum, & Botein, 1990), and nondisadvantaged, depressed mothers (e.g., Cicchetti et al., 2000). For example, Cicchetti, Rogosch, and Toth (2000) evaluated their program based on attachment theory, which sought to increase maternal attunement and sensitive responding to their toddler, seeking to improve the overall quality of mother-child relationship and, hence, interactions. This toddler-mother psychotherapy program was found to be beneficial in preventing a relative decline in IQ among intervention toddlers (Cicchetti et al., 2000), as well as promoting higher rates of secure attachment (Cicchetti, Toth, & Rogosch, 1999), relative to nonintervention control children. These literatures may be useful when considering addiction-violence programming with maltreating parents, as well as batterers who are parents with a dual diagnosis of depression and substance abuse.

In a similar vein for couples, Behavioral Couples Therapy (O'Farrell & Murphy, this volume) includes efforts to increase positive feelings between partners, promote shared activities, and foster the development of communication skills in order to bolster participants' abilities to cope with relationship and general life stressors. O'Farrell and Murphy present clear evidence that their substance abuse-focused intervention has the effect of reducing domestic violence, without any explicit targeting of violence (e.g., defining and identifying the cycle of violence, processing experienced episodes of violence, identifying high-risk situations and triggers for violence). Programs that enhance the relational context for parents and partners who are abusing substances and their children may be an important foundation upon which to build specific dual-focused targets for intervention (e.g., strategies for monitoring irritability when withdrawing from substances in a case of relapse or managing cravings for substances while maintaining a positive child focus).

One unique feature of psychotherapy with child abusers or batterers is that they may be court-involved and intervention may be court-ordered, rather than voluntary. This may compromise internal motivation for change (see also Easton & Sinha, this volume). In the case of child maltreatment, parents who comply with court-ordered substance abuse assessments and treatment recommendations are more likely to have their children returned to them from foster care than noncompliant caretakers (Atkinson & Butler, 1996). Rittner and Dozier (2000) studied the effects of court-ordered substance abuse treatment in CPS cases using casefile review ($N = 447$; 63% adjudicated dependent and subject to court orders). Most judges ordered multiple treatments, including treatment for substance abuse, mental health problems, parenting, monitoring for compliance with treatment, and placement of children with relatives. Compliance with court-ordered treatment appeared to decrease over time, with 52% showing good compliance, attending 50% or more of sessions and no positive drug testing results at six months; this dropped to 39% after 12 months. Further, no significant association was found between treatment compliance and reabuse rates. In predicting reabuse of children, suspected substance abuse was not significant. The findings may have been due, in part, to the way in which substance abuse was documented in case files (i.e., it included caseworkers' suspicions, as well as notations on arrests for possession, police report of paraphernalia at the residence, and substance abuse programs' reports noting substance abuse histories). These authors underscore the need for caseworkers to use standardized substance abuse screenings for both the child's parents, as well as the relatives with whom the child may be placed. Also, caseworkers need to consider carefully how treatment compliance information, as compared to involvement in and treatment success, is used in decision-making about continued supervision. These authors suggest that substance abuse treatment compliance may have been used to evaluate whether to proceed with family reunification, without reevaluating changes in family dynamics, child safety, and comorbid mental illness following treatment. This study highlights the problem of adding challenges (i.e., multiple treatments) to already challenged families.

Encouragingly, a recent collaborative, community-based treatment program, Project Connect, illustrates the benefits of innovative approaches for CPS-families in which parental substance abuse is an identified problem (Olsen, 1995). This program had two primary goals: (1) to reduce the risk of child abuse and assist families in staying together, and (2) to increase the capacity of existing services to respond effectively to these families' needs. Predominantly single, polysubstance abusing parents (66 parents, 176 children) received a myriad of home-based services (e.g., home-based substance abuse assessment and counseling, individual and family counseling, parent education, pediatric nursing services, and linkages with formal substance abuse treatment programs [matched according to program structure, counselor attitudes, and client's motivation to engage in treatment], as well other community resources) for an average of ten months. Monthly coordination committee meetings, consisting of representatives from the state child welfare system, as well as substance abuse and health care providers, were held in order to facilitate inter-agency collaboration and improvements in substance abuse service delivery to families. Pre- and postintervention results indicated significant reductions in risks associated with the habitability of the family home, the mental health of the parent, knowledge of child care, and substance abuse. A comparison of the placement experiences of children whose parents received the intervention (76 children) to children in other state-involved families whose parents similarly suffered from substance abuse, but did not participate in the program (80 children), revealed that the placement rates were roughly equivalent between the two groups. Importantly, however, more children in the Project (45%) were reunified and this occurred more quickly (five versus ten months for the intervention and nonintervention groups, respectively). Owing to the Project parents' decisions to enter residential substance abuse treatment and the shortage of facilities that allow children to remain with their parents, a large percentage of the Project children returning home (76%) experienced a change in their living arrangements. While such dual-focused programs remain an important priority, we now consider the status of treatment for the overlap between domestic violence and substance abuse.

The complexity of overlapping problems raises significant challenges to the currently regarded methods of best practice. More than anything, we need to build the knowledge base about effective practice that encourages greater collaboration among the distinct areas in addiction and relationship violence, given the present system disconnect issues. No professional training can do an equivalent job across so many domains, and we need to rely on the expertise of others in a way that resolves the disconnect between child and adult systems, and substance abuse and violence-related systems, so that service is integrated and, ideally, seamless. It is daunting to conceive of a dual-focused manualized intervention, with demonstrated quality assurance, cost-effective use of resources, and proven program efficacy—typically demonstrated by a randomized control trial and shown to be better than medication alone or some alternative treatment. This challenge is heightened when we consider the literature showing the high comorbidity between Axis I psychiatric conditions, especially depression and post-traumatic stress disorder (PTSD), and substance use disorders (see Flett & Hewitt, this volume; Stewart & Israeli, this volume). In their review of the literature, Stewart and Conrod (in press) conclude that the efficacy of standard substance use disorder (SUD) treatment is less apparent when individuals suffer from comorbid PTSD. Important issues to consider include the functional associations that might underlie the high rates of comorbidity between Axis I disorders and SUDs and, when it comes to treatment, the optimal sequencing of treatment strategies (see also Stewart & Israeli, this volume). In Stewart and Conrod's discussion of investigations that have examined potential psychological mediators of poor treatment outcomes among individuals suffering from such dual disorders, individuals' tendencies toward emotional discharge as a means of coping with emotional distress as a possible pathway to SUD treatment resistance is highlighted. Similar maladaptive coping styles also have been found to predict the perpetration of partner violence among adults receiving treatment for SUDs (Wall & McKee, this volume; Wall & Wekerle, 1999). In order to optimally position clients for success and maintenance of treatment gains, such comorbid problems may need to be addressed prior to targeting the overlap between substance abuse and intimate violence that possibly co-occurs among dually-diagnosed individuals.

As Easton and Sinha (this volume) show, steps are being taken towards adapting a well-established, manualized intervention from Project MATCH and using it as a foundation for developing a dual-focused intervention. While at present, having an Axis I disorder is an exclusion criterion for the Easton and Sinha substance-abusing and battering treatment program, they are considering alternative routes for these clients. It may be that clearly defined different treatment versions for different groups of clients are preferable, as would be indicated by research. Downs and Miller (this volume) are very clear about the paramount need to effectively address the substance-abusing batterer. Whether treating the batterer (Easton & Sinha, this volume) or the couple where there is domestic violence (O'Farrell & Murphy, this volume) and substance abuse problems, relapse-prevention remains a central concern. O'Farrell and Murphy (this volume) clearly demonstrate that rigorous program evaluation is possible within these fields and, as they argue and urge, this should represent an achievable goal for developers of treatments for relationship violence, addiction, and their overlap.

In treating individuals with PTSD, it has been suggested that obstacles to treatment may be related to emotional avoidance and mistrust of the therapist or therapy (Zayfert & Becker, 2000). This may apply to intervention with clients who fall within the addiction-violence equation. One strategy Zayfert and Becker (2000) have adopted is to include a group intervention, in tandem with individual efforts, that is specifically designed to combat low client tolerance for therapy, a salient treatment problem. Approach behavior is shaped by balancing psychoeducational and cognitive restructuring work that is structured with free discussion. The goals are complementary to the individual therapy protocol, serving to habituate fears about being in therapy and providing opportunities for supportive feedback and validation from group facilitators and peers. Attention to targeting motivation may be essential when working with behaviors such as substance abuse and relationship violence.

☐ Intervention Target Outcome: Tailoring Client Problem Behavior and Motivation to Treatment Goals

There would be little argument that healthy behaviors are desirable and that destructive ones should be treated. Different concerns, however, arise by population. For example, it is well documented that substance abuse in both adolescence and young adults can be time-limited, with some youth maturing-out of this problem behavior (e.g., Baer, MacLean & Marlatt, 1998; Jackson, Sher, & Wood, 2000; Moffitt, 1993, 1997; Schulenberg, O'Malley, Bachman, Wadsworth, & Johnston, 1996). Among adolescents and young adults, there are subgroups of individuals for whom their use of substances inevitably represents a progressively debilitating lifespan issue. The same may be true for adolescent dating violence, where the majority of youth engage in verbal abusiveness with their dating partners, while fewer engage in physical and sexual coercion. For the majority of these youth, it is unclear whether engaging in partner aggression would similarly mature into a noncriminal and, largely, nonviolent partnership styles (Wekerle & Wolfe, 1999). There may be a subset of these youth for whom violence would continue to escalate in and across relationships, such that their partnerships would be characterized by a violent dynamic. Given the stage of development and the prognosis for the problem, differing intervention strategies may be indicated. Further, the intervention goal and treatment entry may be better positioned if it is consonant with the client's current motivational level, than if the clinical "change bar" is set too high.

A conceptually and practically sound approach to understanding the processes by which individuals undergo either self-initiated or professionally assisted behavioral change is the stages-of-change model proposed by Prochaska and DiClemente (1982). This model includes five stages of change (Prochaska, DiClemente, & Norcross, 1992). The *precontemplation* stage is one in which the individual has no intention of changing his or her behavior in the near future. While in this stage, individuals are either underaware or unaware of their problems that are quite evident to significant others. Entering treatment at this juncture typically occurs as a result of increased pressure or coercion from others. Any gains made during this stage are usually temporary as "once the pressure is off, however, they often quickly return to their old ways" (Prochaska et al., 1992, p. 1103). The *contemplation* stage occurs when individuals become aware that a problem exists and they contemplate making a change, but a commitment to take action has yet to occur. Usually during this stage, individuals begin to take stock of the perceived benefits and drawbacks associated with modifying their maladaptive behavior patterns. During the *preparation* stage, originally conceptualized as the decision-making stage (Prochaska et al., 1992), individuals intend to take action, having done so unsuccessfully in the recent past. It is during this stage that individuals have generally reduced their problem behavior, but they have not reached a criterion for action (e.g., abstinence). The *action* stage involves the modification of behavior, expectations, and the environment in order to effect behavioral change for a period of one day to six months. The final stage, *maintenance*, involves working toward preventing relapse and reinforcing gains made during the action stage. As applied to the field of addiction, this model is conceptualized as reflecting a spiral pattern during which individuals can progress (and regress) through the various stages of change.

Prochaska et al. (1992) assert that "the most obvious and direct implication of our research is the need to assess the stage of a client's readiness for change and to tailor interventions accordingly" (p. 1110). Given the minimization of perpetrators of violence and the denial of substance abuse problems, we concur with the importance of assessing and matching intervention efforts to a client's internal motivation to change. While this may seem tantamount to declaring most individuals in a stage of precontemplation, variation would be expected given the high relapse rates associated with addiction (e.g., Marlatt & Gordon, 1985) and substantial recidivism rates observed following treatment for relationship violence (e.g., Gondolf, 1997; Wolfe & Wekerle, 1993). The stages-of-change model, which is a dominant approach within the field of addictions, also has been applied to the area of teen dating violence and dating health promotion (e.g., Wolfe, Wekerle, & Scott, 1997).

As discussed by Marlatt (1998), abstinence-oriented approaches have dominated treatment within the field of addictions as "abstinence is almost always required as a precondition for treatment, since most chemical dependence treatment programs refuse to admit patients who are still using drugs" (p. 51). This requirement for abstinence, as a means of maintaining sobriety is, in Marlatt's view, a high-threshold approach that often undermines treatment-seeking behavior. In contrast, harm reduction, which is compatible with a public health approach, recognizes abstinence as an ideal outcome, but accepts alternatives that decrease high risk behaviors that result in harmful consequences. As such, harm reduction is viewed as a low-threshold approach that promotes access to treatment services. To this end, proponents of harm reduction approaches are committed to: (1) reaching out and working collaboratively with target populations in order to develop innovative programs, (2) reducing the stigma associated with help-seeking behavior, and (3) providing a "normalized" approach to understanding harmful and risky behaviors. While the philosophical, political, and clinical implications of harm reduction approaches remain the subject of great debate within the field of addictions they are, nonetheless, emerging as viable, practical, realistic, and humane approaches to treating substance abuse and its concomitant negative behavioral consequences (for a review of recent research, see Marlatt, 1998).

Marlatt and colleagues' Brief Alcohol Screening and Intervention for College Students (BASICS), a harm reduction approach that has been developed specifically for college students, utilizes motivational enhancement interviewing (MET; Miller & Rollnick, 1991) in order to minimize these high risk drinkers' resistance to modifying their hazardous drinking behavior. MET, as a short-term intervention, focuses on six key elements captured by the acronym FRAMES: Feedback, including physical testing results (i.e., urine toxicology screen, blood alcohol levels) that can assist the client in exploring a cost-benefit analysis of their problem behavior moving, for example, from a consideration of good and "not-so-good" things to concerns; Responsibility for their own behavior; Advice on the menu of options available for consideration; Empathy especially regarding the obstacles to change; and promoting Self-efficacy by reviewing past successes, including small or incremental steps and nurturing the belief in personal agency. The efficacy of the BASICS program has been demonstrated (Roberts, Kivlahan, Baer, Neal, & Marlatt, 2000).

Within the field of relationship violence, motivational enhancement interviewing also has been advocated as an intervention tool for working with CPS substance-abusing parents (Hohman, 1998), although research on its effectiveness in this population remains to be seen. Hohman (1998) notes the overlap among social work orientation and MET principles, including client self-determination, respect, dignity, and empowerment, as opposed to a more forceful, direct confrontation that can have the undesirable effect of increasing resistance and maintaining denial. For instance, MET advocates an avoidance of argumentation and negative labeling and, instead, proposes that clinicians roll with the resistance by moving to a less emotionally provocative level of the topic or reflecting the positives and negatives aspects of the issue that the client has raised. The goal-oriented MET interviews may be a good match for the child welfare setting, given that it represents a structured effort at increasing the collaborative nature of a CPS investigation. MET, with its goal of facilitating internally motivated desires for change, may be helpful to the substance-abusing CPS parent in that it may bring into awareness the reality that drugs and alcohol are a problem. This awareness challenges beliefs concerning efficacious parenting, and may serve to confront the ambivalence and fear parents may feel about changing their substance abuse patterns, allowing for an examination of options and the development, step-by-step, of an action plan on how to effect desired changes.

There exists a need for continued support of research designed to develop and test innovative behavioral, pharmacological, and multimodal treatments for addiction and violence problems. In so doing, we need to pay special attention to legal, ethical and confidentiality issues in the interface between research and treatment. It may be valuable to embrace a multipronged approach, recognizing the need for behavior change across multiple domains, taking into account both proximal and long-term goals for treatment. Parallelling the field of addictions, harm reduction approaches have been advocated for treating perpetrators of child abuse, albeit not without controversy (Laws, 1999). With regard to adult partner violence, harm reduction approaches may prove beneficial in moving perpetrators of intimate violence along the continuum toward change (Marlatt, 2001, February, personal communication). There would be consensus, however, among all treatment providers in both the fields of addiction and violence that increased prevention efforts would be a highly desirable corollary intervention goal.

☐ Prevention Programs

While one may construe a short story version of the violence and addiction equation, being tempted, perhaps, to think that substance abusers and violence perpetrators fall into aversive contexts, have aversive interactions with most people, and have aversive personalities, such a stance has little clinical utility as the individual—indeed, the common denominator—is in need of help. The comorbidity of violence and addiction is a magnified indicator of adaptational challenge and the need for professional outreach and prevention. A strong theme throughout this volume is the undeniable need and value to proceed strongly with prevention efforts.

One parenting program, designed to prevent child abuse, does include mothers with substance abuse disorders. Peterson et al.'s (1996) Mom/Kid Trial project reported treatment retention data for mothers who received lifetime diagnoses for alcohol dependence or abuse, marijuana diagnoses, and cocaine diagnoses, indicating that the majority of these substance abusing mothers completed treatment (rates: 64% alcohol; 81% marijuana; 100% cocaine, with overlapping diagnoses noted for most). It is noted that this program has adapted a guided self-change approach to substance abuse, although treatment outcome data remain to be reported. Peterson et al., in their review of the child maltreatment and substance abuse literature, do highlight similar findings suggesting an overlap in suitable intervention targets, including knowledge of child development, punitive parenting, and problems with parental communication and child attachment. These authors call for a greater collaboration among researchers in an effort to provide a more effective and holistic treatment to substance abusing mothers at risk for child maltreatment, noting that few substance abuse residential programs allow children to stay with the mother, nor do they typically provide cognitive behavioral approaches that have shown some effectiveness with maltreating populations (for a review of treatment programs for maltreating parents, see Wolfe & Wekerle, 1993).

Another area for prevention is early intervention with parents of young children, so as to thwart the possibility that maltreated offspring develop substance use problems. For example, the clinical research of David Olds and colleagues (Olds et al., 1997), targets the reduction of child abuse and neglect. Their Nurse Home Visitation Program, which combines parent training, child health, and family support, was originally implemented with low income, single mother families. A randomized trial showed several significant gains for intervention mothers, including decreased child abuse and neglect reports and related variables. At a 15 year follow-up, intervention children were markedly less likely to have run away, been arrested, or have drug and alcohol-related problems. Intervention benefits, however, were substantially mitigated when domestic violence was present. This research shows the efficacy of targeting an important mediator of the relationship between early risk and later violence and substance-related outcomes, namely parenting. This study also suggests, however, that domestic violence may moderate the success of such a prevention program (for reviews of prevention programs, see MacMillan, MacMillan, Offord, Griffith, & MacMillan, 1994a, 1994b; Wekerle & Wolfe, 1993).

The issue of prevention is highlighted by the overlap across the lifespan that is presented in this volume, from adolescents (Pepler et al.), young adults such as college students (Wood & Sher), engaged and newly-wed couples (Leonard), to older adults (Rasmussen Hall & Follette). Wekerle and Wolfe (1993) have identified adolescence, a time when intimate relationships begin to form, and early adulthood, when individuals typically assume parental status as windows of opportunities for prevention efforts (see also Leonard, this volume). The data on normative, community youth presented by Pepler et al. (this volume) points to adolescence as a prime intervention window for a dual-focus on relationship violence (bullying, sexual harassment, teen dating violence) and substance abuse (alcohol and other drugs). It is important to keep in mind the research on high risk samples of adolescents that finds antisocial-conduct disorders to be a risk factor for adolescent drug use and abuse. For example, Clark, Parker, and Lynch (1999) found that child antisocial disorder mediated the relationship between paternal drug abuse and the substance abuse problems of their sons. Cicchetti and Rogosch (1999) point out that, while treatment of antisocial behaviors leading to reduced substance abuse would advance antisocial behaviors to a causal risk factor, it may be an overly unspecific approach to prevention. Given the overlap among problem behaviors in normative and high risk samples, identifying the common risk processes that signal multifinality would be a more coherent approach to prevention.

As Pittman and Wolfe (this volume) advocate, universal prevention efforts delivered in schools and community organizations should begin to consider dual-focused efforts that facilitate youth making connections between substance use and dating aggression, including sexual coercion and unprotected sex. Wide dissemination of information to youth, such as the amount of alcohol consumption leading to exceeding the legal limits and dating behaviors that fall under the criminal law, as well as facilitating skill development in order to support health promotion behaviors (e.g., safety and protection skills for any heightened risk activity) would avoid problems of negative labeling of services. For instance, while Foshee and colleagues delivered their Safe Dates program in the schools and facilitated connections to community resources, few teens sought services outside the school environment (Foshee, 1996; Foshee et al., 1996; Foshee et al., 1998). In short, universal prevention has the advantage among adolescents of promoting a greater "buy in" by school members—students, teachers, guidance counselors, social workers, and administrators—that may have positive benefits to the perceived school climate.

Flanagan and Faison (2001) make an important distinction between zero tolerance and teaching tolerance as policies. The former is focused on the individual and most often is associated with punitive measures (e.g., school expulsion, mandatory community service), and the latter is focused on embracing resolution as part of the public domain, encouraging prosocial involvement of youth bystanders, and peers as counsellors (e.g., peer mediation, cross-curriculum violence education, protected school time for social problem-solving and group cohesion building). This may apply to substance abuse and violence prevention in encouraging peer support for treatment and responsible substance use, as well as recruiting adolescents to tailor and deliver prevention programming to their peers and to younger age children. School youth may be in a position to galvanize prevention efforts toward an inclusive orientation that can transcend social cliques and heighten compassion and social responsibility. Moreover, for youth who come from addiction-violence backgrounds, a heightened sense of mastery and self-efficacy may be achieved in the movement from victim to social advocate (Wolfe et al., 1997). Such prevention efforts, though, may be maximally realized only with the commitment, support, and facilitation of administration across school systems.

Child victims have found ways to function in the maltreating and addicted family, however, these are likely to be very much at odds with functioning in other domains as their lives move on, including to the point of becoming parents themselves. To help prevent maladjustment in these children, we need to help their families. The recommendations stemming from the report of the United States Surgeon General's Conference on Children's Mental Health (USDHHS, 1999) are applicable to most mental health problems, including the overlap between relationship violence and addiction. The report highlights the need to move toward "a community health system that balances health promotion, disease prevention, early detection, and universal access to care. That system must include a balanced research agenda, including basic, biomedical, clinical, behavioral, health services, school-based and community-based prevention and intervention research. . . . Mental healthcare is dispersed across multiple systems. . . . But the first system is the family" (pp. 4–5). Every adult addict, batterer, child abuser, and victim was once a child in a family. We cannot afford to miss opportunities for prevention, early identification, and coordinated services. Be it a child, an adult, or a family, the importance and priority for care of proven quality remains high.

☐ Concluding Comments

Research in addictions is nested within a designated and well-established research support network (e.g., specific funding agencies such as the National Institute on Alcohol Abuse and Alcoholism [NIAAA], and the National Institute on Drug Abuse [NIDA]). For example, in 1993, a program announcement from NIAAA on alcohol and violent behavior was issued. It was situated within a Public Health Service-led national activity for setting priority areas, "Healthy People 2000," where the goal was reducing violent and abusive behavior, including child abuse and domestic violence, and decreasing morbidity and mortality associated with alcohol consumption. In 1996, research on relationships between alcohol and violence was flagged as a NIAAA Special Emphasis Area. In NIAAA's Strategic Plan for 2001–2005, one of its stated seven goals is to further elucidate the relationships between alcohol and violence. In an effort towards achieving this goal, special interests include many of the areas addressed in this volume (e.g., intergenerational linkages, the impact of childhood maltreatment—either direct or indirect—on subsequent alcohol-related behaviors, development of alcohol expectancies related to violence, effects of alcohol on information processing and the perception of potentially aggressive cues, etc.). Such organized encouragement to work on the understanding of and the development of services to those individuals involved in relationship violence and addiction problems is crucial to scholarly advancement. The coming years should be an exciting time for research pertaining to the violence and addiction equation; may the fruitful work continue.

☐ References

Adlaf, E. M., Paglia, A., & Ivis, F. J. (1999). *Drug use among Ontario students 1977–1999: Findings from the OSDUS*. Toronto, Ontario: Addiction Research Foundation. [Also available on the World Wide Web: http://www.camh.net/addiction/OSDUS99].

Administration for Children and Families (ACF) Press Room, United States Department of Health and Human Services (July, 2000). *Abandoned babies—preliminary national estimates.* [Also available on the World Wide Web: http://www.acf.dhhs.gov/news/stats/abandon.htm].

Ainsworth, M. D. S. (1979). Infant-mother attachment. *American Psychologist, 34,* 932–937.

Ainsworth, M. D. S., Blehar, M. C., Waters, E., & Wall, S. (1978). *Patterns of attachment: A psychological study of the strange situation.* Hillsdale, NJ: Erlbaum.

Akin, B. A., & Gregoire, T. K. (1997). Parents' views on child welfare's response to addiction. *Families in Society, July–August,* 393–404.

Atkinson, L., & Butler, S. (1996). Court-ordered assessment: Impact of maternal noncompliance in child maltreatment cases. *Child Abuse and Neglect, 20,* 185–190.

Baer, J. S., MacLean, M. G., & Marlatt, A. G. (1998). Linking etiology and treatment for adolescent substance abuse: Toward a better match. In R. Jessor (Ed.). *New perspectives on adolescent risk behavior* (pp. 182–220). New York: Cambridge University Press.

Bandura, A. (1986). *Social foundations of thought and action: A social cognitive theory.* Englewood Cliffs, NJ: Prentice-Hall.

Bass, E., & Davis, L. (1994). *The courage to heal,* third edition. New York: HarperCollins.

Baxter, B. A., Hinson, R. E., Wall, A-M., & McKee, S. A. (1998). Incorporating culture into the treatment of alcohol abuse and dependence. In S. S. Kazarian & D. R. Evans (Eds.), *Cultural clinical psychology: Theory, research, and practice* (pp. 215–245). New York: Oxford University Press.

Bennett, L. A., Janca, A., Grant, B. F., & Sartorius, N. (1993). Boundaries between normal and pathological drinking: A cross-cultural comparison. *Alcohol Health and Research World, 17,* 190–195.

Bowlby, J. (1969/1982). *Attachment and loss: Vol 1: Attachment* (2nd ed.). New York: Basic.

Bowlby, J. (1972). *Attachment and loss: Vol. 2: Separation, anxiety, and anger.* New York: Basic.

Bowlby, J. (1980). *Attachment and loss: Vol. 3: Loss, sadness, and depression.* New York: Basic.

Bronfrenbrenner, U. (1979). *The experimental ecology of human development.* Cambridge, MA: Harvard University Press.

Caetano, R., & Clark, C. L. (1998). Trends in alcohol-related problems among Whites, Blacks, and Hispanics: 1984-1995. *Alcoholism: Clinical and Experimental Research, 22,* 534–538.

Caetano, R., Cunradi, C. B., Clark, C. L., & Schafer, J. (2000). Intimate partner violence and drinking patterns among White, Black, and Hispanic couples in the U.S. *Journal of Substance Abuse, 11,* 123–138.

Caetano, R., Schafer, J., Clark, C. L., Cunradi, C. B., & Raspberry, K. (2000). Intimate partner violence, acculturation, and alcohol consumption among Hispanic couples in the United States. *Journal of Interpersonal Violence, 15,* 30–45.

Cicchetti, D., & Luthar, S. S. (1999). Special issue: Developmental approaches to substance use and abuse. *Development and Psychopathology, 11.*

Cicchetti, D., & Lynch, M. (1993). Toward an ecological/transactional model of community violence and child maltreatment: Consequences for children's development. *Psychiatry, 56,* 96–118.

Cicchetti, D., & Rogosch, F. A. (1999). Psychopathology as risk for adolescent substance use disorders: A developmental psychopathology perspective. *Journal of Clinical Child Psychology, 28,* 355–365.

Cicchetti, D., Rogosch, F. A., & Toth, S. L. (2000). The efficacy of toddler-parent psychotherapy for fostering cognitive development in offspring of depressed mothers. *Journal of Abnormal Child Psychology, 28,* 135–148.

Cicchetti, D., & Toth, S. L. (1998). The development of depression in children and adolescents. *American Psychologist, 53,* 221–241.

Cicchetti, D., & Toth, S. L. (in press). Special issue: Classification issues in child maltreatment. *Development and Psychopathology.*

Cicchetti, D., Toth, S. L., & Bogosch, E. A. (1999). The efficacy of toddler-parent psychotherapy to increase attachment security in offspring of depressed mothers. *Attachment and Human Development, 1,* 34–66.

Clark, D.B., Parker, A-M., & Lynch, K.G. (1999). Psychopathology and substance-related problems during early adolescence: A survival analysis. *Journal of Clinical Child Psychology, 28,* 333–341.

Cunradi, C. B., Caetano, R., Clark, C. L., & Schafer, J. (1999). Alcohol-related problems and intimate partner violence among White, Black, and Hispanic couples in the U.S. *Alcoholism: Clinical and Experimental Research, 23,* 1492–1501.

Dawson, G., Ashman, S. B., & Carver, L. J. (2000). The role of early experience in shaping behavioral and brain development and its implications for social policy. *Development and Psychopathology, 12,* 695–712.

Day, T. (1995). *The health related costs of violence against women in Canada: The tip of the iceberg.* London, Ontario, Canada: Centre for Research on Violence Against Women and Children.

Dimeff, L. A., Baer, J. S., Kirlahan, D. D., & Marlatt, G. A. (1999). *Brief alcohol screening and intervention for college students (BASICS): A harm reduction approach.* New York: Guilford.

Dinwiddie, S., Heath, A. C., Dunne, M. P., Bucholz, K. K., Madden, P. A. F., Slutske, W. S., Bierut, L. J., Statham, D. B., & Martin, N. G. (2000). Early sexual abuse and lifetime psychopathology: A co-twin-control study. *Psychological Medicine, 30,* 41–52.

Dumas, J. E., & Wekerle, C. (1995). Maternal reports of child behavior problems and personal distress as predictors of dysfunctional parenting. *Development and Psychopathology, 7,* 465–479.

Eisenstat, S., & Bancroft, L. (1999). Domestic violence. *New England Journal of Medicine, 341,* 886–892.

Felitti, V. J., Anda, R. F., Nordenberg, D., Williamson, D. F., Spitz, A. M., Edwards, B. A., Koss, M. P., & Marks, J. S. (1998). Relationship of childhood abuse and household dysfunction to many leading causes of death in adults: The Adverse Childhood Experiences (ACE) study. *American Journal of Preventive Medicine, 14,* 245–258.

Fincham, F. D. (2000). Family violence: A challenge to behavior therapists. *Behavior Therapy, 31,* 685–693.

Flanagan, C. A., & Faison, N. (2001). Youth civic development: Implications of research for social policy and programs. *Social Policy Report, 15,* 3–14.

Foshee, V. A. (1996). Gender differences in adolescent dating abuse prevalence, types, and injuries. *Health Education Research, 11,* 275–286.

Foshee, V. A., Bauman, K. E., Arriaga, X. B., Helms, R. W., Koch, G. G., & Linder, G. F. (1998). An evaluation of Safe Dates, an adolescent dating violence prevention program. *American Journal of Public Health, 88,* 45–50.

Foshee, V. A., Linder, G. F., Bauman, K. E., Langwick, S. A., Arriaga, X. B., Heath, J. L., McMahon, P. M., & Bangdiwala, S. (1996). The Safe Dates Project: Theoretical basis, evaluation design, and selected baseline findings. *American Journal of Preventive Medicine, 12,* 39–47.

Garbarino, J. (1977). The human ecology of child maltreatment: A conceptual model for research. *Journal of Marriage and the Family, 39,* 721–736.

Garbarino, J., Dubrow, N., Kostelny, K., & Pardo, C. (1992). *Children in danger.* San Francisco: Jossey-Bass.

Gliksman, L., Demers, A., Adlaf, E. M., Newton-Taylor, B., & Schmidt, K. (2000). *Canadian Campus Survey 1998.* Toronto, Ontario: Centre for Addiction and Mental Health.

Goldman, M. S., Del Boca, F. K., & Darkes, J. (1999). Alcohol expectancy theory: The application of cognitive neuroscience. In K. E. Leonard & H. T. Blane (Eds.), *Psychological theories of drinking and alcoholism.* (2nd ed., pp. 203–246). New York: Guilford.

Gondolf, E. W. (1997). Patterns of reassault in batterer programs. *Violence and victims, 12,* 373–387.

Grant, B. F. (2000). Estimates of US children exposed to alcohol abuse and dependence in the family. *American Journal of Public Health, 90,* 112–115.

Greenfield, L., Rand, M. R., Craven, D., Klaus, P. A., Ringel, C., Warchol, G., Maston, C., & Fox, J.A. (Eds.). (1998). *Violence by intimates: Analysis of data on crimes by current or former spouses, boyfriends, and girlfriends.* Bureau of Justics Statistics Factbook. Washington, DC: U.S. Department of Justice.

Harwood, H. J., Fountain, D., & Livermore, G. (1998). Economic costs of alcohol abuse and alcoholism. In M. Galanter (Ed.), *Recent developments in alcoholism: Vol. 14. The consequences of alcoholism: Medical neuropsychiatric economic cross cultural* (pp. 307–330). New York: Plenum.

Hohman, M. M. (1998). Motivational interviewing: An intervention tool for child welfare case workers working with substance-abusing parents. *Child Welfare, 77,* 275–289.

Holtzworth-Munroe, A., Rehman, U., & Herron, K. (2000). General and spouse-specific anger and hostility in subtypes of maritally violent men and nonviolent men. *Behavior Therapy, 31,* 603–630.

Jackson, K. M., Sher, K. J., & Wood, P. K. (2000). Trajectories of concurrent substance use disorders:

A developmental, typological approach to comorbidity. *Alcoholism: Clinical and Experimental Research, 24,* 902–913.

Johnston, L. D., O'Malley, P. M., & Bachman, J. G. (2001). *Monitoring the future: National results on adolescent drug use, overview of key findings, 2000* [On-line]. Available: http://www.monitoringthefuture.org.

Josephs, R. A., & Steele, C. M. (1990). The two faces of alcohol myopia: Attentional mediation of psychological stress. *Journal of Abnormal Psychology, 99,* 115–126.

Kaplan, S. J., Pelcovitz, D., & Labruna, V. (1999). Child and adolescent abuse and neglect research: A review of the past 10 years. Part I: Physical and emotional abuse and neglect. *Journal of the American Academy of Child and Adolescent Psychiatry, 38,* 1214–1222.

Kazarian, S. S., & Kazarian, L. Z. (1998). Cultural aspects of family violence. In S. S. Kazarian & D. R. Evans (Eds.), *Cultural clinical psychology: Theory, research, and practice* (pp. 316–347). New York: Oxford University Press.

Kenny, M. C., & McEachern, A. G. (2000). Racial, ethnic, and cultural factors of childhood sexual abuse: A selected review of the literature. *Clinical Psychology Review, 20,* 905–922.

Langhinrichsen-Rohling, J. Huss, M. T., & Ramsey, S. (2000). The clinical utility of batterer typologies. *Journal of Family Violence, 15,* 37–53.

Laws, D. R. (1999). Relapse prevention: The state of the art. *Journal of Interpersonal Violence, 14,* 285–302.

Lipman, E. L., MacMillan, H. L., & Boyle, M. (2001). Childhood abuse and psychiatric disorders among single and married mothers. *American Journal of Psychiatry, 158,* 73–77.

Luthar, S. S., & D'Avanzo, K. (1999). Contextual factors in substance use: A study of suburban and inner-city adolescents. *Development and Psychopathology, 11,* 845–868.

Lyons-Ruth, K., Connell, D., Grunebaum, H., & Botein, S. (1990). Infants at social risk: Maternal depression and family support services as mediators of infant development and security of attachment. *Child Development, 61,* 85–98.

MacAndrew, C. R., & Edgerton, B. (1969). *Drunken comportment: A social explanation.* Chicago: Aldine.

MacMillan, H. L. (2000). Child maltreatment: What we know in the year 2000. *Canadian Journal of Psychiatry, 45,* 702–709.

MacMillan, H. L., MacMillan, J. H., Offord, D. R., Griffith, L., & MacMillan, A. (1994). Primary prevention of child physical abuse and neglect: A critical review. Part I. *Journal of Child Psychology and Psychiatry, 35,* 835–856.

MacMillan, H. L., MacMillan, J. H., Offord, D. R., Griffith, L., & MacMillan, A. (1994b). Primary prevention of child sexual abuse: A criticial review. Part II. *Journal of Child Psychology and Psychiatry, 35,* 857–876.

Maisto, S. A., Carey, K. B., & Bradizza, C. M. (1999). Social learning theory. In K. E. Leonard & H. T. Blane (Eds.), *Psychological theories of drinking and alcoholism* (2nd ed., pp. 106–163). New York: Guilford.

Malik, N. M., & Lindahl, K. M. (1998). Aggression and dominance: The roles of power and culture in domestic violence. *Clinical Psychology: Science and Practice, 5,* 409–423.

Marlatt, G. A. (1998). *Harm reduction: Pragmatic strategies for managing high-risk behaviors.* New York: Guilford.

Marlatt, G. A., & Gordon, J. R. (Eds.). (1985). *Relapse prevention: Maintenance strategies in the treatment of addictive behaviors.* New York: Guilford.

Miller, W. R., & Rollnick, S. (1991). *Motivational interviewing.* New York: Guilford.

Miller-Perrin, C. L., & Perrin, R. D. (1999). *Child maltreatment: An introduction.* Thousand Oaks, CA: Sage.

Milner, J. S. (1993). Social information processing and physical child abuse. *Clinical Psychology Review, 13,* 275–294.

Moffitt, T. E. (1993). Adolescence-limited and life-course persistent antisocial behavior: A developmental taxonomy. *Psychological Review, 100,* 674–701.

Moffitt, T. E. (1997). Adolescence-limited and life-course persistent offending: A complementary pair of developmental theories. In T. P. Thornberry (Ed.), *Developmental theories of crime and delinquency. Advances in criminological theory,* Vol. 7 (pp. 11–54). New Brunswick, NJ: Transaction Publishers.

Office of Applied Studies, Substance Abuse and Mental Health Statistics (2000). *Highlights from the latest OAS report* [On-line]. Available: http://www.drugabusestatistics.samhsa.gov.

Olds, D. L., Eckenrode, J., Henderson, C. R., Jr., Kitzman, H., Powers, J., Cole, R., Sidora, K., Morris, P., Pettitt, L. M., & Luckey, D. (1997). Long-term effects of home visitation on maternal life course and child abuse and neglect. Fifteen-year follow-up of a randomized trial. *Journal of the American Medical Association, 278,* 637–643.

Olsen, L. J. (1995). Services for substance abuse-affected families: The Project Connect experience. *Child and Adolescent Social Work Journal, 12,* 183–195.

Peterson, L., Gable, S., & Saldana, L. (1996). Treatment of maternal addiction to prevent child abuse and neglect. *Addictive Behaviors, 21,* 789–801.

Prochaska, J. C., & DiClemente, C. C. (1982). Transtheoretical therapy: Toward a more integrative model of change. *Psychotherapy: Theory, Research, and Practice, 19,* 276–288.

Prochaska, J. C., DiClemente, C. C., & Norcross, J. C. (1992). In search of how people change: Applications to addictive behaviors. *American Psychologist, 47,* 1102–1114.

Rittner, B., & Dozier, C. D. (2000). Effects of court-ordered substance abuse treatment in child protective services cases. *Social Work, 45,* 131–140.

Roberts, L. J., Kivlahan, D. R., Baer, J. S., Neal, D. J., & Marlatt, G. A. (2000). Individual drinking changes following a brief intervention among college students: Clinical significance in an indicated preventive context. *Journal of Consulting and Clinical Psychology, 68,* 500–505.

Sayette, M. A. (1999) Cognitive theory and research. In K. E. Leonard & H. T. Blane (Eds.), *Psychological theories of drinking and alcoholism* (2nd ed., pp. 247–291). New York: Guilford.

Schulenberg, J., O'Malley, P. M., Bachman, J. G., Wadsworth, K. N., & Johnston, L. D. (1996). Getting drunk and growing up: Trajectories of frequent binge drinking during the transition to young adulthood. *Journal of Studies on Alcohol, 57,* 289–304.

Sedlak, A. J., & Broadhurst, D. D. (1996). *Third national incidence study on child abuse and neglect.* Washington, DC: U.S. Department of Health and Human Services.

Single, E., Robson, L., Xie, X., Rehm, J., Moore, R., Choi, B., Desjardins, S., & Anderson, J. (1996). *The costs of substance abuse in Canada* [On-line]. Available: http://www.cscsa.ca/costhigh.htm.

Stewart, S. H., & Conrod, P. J. (in press). Psychosocial models of functional associations. In P. C. Ouimette & P. J. Brown (Eds.), *PTSD and substance abuse disorder comorbidity: Advances and challenges in research and practice.* Washington, DC: American Psychological Association.

Trocme, N., MacLaurin, B., Fallon, B., Daciuk, J., Billingsly, D., Tourigny, M., Mayer, M., Wright, J., Barter, K., Burford, G., Hornick, J., Sullivan, R., & McKenzie, B. (2001). *Canadian Incidence Study of reported child abuse and neglect: Final report.* Ottawa, Ontario: Minister of Public Works and Government Services Canada.

Tyman, J. (1995). *Inside out.* Saskatoon, Canada: Fifth House.

U.S. Department of Health and Human Services. (1999). *Mental health: A report of the Surgeon General.* Rockville, MD: USDHHS, Center for Mental Health Services, National Institutes of Health, National Institute of Mental Health. [Also available on the World Wide Web: http://www.surgeongeneral.gov/library/mentalhealth]

Wahler, R. G., & Dumas, J. E. (1989). Attentional problems in dysfunctional mother-child interactions: An interbehavioral model. *Psychological Bulletin, 105,* 116–130.

Wall, A-M., & Wekerle, C. (1999, November). Childhood and adult experiences of substance abuse and intimate violence: Does coping style play a role? Paper presented at the annual meeting of the Association for the Advancement of Behaviour Therapy, Toronto, Ontario.

Wang, P. S., Gilman, S. E., Guardino, M., Christiana, J. M., Morselli, P. L., Mickelson, K., & Kessler, R. C. (2000). Initiation of and adherence to treatment for mental disorders: Examination of patient advocate group members in 11 countries. *Medical Care, 38,* 926–936.

Wechsler, H., Dowdall,, G. W., Maenner, G., Gledhill-Hoyt, J., & Lee, H. (1998). Changes in binge drinking and related problems among American college students between 1993 and 1997: Results from the Harvard School of Public Health college alcohol study. *Journal of American College Health, 47,* 57–68.

Wekerle, C., & Wolfe, D. A. (1993). Prevention of child physical abuse and neglect: Promising new directions. *Clinical Psychology Review, 13,* 501–540.

Wekerle, C., & Wolfe, D. A. (1998). Prevention of physical abuse and neglect: Windows of opportunity. In P. K. Trickett & C. Schellenbach (Eds.), *Violence against children in the family and the community* (pp. 339–370). New York: American Psychological Association.

Wekerle, C., & Wolfe, D.A. (1999). Dating violence in mid-adolescence: Theory, significance, and emerging prevention initiatives. *Clinical Psychology Review, 19,* 435–456.

Wolfe, D. A., & Wekerle, C. (1993). Treatment strategies for child physical abuse and neglect: A critical progress report. *Clinical Psychology Review, 13,* 473–500.

Wolfe, D. A., Wekerle, C., & Scott, K. (1997). *Alternatives to violence: Empowering youth to develop healthy relationships.* Thousand Oaks, CA: Sage.

Zayfert, C., & Becker, C. B. (2000). Implementation of empirically supported treatment for PTSD: Obstacles and innovations. *The Behavior Therapist, 23,* 161–168.

INDEX

Aarons, G. A., 136, 137
Aasland, O. G., 101
Abbey, A., 170, 171, 173, 177, 178, 182, 183, 185, 186, 187, 188
Abbott, M. E., 27
Abdelrahman, A., 155
Abel, L., 34
Abraini, J. H., 32
Abrams, D. B., 123, 124, 125, 128, 282, 283, 294
Abrams, K. M., 261
Access to treatment, xiv
Achenbach, T., 86, 155
Acierno, R., 9, 106, 108, 109, 305
Adams, S. L., 221
Adams, W. L., 220, 221, 224, 225, 226
Aday, L. A., 251
Addiction, biological basis and aggression in close relationships, 25–39
Addiction Severity Index, 68
Ades, J., 47
Adesso, V. J., 137
Adinoff, B., 32
Adlaf, E. M., 307, 331, 332
Adolescent risk behavior, prevention and development of healthy nonviolent dating relationships:
alcohol use, 305–307
changing norms, 319
cultural appropriateness, 319–320
dating relationships, 307–309
description and common characteristics, 304–310
emphasizing the positive, 317–318
empowerment, 318–319
keys to healthy relationships, 318
linking alcohol and intimate violence, 311
linking alcohol and sexual activity, 310–311
model programs, 314
prevention programs and adolescent risk behavior, 311–317

Project Northland, 314–315
sexual activity among adolescents, 309–310
Youth Relationship Program, 315–317
Adolescents:
bullying, sexual harassment, dating violence, and substance abuse among adolescents, 153–167
Advisory Commission on Consumer Protection and Quality in the Health Care Industry, 241
Agency for Health Care Planning and Research (AHPCR), 240
Ager, C. R., 226
Ager, J., 106, 111
Ageton, S., 163, 203
Aggression:
bullying, sexual harassment, dating violence, and substance use among adolescents, 153–167
Aguilar-Gaziola, S., 105
Ainsworth, M. D., 48, 51, 52, 76, 330
Akin, B. A., 334
Alanen, Y. O., 37
Albert, D. J., 31
Albert, M. L., 34
Alberta Registry for Child Abuse and Neglect, 212
Alcohol:
acute alcohol and drug intoxication and husband-to-wife physical abuse, 14–15
violence and alcohol: cultural issues and barriers to treatment, 239–252
Alcohol and substance abuse in marital violence and child maltreatment:
acute alcohol effects in marital violence, 207–208
acute alcohol effects relevant to child abuse and neglect, 212
alcohol-child abuse and child neglect relationship, 208–212
alcohol-child abuse relationship, 213–214

Alcohol and substance abuse in marital
    violence and child maltreatment
    (*continued*)
  alcohol-marital violence relationship, 201–
    205
  developmental challenges and alcohol-family
    violence relationship, 200–201
  developmental issues in alcohol use across
    the early adult years, 195, 196–196
  developmental issues in marital and parental
    violence, 196–200
  moderators of alcohol-child abuse/child
    neglect relationship, 212
  moderators of the alcohol-marital violence
    association, 205–207
  summary of alcohol/marital research, 208
Alcohol Dependence Scale (ADS), 204
Alcohol outcome expectancies (AOEs), 129
Aldarondo, E., 265, 263, 264
Alexander, F., 221
Allain, A. N., Jr., 65
Allen, B. A., 204
Allen, J. P., 295
Allers, C. T., 220, 225, 229
Allers, N. T., 220, 225, 229
Alpert, E. J., 277
Al-Rehda, M. R., 294
Alterman, A., 134
American Association of Retired Persons
    (AARP), 220–221
American Association of University Women
    (AAUW), 161
American Psychiatric Association (APA), 75,
    98
  alcohol abuse, defined, 107
  assessment issues, 114
  overlap of substance use disorders with
    psychiatric disorders, 115–116
  PTSD defined, 106
  substance abuse and dependence, 108
Ammerman, R. T., 45, 86
Anda, R. F., 325–326
Anderson, B. K., 173, 177
Anderson, D., 264, 262, 263, 269
Anderson, J., 328
Anderson, J. C., 10, 101, 109
Anderson, K. J., 304, 318
Anderson, L., 137
Anderson, W., 46
Andrews, J. A., 45, 136
Andrews, K., 134
Aneshensel, C., 305, 308
Anglin, M. D., 37
Annis, H. M., 108

Antecedents and correlates of substance
    abuse and relationship violence:
  cultural and community violence, 48
  family violence, 48–50
  interpersonal precursors, 45–46
  psychiatric and personality disorders, 46–47
  relationship violence, 48
  substance abuse, 45
  theoretical perspectives, 47–48
  theories of relationship violence, 50–51
Anthony, J. C., 45
Appel, A. E., 214
Arends, E., 8
Arent, R., 46
Arias, I., 11, 12, 123, 127, 131, 132, 137, 144,
    175, 197, 198, 199, 204
Armenti, N. P., 200
Armor, D. J., 206
Arriaga, X. B., 342
Ary, D., 45
Asdigian, N., 13, 14, 16, 113, 115
Aseltine, R. H., 45, 47
Ashman, S. B., 336
Assaad, J. M., 28, 35
Astin, M. C., 106, 112
Atav, A. S., 320
Atkinson, L., 336
Atkinson, R. M., 221, 225
Atlas, R., 157
Attachment style theory, 76–79
Austin, J. B., 270
Australian National Health and Medical
    Research Council Twin Register, 326
Avakame, E. F., 135
Avery-Leaf, S., 131
Azar, S. T., 48, 85, 89
Azrin, N. H., 294, 295

Babcock, J. C., 72, 73, 77
Bachman, J. G., 169, 170, 196, 332, 339
Bachman, R., 14, 207, 242
Badawy, A., 276
Baer, B. A., 78
Baer, J. S., 339, 340
Baer, P. E., 134
Bagby, M. R., 66
Bail, G., 222
Baker, T., 79
Baldwin, M. W., 77
Balka, E., 46
Ball, S. A., 45, 46, 47, 68
Bammer, G., 4, 209, 210, 213
Bancroft, L., 328

Bandura, A., 123, 124, 125, 126–127, 128, 129, 130, 132, 139, 143, 312, 330
Bangdiwala, S., 342
Bannister, H., 317
Barbour, K. A., 84
Bard, K. A., 207
Barkley, R. A., 34
Barling, J., 11, 12, 131, 134, 197, 198, 199, 204
Barnett, D., 49
Barnett, O. W., 202
Barnum, R., 5, 49
Baron, R. M., 187
Barratt, E. S., 72
Barratt Impulsivity Scale, 72
Barrera, M., 85
Barten, S., 254
Barter, K., 329
Bartholomew, K., 77, 78
Bartholow, B. D., 65
Bartko, J., 32
BASICS program, 340
Bass, E. B., 9, 102, 106, 111, 324
Bates, L., 89
Bates, M., 156, 162
Battered-child syndrome, 2
Batterers:
    borderline male and abusive personality, 73–80
    dysphoric/borderline batterer, 70
    family-only batterer, 70
    treating the addicted male batterer: promising directions for dual-focused programming, 275–289
    typologies of, 69–73
    violent/antisocial batterer, 70
Batterer's Education Program (BEPs), 254, 262, 265
Bauman, K. E., 136, 140, 342
Baumeister, K., 87
Baumeister, R. F., 87
Baumrind, D., 45
Bauserman, R., 115
Baxter, B. A., 334
Bayog, R. D., 294, 295
Bayon, M. C., 85
Beasley, R., 74
Beck, A. T., 103, 288
Beck, J. C., 222
Beck Depression Inventory (BDI), 103, 104
Becker, C. B., 338
Becker, R. L., 242
Becker, S., 106
Beckwith, L., 46
Beeghly, M., 46

Beers, M. H., 222
Begley, C. E., 251
Behavioral Couples Therapy (BCT), 336
Behavioral couples therapy for alcoholism and drug abuse: encountering the problem of domestic violence:
    BCT and partner violence, 295
    BCT and partner violence in treating substance abusing patients, 297–299
    behavioral couples therapy (BCT) treatment methods, 293–299
    conceptualizing interventions, 299–301
    handling partner violence in BCT with alcohol and drug abusing patients, 295–297
    outcome studies of BCT, 294–295
Behavior marital therapy (BMT), 255, 266–270
Belknap, J., 171, 172, 185, 186
Bell, C. C., 49
Belsky, J., 48, 50
Bem, D. J., 37
Benaske, N., 176, 187
Bender, S., 286
Benjack, K. J., 220, 225, 229
Benkelfat, C., 32
Bennett, L., 261, 275, 276, 334
Bennett, L. W., 12, 202
Benoit, D., 3
Ben-Porath, Y., 89, 90
Bensley, L., 305
Benson, D. F., 34
Bentler, P. M., 45, 46, 140
Berbig, L. J., 230
Berndt, T. J., 163
Berne, L. A., 313
Berns, S. B., 267, 269
Bernstein, D. P., 76
Bernstein, M. C., 46
Bernstein, V. J., 46
Bernstein-Lachter, R., 314, 315, 317
Berry, C. J., 134, 135, 176
Berry, E., 104, 105
Bersani, C., 286
Best, C. L., 9, 106, 107, 108, 109, 112, 305
Bibule, S., 31
Bierut, L., 326
Bijl, R., 105
Bijur, P. E., 4
Billingsly, D., 329
Binkoff, J., 282
Biological basis of addiction and aggression in close relationships, 25–39
    assortative mating, 37
    biology and the risk for addictions and aggression, 26

Biological basis of addiction and aggression in close relationships (*continued*)
cue for reward system, 26–28
frontal cortex: executive cognitive function and drug-related aggression, 33–36
genetic risk for addiction and aggression, 37–38
mediating factors of close relationships, 36–38
pain system, 30–31
punishment (threat) system, 28–30
saliency of provocation, 38
satiation system, 32–33
Birchler, G. R., 229, 294, 295
Biro, F. M., 319
Bischof, G. P., 300
Bishop, P., 31
Bissette, G., 32
Bissonnette, M., 107, 137
Bjork, J. M., 138
Black, C., 37
Black, J., 27
Blackson, T. C., 45, 46, 86
Blackwell, P., 46
Blair, K., 179, 186
Blanchard, D. C., 30
Blanchard, R. J., 30
Bland, R. C., 82
Blane, H. T., 12, 74, 75, 205, 206
Blankenship, V., 80
Blankstein, K., 83
Blashfield, R. K., 86
Blatt, S. J., 79
Blazer, D., 221
Blechman, E. A., 90
Blehar, M. C., 76, 330
Bleske, A., 37, 197
Block, J., 46
Bloom, F. E., 27
"Blueprints for Violence Prevention," 314
Blum, R. W., 8
Blumenthal, C., 305
Boden, J., 87
Bodnarchuk, M., 65
Bograd, M., 174, 255
Bohman, M., 37, 38
Boivin, J. F., 37
Bolger, N., 88
Bonarchuk, M., 300
Bond, C. F., 186
Boney-McCoy, S., 106, 287
Bonge, D., 71, 80, 84
Bonsch, A., 45
Bookwala, J., 78
Booth, M. W., 37

Borderline male and abusive personality, 73–80
attachment style theory, 76–79
psychological need for control and power, 79–80
trait anger, hostility, and antisocial personality, 74–76
Borders, S., 8, 104, 105, 117
Borges, G., 105
Botein, S., 336
Botvin, E. M., 312, 313
Botvin, G. J., 312, 313
Boulerice, B., 34
Bowers, T. G., 294
Bowlby, J., 51, 76, 77, 330
Bowlby-Ainsworth attachment theory, 51
Boyatiz, R. E., 80
Boyle, M., 329
Bozarth, M., 27
Bradbury, T. N., 197, 198, 199
Bradizza, C. M., 123, 124, 125, 127, 128, 129, 133, 136–137, 140, 142, 283, 330
Bradley, R. G., 80, 179
Brady, K. T., 106, 112, 116, 117
Brannen, S. J., 299
Bransfield, S. A., 45, 46
Brayden, R. M., 87
Breitenbucher, M., 88
Bremer, D. A., 37
Brennan, K. A., 78
Brennan, P. L., 220, 221, 223, 224, 225, 228, 229
Brent, E. E., 38, 115, 137
Breslau, N., 196
Breslin, F. C., 131, 137, 144
Bridges, K., 134
Bridging the gap: prevention of adolescent risk behaviors and development of healthy nonviolent dating relationships, 304–320
Briere, J., 100, 106, 107, 109, 116
Brill, N., 46
Bristow, M. F., 226
Britten, M. X., 320
Broadhurst, D. D., 325, 331
Brodbelt, S., 179
Brodberry, C., 27
Brody, M. S., 27
Bromet, E. J., 12, 202
Bronfenbrenner, U., 50, 162, 329
Brook, D. W., 135
Brook, J. S., 46, 135
Brookoff, D., 16, 275
Brooks-Gunn, J., 304, 313, 317
Broome, H. L., 221

Broughton, R., 82, 83
Brounstein, P. J., 311, 313, 314
Brown, B. B., 163
Brown, D., 2
Brown, E., 33
Brown, E. D., 295
Brown, G. L., 32
Brown, J., 68
Brown, R., 85
Brown, R. A., 298
Brown, S. A., 136, 137
Brown, T. G., 75, 76, 254
Browne, A., 12, 229, 242
Browne, D. C., 86, 211
Browne, J., 210
Bruce, K., 27, 31
Brumaghim, J. T., 50
Bryan, E., 140
Bryk, A. S., 245
Buchanan, R. G., 221
Bucholz, K. K., 7, 37, 82, 326
Buchsbaum, D. G., 221
Buchsbaum, M. S., 31, 34
Bucky, S. F., 37
Buffalo Newlywed Study (BNS), 197, 206
Buhot, M., 32, 33
Buhrmester, D., 307
Buka, S. L., 105
Bullying, sexual harassment, dating violence,
     and substance use among adolescents:
   aggressive behavior as risk for substance use,
     156–157
   bullying, 158–159
   dating aggression, 159–160
   forms of aggressive behavior, 157–162
   implications and future directions, 164–167
   overlapping problem of adolescent aggres-
     sion and substance use, 154–155
   peer influences in substance use, 162–164
   research program, overview of, 153–154
   sexual harassment, 160–162
   substance use, 154–156
   theoretical framework for considering
     overlap between aggression and substance
     use, 156
Bunney, W. E., 32
Burford, G., 329
Burgess, A. G., 79
Burgess, A. W., 79
Burke, L., 80, 176, 179
Burkhart, B. R., 183
Burklow, K. A., 319
Burleson, J. A., 82
Burns, K., 45, 46
Burns, W. J., 46

Bushman, B. J., 87, 182, 276
Bushman, R., 87
Buss, A. H., 72
Buss, D. M., 68
Buss-Perry Aggression Questionnaire, 72
Butler, A. C., 86
Butler, S., 336
Bybee, D. I., 271
Byrne, C. A., 106, 112, 116

Caddell, J. M., 106
Cado, S., 139
Caetano, R., 184, 241, 242, 243, 332, 333
Cahn, T. S., 85
Cairns, B. D., 154, 157, 163, 165, 166
Cairns, R. B., 154, 157, 163, 165, 166
Calam, R., 105
Calhoun, K., 263
Cami, J., 27
Campbell, B., 47, 205
Campbell, J. A., 255
Campbell, J. C., 106, 111
Campbell, J. L., 183, 187
Campbell, L., 294
Campbell, W. K., 87
Canadian Council on Social Development,
     305
Canadian Incidence Study, 329
Cancil, A., 287
Cano, A., 131
Cantor, R. J., 203
Cantos, A. L., 89
Capaldi, D., 163, 164, 305
Caplan, R., 135
Caplan, T., 75, 76, 254
Cappelleri, J. C., 200
Caraveo-Anduaga, J. J., 105
Carbonari, J. P., 138
Carey, C. M., 139
Carey, K. B., 123, 124, 125, 127, 128, 129, 133,
     136–137, 140, 142, 283, 330
Carlson, B., 10, 176
Carpenter, J. A., 200
Carroll, K. M., 46, 47, 282, 283
Carstensen, L. L., 221, 224, 226
Carver, L. J., 336
Cascardi, M., 131, 262, 263, 265
Cashin, J. R., 170, 171
Caspi, A., 37, 46, 76, 87, 197, 203, 204
Castillo, S., 170
Castro, P., 139
Catalano, R. F., 45, 305
Cate, R. M., 176, 179
Catellier, D., 86, 211

Caton, C., 286
Cattell, R. B., 73
Caudill, B. D., 45
Caulfield, M. B., 137, 144
Cavaiola, A. A., 103
Center for Addiction and Mental Health, 313, 317
Center for Epidemiological Studies Depression scale (CES–D), 102
Center for Substance Abuse Prevention, 313
Center for Substance Abuse Treatment, 241
Center on Addiction and Substance Abuse, 310
Centers for Disease Control (CDC), 305, 308, 309, 311
Chaffin, M., 7, 46, 209, 210, 213
Chamberlain, B., 32
Chambers, W., 103
Chambless, D. L., 109
Chan, A., 295
Chan, Y. C., 88
Chandy, J. M., 8
Chant, H. K., 102
Chapman, C. R., 31
Chapman, K., 173
Charach, A., 157
Chen, H., 286
Chen, K., 169, 171
Chenoweth, R., 140
Chermack, S. T., 170, 181, 182, 276
Chethik, L., 45, 46
Chilamkurti, C., 89
Chilcoat, H. D., 196
Child abuse:
  alcohol and substance abuse in marital abuse and child maltreatment, 195–214
  definition of, 3
  emotional abuse, 3, 4
  epidemiological studies, 6
  forms of, 2
  long-term effects, 8
  neglect, 3, 4
  and personality factors and substance abuse in relationship violence: review and theoretical analysis, 64–91
  physical abuse, 3, 4
  as predictor of adult substance abuse, 8–11
  proportion of perpetrators, 4
  removal from home, 4
  sexual abuse, 3, 4
  and substance-abusing parents, 2–8
  temporal association, 7
  types of, 3
  typologies of abusers and batterers, 69–80
Child Abuse Potential Inventory (CPI), 76, 78, 86

Child Behavior Checklist, 86
Child protective services (CPS), 3
Chin, M. H., 231
Chipperfield, B., 136
Choi, B., 328
Choquette, K. A., 229, 294, 295
Chou, L., 137
Chou, P., 241
Chrestman, K. R., 106, 112
Christensen, M. J., 87
Christiana, J. M., 334
Christiansen, B. A., 137, 140
Christopher, F. S., 176, 179
Christopher, S., 176
Cicchetti, D., 8, 44, 45, 46, 49, 50, 329, 331, 336, 342
Clair, D., 139
Clapp, L., 71, 83
Clare, A. W., 226
Clark, C. L., 184, 241, 242, 243, 332, 333
Clark, D. B., 45, 108, 109, 307, 342
Clark, L. A., 86
Clark, R., 46
Clark, W. B., 171, 196
Claussen, A. H., 46, 54
Clayton, R. R., 135
Clements, M., 199
Clinical and research issues in relationship violence and substance abuse:
  barriers to treatment-help-seeking behavior, access, quality, and diversity, 333–335
  conceptualization of urgent public health issue, 327–331
  identifying, recognizing, and referring, 331–333
  prevention programs, 341–343
  state of evidence on interventions, 335–338
  tailoring client problem behavior and motivation to treatment goals, 338–341
Clinton Administration, 241
Cloniger, C. R., 28, 37, 38
Close relationships:
  biological basis of addiction and aggression in, 25–39
Clum, G. A., 261
Coffey, P., 134, 135
Cognitive social learning models of substance abuse and intimate violence, 123
  applications of social learning theory to alcohol use and abuse and intimate violence: commonalities and points of departure, 127–132
  attentional processes, 125
  coping, 139
  directions for future research, 142–145

efficacy expectancy, 126
empirical validations of social learning theory
    as multivariate framework for understand-
    ing co-occurrence of alcohol use and abuse
    and intimate violence, 140–142
family of origin as critical context for
    observational learning, 134–136
motivational processes, 125
motor reproduction processes, 125
reciprocal determinism, 127, 139–140
retention processes, 125
role of cognition, 126–127, 136–138
self-efficacy expectancies, 138–139
social learning formulations concerning the
    overlap between alcohol use and abuse and
    intimate violence, 132–133
social learning theory: theoretical founda-
    tions and application to alcohol use and
    abuse and intimate violence, 124–133
social learning theory as general model of
    human behavior, 124–127
social learning theory-derived univariate
    investigations on alcohol use and abuse
    and intimate violence, 140
stimulus control of behavior, 126
understanding how social learning mecha-
    nisms influence alcohol consumption and
    intimate violence: critical constructs and
    hypothesized mediating and moderating
    processes, 133–140
Cohall, A., 317
Cohall, R., 317
Cohen, M. A., 202, 203
Cohen, P., 46, 68, 210
Cohen, S., 277
Cohn, E., 173
Cole, R., 341
Coleman, D. H., 201
Coleman, E. M., 106, 112
College students:
    sexual assault and relationship violence:
        examining the role of alcohol and other
        drugs, 169–189
Collins, J. J., 5, 279
Collins, M., 282, 320
Colliver, J. D., 313
Colten, M. E., 45, 47
Composite International Diagnostic Interview
    (CIDI), 102
Cone, J., 85
Conflict Tactics Scale (CTS), 76, 78, 112, 174,
    180, 209, 243, 255, 263, 295, 298
Connell, D., 336
Connelly, C. D., 200
Conner, R. L., 31

Connolly, J., 154, 158, 160, 161, 166
Connors, G. J., 283
Conrod, P. J., 27, 28, 29, 31, 99, 107, 108, 115,
    117
Cook, C., 16, 275
Cooney, N., 282, 283
Cooper, H. M., 182
Cooper, M. L., 89, 107, 129, 139
Copenhaver, M. M., 88
Copenhaver, S., 173, 178
Coping factors, and stress factors, 89–90
Coping strategies and dynamic-maturational
    model of strategic behavior:
    adolescence and adulthood: sexuality and
        integration, 54
    dynamic-maturational model of self-protec-
        tive strategies, 51
    new self-protective strategies in preschool
        years, 53
    school years: variability and integration or
        rigidity and distortion, 53–54
    strategies for eliciting protection in infancy,
        52, 52, 53
Corbett, R., 10
Core Institute, 170
Core Survey, The, 170, 171
Cottler, L. B., 9
Cotton, N. S., 37
Coulter, K. P., 6
Council of Ministers of Education of Canada,
    313
Covington, S. S., 99, 110
Cox, A., 105
Cox, B. J., 29
Cox, N. S., 220, 221, 224, 225, 226
Cox, S. M., 46
Coyle, K., 311, 312, 313, 317
Coyne, A., 230
Coyne, J. C., 114
CPS, 6
Crabbe, J. C., 29
Craig, R. J., 47
Craig, W., 154, 157, 158, 160, 161, 166
Cram, F., 308
Crane, J. B., 37
Craven, D., 242, 328
Creamer, V. A., 136
Crew, B. K., 132, 133, 140, 142
Crittenden, P. M., 44, 48, 49, 51, 52, 54
Cronkite, R. C., 294, 295
Crook, G. M., 138
Crosby, L., 305
Cross-Cultural Applicability (CAR) study, 334
Crossman, R. K., 300
Croughan, J., 102, 105

Crowe, L. C., 183, 186
Crowell, B. A., 221
Crudo, S., 254
Crum, R. M., 6, 7
Crutchfield, C., 312, 318
Cullen, F. T., 171, 172, 173
Cultural differences, xiii–xiv
Cultural issues, violence and alcohol: cultural issues and barriers to treatment, 239–252
Cummings, J. L., 34
Cunradi, C. B., 184, 242, 243, 254, 332, 333
Curran, G. M., 127, 133, 142
Curran, P. J., 196
Curtis, J. R., 221
Cutter, H. S. G., 229, 294, 295

Daciuk, J., 329
Dade County's integrated domestic violence model:
    future directions, 288–289
    substance abuse treatment unit's substance abuse-domestic violence program (SATU-SADV model), 282–288
Dail, P. W., 5, 16
Daly, M., 174, 255, 262
Dancu, C. B., 108
D'Angelo, L. J., 309
Daniels, J. W., 276
Danko, G., 137
Dankwort, J., 270
Dansky, B. S., 106, 107, 108, 112, 116, 117
Darkes, J., 129, 132, 137, 186, 330
Daro, D., 1, 3, 4
Data-gathering methods, 2
Dating:
    dating violence, 153–167
    preventing adolescent risk behaviors and development of healthy nonviolent dating relationships, 304–320
D'Avanzo, K., 330
Davenport, A., 170
Davidovich, J., 275
Davies, J., 263
Davis, C. S., 108
Davis, E. R., 135
Davis, L. J., 221, 324
Davis, T. M., 137
Davis, W. N., 80
Davison, G. C., 84
Dawes, M. A., 86
Dawson, D. A., 241
Dawson, G., 336
Day, N. L., 12, 202

Day, T., 327
DeChant, H. K., 9, 106, 111
DeEskinazi, F. G., 31
Definitional criteria, 2
DeHart, S. S., 220, 224, 225, 226
Deitch, I., 220, 230
De Jong, J., 32
DeKeseredy, W. S., 173, 174, 175
De La Rosa, M., 239
Del Boca, F. K., 129, 132, 137, 330
De Le Torre, R., 27
Dembo, R., 8, 104, 105, 117
Demers, A., 331
Deneault, P., 295
Denton, R., 286
DePanfilis, D., 211
Derman, K. H., 138
DeRogatis, L. R., 9, 76, 102, 104, 106, 111
Dertke, M., 8, 104, 105, 117
Derzon, J. H., 202, 203
Desjardins, S., 328
Developmental psychopathology perspectives on substance abuse and relationship violence, 44–58
    antecedents and correlates of substance abuse and relationship violence, 45–51
    coping strategies and dynamic-maturational model of strategic behavior, 51–54
    failed strategies, 57–58
    substance abuse and relationship violence in a strategic framework, 54–57
Devine, D., 10
De Visser, R., 310
Dewit, D. J., 105
Deykin, E. Y., 105
Diagnostic Interview Schedule (DIS), 102, 105
Diaz, T., 313
Diclemente, C. C., 138, 276, 283, 288, 339
Dielman, T. E., 135
Dierich, A., 32, 33
Diers, L. E., 221, 228, 231
Dietrich, M. S., 87
Dill, L., 9, 102, 106, 111
Dimson, C., 71, 83
Dinero, T. E., 177
Dinwiddie, S. H., 7, 37, 82, 326
Dishion, T., 157, 163, 164, 166, 305
Ditto, B., 27
Djamei, A., 32, 33
Dobash, P., 174
Dobash, R. E., 174, 242, 255, 261, 262
Dobash, R. P., 242, 255, 262
Dobkin, P. L., 45, 46
Dollard, J., 124

Domestic violence:
  and abuse and substance abuse, 11–12
  See also Behavioral couples therapy for
    alcoholism and drug abuse: encountering
    the problem of domestic violence
Dongier, M., 99, 107, 108, 115, 117
Doniger, M., 28, 29
Donovan, D., 282, 283
Donovan, J. E., 204
Dougherty, D. M., 138
Douglas, J. E., 79
Douglass, F. M., IV, 139
Doumas, D., 134, 135
Dowdall, G., 170, 331–332
Doweiko, H. E., 44, 45, 47
Downs, W. R., 6, 8, 9, 10, 11, 12, 76, 99, 102,
    103, 105, 106, 107, 110, 115, 116, 209,
    254, 261, 262–263
Dozier, C. D., 336
Droegmueller, W., 2
Drug Abuse Screening Test (DAST), 72
Dubrow, N., 49, 50, 330
Dudek, B. C., 27
Duff, R. W., 221
Dufort, V., 86, 211
Dufour, M., 241
Dumas, J. E., 330
Dunahoo, C. L., 89, 90
Duncan, R. D., 9, 101, 106, 222
Duncan, S., 136, 155
Duncan, T., 155
Dunedin Multidisciplinary Health and
    Development study, 203
Dunford, E. W., 299
Dunn, M. E., 137
Dunn, N. J., 129, 139
Dunne, M., 37, 326
Dunwiddle, T. V., 27
Dupree, L., 221, 228–229
DuRant, R. H., 309, 310, 313
Dutton, D. G., 65, 69, 71, 74, 77, 79, 80, 83,
    135, 263, 264, 300
Dutton, M. A., 261
Dye, M. L., 89
Dynamic-Maturational Model, 51, 57–58
Dziuba-Leatherman, J., 116, 200

Earleywine, M., 27, 46
Easton, C., 275, 276, 279, 286, 287, 288
Eber, H. W., 73
Ebert, M. H., 32
Eckenrode, J., 200, 341
Eckhardt, C. I., 84, 89

Edelbrock, C., 86, 155
Edgerton, B., 334
Edleson, J. L., 299
Edwall, G. E., 103
Edwards, B. A., 325–326
Egami, Y., 6, 7
Egeland, B., 88
Eggert, M., 33
Ehrensaft, M. K., 264
Eiden, R. D., 46, 85–86, 196
Eisenstat, S., 328
Eisler, R. M., 88
Elder, G. H., 37
Ellickson, P., 317
Ellingson, T., 286
Elliott, D., 107, 132, 133, 140, 141, 142, 203,
    204
Elliott, D. S., 163, 203
Elliott, J. D., 300
Ellis, D. A., 137
Elloran, I., 30
ElSohly, M. A., 178, 187
Elsworth, J., 27
Emans, S. J., 309, 310, 313
Emery, R., 48, 50
Emotional abuse, 3
Endler, N. S., 66
Epidemiological Catchment Area (ECA), 209
Epstein, E. E., 269
Epstein, J. A., 313
Epstein, J. N., 106, 109
Epstein, R., 76, 209
Erdbaugh, J., 288
Erez, E., 172, 185, 186
Erickson, D. J., 47
Eron, L. D., 131, 154, 157, 165
Ervin, F., 32, 38
Ethnicity. *See* Violence and alcohol: cultural
    issues and barriers to treatment
Evans, D. M., 129, 139

Fagan, R. W., 202
Fahy, B., 45, 46
Failed strategies, testing hypotheses drawn
    from Dynamic-Maturational Model, 57–
    58
Faison, N., 342
Fallon, B., 329
Fals-Stewart, W., 266, 293, 294, 295, 298, 299
Famularo, R., 5, 6, 49, 209
Farbakhsh, K., 315, 317
Farber, P. D., 139
Farley, S. C., 132, 133, 140, 142, 202

Farré, M., 27
Farrell, A. D., 312
Farrell, L. E., 298
Farrington, D. P., 154, 155, 157, 162, 165
Faucher, I., 32
Federal Bureau of Investigation (FBI), 169, 172
Feehan, M., 265, 268, 295, 298
Feig, L., 4
Feldman, C. M., 76
Feldman, L., 305, 307
Felitti, V. J., 325–326
Felson, R. B., 132
Fenton, T., 6, 209
Ferguson, L. L., 154
Fergusson, D. M., 7, 8, 10, 210
Fernald, B., 32
Ferrer, H. P., 226
Feuche, N., 47
Fibiger, H. C., 27
Fichtner, R. R., 305, 308, 309
Figueredo, A. J., 49
Fillmore, K. M., 226
Finch, S., 46
Finchman, F. D., 139, 324
Fingold, S. F., 222
Finkel, D., 86
Finkelhor, D., 103, 106, 110, 116, 200, 222, 223, 229, 230
Finlayson, R., 221, 222
Finn, P. R., 27, 31
Finney, J. W., 220, 225, 294, 295
Fischer, E., 7
Fisher, B. S., 171, 172, 173
Fisher, E., 71, 209
Fisher, J. E., 221, 224, 226
Fisher, L., 140
Fitzgerald, H. E., 137
Flanagan, C. A., 342
Flannery, D. J., 139
Fleming, J., 4, 209, 210, 213
Flett, G. L., 66, 69, 74, 82, 83, 84, 85, 88
Floyd, F. J., 294
Flynn, C. A., 82, 83
Flynn, P. M., 45
Foa, E. B., 108
Follette, V. M., 8, 9, 101, 106, 222, 227–228, 229, 231
Follingstad, D. R., 80, 176, 179
Follingstad, D. W., 132
Foo, L., 74, 88, 132, 140, 142, 206
Ford, D. E., 6, 7
Forster, J. L., 317
Foshee, V. A., 136, 308, 342
Fountain, D., 241, 328

Fox, J. A., 328
Foy, D. W., 106, 112, 222
FRAMES, 340
Francione, C. L., 298
Francis, C. R., 73
Fraser, J. S., 262, 263, 270
Freitas, T. T., 295, 298, 299
French, J., 155
Friedman, A. S., 45, 46
Friedmann, P. D., 231
Fromme, K., 137
Frone, M. R., 89, 129, 139
Fullilove, M. R., 106
Fullilove, R. E., III, 106
Furman, W., 307, 308

GABA, 28
Gabarino, J., 329–330
Gable, S., 335, 340, 341
Gaines, R. W., 89
Galbaud du Fort, G., 37
Galimidi, L., 7
Gallagher, P. E., 47
Ganeles, D., 5
Ganiban, J., 49
Ganley, A. L., 270
Garbarino, J., 49, 50
Gariepy, J., 154
Garmezy, N., 48, 50
Garnefski, N., 8
Garrett, J., 90
Garshowitz, M., 83, 88
Gauthier, L. M., 262
Geller, G., 221
Gelles, R. J., 2, 11, 12, 15, 174, 197, 202, 243, 255, 264
Genest, M., 139
Gentile, C., 100
Genung, L., 104, 105
George, L. K., 221
George, W. H., 129, 138, 139, 182, 183, 186
Gerrity, D. A., 180, 186
Gershuny, B. S., 5, 10
Gerstein, D. R., 241, 251
Gessner, J. C., 176
Getreu, A., 104, 105
Giancola, P. R., 25, 34, 36, 181, 276
Giancola, R., 276
Giannini, A. J., 47
Gianoulakis, C., 27, 31
Gibbon, M., 101, 103, 106, 112
Gidycz, C. A., 172, 173, 175, 178, 182
Gifford, E. V., 227–228

Gilbert, N., 171, 173
Gilbert, P., 100, 112
Giles-Sims, J., 262
Gilman, S. E., 334
Gilvarry, E., 313
Glantz, M., 44, 46, 313
Glasgow, D., 105
Gledhill-Hoyt, J., 170, 331–332
Gliksman, L., 331
Glusberg, M., 205
Glynn, P. J., 9
Godley, M., 294, 295
Golant, S. K., 263
Golding, J. M., 226
Goldkamp, J., 282
Goldman, D., 33
Goldman, E., 221
Goldman, M. S., 129, 132, 137, 140, 186, 330
Gomberg, E. S. L., 228
Gondolf, E. W., 69, 71, 280, 286, 339
Gondoli, D. M., 8, 12
Goodchilds, J. D., 182
Goodman, G., 46
Goodman, L. A., 261
Goodwin, D. W., 37
Goodwin, F. K., 32
Goodyear-Smith, F. A., 175
Gordon, A. S., 135
Gordon, J. R., 128, 143, 339
Gordon, T., 27
Gore, S., 45, 47
Gorenstein, E. E., 34
Gorney, B., 254
Gortner, E., 269
Goshko, M., 5, 6, 16, 46, 49, 209
Gothard, S., 79
Gottman, J. M., 72, 73, 77, 82, 267, 269
Gough, R., 316
Gournic, S. J., 182, 186
Goyer, P. F., 32
Graham, J. M., 108
Gralnick, A., 286
Granoff, B. J., 173
Grant, B. F., 1, 241, 325, 334
Grant, M., 101
Grasley, C., 316, 317
Gratch, L. V., 176
Grauerholz, E., 173, 178
Gray, J. A., 31
Greenbaum, P. E., 140
Greenfeld, L., 14
Greenfield, L., 328
Greenfield, S., 6, 7, 286
Greenfield, T., 241

Greening, D., 79
Greenwald, E., 139
Greer, C., 264, 262, 263, 269
Gregoire, T. K., 334
Griffin, M. L., 47
Griffith, L., 342
Grunebaum, H., 336
Grych, J. H., 139
Guagliardo, M. F., 309
Guardino, M., 334
Guidotti, A., 32
Gunderson, J. G., 73
Gupta, A., 31
Gurnack, A., 228
Gustafson, R., 31
Guthrie, P., 69
Guze, S. B., 37
Gwartney-Gibbs, P. A., 175

Haas, A. L., 136, 137
Hagan, J. C., 46
Hahn, M. E., 27
Hahn, N. B., 46
Hall, A. E., 139
Hall, G. C. N., 187
Hall, J. A., 131
Hall, J. G., 134
Halloran, R., 79
Hamberger, K., 69, 80, 286
Hamberger, L. K., 65, 71, 84
Hamby, S. L., 287
Hamilton, C. J., 5
Hammock, G. S., 187
Handlesman, L., 76
Hans, S. L., 46
Hansell, S., 127, 133, 142, 157
Hansen, D. J., 101, 103, 106
Hansen, M., 264, 265, 262
Hanson, R. F., 9, 101, 106, 222
Harburg, E., 135
Harden, P., 32, 34
Hare, R. D., 72
Hare Psychopathy Checklist, 72
Harford, T. C., 196, 241
Harlow, L. L., 37
Harrell, A., 299
Harrington, N. T., 178, 182
Harris, J., 45
Harris, R. A., 27
Harris, T. R., 10, 102, 109, 210, 213
Hart, S., 79
Hart, S. D., 65, 300
Hartgers, C., 45

Hartling, L. M., 88
Hartman, C. R., 79
Hartman, K. A., 134
Hartogers, C., 8
Harvard College Alcohol Study, 170
Harvey, B., 305, 307
Harwood, H. J., 241, 251, 328
Hastings, J. E., 65, 69, 286
Hastings, P. A., 12
Hawkins, D. L., 160, 305, 311
Hawkins, J. D., 45, 305
Hayes, S. C., 227–228
Haygood–Jackson, D., 185
Hayley, D. C., 231
Hazan, C., 77
Healey, K., 261, 262, 270, 276, 277
"Healthy People 2000," 343
Heath, A., 37, 326
Heath, J. L., 342
Hebert, M., 319
Hecaen, H., 34
Hedberg, A. G., 294
Hegedus, A. M., 45, 307
Heidt, E., 101
Heinrichs, T., 5, 16
Heise, L., 222
Hekemian, E., 85, 89
Helms, R. W., 342
Helzer, J. E., 27
Helzer, J. H., 102, 105
Hen, R., 32, 33
Henderson, B. E., 221
Henderson, C. R., 341
Henderson, D. A., 179, 186
Henning, K., 134, 135
Henry J. Kaiser Family Foundation, 307, 310
Henton, J. M., 176, 179
Hepler, N., 312, 318
Herbert, M., 308
Herbison, G. P., 10, 101, 109
Herman, J. L., 261
Hernandez, J. T., 115
Hernandez-Avila, C. A., 82
Herrmann, C. K., 200
Herron, K., 69, 71, 72, 77, 79, 333
Hersen, M., 220, 225, 228
Hervig, L. K., 214
Herzberger, S. D., 131
Hesselbrock, V. M., 37
Hewitt, P. L., 66, 74, 82, 83, 84, 85, 88
Heyman, R. E., 13, 67, 75, 131, 203, 204, 296, 299
Higgins, A. B., 222, 229, 231
High School and Beyond Study, 205

Higley, J. D., 32
Higley, S. B., 32
Hill, H. M., 48
Hill, R. W., 82, 83
Hilton, M. E., 196
Himelein, M. J., 173, 183
Hingson, R., 221
Hinson, R. E., 107, 136, 137, 334
Hirky, A. E., 81, 90
Hirschfield, R. M., 79
Hirschman, R., 187
Hirsh-Pasek, K., 85
Hitz, L., 73
Hoaken, P. N. S., 25, 35, 36, 276
Hobfoll, S. E., 89, 90
Hodges, W. F., 101
Hoff, B. H., 282
Hoffman, J. A., 45
Hoffmann, J. P., 45
Hoffmann, N. G., 103, 220, 224, 225, 226
Hohman, M. M., 340
Hokanson, J. G., 86
Holamon, B., 202
Holden, G. W., 214
Hollenberg, J., 7, 46, 209, 210, 213
Holmes, S. J., 209
Holowaty, P., 305, 307
Holtzworth-Munroe, A., 66, 69, 71, 72, 73, 77, 79, 89, 131, 275, 300, 333
Honbo, K., 137
Hoover, S., 295, 298
Hops, H., 45, 136, 155
Horn, J. P., 48
Horne, L., 105
Hornick, J., 329
Horowitz, H. A., 46, 55
Horowitz, L. M., 77, 78
Horton, A. L., 266
Horwood, J. L., 210
Horwood, L. J., 7, 8, 10
Hosmer, D. W., 248
Hotaling, G. T., 12, 130, 131, 134, 174, 175, 176, 179, 180, 183, 202, 222, 286
Housekamp, B., 222
Houts, R. M., 199
Howard, D. R., 173
Howard, J., 46
Hoyt, D. R., 177
5HT, 32
Huang, J., 46
Huang, Z., 309
Hubbard, R. L., 45
Huesmann, L. R., 154, 157, 165
Hughes, H. M., 48, 73

Hughes, M., 45
Hughes, R., 311, 313
Hughes, S. O., 138
Huizinga, D., 163, 203
Hulbert, D., 131
Hull, J. G., 181, 186
Hulsizer, M. R., 90
Hummer, R. A., 183
Hurt, R. D., 221
Husband, S. D., 47
Huss, M. T., 82, 333
Hussey, D. L., 103, 107
Hussey, J. R., 309
Huston, T. L., 199
Hyer, L., 229
Hyson, M. C., 85

Impairment Index, 206
Initiative to Eliminate Racial and Ethnic
    Disparities in Health, 241
Inn, A., 137
Institute for Survey Research, 242
Insurance, coverage for alcoholism treatment,
    245–251
Interpersonal Dependency Inventory, 79
Intimate partner violence (IPV):
    alcohol problems and, 246–248
    violence and alcohol: cultural issues and
    barriers to treatment, 239–252
Intimate violence:
    cognitive social learning models of substance
    abuse and intimate violence, 123–145
    substance abuse and co-occurring psychiatric
    disorders in victims of intimate violence,
    98–117
Intoxication, acute, alcohol and drug and
    husband–to wife physical abuse, 14–15
Inventory of Drinking Situations (IDS-38),
    108
Inventory of Interpersonal Problems, 78
Ireland, T., 9
Irrational Beliefs Test (IBT), 84
Israeli, A. L., 100, 112
Ito, T. A., 182
Ivis, F. J., 307, 332

Jackson, D. N., 69, 75, 85
Jackson, K. M., 339
Jackson, S. M., 174, 175, 176, 308
Jackson Basic Personality Inventory, 85
Jacob, R. G., 108, 109
Jacob, T., 2, 12, 37, 209

Jacobson, N. S., 72, 73, 77, 82, 267, 269, 300
Jaeger, E., 46
Jalowiec, J., 31
Janca, A., 334
Jang, K. L., 69
Jankowski, M. K., 134, 135
Janoff-Bulman, R., 99, 100, 101, 103, 105, 106,
    109, 116, 117
Jantzen, K., 45
Jatlow, P., 27
Jellinek, M., 5, 6, 16, 46, 49, 209, 295
Jenkins, E. J., 49
Jennings, J. L., 88
Jeremy, R. J., 46
Jessor, J., 204
Jessor, R., 157, 204, 312
Jessor, S., 157, 312
Jimerson, D. C., 32
Jin, L., 231
John, R. S., 74, 134, 135, 206
Johnson, B. L., 266
Johnson, J. G., 68, 210
Johnson, J. H., 78
Johnson, J. L., 45, 46
Johnson, J. R., 90
Johnson, M. P., 11, 264, 270, 271
Johnson, R., 90, 103, 137
Johnson, R. A., 241
Johnson, V., 135, 156, 162
Johnston, L. D., 169, 170, 196, 332, 339
Jones, R. G., 84
Jonik, R., 31
Jory, B., 264, 262, 263, 269
Josephs, R. A., 170, 181, 182, 186, 187, 201,
    330
Jouriles, E. N., 13, 67, 75, 203, 204
Julian, T. W., 202
Jurich, J., 180, 186

Kadden, R., 282, 283
Kaiser, M., 46
Kalaher, S., 85
Kallin, R., 80
Kalmuss, D., 131, 134, 135
Kalof, L., 173
Kalogeras, K., 32
Kandel, D., 134, 163, 169, 171, 196
Kao, C. F., 37
Kaplan, D., 137
Kaplan, H. S., 100, 103, 109
Kaplan, S. J., 5, 335
Karabatsos, G., 177, 178
Karonen, S. L., 32

Karrison, T., 231
Karyl, J., 101
Kasari, C., 46
Kaskutas, L. A., 241
Kass, L. A., 241
Katz, S., 45, 46
Kaufman, J., 134
Kaufman Kantor, G., 13, 14, 16, 101, 113, 115, 201, 202
Kazarian, L. Z., 334
Kazarian, S. S., 334
Keane, T. M., 106
Keeshan, P., 318
Kelleher, K., 7, 46, 209, 210, 213
Keller, L., 286
Kellermann, A., 275
Kelley, M. A., 196
Kelley, M. L., 294, 295
Kelley, S. J., 46, 49
Kelly, K., 173, 174, 175
Kelsey, T., 176
Kemmelmeier, M., 209
Kempe, C., 2
Kendall-Tackett, K. A., 103, 106
Kenny, D. A., 187
Kenny, M. C., 334
Kent, D., 166
Kern, D. E., 9, 102, 106, 111
Kern, J. M., 104, 105, 255, 261, 262
Kesner, J. E., 78
Kessler, R. C., 45, 105, 334
Khavari, K. A., 139
Kiers, H., 68
Killeen, T., 106
Kilpatrick, D. G., 9, 101, 106, 107, 108, 109, 112, 113, 117, 222, 305
Kim, S., 312, 318
King, C. J., 220, 225, 228
Kingston, P., 230
Kinnunen, P., 37
Kinscherff, R., 6, 209
Kirby, D., 311, 312, 313, 317
Kirisci, L., 86
Kirkhart, K., 46
Kitzman, H., 341
Kivlahan, D. R., 340
Klassen, A. D., 10, 102, 109
Klaus, P. A., 328
Klein, W. J., 32
Klevens, J., 85
Klorman, R., 50
Knowles, B. A., 203
Knowles, P. A., 31
Koch, G. G., 342

Koch, W. J., 108
Kofoed, L. L., 221
Kohen, J., 99, 110
Koledin, S., 83
Kolko, D. J., 44, 49, 86
Kolodner, K., 9, 102, 106, 111
Kolody, B., 105
Komorita, S. S., 76, 209
Komro, K. A., 314, 315, 317
Koob, G., 27
Koss, M. P., 49, 172, 173, 175, 176, 177, 178, 182, 186, 222, 325–326
Kostelny, K., 49, 50, 330
Kostens, T., 27
Kotch, J. B., 86, 211
Kouri, E., 276
Kovach, J. A., 99, 106, 110
Koval, J., 176, 179
Kovess, V., 37
Kozeny, J., 134
Krames, L., 69
Kranzler, H. R., 46, 82
Kravitz, J., 222
Kreuger, R. F., 37
Kriem, B., 32
Kristjanson, A. F., 210, 213
Krohn, M., 163, 164
Kropp, P. R., 300
Kropp, R., 65, 300
Kroutil, L. A., 279
Krueger, R. F., 197
Kruesi, M. J., 32
Ku, L., 187
Kubicka, L., 134
Kuck, K., 29
Kuhlman, D. M., 68
Kung, E. M., 312
Kuo, M., 170
Kurdek, L. A., 199
Kurzon, M., 4
Kushner, M. G., 47

Labouvie, R., 196
Labruna, V., 103, 335
Lachs, M., 223
Lacy, W. B., 135
Laidlaw, T., 175
Lairson, D. R., 251
Lake Morgan, L. C., 320
Lammers, J. W., 313
Lane, K. E., 175
Laner, M. R., 179
Lang, A. R., 212

Lang, C., 54
Langeland, W., 45
Langhinrichsen, J., 263
Langhinrichsen-Rohling, J., 82, 134, 135, 139, 333
Langwick, S. A., 342
Lappalainier, J., 33
Largelard, W., 8
Larimer, M. E., 173, 177
Lash, S. J., 88
La Taillade, J. J., 82
Lau, M. A., 30, 35, 36
Lau, R. R., 134
Laudet, A. B., 5
Laughlin, J. E., 80, 179
Laumann-Billings, L., 48, 50
Laursen, B., 304, 308, 318
Lavoie, F., 308, 319
La Voie, L., 8, 104, 105, 117
Lawas, X., 27
Lawrence, E., 197, 198, 199, 262, 263, 265
Laws, D. R., 341
Lawson, M., 275, 276
Lawton, M. J., 221
Le, D. A., 32
Leaper, C., 304, 318
Leber, D., 131
Lee, H., 170, 331–332
Lee, J. E., 170
Lee, W., 12, 15, 276, 282
Lefebvre, L., 316
Leff, J. P., 101, 109
Leff, M., 45, 46
Lefkowitz, M. M., 154, 157, 165
Lehtonen, R., 245
Leichliter, J. S., 171, 178
Leino, E. V., 226
Leitenberg, H., 134, 135, 139, 178, 182, 310
Lejoyeux, M., 47
Lemarquand, D., 25, 27, 31, 32, 33, 33, 276
Lemeshow, S., 248
LeMeur, M., 32, 33
Leo, G. I., 287
Leonard, H., 32
Leonard, K. E., 2, 12, 14, 15, 46, 66, 67, 68, 74, 75, 85–86, 89, 132, 133, 138, 140, 142, 169, 170, 181, 183, 184, 187, 196, 196, 197, 199, 201, 202, 203, 204, 205, 206, 207, 209
Leshner, A., 25
Lesnick, L., 45, 307
Lesser, M. L., 103
Levendosky, A. A., 262
Leventhal, H., 318

Leventhal, J. M., 45
Levine, D. M., 221
Levine-MacCombie, J., 186
Lewis, I. A., 222
Lewis, L. M., 319
Li, F., 163, 164, 305
Liberto, J. G., 221
Lidberg, L., 32
Liepman, M., 282
Liese, B. S., 117
Life Experiences Survey, 78
Lilly, A. A., 32
Lincoln, A. J., 130, 131
Lindahl, K., 199, 334
Linder, G. F., 342
Lindgerg, L. D., 187
Lingenfelter, T., 254
Linnoila, M., 32, 33
Linton, M. A., 173, 178, 186, 311
Lipman, E. L., 329
Lipovsky, J. A., 106
Lipsey, M. W., 202, 203
Litt, M., 282
Litten, R. Z., 295
Livermore, G., 328
Livesley, W. J., 69
Livingston, J. A., 178, 182, 183, 187, 188
Llorente, M., 27
Lloyd, D. A., 102
Lloyd, S., 132, 176, 179
Lockhart, A. B., 31
Loeber, R., 154, 155, 157, 162, 163
Lohr, J. M., 71, 80, 84
Loi, S., 47
Long, J., 33
Longabaugh, R. L., 283
Loranger, A. W., 79
Lott, B., 173
Lottenberg, S., 34
Lowe, J., 295
Lowell, E. S., 90
Lu, C., 171, 172, 173
Luborsky, L., 68
Luchetta, T., 88
Luckey, D., 341
Luckey, J. W., 45
Lukas, S., 137, 276
Lundahl, L. H., 137
Luster, T., 305
Luthar, S. S., 330, 331
Lydum, A. R., 173, 177
Lynch, K. G., 342
Lynch, M., 329
Lynskey, M. T., 7, 8, 210

Lyons-Ruth, K., 336

MacAndrew, C. R., 334
MacDonald, A. B., 108, 109
Macdonald, S., 85
MacEwen, K., 131, 134, 136
MacLaurin, B., 329
MacLean, M. G., 339
MacMillan, A., 342
MacMillan, H. L., 7, 329, 342
MacMillan, J. H., 342
MacMurray, V., 212
Madden, P. A. F., 37, 326
Madhere, S., 48
Maenner, G., 170, 331–332
Magdol, L., 76, 87, 203, 204
Magruder, B., 176
Magruder-Habib, K., 221
Maguin, E., 6, 8, 10, 11, 99, 105, 116, 209
Magura, S., 2, 3, 5, 6, 211
Mahoney, B. S., 179, 186
Maiden, R. P., 242, 298
Maisto, S. A., 123, 124, 125, 127, 128, 129,
    133, 136–137, 138, 140, 142, 283, 330
Maiuro, R. D., 85
Makepeace, J. M., 175, 176, 179
Maker, A. H., 209
Male borderline and abuse personality, 73–80
Malik, N. M., 334
Malik, S., 305, 308
Malinosky–Rummell, R., 101, 103, 106
Malloy, K., 241
Malone, J., 11, 12, 75, 88, 135, 197, 198, 199,
    204, 263, 264, 296
Mandel, F. S., 103
Mandell, W., 135
Mandoki, C. A., 183
Maney, D. W., 179, 186
Mangis, M. W., 173
Mann, S. A., 101, 109
March, J. S., 99
Marcus, J., 46
Margolin, G., 48, 49, 74, 88, 132, 134, 135,
    140, 142, 206
Marital abuse/violence:
    and acute intoxication, drug and alcohol, 14–
    15
    alcohol and substance abuse in marital abuse
    and child maltreatment, 195–214
Markman, H., 131, 199
Marks, J. S., 325–326
Marlatt, A. G., 339
Marlatt, G. A., 128, 143, 340, 341

Marshall, L. L., 134
Martell-Boinske, L., 85
Martin, C., 46
Martin, C. L., 66
Martin, C. S., 27
Martin, J. L., 10, 101, 109
Martin, M. J., 200
Martin, N., 37, 326
Martin, S. E., 14, 207
Martin, T. R., 83, 88
Martin, W. J., 183
Martinez, P., 50
Marwick, C., 277
Mason, A., 80
Masse, L. C., 45, 46
Maston, C., 328
Maton, K. I., 299
Matthews, W. J., 179
May, L. C., 46
Mayer, M., 329
Mayerovitch, J., 27
McAfee, M. P., 182, 186
McAuslan, P., 173, 177, 183
McCance-Katz, E., 27
McCartney, J. R., 225
McCauley, J., 9, 102, 106, 111
McClelland, D. C., 80
McCloskey, K. A., 262, 263, 270
McCloskey, L. A., 49
McCord, J., 163, 166
McCourt, W., 295
McCrady, B., 269, 294
McCrory, M., 254
McCurdy, K., 3, 4
McDougle, C., 27
McDuffie, D., 173, 177, 183
McEachern, A. G., 334
McGue, M., 86
McKay, J. R., 138
McKee, S. A., 107, 136, 137, 334
McKenry, P. C., 78, 202
McKenzie, B., 329
McKenzie, E. B., 270
McLaughlin, F. J., 87
McLaughlin, I. G., 12, 197
McLellan, A. T., 68
McMahon, M., 262
McMahon, P. M., 342
McMaster, L., 161
McNally, R. J., 108
McNamara, G., 45
Medical Expenditure Panel Survey (MEPS),
    240
Meehan, J. C., 69, 71, 72, 77, 79

Meehan, S. M., 27
Mehlman, P. T., 32
Mehta, R. L., 105
Meier, J. H., 73
Meilman, P. W., 170, 171, 178, 185
Meiselman, K. C., 100
Melby, C., 187
Meloy, J. R., 79
Menard, K. S., 185
Mendelson, M., 288
Mendoza, C., 275
Mensutik, C. E., 221
Merikangas, K. R., 105
Merrill, L. L., 214
Meyer, S-L., 79, 261
Meyers, A. R., 221
Meyers, R., 295
Meyer Williams, L., 103, 106
Michael, C., 106
Michael, J. L., 47
Michienzi, T., 100
Michigan Alcoholism Screening Test (MAST), 106, 202
Mickelson, K., 334
Miczerk, K., 276
Midanik, L. T., 171
Mihalic, G. A., 140, 141, 142
Mihalic, S. W., 132, 133, 142, 203, 204
Mikulincer, M., 78
Milgram, G. G., 304
Miller, A., 231
Miller, B., 275
Miller, B. A., 5, 6, 8, 9, 10, 11, 12, 76, 99, 103, 105, 106, 107, 110, 115, 116, 209, 212, 213, 254
Miller, B. C., 305
Miller, G. B., 10
Miller, J. Y., 45, 305
Miller, N., 182
Miller, N. E., 124
Miller, N. S., 47
Miller, P., 137
Miller, P. E., 102
Miller, S. I., 221
Miller, W. R., 276, 287, 288, 340
Miller-Perrin, C. L., 8, 331
Miller-Tutzauer, C., 196
Millon, T., 69, 71, 72
Millon Clinical Multiaxial Inventory (MCMI), 69
Mills, C. S., 173
Milner, J. S., 56, 76, 78, 86, 89, 214, 330
Min, K., 101
Minces, S., 46

Mirin, S. M., 47
Mischel, W., 124
Mock, J., 288
Moeykens, B., 170
Moffitt, T. E., 34, 37, 46, 76, 87, 155, 197, 203, 204, 339
Molgaard, C. A., 221
Molidor, C., 308
Molina, G. B., 319, 320
Molnar, B. E., 105
Monaco, V., 300
Moncher, F. J., 78
Mongeau, P. A., 139
Mongrain, M., 79
Monheit, A. C., 241
Monitoring the Future Study (MTF), 170, 332
Monnier, J., 89, 90
Montgomery, R. P. G., 138
Monti, P., 282
Moore, K. A., 305
Moore, R., 221, 328
Moore-Gurrera, M., 279
Moos, R. H., 220, 221, 223, 224, 225, 228, 229, 294, 295
Morenoff, J., 313
Morey, L. C., 86
Morgan, C. D., 80
Morgenstern, H., 222
Morrel, T. M., 300
Morris, P., 341
Morrison, D. R., 305
Morrow, K. B., 103
Morse, R. M., 221
Morselli, P. L., 334
Morton, D. J., 221
Moss, H., 46
Motoyoshi, M., 226
Mucatel, M., 221
Mudar, P., 5, 89, 129, 139
Mudar, P. J., 209, 212, 213
Mudar, P. S., 76
Muehlenhard, C. L., 173, 178, 186, 311
Mueller, B., 275
Mullen, F. J., 31
Mullen, P., 4, 209, 210, 213
Mullen, P. E., 10, 79, 101, 109
Mulliken, R., 231
Multidimensional Perfectionism Scale, 82
Multidimensional Personality Questionnaire (MPQ), 86
Murdoch, D., 37
Murphy, C. M., 5, 6, 12, 16, 79, 88, 208, 255, 264, 266, 267, 268, 269, 276, 286, 295, 298, 299, 300

Murphy, J. M., 46, 49, 209, 295
Murray, H., 75, 80
Musser, P. H., 299
Muthern, B. O., 196
Myer, S., 286
Myers, B. J., 46

Nagin, D., 154
Nagoshi, C., 137
Najavits, L. M., 106, 116, 117
Nakamura, C. M., 221
Nankkarinen, H., 33
Narcissism Personality Inventory (NPI), 74
National Alcohol and Family Violence Survey
    (NAFVS), 13, 202
National Center on Addiction and Substance
    Abuse, 208, 304, 310, 311
National Center on Child Abuse and Neglect,
    211, 212
National Crime Victimization Study (NCVS),
    11, 14
National Crime Victimization Survey, 207
National Family Violence Study (NFVS), 12, 13
National Family Violence Survey, 201
National Health Interview Survey, 240
National Household Survey on Drug Abuse
    (NHSDA), 1, 331
National Institute of Drug Abuse, 25
National Institute of Mental Health (NIMH), 7
National Institute on Alcohol Abuse and
    Alcoholism, 242
National Institute on Drug Abuse (NIDA), 343
National Longitudinal Study of Adolescent
    Health, 310
National Opinion Research Center, 205
National Organization for Women (NOW), 278
National Survey of College Women, 178
National Task Force on Violence Against
    Women, 278
National Violence Survey, 174
National Women's Study PTSD Module
    (NWS-PTSD), 106, 107, 108, 112
National Youth Survey, 203
Nayak, M. B., 56
Neal, C. J., 173
Neal, D. J., 340
Neale, J. M., 89
Neavins, T. M., 295, 298, 300
Neckerman, H. J., 154
Neff, J. A., 202
Neglect, defined, 3
Neidig, P. H., 131, 134, 135, 139, 296, 299
Neilsen, J., 37
Nelson, C. B., 45

Nelson, H., 294
Nemeroff, C., 32
Nerney, M., 231
Neurobiology and behavior, 56–57
Newcomb, M. D., 45, 46, 140
Newlove, T., 79
Newman, D. L., 46
Newton–Taylor, B., 331
New York State Central Registry for Child
    Abuse and Neglect, 210
NIAAA, 241, 343
Niaura, R. S., 30, 123, 124, 125, 128, 283
Nicholson, M. E., 179, 186
Nirenberg, T., 282
Nitz, K., 309, 311, 313
Nixon, J. M., 101, 109
Noel, N., 294
Noller, P., 78
Norcross, J. C., 276, 339
Nordenberg, D., 325–326
North Carolina Central Registry of Child
    Abuse and Neglect, 211
Northridge, M., 317

O'Brien, C. P., 68
O'Brien, K., 16, 275
O'Connell, P., 158
O'Connor, M. J., 46
Oei, T. P., 138
Oeltmann, J. E., 309
O'Farrell, C. M., 298
O'Farrell, T. J., 12, 138, 208, 229, 255, 264, 265,
    266, 267, 268, 269, 293, 294, 295, 298
Office of Applied Studies, 331
Offord, D. R., 342
Ogland-Hand, S. M., 106, 112
Ogloff, J. P., 65, 300
O'Hara, P., 305, 308, 309
O'Keefe, M., 132, 133, 140, 142, 305, 308
Older adults, substance abuse and
    interpersonal violence in, 220–232
Oldham, J. M., 47, 79
Olds, D. L., 341
O'Leary, D., 286
O'Leary, K. D., 11, 12, 13, 49, 67, 75, 79, 88,
    89, 123, 124, 125, 127, 130, 131, 132, 133,
    135, 137, 141, 142, 144, 175, 179, 183,
    184, 187, 197, 198, 199, 203, 204, 261,
    262, 263, 264, 265, 296, 299, 300
Oliver, J. M., 85
Olsen, L. J., 337
Olson, K., 8
Olson, R. E., 47
Olson, S., 275

O'Malley, P. M., 169, 170, 196, 332, 339
O'Neill, S., 295, 298, 299
Ontario Student Drug Use Survey (OSDUS), 307, 332
Orme, T. C., 5, 208
Orn, H., 82
Oros, C. J., 172
Orvaschel, H., 103
Oslin, D. W., 221
Oster, R., 305, 308, 309
O'Sullivan, C., 261, 262, 270, 276, 277
Ott, P. J., 45
Ouimette, P. C., 106, 112
Ouslander, J. G., 222
Outlaw, M. C., 185
Overlap between relationship violence and substance abuse, 1–16
   acute alcohol and drug intoxication and husband-to-wife physical abuse, 14–15
   child abuse and substance-abusing parents, 2–8
   child abuse as predictor of adult substance abuse, 8–11
   habitual substance use and husband-to-wife physical abuse, 12–14
   substance abuse and abuse and domestic violence, 11–12
Overpeck, M. D., 4
Ozaki, N., 33

Padina, R. J., 135
Paganini-Hill, A., 221
Paglia, A., 332
Pahkinen, E. J., 245
Paikoff, R. L., 313, 317
Palmer, S., 85
Panek, D. D., 12
Panksepp, J., 31
Panzer, P. G., 106
Pardo, C., 49, 50, 330
Parental Punitiveness Scale (PPS), 76, 209
Parental substance abuse, 3
   child abuse fatalities, 4
   prenatal substance abuse, 3
Parkas, K., 46
Parker, A. M., 342
Parker, J. L., 32
Parkinson, D. K., 12, 48, 202
Parris, D., 305, 308, 309
Partner violence, treating dual problems of partner violence and substance abuse, 254–271
Partridge, M. F., 54
Pathe, M., 79

Patterson, A., 254
Patterson, G. R., 124, 157
Paulhus, D. L., 66
Paykel, E. S., 86
Paymar, M., 261, 262, 264, 282
Peddecord, K. M., 221
Pelcovitz, D., 5, 103, 335
Pelham, W. E., 212
Pence, E., 261, 262, 263, 264, 269, 270, 282
Pendelton, B., 286
Penhale, B., 230
Pepler, D. J., 154, 157, 158, 160, 161, 166
Pernanen, K., 14, 201, 207
Perrin, R. D., 8, 331
Perry, C. L., 314, 315, 317
Perry, D. G., 138
Perry, L. C., 138
Perry, M., 72
Personality, stress, and coping model, 81
   depression *versus* egotism in abusiveness, 87
   hostile, depressive personality, 85–87
   perfectionistic overcontrol and abusiveness, 82–85
   psychopathy, 82
Personality Disorder Examination, 79
Personality factors:
   broad scope of, 65–75
   dimensional *versus* categorical approaches, 68–69
   distal *versus* proximal personality factors, 66–68
   models and conceptualizations of role of, 65–69
Personality factors and substance abuse in relationship violence and child abuse: review and theoretical analysis:
   attachment style theory, 76–79
   borderline male and abusive personality, 73–80
   broad scope of personality factors, 65–66
   coping factors, 89–90
   dimensional *versus* categorical approaches, 68–69
   distal *versus* proximal personality factors, 66–68
   models and conceptualizations of the role of personality, 65–69
   personality, stress, and coping model, 81–87
   psychological need for control and power, 79–80
   stress factors, 88–90
   trait anger, hostility, and antisocial personality, 74–76
   typologies of batterers and child abusers, 69–73

Personality Research Form-Version E (PRF), 75
Peters, K., 37
Peterson, C., 209
Peterson, I., 10
Peterson, J., 27, *30*, 31
Peterson, J. B., 25, 26, 32, 34, 35, 36
Peterson, L., 2, 5, 263, 335, 340, 341
Peterson, R. A., 108
Pettitt, L. M., 341
Pfefferbaum, B., 47
Phillips, A. C., 27
Phillips, T. J., 27
Physical abuse, of children, defined, 3
Pickering, R., 241
Pierre, N., 313
Pihl, R. O., 25, 26, 27, 28, 29, 30, *30*, 31, 32,
    33, *33*, 34, 35, *35*, 36, 37, 38, 99, 107, 108,
    115, 117, 276
Pillemer, K. A., 197, 223, 230
Pistole, M. C., 77
Pittman, A. L., 311, 312, 316
Plass, M. S., 176
Platt, J. J., 47
Pleck, J. H., 187
Plotnick, S., 32
Poitrast, F. G., 5, 6, 16, 46, 49, 209
Poland, M. L., 106, 111
Poland, R. E., 32
Polich, J. M., 206
Poling, J., 46, 82
Pollak, S. D., 50
Pollock, V. E., 182
Polusny, M. A., 8, 9, 101, 106, 229
Pope, H., 276
Poulin, F., 163, 166
Poulos, C. X., 32
Poverty, 3
Powers, J. L., 200, 341
Present State Examination (PSE), 101
Presley, C. A., 170, 171, 178
Price, L., 27
Pringle, J., 100, 112
Prochaska, J. C., 339
Prochaska, J. O., 276
Project Connect, 337
Project MATCH, 283, 338
Project Northland, 316–317
Pryzbeck, T. R., 27
Psychiatric disorders, co-occurring disorders
    and substance abuse in victims of
    intimate violence, 98–117
PTSD:
    substance abuse and co-occurring psychiatric
        disorders in victims of intimate violence,
        98–117

PTSD Symptom Self-Report Scale (PSS–SR),
    108
Public health issues:
    addictions, xiii
    child maltreatment, xiii
    domestic violence, xiii
Puig-Antich, J., 103
Purcell, R., 79
Putnam, F. W., 44, 49

Quadrel, M. J., 134
Quigley, B. M., 14, 15, 132, 133, 138, 199,
    204, 206, 207
Quinlan, D. M., 79
Quinn, D., 5, 6, 16, 46, 49, 209
Quirk, A., 47

Radloff, L., 102
Rahdert, E., 313
Raimo, E. B., 105
Raine, A., 31, 34
Ramboz, S., 32, 33
Ramsey, S., 298, 333
Ramsey-Klawsnik, H., 230
Rand, M. R., 242, 328
Raskin, G., 5, 10, 140
Raskin, R., 74
Raskin White, R. H., 127, 133, 142
Raspberry, K., 242, 243, 333
Ratcliff, K. S., 102, 105
Raudenbush, S. W., 245
Rawlings, R., 32
Recupero, P. R., 298
Rehm, J., 328
Rehman, U., 333
Reich, T., 37
Reichman, J., 29
Reichman, W. E., 230
Reid, H., 282
Reid, J. B., 157
Reilly, M. E., 173
Reiss, S., 108
Reitzel-Jaffe, D., 316
Relationship abuse, overlap with substance
    abuse, 1–16
Relationship violence, xiii
    clinical and research issues in relationship
        violence and substance, 324–343
    developmental psychopathology perspectives
        on substance abuse and, 44–58
    and personality factors and substance abuse
        and child abuse: review and theoretical
        analysis, 64–91

sexual assault and relationship violence among college students: examining the role of alcohol and other drugs, 169–189

Rennison, C. M., 1, 11, 277

Rescorla, L., 85

Resick, P. A., 229

Resnick, H. S., 9, 101, 106, 107, 108, 109, 112, 117, 222, 305

Resnick, M. D., 8

Reuben, D. B., 222

Revised Conflict Tactic Scale, 287

Rhodes, N. R., 270

Rhodes, T., 47

Richardson, D., 183, 187

Richman, J. A., 196

Richters, J. E., 50

Ries, R., 286

Riggs, D. S., 108, 127, 130, 131, 132, 133, 137, 141, 142, 144, 179, 183, 184, 187

Rimmer, J., 5, 208

Rind, B., 115

Rindels, B., 254

Ringel, C., 328

Risser, D., 45

Rittner, B., 336

Rivera, F., 275

Roberts, A., 275

Roberts, L. J., 89, 196, 197, 340

Roberts, N., 78

Robin, R., 33

Robins, L. N., 102, 105, 209

Robinson, L., 277

Robinson, R. R., 85, 89

Robitaille, L., 308, 319

Robson, L., 328

Rodgers, K., 11, 12, 14

Rodning, C., 46

Rodriguez, G., 155

Roel, J. P., 314

Rogers, K., 169

Rogers, S. M., 187

Rogers, W., 222

Rogosch, F. A., 44, 45, 46, 331, 336, 342

Rohrbeck, C. A., 85

Rohsenow, D. J., 10, 137, 282

Roiphe, K., 171, 173

Roizen, J., 2, 177, 184

Roland, E. J., 279

Rollnick, S., 340

Rollstin, A. O., 255, 261, 262

Romans, S. E., 10, 101, 109

Rooijen, L., 209

Room, R., 241

Roosa, M., 49

Roscoe, B., 176, 187

Rose, P., 134

Rosenbaum, A., 11, 12, 49, 197, 198, 199, 204

Rosenberg, D., 88

Rosenberg, H., 222

Rosenberg, M., 79, 103

Rosenberg, S. E., 78

Rosenberg Self–Esteem Scale, 79, 103, 104

Rosenstein, D. S., 46, 55

Rosenthal, D. A., 310

Rosenthal, S. L., 319

Rospenda, K. M., 196

Ross, D., 37

Ross, L. T., 173, 177, 183

Ross, R. K., 221

Rostain, J. C., 32

Roth, J., 304

Roth, R., 27

Roth, Z., 134

Rothbaum, B. O., 108

Rothfleisch, J., 34, *35*

Rothschild, B., 71, 83

Rotter, J. B., 124

Rotunda, R. J., 267, 268, 269

Rounsaville, B. J., 46, 47, 82, 283

Roy, A., 32

Ruback, R. B., 185

Rubin, A., 299

Rubinow, D. R., 32

Runtz, M., 100, 106, 109, 116

Rushe, R. H., 82

Rushforth, N., 275

Russakoff, L. M., 79

Russell, M., 89, 107, 129, 139

Russell, R., 27

Russo, N. F., 222

Rutgers Health and Human Development project, 196

Rutter, M., 48

Ryan, C. M., 12, 202

Ryan, J., 155

Rychtarik, R., 288

Ryden, J., 9, 102, 106, 111

Sacchitelle, C., 45, 46

Safe Dates, 342

Saladin, M., 106, 117

Salamone, S. J., 178, 187

Saldana, L., 335, 340, 341

Saltzman, H., 310

Saltzman, L. E., 242

Salzinger, S., 5, 68, 103, 210

Samios, M., 175

Samoluk, S. B., 107, 108, 109, 117

Sampling procedures, 2

Sampson, R. J., 313
Sandin, E., 89
Sandler, I. N., 49
Saner, H., 317
Santor, D. A., 100, 112
Sarason, I. G., 78
Sartorius, N., 334
Sas, L., 100, 109
Saudou, F., 32, 33
Saunders, B. E., 9, 101, 106, 107, 108, 109, 112, 222, 305
Saunders, D. G., 65, 71, 266
Saunders, J. B., 101
Saunders, K., 77
Sayette, M. A., 181, 182, 330
Scarce, M., 172
Schafer, J., 184, 241, 242, 243, 332, 333
Schaie, K. W., 226
Schechter, M. D., 27
Schechter, S., 255
Schedule for Affective Disorders and Schizophrenia for Children (Kiddie-SADS), 103
Scheidt, D. M., 10
Scheidt, P. C., 4
Schiff, M., 103
Schinke, S. P., 313
Schlee, K. A., 262, 263, 265
Schluter, D. T., 202
Schmeidler, J., 8, 104, 105, 117
Schmidt, L., 251
Schmits, R. E., 221
Schmitt, D., 46
Schneider, B., 45
Schnoll, S. H., 221
Schnurr, P. P., 9, 108, 109
Schoder, J., 305
Schonfeld, L., 221
Schottenfeld, R. S., 45, 68
Schroeder, A. F., 9, 102, 106, 111
Schroeder, M. L., 69
Schuckit, M. A., 45, 105, 134
Schulenberg, J., 196, 339
Schuller, R. A., 12
Schutte, K., 221, 224, 228
Scott, K., 312, 316, 339, 343
Searles, J. S., 38, 134
Sebastian, J. A., 132
Sebring, P., 205
Sedlak, A. J., 325, 331
Seefeldt, L., 49
Segal, D. L., 220, 225, 228
Sege, R. D., 277
Segrist, A. E., 180, 186
Segu, L., 32, 33

Séguin, J., 28, 34
Segura, J., 27
Self-Report Early Delinquency Scale, 155
Selzer, M., 72, 106, 202, 209, 288
Senchak, M., 12, 14, 67, 68, 74, 75, 132, 133, 138, 140, 142, 169, 183, 197, 203, 204, 206
Sengstock, M., 223, 230
Seraganian, P., 75, 76, 254
Severson, K., 225
Sexual abuse, defined, 3
Sexual assault and relationship violence among college students: examining the role of alcohol and other drugs, 169
    administration and institutional responses, 185
    alcohol and dating violence, 183–184
    alcohol and sexual aggression, 182–183
    implications for preventive interventions, 185–186
    policy and prevention implications, 184–185
    potential explanations for relations among substance use, sexual assault, and relationship violence, 180–186
    prevalence and incidence of substance abuse, sexual assault, and relationship violence among college students, 170–177
    relations among substance use, sexual assault, and relationship violence, 177–180
    relationship violence among college students, 174–177
    sexual assault among college students, 172–174
    sexual assault and relationship violence among college students, 171–172
    substance abuse and abuse among college students, 170–171
    substance abuse and relationship violence among college students, 179–180
    substance abuse and sexual assault among college students, 177–179
    unresolved issues and future research priorities, 186–189
Sexual Experiences Survey (SES), 172
Sexual harassment, bullying, sexual harassment, dating violence, and substance abuse among adolescents, 153–167
Seymour, F. W., 308
Shaffer, J. N., 185
Shah, R. Z., 5, 16
Shaken Baby Syndrome, 329
Shamai, M., 264, 265, 262, 263, 264
Shapiro, J., 46
Shaver, P. R., 77, 78

Shaw, S. R., 106, 116
Shedler, J. S., 46
Sheikh, J. I., 222
Shen, H., 241, 242
Shepard, M. F., 255, 262, 263, 269, 270
Sher, K. J., 5, 10, 38, 47, 65, 115, 137, 140, 339
Sherrod, K. B., 87
Shestowsky, J., 27
Shields, N., 76, 254
Shiffman, S., 47
Shoemaker, C., 226
Shook, N. J., 180, 186
Shope, J. T., 135
Short, J. W., 82
Short Michigan Alcoholism Screening Test
    (SMAST), 72, 209
Shortt, J. W., 269
Shortt, L., 305, 307
Shrier, L. A., 309, 310, 313
Shulman, I. D., 29
Sidora, K., 341
Siegle, J. M., 78
Sierra, M., 85
Sieving, R. E., 317
Sigelman, C. K., 134, 135, 176
Sigman, M., 46
Sigvardsson, S., 37, 38
Silva, P. A., 37, 46, 76, 87, 155, 197, 203, 204
Silver, H., 2
Silverman, F., 2
Silvern, L., 101
Simon, R., 286
Singer, L., 46
Singer, M., 103, 107, 139
Single, E., 328
Singleton, M., 205
Sinha, R., 275, 276, 279, 286, 287, 288
Sisson, R. W., 294, 295
Sixteen Personality Factor Questionnaire, 73
Skinner, H. A., 72, 204
Skinner, J. B., 107, 129, 139
Skodol, A. E., 47
Skorina, J. K., 110
Skowronski, K. J., 131
Slater, C. H., 251
Sleutel, M. R., 255, 262, 267
Sloan, J. J., 171, 172, 173
Sloan, M. P., 73
Slutske, W., 37, 326
Small, S. A., 305
Smart, L., 87
Smith, A. M., 310
Smith, B. E., 320
Smith, C., 166, 222, 261, 262, 270, 276, 277
Smith, G., 5, 6, 16, 46, 49, 137, 140, 209

Smith, M., 106
Smith, S. E., 38
Smutzler, N., 89, 131
Smyth, N. J., 5, 47, 76, 209, 212, 213
Sobell, L. C., 287
Sobell, M. B., 287
Sobrie, P., 32
Social learning theory (SLT):
    cognitive social learning models of substance
        abuse and intimate violence, 123–145
Socioeconomic status (SES), 2
Solomon, J., 47
Somes, G., 275
Sonerstein, F. L., 187
Sorenson, S., 241, 305, 308
Sorenson, S. B., 242
Spaccarelli, S., 49
Speer, D. C., 228–229
Spencer, B., 205
Spencer, G. A., 320
Spieker, S. J., 305
Spielberger, C. D., 72, 74, 75
Spielberger's State-Trait Anger Inventory, 74,
    75
Spielberger Trait Anger Inventory, 72
Spitz, A. M., 325–326
Spitzer, R. L., 101, 103, 106, 112
Spoont, M. R., 32
Spracklen, K., 163, 164, 305
Spring, S., 254
Stabenau, J. R., 37
Stacy, A. W., 140
Stambul, H. B., 206
Stanford, E. P., 221
Stanley, J., 34
Starek, J., 101
Stark, M. J., 47
Starzomski, A., 74, 77
Statham, D., 37, 326
Steele, B., 2
Steele, C. M., 170, 181, 182, 186, 187, 201, 330
Steer, R. A., 103
Stein, J. A., 76
Sterman, L., 223
Stets, J. E., 11, 174, 175, 179, 186
Stetson, B. A., 136
Stewart, S. H., 8, 27, 28, 29, 31, 99, 100, 101,
    102, 103, 106–107, 108, 109, 115, 117
Stewart Fahs, P. S., 320
Stigler, M., 317
Stith, S. M., 132, 133, 140, 142, 202, 300
Stoddard, J., 31, 34
Stokes, E. J., 221
Stoltenberg, C. D., 74
Stone, B. K., 90

Stone, K., 5, 49

Stoolmiller, M., 305

Storaasli, R., 71, 83

Stout, R., 294

Stouthamer-Loeber, M., 154, 155, 157, 162

Straatman, 316

Strachan, C. E., 80

Strack, R., 313

Straus, M. A., 2, 11, 12, 13, 101, 112, 130, 131, 132, 174, 175, 197, 200, 201, 202, 243, 255, 265, 263, 264, 287, 295

Strauss, M. A., 76, 131

Stress factors, coping factors, 89–90

Strickler, W. L. A., 36

Stroot, E., 137

Strosahl, K. D., 227–228

Struckman-Johnson, C., 173

Struckman-Johnson, D., 173

Structured Clinical Interview for DSM-III-R (SCID), 101

Stuart, G. L., 66, 67, 69, 71–72, 72, 73, 77, 79, 275, 298

Stuart, G. W., 79

"Study of Child Maltreatment in Alcohol Abusing Families," 211

Stumpf, J., 316

Stuss, D., 34

Substance abuse, xiii

and abuse and domestic violence, 11–12

and alcohol in marital violence and child maltreatment, 195–214

bullying, sexual harassment, dating violence, and substance use among adolescents, 153–167

cognitive social learning models of substance abuse and intimate violence, 123–145

and co-occurring psychiatric disorders in victims of intimate violence, 98–117

developmental psychopathology perspectives and relationship violence, 44–58

habitual substance use and husband-to-wife physical abuse, 12–14

overlap with relationship abuse, 1–16

and personality factors in relationship violence and child abuse: review and theoretical analysis, 64–91

treating dual problems of partner violence and substance abuse, 254–271

See also Parental substance abuse

Substance abuse and co-occurring psychiatric disorders in victims of intimate violence:

assessment issues, 114–115

assessment of comorbidity and functional relations, 114

clinical implications, 116–117

conceptual and methodological issues, 113–116

depression, 101–105, 111–112

individual differences, 116

nature of violence exposure, 116

posttraumatic stress disorder, 106–109, 112–113

sexual dysfunction, 109–111

specificity of overlap of substance use disorders with particular psychiatric disorders, 115–116

substance abuse and psychiatric disorders in victims of parent-to-child violence, 101–111

substance abuse and psychiatric disorders in victims of partner-to-partner violence, 111–113

theoretical perspectives-trauma theory, 99–101

third variable issues, 115

trauma theory-theoretical perspective, 99–101

Substance abuse and interpersonal violence in older adults, 220–232

alcohol abuse and prevalence, 221

assessment and diagnosis, 224–225

categorization and definition in research studies, 224

clinical and research issues, 230–232

definition of older adult, 220–221

experiential avoidance (EA), 227–228

illicit drug abuse and prevalence, 222

interpersonal violence as avoidance, 229–230

interpersonal violence prevalence, 222–223

methodological considerations, 223–227

prescription medication abuse and prevalence, 221–222

relationship between substance abuse and interpersonal violence, 227–230

research, 225–227

substance abuse as avoidance, 228–229

substance abuse prevalence, 221–222

theoretical conceptualization, 227–228

Substance abuse and psychiatric disorders in victims of parent-to-child violence:

depression, 101–105

posttraumatic stress disorder, 106–109

sexual dysfunction, 109–111

Substance abuse and psychiatric disorders in victims of partner-to-partner violence:

depression, 111–112

posttraumatic stress disorder, 112–113

Substance abuse and relationship violence in a strategic framework:

neurobiology behavior, 56–57

strategic function of drug use and abuse, 55

strategies associated with substance abuse

and interpersonal violence, 54
typing behavior, strategies, and development
   to substance abuse, 55
typing behavior and strategies to interper-
   sonal violence, 55–56
Succop, P. A., 319
Sugarman, D. B., 12, 134, 174, 175, 176, 179,
   180, 183, 202, 286, 287
Sugland, B. W., 305
Suiter, J., 197
Suitor, J., 230
Sullivan, C. M., 271
Sullivan, R., 329
Sultan, F. E., 109
Susman, V. L., 79
Suter, N., 241
Sutker, P. B., 65
Sutton, D., 311, 313
Suzanne, S., 275, 276, 279, 286, 287
Swaim, R. C., 45, 46
Swales, P. J., 222
Swedo, S., 32
Sweet, S., 12
Swendsen, J. D., 105
Swinson, R. P., 29
Syers, M. A., 299
Symptom Checklist-86-Revised (SCL-86-R),
   76, 104
Symptom Checklist (SCL-22), 102, 111

Tabrizi, M. A., 103
Takayama, J. I., 6
Taradash, A., 154, 160
Tarrant, N., 77
Tarter, R. E., 45, 46, 65, 134
Tate, S. R., 136, 137
Tatsuoka, M. M., 73
Taub, P. T., 32
Taylor, C. B., 222
Taylor, J., 27
Taylor, K. L., 106
Taylor, S. P., 108, 170, 181, 182, 201
Tedeschi, J. T., 132
Tellegen, L. A., 86
Tennen, H., 46, 82
Teran, L., 319, 320
Terr, L. C., 100, 101, 106, 116
Terry, H., 74, 226
Testa, M., 9, 178, 182, 183, 187, 188
Thematic Apperception Test (TAT), 80
Thoenness, N., 79, 261
Thomas, C. E., 99, 100, 101, 103, 105, 106,
   109, 116, 117
Thomas, J., 228

Thomas, M., 311, 313
Thompson, T., 16, 275
Thorn, G., 134, 135, 139
Thornberry, T., 163, 164
Thornquist, M., 68
Tildesley, E., 45
Tjaden, P., 79, 261
Tohen, M., 286
Tokola, R., 32
Tolin, D. F., 71, 80
Tolman, R. M., 12, 202, 308
Tolson, R. L., 221
Tomko, L. A., 45, 46
Tonigan, S. J., 288
Tontodonato, P., 132, 133, 140, 142
Toth, S. L., 336
Tourigny, M., 329
Trafficking Victims Protection Act of 2000, 278
Trauma Symptom Checklist-36 (TSC-36), 107
Treating dual problems of partner violence
      and substance abuse:
   Behavioral Couples Therapy (BCT), 269
   behavioral marital therapy, 266–268
   behavior marital therapy (BMT), 266–270
   changes of definitions and views of partner
      abuse over time, 261–261
   classical family systems theories, 262–263
   combining treatment for partner violence
      and substance abuse, 265–270
   defining violence, 255
   differential philosophies and conceptual
      approaches for addressing partner abuse,
      261–265
   distinction between common couple violence
      and patriarchal terrorism, 264–265
   family systems theories, relationship coun-
      seling, and substance abuse, 265–266
   feminist theories, 261–262
   fitting services to needs of client, 270
   incorporating relationship counseling into
      cases of partner violence, 264–263
   intimate justice theory, 264
   objective and subjective definitions of partner
      violence, 255–261
   use of relationship counseling, 263–264
   using behavioral marital therapy, 268–270
Treating the addicted male batterer:
      promising directions for dual–focused
      programming:
   criminal justice issues affecting batterer
      interventions, 276–278
   Dade County's integrated domestic violence
      model, 282
   diversion programs and conditions of
      probation, 278–279

Treating the addicted male batterer
(*continued*)
domestic violence legislation, 277–278
policies regarding substance use at the time
of alleged offense, 281
treatment compliance and treatment out-
come, 279–280
treatment models for male batterers, 281–288
Treister, L., 305, 308
Tremblay, R., 28, 34, 45, 46, 154
Trickett, P. K., 44, 48, 49
Triffleman, E., 46
Trocme, N., 329
Tromovitch, P., 115
Tronick, E., 46
Trued, S., 221
Trull, T. J., 65, 69
Tryee, A., 11, 135
Tsianos, D., 107
Turlington, S., 82, 83
Turnbull-Donovan, W., 83
Turner, A. P., 173, 177
Turner, C. F., 187
Turner, J. A., 221
Turner, R. J., 102
Tweed, R. G., 71, 77
Twentyman, C. T., 85, 89
Tyler, K. A., 177
Tyman, J., 324
Typologies of batterers and child abusers, 69–
73
Tyree, A., 12, 75, 88, 197, 198, 199, 204

Ugena, B., 27
Ullman, S. E., 177, 178
Unger, J. B., 319, 320
United States Advisory on Child Abuse and
Neglect, 4
United States Bureau of Justice, 172, 173, 277
United States Census Bureau, 221, 240–241,
251
United States Department of Education, 205
United States Department of Health and
Human Services (USDHHS), 1, 4, 6, 200,
211, 212, 220, 309, 312, 317, 325, 343
United States General Accounting Office, 222
Upchurch, D. M., 241, 242
Ureno, A., 78

Vaccaro, D., 45
Valois, R. F., 309, 312
Van Eenwyk, J., 305
Van Erp, A., 276

Van Hasselt, V. B., 220, 225, 228
Van Hutton, V., 12, 208, 266, 268, 295, 298
Van Kammen, W., 154, 155, 157, 162
Van Praag, H. M., 289
Van Rooijen, L., 72
Vanyukov, M., 46
Vargo, M., 48
Vassileva, J., 27
Veblen-Mortenson, S., 314, 315, 317
Vega, W. A., 105
Veniegas, R., 30
Veronen, L. J., 106
Victims of Trafficking and Violence
Prevention Act of 2000, 278
Vieth, A., 65
Vik, P. W., 136, 137
Villasenor, V. S., 78
Villeponteaux, L. A., 106
Vincent, M., 313
Vinokur, A., 72, 209
Vinton, L., 223, 231
Violence Against Women Act (VAWA), 277,
278
Violence Against Women (VAW), 11, 12
Violence and alcohol: cultural issues and
barriers to treatment:
access to health care for ethnic Americans,
240–241
alcohol treatment, 241
analysis of 1995 National Couples Study:
ethnicity, alcohol, and intimate partner
violence, 242–251
black couples, 248–249
female-to-male partner (FMPV), 243
health insurance and alcohol treatment
coverage by couple ethnicity, 248
Hispanic couples, 249–250
insurance and alcoholism treatment coverage
in pooled sample of couples, 245–246
intimate partner violence, 241–242
male-to-female partner (MFPV), 243
mixed ethnicity couples, 250–251
predictors of health insurance coverage: role
of alcohol problems, intimate partner
violence, income, and neighborhood
characteristics, 246–248
white couples, 250
Virkkunen, M., 32, 33
Vitaliano, P. P., 85
Vitaro, F., 45
Vivian, D., 261, 263, 264, 296
Vogel, R. E., 183
Vogel-Sprott, M., 136
Vogeltanz, N. D., 10, 102, 109, 210, 213, 221,
228, 231

Von Knorring, A., 38
Vredenburg, K., 69

Wachowiak, D. G., 183
Wadsworth, K. N., 196, 339
Waelde, L., 101
Wagner, B. C., 85
Wahler, R. G., 330
Walder, L. O., 154, 157, 165
Waldner-Haugrud, L. K., 176
Walitzer, K. S., 38, 115, 137
Walker, L. E., 112, 229
Wall, A-M., 45, 107, 137, 139, 324–343
Wall, S., 76, 330
Wallace, J., 66
Wallace, R., 106
Waller, J., 106, 111, 309
Walsh, C., 7
Walsh, J. F., 308
Walsh, M., 31
Walter, J., 231
Walters, E. E., 105
Waltz, J., 72, 73, 77, 82, 300
Wambold, P. M., 179, 186
Wang, C. T., 1
Wang, P. S., 334
Wanner, E., 80
Warchol, G., 328
Ward, C., 288
Ward, S. K., 173
Warnecke, L. B., 28
Warner, L. A., 45
Warr, M., 163
Washburn, M., 8, 104, 105, 117
Washousky, R. C., 47
Waskel, S. A., 221
Waters, E., 76, 330
Watson, D., 86
Wauchope, B. A., 200
Weaver, T. L., 261
Webb, J. A., 134
Webster, B. A., 298
Webster-Stratton, C., 49, 209
Wechsler, H., 170, 331–332
Wehner, E., 308
Weiland, D., 282
Weiler, J. L., 9
Weinbaum, D., 155
Weinberg, N. Z., 44, 46, 135, 313
Weiner, M., 103
Weinick, R. M., 241
Weinraub, M., 46
Weinstein, S., 12, 15, 276, 282
Weisner, C., 241, 251

Weiss, R., 286
Weiss, R. D., 47, 106, 116, 117
Weiss, R. J., 138
Wekerle, C., 2, 3, 8, 45, 49, 100, 107, 109, 137,
    139, 160, 305, 311, 312, 315, 316, 317,
    324–343
Welchans, S., 1, 11, 277
Welte, J., 276
Werk, A., 75, 76, 254
West, H., 228–229
Westat, 4, 5, 245
Westlund, K. N., 31
WesVar Complex Samples, 248
Whalen, M., 255, 261
Wharton, R., 5, 49
Whipple, E. E., 49, 209
Whitbeck, L. B., 177
White, H. R., 156, 157, 162
White, J. W., 175, 176
White, K. S., 312
White, M., 282
White, S., 173
Whiteman, M., 46
Whitfield, J., 37
Whitman, M., 135
Widiger, T. A., 69
Widom, C. S., 2, 5, 9, 131, 134
Wieczorek, W., 276
Wiens, A. N., 221
Wilder-Padilla, S., 37
Wileman, B., 270
Wileman, R., 270
Wiles, K. A., 134, 135, 176
Williams, C., 16, 275, 314, 315, 317
Williams, J., 101, 103, 106, 112, 228–229
Williams, K., 173
Williams, L., 104, 105, 139
Williams, O. J., 242
Williams, S., 318
Williams, V., 304, 308, 318
Williamson, D. F., 325–326
Willis, S. L., 226
Willis, W. D., 31
Wills, T. A., 45, 47, 81, 90
Wilsnack, R. W., 196, 210, 213, 221, 228, 231
Wilsnack, S. C., 10, 102, 109, 196, 210, 213,
    221, 228, 231, 254
Wilson, D. B., 202, 203
Wilson, K. G., 227–228
Wilson, M., 174, 255, 262
Wilt, S., 275
Windle, M., 10, 38, 107, 156, 157, 196
Windle, R. C., 10
Wing, J. K., 101, 109
Winger, G., 27

Winkler, K., 106
Winsor, J., 86, 211
Winter, D. G., 80
Wirtz, P. W., 283
Wise, R., 27, 31
Wish, E. D., 104, 105
Wisniewski, N., 172, 173, 175, 178, 182
Wittchen, H-U., 105
Wolf, R. S., 230
Wolfe, D. A., 2, 3, 8, 49, 87, 100, 109, 131,
    132, 160, 305, 311, 312, 315, 316, 317,
    339, 341, 342, 343
Wolfe, E., 6
Wolfe, J., 106, 112
Wolfe, V. V., 100
Wolkenstein, B. H., 223
Wolock, I., 2, 3, 6, 211
Wolter, K. M., 245
Wonderlich, S. A., 210, 213
Wong, M., 7
Wood, J. M., 211
Wood, M. D., 140
Wood, P. B., 47
Wood, P. K., 38, 115, 137, 140, 339
Woods, E. R., 309, 310
Woods, M. G., 229
Woody, G. E., 68
World Health Organization (WHO), 101, 102
Wright, J., 329
Wright, S., 132

Xie, X., 328

Yamaguchi, K., 196
Yamashita, T., 46

Yllo, K. A., 262
YM Magazine, 307, 310
Young, R. M., 138
Young, S. N., 32, 38
Youth Relationships Program, 316
Youth Risk Behavior Surveillance, 305
Youth Risk Behavior Survey, 310, 311
Youth Self-Report Questionnaire, 155
Yuan, J., 179, 186

Zacchia, C., 30
Zacker, J., 207
Zawacki, T., 183
Zayfert, C., 338
Zdaniuk, B., 78
Zeena, T. H., 105
Zeffren, M. J., 222
Zegree, J. B., 85
Zeichner, A., 30, 34, 36, 276
Zeigler, S., 157
Zeiss, A. M., 221, 224, 226
Zelazo, P. D., 34, 35
Zellman, G. L., 182
Zhang, L., 276
Zigler, E., 134
Zohar, A. H., 79
Zrull, M. C., 82, 83
Zucker, R. A., 137
Zuckerman, A., 88
Zuckerman, M., 68
Zuravin, S. J., 211
Zuroff, D. C., 79
Zweben, A., 283, 288
Zweig, J. M., 311, 313, 314
Zwick, W., 282